SOUND AND SENSE: A TEXT ON LAW AND LITERATURE

By

Jerry J. Phillips
Professor of Law,
University of Tennessee

Judy M. Cornett
Associate Professor of Law,
University of Tennessee

Mat #40064723

Cover art by Joseph Gentry Stinnett

COPYRIGHT © 2003

COPYRIGHT © 2003 By West, a Thomson business
        610 Opperman Drive
        P.O. Box 64526
        St. Paul, MN 55164–0526
        1–800–328–9352

Printed in the United States of America

ISBN 0–314–26488–4

 TEXT IS PRINTED ON 10% POST CONSUMER RECYCLED PAPER

To Anne C. Phillips

J.J.P.

To my father, William McKinley Cornett

J.M.C.

*

Introduction

Just as there are many reasons to teach Law and Literature, so there are many ways to teach it. We hope this book will support many ways of teaching Law and Literature.

This book grew out of the co-authors' seven years of co-teaching a 3-hour elective course in Law and Literature at the University of Tennessee College of Law. Those seven years of co-teaching grew out of a single lunchtime conversation in which one co-teacher—who was then teaching the course alone—complained to the other that her Law and Literature students had been unable to analyze the opening passage of BLEAK HOUSE. The students were either uninterested in or unable to discuss the rhetorical structure and readerly effects of those wonderful initial pages.

This complaint about BLEAK HOUSE led in turn to a discussion of the King James Bible as a major ingredient in the stylistic sensibilities of many of those in our generation. (Both of us are natives of East Tennessee who, after some academic sojourns, returned home to teach law.) Sadly, we concluded that the proliferation of new translations of the Bible, beginning in the 1950's, had deprived our students of the familiarity with the rhythms and structures that molded the literary sensibilities of writers like Charles Dickens, Abraham Lincoln, and Eudora Welty. We also decided on the spot to co-teach Law and Literature the following year, using only the King James Bible as a text.

That experiment lasted several largely successful years, but we gradually found ourselves realizing the usefulness of bringing in a wider variety of literature, especially those classics like Milton and Shakespeare, whose works themselves so clearly adumbrate and reflect the influence of the King James Bible. Of course, the Judeo-Christian tradition is not the only source of good literature, and we have included a number of selections from other traditions.

What we have strived for in our course—and what we hope is reflected in this work—is an attention, not just to *themes* relative to law but to *rhetorical* considerations that permeate written expression of all kinds, including law. For law, in our view, is preeminently a linguistic discipline, and students engage with law primarily on a linguistic level. In our Law and Literature course, we hope, students explore the capacities of language to embody their analyses, their emotions, and their ethics.

Our emphasis on the rhetorical as well as the thematic accounts both for the title of the book and its structure. SOUND AND SENSE we chose as our title because of the intimate connection between sound and sense. The Duchess may have had it right when she said, "Take care of sense and the sounds will take care of themselves." But you never know about Lewis Carroll and ALICE IN WONDERLAND, where nothing is ever quite what it seems to be. Alexander Pope more likely reflects the true relation of sound and sense: "The sound must seem an echo to the sense." Or, as Hamlet put it, the purpose of the play "was and is, to hold, as it were, the mirror up to nature."

When we use the term "sense," we refer to all of the senses. In fact, it is very difficult to know where one sense leaves off, and another picks up. We make no distinction between intelligence and sensibility when we use the term sense.

When we use the term "sound," we refer most commonly to the magic of the spoken word. We encourage our students to read aloud with the same kind of facility that they often acquire when they talk. The meanings of the words they use must be carefully weighed. Thereby the sense of the word becomes inextricably bound up in its sound. This wedding of sound and sense will carry over into writing.

We have arranged the materials according to genre—speeches, essays, stories, plays, and poetry—and this order can be followed by those choosing to emphasize rhetoric. For those wishing to take a thematic approach, the thematic index in the Teacher's Manual will allow teachers to assign works across genres.

The hardest choice facing us from the beginning was in deciding what materials to include in this book. The cornucopia of great material is simply overwhelming. Many of our generous colleagues from around the country shared with us their ideas and suggestions. We tried to include as broad a spectrum of materials as we could, realizing that teachers who use our book will supplement the materials with their own favorites. We relied heavily on materials that have worked well for us in class. We have kept our own comments to a minimum, hoping that the questions following many of the selections will sufficiently stimulate thought and discussion.

Readers will notice that many of the materials in this book lack any explicit legal theme. This choice was deliberate, reflecting our belief that the discipline of law is as broad as lived life. From a pedagogical standpoint, our students have reported that re-encountering nonlegal literature refreshes them, enabling them to see more clearly their emerging identities as lawyers.

The case method of law study, at its best, is a technique for discovering what is problematic in law and life. *See* James Boyd White, *quoted in* Carol M. Parker, *A Liberal Education in Law*, 1 J. OF ASSN. OF LEGAL WRITING DIRECTORS 130, 131–32 (2002). Carried to its proper extension, law study involves a capacity for negative capability, as Keats called it— "When man is capable of being in uncertainties, mysteries, doubts, without any irritable reaching after fact and reason," a capability "which Shakespeare possessed so enormously" (letter of Keats, Hampstead 21 Dec. 1817). As Steven L. Winter put it:

> Despite our lofty ambitions, it is becoming increasingly obvious that our objectivist tools are unequal to the task

of mastering the uncertainty and complexity of the human experience that we seek to regulate. To manage better, we first need to rediscover human reason in all its imaginative capacity. We must learn to appreciate and use what [Wallace] Stevens calls the "disposition to metaphor" if we are to have "humane law within the limits of human imagination."

Book Review, 105 HARV. L. REV. 745, 749 (1991). Thus the vital importance of studying literature to understand law.

JERRY J. PHILLIPS
JUDY M. CORNETT

*

Acknowledgments

We want to thank our many colleagues around the country who have given us moral and practical support in the preparation of this text. Many people have shared with us syllabi from their law and literature courses, ideas regarding particularly useful materials, suggestions on how to structure the course, and so on. We incorporated many of these thoughts into this text and into the accompanying teacher's manual. Thank you to the following: George Anastaplo, Maxwell Bloomfield, Nancy L. Cook, George Dargo, Martha Duncan, Jack Edmonds, Neal Feigenson, Robert L. Felix, Robert A. Ferguson, Paul J. Heald, Perry Hodges, Michael H. Hoffheimer, Nicole Lally, David J. Leibson, Mari J. Matsuda, Norval Morris, Henry Ordower, Carol Parker, Judith Resnik, Phoebe Smith, Debora Threedy, Judy Scales-Trent, Penny Tschantz, Margaret V. Turano, Marilyn R. Walter, James Boyd White, Scott E. Wood, and Joan H. Worley.

We also want to thank our research assistants, Allison Bussell, Class of 2004, and Sally Little, Class of 2003, for their unflagging assistance. We also wish to thank the following members of the University of Tennessee College of Law secretarial staff who so faithfully assisted in producing this work: Neal Fischer, Sonya Fowler, Lorenza Houser, Pat McNeil, Stephanie Swain, and Wendy Vermillion. Thanks are also due to Teresa Peterson, Fiscal and Financial Manager of the College of Law, for her invaluable assistance in securing copyright permissions, and to the staff of the College of Law Business Office: C.J. Ottinger, Joyce Satterfield, and Angel Akin.

We also especially thank our dean, Thomas C. Galligan, Jr., for his material and moral support of this book.

Most of all, we thank our students in Law and Literature throughout the years, without whom this book would not have been possible.

J.J.P.
J.M.C.

*

Permissions

The following works are reprinted here by permission as follows:

Excerpt from CLARENCE DARROW: A SENTIMENTAL REBEL, by Arthur and Lila Weinberg (New York: G.P. Putnam's Sons, 1980). Copyright © 1980 by Arthur and Lila Weinberg. Reprinted with permission of Lila Weinberg.

James Dempsey, *The Apple Falls Close to the Tree*, from THE ART OF SUMMATION, ED. M. BLOCK, copyright 1963, by permission of the New York State Trial Lawyers Association, Inc.

Excerpt from GERALD GUNTHER, LEARNED HAND (hardover Knopf 1994; paperback Harvard 1995) copyright 1994 by Usingen Corporation, reprinted by permission of Barbara Gunther.

Excerpt from DAVID HERBERT DONALD, LINCOLN, copyright 1995 by David Herbert Donald, by permission of David Herbert Donald.

Excerpt from "Uncommon Predicates: Notes on Lincoln's Second Inaugural Address," copyright 1997 by The Society for Values in Higher Education and The University of Tennessee, Knoxville, by permission of SOUNDINGS: AN INTERDISCIPLINARY JOURNAL.

Reprinted by arrangement with the Estate of Martin Luther King Jr., c/o Writers House as agent for the proprietor New York, NY
I Have a Dream
Copyright 1963 Dr. Martin Luther King Jr., copyright renewed 1991 Coretta Scott King
Letter from Birmingham Jail
Copyright 1963 Dr. Martin Luther King Jr., copyright renewed 1991 Coretta Scott King
Drum Major Instinct
Copyright 1968 Dr. Martin Luther King Jr., copyright renewed 1996 Coretta Scott King

Grandmother Twylah Nitsch, *She Whose Voice Rides on the Wind*. Copyright © 1995 by Beth Benatovich Berenson. From "She Whose Voice Rides on the Wind" by Grandmother Twylah Nitsch in WHAT WE KNOW SO FAR: WISDOM AMONG WOMEN, edited by Beth Benatovich. Reprinted by permission of St. Martin's Press, LLC.

Gao Xingjian, *The Case for Literature*, © The Nobel Foundation 2000, reprinted by permission of the Nobel Foundation.

*

Summary of Contents

CHAPTER 4

PLAYS

CHAPTER 5

POEMS

Table of Contents

CHAPTER 3

STORIES

CHAPTER 4

PLAYS

CHAPTER 5

POEMS

Table of Cases

The principal cases are in bold type. Cases cited or discussed in the text are roman type. References are to pages. Cases cited in principal cases and within other quoted materials are not included.

*

SOUND AND SENSE: A TEXT ON LAW AND LITERATURE

*

Chapter 1

SPEECHES

A. INTRODUCTION

Speeches are made to an audience, and depend heavily on audience response. A speech has a dual character: as delivered, with all the context provided by time, place, vocal quality, and nonverbal content; and as written, with all the characteristics of a text, escaping (some would say transcending) the time, place, and context of the speech as delivered. Speeches that are republished in textual form may come to be thought of as something else, such as Learned Hand's essay *On Liberty* in the next section. If we are lucky enough to have an audio or audiovisual record of a speech as delivered, such as Martin Luther King Jr.'s "I Have a Dream," we can imagine the original context of the speech and compare it with its textual incarnation. Of course, the audiovisual record of the speech is itself an incarnation of the speech as delivered and cannot replicate exactly the lived experience of it.

Robertson Davies, in his essay *Ham and Tongue* (1977), remarks that public speeches are rarely examined as if they were literary creations. The context of a speech "is frequently chewed over, but the manner in which it is delivered, and the circumstances of its delivery go undiscussed." He laments the "North American Myth of Sincerity, a myth which suggests that anything done skillfully, or with accomplishment, is of less worth than what is botched." There is only one way to make a speech, he says, "and that is to have something to say, and to say it as clearly as you can, in a fashion that does not insult or patronize your hearers." He emphasizes the importance of vocabulary. "I would rather listen to somebody who loved meanings better than words themselves, a speaker who would remain silent rather than use a word he did not truly know."

One feature that often characterizes speeches is the way in which the speaker responds to the audience, and the audience responds to the speaker. Darrow's final arguments to the jury in the two *Sweet* cases are paradigms of this feature. It is intriguing to reflect on the modulations of voice and the shifts of emphasis that Darrow must have made in response to his sense of the mood of the jury in these cases. In Mark

1

Antony's address to the crowd on the death of Julius Caesar, one can sense the crowd's shift of mood in response to Antony's exhortations.

Speeches are the backbone of the lawyer's profession, whether in addressing a jury, a judge, a client, or another lawyer. The essence of the good speech is the ability of the speaker to judge and respond to her audience. Careful preparation is essential, but the presentation must always remain fluid. The great Maria Callas said that she memorized her operatic parts down to the last detail of inflection and movement on stage. But when she began to perform, she said, her artistic instinct took over and she brushed all her preparation aside into the subconscious. So it is with the great speech. How effectively one speaks a speech— whether one's own or that of another—depends on how well one reads the audience and the situation.

Blake Robison, Head of the University of Tennessee Theatre Department and Artistic Director of the Clarence Brown Theatre at the University of Tennessee, was a guest lecturer in the authors' course on law and theatre in the spring of 2001. In that lecture he listed the five steps for method acting. The actor must persistently ask herself, both in each line and for the whole play:

Who am I?

Where am I?

What are my character's circumstances?

What do I want my audience to do?

How do I get them to do it?

Do the speakers in this chapter effectively ask themselves these questions? Do lawyers?

B. ARGUMENTS

Clarence Darrow was hired in 1925 to represent several African–Americans accused of conspiracy to commit murder. Dr. Ossian H. Sweet, a successful doctor, bought a house in a white Detroit neighborhood for himself and his wife and child. Dr. Sweet anticipated trouble, because other blacks moving into white neighborhoods in the Detroit area had been intimidated by white vigilante groups and forced to move out. When Dr. Sweet moved in, he brought with him nine black friends, armed with guns and ammunition. He left the child with relatives.

A large crowd gathered in front of the Sweet house on the first night of their residency, but there was no violence. On the second night the crowd gathered and began throwing rocks at the Sweet house and yelling threats. At some point during the disturbance, shots were fired, and a white man named Breiner was killed in the street. The police, who were already present at the scene, quickly arrested all eleven occupants of the Sweet residence and charged them with murder.

The jury deliberated for 46 hours, but were unable to agree. The judge declared a mistrial.

Several months later the prosecution brought a murder charge against one of the blacks, Henry Sweet, the brother of Dr. Ossian Sweet. Once again Clarence Darrow was hired to defend. The following are excerpts from Darrow's closing argument to the jury in the second case.

CLOSING ARGUMENT OF CLARENCE DARROW
IN THE CASE OF

PEOPLE v. HENRY SWEET
In the Recorder's Court
Detroit, Michigan

Before
The Honorable Frank Murphy
[*later a justice of the United States Supreme Court*].
May 11, 1926

[This text comes from the transcript published in 1927 by the National Association for the Advancement of Colored People, which had underwritten the defense of Henry Sweet.]

MR. DARROW: If the Court please, Gentlemen of the Jury: You have listened so long and patiently that I do not know whether you are able to stand much more. I want to say, however, that while I have tried a good many cases in the forty-seven or forty-eight years that I have lived in court houses, that in one way this has been one of the pleasantest trials I have ever been in. The kindness and the consideration of the Court is such as to make it easy for everybody, and I have seldom found as courteous, gentlemanly and kindly opponents as I have had in this case. I appreciate their friendship. Lawyers are apt to look at cases from different standpoints, and I sometimes find it difficult to understand how a lawyer on the other side can think as he thinks and say what he says. I, being an extremely reasonable man and entirely free from all kinds of prejudices myself, find this hard to comprehend.

I shall begin about where my friend Mr. Moll [*Assistant Wayne County Prosecutor Lester Moll*] began yesterday. He says lightly, gentlemen, that this isn't a race question. This is a murder case. We don't want any prejudice; we don't want the other side to have any. Race and color have nothing to do with this case. This is a case of murder.

Now, let's see; I am going to try to be as fair as I can with you gentlemen; still I don't mind being watched at that. I just want you to give such consideration to what I say as you think it is worth. I insist that there is nothing but prejudice in this case; that if it was reversed and eleven white men had shot and killed a black while protecting their home and their lives against a mob of blacks, nobody would have dreamed of having them indicted. I know what I am talking about, and so do you. They would have been given medals instead.

Eleven colored men and one woman are in this indictment, tried by twelve jurors, gentlemen. Every one of you are white, aren't you? At least you all think so. We haven't one colored man on this jury. We couldn't get one. One was called and he was disqualified. You twelve white men are trying a colored man on race prejudice. Now, let me ask you whether you are not prejudiced. I want to put this square to you, gentlemen. I haven't any doubt but that every one of you are prejudiced against colored people. I want you to guard against it. I want you to do all you can to be fair in this case, and I believe you will. A number of you people have answered the question that you are acquainted with colored people. One juror I have in mind, who is sitting here, said there were two or three families living on the street in the block where he lives, and he had lived there for a year or more, but he didn't know their names and had never met them. Some of the rest of you said that you had employed colored people to work for you, are even employing them now. All right.

You have seen some of the colored people in this case. They have been so far above the white people that live at the corner of Garland and Charlevoix [*in eastern Detroit, where the shooting occurred*] that they can't be compared, intellectually, morally and physically, and you know it. How many of you jurors, gentlemen, have ever had a colored person visit you in your home? How many of you have ever visited in their homes? How many of you have invited them to dinner at your house? Probably not one of you. Now, why, gentlemen?

There isn't one of you men but what know just from the witnesses you have seen in this case that there are colored people who are intellectually the equal of all of you. Am I right? Colored people living right here in the City of Detroit are intellectually the equals and some of them superior to most of us. Is that true? Some of them are people of more character and learning than most of us. I have a picture in my mind of the first witness we put on the stand—Mrs. Spalding. Modest, intelligent, beautiful; the beauty in her face doesn't come from powder or paint, or any artificial means, but has to come from within; kindly, human feeling. You couldn't forget her. I couldn't forget her. You seldom have seen anybody of her beauty and her appearance. She has some colored blood in her veins. Compare her with the teacher who for ten years has taught high school on what she called the corner of Garland and "Gote" [Goethe] Street. Compare the two.

Now, why don't you individually, and why don't I, and why doesn't every white person whose chances have been greater and whose wealth is larger, associate with them? There is only one reason, and that is prejudice. Can you give any other reason for it? They would be intellectual companions. They have good manners. They are clean. They are all of them clean enough to wait on us, but not clean enough to associate with. Is there any reason in the world why we don't associate with them excepting prejudice? Still none of us want to be prejudiced. I think not one man of this jury wants to be prejudiced. It is forced into us almost from our youth until somehow or other we feel we are superior to these people who have black faces.

Now, gentlemen, I say you are prejudiced. I fancy every one of you are, otherwise you would have some companions amongst these colored people. You will overcome it, I believe, in the trial of this case. But they tell me there is no race prejudice, and it is plain nonsense, and nothing else. Who are we, anyway? A child is born into this world without any knowledge of any sort. He has a brain which is a piece of putty; he inherits nothing in the way of knowledge or of ideas. If he is white, he knows nothing about color. He has no antipathy to the black.

The black and the white both will live together and play together, but as soon as the baby is born we begin giving him ideas. We begin planting seeds in his mind. We begin telling him he must do this and he must not do that. We tell him about race and social equality and the thousands of things that men talk about until he grows up. It has been trained into us, and you, gentlemen, bring that feeling into this jury box, and that feeling which is a part of your life long training.

You need not tell me you are not prejudiced. I know better. We are not very much but a bundle of prejudices anyhow. We are prejudiced against other people's color. Prejudiced against other men's religion; prejudiced against other people's politics. Prejudiced against people's looks. Prejudiced about the way they dress. We are full of prejudices. You can teach a man anything beginning with the child; you can make anything out of him, and we are not responsible for it. Here and there some of us haven't any prejudices on some questions, but if you look deep enough you will find them; and we all know it.

All I hope for, gentlemen of the jury, is this: That you are strong enough, and honest enough, and decent enough to lay it aside in this case and decide it as you ought to. And I say, there is no man in Detroit that doesn't know that these defendants, everyone of them, did right. There isn't a man in Detroit who doesn't know that the defendant did his duty, and that this case is an attempt to send him and his companions to prison because they defended their constitutional rights. It is a wicked attempt, and you are asked to be a party to it. You know it. I don't need to talk to this jury about the facts in this case. There is no man who can read or can understand that does not know the facts. Is there prejudice in it?

. . . .

Mr. Moll took particular pains to say to you, gentlemen, that these eleven people here are guilty of murder; he calls this a cold-blooded, deliberate and premeditated murder; that is, they were there to kill. That was their purpose. Eleven, he said. I am not going to discuss the case of all of them just now, but I am starting where he started. He doesn't want any misunderstanding.

Amongst that eleven is Mrs. Sweet. The wife of Dr. Sweet, she is a murderer, gentlemen? The State's Attorney said so, and the Assistant State's Attorney said so. The State's Attorney would have to endorse it because he, himself, stands by what his assistant says. Pray, tell me what has Mrs. Sweet done to make her a murderer? She is the wife of

Dr. Sweet. She is the mother of his little baby. She left the child at her mother's home while she moved into this highly cultured community near Goethe Street. Anyhow, the baby was to be safe; but she took her own chance, and she didn't have a gun; none was provided for her. Brother Toms drew from the witnesses that there were ten guns, and ten men. He didn't leave any for her. Maybe she had a pen knife, but there is no evidence on that question. What did she do, gentlemen? She is put down here as a murderer. She wasn't even upstairs. She didn't even look out of a window. She was down in the back kitchen cooking a ham to feed her family and friends, and a white mob came to drive them out of their home before the ham was served for dinner. She is a murderer, and all of these defendants who were driven out of their home must go to the penitentiary for life if you can find twelve jurors somewhere who have enough prejudice in their hearts, and hatred in their minds.

Now, that is this case, gentlemen, and that is all there is to this case. Take the hatred away, and you have nothing left. Mr. Moll says that this is a case between Breiner [*Leon Breiner, the victim*] and Henry Sweet.

MR. MOLL: No, I did not say any such thing.

MR. DARROW: Well, let me correct it. He says that he holds a brief for Breiner. That is right; isn't it.

MR. MOLL: That is right.

MR. DARROW: Well, I will put it just as it is, he holds a brief for Breiner, this Prosecuting Attorney. He is wrong. If he holds a brief for Breiner, he should throw it in the stove. It has no place in a court of justice. The question here is whether these defendants or this defendant is guilty of murder. It has nothing to do with Breiner.

He says that I wiggled and squirmed every time they mentioned Breiner. Well, now, I don't know. Did I? Maybe I did. I didn't know it. I have been around court rooms so long that I fancy I could listen to anything without moving a hair. Maybe I couldn't. And, I rather think my friend is pretty wise. He said that I don't like to hear them talk about Breiner. I don't, gentlemen, and I might have shown it. This isn't the first case I was ever in. I don't like to hear the State's Attorney talk about the blood of a victim. It has such a mussy sound. I wish they would leave it out. I will be frank with you about it. I don't think it has any place in a case. I think it tends to create prejudice and feeling and it has no place, and it is always dangerous. And perhaps—whether I showed it or not, my friend read my mind. I don't like it.

Now, gentlemen, as he talked about Breiner, I am going to talk about him, and it isn't easy, either. It isn't easy to talk about the dead, unless you "slobber" over them and I am not going to "slobber" over Breiner. I am going to tell you the truth about it. Why did he say that he held a brief for Breiner, and ask you to judge between Breiner and Henry Sweet? You know why he said it. To get a verdict, gentlemen.

That is why he said it. Had it any place in this case? Henry Sweet never knew that such a man lived as Breiner. Did he? He didn't shoot at him. Somebody shot out into that crowd and Breiner got it. Nobody had any feeling against him.

But who was Breiner, anyway? I will tell you who he was. I am going to measure my words when I state it, and I am going to make good before I am through in what I say. Who was he? He was a conspirator in as foul a conspiracy as was ever hatched in a community; in a conspiracy to drive from their homes a little family of black people and not only that, but to destroy these blacks and their home. Now, let me see whether I am right. What do we know of Breiner? He lived two blocks from the Sweet home. On the 14th day of July, seven hundred people met at the schoolhouse and the schoolhouse was too small, and they went out into the yard. This school house was across the street from the Sweet house.

Every man in that community knew all about it. Every man in that community understood it. And in that schoolhouse a man rose and told what they had done in his community; that by main force they had driven Negro families from their homes, and that when a Negro moved to Garland Street, their people would be present to help. That is why Mr. Breiner came early to the circus on the 9th. He went past that house, back and forth, two or three times that night. Any question about that? Two or three times that night he wandered past that house. What was he doing? "Smoking his pipe." What were the rest of them doing? They were a part of a mob and they had no rights, and the Court will tell you so, I think. And, if he does, gentlemen, it is your duty to accept it.

Was Breiner innocent? If he was, every other man there was innocent. He left his home. He had gone two or three times down to the corner and back. He had come to Dove's steps where a crowd had collected and peacefully pulled out his pipe and begun to smoke until the curtain should be raised. You know it. Why was he there? He was there just the same as the Roman populace were wont to gather at the Colosseum where they brought out the slaves and the gladiators and waited for the lions to be unloosed. That is why he was there. He was there waiting to see these black men driven from their homes, and you know it; peacefully smoking his pipe, and as innocent a man as ever scuttled a ship. No innocent people were there. What else did Breiner do? He sat there while boys came and stood in front of him not five feet away, and stoned these black people's homes, didn't he? Did he raise his hand? Did he try to protect any of them? No, no. He was not there for that. He was there waiting for the circus to begin.

Gentlemen, it is a reflection upon anybody's intelligence to say that everyone did not know why this mob was there. You know! Everyone of you know why. They came early to take their seats at the ringside. Didn't they? And Breiner sat at one point where the stones were thrown, didn't he? Was he a member of that mob? Gentlemen, that mob was bent not only on making an assault upon the rights of the owners of that house, not only making an assault upon their persons and their property, but they were making an assault on the constitution and the laws of the nation, and the state under which they live. They were like Samson in the temple, seeking to tear down the pillars of the structure. So that blind prejudices and their bitter hate would rule supreme in the City of Detroit. Now, that was the case.

Gentlemen, does anybody need to argue to you as to why those people were there? Was my friend Moll even intelligent when he told you that this was a neighborly crowd? I wonder if he knows you better than I do. I hope not. A neighborly crowd? A man who comes to your home and puts a razor across your windpipe, or who meets you on the street and puts a dagger through your heart is as much a neighbor as these conspirators and rioters were who drove these black people from their home. Neighbors, eh? Visiting? Bringing them greetings and good cheer! Our people were newcomers. They might have needed their larder stocked. It was a hot night. The crowd probably brought them ice cream and soda, and possibly other cold drinks. Neighbors? Gentlemen—neighbors? They were neighbors in the same sense that a nest of rattlesnakes are neighbors when you accidentally put your foot upon them. They are neighbors in the sense that a viper is a neighbor when you warm it in your bosom and it bites you. And every man who knows anything about this case knows it. You know what the purpose was.

. . . .

It was bad enough for a mob, by force and violation of law, to attempt to drive these people from their house, but gentlemen, it is worse to send them to prison for life for defending their home. . . .

Let me ask you this question, gentlemen: Mr. Moll says that these colored people had a perfect right to live in that house. Still he did not waste any sympathy on the attempt to drive them out. He did not say it was an outrage to molest them. Oh, no, he said they had a perfect right to live in that house. But the mob met there to drive them out. That is exactly what they did, and they have lied, and lied, and lied to send these defendants to the penitentiary for life, so that they will not go back to their home.

Now, you know that the mob met there for that purpose. They violated the constitution and the law, they violated every human feeling, and threw justice and mercy and humanity to the winds, and they made a murderous attack upon their neighbor because his face was black. Which is the worse, to do that or lie about it? In describing this mob, I heard the word "few" from the State's witnesses so many times that I could hear it in my sleep, and I presume that when I am dying I will hear that "few," "few," "few" stuff that I heard in Detroit from people who lied and lied and lied. What was this "few"? And who were they, or how did they come there? I can't tell you about every one of these witnesses, but I can tell you about some of them. . . .

Are the people who live around the corner of Charlevoix and Garland worse than other people? There isn't one of you who doesn't know that they lied. There isn't one of you who does not know that they tried to drive those people out and now are trying to send them to the penitentiary so that they can't move back; all in violation of the law, and are trying to get you to do the job. Are they worse than other people? I don't know as they are. How much do you know about prejudice? Race prejudice. Religious prejudice. These feelings that have divided men and caused them to do the most terrible things. Prejudices have burned men at the stake, broken them on the rack, torn every joint apart, destroyed people by the million. Men have done this on account of some terrible prejudice which even now is reaching out to undermine this republic of ours and to destroy the freedom that has been the most cherished part of our institutions.

These witnesses honestly believe that they are better than blacks. I do not. They honestly believe that it is their duty to keep colored people out. They honestly believe that the blacks are an inferior race and yet they look at themselves, I don't know how they can. If they had one colored family up there, some of the neighbors might learn how to pronounce "Goethe." It would be too bad to spread a little culture in that vicinity. They might die. They are possessed with that idea and that fanaticism, and when people are possessed with that they are terribly cruel. They don't stand alone. Others have done the same thing. Others will do the same thing so long as this weary old world shall last. They may do it again, but, gentlemen, they ought not to ask you to do it for them. That is a pretty dirty job to turn over to a jury, and they ought not to expect you to do it.

. . . .

Was there a crowd at that corner on that fatal night? Let me see what their witnesses say, if we can find out. Not one of them has told the truth, excepting as we dragged it from them. Mr. Dove lives right across the street from the Sweet house. He said he got home from his work and went out on his porch, and his wife and baby went with him. And there were two other people upstairs, and they were all there present at roll call, not only on the 9th but on the 8th. It was a warm evening and they got there in time for the shooting.

How hard it was to pry out of them that they went there on account of the colored people who had moved in across the way! You people are not lawyers. You do not know how hard it was to make them admit the truth. It is harder to pull the truth out of a reluctant witness than to listen to them lie. They were there on the porch for everything on earth except to see the slaughter. Still, they finally admitted that curiosity took them there, just curiosity. Curiosity over what? A black man had driven up to the house two small trucks containing a bed and a stove and a few chairs and a few clothes, and he was going to live in that community. That is why their witnesses went to that corner that night and reluctantly they admitted it.

Dove said that there were about ten or fifteen people in front of his house, and that Leon Breiner was sitting there on the lawn; and a number of other people standing there, too. Mrs. Dove said there were two over there and that she did not see Breiner, or anybody else, and the people upstairs weren't there, and the two roomers weren't there, although all of them have testified that they were present.

Here is another witness, Abbie Davis. She testified that she went down around the corner where everybody else went; we have had about ten or fifteen who went around that corner and each one said that no one else was there. She said, as I remember it, there were probably about twenty people on the street. And I asked: How, many in front of the Dove house? She didn't see any, though she was right across the street.

Let us take the corner of Charlevoix, where the school house stands, with the Sweet house on the other side. How many were there? Schuknecht, the officer [*Norton Schuknecht, a witness for the prosecution*], said that he stood on that corner all the evening. Schuknecht said that fifteen or twenty were standing there, and some other witnesses put it higher.

Miss Stowell,—Miss Stowell—do you see her? I do. S-t-o-w-e-l-l. You remember, gentlemen, that she spelled it for us. I can spell that in my sleep, too. I can spell it backwards. Well, let me recall her to you. She teaches school at the corner of Garland and "Gother" Street; fifteen years a high school teacher, and, in common with all the other people in the community, she called it "Gother" Street.

She came down to the apartment building, opposite the Sweet house that night to see about a picnic. She left just before the picnic began. She said she sat on the porch with Draper and his wife and made arrangements for the children to go to the picnic and she thought their boy was there, too.

Now, you remember Draper. Draper was a long, lean, hungry-looking duck.... He said he paced up and down in front of his house. He didn't see much of anything. I asked him where his boy was. Well, he thought his boy was part of the time out on that porch. Were you there? "No." Was your wife there? "No." Now, part of the time the boy was there. Well, now, Miss S-t-o-w-e-l-l said that they were all there. She was there all right. Nobody was on the street in front of them. She sat right there.

And they called this fellow Belcher, the man who is so good to his wife. His wife had gone away—not for good—either for her good or his—to visit a sick friend that belonged to her lodge. And, as soon as she got out of the house Belcher started down to the corner across from the Sweet house and got restless and uneasy. Maybe he is telling the truth. I have a theory that might account for his telling the truth, but it is not the theory of the State. He paced up and down the block for half an hour looking over the street cars to see if, perchance, his wandering wife might return. She was accustomed to going out of nights, and the cars stopped at their door. It wasn't dark. The corner of Garland and Charlevoix is inhabited by very fine people who have an "improvement club" so as to keep it in proper condition for their children. I don't see why he was so restless about his wife; whatever it was, for more than half an hour, he was pacing back and forth; probably nearer an hour. He didn't see anybody else. He didn't see Draper.

He did see a policemen, but that is all; but, Miss S-t-o-w-e-l-l didn't see him. Didn't see anything, but looked over at the other side to the schoolhouse yard, and what did she see? "Well, there were fifty or one hundred people around there." So, I don't know as I should complain so much about her. She came nearer to telling the truth about that than any other witness called by the State; a good deal nearer. She looked across the street and saw fifty or one hundred people, but she saw nobody on the sidewalk and it was seething with people who weren't even there, and when she went away she didn't look around the corners, and didn't know who were there. Wonderful witness, that woman.

Are there any two of their witnesses that have agreed on any fact? She says fifty or one hundred. What did the policeman say? There were about eight policemen standing around there to protect a colored family. Two of them were from Tennessee. That ought to have helped some. I don't know where the rest came from. Some them seemed to come from some institution, judging by the way they talked. Do you remember the fellow that said he was parading all the evening along the one sidewalk next to his house? Right along here. Didn't see anybody. Didn't know whether anybody was over there in the schoolhouse-yard, and he said "there might have been four." Now, he is one, isn't he?

Here is another policeman, parading all the evening on this short beat. He came pretty nearly down to the corner. Nobody was on this corner. Was there anybody on the schoolhouse-yard? "There might have been four." Four, gentlemen. I wouldn't say this man lied. It takes some mentality to lie. An idiot can't lie. It takes mentality because it implies a design, and those two people had no design or anything else. Now, I won't say the same about Schuknecht. He has some mentality; some; just some. He said "there were probably one hundred and fifty around there." The next man—what is the name of the next policeman?

MR. TOMS [*Wayne County Prosecutor Robert M. Toms*]: Schellenberger [*Paul Schellenberger, also a witness for the prosecution*].

MR. DARROW: Schellenberger. He said "there were forty or fifty," but he finally admitted that he said "one hundred and fifty" on the former trial. You can fix it the way you want it. Let me tell you this: Every witness the State put on told how the policemen were always keeping the crowd moving, didn't they? They were always driving people along and not permitting them to congregate, didn't they? Who were these people and where did they come from? No two witnesses on the part of the State have agreed about anything.

. . . .

Now they put another witness on the stand. Everybody in that vicinity belonged to the improvement club. I am going to mention this again, but I just want to speak about one thing in connection with that club. Mr. Andrews came here, and you remember my prying out and surprising myself with my good luck, because when a lawyer gets something he wants, he doesn't at all feel that he was clever. He just worms around until he gets it, that's all. I asked:—Did you belong? He said he did. How many were at the meeting of the Improvement Club at the schoolhouse? "Oh, seven or eight hundred." That is their witness. They began in the schoolhouse and there wasn't room enough to hold them, and they went out in the yard. . . .

What did the speaker at the meeting say? "Well, one of them was very radical." He was? "Yes." What did he say? "He said he advocated violence. They told what they had done up there on Tireman street, where they had driven Dr. Carter [*Dr. Alexander Turner*] out, and they wouldn't have him, and he said, whenever you undertake to do something with this Negro question down here, we will support you." Gentlemen, are you deaf or dumb or blind, or just prejudiced, which means all three of them? No person with an ounce of intelligence could have any doubt about the facts in this case. . . .

On the eve of the Sweet family moving into their home, and on the corner of the street where their home was located and in a public school house, not in the South but in Detroit. Six or seven hundred neighbors in this community listened to a speaker advocating the violation of the constitution and the laws, and calling upon the people to assemble with violence and force and drive these colored people from their homes. Seven hundred people there, and only one man told it.

Let me say something else about it, gentlemen. There were present at that meeting two detectives, sent by the Police Department to make a report. Officer Schuknecht said that he had heard about the formation of that "Improvement Club" and the calling of that meeting, and the purchase of that house by colored people, and he wanted to watch it. So he sent two detectives there. They heard this man make a speech that would send any black man to jail, that would have sent any political crusader to jail. They heard the speaker urge people to make an assault upon life and property; to violate the constitution and the law; to take things in their own hands and promise that an organization would stand back of them.

Why was he not arrested? Gentlemen, in a schoolyard paid for by your taxes; paid for by the common people, of every color, and every nationality, and every religion, that man stood there and harangued a mob and urged them to violence and crime in the presence of the officers of this city, and nothing was done about it. Didn't everybody in the community know it? Everybody! Didn't Schuknecht know it? He sent the detective there for that purpose. And what else did Andrews say? He said the audience applauded this mad and criminal speech, and he applauded, too.

And yet, you say that eleven poor blacks penned in a house for two days, with a surging mob around them, and knowing the temper of that community; and knowing all about what had happened in the past; reading the Mayor's proclamation, and seeing who was there, and knowing what occurred in the school house, waiting through the long night of the 8th and through the day of the 9th, walled in with the mob into the night of the 9th, until the stones fell on the roof, and windows were knocked out; and yet, gentlemen, you are told that they should have waited until their blood should be shed, even until they were dead, and liberty should be slain with them. How long, pray, must an intelligent American citizen wait in the City of Detroit, with all this history before them? And, then, gentlemen, after all that, these poor blacks are brought back into a court of justice and twelve jurors are asked to send them to prison for life.

I want to talk to you a little more about who was around that house, and why, and what they were doing, and how many there were. You may remember a man named Miller. This man Miller expressed it pretty well. I suppose I prodded him quite a bit. I asked—what was the organization for? "Oh, we want to protect the place." Against what? "Oh, well, generally." You can't make it more definite? "Yes, against undesirables." Who do you mean by "undesirables?" "Oh, people we don't want," and so on and so forth. Finally, he said, "against Negroes." I said: Anybody else? He thought awhile, and he said: "Well, against Eyetalians." He didn't say "Italians." He hadn't got that far along yet, but he said "Eye-talians." Of course, there was a Syrian merchant running the store on the corner, so Syrians evidently didn't count. By the way, we haven't seen that Syrian or heard from him. He must have done a fine business that night. He should have seen something. They were not prejudiced much about Syrians. They want to keep it American, Miller says. I asked him who the undesirables were, and the first are Negroes, and the second, Eye-talians.

Well, now, gentlemen, just by the way of passing, words are great things, you know. You hear some fellow who wants more money than you want, and he calls himself a one-hundred percent American. Probably he doesn't know what the word American means. But he knows what he wants. You hear some fellow who wants something else talking about Americanism. I don't know where Miller came from; about how early or how late an arrival he is in America. The only real Americans that I know about are the Indians, and we killed most of them and pensioned the rest....

I guess that the ancestors of my clients got here long before Miller's did. They have been here for more than three hundred years; before the Pilgrims landed, the slave ships landed, gentlemen. They are Americans and have given life and blood on a thousand different kinds of fields for America and have given their labor for nothing, for America. They are Americans. Mr. Miller doesn't know it. He thinks he is the only kind of American. The Negroes and Eye-talians don't count. Of course, he doesn't like them. Mr. Miller doesn't know that it was an Eye-talian that discovered this land of ours. Christopher Columbus was an "Eye-talian," but he isn't good enough to associate with Miller. None of the people of brains and courage and intelligence, unless they happen to live around those four corners, are good enough, and there are no brains and intelligence, and so forth, to spare around those corners. If there ever was they have been spared. These are the kind of prejudices that make up the warp and woof of this case.

Gentlemen, lawyers are very intemperate in their statements. My friend, Moll, said that my client here was a coward. A coward, gentlemen. Here, he says, were a gang of gunmen, and cowards—shot Breiner through the back. Nobody saw Breiner, of course. If he had his face turned toward the house, while he was smoking there, waiting for the shooting to begin, it wasn't our fault. It wouldn't make any difference which way he turned. I suppose the bullet would have killed him just the same, if he had been in the way of it. If he had been at home, it would not have happened.

Who are the cowards in this case? Cowards, gentlemen! Eleven people with black skins, eleven people, gentlemen, whose ancestors did not come to America because they wanted to, but were brought here in slave ships, to toil for nothing, for the whites—whose lives have been taken in nearly every state in the Union,—they have been victims of riots all over this land of the free. They have had to take what is left after everybody else has grabbed what he wanted. The only place where he has been put in front is on the battlefield. When we are fighting we give him a chance to die, and the best chance. But, everywhere else, he has been food for the flames, and the ropes, and the knives, and the guns and hate of the white, regardless of law and liberty, and the common sentiments of justice that should move men. Were they cowards? No, gentlemen, they may have been gunmen. They may have tried to murder, but they were not cowards.

Eleven people, knowing what it meant, with the history of the race behind them, with the picture of Detroit in front of them; with the memory of Turner and Bristol [*Alexander Turner and Vollington Bristol, two Blacks driven out of their homes earlier in the summer of 1925*]; with the Mayor's proclamation still fresh on paper with the knowledge of shootings and killings and insult and injury without end, eleven of them go into a house, gentlemen, with no police protection, in the face of a mob, and the hatred of a community, and take guns and ammunition and fight for their rights, and for your rights and for mine, and for the rights of every being that lives. They went in and faced a mob seeking to tear them to bits. Call them something besides cowards.

The cowardly curs were in the mob gathered there with the backing of the law. A lot of children went in front and threw the stones. They stayed for two days and two nights in front of this home and by their threats and assault were trying to drive the Negroes out. Those were the cowardly curs, and you know it. I suppose there isn't any ten of them that would come out in the open daylight against those ten. Oh, no, gentlemen, their blood is too pure for that. They can only act like a band of coyotes baying some victim who has no chance.

And then my clients are called cowards. All right, gentlemen, call them something else. These blacks have been called many names along down through the ages, but there have been those through the sad years who believed in justice and mercy and charity and love and kindliness, and there have been those who believed that a black man should have some rights, even in a country where he was brought in chains. There are those even crazy enough to hope and to dream that sometime he will come from under this cloud and take his place amongst the people of the world. If he does, it will be through his courage and his culture. It will be by his intelligence and his scholarship and his effort, and I say, gentlemen of the jury, no honest, right feeling man, whether on a jury, or anywhere else, would place anything in his way in this great struggle behind him and before him.

. . . .

Let us be honest about it. There are people who buy themselves a little home and think the value of it would go down if colored people come. Perhaps it would. I don't know. I am not going to testify in this case. It may go down and it may go up. It will probably go down for some purposes and go up for others. I don't know. Suppose it does? What of it? I am sorry for anybody whose home depreciates in value. Still, you cannot keep up a government for the purpose of making people's homes valuable. Noise will depreciate the value of a house, and sometimes a street car line will do it. A public school will do it. People do not like a lot of children around their house. That is one reason why they send them to school. You cannot get as much for your property. Livery stables used to do it; garages do it now. Any kind of noise will do it. No man can buy a house and be sure that somebody will not depreciate its value. Something may enhance its value, of course. We are always willing to take the profit, but not willing to take the loss. Those are incidents of civilization. We get that because we refuse to live with our fellowman, that is all.

Look at the Negro's side of it. You remember Dancy. Did you ever see a brighter man than he? Compare him with Miller. Compare him with Miss S-t-o-w-e-l-l. Compare him with Andrews. Compare him with anybody on their side of this case. There isn't any comparison. Dancy is colored. He is the head of the Urban League, branch of the association of charities. His business is to look after the poor blacks, the ones who need it.

He told you how hard it was for colored people to find homes. Do I need to say anything about it? You, gentlemen, are here and you want to do right. Are any of you going to invite colored people to live next door to you? No. Would it hurt you? Not at all. Prejudice is so deep that it might affect the value of your property for sale purposes. Let me ask you, would not any of you like to meet Dancy? Who would you rather meet for companionship and association and fellowship, Dancy or some of the gophers up around "Goffee" Street as some call it? I know who you would rather meet.

. . . .

What are you, gentlemen? And what am I? I don't know. I can only go a little way toward the source of my own being. I know my father and I know my mother. I knew my great-grandmothers and my grandfathers on both sides, but I didn't know my great-grandfathers and great-grandmothers on either side, and I don't know who they were. All that a man can do in this direction is but little. He can only slightly raise the veil that hangs over all the past. He can peer into the darkness just a little way and that is all. I know that somewhere around 1600, as the record goes, some of my ancestors came from England. Some of them. I don't know where all of them came from, and I don't think any human being knows where all his ancestors came from. But back of that, I can say nothing. What do you know of yours?

. . . .

Gentlemen, I wonder who we are anyhow, to be so proud about our ancestry? We had better try to do something to be proud of ourselves; we had better try to do something kindly, something humane, to some human being, than to brag about our ancestry, of which none of us know anything.

. . . .

Imagine yourselves colored, gentlemen. Imagine yourselves back in the Sweet house on that fatal night. That is the only right way to treat this case, and the court will tell you so. Would you move there? Where would you move? Dancy says there were six or seven thousand colored people here sixteen years ago. And seventy-one thousand five years ago. Gentlemen, why are they here? They came here as you came here, under the laws of trade and business, under the instincts to live; both the white and the colored, just the same; the instincts of all animals to propagate their kind, the feelings back of life and on which life depends. They came here to live. Your factories were open for them. Mr. Ford hired them. The automobile companies hired them. Everybody hired them. They were all willing to give them work, weren't they? Every one of them.

You and I are willing to give them work, too. We are willing to have them in our houses to take care of the children and do the rough work that we shun ourselves. They are not offensive, either. We invited them; pretty nearly all the colored population has come to Detroit in the last fifteen years; most of them, anyhow. . . .

The colored people must live somewhere. Everybody is willing to have them live somewhere else. The people at the corner of Garland and Charlevoix would be willing to have them go to some other section. They would be willing to have them buy a place up next to Mrs. Dodge's house; but most of them haven't got money enough to do that; none that I know of. Everybody would be willing to have them go somewhere else.

Somewhere they must live. Are you going to kill them? Are you going to say that they can work, but they can't get a place to sleep? They can toil in the mill, but can't eat their dinner at home. We want them to build automobiles for us, don't we? We even let them become our chauffeurs. Oh, gentlemen, what is the use! You know it is wrong. Everyone of you know it is wrong. You know that no man in conscience could blame a Negro for almost anything. Can you think of these people without shouldering your own responsibility? Don't make it harder for them, I beg you.

They sent four policemen in the morning to help this little family move in. They had a bedstead, a stove and some bedding, ten guns and some ammunition, and they had food to last them through a siege. I feel that they should have taken less furniture and more food and guns.

. . . .

Now, let us get to the bare facts in this case. The City of Detroit had the police force there to help these people move into their home. When they unloaded their goods, men and women on the street began going from house to house. This club got busy. They went from house to house to sound the alarm, "the Negroes are coming," as if a foreign army was invading their homes; as if a wild beast had come down out of the mountains in the olden times.

I am not going over it fully. Two attractive, clever girls, who have color in their faces, without using paint, stayed at the Sweets' that night, the 8th, because they did not dare go home. Can you imagine those colored people? They didn't dare move without thinking of their color. Where we go into a hotel unconsciously, or a church, if we choose, they do not. Of course, colored people belong to a church, and they have a Y.M.C.A. That is, a Jim Crow Y.M.C.A. The black Christians cannot mix with the white Christians. They will probably have a Jim Crow Heaven where the white angels will not be obliged to meet the black angels, except as servants.

These girls went out to the Sweets' house and were marooned, and did not dare to go home on account of the crowd on the streets. Was there a crowd? Schuknecht says there were more on the streets on the 8th than the 9th. Of course, I don't believe him, but he says there were more automobiles on the 9th. The papers had advertised that the colored people had come, and over on Tireman Avenue they were busy gathering the clans to help out the Nordic brother of Charlevoix and Garland.

On the 9th, what happened? I have told you something about the crowd. Are our witnesses telling the truth, or are they lying? . . .

. . . .

I will call your attention a minute to witnesses we have brought here. Those two were white. There is another white witness. That is this motherly, attractive, Mrs. Hinteys; I don't worry about her at all. My friends of the prosecution tried to say some things about her, not so very unkindly. I don't know as I would say unkindly at all, but rather arouse suspicion in your minds as to the truth of her story . . . .

. . . .

Is the old lady telling the truth? She is the kind we don't see as much of now as we once did see. She is the working woman. Of course, you don't see them very much except when you come in the house and visit the kitchen. But I am older than most of you, I guess, than any of you. Anyway, I have seen them. A woman with a fine face. She probably would have called that "Goethy" Street, like the rest, because she hasn't much education. She isn't like the rest of the mob. A fine, honest face. She knew exactly what she was talking about and she told the truth. As I looked at her on the witness stand, it seemed to me that I could see through her face; her face covered with the scars of life, and fight, and hard work, to the inward beauty that shone through it. I could almost feel the years slipping away from me and leaving me a boy again in the simple country town where I was born; I could see my mother and her companions who swept their own houses, did their own washing and baked their own bread and made clothes for the children; they were kind, simple, human and honest.

There isn't a man on this jury who could be persuaded to believe that this woman wasn't honest. She said there were five hundred people on the corner alone. Is there any doubt about that? She said "more than five hundred." She said "twice as many as there are in this room."

Now let's see what Schuknecht said, and then I shall skip a little. I know you wish I would skip a lot more. There were certain things that did happen that night, weren't there? There was a crowd there. They began coming as the dusk gathered. They don't work in the daylight; not those fellows. They are too good for daylight work. They came as the dusk gathered. They came in taxis and automobiles and on foot. They came on every street that centered at Charlevoix; they came down the sidewalk and over across the street, where they gathered in that schoolyard; the schoolyard, gentlemen, of all the places on earth; the schoolyard where they made their deadly assault upon justice and honesty and law, and they were gathered there five hundred strong. Still this was no doubt the only occasion that most of them had ever needed a schoolhouse.

Schuknecht stood out in front, didn't he? He had this in charge. I don't need to go beyond the witnesses who appeared here for the State. He stood there on that corner, in front of the schoolhouse....

. . . .

What was Schuknecht doing? Now, gentlemen, let us see about that again. I never say much about policemen.

MR. TOMS: What was that?

MR. DARROW: I never say much about policemen. Do I?

MR. TOMS: That is what you said, but I couldn't believe it.

MR. DARROW: I am going to be very easy on Schuknecht. I have often seen good policemen. I mean, good men who were policemen. But, now, Schuknecht said that he had this matter in his charge. Didn't he? He stood right there on the corner. He did wander a little bit, but not much; inside of the block all the time, knowing that the whole responsibility rested on him. He had eight men early in that evening besides himself; and another officer. That made ten; and then as the night wore on, and the darkness began to gather, the darkness and the crowd came down together on those four corners.

They sent for two more policemen. Then they put policemen on the four corners a block away and blocked the street. For what? There wasn't any crowd there. Nobody says it was a crowd, unless they are lying; just a "few"; a "few"; and they blocked the streets. Gentlemen, none of you look like you were born yesterday. Maybe you were; I cannot tell. And then a little later, what happened? They sent for two more policemen. At the station they had twenty or thirty in reserve waiting for a riot call. Didn't they? They had ten or twelve policemen, twenty or thirty waiting for a riot call, and they sent up for two more, in a hurry, and they hustled down.

And then two policemen were sent to the top of that flat across the way, where they could "view the landscape" o'er the highest point of vantage, which, of course, would be used to protect the civilization and culture of Charlevoix Avenue; and they had just got started to go to the top of the flat when they sent for six more.

Gentlemen, six more policemen, making some fifteen or eighteen policemen around that corner. Was there any need of it? It was perfectly peaceful. Only four people on the schoolhouse grounds, according to some of them. Nothing doing. All quiet on the Potomac; warm summer evening, and the children lying on the lawn. Children, gentlemen, children. There might have been some children earlier in the evening, but they had all been gathered under their mothers' wings before that time, and most of the women had disappeared. Just before these fatal shots were fired. Why were the policemen there?

. . . .

Gentlemen, supposing you return a verdict of not guilty in this case, which you will; I would be ashamed to think you would not; what would happen if this man and his wife and his child, moved into that house? They have the same right to go to that house that you have to your home, after your services are done. What will happen? Don't you know? What did Schuknecht say? Eight or ten policemen were standing around that house for two days and two nights. A menacing crowd was around them, wasn't there? The police were protecting them. Did one policeman ever go to one person in that crowd and say: "What are you here for?"

. . . .

Schuknecht was standing there; five or six others were standing there, weren't they, gentlemen? Let us see how closely they were guarding the house. They did nothing. They heard no stones thrown against that house; not one of them; and yet they were not twenty feet away. The State brought here some twenty stones gathered next morning from the house and yard, and nobody knows how many more there were. Gentlemen, a roof slopes at an incline of forty-five degrees, or about that. You can get the exact figures if you want them. Imagine some one throwing stones against the roof. How many of them would stay there, or how many of them would stay in the immediate yard, and how many of them would be left there after the mob had finished and sought to protect itself, and the police and crowd had gathered them up, the police force which was responsible for this tragedy? None of them heard a stone, and yet they were there to protect that home. None of them heard the broken glass, but they were there to protect that home. None of them saw two men come in a taxi, except one who hesitated and finally admitted that it seemed as if he did; but none of the rest. Gentlemen, you could have looted that house and moved it away and the police would never have known it. That is the way these people were protected.

[Break for lunch.]

. . . .

Oh, they say, there is nothing to justify this shooting; it was an orderly, neighborly crowd; an orderly, neighborly crowd. They came there for a purpose and intended to carry it out. How long, pray, would these men wait penned up in that house? How long would you wait? The very presence of the crowd was a mob, as I believe the Court will tell you.

Suppose a crowd gathers around your house; a crowd which doesn't want you there; a hostile crowd, for a part of two days and two nights, until the police force of the city is called in to protect you. How long, tell me, are you going to live in that condition with a mob surrounding your house and the police-force standing in front of it? How long should these men have waited? I can imagine why they waited as long as they did. You wouldn't have waited. Counsel say they had just as good reason to shoot on the 8th as on the 9th. Concede it. They did not shoot. They waited and hoped and prayed that in some way this crowd would pass them by and grant them the right to live.

The mob came back the next night and the colored people waited while they were gathering; they waited while they were coming from every street and every corner, and while the officers were supine and helpless and doing nothing. And they waited until dozens of stones were thrown against the house on the roof, probably—don't know how many. Nobody knows how many. They waited until the windows were broken before they shot. Why did they wait so long? I think I know. How much chance had these people for their life after they shot; surrounded by a crowd, as they were? They would never take a chance unless they thought it was necessary to take the chance. Eleven black people penned up in the face of a mob. What chance did they have?

Suppose they shot before they should. What is the theory of counsel in this case? Nobody pretends there is anything in this case to prove that our client Henry fired the fatal shot. There isn't the slightest. It wasn't a shot that would fit the gun he had. The theory of this case is that he was a part of a combination to do something. Now, what was that combination, gentlemen? Your own sense will tell you what it was. Did they combine to go there and kill somebody? Were they looking for somebody to murder?

Dr. Sweet scraped together his small earnings by his industry and put himself through college, and he scraped together his small earnings of three thousand dollars to buy that home because he wanted to kill somebody? It is silly to talk about it. He bought that home just as you buy yours, because he wanted a home to live in, to take his wife and to raise his family. There is no difference between the love of a black man for his offspring and the love of a white. He and his wife had the same feeling of fatherly and motherly affection for their child that you gentlemen have for yours, and that your father and mother had for you. They bought that home for that purpose; not to kill somebody.

They might have feared trouble, as they probably did, and as the evidence shows that every man with a black face fears it, when he moved into a home that is fit for a dog to live in. It is part of the curse that, for some inscrutable reason, has followed the race—if you call it a race—and which curse, let us hope, sometime the world will be wise enough and decent enough and human enough to wipe out.

They went there to live. They knew the dangers. Why do you suppose they took these guns and this ammunition and these men there? Because they wanted to kill somebody? It is utterly absurd and crazy. They took them there because they thought it might be necessary to defend their home with their lives and they were determined to do it. They took guns there that in case of need they might fight, fight even to death for their home, and for each other, for their people, for their race, for their rights under the Constitution and the laws under which all of us live; and unless men and women will do that, we will soon be a race of slaves, whether we are black or white. "Eternal vigilance is the price of liberty," and it has always been so and always will be. Do you suppose they were in there for any other purpose? Gentlemen, there isn't a chance that they took arms there for anything else.

They did go there knowing their rights, feeling their responsibility, and determined to maintain those rights if it meant death to the last man and the last woman, and no one could do more. No man lived a better life or died a better death than fighting for his home and his children, for himself, and for the eternal principles upon which life depends. Instead of being here under indictment, for murder, they should be honored for the brave stand they made, for their rights and ours. Some day, both white and black, irrespective of color, will honor the memory of these men, whether they are inside prison-walls or outside, and will recognize that they fought not only for themselves, but for every man who wishes to be free.

Did they shoot too quick? Tell me just how long a man needs wait for a mob? The Court, I know, will instruct you on that. How long do you need to wait for a mob?

. . . .

This isn't a case of a man who trespasses upon the ground of some other man and is killed. It is the case of an unlawful mob, which in itself is a crime; a mob bent on mischief; a mob that has no rights. They are too dangerous. It is like a fire. One man may do something. Two will do much more; three will do more than three times as much; a crowd will do something that no man ever dreamed of doing. The law recognizes it. It is the duty of every man—I don't care who he is, to disperse a mob. It is the duty of the officers to disperse them. It was the duty of the inmates of the house, even though they had to kill somebody to do it. Now, gentlemen, I wouldn't ask you to take the law on my statement. The Court will tell you the law. A mob is a criminal combination of itself. Their presence is enough. You need not wait until it spreads. It is there, and that is enough. There is no other law; there hasn't been for years, and it is the law which will govern this case.

. . . .

Here is Henry Sweet, the defendant in this case, a boy. How many of you know why you are trying him? What had he to do with it? Why is he in this case? A boy, twenty-one years old, working his way through college, and he is just as good a boy as the boy of any juror in this box; just as good a boy as you people were when you were boys, and I submit to you, he did nothing whatever that was wrong.

Of course, we lawyers talk and talk and talk, as if we feared results. I don't mean to trifle with you. I always fear results. When life or liberty is in the hands of a lawyer, he realizes the terrible responsibility that is on him, and he fears that some word will be left unspoken, or some thought will be forgotten. I would not be telling you the truth if I told you that I did not fear the result of this important case; and when my judgment and my reason come to my aid and take counsel with my fears, I know, and I feel perfectly well that no twelve American jurors, especially in any northern land, could be brought together who would dream of taking a boy's life or liberty under circumstances like this. That is what my judgment tells me, but my fears perhaps cause me to go further and to say more when I should not have said as much.

Now, let me tell you when a man has the right to shoot in self-defense, and in defense of his home; not when these vital things in life are in danger, but when he thinks they are. These despised blacks did not need to wait until the house was beaten down above their heads. They didn't need to wait until every window was broken. They didn't need to wait longer for that mob to grow more inflamed. There is nothing so dangerous as ignorance and bigotry when it is unleashed as it was here. The Court will tell you that these inmates of this house had the right to decide upon appearances, and if they did, even though they were mistaken they are not guilty. I don't know but they could safely have stayed a little longer. I don't know but it would have been well enough to let this mob break a few more window-panes. I don't know but it would have been better and been safe to have let them batter down the house before they shot. I don't know.

How am I to tell, and how are you to tell? You are twelve white men, gentlemen. You are twelve men sitting here eight months after all this occurred, listening to the evidence, perjured and otherwise, in this court, to tell whether they acted too quickly or too slowly. A man may be running an engine out on the railroad. He may stop too quickly or too slowly. In an emergency he is bound to do one or the other, and the jury a year after, sitting in cold blood, may listen to the evidence and say that he acted too quickly. What do they know about it? You must sit out there upon a moving engine with your hand on the throttle and facing danger and must decide and act quickly. Then you can tell.

Cases often occur in the courts, which doesn't speak very well for the decency of courts, but they have happened, where men have been shipwrecked at sea, a number of the men having left the ship and gone into a small boat to save their lives; they have floated around for hours and tossed on the wild waves of an angry sea; their food disappearing, the boat heavy and likely to sink and no friendly sail in sight—What are they to do? Will they throw some of their companions off the boat and save the rest? Will they eat some to save the others? If they kill anybody, it is because they want to live. Every living thing wants to live. The strongest instinct in life is to keep going. You have seen a tree upon a rock send a shoot down for ten or fifteen or twenty feet, to search for water, to draw it up, that it may still survive; it is a strong instinct with animals and with plants, with all sentient things, to keep alive.

Men are out in a boat, in an angry sea, with little food, and less water. No hope in sight. What will they do? They throw a companion overboard to save themselves, or they kill somebody to save themselves. Juries have come into court and passed on the question of whether they should have waited longer, or not. Later, the survivors were picked up by a ship and perhaps, if they had waited longer, all would have been saved; yet a jury, months after it was over, sitting safely in their jury box, pass upon the question of whether they acted too quickly or not.

Can they tell? No. To decide that case, you must be in a small boat, with little food and water; in a wild sea, with no sail in sight, and drifting around for hours or days in the face of the deep, beset by hunger and darkness and fear and hope. Then you can tell; but, no man can tell without it. It can't be done, gentlemen, and the law says so, and this Court will tell you so.

. . . .

The first instinct a man has is to save his life. He doesn't need to experiment. He hasn't time to experiment. When he thinks it is time to save his life, he has the right to act. There isn't any question about it. It has been the law of every English speaking country so long as we have had law. Every man's home is his castle, which even the King may not enter. Every man has a right to kill to defend himself or his family, or others, either in the defense of the home or in the defense of themselves.

So far as that branch of the case is concerned, there is only one thing that this jury has a right to consider, and that is whether the defendants acted in honest fear of danger. That is all. Perhaps they could have safely waited longer. I know a little about psychology. If I could talk to a man long enough, and not too long, and he talk to me a little, I could guess fairly well what is going on in his head, but I can't understand the psychology of a mob, and neither can anybody else. We know it is unreasoning. We know it is filled with hatred. We know it is cruel. We know it has no heart, no soul, and no pity. We know it is as cruel as the grave. No man has a right to stop and dicker while waiting for a mob.

. . . .

What do you think about it? Suppose you were black. Do you think you would forget it even in your dreams? Or would you have black dreams? Suppose you had to watch every point of contact with your neighbor and remember your color, and you knew your children were growing up under this handicap. Do you suppose you would think of anything else?

Well, gentlemen, I imagine that a colored man would think of that before he would think of where he could get bootleg whiskey, even. Do you suppose this boy coming in here didn't know all about the conditions, and did not learn all about them? Did he not know about Detroit? Do you suppose he hadn't read the story of his race? He is intelligent. He goes to school. He would have been a graduate now, except for this long hesitation, when he is waiting to see whether he goes back to college or goes to jail. Do you suppose that black students and teachers are discussing it?

Anyhow, gentlemen, what is the use? The jury isn't supposed to be entirely ignorant. They are supposed to know something. These black people were in the house with the black man's psychology, and with the black man's fear, based, on what they had heard and what they had read and what they knew. I don't need to go far. I don't need to travel to Florida. I don't even need to talk about the Chicago riots. The testimony showed that in Chicago a colored boy on a raft had been washed to a white bathing beach, and men and boys of my race stoned him to death. A riot began, and some hundred and twenty were killed.

. . . .

I was told there had not been a lynching of a colored man in thirty years or more in Michigan. All right. Why, I can remember when the early statesmen of Michigan cared for the colored man and when they embodied the rights of the colored men in the constitution and statutes. I can remember when they laid the foundation that made it possible for a man of any color or any religion, or any creed, to own his home wherever he could find a man to sell it. I remember when civil rights laws were passed that gave the Negro the right to go where the white man went and as he went. There are some men who seem to think those laws were wrong. I do not. Wrong or not, it is the law, and if you were black you would protest with every fiber of your body your right to live.

Michigan used to protect the rights of colored people. There were not many of them here, but they have come in the last few years, and with them has come prejudice. Then, too, the southern white man has followed his black slave. But that isn't all. Black labor has come in competition with white. Prejudices have been created where there was no prejudice before. We have listened to the siren song that we are a superior race and have superior rights, and that the black man has none.

It is a new idea in Detroit that a colored man's home can be torn down about his head because he is black. There are some eighty thousand blacks here now, and they are bound to reach out. They have reached out in the past, and they will reach out in the future. Do not make any mistake, gentlemen. I am making no promises. I know the instinct for life. I know it reaches black and white alike. I know that you cannot confine any body of people to any particular place, and, as the population grows, the colored people will go farther. I know it, and you must change the law or you must take it as it is, or you must invoke the primal law of nature and get back to clubs and fists, and if you are ready for that, gentlemen, all right, but do it with your eyes open. That is all I care for. You must have a government of law or blind force, and if you are ready to let blind force take the place of law, the responsibility is on you, not on me.

Now, let us see what has happened here. So far as I know, there had been nothing of the sort happened when Dr. Sweet bought his home. He took an option on it in May, and got his deed in June; and in July, in that one month, while he was deliberating on moving, there were three cases of driving Negro families out of their homes in Detroit. This was accomplished by stones, clubs, guns and mobs.

. . . .

They determined to move in and to take nine men with them. What would you have done, gentlemen? If you had courage, you would have done as Dr. Sweet did. You would have been crazy or a coward if you hadn't. Would you have moved in alone? No, you would not have gone alone. You would have taken your wife. If you had a brother or two, you would have taken them because you would know, that you could rely on them, and you would have taken those nearest to you. And you would have moved in just as Dr. Sweet did. Wouldn't you? He didn't shoot the first night. He didn't look for trouble. He kept his house dark so that the neighbors wouldn't see him. He didn't dare have a light in his house, gentlemen, for fear of the neighbors. Noble neighbors, who were to have a colored family in their neighborhood. He had the light put out in the front part of the house, so as not to tempt any of the mob to violence.

Now, let us go back a little. What happened before this? I don't need to go over the history of the case. Everybody who wants to understand knows it, and many who don't want to understand it. As soon as Dr. Sweet bought this house, the neighbors organized the "Water Works Park Improvement Association." They made a constitution and by-laws. You may read the constitution and by-laws of every club, whether it is the Rotary Club or the—I was trying to think of some other club, but I can't. Whatever the club, it must always have a constitution and by-laws. These are all about the same. You cannot tell anything about a man by the church he belongs to. You can't tell anything about him by the kind of clothes he wears. You can't tell anything about him by any of these extraneous matters, and you can't tell anything about an association from the by-laws. Not a thing. I belonged to associations in my time. As far as I can remember, they all had by-laws.

MR. TOMS: All of them have the same by-laws?

MR. DARROW: Yes, all have the same. They are all of them engaged in the work of uplifting humanity, and humanity still wants to stay down. All engaged in the same work, according to their by-laws, gentlemen. So, the "Water Works Park Improvement Club" had by-laws. They were going to aid the police. They didn't get a chance to try to aid them until that night. They were going to regulate automobile traffic. They didn't get any chance to regulate automobile traffic until that night. They were going to protect the homes and make them safe for children.

The purpose was clear, and every single member reluctantly said that they joined it to keep colored people out of the district. They might have said it first as well as last. People, even in a wealthy and aristocratic neighborhood like Garland and Charlevoix, don't give up a dollar without expecting some profit; not a whole dollar. Sometimes two in one family, the husband and wife, joined.

They got in quick. The woods were on fire. Something had to be done, as quick as they heard that Dr. Sweet was coming; Dr. Sweet, who had been a bellhop on a boat, and a bellhop in hotels, and fired furnaces and sold popcorn and has worked his way with his great handicap through school and through college, and graduated as a doctor, and gone to Europe and taken another degree; Dr. Sweet, who knew more than any man in the neighborhood ever would know or ever want to know. He deserved more for all he had done. When they heard he was coming, then it was time to act, and act together, for the sake of their homes, their families and their firesides, and so they got together. They didn't wait. A meeting was called in the neighborhood; we haven't a record of that, but we have a record of another one.

And then, what happened after that? Let me read you, not from the books of any organization; not from colored people; from what I have learned is a perfectly respectable paper, so far as papers go, the *Detroit Free Press*.

MR. TOMS: *Free Press*, the best morning paper.

MR. DARROW: And the only real Free Press that I ever heard of. On July 12th, gentlemen, a month after Dr. Sweet had bought his home, this appears in the paper, the headlines: "Stop Rioting." "Smith Pleads with Citizens. Detroit Faces Shame and Disgrace as the Result of Fighting, he states." "Negro, held for shooting youth, vacates residence under police guard."

Here is the story, not published in colored papers:

"While Detroit police were anticipating further outbreaks near the homes occupied by Negroes in white residential areas and had full complements of reserves in readiness to deal with any situation that might arise, Mayor John W. Smith late yesterday issued a statement asking the public to see that the riots 'do not grow into a condition which will be a lasting stain on the reputation of Detroit as a law-abiding community.'

"The storm centers are considered to be American and Tireman Avenues where Vollington A. Bristol, Negro undertaker still occupies the home he recently purchased there in the teeth of demonstrations on three successive nights and a residence on Prairie Avenue, near Grand River Avenue.

ONE NEGRO MOVES

"John W. Fletcher, 9428 Stoepel Avenue, two blocks from Livernois and Plymouth Avenue, the Negro who is to be charged with causing grievous bodily harm in connection with the shooting of a white youth, Leonard Paul, 15 years old, 9567 Prairie Avenue, Friday night, relieved the situation in his district by moving out yesterday after less than forty-eight hours tenancy. Six patrolmen, under Lieutenant A.R. Saal of the Petosky Avenue Station, were at hand as Fletcher moved his furniture over his brick-strewn lawn from the house in which not one window remained whole."

Gentlemen, what kind of feeling does it give a white man? It makes me ashamed of my race. Now, to go on:

"There was no trouble.

"Latest reports from Receiving Hospital indicates that the youth, Paul, who was twice shot in the hip by Fletcher, according to the latter's alleged statement, is still in a serious condition.

"Although no demonstrations were held up to a late hour last night, police guards will be maintained for an indefinite period about the three homes, it was announced. Two of the houses have been purchased and occupied by Negro families, and negotiations are under way for the purchase of the third by a Negro, according to rumors which have reached the police. The latter is on Prairie Avenue.

"The police armored car, which was conditioned early last week and has been held in readiness in case of trouble, last night was moved near the scene of the recent disturbances. It will remain for the present in the vicinity of Tireman and American Avenues. Every available policeman and detective, and fifty deputy sheriffs also have been detailed to the locality.

"A meeting, attended by more than ten thousand persons, was held on West Fourth Street, a mile west of Lincoln Park Village last night. A speaker from Tennessee advocated laws to compel Negroes to live only in certain quarters of the city."

I don't know whether he was one of the policemen who was up at the Sweet house. This speaker was from Tennessee.

"The only incident noted occurred when Bristol left this house. As he greeted Sergeant Welsh and two officers who stood on guard, an automobile passed by and swerved towards the pavement where the Negro was. The latter jumped back hurriedly, and the car kept on its way."

Mayor Smith's statement is as follows:

"Recent incidents of violence and attempted violence in connection with racial disagreements constitute a warning to the people of Detroit which they cannot afford to ignore. They are to be deplored, and it is a duty which rests as much upon the citizenry as upon the public officials to see that they do not grow into a condition which will be a lasting stain upon the reputation of Detroit as a law-abiding community.

"The police department can have but one duty in connection with all such incidents,—that is, to use its utmost endeavors to prevent the destruction of life and property. In the performance of this duty, I trust that every police officer will be unremitting in his efforts. The law recognizes no distinction in color or race. On all occasions when the emotions are deeply stirred by controversy, the persons affected on all sides of the dispute are likely to feel that the police or other controlling force are siding against them. I hope and believe that the police during the recent attempts to preserve law and order have done so impartially.

"With the police department doing its utmost to preserve order, there is always the possibility that uncontrolled elements may reach such proportions that even these efforts will not be completely effectual. It is that fact that calls for earnest cooperation by all good citizens at this time. Curiosity seekers who go to scenes of threatened disorder add immeasurably to the problem of preserving order. Thus, the persons innocent of ill intentions are likely to be chiefly responsible for inexcusable incidents.

"The condition which faces Detroit is one which faced Washington, East St. Louis, Chicago and other large cities. The result in those cities was one which Detroit must avoid, if possible. A single fatal riot would injure this city beyond remedy.

"The avoidance of further disorder belongs to the good sense of the leaders of thought in both white and colored races. The persons either white or colored who attempt to urge their fellows on to disorder and crime are guilty of the most serious offense upon the statute books. It is clear that a thoughtless individual of both races constitutes the nucleus in each disorder, and it is equally clear that the inspiration for their acts comes from malign influences which are willing to go even to the limits of bloodshed to gain their ends. The police are expected to inquire and prosecute any persons active in organizing such disorder or inciting a riot. The rest of the duty for preserving order lies with the individual citizens—by refraining from adding to the crowds in districts where danger exists, from refraining from discussion which may have a tendency to incite disorder, and finally to rebuke at once the individual agitators who are willing to risk human life, destroy property, and ruin their city's reputation.''

That is the Mayor's proclamation. The newspaper adds this: ''To maintain the high standard of the residential district between Jefferson and Mack Avenues, a meeting has been called by the Water Works Improvement Association for Thursday night in the Howe School auditorium. Men and women of the district, which includes Cadillac, Hurlburt, Bewick, Garland, St. Clair, and Harding Avenues, are asked to 'attend in self-defense.' ''

I shall not talk to you much longer. I am sorry I have talked so long. But this case is close to my heart. These colored people read this story in the paper. Do I need to go anywhere else to find the feeling of peril over the question of color? Dr. Sweet had to face the same proposition....

. . . .

Who are these people who were in this house? Were they people of character? Were they people of standing? Were they people of intelligence?

First, there was Doctor Sweet. Gentlemen, a white man does pretty well when he does what Doctor Sweet did. A white boy who can start in with nothing, and put himself through college, study medicine, taking post graduate work in Europe, earning every penny of it as he goes along, shoveling snow and coal, and working as a bellhop, on boats, working at every kind of employment that he can get to make his way, is some fellow.

But, Dr. Sweet has the handicap of the color of his face. And there is no handicap more terrible than that. Supposing you had your choice, right here this minute, would you rather lose your eyesight or become colored? Would you rather lose your hearing or be a Negro? Would you rather go out there on the street and have your leg cut off by a street car, or have a black skin?

I don't like to speak of it; I do not like to speak of it in the presence of these colored people, whom I have always urged to be as happy as they can. But, it is true, life is a hard game, anyhow. But, when the cards are stacked against you, it is terribly hard. And they are stacked against a race for no reason but that they are black.

Who are these men who were in this house? There was Doctor Sweet. There was his brother, who was a dentist. There was this young boy who worked his way for three years through college, with a little aid from his brother, and who was on his way to graduate. Henry's future is now in your hands. There was his companion, who was working his way through college,—all gathered in that house.

Were they hoodlums? Were they criminals? Were they anything except men who asked for a chance to live; who asked for a chance to breathe the free air and make their own way, earn their own living, and get their bread by the sweat of their brow?

I will read to you what the Mayor said. I will call your attention to one sentence in it again, and then let us see what the mob did. This was the Mayor of your City, whose voice should be heard, who speaks of the danger that is imminent to this city and to every other city in the north, a danger that may bear fruit at any time; and he called the attention of the public of this city to this great danger, gentlemen. And, I want to call your attention to it. Here is what he said:

> "The avoidance of further disorder belongs to the good sense of the leaders of thought of both white and colored races. The persons, either white or colored, who attempt to urge their fellows to disorder and crime, are guilty of the most serious offences upon the statute books."

. . . .

Gentlemen, these black men shot. Whether any bullets from their guns hit Breiner, I do not care. I will not discuss it. It is passing strange that the bullet that went through him, went directly through, not as if it was shot from some higher place. It was not the bullet that came from Henry Sweet's rifle; that is plain. It might have come from the house; I do not know, gentlemen, and I do not care. There are bigger issues in this case than that. The right to defend your home, the right to defend your person, is as sacred a right as any human being could fight for, and as sacred a cause as any jury could sustain.

That issue not only involves the defendants in this case, but it involves every man who wants to live, every man who wants freedom to work and to breathe; it is an issue worth fighting for, and worth dying for, it is an issue worth the attention of this jury, who have a chance that is given to few juries to pass upon a real case that will mean something in the history of a race.

These men were taken to the police station. Gentlemen, there was never a time that these black men's rights were protected in the least; never once. They had no rights—they are black. They were to be driven out of their home, under the law's protection. When they defended their home, they were arrested and charged with murder. They were taken to a police station, manacled. And they asked for a lawyer. And, every man, if he has any brains at all, asks for a lawyer when he is in the hands of the police. If he does not want to have a web woven around him, to entangle or ensnare him, he will ask for a lawyer. And, the lawyer's first aid to the injured always is, "Keep your mouth shut." It is not a case of whether you are guilty or not guilty. That makes no difference. "Keep your mouth shut." The police grabbed them, as is their habit. They got the County Attorney to ask questions.

What did they do? They did what everybody does, helpless, alone, and unadvised. They did not know, even, that anybody was killed. At least there is no evidence that they knew. But, they knew that they had been arrested for defending their own rights to live; and they were there in the hands of their enemies; and they told the best story they could think of at the time,—just as ninety-nine men out of a hundred always do. Whether they are guilty or not guilty makes no difference. But lawyers, and even policemen, should have protected their rights.

Some things that these defendants said were not true, as is always the case. The prosecutor read a statement from this boy, which is conflicting. In two places he says that he shot "over them." In another he said that he shot "at them." He probably said it in each place but the reporter probably got one of them wrong. But Henry makes it perfectly explicit, and when you go to your jury room and read it all, you will find that he does. In another place he said he shot to defend his brother's home and family. He says that in two or three places. You can also find he said that he shot so that they would run away, and leave them to eat their dinner. They are both there. These conflicting statements you will find in all cases of this sort. You always find them, where men have been sweated, without help, without a lawyer, groping around blindly, in the hands of the enemy, without the aid of anybody to protect their rights. Gentlemen, from the first to the last, there has not been a substantial right of these defendants that was not violated.

We come now and lay this man's case in the hands of a jury of our peers—the first defense and the last defense is the protection of home and life as provided by our law. We are willing to leave it here. I feel, as I look at you, that we will be treated fairly and decently, even understandingly and kindly. You know what this case is. You know why it is. You know that if white men had been fighting their way against colored men, nobody would ever have dreamed of a prosecution. And you know that, from the beginning of this case to the end, up to the time you write your verdict, the prosecution is based on race prejudice and nothing else.

. . . .

Gentlemen, you were called into this case by chance. It took us a week to find you, a week of culling out prejudice and hatred. Probably we did not cull it all out at that; but we took the best and the fairest that we could find. It is up to you.

Your verdict means something in this case: It means something, more than the fate of this boy. It is not often that a case is submitted to twelve men where the decision may mean a milestone in the progress of the human race. But this case does. And, I hope and I trust that you have a feeling of responsibility that will make you take it and do your duty as citizens of a great nation, and, as members of the human family, which is better still.

Let me say just a parting word for Henry Sweet, who has well nigh been forgotten. I am serious, but it seems almost like a reflection upon this jury to talk as if I doubted your verdict. What has this boy done? This one boy now that I am culling out from all of the rest, and whose fate is in your hands,—can you tell me what he has done? Can I believe myself? Am I standing in a Court of Justice, where twelve men on their oaths are asked to take away the liberty of a boy twenty-one years of age, who has done nothing more than what Henry Sweet has done?

Gentlemen, you may think he shot too quick; you may think he erred in judgment; you may think that Doctor Sweet should not have gone there, prepared to defend his home. But, what of this case of Henry Sweet? What has he done? I want to put it up to you, each one of you, individually. Doctor Sweet was his elder brother. He had helped Henry through school. He loved him. He had taken him into his home. Henry had lived with him and his wife; he had fondled his baby. The doctor had promised Henry money to go through school. Henry was getting his education, to take his place in the world, gentlemen—and this is a hard job. With his brother's help, he had worked himself through college up to the last year. The doctor had bought a home. He feared danger. He moved in with his wife and he asked this boy to go with him. And this boy went to help defend his brother, and his brother's wife and his child and his home.

Do you think more of him or less of him for that? I never saw twelve men in my life—and I have looked at a good many faces of a good many juries—I never saw twelve men in my life, that, if you could get them to understand a human case, were not true and right.

Should this boy have gone along and helped his brother? Or, should he have stayed away? What would you have done? And yet, gentlemen, here is a boy, and the President of his College came all the way here from Ohio to tell you what he thinks of him. His teachers have come here, from Ohio, to tell you what they think of him. The Methodist Bishop has come here to tell you what he thinks of him.

So, gentlemen, I am justified in saying that this boy is as kindly, as well disposed, as decent a man as any one of you twelve. Do you think he ought to be taken out of his school and sent to the penitentiary? All right, gentlemen, if you think so, do it. It is your job, not mine. If you think so, do it. But if you do, gentlemen, if you should ever look into the face of your own boy, or your own brother, or look into your own heart, you will regret it in sackcloth and ashes. You know, if he committed any offense, it was being loyal and true to his brother whom he loved. I know where you will send him, and it will not be to the penitentiary.

Now, gentlemen, just one more word, and I am through with this case. I do not live in Detroit. But I have no feeling against this city. In fact, I shall always have the kindest remembrance of it, especially if this case results as I think and feel that it will. I am the last one to come here to stir up race hatred, or any other hatred. I do not believe in the law of hate. I may not be true to my ideals always, but I believe in the law of love, and I believe you can do nothing with hatred. I would like to see a time when man loves his fellow man, and forgets his color or his creed. We will never be civilized until that time comes.

I know the Negro race has a long road to go. I believe the life of the Negro race has been a life of tragedy, of injustice, of oppression. The law has made him equal, but man has not. And, after all, the last analysis is, what has man done?—and not what has the law done? I know there is a long road ahead of him, before he can take the place which I believe he should take. I know that before him there is suffering, sorrow, tribulation and death among the blacks, and perhaps the whites. I am sorry. I would do what I could to avert it. I would advise patience; I would advise toleration; I would advise understanding; I would advise all of those things which are necessary for men who live together.

Gentlemen, what do you think is your duty in this case? I have watched, day after day, these black, tense faces that have crowded this court. These black faces that now are looking to you twelve whites, feeling that the hopes and fears of a race are in your keeping.

This case is about to end, gentlemen. To them, it is life. Not one of their color sits on this jury. Their fate is in the hands of twelve whites. Their eyes are fixed on you, their hearts go out to you, and their hopes hang on your verdict.

This is all. I ask you, on behalf of this defendant, on behalf of these helpless ones who turn to you, and more than that,—on behalf of this great state, and this great city which must face this problem, and face it fairly—I ask you, in the name of progress and of the human race, to return a verdict of not guilty in this case!

[The jury returned a verdict of not guilty.]

Notes

1. *Causation.* There is some indication that the fatal shot may not have come from the Sweet house. Why does Darrow downplay this issue?

2. *Analogy.* Darrow analogizes the Sweets to the passengers in a boat lost at sea. How long, he asks, must the passengers wait before attacking one another to sustain life? Is this a fair analogy to the Sweet situation? Why do you think Darrow made the analogy?

3. *The Tone of the Arguments.* To describe the *Sweet* speeches as confrontational is an understatement. Is this an effective method of presentation here? Compare the style of Mark Antony's speech in *Julius Caesar,* given below.

Each of the *Sweet* closing arguments was about seven hours long. Many of Darrow's arguments in other cases were longer. There is considerable repetition in the *Sweet* arguments. What is the effect of the length and repetition?

Darrow was a white man representing blacks before a jury of white men. He addressed the racial issues explicitly. Was Darrow's approach necessary?

Was it effective? Is his discourse on race relations dated? Are any aspects of it still valid?

Select a passage from the closing argument for class presentation. Explain the reasons for the tone of your presentation (emphases, pauses, voice modulations, etc.).

4. *The State's Reply.* Part of the argument of Attorney General Toms, state prosecutor, in the Henry Sweet case, is given by Arthur and Lila Weinberg in their biography, CLARENCE DARROW: A SENTIMENTAL REBEL (1980), at 347–48:

> Toms spoke for the prosecution. He took Darrow to task for characterizing most of the state's witnesses as "liars and cowardly curs.... We rather thought we had pretty decent people here in Detroit, but it took a Chicago lawyer to come here and tell us that the people of a whole neighborhood of our city are liars and cowardly curs."
>
> He asked the jury not to get "switched off" into philosophical speculations. "Let's not be persuaded into solving the Negro problem," he said. "It is not our place to decide if the Negro's ancestors have been rightly treated. We are here to learn why one man was killed, and for no other reason."
>
> "When Mr. Darrow says the Negro is in the hands of the enemy when he is in the hands of the police he isn't helping to solve the race problem. That doesn't fit his theory that man's love for his fellowman is the basis for the solution.
>
> "I do know we have got to occupy the same land together; we have got to be citizens of this land together. It's got to be done by mutual charity and forbearance, and by giving the colored man a chance by education to learn law.
>
> "I can't compete with this emotionalist from Chicago, neither verbally nor emotionally, but if you stick to the facts I have no fear of the outcome.
>
> "It takes more than Darrow's enunciation to make liars out of the whole neighborhood. Because people do not agree it does not mean they are testifying falsely. When 71 people, months after an event, cannot agree on every detail are they forever to be branded as liars?" Toms asked.
>
> "Remember, I admit that Dr. Sweet had a right to buy that house, where the trouble occurred. I grant he had the right to defend it against attack. But I also claim the right of people in the neighborhood to sit on their porches. I claim that citizens may exercise their rights without being shot at while doing so."
>
> Three hours and thirty-five minutes after the jury began deliberations, they reached a verdict. Toms's face flushed as the jury filed into the courtroom. Darrow gripped the arms of his chair. The foreman read, "Not guilty."

5. *Sequelae.* Arthur and Lila Weinberg, *supra* at 348–49, conclude their discussion of the *Sweet* cases:

To Judge Murphy, hearing Darrow's final summation was "the greatest experience" in his life. Although the judge saw his role in the Sweet case as merely "enforcing legal equality," Darrow felt that "it was the first time in all my career where a judge really tried to help, and displayed a sympathetic interest in saving poor devils from the extreme forces of the law, rather than otherwise."

Clarence "never mouths Christianity but always practices it," commented Judge Murphy.

The cost to the NAACP of both trials totaled $37,849. The organization published the complete text of Darrow's plea in the second trial because "of its historical, legal, and humanitarian value."

For more than a year the possibility of another trial haunted the defense. Finally, on July 21, 1927, the prosecutor moved to dismiss all charges against all defendants. The eleven blacks were free at last.

The Sweets never went back together to their home at Garland and Charlevoix. Tragedy stalked them the remainder of their years. Gladys and the child both died of tuberculosis within two years of Henry's acquittal. Fourteen years later Henry also fell victim to the disease. Ossian, twice married and twice divorced after Gladys's death, did move back to the house in 1930 and remained there for twenty-one years. In 1934 he ran as a Republican candidate for the State Senate, and in 1950 as a Democratic candidate for the U.S. Congress. He was defeated both times. He had two more court experiences: first, when he was fined for selling cigarettes without a license in a pharmacy he owned; later, to fight a paternity suit. Suffering intense pain from arthritis, Ossian fatally shot himself on March 19, 1960.

There was a short-lived utopia following Murphy's dismissal of the other charges. The badly bruised relationship between the whites and blacks seemed to have been mollified by the verdict, and for a time incidents between the two races decreased. Toms believed that whites would now be more inclined to recognize the inherent right of blacks to live where they chose.

Darrow said, "Prejudices have to be reckoned with as much as facts. And the whites cannot be held responsible for their prejudices for all of us are products of environment...." He cautioned blacks to "remember that it takes a long time to overcome habits and prejudices. Their progress is bound to be slow, but I feel that it will be sure. It will come by mutual understandings and consideration rather than legislation. I believe that the outcome of this case will be a benefit to the whites and the black men alike."

The optimism expressed by Darrow, Toms, and the judge was premature. The bitter riots of 1943 and 1967 in Detroit opened old wounds and created new ones. Darrow's concluding words in the second Sweet trial were ironic—and prophetic—commentaries.

The law had made the Negro equal, Darrow said then, "but man has not. And after all, the last analysis is, what has man done?—and not what has the law done? I know there is a long road ahead of him, before he can take the place which I believe he should take. I know that before him there is suffering, sorrow, tribulation and death among the blacks, and perhaps the whites. I am sorry. I would do what I could to avert it. I would advise patience; I would advise toleration; I would advise understanding; I would advise all of those things which are necessary for men who live together."

6. *The Present.* In August 2002 Dennis Archer was named president-elect of the 400,000–member American Bar Association. In 2003, he will become the first African–American president of that organization. Dennis Archer served as Mayor of Detroit from 1994–2001. How does Darrow's argument in the *Sweet* case foreshadow this development?

7. *Prejudice.* Darrow confronts his audience with observations about their racial prejudices. Does Darrow's argument reveal any prejudices of his own? Or must we attribute everything in the argument to Darrow's strategy as an advocate? What was the rhetorical purpose behind his repeated spelling of Ms. Stowell's name? Or his repeated (and varied) invocations of the witnesses' (mis)pronunciations of Goethe Street?

* * *

Besides being a consummate lawyer, Clarence Darrow was a highly sought-after lecturer. Although there are very fine recordings of his great contemporary, the tenor Enrico Caruso (1873–1921), there are no good recordings of any of the speeches of Clarence Darrow (1857–1938).

Arthur Weinberg, in *Attorney For the Damned* (1989), has collected many of Darrow's outstanding trial arguments and lectures, including his 1902 Chicago address on crime and criminals, his 1912 John Brown speech, many of his labor case arguments, and his arguments in the Leopold and Loeb case in 1924 and the Scopes trial in 1925.

The warden of the Cook County Jail, Chicago, knew Darrow as a criminologist, lawyer, and writer, and invited him to speak to the Cook County Jail prisoners in 1902. The following is the speech which Darrow gave to the inmates in response to that invitation.

ADDRESS TO THE PRISONERS IN THE COOK COUNTY JAIL
Clarence Darrow

If I looked at jails and crimes and prisoners in the way the ordinary person does, I should not speak on this subject to you. The reason I talk to you on the question of crime, its cause and cure, is because I really do not in the least believe in crime. There is no such thing as a crime as the word is generally understood. I do not believe there is any sort of distinction between the real moral condition of the people in and out of jail. One is just as good as the other. The people here can no more help being here than the people outside can avoid being outside. I do not believe that people are in jail because they deserve to be. They are in jail simply because they cannot avoid it on account of circumstances which are entirely beyond their control and for which they are in no way responsible.

I suppose a great many people on the outside would say I was doing you harm if they should hear what I say to you this afternoon, but you cannot be hurt a great deal anyway, so it will not matter. Good people outside would say that I was really teaching you things that were calculated to injure society, but it's worthwhile now and then to hear something different from what you ordinarily get from preachers and the like. These will tell you that you should be good and then you will get rich and be happy. Of course we know that people do not get rich by being good, and that is the reason why so many of you people try to get rich some other way, only you do not understand how to do it quite as well as the fellow outside.

There are people who think that everything in this world is an accident. But really there is no such thing as an accident. A great many folks admit that many of the people in jail ought not to be there, and many who are outside ought to be in. I think none of them ought to be here. There ought to be no jails, and if it were not for the fact that the people on the outside are so grasping and heartless in their dealings with the people on the inside, there would be no such institution as jails.

I do not want you to believe that I think all you people here are angels. I do not think that. You are people of all kinds, all of you doing the best you can, and that is evidently not very well—you are people of all kinds and conditions and under all circumstances. In one sense everybody is equally good and equally bad. We all do the best we can under the circumstances. But as to the exact things for which you are sent here, some of you are guilty and did the particular act because you needed the money. Some of you did it because you are in the habit of doing it, and some of you because you are born to it, and it comes to be as natural as it does, for instance, for me to be good.

Most of you probably have nothing against me, and most of you would treat me the same as any other person would; probably better than some of the people on the outside would treat me, because you think I believe in you and they know I do not believe in them. While you would not have the least thing against me in the world you might pick my pockets. I do not think all of you would, but I think some of you would. You would not have anything against me, but that's your profession, a few of you. Some of the rest of you, if my doors were unlocked, might come in if you saw anything you wanted—not out of malice to me, but because that is your trade. There is no doubt there are quite a number of people in this jail who would pick my pockets. And still I know this, that when I get outside pretty nearly everybody picks my pocket. There may be some of you who would hold up a man on the street, if you did not happen to have something else to do, and needed the money; but when I want to light my house or my office, the gas company holds me up. They charge me one dollar for something that is worth twenty-five cents, and still all these people are good people; they are pillars of society and support the churches, and they are respectable.

When I ride on the street cars, I am held up—I pay five cents for a ride that is worth two and a half cents, simply because a body of men have bribed the city council and the legislature, so that all the rest of us have to pay tribute to them.

If I do not wish to fall into the clutches of the gas trust and choose to burn oil instead of gas, then good Mr. Rockefeller holds me up, and he uses a certain portion of his money to build universities and support churches which are engaged in telling us how to be good.

Some of you are here for obtaining property under false pretenses— yet I pick up a great Sunday paper and read the advertisements of a merchant prince—" 'Shirt waists for 39 cents, marked down from $3.00.' "

When I read the advertisements in the paper I see they are all lies. When I want to get out and find a place to stand anywhere on the face of the earth, I find that it has all been taken up long ago before I came here, and before you came here, and somebody says, " 'Get off, swim into the lake, fly into the air; go anywhere, but get off.' " That is because these people have the police and they have the jails and judges and the lawyers and the soldiers and all the rest of them to take care of the earth and drive everybody off that comes in their way.

A great many people will tell you that all this is true, but that it does not excuse you. These facts do not excuse some fellow who reaches into my pocket and takes out a five dollar bill; the fact that the gas company bribes the members of the legislature from year to year, and fixes the law, so that all you people are compelled to be " 'fleeced' " whenever you deal with them; the fact that the street car companies and the gas companies have control of the streets and the fact that the landlords own all the earth, they say, has nothing to do with you.

Let us see whether there is any connection between the crimes of the respectable classes and your presence in the jail. Many of you people are in jail because you have really committed burglary. Many of you, because you have stolen something; in the meaning of the law, you have taken some other person's property. Some of you have entered a store and carried off a pair of shoes because you did not have the price. Possibly some of you have committed murder. I cannot tell what all of you did. There are a great many people here who have done some of these things who really do not know themselves why they did them. I think I know why you did them—every one of you; you did these things because you were bound to do them. It looked to you at the time as if you had a chance to do them or not, as you saw fit, but still after all you had no choice. There may be people here who had some money in their pockets and who still went out and got some more money in a way society forbids. Now you may not yourselves see exactly why it was you did this thing, but if you look at the question deeply enough and carefully enough you would see that there were circumstances that drove you to do exactly the thing which you did. You could not help it any more than we outside can help taking the positions that we take. The reformers who tell you to be good and you will be happy, and the people on the outside who have property to protect—they think that the only way to do it is by building jails and locking you up in cells on week days and praying for you Sundays.

I think that all of this has nothing whatever to do with right conduct. I think it is very easily seen what has to do with right conduct. Some so-called criminals—and I will use this word because it is handy, it means nothing to me—I speak of the criminals who get caught as distinguished from the criminals who catch them—some of these so-called criminals are in jail for the first offenses, but nine-tenths of you are in jail because you did not have a good lawyer and of course you did not have a good lawyer because you did not have enough money to pay a good lawyer. There is no very great danger of a rich man going to jail.

Some of you may be here for the first time. If we would open the doors and let you out, and leave the laws as they are today, some of you would be back tomorrow. This is about as good a place as you can get anyway. There are many people here who are so in the habit of coming that they would not know where else to go. There are people who are born with the tendency to break into jail every chance they get, and they cannot avoid it. You cannot figure out your life and see why it was, but still there is a reason for it, and if we were all wise and knew all the facts we could figure it out.

In the first place, there are a good many more people who go to jail in the winter time than in summer. Why is this? Is it because people are more wicked in winter? No, it is because the coal trust begins to get in its grip in the winter. A few gentlemen take possession of the coal, and unless the people will pay $7 or $8 a ton for something that is worth $3, they will have to freeze. Then there is nothing to do but break into jail, and so there are many more in jail in the winter than in summer. It costs more for gas in the winter because the nights are longer, and people go to jail to save gas bills. The jails are electric lighted. You may not know it, but these economic laws are working all the time, whether we know it or do not know it.

There are more people go to jail in hard times than in good times— few people comparatively go to jail except when they are hard up. They go to jail because they have no other place to go. They may not know why, but it is true all the same. People are not more wicked in hard times. That is not the reason. The fact is true all over the world that in hard times more people go to jail than in good times, and in winter more people go to jail than in summer. Of course it is pretty hard times for people who go to jail at any time. The people who go to jail are almost always poor people—people who have no other place to live first and last. When times are hard then you find large numbers of people who go to jail who would not otherwise be in jail.

Long ago Mr. Buckle, who was a great philosopher and historian, collected facts and he showed that the number of people who are arrested increased just as the price of food increased. When they put up the price of gas ten cents a thousand I do not know who will go to jail, but I do know that a certain number of people will go. When the meat combine raises the price of beef I do not know who is going to jail, but I know that a large number of people are bound to go. Whenever the Standard Oil Company raises the price of oil, I know that a certain number of girls who are seamstresses, and who work night after night long hours for somebody else, will be compelled to go out on the streets and ply another trade, and I know that Mr. Rockefeller and his associates are responsible and not the poor girls in the jails.

First and last, people are sent to jail because they are poor. Sometimes, as I say, you may not need money at the particular time, but you wish to have thrifty forehanded habits, and do not always wait until you are in absolute want. Some of you people are perhaps plying the trade, the profession, which is called burglary. No man in his right senses will go into a strange house in the dead of night and prowl around with a dark lantern through unfamiliar rooms and take chances of his life if he has plenty of the good things of the world in his own home. You would not take any such chances as that. If a man had clothes in his clothes-press and beefsteak in his pantry, and money in the bank, he would not navigate around nights in houses where he knows nothing about the premises whatever. It always requires experience and education for this profession, and people who fit themselves for it are no more to blame than I am for being a lawyer. A man would not hold up another man on the street if he had plenty of money in his own pocket. He might do it if he had one dollar or two dollars, but he wouldn't if he had as much money as Mr. Rockefeller has. Mr. Rockefeller has a great deal better hold-up game than that.

The more that is taken from the poor by the rich, who have the chance to take it, the more poor people there are who are compelled to resort to these means for a livelihood. They may not understand it, they may not think so at once, but after all they are driven into that line of employment.

There is a bill before the legislature of this State to punish kidnaping of children with death. We have wise members of the legislature. They know the gas trust when they see it and they always see it—they can furnish light enough to be seen, and this legislature thinks it is going to stop kidnaping of children by making a law punishing kidnapers of children with death. I don't believe in kidnaping children, but the legislature is all wrong. Kidnaping children is not a crime, it is a profession. It has been developed with the times. It has been developed with our modern industrial conditions. There are many ways of making money—many new ways that our ancestors knew nothing about. Our ancestors knew nothing about a billion dollar trust; and here comes some poor fellow who has no other trade and he discovers the profession of kidnaping children.

This crime is born, not because people are bad; people don't kidnap other people's children because they want the children or because they are devilish, but because they see a chance to get some money out of it. You cannot cure this crime by passing a law punishing by death kidnapers of children. There is one way to cure it. There is one way to cure all these offenses, and that is to give the people a chance to live. There is no other way, and there never was any other way since the world began, and the world is so blind and stupid that it will not see. If every man and woman and child in the world had a chance to make a decent, fair, honest living, there would be no jails, and no lawyers and no courts. There might be some persons here or there with some peculiar formation of their brain, like Rockefeller, who would do these things simply to be doing them; but they would be very, very few, and those should be sent to a hospital and treated, and not sent to jail, and they would entirely disappear in the second generation, or at least in the third generation.

I am not talking pure theory. I will just give you two or three illustrations.

The English people once punished criminals by sending them away. They would load them on a ship and export them to Australia. England was owned by lords and nobles and rich people. They owned the whole earth over there, and the other people had to stay in the streets. They could not get a decent living. They used to take their criminals and send them to Australia—I mean the class of criminals who got caught. When these criminals got over there, and nobody else had come, they had the whole continent to run over, and so they could raise sheep and furnish their own meat, which is easier than stealing it; these criminals then became decent, respectable people because they had a chance to live. They did not commit any crimes. They were just like the English people who sent them there, only better. And in the second generation the descendants of those criminals were as good and respectable a class of people as there were on the face of the earth, and then they began building churches and jails themselves.

A portion of this country was settled in the same way, landing prisoners down on the southern coast; but when they got here and had a whole continent to run over and plenty of chances to make a living, they became respectable citizens, making their own living just like any other citizen in the world; but finally these descendants of the English aristocracy, who sent the people over to Australia, found out they were getting rich, and so they went over to get possession of the earth as they always do, and they organized land syndicates and got control of the land and ores, and then they had just as many criminals in Australia as they did in England. It was not because the world had grown bad; it was because the earth had been taken away from the people.

Some of you people have lived in the country. It's prettier than it is here. And if you have ever lived on a farm you understand that if you put a lot of cattle in a field, when the pasture is short they will jump over the fence; but put them in a good field where there is plenty of pasture, and they will be law-abiding cattle to the end of time. The human animal is just like the rest of the animals, only a little more so. The same thing that governs in the one governs in the other.

Everybody makes his living along the lines of least resistance. A wise man who comes into a country early sees a great undeveloped land. For instance, our rich men twenty-five years ago saw that Chicago was small and knew a lot of people would come here and settle, and they readily saw that if they had all the land around here it would be worth a good deal, so they grabbed the land. You cannot be a landlord because somebody has got it all. You must find some other calling. In England and Ireland and Scotland less than five percent own all the land there is, and the people are bound to stay there on any kind of terms the landlords give. They must live the best they can, so they develop all these various professions—burglary, picking pockets and the like.

Again, people find all sorts of ways of getting rich. These are diseases like everything else. You look at people getting rich, organizing trusts, and making a million dollars, and somebody gets the disease and he starts out. He catches it just as a man catches the mumps or the measles; he is not to blame, it is in the air. You will find men speculating beyond their means, because the mania of money-getting is taking possession of them. It is simply a disease; nothing more, nothing less. You cannot avoid catching it; but the fellows who have control of the earth have the advantage of you. See what the law is; when these men get control of things, they make the laws. They do not make the laws to protect anybody; courts are not instruments of justice; when your case gets into court it will make little difference whether you are guilty or innocent; but it's better if you have a smart lawyer. And you cannot have a smart lawyer unless you have money. First and last it's a question of money. Those men who own the earth make the laws to protect what they have. They fix up a sort of fence or pen around what they have, and they fix the law so the fellow on the outside cannot get in. The laws are really organized for the protection of the men who rule the world. They were never organized or enforced to do justice. We have no system for doing justice, not the slightest in the world.

Let me illustrate: Take the poorest person in this room. If the community had provided a system of doing justice the poorest person in this room would have as good a lawyer as the richest, would he not? When you went into court you would have just as long a trial, and just as fair a trial as the richest person in Chicago. Your case would not be tried in fifteen or twenty minutes, whereas it would take fifteen days to get through with a rich man's case.

Then if you were rich and were beaten your case would be taken to the Appellate Court. A poor man cannot take his case to the Appellate Court; he has not the price; and then to the Supreme Court, and if he were beaten there he might perhaps go to the United States Supreme Court. And he might die of old age before he got into jail. If you are poor, it's a quick job. You are almost known to be guilty, else you would not be there. Why should anyone be in the criminal court if he were not guilty? He would not be there if he could be anywhere else. The officials have no time to look after these cases. The people who are on the outside, who are running banks and building churches and making jails, they have no time to examine 600 or 700 prisoners each year to see whether they are guilty or innocent. If the courts were organized to promote justice, the people would elect somebody to defend all these criminals, somebody as smart as the prosecutor—and give him as many detectives and as many assistants to help, and pay as much money to defend you as to prosecute you. We have a very able man for State's Attorney, and he has many assistants, detectives, and policemen without end, and judges to hear the cases—everything handy.

Most of our criminal code consists in offenses against property. People are sent to jail because they have committed a crime against property. It is of very little consequence whether one hundred people more or less go to jail who ought not to go—you must protect property, because in this world property is of more importance than anything else.

How is it done? These people who have property fix it so they can protect what they have. When somebody commits a crime it does not follow that he has done something that is morally wrong. The man on the outside who has committed no crime may have done something. For instance: to take all the coal in the United States and raise the price two dollars or three dollars when there is no need of it, and thus kills thousands of babies and send thousands of people to the poorhouse and tens of thousands to jail, as is done every year in the United States—this is a greater crime than all the people in our jails ever committed, but the law does not punish it. Why? Because the fellows who control the earth make the laws. If you and I had the making of the laws, the first thing we would do would be to punish the fellow who gets control of the earth. Nature put this coal in the ground for me as well as for them and nature made the prairies up here to raise wheat for me as well as for them, and then the great railroad companies came along and fenced it up.

Most all of the crimes for which we are punished are property crimes. There are a few personal crimes, like murder—but they are very few. The crimes committed are mostly against property. If this punishment is right the criminals must have a lot of property. How much money is there in this crowd? And yet you are all here for crimes against property. The people up and down the Lake Shore have not committed crime, still they have so much property they don't know what to do with it. It is perfectly plain why these people have not committed crimes against property; they make the laws and therefore do not need to break them. And in order for you to get some property you are obliged to break the rules of the game. I don't know but what some of you may have had a very nice chance to get rich by carrying the hod for one dollar a day, twelve hours. Instead of taking that nice, easy profession, you are a burglar. If you had been given a chance to be a banker you would rather follow that. Some of you may have had a chance to work as a switchman on a railroad where you know, according to statistics, that you cannot live and keep all your limbs more than seven years, and you get fifty dollars a month for taking your lives in your hands, and instead of taking that lucrative position you choose to be a sneak thief, or something like that. Some of you made that sort of chance. I don't know which I would take if I was reduced to this choice. I have an easier choice.

I will guarantee to take from this jail, or any jail in the world, five hundred men who have been the worst criminals and law breakers who ever got into jail, and I will go down to our lowest streets and take five hundred of the most hardened prostitutes, and go out somewhere where there is plenty of land, and will give them a chance to make a living, and they will be as good people as the average in the community.

There is a remedy for the sort of condition we see here. The world never finds it out, or when it does find it out it does not enforce it. You may pass a law punishing every person with death for burglary, and it will make no difference. Men will commit it just the same. In England there was a time when one hundred different offenses were punishable with death, and it made no difference. The English people strangely found out that so fast as they repealed the severe penalties and so fast as they did away with punishing men by death, crime decreased instead of increased; that the smaller the penalty the fewer the crimes.

Hanging men in our county jails does not prevent murder. It makes murderers.

And this has been the history of the world. It's easy to see how to do away with what we call crime. It is not so easy to do it. I will tell you how to do it. It can be done by giving the people a chance to live—by destroying special privileges. So long as big criminals can get the coal fields, so long as the big criminals have control of the city council and get the public streets for street cars and gas rights, this is bound to send thousands of poor people to jail. So long as men are allowed to monopolize all the earth, and compel others to live on such terms as these men see fit to make, then you are bound to get into jail.

The only way in the world to abolish crime and criminals is to abolish the big ones and the little ones together. Make fair conditions of life. Give men a chance to live. Abolish the right of private ownership of land, abolish monopoly, make the world partners in production, partners in the good things of life. Nobody would steal if he could get something of his own some easier way. Nobody will commit burglary when he has a house full. No girl will go out on the streets when she has a comfortable place at home. The man who owns a sweatshop or a department store may not be to blame himself for the condition of his girls, but when he pays them five dollars, three dollars, and two dollars a week, I wonder where he thinks they will get the rest of their money to live. The only way to cure these conditions is by equality. There should be no jails. They do not accomplish what they pretend to accomplish. If you would wipe them out, there would be no more criminals than now. They terrorize nobody. They are a blot upon civilization, and a jail is an evidence of the lack of charity of the people on the outside who make the jails and fill them with the victims of their greed.

Notes

1. *Publication.* Darrow had his address printed in pamphlet form. In his Preface, Darrow wrote: "Some of my good friends have insisted that while my theories are true, I should not have given them to the inmates of a jail. Realizing the force of the suggestion that the truth should not be spoken to all people, I have caused these remarks to be printed on rather good paper and in a somewhat expensive form. In this way the truth does not become cheap and vulgar, and is only placed before those whose intelligence and affluence will prevent their being influenced by it."

The price of the pamphlet? Five cents, the same as a streetcar ride.

2. *Method Acting.* Who was Darrow's intended audience? What was his strategy?

3. *Truth.* Darrow makes a number of pithy assertions in the address— for example, "There is no very great danger of a rich man going to jail" and "We have no system for doing justice, not the slightest in the world." In what sense were these statements true when and where Darrow made them? Are they (still) true here and now?

4. *This Land is Your Land.* Darrow says, "Nature put this coal in the ground for me as well as for them and nature made the prairie up here to raise wheat for me as well as for them, and then the great railroad companies came along and fenced it up." How does Darrow's assessment compare with that of the great folk singer, Woody Guthrie (1912–1967) in "This Land Is Your Land," first recorded in the 1940's? Are the lawyer and the folk singer part of the same tradition?

5. *Propriety.* Do you agree with Darrow's friends that he should not have given this speech to a group of prisoners? Who would be an appropriate audience for his remarks then and today? Darrow is the subject of a Federal Bureau of Investigation memorandum from R.E. Joseph to Clyde Tolson, Deputy Director, dated June 24, 1936. Joseph notes that Darrow's article, "How to Select a Jury," which had just been published in the May 1936 issue of *Esquire*, "might be helpful to the Director [J. Edgar Hoover] in making future addresses, at which time he might desire to point out how unscrupulous criminal lawyers stimulate disrespect for law and influence crime conditions." (Available at *<http://foia.fbi.gov/darrow.htm>*). Could the same be said for the "Address to the Prisoners of the Cook County Jail"?

* * *

In M. Block, The Art of Summation at 101–02 (1962), James Dempsey presents a model closing argument for plaintiffs' attorneys in a child wrongful death case:

THE APPLE FALLS CLOSE TO THE TREE
James Dempsey

Now, as to children. It seems to me that there is a very definite approach because the hardest thing in the world is to establish the value of the life of a child to a bereaved family. A two-year-old child; five-year-old child; ten- or twelve-year-old child—the jury is supposed to assess pecuniary damages when they know, of course, that at that age the child is a financial liability.

So, I suggest this kind of an approach. "There is an old saying—and bear in mind that you cannot see, you never have seen and you never will see this child. The law forbids me to introduce into evidence the photograph of this child. Yet, you are called upon to find damages for the loss of this child, who to you is an unknown individual. The old saying is this, 'the apple falls close to the tree.' What does it mean? You have seen the mother; you have seen the father and although you will never see this child, by seeing the mother and the father you can get some estimate of the blood that was in this child's veins before the child died.

"There are people who put their money in the bank; there are people who put their money into property; into stocks, into bonds; but there are other people who put their money into their children. Their savings, the results of their sacrifice, the result of their every living thought, they put that into their children. Not that they expect ever to get anything back from their children, not that they are concerned with money received but because they are their children.

"In the early morning of life from the time that the child gets out of the crib and first begins his faltering steps across the floor, from the time the child rises from the crib and endeavors to walk, whose strong sustaining hand lifts that child to its feet and helps the child across the living room floor? The hand of the father, the hand of the mother, that is the strong hand, the hand of the parents that starts the child out in the pathway of life. But as life goes on, the morning sun goes to sunset, and at that time in life, the father, the mother has come to the evening tide of their days and at that point, when the steps of the father and the mother are faltering and heavy, what hand goes out to help them? The hand of that child, grown to manhood, at the time the parents need the help of the child, the hand of that child is there.

"Well, these parents will not have that hand. It is up to you to decide. You must realize that in the days of their extremity they will not have the help of this boy whose life has been lost at this tragic time."

Notes

1. *The Closing Argument.* Compare and contrast the techniques of Darrow and Dempsey in their closing arguments, given above.

2. *The Set Argument.* Is it offensive that Dempsey's argument is usable in any child wrongful death case? In that regard, Darrow's arguments in the first and second *Sweet* cases bore considerable similarity. His labor defense arguments also tended to follow a pattern, *i.e.,* the defense of the labor movement as a whole was at stake.

3. *The Mercenary Motive.* Is it offensive that Dempsey was making his argument for the sake of money (for himself and his client)? Could Dempsey be genuinely concerned about the fate of a deceased child whom he had never met? Does it matter whether or not he felt such concern?

C. PATRIOTISM

Patriotism having become one of our topics. Johnson suddenly uttered, in a strong, determined tone, an apothegm, at which many will start: "Patriotism is the last refuge of a scoundrel!" But let it be considered, that he did not mean a real and generous love of our country, but that pretended patriotism which so many, in all ages and countries, have made a cloak for self-interest. I maintained that certainly all patriots are not scoundrels.

April 7, 1775. JAMES BOSWELL, LIFE OF JOHNSON (1791).

That man is little to be envied whose patriotism will not gain force upon the plain of Marathon, or whose piety will not grow warmer among the ruins of Iona.

SAMUEL JOHNSON, JOURNEY TO THE WESTERN ISLANDS (1775)

WILLIAM SHAKESPEARE
JULIUS CAESAR
Act III Scene 2

ALL

Live, Brutus, live, live!

FIRST PLEBEIAN

Bring him with triumph home unto his house.

SECOND PLEBEIAN

Give him a statue with his ancestors.

THIRD PLEBEIAN

Let him be Caesar.

FOURTH PLEBEIAN

Caesar's better parts

Shall be crown'd in Brutus.

FIRST PLEBEIAN

We'll bring him to his house with shouts and clamors.

BRUTUS

My countrymen—

SECOND PLEBEIAN

Peace! Silence! Brutus speaks.

FIRST PLEBEIAN

Peace, ho!

BRUTUS

Good countrymen, let me depart alone,
And, for my sake, stay here with Antony.
Do grace to Caesar's corse, and grace his speech
Tending to Caesar's glories, which Mark Antony,
By our permission, is allow'd to make.
I do entreat you, not a man depart,
Save I alone, till Antony have spoke.
Exit.

FIRST PLEBEIAN

Stay, ho, and let us hear Mark Antony.

THIRD PLEBEIAN

Let him go up into the public chair;
We'll hear him. Noble Antony, go up.

ANTONY

For Brutus' sake, I am beholding to you.

[Goes into the pulpit.]

FOURTH PLEBEIAN

What does he say of Brutus?

THIRD PLEBEIAN

He says, for Brutus' sake,
He finds himself beholding to us all.

FOURTH PLEBEIAN

"Twere best he speak no harm of Brutus here."

FIRST PLEBEIAN

This Caesar was a tyrant.

THIRD PLEBEIAN

Nay, that's certain.
We are blest that Rome is rid of him.

SECOND PLEBEIAN

Peace! Let us hear what Antony can say.

ANTONY

You gentle Romans—

ALL

Peace, ho! Let us hear him.

ANTONY

Friends, Romans, countrymen, lend me your ears!
I come to bury Caesar, not to praise him.
The evil that men do lives after them,
The good is oft interred with their bones;
So let it be with Caesar. The noble Brutus
Hath told you Caesar was ambitious;
If it were so, it was a grievous fault,
And grievously hath Caesar answer'd it.
Here, under leave of Brutus and the rest—
For Brutus is an honorable man;
So are they all, all honorable men—
Come I to speak in Caesar's funeral.
He was my friend, faithful and just to me;
But Brutus says he was ambitious,
And Brutus is an honorable man.
He hath brought many captives home to Rome,
Whose ransoms did the general coffers fill.
Did this in Caesar seem ambitious?
When that the poor have cried, Caesar hath wept;
Ambition should be made of sterner stuff:
Yet Brutus says he was ambitious,
And Brutus is an honorable man.
You all did see that on the Lupercal
I thrice presented him a kingly crown,
Which he did thrice refuse. Was this ambition?
Yet Brutus says he was ambitious,
And sure he is an honorable man.
I speak not to disprove what Brutus spoke,
But here I am to speak what I do know.
You all did love him once, not without cause;
What cause withholds you then to mourn for him?
O judgement, thou art fled to brutish beasts,
And men have lost their reason. Bear with me;
My heart is in the coffin there with Caesar,
And I must pause till it come back to me.

[He weeps.]

FIRST PLEBEIAN

Methinks there is much reason in his sayings.

SECOND PLEBEIAN

If thou consider rightly of the matter,
Caesar has had great wrong.

THIRD PLEBEIAN

Has he, masters?

I fear there will a worse come in his place.

FOURTH PLEBEIAN

Mark'd ye his words? He would not take the crown;
Therefore 'tis certain he was not ambitious.

FIRST PLEBEIAN

If it be found so, some will dear abide it.

SECOND PLEBEIAN

Poor soul, his eyes are red as fire with weeping.

THIRD PLEBEIAN

There's not a nobler man in Rome than Antony.

FOURTH PLEBEIAN

Now mark him, he begins again to speak.

ANTONY

But yesterday the word of Caesar might
Have stood against the world. Now lies he there,
And none so poor to do him reverence.
O masters! If I were disposed to stir
Your hearts and minds to mutiny and rage,
I should do Brutus wrong and Cassius wrong,
Who, you all know, are honorable men.
I will not do them wrong; I rather choose
To wrong the dead, to wrong myself and you,
Than I will wrong such honorable men.
But here's a parchment with the seal of Caesar;
I found it in his closet, 'tis his will.

[Shows the will.]

Let but the commons hear this testament—
Which, pardon me, I do not mean to read—
And they would go and kiss dead Caesar's wounds
And dip their napkins in his sacred blood,
Yea, beg a hair of him for memory,
And, dying, mention it within their wills,
Bequeathing it as a rich legacy
Unto their issue.

FOURTH PLEBEIAN

We'll hear the will. Read it, Mark Antony.

ALL

The will, the will! We will hear Caesar's will.

ANTONY

Have patience, gentle friends, I must not read it;
It is not meet you know how Caesar loved you.
You are not wood, you are not stones, but men;
And, being men, hearing the will of Caesar,
It will inflame you, it will make you mad.
'Tis good you know not that you are his heirs,
For if you should, O, what would come of it!

FOURTH PLEBEIAN

Read the will; we'll hear it, Antony.
You shall read us the will, Caesar's will.

ANTONY

Will you be patient? Will you stay awhile?
I have o'ershot myself to tell you of it.
I fear I wrong the honorable men
Whose daggers have stabb'd Caesar; I do fear it.

FOURTH PLEBEIAN

They were traitors. Honorable men!

ALL

The will! The testament!

SECOND PLEBEIAN

They were villains, murtherers. The will!
Read the will!

ANTONY

You will compel me then to read the will?
Then make a ring about the corse of Caesar,
And let me show you him that made the will.
Shall I descend? And will you give me leave?

ALL

Come down.

SECOND PLEBEIAN

Descend.

[He comes down from the pulpit.]

THIRD PLEBEIAN

You shall have leave.

FOURTH PLEBEIAN

A ring, stand round.

FIRST PLEBEIAN

Stand from the hearse, stand from the body.

SECOND PLEBEIAN

Room for Antony, most noble Antony.

ANTONY

Nay, press not so upon me, stand far off.

ALL

Stand back; room, bear back!

ANTONY

If you have tears, prepare to shed them now.
You all do know this mantle. I remember
The first time ever Caesar put it on;
'Twas on a summer's evening, in his tent,
That day he overcame the Nervii.
Look, in this place ran Cassius' dagger through;
See what a rent the envious Casca made;
Through this the well-beloved Brutus stabb'd;
And as he pluck'd his cursed steel away,
Mark how the blood of Caesar follow'd it,
As rushing out of doors, to be resolved
If Brutus so unkindly knock'd, or no;
For Brutus, as you know, was Caesar's angel.
Judge, O you gods, how dearly Caesar loved him!
This was the most unkindest cut of all;
For when the noble Caesar saw him stab,
Ingratitude, more strong than traitors' arms,
Quite vanquish'd him. Then burst his mighty heart,
And, in his mantle muffling up his face,
Even at the base of Pompey's statue,
Which all the while ran blood, great Caesar fell.
O, what a fall was there, my countrymen!
Then I, and you, and all of us fell down,
Whilst bloody treason flourish'd over us.
O, now you weep, and I perceive you feel
The dint of pity. These are gracious drops.
Kind souls, what weep you when you but behold
Our Caesar's vesture wounded? Look you here,
Here is himself, marr'd, as you see, with traitors.

[He lifts Caesar's mantle.]

FIRST PLEBEIAN

O piteous spectacle!

SECOND PLEBEIAN

O noble Caesar!

THIRD PLEBEIAN

O woeful day!

FOURTH PLEBEIAN

O traitors, villains!

FIRST PLEBEIAN

O most bloody sight!

SECOND PLEBEIAN

We will be revenged.

ALL

Revenge! About! Seek! Burn! Fire! Kill!
Slay! Let not a traitor live!

ANTONY

Stay, countrymen.

FIRST PLEBEIAN

Peace there! Hear the noble Antony.

SECOND PLEBEIAN

We'll hear him, we'll follow him, we'll die with him.

ANTONY

Good friends, sweet friends, let me not stir you up
To such a sudden flood of mutiny.
They that have done this deed are honorable.
What private griefs they have, alas, I know not,
That made them do it. They are wise and honorable,
And will, no doubt, with reasons answer you.
I come not, friends, to steal away your hearts.
I am no orator, as Brutus is;
But, as you know me all, a plain blunt man,
That love my friend, and that they know full well
That gave me public leave to speak of him.
For I have neither wit, nor words, nor worth,
Action, nor utterance, nor the power of speech,
To stir men's blood. I only speak right on;
I tell you that which you yourselves do know;

Show you sweet Caesar's wounds, poor dumb mouths,
And bid them speak for me. But were I Brutus,
And Brutus Antony, there were an Antony
Would ruffle up your spirits and put a tongue
In every wound of Caesar that should move
The stones of Rome to rise and mutiny.

ALL

We'll mutiny.

FIRST PLEBEIAN

We'll burn the house of Brutus.

THIRD PLEBEIAN

Away, then! Come, seek the conspirators.

ANTONY

Yet hear me, countrymen; yet hear me speak.

ALL

Peace, ho! Hear Antony, most noble Antony!

ANTONY

Why, friends, you go to do you know not what.
Wherein hath Caesar thus deserved your loves?
Alas, you know not; I must tell you then.
You have forgot the will I told you of.

ALL

Most true, the will! Let's stay and hear the will.

ANTONY

Here is the will, and under Caesar's seal.
To every Roman citizen he gives,
To every several man, seventy-five drachmas.

SECOND PLEBEIAN

Most noble Caesar! We'll revenge his death.

THIRD PLEBEIAN

O royal Caesar!

ANTONY

Hear me with patience.

ALL
Peace, ho!

ANTONY

Moreover, he hath left you all his walks,
His private arbors, and new-planted orchards,
On this side Tiber; he hath left them you,
And to your heirs forever—common pleasures,
To walk abroad and recreate yourselves.
Here was a Caesar! When comes such another?

FIRST PLEBEIAN

Never, never. Come, away, away!
We'll burn his body in the holy place
And with the brands fire the traitors' houses.
Take up the body.

SECOND PLEBEIAN

Go fetch fire.

THIRD PLEBEIAN

Pluck down benches.

FOURTH PLEBEIAN

Pluck down forms, windows, anything.

Exeunt Plebeians [with the body].

ANTONY

Now let it work. Mischief, thou art afoot,
Take thou what course thou wilt.

Notes

1. *Julius Caesar.* Rome was in a period of political turmoil in the last century B.C. The situation may be compared to that preceding the French Revolution of 1789. Both situations veered toward political chaos, and invited the intervention of a strong man.

Sulla, a powerful and able general, assumed the office of dictator after civil war broke out following the war with Pontus of Asia Minor in 88 B.C. He voluntarily resigned his dictatorship in 79 B.C., but not before making radical changes that weakened the established form of Roman government. After Sulla's death in 78 B.C., rivalry developed between two other powerful generals, Pompey and Julius Caesar. Pompey was aligned with the Senate, which demanded in 49 B.C. that Caesar disband his army. Instead of doing so, Caesar illegally crossed the Rubicon River between Gaul and Italy, marched on Rome, overthrew the government, and declared himself the supreme ruler of the Roman Empire.

Caesar considered himself a benevolent despot, and he put into effect many progressive reforms in his brief reign, 49–44 B.C. But on the Ides of March, 44 B.C., he was stabbed to death in the Senate by a group of conspirators, and Rome was once more plunged into civil war. See generally 1 T. WALTER WALLBANK AND ALISTAIR M. TAYLOR, CIVILIZATION PAST AND PRESENT 139–41 (1960).

2. *Subject and Style.* Compare Mark Antony's speech to the plebeians with that of Darrow to the jury in the second *Sweet* case. Are the audiences, as perceived by the speakers, similar? Are the speakers' styles similar? Their goals?

BRUCE TO HIS MEN AT BANNOCKBURN
Robert Burns

Tune—*Hey, tuttie taitie.*

Scots, wha hae wi' Wallace bled,
Scots, wham Bruce has often led,
Welcome to your gory bed,
    Or to victorie!

Now's the day, and now's the hour;
See the front of battle lour;
See approach proud Edward's power—
    Chains and slaverie!

Wha will be a traitor-knave?
Wha can fill a coward's grave?
Wha sae base as be a slave?
    Let him turn and flee!

Wha for Scotland's king and law
Freedom's sword will strongly draw,
Freeman stand, or freeman fa',
    Let him follow me!

By oppression's woes and pains!
By your sons in servile chains!
We will drain our dearest veins,
    But they shall be free!

Lay the proud usurpers low!
Tyrants fall in ev'ry foe!
Liberty's in ev'ry blow!—
    Let us do or die!

Notes

1. *The Bruce.* Robert the Bruce was a descendant of a long line of Bruces (variant of Bruis, Braose, Breaux and Brus) who came over to England with the Norman Conquest in 1066. Robert the Bruce (le Brus), the most famous of the Bruces, became king of Scotland in 1305.

The following is an account of the Battle of Bannockburn, as set forth in 3 ENCYCLOPEDIA BRITANNICA 354–55 (1910):

    The famous battle of Bannockburn (24th June 1314) was fought for the relief of Stirling Castle, which was besieged by the Scottish forces under Robert Bruce. The English governor of Stirling had promised that, if he were not relieved by that date, he would surrender the castle, and Edward II. hastily collected an army in the northern and midland counties of England. Bruce made no attempt to defend the border, and selected his defensive position on the Bannock Burn, 2½ m. S. of Stirling. His front was covered by the marshy bed of the stream, his left flank by its northerly bend towards the Forth, his right by a group of woods, behind which, until the English army appeared, the Scots concealed themselves.... On the 23rd the van of the army of Edward, which numbered about 60,000 against the 40,000 of the Scots, appeared to the south of the burn and at once despatched two bodies of men towards Stirling, the first by the direct road, the other over the lower Bannock Burn near its junction with the Forth. The former was met by the Scottish outpost on the road, and here occurred the famous single combat in which Robert Bruce, though not fully armed for battle, killed Sir Henry Bohun.... The English army assembled for battle on the following day. Early on St. John's day the Scottish army took up its assigned positions.... The reserve under Bruce consisted of a corps of pikemen and a squadron of 500 chosen men-at-arms under Sir Robert Keith, the marischal of Scotland. The line of the defenders was unusually dense; Edward, in forming up on an equal front with greatly superior numbers, found his army almost hopelessly cramped.... The attack of the English failed to make any gap in the line of defence, many knights and men-at-arms were injured ..., and the battle became a *mêlée*, the Scots, with better fortune than at Falkirk and Flodden, presenting always an impenetrable hedge of spears, the English, too stubborn to draw off, constantly trying in vain to break it down.... Bruce threw his infantry reserve into the battle, the arrows of the English archers wounded the men-at-arms of their own side, and the remnants of the leading line were tired and disheartened when the final impetus to their rout was given by the historic charge of the "gillies," some thousands of Scottish camp-followers who suddenly emerged from the woods, blowing horns, waving such weapons as they possessed, and holding aloft improvised banners. Their cries of "slay, slay!" seemed to the wearied English to betoken the advance of a great reserve, and in a few minutes the whole English army broke and fled in disorder down the slope. Many perished in the burn, and the demoralized fugitives were hunted by the peasantry until they re-crossed the English border. One earl, forty-two barons and bannerets, two hundred knights, seven hundred esquires and probably 10,000 foot were killed in the battle and the pursuit. One earl, twenty-two barons and bannerets and sixty-eight knight fell into the hands of the victors, whose total loss of 4000 men included, it is said, only two knights.

WILLIAM SHAKESPEARE
HENRY V
Act IV Scene 3

Battle of Agincourt

Enter GLOUCESTER, BEDFORD, EXETER, ERPINGHAM, with all his host: SALISBURY and WESTMORELAND

GLOUCESTER

Where is the king?

BEDFORD

The king himself is rode to view their battle.

WESTMORELAND

Of fighting men they have full three score thousand.

EXETER

There's five to one; besides, they all are fresh.

SALISBURY

God's arm strike with us! 'tis a fearful odds.
God be wi' you, princes all; I'll to my charge:
If we no more meet till we meet in heaven,
Then, joyfully, my noble Lord of Bedford,
My dear Lord Gloucester, and my good Lord Exeter,
And my kind kinsman, warriors all, adieu!

BEDFORD

Farewell, good Salisbury; and good luck go with thee!

EXETER

Farewell, kind lord; fight valiantly to-day:
And yet I do thee wrong to mind thee of it,
For thou art framed of the firm truth of valour.

Exit SALISBURY

BEDFORD

He is full of valour as of kindness;
Princely in both.

Enter the KING

WESTMORELAND

O that we now had here
But one ten thousand of those men in England
That do no work to-day!

KING HENRY V

What's he that wishes so?
My cousin Westmoreland? No, my fair cousin:
If we are mark'd to die, we are now
To do our country loss; and if to live,
The fewer men, the greater share of honour.

God's will! I pray thee, wish not one man more.
By Jove, I am not covetous for gold,
Nor care I who doth feed upon my cost;
It yearns me not if men my garments wear;
Such outward things dwell not in my desires:
But if it be a sin to covet honor,
I am the most offending soul alive.
No, faith, my coz, wish not a man from England:
God's peace! I would not lose so great an honor
As one man more, methinks, would share from me
For the best hope I have. O, do not wish one more!
Rather proclaim it, Westmoreland, through my host,
That he which hath no stomach to this fight,
Let him depart; his passport shall be made
And crowns for convoy put into his purse:
We would not die in that man's company
That fears his fellowship to die with us.
This day is called the feast of Crispian:
He that outlives this day, and comes safe home,
Will stand a tip-toe when the day is named,
And rouse him at the name of Crispian.
He that shall live this day, and see old age,
Will yearly on the vigil feast his neighbors,
And say 'To-morrow is Saint Crispian:'
Then will he strip his sleeve and show his scars.
And say 'These wounds I had on Crispin's day.'
Old men forget: yet all shall be forgot,
But he'll remember with advantages
What feats he did that day: then shall our names.
Familiar in his mouth as household words,
Harry the king, Bedford and Exeter,
Warwick and Talbot, Salisbury and Gloucester,
Be in their flowing cups freshly remember'd.
This story shall the good man teach his son;
And Crispin Crispian shall ne'er go by,
From this day to the ending of the world,
But we in it shall be remember'd;
We few, we happy few, we band of brothers;
For he to-day that sheds his blood with me
Shall be my brother; be he ne'er so vile,
This day shall gentle his condition:
And gentlemen in England now a-bed
Shall think themselves accursed they were not here,
And hold their manhoods cheap whiles any speaks
That fought with us upon Saint Crispin's day.

Notes

1. *Agincourt.* From 1 ENCYCLOPEDIA BRITANNICA 375–76 (1910), an account of the famous battle on St. Crispin's day in 1415:

The battle was fought in the defile formed by the wood of Agincourt and that of Tramecourt, at the northern exit of which the army under d'Albret, constable of France, had placed itself so as to bar the way to Calais against the English forces which had been campaigning on the Somme. The night of the 24th of October was spent by the two armies on the ground, and the English had but little shelter from the heavy rain which fell. Early on the 25th, St Crispin's day, Henry arrayed his little army (about 1000 men-at-arms, 6000 archers, and a few thousands of other foot). It is probable that the usual three "battles" were drawn up in line, each with its archers on the flanks and the dismounted men-at-arms in the centre; the archers being thrown forward in wedge-shaped salients.... The French, on the other hand, were drawn up in three lines, each line formed in deep masses. They were at least four times more numerous than the English, but restricted by the nature of the ground to the extent of front, they were unable to use their full weight (cf. Bannockburn); further, the deep mud prevented their artillery from taking part, and the crossbowmen were as usual relegated to the rear of the knights and men-at-arms.... For three hours after sunrise there was no fighting; then Henry, finding that the French would not advance, moved his army farther into the defile. The archers fixed the pointed stakes, which they carried to ward off cavalry charges, and opened the engagement with flights of arrows. The chivalry of France, undisciplined and careless of the lesson of Crécy and Poitiers, was quickly stung into action, and the French mounted men charged, only to be driven back into confusion. The constable himself headed the leading line of dismounted men-at-arms; weighted with their armour, and sinking deep into the mud with every step, they yet reached and engaged the English men-at-arms; for a time the fighting was severe. The thin line of the defenders was borne back and King Henry was almost beaten to the ground. But at this moment the archers, taking their hatchets, swords or other weapons, penetrated the gaps in the now disordered French, who could not move to cope with their unarmoured assailants, and were slaughtered or taken prisoners to a man. The second line of the French came on, only to be engulfed in the *mêlée*; its leaders, like those of the first line, were killed or taken, and the commanders of the third sought and found their death in the battle, while their men rode off to safety. The closing scene of the battle was a half-hearted attack made by a body of fugitives, which led merely to the slaughter of the French prisoners, which was ordered by Henry because he had not enough men both to guard them and to meet the attack. The slaughter ceased when the assailants drew off. The total loss of the English is stated at thirteen men-at-arms (including the duke of York, grandson of Edward III.) and about 100 of the foot. The French lost 5000 of noble birth killed, including the constable, 3 dukes, 5 counts and 90 barons; 1000 more were taken prisoners, amongst them the duke of Orleans (the Charles d'Orléans of literature).

2. *A Comparison of the Imagined Speeches at Bannockburn and Agincourt.* Bobby Burns (1759–1796), the unsurpassed poet-hero of Scotland, is renowned for his poems. Who can dream of meeting with or parting from an

old friend without recalling his *Auld Lang Syne?* What man of the people does not know Burns's *A Man's A Man For A' That?*

Bruce to His Men at Bannockburn, like many of Burns's poems, was written to be sung, this one to the accompaniment of the surly bagpipe. The lilt of the poem is light and jolly, with a four-foot line that sounds like a children's rhyme. But the theme of the poem is sombre indeed.

Henry's speech at Agincourt, as imagined by Shakespeare, is light-hearted, almost bantering. Who needs one more man, he asks, when every man who fights here today will be a hero forever? Why share the glory?

It sounds as if all the people assembled at Agincourt are close friends: my cousin Westmoreland, Bedford, Exeter, Warwick, Talbot, Salisbury, Gloucester. "For he today who sheds his blood with me shall be my brother."

Both the Bruce and Henry would flush out cowards. Says the Bruce, "Wha sae base as be a slave? Let him turn and flee!" And Henry: "He which hath no stomach to this fight, let him depart; his passport shall be made and crowns for convoy put into his purse. We would not die in that man's company that fears his fellowship to die with us."

Henry's speech, like that of Antony in *Julius Caesar,* begins quietly, almost conversationally, and rises to a thundering crescendo at the end.

The Bruce's speech, on the other hand, is sung to a ditty, "Hey, tuttie taitie." The tempo never changes. The presentation remains monotonic throughout.

Which speech is more bloodcurdling? Which is more patriotic?

* * *

The life of Patrick Henry is described in 13 ENCYCLOPEDIA BRITANNICA 300–01 (1910):

HENRY, PATRICK (1736–1799), American statesman and orator, was born at Studley, Hanover County, Virginia, on the 29th of May 1736. He was the son of John Henry, a well-educated Scotsman, among whose relatives was the historian William Robertson, and who served in Virginia as county surveyor, colonel and judge of a county court. His mother was one of a family named Winston, of Welsh descent, noted for conversational and musical talent. At the age of ten Patrick was making slow progress in the study of reading, writing and arithmetic at a small country school, when his father became his tutor and taught him Latin, Greek and mathematics for five years, but with limited success. His school days being then terminated, he was employed as a store-clerk for one year. Within the seven years next following he failed twice as a store-keeper and once as a farmer; but in the meantime acquired a taste for reading, of history especially, and read and re-read the history of Greece and Rome, of England, and of her American colonies. Then, poor but not discouraged, he resolved to be a lawyer, and after reading *Coke upon Littleton* and the Virginia laws for a few weeks only, he strongly impressed one of his examiners, and was admitted to the bar at the age of twenty four, on condition that he spend more time in study before beginning to practice. He rapidly acquired a considerable practice, his fee books shewing that for the first three years he charged fees in 1185 cases.

Then in 1763 was delivered his speech in "The Parson's Cause"—a suit brought by a clergyman, Rev. James Maury, in the Hanover County Court, to secure restitution for money considered by him to be due or account of his salary (16,000 pounds of tobacco by law) having been paid in money calculated at a rate less than the current market price of tobacco. This speech, which, according to reports, was extremely radical and denied the right of the king to disallow acts of the colonial legislature, made Henry the idol of the common people of Virginia and procured for him an enormous practice. In 1765 he was elected a member of the Virginia legislature, where he became in the same year the author of the "Virginia Resolutions," which were no less than a declaration of resistance to the Stamp Act and an assertion of the right of the colonies to legislate for themselves independently of the control of the British parliament, and gave a most powerful impetus to the movement resulting in the War of Independence. In a speech urging their adoption appear the often-quoted words: "Tarquin and Caesar had each his Brutus, Charles the First his Cromwell, and George the Third [here he was interrupted by cries of "Treason"] and George the Third may profit by their example! If *this* be treason, make the most of it." Until 1775 he continued to sit in the House of Burgesses, as a leader during all that eventful period. He was prominent as a radical in all measures in opposition to the British government, and was a member of the first Virginia committee of correspondence. In 1774 and 1775 he was a delegate to the Continental Congress and served on three of its most important committees: that on colonial trade and manufactures, that for drawing up an address to the king, and that for stating the rights of the colonies. In 1775, in the second revolutionary convention of Virginia, Henry, regarding war as inevitable, presented resolutions for arming the Virginia militia. The more conservative members strongly opposed them as premature, whereupon Henry supported them in a speech familiar to the American school-boy for several generations following, closing with the words, "Is life so dear or peace so sweet as to be purchased at the price of chains and slavery? Forbid it, Almighty God! I know not what course others may take, but as for me, give me liberty or give me death!" The resolutions were passed and their author was made chairman of the committee for which they provided. The chief command of the newly organized army was also given to him, but previously, at the head of a body of militia, he had demanded satisfaction for powder removed from the public store by order of Lord Dunmore, the royal governor, with the result that £330 was paid in compensation. But his military appointment required obedience to the Committee of Public Safety and this body, largely dominated by Edmund Pendleton, so restrained him from active service that he resigned on the 28th of February 1776. In the Virginia convention of 1776 he favoured the postponement of a declaration of independence, until a firm union of the colonies and the friendship of France and Spain had been secured. In the same convention he served on the committee which drafted the first constitution for Virginia, and was elected governor of the State—to which office he was re-elected in 1777 and 1778, thus serving as long as the new constitution allowed any man to serve continuously. As governor he gave Washington able support and sent out the expedition under George Rogers Clark into the Illinois country. In 1778 he was chosen a delegate to Congress, but declined to serve. From 1780 to 1784 and from 1787 to 1790 he was again a member of his State legislature; and from 1784 to 1786 was again governor. Until 1786 he was a leading advocate of a stronger central government but when chosen a delegate to the Philadelphia constitutional convention of 1787, he had become cold in the cause and declined to serve. Moreover, in the state convention called to decide whether Virginia should ratify the Federal Constitution he led the opposition, contending that the proposed Constitution, because of its centralizing character, was dangerous to the liberties of the country. This change of attitude is thought to have been due chiefly to his suspicion of the North aroused by John Jay's proposal to surrender to Spain for twenty-five or thirty years the navigation of the Mississippi. From 1794 until his death he declined in succession the following offices: United States Senator (1794), secretary of state in Washington's cabinet (1795), chief justice of the United States Supreme Court (1795), governor of Virginia (1796), to which office he had been elected by the Assembly, and envoy to France (1799). In 1799, however, he consented to serve again in his State legislature, where he wished to combat the Virginia Resolutions; he never took his seat, since he died, on his Red Hill estate in Charlotte County, Virginia, on the 6th of June of that year. Henry was twice married, first to Sarah Skelton, and second to Dorothea Spotswood Dandridge, a grand-daughter of Governor Alexander Spotswood.

GIVE ME LIBERTY OR GIVE ME DEATH
Patrick Henry
March 23, 1775

No man thinks more highly than I do of the patriotism, as well as abilities, of the very worthy gentlemen who have just addressed the house. But different men often see the same subject in different lights; and, therefore, I hope it will not be thought disrespectful to those gentlemen if, entertaining as I do opinions of a character very opposite to theirs, I shall speak forth my sentiments freely and without reserve. This is no time for ceremony. The question before the house is one of awful moment to this country. For my own part, I consider it as nothing less than a question of freedom or slavery; and in proportion to the magnitude of the subject ought to be the freedom of the debate. It is only in this way that we can hope to arrive at the truth, and fulfill the great responsibility which we hold to God and our country. Should I keep back my opinions at such a time, through fear of giving offense, I should consider myself as guilty of treason towards my country, and of an act of disloyalty toward the Majesty of Heaven, which I revere above all earthly kings.

Mr. President, it is natural to man to indulge in the illusions of hope. We are apt to shut our eyes against a painful truth, and listen to the song of that siren till she transforms us into beasts. Is this the part of wise men, engaged in a great and arduous struggle for liberty? Are we disposed to be of the numbers of those who, having eyes, see not, and, having ears, hear not, the things which so nearly concern their temporal salvation? For my part, whatever anguish of spirit it may cost, I am willing to know the whole truth, to know the worst, and to provide for it.

I have but one lamp by which my feet are guided, and that is the lamp of experience. I know of no way of judging of the future but by the past. And judging by the past, I wish to know what there has been in the conduct of the British ministry for the last ten years to justify those hopes with which gentlemen have been pleased to solace themselves and the House. Is it that insidious smile with which our petition has been lately received?

Trust it not, sir; it will prove a snare to your feet. Suffer not yourselves to be betrayed with a kiss. Ask yourselves how this gracious reception of our petition comports with those warlike preparations which cover our waters and darken our land. Are fleets and armies necessary to a work of love and reconciliation? Have we shown ourselves so unwilling to be reconciled that force must be called in to win back our love? Let us not deceive ourselves, sir. These are the implements of war and subjugation; the last arguments to which kings resort. I ask gentlemen, sir, what means this martial array, if its purpose be not to force us to submission? Can gentlemen assign any other possible motive for it? Has Great Britain any enemy, in this quarter of the world, to call for all this accumulation of navies and armies? No, sir, she has none. They are meant for us: they can be meant for no other. They are sent over to bind and rivet upon us those chains which the British ministry have been so long forging. And what have we to oppose to them? Shall we try argument? Sir, we have been trying that for the last ten years. Have we anything new to offer upon the subject? Nothing. We have held the subject up in every light of which it is capable; but it has been all in vain. Shall we resort to entreaty and humble supplication? What terms shall we find which have not been already exhausted? Let us not, I beseech you, sir, deceive ourselves. Sir, we have done everything that could be done to avert the storm which is now coming on. We have petitioned; we have remonstrated; we have supplicated; we have prostrated ourselves before the throne, and have implored its interposition to arrest the tyrannical hands of the ministry and Parliament. Our petitions have been slighted; our remonstrances have produced additional violence and insult; our supplications have been disregarded; and we have been spurned, with contempt, from the foot of the throne! In vain, after these things, may we indulge the fond hope of peace and reconciliation.

There is no longer any room for hope. If we wish to be free—if we mean to preserve inviolate those inestimable privileges for which we have been so long contending—if we mean not basely to abandon the noble struggle in which we have been so long engaged, and which we have pledged ourselves never to abandon until the glorious object of our contest shall be obtained—we must fight! I repeat it, sir, we must fight! An appeal to arms and to the God of hosts is all that is left us! They tell us, sir, that we are weak; unable to cope with so formidable an adversary. But when shall we be stronger? Will it be the next week, or the next year? Will it be when we are totally disarmed, and when a British guard shall be stationed in every house? Shall we gather strength by irresolution and inaction? Shall we acquire the means of effectual resistance by lying supinely on our backs and hugging the delusive phantom of hope, until our enemies shall have bound us hand and foot? Sir, we are not weak if we make a proper use of those means which the God of nature hath placed in our power. The millions of people, armed in the holy cause of liberty, and in such a country as that which we possess, are invincible by any force which our enemy can send against us. Besides, sir, we shall not fight our battles alone. There is a just God who presides over the destinies of nations, and who will raise up friends to fight our battles for us. The battle, sir, is not to the strong alone; it is to the vigilant, the active, the brave. Besides, sir, we have no election. If we were base enough to desire it, it is now too late to retire from the contest. There is no retreat but in submission and slavery! Our chains are forged! Their clanking may be heard on the plains of Boston! The war is inevitable—and let it come! I repeat it, sir, let it come.

It is in vain, sir, to extenuate the matter. Gentlemen may cry, Peace, Peace—but there is no peace. The war is actually begun! The next gale that sweeps from the north will bring to our ears the clash of resounding arms! Our brethren are already in the field! Why stand we here idle? What is it that gentlemen wish? What would they have? Is life so dear, or peace so sweet, as to be purchased at the price of chains and slavery? Forbid it, Almighty God! I know not what course others may take; but as for me, give me liberty or give me death!

Notes

1. *The Cadence of Patrick Henry's Speech to the Virginia Revolutionary Convention in 1775.* We will later study portions of the King James Bible. When we do, remember Patrick Henry's cadence, and that of Lincoln and Martin Luther King, Jr. given in this chapter, and compare them to the cadence of the King James Bible.

2. *Terrorism and Patriotism.* After the terrorist attacks in the United States on September 11, 2001, American flags spontaneously appeared on vehicles and buildings all over the nation. What do you think the flag-displayers were trying to say? To whom? How do you think the flag displays were understood by observers?

Compare and contrast the September 11 attacks to the Japanese attack on Pearl Harbor on December 7, 1941. President Roosevelt described December 7 as "a date which will live in infamy." Signs reading "Remember Pearl Harbor" appeared all over the nation.

Are there some acts that are intolerable even during time of war? How can one tell when the line between the tolerable and the intolerable has been crossed? On which side of the line is bombing nonmilitary civilians? Use of nuclear weapons? Sherman's march through Georgia? Assassination? Germ warfare? Does your answer depend on whether the enemy has committed such acts first?

* * *

LEARNED HAND: THE MAN AND THE JUDGE
Gerald Gunther

Until the final year of World War II, Hand, despite his thirty-five years on the federal bench, was not a widely known public figure: most Americans had never heard of the judge with the unusual name. Not until one Sunday afternoon in May 1944 did Hand utter words that would catapult him into popular fame. On May 21, 1944, Hand was one of the speakers at the annual "I Am an American Day" ceremony in New York City's Central Park, where 150,000 newly naturalized citizens were to swear their oaths of allegiance. He had been asked to make a few remarks and then lead the assemblage in the Pledge of Allegiance. Hand had always dreaded extemporaneous speaking, and in this instance as usual he spent some time writing out his talk ahead of time. His brief speech, little noticed at the time of the gathering, proved to be long remembered. More than any other statement he ever made, this address spread his reputation far beyond the legal profession and assured him nationwide fame.

The speech was heard by the largest audience ever gathered in New York City. (In addition to the 150,000 new citizens, more than a million others, no doubt attracted by the mild, sunny summer weather and by the promise of Broadway entertainment, heard the proceedings over loudspeakers scattered throughout the park.) Under "an almost cloudless blue sky," nearly one and a half million people attended the ceremony. Patriotism was at its zenith. The fortunes of the war had clearly turned in the Allies' favor, and anticipation of an impending invasion of Nazi-held Northern Europe was in the air. New York Mayor Fiorello La Guardia's welcoming remarks expressed the mood: "We are set for it. We are waiting. Nobody knows when it will come. But we have the utmost confidence in our commander.... Whenever it comes we will back those men and give them everything we've got." A little more than two weeks later, on D-day, June 6, the invasion began.

The crowd that heard Hand's words must have been fatigued by the time he rose to speak, well after four o'clock in the afternoon. The first members of the gathering throng, many bringing picnic lunches, had begun to fill the park at ten-thirty in the morning. The program began at two-thirty, with occasional relief from the extensive speech-making supplied by the music of three bands and performances by the casts of several Broadway musicals, from *Carmen Jones* to *Oklahoma!* New York's New Deal senator, Robert F. Wagner, delivered the longest speech, outlining a program of "American ideals" that should guide the nation after victory. Remarks by a number of city officials and by clergymen of three major faiths added to the festive occasion.

. . . .

Hand's brief words garnered no immediate acclaim whatever. The front-page coverage of the occasion in the next day's *New York Times* quoted at length from Senator Wagner's speech and more briefly from the other addresses, but printed not a word of what Hand had said. Yet within a few weeks, Hand's remarks about "the spirit of liberty" were the subject of enormous publicity.

There would have been no public attention to Hand's speech had the Central Park ceremonies not been broadcast by New York City's municipal radio station, WNYC. Philip Hamburger, a staff member at *The New Yorker,* tuned his radio to WNYC that afternoon, hoping to find the classical music that was the staple of the station's programming. Instead, he heard the "I Am an American Day" ceremonies. He was deeply impressed by Hand's eloquence. Discovering the next morning that "not a newspaper in town quoted [the] remarks," as he reported later, he called Hand's chambers and went to the Foley Square Courthouse to borrow Hand's typescript of his speech and to speak briefly with the judge.

Hamburger was one of the writers of the "Talk of the Town" segment that begins each issue of *The New Yorker.* For the June 10, 1944, issue, he wrote a short, chatty essay, "Notes on Freedom," in which he reported on his brief talk with Hand and quoted some excerpts from the speech. While the readership of *The New Yorker* was a good deal larger than that of the law reviews and the court reports in which Hand's prose usually appeared, it did not by itself guarantee the enormous attention Hand's remarks ultimately received. Several weeks later, *The New York Times* made amends for its initial neglect by printing the speech in full in its Sunday magazine. The next day, *Life* magazine also printed the full text, calling it "a new stone in the edifice of American oratory. It is not in the great Webster tradition, but in the greater, simpler tradition of Lincoln." *Reader's Digest* quickly followed suit, assuring Hand an even larger audience.

The surge of publicity was not yet at an end. More than two years later, Philip Hamburger wrote a splendid biographical profile of Hand that appeared as a feature article in *Life's* November 4, 1946, issue. Prominently featured next to the title, "The Great Judge," and facing a full-page photo of Hand was a bold-faced paragraph entitled "The Spirit of Liberty," quoting Hand's definition. Hand, who had so often scorned the capacity of modern mass culture to homogenize tastes, suddenly found himself a folk hero; he received far more mail about this single brief address than about any of his opinions or other speeches. He had written his address hastily, spurred by a sense of duty that stemmed from his ongoing participation, since 1941, in Mayor La Guardia's committee to celebrate "I Am an American Day," on which Hand had served through most of the war years—in large part because his son-in-law Newbold Morris, his daughter Constance's husband, served in the La Guardia administration as president of the city council. Moreover, the Conference of Senior Circuit Judges had implemented an earlier congressional resolution by passing one of its own in September 1942, urging all federal judges to emphasize the importance of naturalization proceedings, which were seen as vital to furthering wartime patriotism. Thus, when Hand was asked in 1944 to administer the Pledge of Allegiance, he did not feel free to turn down the invitation. Though he did not think that he was composing a memorable speech, and was puzzled and surprised by all the acclaim, he occasionally confessed that he actually enjoyed it. And as public acclaim for the address mounted, he found it increasingly difficult to insist that his remarks "did not seem to ... have great quality." Writing to his friend the drama critic John Mason Brown, Hand commented on the praise: "I suppose if I say that it seemed to me so extravagant as to be silly, it would only be put down to false modesty; so consider it unsaid." A year later, in response to another enthusiastic letter from Brown, Hand confessed, "[Y]ou please me absurdly, in spite of your wild Bacchanalian madness." He could no longer deny the enormous public attention that Hamburger's efforts had brought him. He referred to himself as "[a]n old gent whom a pleasant chap from *The New Yorker* put on the front page and pushed into a publicity which, in accordance with the nature of that Beast, has rolled up into a snowball. Why not all draw a deep breath and relax?"

Only a few of those who complimented Hand on his remarks had actually heard them in person. Among them was the secretary of the New York City Bar Association, who told him, "I felt ... that we were listening to an address by you that perhaps will be as memorable as that called 'The Gettysburg Address,'" a comparison that reverberated in ensuing years. The president of the Virginia State Bar Association also insisted, "For simplicity and beauty, [your speech] rivals Lincoln's Gettysburg Address." An old acquaintance told Hand that she had first learned of the address when her cook came home from Central Park and told her "what [Hand] said to her (to *her*!) and how much it would always mean." A particularly perceptive acquaintance hoped that Hand would truly accept and take satisfaction in the applause, because of its importance in Hand's "unending quest for validation."

Hand, though never without misgivings, relished this applause. As he wrote to a friend, Harry King:

> [L]ike nearly everybody else, I adore applause and so I "lapped up" this. If a man says he doesn't, he lies. Still, I felt ashamed that I liked it so much. I suppose nobody who has any sense, when he gets into bed, pulls up the bedclothes, and thinks over his past life, does not feel a shudder at the recollection of the times when he has been a coward, or a liar, or a weakling, or an ass. So I feel, when people like you say what you [do], as though it was only by a streak of luck that folks have not found me out. But I am glad they never have, and if I can continue to play you along, I shall do it.

Hand was especially touched by reports of how much his speech meant to servicemen, including a navy officer who carried a copy of the speech in his uniform and read it out loud to anyone who would listen until the magazine clipping fell apart. But no one saw the irony of Hand's newfound fame more clearly than Louis Henkin. Writing to Hand from his post in France, Henkin reported that he had read Hand's remarks in both *Life* and in the *Reader's Digest* and that he was very impressed—"proud of the old boss, as if I had something to do with it."

But what struck me, enough to say it aloud to some "Looey" up here, was the fact that here you are at near 73, gaining popular acclaim for a few hundred words you dashed off some evening when the deadline began to oppress you. And for 35 years you worked your work and lived your life as Judge Learned Hand, so that someone on the Court in Washington once told me I was working for "the greatest living Judge of the English speaking world." And to our great citizens of the Republic, Learned Hand was probably a character out of a New Amsterdam folk tale, or an old English description of a local village scribe! . . . But I'm still pleased.

The strongly favorable response to Hand's Central Park speech was to some extent paradoxical. Hand, for decades an agnostic, delivered an address with notable religious overtones, including an invocation of Jesus Christ. The speech was unusual, moreover, in its plea for equal respect for all members of the community, with its reference to "a kingdom where the least shall be heard and considered side by side with the greatest." But Hand's dominant theme was in his claim that the spirit of liberty was skeptical. After all, his remarks were delivered in the midst of war, at a time when unquestioning loyalty to the cause was considered every American's duty. Yet here was a federal judge at an important patriotic ceremony admiring the "spirit which is not too sure that it is right." Even at a time when the survival of democracies was at issue, he adhered to his commitment to the doubting spirit. Skepticism and doubt are not fashionable traits in the midst of battle, but his forceful eloquence and praise of doubt even amid clamors for certainty struck a responsive chord with a large audience.

THE SPIRIT OF LIBERTY
Learned Hand
May 21, 1944

We have gathered here to affirm a faith, a faith in a common purpose, a common conviction, a common devotion. Some of us have chosen America as the land of our adoption; the rest have come from those who did the same. For this reason we have some right to consider ourselves a picked group, a group of those who had the courage to break from the past and brave the dangers and the loneliness of a strange land. What was the object that nerved us, or those who went before us, to this choice? We sought liberty; freedom from oppression, freedom from want, freedom to be ourselves. This then we sought; this we now believe that we are by way of winning. What do we mean when we say that first of all we seek liberty? I often wonder whether we do not rest our hopes too much upon constitutions, upon laws, and upon courts. These are false hopes; believe me, these are false hopes. Liberty lies in the hearts of men and women; when it dies there, no constitution, no law, no court can save it; no constitution, no law, no court can even do much to help it.

While it lies there, it needs no constitution, no law, no court to save it. And what is this liberty which must lie in the hearts of men and women? It is not the ruthless, the unbridled will; it is not freedom to do as one likes. That is the denial of liberty, and leads straight to its overthrow. A society in which men recognize no check upon their freedom soon becomes a society where freedom is the possession of only a savage few; as we have learned to our sorrow.

What, then, is the spirit of liberty? I cannot define it; I can only tell you my own faith. The spirit of liberty is the spirit which is not too sure that it is right; the spirit of liberty is the spirit which seeks to understand the minds of other men and women; the spirit of liberty is the spirit which weighs their interest alongside its own without bias; the spirit of liberty remembers that not even a sparrow falls to earth unheeded; the spirit of liberty is the spirit of him who, near two thousand years ago, taught mankind that lesson it has never learned, but has never quite forgotten; that there may be a kingdom where the least shall be heard and considered side by side with the greatest. And now in that spirit, that spirit of an America which has never been, and which may never be—nay, which never will be except as the conscience and courage of Americans create it—yet in the spirit of America which lies hidden in some form in the aspirations of us all; in the spirit of that America for which our young men are at this moment fighting and dying; in that spirit of liberty and of America I ask you to rise and with me pledge our faith in the glorious destiny of our beloved country.

Notes

1. *Civil Liberties*. Do you agree with Hand's definition of liberty? How is Hand's "liberty" related to the "civil liberties" viewed by some as under attach by measures taken as part of the so-called War on Terrorism? Gerald Gunther in his monumental biography, LEARNED HAND: THE MAN AND THE JUDGE 562–66 (1994), opines that, had Hand been appointed to the U.S. Supreme Court by Franklin Roosevelt, he would have sided with Justice Frankfurter, who generally believed that the Court should not intervene to protect individual rights from majority decisionmaking. How does this position square with Hand's speech?

2. *Braveheart*. At the end of the Mel Gibson movie, *Braveheart*, William Wallace utters his last anguished word: "FREEDOM!" Does Wallace mean the same thing by this word as Hand meant by "liberty"? How does Hand's definition of liberty compare to that of Patrick Henry?

D. THE CIVIL WAR

The seeds of the American Civil War were implacably sown in the United States Constitution, where slavery was explicitly recognized as part of the American system of democracy. As John Brown said at his trial in 1859, the shedding of blood was necessary to the resolution of the great problem of slavery. Within two years after his death, the country began its four-year bath of blood.

Abraham Lincoln out of Illinois was as unexpected as Shakespeare out of Elizabethan England or John Lennon and Paul McCartney out of post-War Liverpool. He favored first and foremost the preservation of the Union, and only gradually began to see the inevitability and desirability of equality for the African-American.

Lincoln's speeches are unsurpassed in American political life. He managed to reach beyond the politics of the time.

ADDRESS AT COOPER INSTITUTE
Abraham Lincoln
New York City
February 27, 1860

MR. PRESIDENT AND FELLOW–CITIZENS: The facts with which I shall deal this evening are mainly old and familiar; nor is there anything new in the general use I shall make of them. If there shall be any novelty, it will be in the mode of presenting the facts, and the inferences and observations following that presentation.

In his speech last autumn, at Columbus, Ohio, as reported in "The New York Times," Senator Douglas said: *"Our fathers, when they framed the Government under which we live, understood this question just as well, and even better, than we do now."*

I fully indorse this, and I adopt it as a text for this discourse. I so adopt it because it furnishes a precise and an agreed starting point for a discussion between Republicans and that wing of the Democracy headed by Senator Douglas. It simply leaves the inquiry: *"What was the understanding those fathers had of the question mentioned?"*

What is the frame of Government under which we live?

The answer must be: "The Constitution of the United States." That Constitution consists of the original, framed in 1787, (and under which the present government first went into operation,) and twelve subsequently framed amendments, the first ten of which were framed in 1789.

Who were our fathers that framed the Constitution? I suppose the "thirty-nine" who signed the original instrument may be fairly called our fathers who framed that part of the present Government. It is almost exactly true to say they framed it, and it is altogether true to say they fairly represented the opinion and sentiment of the whole nation at that time. Their names, being familiar to nearly all, and accessible to quite all, need not now be repeated.

I take these "thirty-nine" for the present, as being "our fathers who framed the Government under which we live."

What is the question which, according to the text, those fathers understood "just as well, and even better than we do now?"

It is this: Does the proper division of local from federal authority, or anything in the Constitution, forbid our *Federal Government* to control as to slavery in *our Federal Territories?*

Upon this, Senator Douglas holds the affirmative, and Republicans the negative. This affirmation and denial form an issue; and this issue—this question—is precisely what the text declares our fathers understood "better than we."

Let us now inquire whether the "thirty-nine," or any of them, ever acted upon this question; and if they did, how they acted upon it—how they expressed that better understanding?

In 1784, three years before the Constitution—the United States then owning the Northwestern Territory, and no other, the Congress of the Confederation had before them the question of prohibiting slavery in that Territory; and four of the "thirty-nine," who afterward framed the Constitution, were in that Congress, and voted on that question. Of these, Roger Sherman, Thomas Mifflin, and Hugh Williamson voted for the prohibition, thus showing that, in their understanding, no line dividing local from federal authority, nor anything else, properly forbade the Federal Government to control as to slavery in federal territory. The other of the four—James M'Henry—voted against the prohibition, showing that, for some cause, he thought it improper to vote for it.

In 1787, still before the Constitution, but while the Convention was in session framing it, and while the Northwestern Territory still was the only territory owned by the United States, the same question of prohibiting slavery in the territory again came before the Congress of the Confederation; and two more of the "thirty-nine" who afterward signed the Constitution, were in that Congress, and voted on the question. They were William Blount and William Few; and they both voted for the prohibition—thus showing that, in their understanding, no line dividing local from federal authority, nor anything else, properly forbade the Federal Government to control as to slavery in federal territory. This time the prohibition became a law, being part of what is now well known as the Ordinance of '87.

The question of federal control of slavery in the territories, seems not to have been directly before the Convention which framed the original Constitution; and hence it is not recorded that the "thirty-nine," or any of them, while engaged on that instrument, expressed any opinion of that precise question.

In 1789, by the first Congress which sat under the Constitution, an act was passed to enforce the Ordinance of '87, including the prohibition of slavery in the Northwestern Territory. The bill for this act was reported by one of the "thirty-nine," Thomas Fitzsimmons, then a member of the House of Representatives from Pennsylvania. It went through all its stages without a word of opposition, and finally passed both branches without yeas and nays, which is equivalent to an unanimous passage. In this Congress there were sixteen of the thirty-nine fathers who framed the original Constitution. They were John Langdon, Nicholas Gilman, Wm. S. Johnson, Roger Sherman, Robert Morris, Thos. Fitzsimmons, William Few, Abraham Baldwin, Rufus King, William

Paterson, George Clymer, Richard Bassett, George Read, Pierce Butler, Daniel Carroll, James Madison.

This shows that, in their understanding, no line dividing local from federal authority, nor anything in the Constitution, properly forbade Congress to prohibit slavery in the federal territory; else both their fidelity to correct principle, and their oath to support the Constitution, would have constrained them to oppose the prohibition.

Again, George Washington, another of the "thirty-nine," was then President of the United States, and, as such, approved and signed the bill; thus completing its validity as a law, and thus showing that, in his understanding, no line dividing local from federal authority, nor anything in the Constitution, forbade the Federal Government to control as to slavery in federal territory.

No great while after the adoption of the original Constitution, North Carolina ceded to the Federal Government the country now constituting the State of Tennessee; and a few years later Georgia ceded that which now constitutes the States of Mississippi and Alabama. In both deeds of cession it was made a condition by the ceding States that the Federal Government should not prohibit slavery in the ceded country. Besides this, slavery was then actually in the ceded country. Under these circumstances, Congress, on taking charge of these countries, did not absolutely prohibit slavery within them. But they did interfere with it— take control of it—even there, to a certain extent. In 1798, Congress organized the Territory of Mississippi. In the act of organization, they prohibited the bringing of slaves into the Territory, from any place without the United States, by fine, and giving freedom to slaves so brought. This act passed both branches of Congress without yeas and nays. In that Congress were three of the "thirty-nine" who framed the original Constitution. They were John Langdon, George Read and Abraham Baldwin. They all, probably, voted for it. Certainly they would have placed their opposition to it upon record, if, in their understanding, any line dividing local from federal authority, or anything in the Constitution, properly forbade the Federal Government to control as to slavery in federal territory.

In 1803, the Federal Government purchased the Louisiana country. Our former territorial acquisitions came from certain of our own States; but this Louisiana country was acquired from a foreign nation. In 1804, Congress gave a territorial organization to that part of it which now constitutes the State of Louisiana. New Orleans, lying within that part, was an old and comparatively large city. There were other considerable towns and settlements, and slavery was extensively and thoroughly intermingled with the people. Congress did not, in the Territorial Act, prohibit slavery; but they did interfere with it—take control of it—in a more marked and extensive way than they did in the case of Mississippi. The substance of the provision therein made, in relation to slaves, was:

First. That no slave should be imported into the territory from foreign parts.

Second. That no slave should be carried into it who had been imported into the United States since the first day of May, 1798.

Third. That no slave should be carried into it, except by the owner, and for his own use as a settler; the penalty in all the cases being a fine upon the violator of the law, and freedom to the slave.

This act also was passed without yeas and nays. In the Congress which passed it, there were two of the "thirty-nine." They were Abraham Baldwin and Jonathan Dayton. As stated in the case of Mississippi, it is probable they both voted for it. They would not have allowed it to pass without recording their opposition to it, if, in their understanding, it violated either the line properly dividing local from federal authority, or any provision of the Constitution.

In 1819–20, came and passed the Missouri question. Many votes were taken, by yeas and nays, in both branches of Congress, upon the various phases of the general question. Two of the "thirty-nine"—Rufus King and Charles Pinckney—were members of that Congress. Mr. King steadily voted for slavery prohibition and against all compromises, while Mr. Pinckney as steadily voted against slavery prohibition and against all compromises. By this, Mr. King showed that, in his understanding, no line dividing local from federal authority, nor anything in the Constitution, was violated by Congress prohibiting slavery in federal territory; while Mr. Pinckney, by his votes, showed that, in his understanding, there was some sufficient reason for opposing such prohibition in that case.

The cases I have mentioned are the only acts of the "thirty-nine," or of any of them, upon the direct issue, which I have been able to discover.

To enumerate the persons who thus acted, as being four in 1784, two in 1787, seventeen in 1789, three in 1798, two in 1804, and two in 1819–20—there would be thirty of them. But this would be counting John Langdon, Roger Sherman, William Few, Rufus King, and George Read, each twice, and Abraham Baldwin, three times. The true number of those of the "thirty-nine" whom I have shown to have acted upon the question, which, by the text, they understood better than we, is twenty-three, leaving sixteen not shown to have acted upon it in any way.

Here, then, we have twenty-three out of our thirty-nine fathers "who framed the Government under which we live," who have, upon their official responsibility and their corporal oaths, acted upon the very question which the text affirms they "understood just as well, and even better than we do now;" and twenty-one of them—a clear majority of the whole "thirty-nine"—so acting upon it as to make them guilty of gross political impropriety and wilful perjury, if, in their understanding, any proper division between local and federal authority, or anything in the Constitution they had made themselves, and sworn to support, forbade the Federal Government to control as to slavery in the federal territories. Thus the twenty-one acted; and, as actions speak louder than words, so actions, under such responsibility, speak still louder.

Two of the twenty-three voted against Congressional prohibition of slavery in the federal territories, in the instances in which they acted upon the question. But for what reasons they so voted is not known. They may have done so because they thought a proper division of local from federal authority, or some provision or principle of the Constitution, stood in the way; or they may, without any such question, have voted against the prohibition, on what appeared to them to be sufficient grounds of expediency. No one who has sworn to support the Constitution, can conscientiously vote for what he understands to be an unconstitutional measure, however expedient he may think it; but one may and ought to vote against a measure which he deems constitutional, if, at the same time, he deems it inexpedient. It, therefore, would be unsafe to set down even the two who voted against the prohibition, as having done so because, in their understanding, any proper division of local from federal authority, or anything in the Constitution, forbade the Federal Government to control as to slavery in federal territory.

The remaining sixteen of the "thirty-nine," so far as I have discovered, have left no record of their understanding upon the direct question of federal control of slavery in the federal territories. But there is much reason to believe that their understanding upon that question would not have appeared different from that of their twenty-three compeers, had it been manifested at all.

For the purpose of adhering rigidly to the text, I have purposely omitted whatever understanding may have been manifested by any person, however distinguished, other than the thirty-nine fathers who framed the original Constitution; and, for the same reason, I have also omitted whatever understanding may have been manifested by any of the "thirty-nine" even, on any other phase of the general question of slavery. If we should look into their acts and declarations on those other phases, as the foreign slave trade, and the morality and policy of slavery generally, it would appear to us that on the direct question of federal control of slavery in federal territories, the sixteen, if they had acted at all, would probably have acted just as the twenty-three did. Among that sixteen were several of the most noted anti-slavery men of those times— as Dr. Franklin, Alexander Hamilton and Gouverneur Morris—while there was not one now known to have been otherwise, unless it may be John Rutledge, of South Carolina.

The sum of the whole is, that of our thirty-nine fathers who framed the original Constitution, twenty-one—a clear majority of the whole— certainly understood that no proper division of local from federal authority, nor any part of the Constitution, forbade the Federal Government to control slavery in the federal territories; while all the rest probably had the same understanding. Such, unquestionably, was the understanding of our fathers who framed the original Constitution; and the text affirms that they understood the question "better than we."

But, so far, I have been considering the understanding of the question manifested by the framers of the original Constitution. In and by the original instrument, a mode was provided for amending it; and, as I have already stated, the present frame of "the Government under which we live" consists of that original, and twelve amendatory articles framed and adopted since. Those who now insist that federal control of slavery in federal territories violates the Constitution, point us to the provisions which they suppose it thus violates; and, as I understand, they all fix upon provisions in these amendatory articles, and not in the original instrument. The Supreme Court, in the Dred Scott case, plant themselves upon the fifth amendment, which provides that no person shall be deprived of "life, liberty or property without due process of law;" while Senator Douglas and his peculiar adherents plant themselves upon the tenth amendment, providing that "the powers not delegated to the United States by the Constitution," "are reserved to the States respectively, or to the people."

Now, it so happens that these amendments were framed by the first Congress which sat under the Constitution—the identical Congress which passed the act already mentioned, enforcing the prohibition of slavery in the Northwestern Territory. Not only was it the same Congress, but they were the identical, same individual men who, at the same session, and at the same time within the session, had under consideration, and in progress toward maturity, these Constitutional amendments, and this act prohibiting slavery in all the territory the nation then owned. The Constitutional amendments were introduced before, and passed after the act enforcing the Ordinance of '87; so that, during the whole pendency of the act to enforce the Ordinance, the Constitutional amendments were also pending.

The seventy-six members of that Congress, including sixteen of the framers of the original Constitution, as before stated, were preeminently our fathers who framed that part of "the Government under which we live," which is now claimed as forbidding the Federal Government to control slavery in the federal territories.

Is it not a little presumptuous in any one at this day to affirm that the two things which that Congress deliberately framed, and carried to maturity at the same time, are absolutely inconsistent with each other? And does not such affirmation become impudently absurd when coupled with the other affirmation from the same mouth, that those who did the two things, alleged to be inconsistent, understood whether they really were inconsistent better than we—better than he who affirms that they are inconsistent?

It is surely safe to assume that the thirty-nine framers of the original Constitution, and the seventy-six members of the Congress which framed the amendments thereto, taken together, do certainly include those who may be fairly called "our fathers who framed the Government under which we live." And so assuming, I defy any man to show that any one of them ever, in his whole life, declared that, in his understanding, any proper division of local from federal authority, or any part of the Constitution, forbade the Federal Government to control as to slavery in the federal territories. I go a step further. I defy any one to show that any living man in the whole world ever did, prior to the beginning of the present century, (and I might almost say prior to the beginning of the last half of the present century,) declare that, in his understanding, any proper division of local from federal authority, or any part of the Constitution, forbade the Federal Government to control as to slavery in the federal territories. To those who now so declare, I give, not only "our fathers who framed the Government under which we live," but with them all other living men within the century in which it was framed, among whom to search, and they shall not be able to find the evidence of a single man agreeing with them.

Now, and here, let me guard a little against being misunderstood. I do not mean to say we are bound to follow implicitly in whatever our fathers did. To do so, would be to discard all the lights of current experience—to reject all progress—all improvement. What I do say is, that if we would supplant the opinions and policy of our fathers in any case, we should do so upon evidence so conclusive, and argument so clear, that even their great authority, fairly considered and weighed, cannot stand; and most surely not in a case whereof we ourselves declare they understood the question better than we.

If any man at this day sincerely believes that a proper division of local from federal authority, or any part of the Constitution, forbids the Federal Government to control as to slavery in the federal territories, he is right to say so, and to enforce his position by all truthful evidence and fair argument which he can. But he has no right to mislead others, who have less access to history, and less leisure to study it, into the false belief that "our fathers, who framed the Government under which we live," were of the same opinion—thus substituting falsehood and deception for truthful evidence and fair argument. If any man at this day sincerely believes "our fathers who framed the Government under which we live," used and applied principles, in other cases, which ought to have led them to understand that a proper division of local from federal authority or some part of the Constitution, forbids the Federal Government to control as to slavery in the federal territories, he is right to say so. But he should, at the same time, brave the responsibility of declaring that, in his opinion, he understands their principles better than they did themselves; and especially should he not shirk that responsibility by asserting that they "understood the question just as well, and even better, than we do now."

But enough! *Let all who believe that "our fathers, who framed the Government under which we live, understood this question just as well, and even better, than we do now," speak as they spoke, and act as they acted upon it. This is all Republicans ask—all Republicans desire—in relation to slavery. As those fathers marked it, so let it be again marked, as an evil not to be extended, but to be tolerated and protected only because of and so far as its actual presence among us makes that toleration and protection a necessity. Let all the guaranties those fathers gave it, be, not grudgingly, but fully and fairly maintained.* For this

Republicans contend, and with this, so far as I know or believe, they will be content.

And now, if they would listen—as I suppose they will not—I would address a few words to the Southern people.

I would say to them:—You consider yourselves a reasonable and a just people; and I consider that in the general qualities of reason and justice you are not inferior to any other people. Still, when you speak of us Republicans, you do so only to denounce us as reptiles, or, at the best, as no better than outlaws. You will grant a hearing to pirates or murderers, but nothing like it to "Black Republicans." In all your contentions with one another, each of you deems an unconditional condemnation of "Black Republicanism" as the first thing to be attended to. Indeed, such condemnation of us seems to be an indispensable prerequisite—license, so to speak—among you to be admitted or permitted to speak at all. Now, can you, or not, be prevailed upon to pause and to consider whether this is quite just to us, or even to yourselves? Bring forward your charges and specifications, and then be patient long enough to hear us deny or justify.

You say we are sectional. We deny it. That makes an issue; and the burden of proof is upon you. You produce your proof; and what is it? Why, that our party has no existence in your section—gets no votes in your section. The fact is substantially true; but does it prove the issue? If it does, then in case we should, without change of principle, begin to get votes in your section, we should thereby cease to be sectional. You cannot escape this conclusion; and yet, are you willing to abide by it? If you are, you will probably soon find that we have ceased to be sectional, for we shall get votes in your section this very year. You will then begin to discover, as the truth plainly is, that your proof does not touch the issue. The fact that we get no votes in your section, is a fact of your making, and not of ours. And if there be fault in that fact, that fault is primarily yours, and remains so until you show that we repel you by some wrong principle or practice. If we do repel you by any wrong principle or practice, the fault is ours; but this brings you to where you ought to have started—to a discussion of the right or wrong of our principle. If our principle, put in practice, would wrong your section for the benefit of ours, or for any other object, then our principle, and we with it, are sectional, and are justly opposed and denounced as such. Meet us, then, on the question of whether our principle, put in practice, would wrong your section; and so meet us as if it were possible that something may be said on our side. Do you accept the challenge? No! Then you really believe that the principle which "our fathers who framed the Government under which we live" thought so clearly right as to adopt it, and indorse it again and again, upon their official oaths, is in fact so clearly wrong as to demand your condemnation without a moment's consideration.

Some of you delight to flaunt in our faces the warning against sectional parties given by Washington in his Farewell Address. Less than eight years before Washington gave that warning, he had, as President of the United States, approved and signed an act of Congress, enforcing the prohibition of slavery in the Northwestern Territory, which act embodied the policy of the Government upon that subject up to and at the very moment he penned that warning; and about one year after he penned it, he wrote Lafayette that he considered that prohibition a wise measure, expressing in the same connection his hope that we should at some time have a confederacy of free States.

Bearing this in mind, and seeing that sectionalism has since arisen upon this same subject, is that warning a weapon in your hands against us, or in our hands against you? Could Washington himself speak, would he cast the blame of that sectionalism upon us, who sustain his policy, or upon you who repudiate it? We respect that warning of Washington, and we commend it to you, together with his example pointing to the right application of it.

But you say you are conservative—eminently conservative—while we are revolutionary, destructive, or something of the sort. What is conservatism? Is it not adherence to the old and tried, against the new and untried? We stick to, contend for, the identical old policy on the point in controversy which was adopted by "our fathers who framed the Government under which we live"; while you with one accord reject, and scout, and spit upon that old policy, and insist upon substituting something new. True, you disagree among yourselves as to what that substitute shall be. You are divided on new propositions and plans, but you are unanimous in rejecting and denouncing the old policy of the fathers. Some of you are for reviving the foreign slave trade; some for a Congressional Slave-Code for the Territories; some for Congress forbidding the Territories to prohibit Slavery within their limits; some for maintaining Slavery in the Territories through the judiciary; some for the "gur-reat pur-rinciple" that "if one man would enslave another, no third man should object," fantastically called "Popular Sovereignty"; but never a man among you in favor of federal prohibition of slavery in federal territories, according to the practice of "our fathers who framed the Government under which we live." Not one of all your various plans can show a precedent or an advocate in the century within which our Government originated. Consider, then, whether your claim of conservatism for yourselves, and your charge of destructiveness against us, are based on the most clear and stable foundations.

Again, you say we have made the slavery question more prominent than it formerly was. We deny it. We admit that it is more prominent, but we deny that we made it so. It was not we, but you, who discarded the old policy of the fathers. We resisted, and still resist, your innovation; and thence comes the greater prominence of the question. Would you have that question reduced to its former proportions? Go back to that old policy. What has been will be again, under the same conditions. If you would have the peace of the old times, readopt the precepts and policy of the old times.

You charge that we stir up insurrections among your slaves. We deny it; and what is your proof? Harper's Ferry! John Brown!! John Brown was no Republican; and you have failed to implicate a single Republican in his Harper's Ferry enterprise. If any member of our party is guilty in that matter, you know it or you do not know it. If you do know it, you are inexcusable for not designating the man and proving the fact. If you do not know it, you are inexcusable for asserting it, and especially for persisting in the assertion after you have tried and failed to make the proof. You need not be told that persisting in a charge which one does not know to be true, is simply malicious slander.

Some of you admit that no Republican designedly aided or encouraged the Harper's Ferry affair; but still insist that our doctrines and declarations necessarily lead to such results. We do not believe it. We know we hold to no doctrine, and make no declaration, which were not held to and made by "our fathers who framed the Government under which we live." You never dealt fairly by us in relation to this affair. When it occurred, some important State elections were near at hand, and you were in evident glee with the belief that, by charging the blame upon us, you could get an advantage of us in those elections. The elections came, and your expectations were not quite fulfilled. Every Republican man knew that, as to himself at least, your charge was a slander, and he was not much inclined by it to cast his vote in your favor. Republican doctrines and declarations are accompanied with a continual protest against any interference whatever with your slaves, or with you about your slaves. Surely, this does not encourage them to revolt. True, we do, in common with "our fathers, who framed the Government under which we live," declare our belief that slavery is wrong; but the slaves do not hear us declare even this. For anything we say or do, the slaves would scarcely know there is a Republican party. I believe they would not, in fact, generally know it but for your misrepresentations of us, in their hearing. In your political contests among yourselves, each faction charges the other with sympathy with Black Republicanism; and then, to give point to the charge, defines Black Republicanism to simply be insurrection, blood and thunder among the slaves.

Slave insurrections are no more common now than they were before the Republican party was organized. What induced the Southampton insurrection, twenty-eight years ago, in which, at least, three times as many lives were lost as at Harper's Ferry? You can scarcely stretch your very elastic fancy to the conclusion that Southampton was "got up by Black Republicanism." In the present state of things in the United States, I do not think a general, or even a very extensive slave insurrection, is possible. The indispensable concert of action cannot be attained. The slaves have no means of rapid communication; nor can incendiary freemen, black or white, supply it. The explosive materials are everywhere in parcels; but there neither are, nor can be supplied, the indispensable connecting trains.

Much is said by Southern people about the affection of slaves for their masters and mistresses; and a part of it, at least, is true. A plot for

an uprising could scarcely be devised and communicated to twenty
individuals before some one of them, to save the life of a favorite master
or mistress, would divulge it. This is the rule; and the slave revolution in
Hayti was not an exception to it, but a case occurring under peculiar
circumstances. The gunpowder plot of British history, though not connected with slaves, was more in point. In that case, only about twenty
were admitted to the secret; and yet one of them, in his anxiety to save a
friend, betrayed the plot to that friend, and, by consequence, averted the
calamity. Occasional poisonings from the kitchen, and open or stealthy
assassinations in the field, and local revolts extending to a score or so,
will continue to occur as the natural results of slavery; but no general
insurrection of slaves, as I think, can happen in this country for a long
time. Whoever much fears, or much hopes for such an event, will be alike
disappointed.

In the language of Mr. Jefferson, uttered many years ago, "It is still
in our power to direct the process of emancipation, and deportation,
peaceably, and in such slow degrees, as that the evil will wear off
insensibly; and their places be, pari passu, filled up by free white
laborers. If, on the contrary, it is left to force itself on, human nature
must shudder at the prospect held up."

Mr. Jefferson did not mean to say, nor do I, that the power of
emancipation is in the Federal Government. He spoke of Virginia; and,
as to the power of emancipation, I speak of the slaveholding States only.
The Federal Government, however, as we insist, has the power of
restraining the extension of the institution—the power to insure that a
slave insurrection shall never occur on any American soil which is now
free from slavery.

John Brown's effort was peculiar. It was not a slave insurrection. It
was an attempt by white men to get up a revolt among slaves, in which
the slaves refused to participate. In fact, it was so absurd that the slaves,
with all their ignorance, saw plainly enough it could not succeed. That
affair, in its philosophy, corresponds with the many attempts, related in
history, at the assassination of kings and emperors. An enthusiast
broods over the oppression of a people till he fancies himself commissioned by Heaven to liberate them.

He ventures the attempt, which ends in little else than his own
execution. Orsini's attempt on Louis Napoleon, and John Brown's attempt at Harper's Ferry were, in their philosophy, precisely the same.
The eagerness to cast blame on old England in the one case, and on New
England in the other, does not disprove the sameness of the two things.

And how much would it avail you, if you could, by the use of John
Brown, Helper's Book, and the like, break up the Republican organization? Human action can be modified to some extent, but human nature
cannot be changed. There is a judgment and a feeling against slavery in
this nation, which cast at least a million and a half of votes. You cannot
destroy that judgment and feeling—that sentiment—by breaking up the
political organization which rallies around it. You can scarcely scatter

and disperse an army which has been formed into order in the face of your heaviest fire; but if you could, how much would you gain by forcing the sentiment which created it out of the peaceful channel of the ballot-box, into some other channel? What would that other channel probably be? Would the number of John Browns be lessened or enlarged by the operation?

But you will break up the Union rather than submit to a denial of your Constitutional rights.

That has a somewhat reckless sound; but it would be palliated, if not fully justified, were we proposing, by the mere force of numbers, to deprive you of some right, plainly written down in the Constitution. But we are proposing no such thing.

When you make these declarations, you have a specific and well-understood allusion to an assumed Constitutional right of yours, to take slaves into the federal territories, and to hold them there as property. But no such right is specifically written in the Constitution. That instrument is literally silent about any such right. We, on the contrary, deny that such a right has any existence in the Constitution, even by implication.

Your purpose, then, plainly stated, is, that you will destroy the Government, unless you be allowed to construe and enforce the Constitution as you please, on all points in dispute between you and us. You will rule or ruin in all events.

This, plainly stated, is your language. Perhaps you will say the Supreme Court has decided the disputed Constitutional question in your favor. Not quite so. But waiving the lawyer's distinction between dictum and decision, the Court have decided the question for you in a sort of way. The Court have substantially said, it is your Constitutional right to take slaves into the federal territories, and to hold them there as property. When I say the decision was made in a sort of way, I mean it was made in a divided Court, by a bare majority of the Judges, and they not quite agreeing with one another in the reasons for making it; that it is so made as that its avowed supporters disagree with one another about its meaning, and that it was mainly based upon a mistaken statement of fact—the statement in the opinion that "the right of property in a slave is distinctly and expressly affirmed in the Constitution."

An inspection of the Constitution will show that the right of property in a slave is not "*distinctly* and *expressly* affirmed" in it. Bear in mind, the Judges do not pledge their judicial opinion that such right is *impliedly* affirmed in the Constitution; but they pledge their veracity that it is "*distinctly* and *expressly*" affirmed there—"distinctly," that is, not mingled with anything else—"expressly," that is, in words meaning just that, without the aid of any inference, and susceptible of no other meaning.

If they had only pledged their judicial opinion that such right is affirmed in the instrument by implication, it would be open to others to show that neither the word "slave" nor "slavery" is to be found in the Constitution, nor the word "property" even, in any connection with language alluding to the things slave, or slavery, and that wherever in that instrument the slave is alluded to, he is called a "person";—and wherever his master's legal right in relation to him is alluded to, it is spoken of as "service or labor which may be due,"—as a debt payable in service or labor. Also, it would be open to show, by contemporaneous history, that this mode of alluding to slaves and slavery, instead of speaking of them, was employed on purpose to exclude from the Constitution the idea that there could be property in man.

To show all this, is easy and certain.

When this obvious mistake of the Judges shall be brought to their notice, is it not reasonable to expect that they will withdraw the mistaken statement, and reconsider the conclusion based upon it?

And then it is to be remembered that "our fathers, who framed the Government under which we live"—the men who made the Constitution—decided this same Constitutional question in our favor, long ago—decided it without division among themselves, when making the decision; without division among themselves about the meaning of it after it was made, and, so far as any evidence is left, without basing it upon any mistaken statement of facts.

Under all these circumstances, do you really feel yourselves justified to break up this Government, unless such a court decision as yours is, shall be at once submitted to as a conclusive and final rule of political action? But you will not abide the election of a Republican President! In that supposed event, you say, you will destroy the Union; and then, you say, the great crime of having destroyed it will be upon us! That is cool. A highwayman holds a pistol to my ear, and mutters through his teeth, "Stand and deliver, or I shall kill you, and then you will be a murderer!"

To be sure, what the robber demanded of me—my money—was my own; and I had a clear right to keep it; but it was no more my own than my vote is my own; and the threat of death to me, to extort my money, and the threat of destruction to the Union, to extort my vote, can scarcely be distinguished in principle.

A few words now to Republicans. *It is exceedingly desirable that all parts of this great Confederacy shall be at peace, and in harmony, one with another. Let us Republicans do our part to have it so. Even though much provoked, let us do nothing through passion and ill temper. Even though the southern people will not so much as listen to us, let us calmly consider their demands, and yield to them if, in our deliberate view of our duty, we possibly can.* Judging by all they say and do, and by the subject and nature of their controversy with us, let us determine, if we can, what will satisfy them.

Will they be satisfied if the Territories be unconditionally surrendered to them? We know they will not. In all their present complaints against us, the Territories are scarcely mentioned. Invasions and insurrections are the rage now. Will it satisfy them, if, in the future, we have nothing to do with invasions and insurrections? We know it will not. We so know, because we know we never had anything to do with invasions and insurrections; and yet this total abstaining does not exempt us from the charge and the denunciation.

The question recurs, what will satisfy them? Simply this: We must not only let them alone, but we must, somehow, convince them that we do let them alone. This, we know by experience, is no easy task. We have been so trying to convince them from the very beginning of our organization, but with no success. In all our platforms and speeches we have constantly protested our purpose to let them alone; but this has had no tendency to convince them. Alike unavailing to convince them, is the fact that they have never detected a man of us in any attempt to disturb them.

These natural, and apparently adequate means all failing, what will convince them? This, and this only: cease to call slavery *wrong*, and join them in calling it *right*. And this must be done thoroughly—done in *acts* as well as in *words*. Silence will not be tolerated—we must place ourselves avowedly with them. Senator Douglas's new sedition law must be enacted and enforced, suppressing all declarations that slavery is wrong, whether made in politics, in presses, in pulpits, or in private. We must arrest and return their fugitive slaves with greedy pleasure. We must pull down our Free State constitutions. The whole atmosphere must be disinfected from all taint of opposition to slavery, before they will cease to believe that all their troubles proceed from us.

I am quite aware they do not state their case precisely in this way. Most of them would probably say to us, "Let us alone, do nothing to us, and say what you please about slavery." But we do let them alone—have never disturbed them—so that, after all, it is what we say, which dissatisfies them. They will continue to accuse us of doing, until we cease saying.

I am also aware they have not, as yet, in terms, demanded the overthrow of our Free-State Constitutions. Yet those Constitutions declare the wrong of slavery, with more solemn emphasis, than do all other sayings against it; and when all these other sayings shall have been silenced, the overthrow of these Constitutions will be demanded, and nothing be left to resist the demand. It is nothing to the contrary, that they do not demand the whole of this just now. Demanding what they do, and for the reason they do, they can voluntarily stop nowhere short of this consummation. Holding, as they do, that slavery is morally right, and socially elevating, they cannot cease to demand a full national recognition of it, as a legal right, and a social blessing.

Nor can we justifiably withhold this, on any ground save our conviction that slavery is wrong. If slavery is right, all words, acts, laws, and constitutions against it, are themselves wrong, and should be silenced, and swept away. If it is right, we cannot justly object to its nationality—its universality; if it is wrong, they cannot justly insist upon its extension—its enlargement. All they ask, we could readily grant, if we thought slavery right; all we ask, they could as readily grant, if they thought it wrong. Their thinking it right, and our thinking it wrong, is the precise fact upon which depends the whole controversy. Thinking it right, as they do, they are not to blame for desiring its full recognition, as being right; but, thinking it wrong, as we do, can we yield to them? Can we cast our votes with their view, and against our own? In view of our moral, social, and political responsibilities, can we do this?

Wrong as we think slavery is, we can yet afford to let it alone where it is, because that much is due to the necessity arising from its actual presence in the nation; but can we, while our votes will prevent it, allow it to spread into the National Territories, and to overrun us here in these Free States? If our sense of duty forbids this, then let us stand by our duty, fearlessly and effectively. Let us be diverted by none of those sophistical contrivances wherewith we are so industriously plied and belabored—contrivances such as groping for some middle ground between the right and the wrong, vain as the search for a man who should be neither a living man nor a dead man—such as a policy of "don't care" on a question about which all true men do care—such as Union appeals beseeching true Union men to yield to Disunionists, reversing the divine rule, and calling, not the sinners, but the righteous to repentance—such as invocations to Washington, imploring men to unsay what Washington said, and undo what Washington did.

Neither let us be slandered from our duty by false accusations against us, nor frightened from it by menaces of destruction to the Government nor of dungeons to ourselves. *LET US HAVE FAITH THAT RIGHT MAKES MIGHT, AND IN THAT FAITH, LET US, TO THE END, DARE TO DO OUR DUTY AS WE UNDERSTAND IT.*

Notes

1. *The Cooper Institute Speech.* David Herbert Donald, in his superb biography, LINCOLN (1995), describes the origin and delivery of Lincoln's 1860 speech at the Cooper Institute:

> Shrewdly Lincoln recognized that his own chances against these better-known rivals could best be advanced not by an open announcement of his candidacy but by small, private moves to consolidate his strength and expand his influence. To ensure wider circulation of his ideas, he took an active role in compiling and preserving his 1858 debates with Douglas. With the assistance of Henry C. Whitney he collected the reports of his speeches that appeared in the *Chicago Press and Tribune* and those of Douglas in the *Chicago Times*. These he carefully pasted in a large scrapbook, which he hoped to have published. After plans for having a book printed in Springfield failed, he turned over the project to Follett, Foster & Company of Columbus, Ohio, which shortly before the national nominating conventions of 1860 issued a 268–page book titled *Political Debates Between Hon. Abraham Lincoln and Hon. Stephen A. Douglas, in the Celebrated Campaign of 1858, in Illinois*. It immediately became a best-seller.

In December 1859, Lincoln made another quiet move to gain broader recognition by preparing an autobiography for campaign purposes. Jesse W. Fell, a Bloomington politician, forwarded a request from Joseph J. Lewis, of the *Chester County (Pennsylvania) Times*, for biographical information he could use in preparing an article on Lincoln. Lincoln complied with a terse sketch that reviewed his homespun beginnings, summarized his public career, and ended: "If any personal description of me is thought desirable, it may be said, I am, in height, six feet, four inches, nearly; lean in flesh, weighing, on an average, one hundred and eighty pounds; dark complexion, with coarse black hair, and grey eyes—no other marks or brands recollected." This he sent to Fell, noting, "There is not much of it, for the reason, I suppose, that there is not much of me." Lewis evidently found the sketch meager, for he embroidered it with remarks on Lincoln's oratorical gifts and on his long record of support for a protective tariff, so dear to Pennsylvanians. His article, widely copied in other Republican newspapers, was the first published biography of Lincoln.

An even stronger indication of Lincoln's growing interest in a presidential race was the alacrity with which he accepted an invitation from New York to lecture at Henry Ward Beecher's Plymouth Church in Brooklyn in February 1860. Knowing that he would appear before a sophisticated Eastern audience, he promptly began more careful research and preparation than for any other speech of his life. He also ordered a brand-new black suit for the occasion, for which he paid the local tailors, Woods & Henckle, $100.

By the time he arrived in the East, sponsorship of the address had been taken over by the Young Men's Central Republican Union, a body that included sixty-five-year-old William Cullen Bryant, forty-nine-year-old Horace Greeley, and other such youths, who were organizing a stop-Seward movement. Lincoln's was the third in a series of lectures—following addresses by Frank Blair, the Missouri anti-slavery leader, and Cassius M. Clay, the Kentucky abolitionist—designed, according to the sponsors, "to call out our better, but busier citizens, who never attend political meetings." Without informing Lincoln, the Young Republicans also shifted the lecture from Brooklyn to the Cooper Union in Manhattan. Learning of the change after he arrived and registered at the Astor House, Lincoln spent his first day in New York revising his address, so as to make it more suitable for a general political audience than for a religious congregation.

On Monday, February 27, escorted by several of the Young Republicans, he caught a glimpse of Broadway and had his photograph, which he had called his "shadow," taken at Mathew B. Brady's studio, where he exchanged pleasantries with George Bancroft. "I am on my way to Massachusetts," Lincoln told the historian, "where I have a son at school, who, if report be true, already knows much more than his father." The portrait Brady produced after this sitting was a work of art; he retouched the negative in order to correct Lincoln's left eye that seemed to be roving upward and eliminated harsh lines from his face to show an almost handsome, statesmanlike image.

That night, after a warm introduction by Bryant, Lincoln appeared before a capacity audience at the Cooper Union. Many of his listeners expected "something weird, rough, and uncultivated," George Haven Putnam remembered, and Lincoln's appearance did nothing to undeceive them. "The long, ungainly figure, upon which hung clothes that, while new for the trip, were evidently the work of an unskilled tailor; the large feet; the clumsy hands, of which ... the orator seemed to be unduly conscious; the long, gaunt head capped by a shock of hair that seemed not to have been thoroughly brushed out," Putnam continued, "made a picture which did not fit in with New York's conception of a finished statesman." Equally disconcerting was Lincoln's voice, for it was high and piercing in tone at the outset.

But the speech that he delivered, reading carefully and soberly from sheets of blue foolscap, quickly erased the impression of a crude frontiersman. It was a masterful exploration of the political paths open to the nation. In the first third of the address Lincoln closely examined Douglas's contention that popular sovereignty was simply a continuation of a policy initiated by the Founding Fathers. After digging through the records of the Constitutional Convention and the debates in the earliest Congresses, he was able to show that of the thirty-nine signers of the Constitution, at least twenty-one demonstrated by their votes that the federal government had the power to control slavery in the national territories; other noted antislavery men, like Benjamin Franklin, Alexander Hamilton, and Gouverneur Morris, should probably be added to that list, though they were not called to vote on this specific question. This minutely detailed record confirmed a position that Lincoln had been arguing for years: that prior to Douglas's introduction of the Kansas-Nebraska Act it was impossible "to show that any living man in the whole world ever did ... declare that ... the Constitution forbade the Federal Government to control as to slavery in the federal territories."

Next Lincoln examined the Southern position, though he had little hope that his arguments would be heard, much less heeded, in that section. Nevertheless, he seized the opportunity to argue that the Republicans were the true conservatives on questions relating to slavery; they adhered "to the old and tried, against the new and untried," while Southern fire-eaters "with one accord reject, and scout, and spit upon that old policy." This gave him a welcome opening to explain the Republican attitude toward the raid that John Brown and a handful of zealous followers had staged in October 1859 on Harpers Ferry, Virginia. At that time Lincoln denounced Brown's attempt to stir up an insurrection among the slaves as "wrong for two reasons. It was a violation of law and it was, as all such attacks must be, futile as far as any effect it might have on the extinction of a great evil." Though he had paid tribute to Brown's "great courage, rare unselfishness" and sympathized with his hatred of slavery, he concluded that the old abolitionist was "insane." Now he took the offensive, pointing out that Brown's raid was not a slave insurrection but "an attempt by white men to get up a revolt among slaves, in which the slaves refused to participate"; further, he pointed out, Southerners after an elaborate congressional investigation had failed to implicate a single Republican in it. Southern efforts to capitalize on John Brown's raid were simply additional evidence of their determination to "rule or ruin in all events." More recently Southerners had gone so far as to announce that if a Republican was elected President in 1860 the Union would be dissolved and the fault would be the North's. "That is cool," Lincoln exclaimed. "A highwayman holds a pistol to my ear, and mutters through his teeth, 'Stand and deliver, or I shall kill you, and then you will be a murderer!' "

What should Northerners do? Avoiding both the moral indifference with which Douglas approached the slavery issue and the proslavery zeal of the Southern radicals, Republicans should fearlessly and effectively persist in excluding slavery from the national territories, confining it to the states where it already existed. "Neither let us be slandered from our duty by false accusations against us, nor frightened from it by menaces of destruction to the Government nor of dungeons to ourselves," Lincoln announced in his spine-tingling peroration. "Let us have faith that right makes might, and in that faith, let us, to the end, dare to do our duty as we understand it."

As a speech, it was a superb performance. The audience frequently applauded during the delivery of the address, and when Lincoln closed, the crowd cheered and stood, waving handkerchiefs and hats. Noah Brooks, then working for the *New York Tribune,* exclaimed: "He's the greatest man since St. Paul," and a student at the Harvard Law School, trained to master his emotions, told his father, "It was the best speech I ever heard." The next day four New York papers printed the address in full. Bryant in the *New York Evening Post* called it forcible and "most logically and convincingly stated." Greeley, less restrained, announced: "Mr. Lincoln is one of Nature's orators, using his rare powers solely and effectively to elucidate and to convince, though their inevitable effect is to delight and electrify as well." Immediately published in pamphlet form, the Cooper Union address was issued and reissued as a Republican tract by the *New York Tribune,* the *Chicago Press and Tribune,* the *Detroit Tribune,* and the *Albany Evening Journal.*

It was also a superb political move for an unannounced presidential aspirant. Appearing in Seward's home state, sponsored by a group largely loyal to Chase, Lincoln shrewdly made no reference to either of these Republican rivals for the nomination. Recognizing that if the Republicans were going to win in 1860 they needed the support of men who had voted for Fillmore in the previous election, Lincoln in his Cooper Union address stressed his conservatism. He did not mention his house-divided thesis or Seward's irrepressible-conflict prediction; Republicans were presented as a party of moderates who were simply trying to preserve the legacy of the Founding Fathers against the radical assaults of the proslavery element. Even Lincoln's language contributed to the effect he sought; the careful structure of the speech, the absence of incendiary rhetoric, even the laborious recital of the voting records of the Founding Fathers, all suggested reasonableness and stability, not wide-eyed fanaticism. In short, it was, as one of the sponsors wrote, an enormous success. Sending Lincoln the agreed-upon fee of $200, he added, "I would that if were $200,000 for you are worthy of it."

2. *That is Cool.* Towards the end of his Cooper Institute speech, Lincoln chides the Southerners:

> But you will not abide the election of a Republican president! In that supposed event, you say, you will destroy the Union; and then, you say, the great crime of having destroyed it will be upon us! That is cool. A highwayman holds a pistol to my ear, and mutters through his teeth, "Stand and deliver, or I shall kill you, and then you will be a murderer!"

"That is cool" sounds very modern. Please determine the vernacular meaning of that phrase as used in 1860, and whether that meaning has influenced the present-day meaning of the phrase.

3. *Article IV.* Why did Lincoln not discuss Art. IV, sec. 3, paragraph 2, of the United States Constitution, which gives Congress the power to make "all needful Rules and Regulations" in regard to U.S. territories?

4. *Logic.* Lincoln uses logical reasoning to make each of his points. Try charting the logical structure of the speech. At which points is his logic most susceptible to challenge? Have you heard any recent political speeches that rely primarily upon logic for their effect?

5. *Effect.* As Donald notes, this speech caused a sensation as delivered. What effect did the written speech have upon you? Compare your reaction to the Cooper Institute Address with your reactions to "The Gettysburg Address" and "I Have a Dream," *infra.*

THE GETTYSBURG ADDRESS
Abraham Lincoln

NATIONAL CEMETERY
GETTYSBURG, PENNSYLVANIA
November 19, 1863

Four score and seven years ago our fathers brought forth on this continent, a new nation, conceived in liberty, and dedicated to the proposition that all men are created equal.

Now we are engaged in a great civil war, testing whether that nation, or any nation so conceived and so dedicated, can long endure. We are met on a great battlefield of that war. We have come to dedicate a portion of that field as a final resting place for those who here gave their lives that that nation might live. It is altogether fitting and proper that we should do this.

But, in a larger sense, we cannot dedicate, we cannot consecrate, we cannot hallow this ground. The brave men, living and dead, who struggled here have consecrated it far above our poor power to add or detract. The world will little note nor long remember what we say here, but it can never forget what they did here. It is for us, the living, rather, to be dedicated here to the unfinished work which they who fought here have thus far so nobly advanced. It is rather for us to be here dedicated to the great task remaining before us—that from these honored dead we take increased devotion to that cause for which they gave the last full measure of devotion—that we here highly resolve that these dead shall not have died in vain—that this nation, under God, shall have a new birth of freedom—and that government of the people, by the people, for the people, shall not perish from the earth.

Notes

1. *The Gettysburg Address(es).* Perhaps no speech is more widely known among American school children than Lincoln's *Gettysburg Address.* The version printed here, however, is only one of several versions of the speech. Two drafts of the speech—differing from one another and from this version—are available in holograph form on the website of the Library of Congress, *<http://www.loc.gov/exhibits/gadd/gadrft.html>*(visited December 1, 2002). Compare these versions to the version printed here (the "Bliss" version) and discuss whether these differences in wording change the meaning or effect of the speech. Reading the various versions aloud may be enlightening.

2. *The Occasion.* The Battle of Gettysburg (July 1–3, 1863) was a turning point in the American Civil War. It marked the defeat of Lee's attempt to invade Pennsylvania and reach Washington. Moreover, the manpower and psychological drain on the Southern cause as a result of this loss was inestimable.

The occasion for the speech was to dedicate the new Gettysburg national cemetery, and to commemorate the war dead. The principal speaker was Edward Everett, an eminent scholar, statesman, and theologian, who spoke for two hours. President Lincoln was invited to make a few remarks as a courtesy. His speech lasted about three minutes.

Everett's speech, however, was little noted nor long remembered, while Lincoln's will never be forgotten. There Lincoln shifted the focus and purpose of war, from preservation of the Union to emancipation of the slave. Drawing on the Declaration of Independence, rather than the Constitution, he breathtakingly declared that this nation was conceived in liberty and "dedicated to the proposition that all men are created equal." After this speech, the position of the South became morally indefensible in the eyes of Britain, of Europe, and of the world.

3. *The Style.* Gary Wills, in his little book *Lincoln At Gettysburg* (1992), notes the similarities between Lincoln's speech and a Greek oration in praise of the war dead. The speech is impersonal, urging its hearers on to higher levels of patriotism. Ronald C. White, in his book *Lincoln's Greatest Speech* (2002), notes how Lincoln in this speech, as well as others, has a structure beginning in the past, moving to the present, and finally looking to the future. This speech has the flow of the movement of life.

In the note after Lincoln's *Second Inaugural Address*, which follows, the commentator indicates that *The Gettysburg Address* is particularly characterized by the use of sets of threes: a new nation, conceived in liberty, and dedicated; that nation, or any nation, can long endure; we cannot dedicate, we cannot consecrate, we cannot hallow; and on to the soaring climax of:

that from, that we here, that this nation; and ending with the ringing double triplet—and that government—of the people—by the people—for the people—shall not perish—from this earth—

What was Lincoln trying to accomplish by this repeated, pervasive use of triplets? Was he appealing to that strong Christian symbol, the trinity? Or was he echoing the Pauline doctrine of faith, hope, and charity—the greatest of these being charity? However the speech is described, its Biblical overtones are unmistakable—just as they are in *The Second Inaugural Address.*

SECOND INAUGURAL ADDRESS
Abraham Lincoln
Washington, D.C.
March 4, 1865

At this second appearing to take the oath of the presidential office, there is less occasion for an extended address than there was at the first. Then a statement, somewhat in detail, of a course to be pursued, seemed fitting and proper. Now, at the expiration of four years, during which public declarations have been constantly called forth on every point and phase of the great contest which still absorbs the attention, and engrosses the energies of the nation, little that is new could be presented. The progress of our arms, upon which all else chiefly depends, is as well known to the public as to myself; and it is, I trust, reasonably satisfactory and encouraging to all. With high hope for the future, no prediction in regard to it is ventured.

On the occasion corresponding to this four years ago, all thoughts were anxiously directed to an impending civil war. All dreaded it—all sought to avert it. While the inaugural address was being delivered from this place, devoted altogether to *saving* the Union without war, insurgent agents were in the city seeking to *destroy* it without war—seeking to dissolve the Union, and divide effects, by negotiation. Both parties deprecated war; but one of them would *make* war rather than let the nation survive; and the other would *accept* war rather than let it perish. And the war came.

One eighth of the whole population were colored slaves, not distributed generally over the Union, but localized in the Southern part of it. These slaves constituted a peculiar and powerful interest. All knew that this interest was, somehow, the cause of the war. To strengthen, perpetuate, and extend this interest was the object for which the insurgents would rend the Union, even by war; while the government claimed no right to do more than to restrict the territorial enlargement of it. Neither party expected for the war, the magnitude, or the duration, which it has already attained. Neither anticipated that the *cause* of the conflict might cease with, or even before, the conflict itself should cease. Each looked for an easier triumph, and a result less fundamental and astounding. Both read the same Bible, and pray to the same God; and each invokes His aid against the other. It may seem strange that any men should dare to ask a just God's assistance in wringing their bread from the sweat of other men's faces; but let us judge not that we be not judged. The prayers of both could not be answered; that of neither has been answered fully. The Almighty has his own purposes. "Woe unto the world because of offences! for it must needs be that offences come; but woe to that man by whom the offence cometh!" If we shall suppose that American Slavery is one of those offences which, in the providence of God, must needs come, but which, having continued through His appointed time, He now wills to remove, and that He gives to both North and South, this terrible war, as the woe due to those by whom the offence came, shall we discern therein any departure from those divine attributes which the believers in a Living God always ascribe to Him? Fondly do we hope—fervently do we pray—that this mighty scourge of war may speedily pass away. Yet, if God wills that it continue, until all the wealth piled by the bond-man's two hundred and fifty years of unrequited toil shall be sunk, and until every drop of blood drawn with the lash, shall be paid by another drawn with the sword, as was said three thousand years ago, so still it must be said, "the judgments of the Lord, are true and righteous altogether."

With malice toward none; with charity for all; with firmness in the right, as God gives us to see the right, let us strive on to finish the work we are in; to bind up the nation's wounds; to care for him who shall have borne the battle, and for his widow, and his orphan—to do all which may achieve and cherish a just and lasting peace, among ourselves, and with all nations.

Notes

1. *The Second Inaugural Address.* One writer, in 80 SOUNDINGS 154–59 (Spring 1997), describes this speech as follows:

> Lincoln delivered his Second Inaugural Address slightly over a month before the Confederate surrender at Appomattox on April 9, 1865, and about six weeks before his assassination on April 14. A sense of tragedy and deep sadness hung heavily over the President, mixed with the hope that the war might soon be over. There is a pervasive fatalism in the speech, and perhaps a presentiment of his own approaching death.

> The Second Inaugural Address merits comparison with the Gettysburg Address of 1863. At Gettysburg Lincoln spoke in a powerful, solemn, positive manner that captured the conscience of the nation for all time. There he spoke in a triplet meter, reflecting, it might be suggested, the religious concept of Trinity. The speech was short, ending in one of the best-known phrases in American history—"that government of the people, by the people, for the people, shall not perish from the earth."

> The Gettysburg Address has received widespread acclaim. The Second Inaugural Address has received nothing approaching similar recognition. Yet in many ways the Second Inaugural Address equals or surpasses that at Gettysburg. Perhaps the sober metaphysics of the

Second Inaugural Address has obscured its greatness in the popular mind.

Like the Gettysburg Address, the Second Inaugural is short, and it ends in a series of unforgettable prepositional phrases:

> With malice toward none; with charity for all; with firmness in the right, as God gives us to see the right, let us strive on to finish the work we are in; to bind up the nation's wounds; to care for him who shall have borne the battle, and for his widow, and his orphan—to do all which may achieve and cherish a just and a lasting peace, among ourselves, and with all nations.

While the Gettysburg Address resounds in threes, the Second Inaugural Address is marked by a steady, implacable rhythm that seems closer to the iambic. The speech begins sharply, as a kind of clarion call, "Fellow Countrymen." But the iambic soon asserts itself:

At this second appearing
> to take the oath
>> of the presidential office....

And it continues, despite interruptions, to Lincoln's closing words:

> achieve and cherish
>> a just and lasting peace
>>> among ourselves
>>>> and with all nations.

What was Lincoln trying to achieve here? The linked stresses of the dominant meter are consonant with his underlying theme. He would "bind up the nation's wounds" to reunite North and South into a single whole: one nation.

There is about the entire speech a stasis that fixes the speaker and listener in a timeless moment. Stationary "ing" words appear throughout: "At this second appearing," "fitting and proper," "encouraging to all," and so on. Verbs of the passive voice, conveying the sense of an action that is at once impersonal and public, witnessed, shared, and suffered by all, are everywhere: "to be pursued," "could not be answered," "is as well known," "is ventured," and so on. After four dreadful years, the President is calling for the war and for time to stop, and for the nation to take account of itself.

A vast impersonality undergirds the stasis. Prepositional phrases occur with great frequency and give the speech a distended quality. Something is happening to which we are all, North and South, party, but there is no thought or talk of controlling this happening or its outcome. There is frequent use of the impersonal pronoun. Lincoln seldom refers to himself, or indeed to anyone else, as an actor in the drama.

He uses metonymy with curious impersonal power. There is only one true metonym in the speech: "The progress of our arms." But a metonymic quality runs throughout: thus, the second "appearing" to take the "oath" of the presidential "office"; the "energies" of the nation; the "Union"; the "peculiar and powerful interest" of slavery; and so on.

Perhaps the most dramatic quasi-metonymic device occurs at the end of the second paragraph: "Both parties deprecated war; but one of them would *make* war rather than let the nation survive; and the other would *accept* war rather than let it perish. And the war came." The simple, impersonal monosyllabic conjunctive sentence, "And the war came," sounds like the booming of cannons: a giant, personified beast, slouching toward Fort Sumter.

Lincoln, like all the greatest writers, uses literacy devices with extraordinary effect. The war, impersonal as it is, is yet deadly familiar. He concludes by urging the nation not just to care for the veterans, both North and South, but "for him who shall have borne the battle"—the "him" being as personal as your own brother.

The speech is filled with marvelous, complex, alliterative, assonant periodic sentences that depersonalize and elevate the occasion: "Now, at the expiration of four years...," "To strengthen, perpetuate, and extend this interest...," "If we shall suppose that American Slavery ..." (not just Southern slavery), "Yet, if God wills that it continue ...," and the incomparable last paragraph-sentence, "With malice toward none; with charity for all. ..."

Lincoln was a lawyer, and he thought and spoke like a lawyer. His First Inaugural and Cooper Institute speeches are brilliant examples of legal argumentation. The Second Inaugural Address is no less so, though in a more muted manner. The organization of the speech reads like a dispassionate legal brief. There is an introduction, a recounting of the origin of the war and its consequences, and then the challenge of the future. Abstract legal terminology occurs throughout. Both "parties" deprecated war. But the insurgent agents sought to "dissolve the Union, and divide effects, by negotiation." All knew that the "peculiar" interest of slavery was somehow the cause of the war. The government claimed "no right to do more than to restrict the territorial enlargement" of this interest.

The most outstanding feature of the Address is its grandly abstract religious symbolism, which appears most prominently in the third paragraph of the speech. This paragraph is equal in length to the combined length of the other three paragraphs. It begins in the past tense, tracing the history, the causes, and the course of the war. Then, a third of the way through, it shifts abruptly and dramatically to the present tense with the remarkable and inescapable irony of the case: "Both read the same Bible, and pray to the same God; and each invokes His aid against the other." There follow a series of Biblical references: "wringing their bread from the sweat of other men's faces" (cf. Gen. 3.19); "let us judge not that we be not judged" (Matt. 7.1); "Woe unto the world because of offences!" (Matt. 18.17); and "the judgments of the Lord are true and righteous altogether" (Psalms 19.19).

These Biblical references set the tone for the unanswered and unanswerable central question of the speech:

If we shall suppose that American Slavery is one of those offences which, in the providence of God, must needs come, but which, having continued through His appointed time, He now wills to remove, and that He gives to both North and South, this terrible war, as the woe due to those by whom the offence came, shall we discern therein any departure from those divine attributes which the believers in a Living God always ascribe to Him?

One is reminded here of a multitude of Biblical texts. Why did Judas betray his Master? Luke says simply: "Then entered Satan into Judas surnamed Iscariot" (22.3). Thus the Lord spoke to Isaiah. "I form the light, and create darkness: I make peace, and create evil: I the Lord do all these things" (Isaiah 45.7). And so the prayer: "And lead us not into temptation" (Matthew 6.13). Job "was perfect and upright, and one that feared God and eschewed evil" (Job 1.6). But there was a day "when the sons of God came to present themselves before the Lord, and Satan came also among them" (Job 1.6). Now the serpent, "more subtil than any beast of the field which the Lord God had made," said unto Eve, "for God doth know that in the day ye eat thereof, then your eyes shall be opened, and ye shall be as gods, knowing good and evil" (Genesis 3.1,5). And the Lord God said, "Behold, the man is become as one of us, to know good and evil" (Genesis 3.22). As Milton put it, the story of the fall is told to "justify the ways of God to men" (*Paradise Lost 1.22*). Lincoln was intimately familiar with such hard places as these—both in the Bible and in his own life.

With magnificent ambiguity, Lincoln begins that central question *"If we shall suppose"*—with the subjunctive "if" and "suppose" surrounding the imperative "shall." Having posed the question, he does not, and cannot, answer it directly, anymore than Job could explain his tribulations, or than we can explain Judas's motivation, or than anyone can explain the temptation of the tree in the midst of the garden of Eden. So he answers indirectly, with the serenity and faith that have always characterized true believers in a living God: "[T]he judgements of the Lord are true and righteous altogether." It is this serenity and faith that enable him to conclude "with malice toward none," and "with charity for all."

The third and fourth paragraphs whipsaw between fatalism and free will, steel firmness and gentle charity. First the fatalism, contained in the above-quoted sentence, followed by the firm resolve that if God wills the war to continue, then the North is prepared to fight as long as necessary and at whatever price, to bring down the insidious evil of American slavery. These powerful, fatalistic, bellicose statements are immediately followed by one of the most humane statements in all of literature—especially, coming as it does, from the President who has waged "this mighty scourge of war" for four excruciating years: "With malice toward none; with charity for all.... let us ... bind up the nation's wounds."

Seldom have sound and meaning been so successfully bound together as in the Second Inaugural Address. Here President Lincoln states his credo: of fatalism, of extraordinary force of character, of nobility, and of boundless love for humankind. This speech is unsurpassed in the annals of American literature. It is fashioned neither of patriotism, nor of sorrow, nor of jubilation, nor of any particular emotion. It takes us outside ourselves, and onto a higher plane than we ever thought we could attain.

2. *Providence. See* C.G. Jung, "Answer to Job," *in* 11 THE COLLECTED WORKS OF C.G. JUNG 355–470 (R.F.C. Hull, trans., Princeton UP 2d ed. 1969).

E. THE CIVIL RIGHTS MOVEMENT

The fabric of American society seemed about to unravel in the 1960s, and politics seemed about to spin out of control. The highly divisive war in Vietnam escalated. John F. Kennedy was assassinated in 1963. Martin Luther King, Jr. was assassinated in April 1968, and Robert Kennedy was assassinated in June of the same year. Student demonstrations and race riots spread across the country. Watergate was waiting to happen.

Yet, through all this turmoil, the United States Congress from 1964 through 1968 enacted some of the most far-reaching, progressive civil rights legislation in the history of the nation. President Lyndon Johnson, the Vietnam war hawk, must be given substantial credit for this historic development. So must the United States Supreme Court, through its preparatory probings in the area. But at the moral and political center of the civil rights movement stood a Southern black minister, Martin Luther King, Jr.

THE DRUM MAJOR INSTINCT
Martin Luther King, Jr.

This morning I would like to use as a subject from which to preach: "The Drum Major Instinct." And our text for the morning is taken from a very familiar passage in the tenth chapter as recorded by Saint Mark. Beginning with the thirty-fifth verse of that chapter, we read these words: "And James and John, the sons of Zebedee, came unto him saying, 'Master, we would that thou shouldest do for us whatsoever we shall desire.' And he said unto them, 'What would ye that I should do for you?' And they said unto him, 'Grant unto us that we may sit, one on thy right hand, and the other on thy left hand, in thy glory.' But Jesus said unto them, 'Ye know not what ye ask: Can ye drink of the cup that I drink of? and be baptized with the baptism that I am baptized with?' And they said unto him, 'We can.' And Jesus said unto them, 'Ye shall indeed drink of the cup that I drink of, and with the baptism that I am baptized withal shall ye be baptized: but to sit on my right hand and on my left hand is not mine to give; but it shall be given to them for whom it is prepared.' "

And then Jesus goes on toward the end of that passage to say, "But so shall it not be among you: but whosoever will be great among you, shall be your servant: and whosoever of you will be the chiefest, shall be servant of all.'' The setting is clear. James and John are making a specific request of the master. They had dreamed, as most of the Hebrews dreamed, of a coming king of Israel who would set Jerusalem free and establish his kingdom on Mount Zion, and in righteousness rule the world. And they thought of Jesus as this kind of king. And they were thinking of that day when Jesus would reign supreme as this new king of Israel. And they were saying, ''Now when you establish your kingdom, let one of us sit on the right hand and the other on the left hand of your throne.''

Now very quickly, we would automatically condemn James and John, and we would say they were selfish. Why would they make such a selfish request? But before we condemn them too quickly, let us look calmly and honestly at ourselves, and we will discover that we too have those same basic desires for recognition, for importance. That same desire for attention, that same desire to be first. Of course, the other disciples got mad with James and John, and you could understand why, but we must understand that we have some of the same James and John qualities. And there is deep down within all of us an instinct. It's a kind of drum major instinct—a desire to be out front, a desire to lead the parade, a desire to be first. And it is something that runs the whole gamut of life.

And so before we condemn them, let us see that we all have the drum major instinct. We all want to be important, to surpass others, to achieve distinction, to lead the parade. Alfred Adler, the great psychoanalyst, contends that this is the dominant impulse. Sigmund Freud used to contend that sex was the dominant impulse, and Adler came up with a new argument saying that this quest for recognition, this desire for attention, this desire for distinction is the basic impulse, the basic drive of human life—this drum major instinct.

And you know, we begin early to ask life to put us first. Our first cry as a baby was a bid for attention. And all through childhood the drum major impulse or instinct is a major obsession. Children ask life to grant them first place. They are a little bundle of ego. And they have innately the drum major impulse or the drum major instinct.

Now in adult life, we still have it, and we really never get by it. We like to do something good. And you know, we like to be praised for it. Now if you don't believe that, you just go on living life, and you will discover very soon that you like to be praised. Everybody likes it, as a matter of fact. And somehow this warm glow we feel when we are praised or when our name is in print is something of the vitamin A to our ego. Nobody is unhappy when they are praised, even if they know they don't deserve it and even if they don't believe it. The only unhappy people about praise is when that praise is going too much toward somebody else. But everybody likes to be praised because of this real drum major instinct.

Now the presence of the drum major instinct is why so many people are ''joiners.'' You know, there are some people who just join everything.

And it's really a quest for attention and recognition and importance. And they get names that give them that impression. So you get your groups, and they become the "Grand Patron," and the little fellow who is henpecked at home needs a chance to be the "Most Worthy of the Most Worthy" of something. It is the drum major impulse and longing that runs the gamut of human life. And so we see it everywhere, this quest for recognition. And we join things, overjoin really, that we think that we will find that recognition in.

Now the presence of this instinct explains why we are so often taken by advertisers. You know, those gentlemen of massive verbal persuasion. And they have a way of saying things to you that kind of gets you into buying. In order to be a man of distinction, you must drink this whiskey. In order to make your neighbors envious, you must drive this type of car. In order to be lovely to love you must wear this kind of lipstick or this kind of perfume. And you know, before you know it, you're just buying that stuff. That's the way the advertisers do it.

I got a letter the other day, and it was a new magazine coming out. And it opened up, "Dear Dr. King: As you know, you are on many mailing lists. And you are categorized as highly intelligent, progressive, a lover of the arts and the sciences, and I know you will want to read what I have to say." Of course I did. After you said all of that and explained me so exactly, of course I wanted to read it.

But very seriously, it goes through life; the drum major instinct is real. And you know what else it causes to happen? It often causes us to live above our means. It's nothing but the drum major instinct. Do you ever see people buy cars that they can't even begin to buy in terms of their income? You've seen people riding around in Cadillacs and Chryslers who don't earn enough to have a good T–Model Ford. But it feeds a repressed ego.

You know, economists tell us that your automobile should not cost more than half of your annual income. So if you make an income of five thousand dollars, your car shouldn't cost more than about twenty-five hundred. That's just good economics. And if it's a family of two, and both members of the family make ten thousand dollars, they would have to make out with one car. That would be good economics, although it's often inconvenient. But so often, haven't you seen people making five thousand dollars a year and driving a car that costs six thousand? And they wonder why their ends never meet. That's a fact.

Now the economists also say that your house shouldn't cost—if you're buying a house, it shouldn't cost more than twice your income. That's based on the economy and how you would make ends meet. So, if you have an income of five thousand dollars, it's kind of difficult in this society. But say it's a family with an income of ten thousand dollars, the house shouldn't cost much more than twenty thousand. Well, I've seen folk making ten thousand dollars, living in a forty- and fifty-thousand-dollar house. And you know they just barely make it. They get a check every month somewhere, and they owe all of that out before it comes in. Never have anything to put away for rainy days.

But now the problem is, it is the drum major instinct. And you know, you see people over and over again with the drum major instinct taking them over. And they just live their lives trying to outdo the Joneses. They got to get this coat because this particular coat is a little better and a little better-looking than Mary's coat. And I got to drive this car because it's something about this car that makes my car a little better than my neighbor's car. I know a man who used to live in a thirty-five-thousand-dollar house. And other people started building thirty-five-thousand-dollar houses, so he built a seventy-five-thousand-dollar house. And then somebody else built a seventy-five-thousand-dollar house, and he built a hundred-thousand-dollar house. And I don't know where he's going to end up if he's going to live his life trying to keep up with the Joneses.

There comes a time that the drum major instinct can become destructive. And that's where I want to move now. I want to move to the point of saying that if this instinct is not harnessed, it becomes a very dangerous, pernicious instinct. For instance, if it isn't harnessed, it causes one's personality to become distorted. I guess that's the most damaging aspect of it: what it does to the personality. If it isn't harnessed, you will end up day in and day out trying to deal with your ego problem by boasting. Have you ever heard people that—you know, and I'm sure you've met them—that really become sickening because they just sit up all the time talking about themselves. And they just boast and boast and boast, and that's the person who has not harnessed the drum major instinct.

And then it does other things to the personality. It causes you to lie about who you know sometimes. There are some people who are influence peddlers. And in their attempt to deal with the drum major instinct, they have to try to identify with the so-called big-name people. And if you're not careful, they will make you think they know somebody that they don't really know. They know them well, they sip tea with them, and they this-and-that. That happens to people.

And the other thing is that it causes one to engage ultimately in activities that are merely used to get attention. Criminologists tell us that some people are driven to crime because of this drum major instinct. They don't feel that they are getting enough attention through the normal channels of social behavior, and so they turn to anti-social behavior in order to get attention, in order to feel important. And so they get that gun, and before they know it they rob a bank in a quest for recognition, in a quest for importance.

And then the final great tragedy of the distorted personality is the fact that when one fails to harness this instinct, he ends up trying to push others down in order to push himself up. And whenever you do that, you engage in some of the most vicious activities. You will spread evil, vicious, lying gossip on people, because you are trying to pull them down in order to push yourself up. And the great issue of life is to harness the drum major instinct.

Now the other problem is, when you don't harness the drum major instinct—this uncontrolled aspect of it—is that it leads to snobbish exclusivism. And you know, this is the danger of social clubs and fraternities—I'm in a fraternity; I'm in two or three—for sororities and all of these, I'm not talking against them. I'm saying it's the danger. The danger is that they can become forces of classism and exclusivism where somehow you get a degree of satisfaction because you are in something exclusive. And that's fulfilling something, you know—that I'm in this fraternity, and it's the best fraternity in the world, and everybody can't get in this fraternity. So it ends up, you know, a very exclusive kind of thing.

And you know, that can happen with the church; I know churches get in that bind sometimes. I've been to churches, you know, and they say, "We have so many doctors, and so many school teachers, and so many lawyers, and so many businessmen in our church." And that's fine, because doctors need to go to church, and lawyers, and businessmen, teachers—they ought to be in church. But they say that—even the preacher sometimes will go all through that—they say that as if the other people don't count. And the church is the one place where a doctor ought to forget that he's a doctor. The church is the one place where a Ph.D. ought to forget that he's a Ph.D. The church is the one place that the school teacher ought to forget the degree she has behind her name. The church is the one place where the lawyer ought to forget that he's a lawyer. And any church that violates the "whosoever will, let him come" doctrine is a dead, cold church, and nothing but a little social club with a thin veneer of religiosity.

When the church is true to its nature, it says, "Whosoever will, let him come." And it does not propose to satisfy the perverted uses of the drum major instinct. It's the one place where everybody should be the same, standing before a common master and savior. And a recognition grows out of this—that all men are brothers because they are children of a common father.

The drum major instinct can lead to exclusivism in one's thinking and can lead one to feel that because he has some training, he's a little better than that person who doesn't have it. Or because he has some economic security, that he's a little better than that person who doesn't have it. And that's the uncontrolled, perverted use of the drum major instinct.

Now the other thing is, that it leads to tragic—and we've seen it happen so often—tragic race prejudice. Many who have written about this problem—Lillian Smith used to say it beautifully in some of her books. And she would say it to the point of getting men and women to see the source of the problem. Do you know that a lot of the race problem grows out of the drum major instinct? A need that some people have to feel superior. A need that some people have to feel that they are first, and to feel that their white skin ordained them to be first. And they have said it over and over again in ways that we see with our own eyes. In fact, not too long ago, a man down in Mississippi said that God was a charter member of the White Citizens Council. And so God being the charter member means that everybody who's in that has a kind of divinity, a kind of superiority.

And think of what has happened in history as a result of this perverted use of the drum major instinct. It has led to the most tragic prejudice, the most tragic expressions of man's inhumanity to man.

I always try to do a little converting when I'm in jail. And when we were in jail in Birmingham the other day, the white wardens and all enjoyed coming around the cell to talk about the race problem. And they were showing us where we were so wrong demonstrating. And they were showing us where segregation was so right. And they were showing us where intermarriage was so wrong. So I would get to preaching, and we would get to talking—calmly, because they wanted to talk about it. And then we got down one day to the point—that was the second or third day—to talk about where they lived, and how much they were earning. And when those brothers told me what they were earning, I said, "Now, you know what? You ought to be marching with us. You're just as poor as Negroes." And I said, "You are put in the position of supporting your oppressor, because through prejudice and blindness, you fail to see that the same forces that oppress Negroes in American society oppress poor white people. And all you are living on is the satisfaction of your skin being white, and the drum major instinct of thinking that you are somebody big because you are white. And you're so poor you can't send your children to school. You ought to be out here marching with every one of us every time we have a march."

Now that's a fact. That the poor white has been put into this position, where through blindness and prejudice, he is forced to support his oppressors. And the only thing he has going for him is the false feeling that he's superior because his skin is white—and can't hardly eat and make his ends meet week in and week out.

And not only does this thing go into the racial struggle, it goes into the struggle between nations. And I would submit to you this morning that what is wrong in the world today is that the nations of the world are engaged in a bitter, colossal contest for supremacy. And if something doesn't happen to stop this trend, I'm sorely afraid that we won't be here to talk about Jesus Christ and about God and about brotherhood too many more years. If somebody doesn't bring an end to this suicidal thrust that we see in the world today, none of us are going to be around, because somebody's going to make the mistake through our senseless blunderings of dropping a nuclear bomb somewhere. And then another one is going to drop. And don't let anybody fool you, this can happen within a matter of seconds. They have twenty-megaton bombs in Russia right now that can destroy a city as big as New York in three seconds, with everybody wiped away, and every building. And we can do the same thing to Russia and China.

But this is why we are drifting. And we are drifting there because nations are caught up with the drum major instinct. "I must be first." "I must be supreme." "Our nation must rule the world." And I am sad to say that the nation in which we live is the supreme culprit. And I'm going to continue to say it to America, because I love this country too much to see the drift that it has taken.

God didn't call America to do what she's doing in the world now. God didn't call America to engage in a senseless, unjust war as the war in Vietnam. And we are criminals in that war. We've committed more war crimes almost than any nation in the world, and I'm going to continue to say it. And we won't stop it because of our pride and our arrogance as a nation.

But God has a way of even putting nations in their place. The God that I worship has a way of saying, "Don't play with me." He has a way of saying, as the God of the Old Testament used to say to the Hebrews, "Don't play with me, Israel. Don't play with me, Babylon. Be still and know that I'm God. And if you don't stop your reckless course, I'll rise up and break the backbone of your power." And that can happen to America. Every now and then I go back and read Gibbons' *Decline and Fall of the Roman Empire*. And when I come and look at America, I say to myself, the parallels are frightening.

And we have perverted the drum major instinct. But let me rush on to my conclusion, because I want you to see what Jesus was really saying. What was the answer that Jesus gave these men? It's very interesting. One would have thought that Jesus would have condemned them. One would have thought that Jesus would have said, "You are out of your place. You are selfish. Why would you raise such a question?"

But that isn't what Jesus did; he did something altogether different. He said in substance, "Oh, I see, you want to be first. You want to be great. You want to be important. You want to be significant. Well, you ought to be. If you're going to be my disciple, you must be." But he reordered priorities. And he said, "Yes, don't give up this instinct. It's a good instinct if you use it right. It's a good instinct if you don't distort it and pervert it. Don't give it up. Keep feeling the need for being important. Keep feeling the need for being first. But I want you to be first in love. I want you to be first in moral excellence. I want you to be first in generosity. That is what I want you to do."

And he transformed the situation by giving a new definition of greatness. And you know how he said it? He said, "Now brethren, I can't give you greatness. And really, I can't make you first." This is what Jesus said to James and John. "You must earn it. True greatness comes not by favoritism, but by fitness. And the right hand and the left are not mine to give, they belong to those who are prepared."

And so Jesus gave us a new norm of greatness. If you want to be important—wonderful. If you want to be recognized—wonderful. If you want to be great—wonderful. But recognize that he who is greatest among you shall be your servant. That's a new definition of greatness. And this morning, the thing that I like about it: by giving that definition of greatness, it means that everybody can be great, because everybody can serve. You don't have to have a college degree to serve. You don't have to make your subject and your verb agree to serve. You don't have to know about Plato and Aristotle to serve. You don't have to know Einstein's theory of relativity to serve. You don't have to know the second theory of thermodynamics in physics to serve. You only need a heart full of grace, a soul generated by love. And you can be that servant.

I know a man—and I just want to talk about him a minute, and maybe you will discover who I'm talking about as I go down the way because he was a great one. And he just went about serving. He was born in an obscure village, the child of a poor peasant woman. And then he grew up in still another obscure village, where he worked as a carpenter until he was thirty years old. Then for three years, he just got on his feet, and he was an itinerant preacher. And he went about doing some things. He didn't have much. He never wrote a book. He never held an office. He never had a family. He never owned a house. He never went to college. He never visited a big city. He never went two hundred miles from where he was born. He did none of the usual things that the world would associate with greatness. He had no credentials but himself.

He was only thirty-three when the tide of public opinion turned against him. They called him a rabble-rouser. They called him a trouble-maker. They said he was an agitator. He practiced civil disobedience; he broke injunctions. And so he was turned over to his enemies and went through the mockery of a trial. And the irony of it all is that his friends turned him over to them. One of his closest friends denied him. Another of his friends turned him over to his enemies. And while he was dying, the people who killed him gambled for his clothing, the only possession that he had in the world. When he was dead he was buried in a borrowed tomb, through the pity of a friend.

Nineteen centuries have come and gone and today he stands as the most influential figure that ever entered human history. All of the armies that ever marched, all the navies that ever sailed, all the parliaments that ever sat, and all the kings that ever reigned put together have not affected the life of man on this earth as much as that one solitary life. His name may be a familiar one. But today I can hear them talking about him. Every now and then somebody says, "He's King of Kings." And again I can hear somebody saying, "He's Lord of Lords." Somewhere else I can hear somebody saying, "In Christ there is no East nor West." And then they go on and talk about, "In Him there's no North and South, but one great Fellowship of Love throughout the whole wide world." He didn't have anything. He just went around serving and doing good.

This morning, you can be on his right hand and his left hand if you serve. It's the only way in.

Every now and then I guess we all think realistically about that day when we will be victimized with what is life's final common denominator—that something that we call death. We all think about it. And every now and then I think about my own death and I think about my own funeral. And I don't think of it in a morbid sense. And every now and then I ask myself, "What is it that I would want said?" And I leave the word to you this morning.

If any of you are around when I have to meet my day, I don't want a long funeral. And if you get somebody to deliver the eulogy, tell them not to talk too long. And every now and then I wonder what I want them to say. Tell them not to mention that I have a Nobel Peace Prize—that isn't important. Tell them not to mention that I have three or four hundred other awards—that's not important. Tell them not to mention where I went to school.

I'd like somebody to mention that day that Martin Luther King, Jr., tried to give his life serving others. I'd like for somebody to say that day that Martin Luther King, Jr., tried to love somebody. I want you to say that day that I tried to be right on the war question. I want you to be able to say that day that I did try to feed the hungry. And I want you to be able to say that day that I did try in my life to clothe those who were naked. I want you to say on that day that I did try in my life to visit those who were in prison. I want you to say that I tried to love and serve humanity.

Yes, if you want to say that I was a drum major, say that I was a drum major for justice. Say that I was a drum major for peace. I was a drum major for righteousness. And all of the other shallow things will not matter. I won't have any money to leave behind. I won't have the fine and luxurious things of life to leave behind. But I just want to leave a committed life behind.

And that's all I want to say . . . if I can help somebody as I pass along, if I can cheer somebody with a word of song, if I can show somebody he's traveling wrong, Then my living will not be in vain.

Yes, Jesus, I want to be on your right or your left side, not for any selfish reason. I want to be on your right or your left side, not in terms of some political kingdom or ambition. But I just want to be there in love and in justice and in truth and in commitment to others, so that we can make of this old world a new world.

Notes

1. *Martin Luther King, Jr. the Preacher. The Drum Major Instinct* was delivered by Dr. King as a sermon at Ebenezer Baptist Church in Atlanta, Georgia on February 4, 1968, two months before his assassination. Dr. King was a riveting preacher. This sermon, as well as other sermons and speeches by Dr. King, are recorded and should be heard to appreciate the effectiveness of his delivery.

2. *Me First.* In this sermon Dr. King turns ambition on its head. Is his formula practical? At one point in the sermon Dr. King says: "True greatness comes not by favoritism, but by fitness." Is this statement consonant with the idea that the first shall be last, and the last first?

I HAVE A DREAM
Martin Luther King, Jr.

I am happy to join with you today in what will go down in history as the greatest demonstration for freedom in the history of our nation.

Five score years ago, a great American, in whose symbolic shadow we stand today, signed the Emancipation Proclamation. This momentous decree came as a great beacon of hope to millions of Negro slaves, who had been seared in the flames of withering injustice. It came as a joyous daybreak to end the long night of their captivity. But one hundred years later, the Negro is still not free. One hundred years later, the life of the Negro is still sadly crippled by the manacles of segregation and the chains of discrimination.

One hundred years later, the Negro lives on a lonely island of poverty in the midst of a vast ocean of material prosperity. One hundred years later, the Negro is still languishing in the corners of American society and finds himself an exile in his own land. So we have come here today to dramatize a shameful condition.

In a sense we have come to our Nation's Capital to cash a check. When the architects of our great republic wrote the magnificent words of the Constitution and the Declaration of Independence, they were signing a promissory note to which every American was to fall heir.

This note was a promise that all men, yes, black men as well as white men, would be guaranteed the inalienable rights of life, liberty, and the pursuit of happiness.

It is obvious today that America has defaulted on this promissory note insofar as her citizens of color are concerned. Instead of honoring this sacred obligation, America has given the Negro people a bad check, a check that has come back marked "insufficient funds."

But we refuse to believe that the bank of justice is bankrupt. We refuse to believe that there are insufficient funds in the great vaults of opportunity of this nation. So we have come to cash this check, a check that will give us upon demand the riches of freedom and security of justice.

We have also come to this hallowed spot to remind America of the fierce urgency of now. This is not time to engage in the luxury of cooling off or to take the tranquilizing drug of gradualism.

Now is the time to make real the promise of democracy.

Now is the time to rise from the dark and desolate valley of segregation to the sunlit path of racial justice.

Now is the time to lift our nation from the quicksands of racial injustice to the solid rock of brotherhood.

Now is the time to make justice a reality to all of God's children.

It would be fatal for the nation to overlook the urgency of the moment and to underestimate the determination of its colored citizens. This sweltering summer of the Negro's legitimate discontent will not pass until there is an invigorating autumn of freedom and equality. Nineteen sixty-three is not an end but a beginning. Those who hope that the Negro needed to blow off steam and will now be content will have a rude awakening if the nation returns to business as usual.

There will be neither rest nor tranquility in America until the Negro is granted his citizenship rights. The whirlwinds of revolt will continue to shake the foundations of our nation until the bright day of justice emerges.

But there is something that I must say to my people who stand on the warm threshold which leads into the palace of justice. In the process of gaining our rightful place we must not be guilty of wrongful deeds.

Let us not seek to satisfy our thirst for freedom by drinking from the cup of bitterness and hatred. We must ever conduct our struggle on the high plane of dignity and discipline. We must not allow our creative protest to degenerate into physical violence. Again and again we must rise to the majestic heights of meeting physical force with soul force.

The marvelous new militancy which has engulfed the Negro community must not lead us to a distrust of all white people, for many of our white brothers, as evidenced by their presence here today, have come to realize that their destiny is tied up with our destiny. They have come to realize that their freedom is inextricably bound to our freedom. We cannot walk alone.

And as we walk, we must make the pledge that we shall always march ahead. We cannot turn back. There are those who are asking the devotees of civil rights, "When will you be satisfied?" We can never be satisfied as long as the Negro is the victim of the unspeakable horrors of police brutality.

We can never be satisfied as long as our bodies, heavy with the fatigue of travel, cannot gain lodging in the motels of the highways and the hotels of the cities.

We cannot be satisfied as long as the Negro's basic mobility is from a smaller ghetto to a larger one.

We can never be satisfied as long as our children are stripped of their selfhood and robbed of their dignity by signs stating "for whites only."

We cannot be satisfied as long as a Negro in Mississippi cannot vote and a Negro in New York believes he has nothing for which to vote.

No, no we are not satisfied and we will not be satisfied until justice rolls down like waters and righteousness like a mighty stream.

I am not unmindful that some of you have come here out of your trials and tribulations. Some of you have come fresh from narrow jail cells. Some of you have come from areas where your quest for freedom left you battered by storms of persecutions and staggered by the winds of police brutality.

You have been the veterans of creative suffering. Continue to work with the faith that unearned suffering is redemptive.

Go back to Mississippi, go back to Alabama, go back to South Carolina, go back to Georgia, go back to Louisiana, go back to the slums and ghettos of our modern cities, knowing that somehow this situation can and will be changed.

Let us not wallow in the valley of despair. I say to you today, my friends, that even though we face the difficulties of today and tomorrow, I still have a dream. It is a dream deeply rooted in the American dream.

I have a dream that one day this nation will rise up and live out the true meaning of its creed. We hold these truths to be self-evident, that all men are created equal.

I have a dream that one day on the red hills of Georgia the sons of former slaves and the sons of former slave owners will be able to sit down together at the table of brotherhood.

I have a dream that one day, even the state of Mississippi, a state sweltering with the heat of oppression, will be transformed into an oasis of freedom and justice.

I have a dream that my four little children will one day live in a nation where they will not be judged by the color of their skin but by the content of their character.

I have a dream today!

I have a dream that one day down in Alabama, with its vicious racists, with its governor having his lips dripping with the words of interposition and nullification; that one day right down in Alabama little black boys and black girls will be able to join hands with little white boys and white girls as sisters and brothers.

I have a dream today!

I have a dream that one day every valley shall be exalted, and every hill and every mountain shall be made low, the rough places will be made plain and the crooked places will be made straight, and the glory of the Lord shall be revealed and all flesh shall see it together.

This is our hope. This is the faith that I will go back to the South with. With this faith we will be able to hew out of the mountain of despair a stone of hope.

With this faith we will be able to transform the jangling discords of our nation into a beautiful symphony of brotherhood.

With this faith we will be able to work together, to pray together, to struggle together, to go to jail together, to climb up for freedom together, knowing that we will be free one day.

This will be the day when all of God's children will be able to sing with new meaning, "My country 'tis of thee, sweet land of liberty, of thee I sing. Land where my fathers died, land of the Pilgrim's pride, from every mountainside, let freedom ring!"

And if America is to be a great nation, this must become true. So let freedom ring from the hilltops of New Hampshire. Let freedom ring from the mighty mountains of New York.

Let freedom ring from the heightening Alleghenies of Pennsylvania.

Let freedom ring from the snow-capped Rockies of Colorado.

Let freedom ring from the curvaceous slopes of California.

But not only that, let freedom ring from Stone Mountain of Georgia.

Let freedom ring from Lookout Mountain of Tennessee.

Let freedom ring from every hill and molehill of Mississippi and every mountainside.

And when this happens, when we let freedom ring, when we let it ring from every village and every hamlet, from every state and every city, we will be able to speed up that day when all of God's children, black men and white men, Jews and Gentiles, Protestants and Catholics, will be able to join hands and sing in the words of the old spiritual, "Free at last, free at last. Thank God Almighty, we are free at last."

Notes

1. *March on Washington.* Dr. King's *I Have A Dream* speech, delivered in front of the Lincoln Memorial on August 28, 1963, has become immortalized in American culture. The speech was videotaped, and should be available in all law school libraries.

2. *A Dream.* What different meanings does the word "dream" have? Which of these meanings did Dr. King intend to incorporate into his speech?

Has Dr. King's dream come true?

3. *Commerce.* Dr. King uses a metaphor from commercial law. Is this metaphor surprising? Appropriate? Effective? Explain.

4. *A Letter From A Birmingham Jail.* While serving time in a Birmingham jail for his involvement in civil rights activities, he wrote an open letter in April 1963 to his fellow clergymen, many of whom had expressed concern over his nonviolent resistance to law as illegal and likely to lead to civil disturbances. An excerpt from the poignant, very personal letter is given here.

You express a great deal of anxiety over our willingness to break laws. This is certainly a legitimate concern. Since we so diligently urge people to obey the Supreme Court's decision of 1954 outlawing segregation in the public schools, at first glance it may seem rather paradoxical for us consciously to break laws. One may well ask: "How can you advocate breaking some laws and obeying others?" The answer lies in the fact that there are two types of laws: there are *just* and there are *unjust laws.* One has not only a legal but a moral responsibility to obey just laws. Conversely, one has a moral responsibility to disobey unjust laws. I would agree with St. Augustine that "an unjust law is no law at all."

Now, what is the difference between the two? How does one determine whether a law is just or unjust? A just law is a man-made code that squares with the moral law or the law of God. An unjust law is a code that is out of harmony with the moral law. To put it in the terms of St. Thomas Aquinas: An unjust law is a human law that is not rooted in eternal law and natural law. Any law that uplifts human personality is just. Any law that degrades human personality is unjust. All segregation statutes are unjust because segregation distorts the soul and damages the personality. It gives the segregator a false sense of superiority and the segregated a false sense of inferiority. Segregation, to use the terminology of the Jewish philosopher Martin Buber, substitutes an "I-it" relationship for an "I-thou" relationship and ends up relegating persons to the status of things. Hence segregation is not only politically, economically and sociologically unsound, but it is morally wrong and sinful. Paul Tillich said that sin is separation. Is not segregation an existential expression of man's tragic separation, his awful estrangement, his terrible sinfulness? Thus it is that I can urge men to obey the 1954 decision of the Supreme Court, for it is morally right; and I can urge them to disobey segregation ordinances, for they are morally wrong.

F.   THE SITUATIONALLY DEPRIVED

One can be deprived by the situation, or the circumstances in which one finds oneself, of the opportunity to go forward. *See* PATRICIA MEYER SPACKS, GOSSIP 209 (1985). One likes to believe that she can do something about those circumstances. John Milton wrote an epic poem, *Paradise Lost,* to vindicate free will, but it is remarkable that throughout the poem God appears to be in control of all events that happen, including the sinful acts of Satan. Some would call this situation a paradox. Others would call it an antinomy.

WILLIAM SHAKESPEARE
THE MERCHANT OF VENICE
Act III Scene 1

[Antonio, in financial straits, borrows money from the Jewish money lender Shylock, to be paid back when Antonio's ships come in. If Antonio defaults, Shylock will exact a pound of flesh as a forfeiture, to be carved by Shylock from Antonio's body.

News arrives that the first of Antonio's ships has foundered at sea. Suddenly the threat of the forfeiture becomes a distinct possibility.

Salerio, a friend of Antonio, sounds out Shylock about the seriousness of his intent to exact the pound of flesh. Shylock, having just lost his daughter, who eloped with a Christian taking all Shylock's ready cash and jewels when she left, is in no mood to be Christianly.]

SHYLOCK

There I have another bad match! A bankrupt, a prodigal, who dare scarce show his head on the Rialto, a beggar, that was used to come so smug upon the mart! Let him look to his bond. He was wont to call me usurer; let him look to his bond. He was wont to lend money for a Christian courtesy; let him look to his bond.

SALERIO

Why, I am sure, if he forfeit, thou wilt not take his flesh! What's that good for?

SHYLOCK

To bait fish withal; if it will feed nothing else, it will feed my revenge. He hath disgraced me and hindered me half a million, laughed at my losses, mocked at my gains, scorned my nation, thwarted my bargains, cooled my friends, heated mine enemies—and what's his reason? I am a Jew. Hath not a Jew eyes? Hath not a Jew hands, organs, dimensions, senses, affections, passions? Fed with the same food, hurt with the same weapons, subject to the same diseases, healed by the same means, warmed and cooled by the same winter and summer, as a Christian is? If you prick us, do we not bleed? If you tickle us, do we not laugh? If you poison us, do we not die? And if you wrong us, shall we not revenge? If we are like you in the rest, we will resemble you in that. If a Jew wrong a Christian, what is his humility? Revenge. If a Christian wrong a Jew, what should his sufferance be by Christian example? Why, revenge! The villainy you teach me, I will execute, and it shall go hard but I will better the instruction.

Notes

1. *The Tone.* How should Shylock's famous speech, "Hath not a Jew eyes?" be read? Present the speech in three distinctly different ways, and for each presentation explain: who you are; where you are; what your circumstances are; whom you are trying to persuade; and how you intend to accomplish your goal.

2. *Portia.* If ever there were a woman who stood the concept of the "situationally deprived" on its head, it is Portia. While she is but a "mere woman," she outsmarts all the men with whom she comes in contact in *The Merchant of Venice.*

In order to help Antonio's dear friend, her lover Bassanio, Portia appears disguised as Bellario, a lawyer from Padua, to address the legality of the bond, in which Antonio has pledged a "pound of flesh" as security for the loan from Shylock.

Act IV Scene 1

PORTIA

Is your name Shylock?

SHYLOCK

Shylock is my name.

PORTIA

Of a strange nature is the suit you follow,
Yet in such rule that the Venetian law
Cannot impugn you as you do proceed.
[To Antonio]
You stand within his danger, do you not?

ANTONIO

Ay, so he says.

PORTIA

Do you confess the bond?

ANTONIO

I do.

PORTIA

Then must the Jew be merciful.

SHYLOCK

On what compulsion must I? Tell me that.

PORTIA

The quality of mercy is not strain'd.
It droppeth as the gentle rain from heaven
Upon the place beneath. It is twice blest:
It blesseth him that gives and him that takes.
'Tis mightiest in the mightiest; it becomes
The thronèd monarch better than his crown.
His sceptre shows the force of temporal power,

The attribute to awe and majesty
Wherein doth sit the dread and fear of kings;
But mercy is above this sceptred sway.
It is enthronèd in the hearts of kings;
It is an attribute to God himself;
And earthly power doth then show likest God's
When mercy seasons justice. Therefore, Jew,
Though justice be thy plea, consider this:
That in the course of justice none of us
Should see salvation. We do pray for mercy,
And that same prayer doth teach us all to render
The deeds of mercy. I have spoke thus much
To mitigate the justice of thy plea,
Which, if thou follow, this strict court of Venice
Must needs give sentence 'gainst the merchant there.

SHYLOCK

My deeds upon my head! I crave the law,
The penalty and forfeit of my bond.

Having demanded enforcement of his contract according to the letter of the law, Shylock is hoist by his own petard when Portia opines that he cannot have his pound of flesh since obtaining it would also forfeit Antonio's blood, which the contract does not call for. Portia's speech here, "The quality of mercy is not strained," is one of the most famous speeches in all Shakespeare. In it, Portia uses a Christian argument to try to persuade Shylock. How effective could her argument be? What is Shakespeare's point here?

* * *

American women were agitating for the right to vote even prior to the Civil War. In her *History of Women's Suffrage*, Frances D. Gage recalls the Akron Convention on Women's Suffrage, in May of 1851. Frances D. Gage, 1 HISTORY OF WOMEN'S SUFFRAGE 1848–1861, at 115–17 (Eliz. Cady Stanton, Susan B. Anthony, and Matilda Joslyn Gage, eds., reprint ed. 1985). Gage was presiding at the podium when she saw "a tall, gaunt black woman in a gray dress and white turban, surmounted with an uncouth sun-bonnet, march deliberately into the church, walk with the air of a queen up the aisle, and take her seat upon the pulpit steps. A buzz of disapprobation was heard all over the house.... [O]ld Sojourner, quiet and reticent as the 'Lybian Statue,' sat crouched against the wall on the corner of the pulpit stairs, her sun-bonnet shading her eyes, her elbows on her knees, her chin resting upon her broad, hard palms." At this time, Sojourner Truth had already embarked on her career as an itinerant minister, and she listened to the discourse of some of the ministers from established churches who addressed the convention:

> ... Methodist, Baptist, Episcopal, Presbyterian, and Universalist ministers came in to hear and discuss the resolutions presented. One

claimed superior rights and privileges for man, on the ground of "superior intellect"; another, because of the "manhood of Christ; if God had desired the equality of woman, He would have given some token of His will through the birth, life, and death of the Saviour." Another gave us a theological view of the "sin of our first mother."

There were very few women in those days who dared to "speak in meeting"; and the August teachers of the people were seemingly getting the better of us, while the boys in the galleries, and the sneerers among the pews, were hugely enjoying the discomfiture, as they supposed, of the "strong-minded." Some of the tender-skinned friends were on the point of losing dignity, and the atmosphere betokened a storm. When, slowly from her seat in the corner rose Sojourner Truth, who, till now, had scarcely lifted her head. "Don't let her speak!" gasped half a dozen in my ear. She moved slowly and solemnly to the front, laid her old bonnet at her feet, and turned her great speaking eyes to me. There was a hissing sound of disapprobation above and below. I rose and announced "Sojourner Truth," and begged the audience to keep silence for a few moments.

The tumult subsided at once, and every eye was fixed on this almost Amazon form, which stood nearly six feet high, head erect, and eyes piercing the upper air like one in a dream. At her first word there was a profound hush. She spoke in deep tones, which, though not loud, reached every ear in the house, and away through the throngs at the doors and windows.

The speech Gage recorded has come down to us by the title "Ain't I a Woman?" from its refrain.

AIN'T I A WOMAN?
Sojourner Truth

Well, children, where there is so much racket there must be something out of kilter. I think that 'twixt the negroes of the South and the women at the North, all talking about rights, the white men will be in a fix pretty soon.' But what's all this here talking about?

That man over there says that women need to be helped into carriages, and lifted over ditches, and to have the best place everywhere. Nobody ever helps me into carriages, or over mud-puddles, or gives me any best place! And ain't I a woman? Look at me! Look at my arm! I have ploughed and planted, and gathered into barns, and no man could head me! And ain't I a woman? I could work as much and eat as much as a man—when I could get it—and bear the lash as well! And ain't I a woman? I have borne thirteen children, and seen most all sold off to slavery, and when I cried out with my mother's grief, none but Jesus heard me! And ain't I a woman?

Then they talk about this thing in the head; what's this they call it? [Gage reports that a member of the audience whispers, "intellect."] That's it, honey. What's that got to do with women's rights or negroes' rights? If my cup won't hold but a pint, and yours holds a quart, wouldn't you be mean not to let me have my little half measure full? [Here, says Gage, "she pointed her significant finger, and sent a keen glance at the minister who had made the argument. The cheering was long and loud."]

Then that little man in black there, he says women can't have as much rights as men, 'cause Christ wasn't a woman! Where did your Christ come from? [Here, according to Gage, "Rolling thunder couldn't have stilled that crowd, as did those deep, wonderful tones, as she stood there with outstretched arms and eyes of fire."] Where did your Christ come from? From God and a woman! Man had nothing to do with Him.

If the first woman God ever made was strong enough to turn the world upside down all alone, these women together ought to be able to turn it back, and get it right side up again! And now they is asking to do it, the men better let them. ["Long continued cheering," says Gage at this point.]

Obliged to you for hearing me, and now old Sojourner ain't got nothing more to say.

Notes

1. *Response.* Gage sums up the effect of the speech:

Amid roars of applause, she returned to her corner, leaving more than one of us with streaming eyes, and hearts beating with gratitude. She had taken us up in her strong arms and carried us safely over the slough of difficulty turning the whole tide in our favor. I have never in my life seen anything like the magical influence that subdued the mobbish spirit of the day, and turned the sneers and jeers of an excited crowd into notes of respect and admiration. Hundreds rushed up to shake hands with her, and congratulate the glorious old mother....

2. *Sojourner Truth.* Sojourner Truth was born into slavery as Isabella Baumfree in 1797 in upstate New York. Emancipated when New York abolished slavery in the 1820's, she travelled to New York City and later to Northampton, Massachusetts, where she became active in an abolitionist community including Frederick Douglass and William Lloyd Garrison. She changed her name to Sojourner Truth in 1843 as the result of a spiritual experience that also led her to become an itinerant preacher. Thereafter, she travelled and spoke extensively, dying in 1883 in Battle Creek, Michigan.

She once spoke at an anti-slavery meeting in an area of the Midwest which had been devastated by an invasion of weevils that attacked and destroyed the wheat crop. The weevils ate the heart out of each kernel, leaving an empty husk behind. Having toured the area before her speech, she allegedly told the crowd that the United States Constitution was like the weevil-infested wheat—the Constitution looked good, but "there is a little weevil in it." *See* LERONE BENNETT, JR., BEFORE THE MAYFLOWER: A HISTORY OF BLACK AMERICA 182 (6th ed. 1988).

* * *

Elizabeth Cady Stanton (1815–1902) was one of the pioneers of the women's movement in the United States. Along with her friend, Susan B. Anthony, she worked tirelessly for half a century to secure women's civil and political rights. She was the driving force behind the Seneca Falls Convention of 1848, a founding event of the women's movement. An abolitionist as well as a suffragist, after the Civil War she split with other feminists over the issue of suffrage for liberated African-Americans. Stanton argued for universal adult suffrage, while more conservative suffragists agreed that first priority should be given to securing voting rights for male African-Americans. Conservative suffragists also disagreed with Stanton's more radical feminism, as reflected in her *Woman's Bible*, which rewrote the Bible to make it more fair to women. Neither she nor Anthony lived to see the ratification of the Nineteenth Amendment, giving women the right to vote, in 1920. She gave the following address, often entitled "The Male Element," at the 1868 Woman's Suffrage Convention in Washington, D.C.

THE MALE ELEMENT
Elizabeth Cady Stanton

I urge a sixteenth amendment, because "manhood suffrage," or a man's government, is civil, religious, and social disorganization. The male element is a destructive force, stern, selfish, aggrandizing, loving war, violence, conquest, acquisition, breeding in the material and moral world alike discord, disorder, disease, and death. See what a record of blood and cruelty the pages of history reveal! Through what slavery, slaughter, and sacrifice, through what inquisitions and imprisonments, pains and persecutions, black codes and gloomy creeds, the soul of humanity has struggled for the centuries, while mercy has veiled her face and all hearts have been dead alike to love and hope!

The male element has held high carnival thus far; it has fairly run riot from the beginning, overpowering the feminine element everywhere, crushing out all the diviner qualities in human nature, until we know but little of true manhood and womanhood, of the latter comparatively nothing, for it has scarce been recognized as a power until within the last century. Society is but the reflection of man himself, untempered by woman's thought; the hard iron rule we feel alike in the church, the state, and the home. No one need wonder at the disorganization, at the fragmentary condition of everything, when we remember that man, who represents but half a complete being, with but half an idea on every subject, has undertaken the absolute control of all sublunary matters.

People object to the demands of those whom they choose to call the strong-minded, because they say "the right of suffrage will make the women masculine." That is just the difficulty in which we are involved today. Though disfranchised, we have few women in the best sense; we have simply so many reflections, varieties, and dilutions of the masculine gender. The strong, natural characteristics of womanhood are repressed and ignored in dependence, for so long as man feeds woman she will try to please the giver and adapt herself to his condition. To keep a foothold in society, woman must be as near like man as possible, reflect his ideas, opinions, virtues, motives, prejudices, and vices. She must respect his statutes, though they strip her of every inalienable right, and conflict with that higher law written by the finger of God on her own soul.

She must look at everything from its dollar-and-cent point of view, or she is a mere romancer. She must accept things as they are and make the best of them. To mourn over the miseries of others, the poverty of the poor, their hardships in jails, prisons, asylums, the horrors of war, cruelty, and brutality in every form, all this would be mere sentimentalizing. To protest against the intrigue, bribery, and corruption of public life, to desire that her sons might follow some business that did not involve lying, cheating, and a hard, grinding selfishness, would be arrant nonsense.

In this way man has been molding woman to his ideas by direct and positive influences, while she, if not a negation, has used indirect means to control him, and in most cases developed the very characteristics both in him and herself that needed repression. And now man himself stands appalled at the results of his own excesses, and mourns in bitterness that falsehood, selfishness, and violence are the law of life. The need of this hour is not territory, gold mines, railroads, or specie payments but a new evangel of womanhood, to exalt purity, virtue, morality, true religion, to lift man up into the higher realms of thought and action.

We ask woman's enfranchisement, as the first step toward the recognition of that essential element in government that can only secure the health, strength, and prosperity of the nation. Whatever is done to lift woman to her true position will help to usher in a new day of peace and perfection for the race.

In speaking of the masculine element, I do not wish to be understood to say that all men are hard, selfish, and brutal, for many of the most beautiful spirits the world has known have been clothed with manhood; but I refer to those characteristics, though often marked in woman, that distinguish what is called the stronger sex. For example, the love of acquisition and conquest, the very pioneers of civilization, when expended on the earth, the sea, the elements, the riches and forces of nature, are powers of destruction when used to subjugate one man to another or to sacrifice nations to ambition.

Here that great conservator of woman's love, if permitted to assert itself, as it naturally would in freedom against oppression, violence, and war, would hold all these destructive forces in check, for woman knows the cost of life better than man does, and not with her consent would one drop of blood ever be shed, one life sacrificed in vain.

With violence and disturbance in the natural world, we see a constant effort to maintain an equilibrium of forces. Nature, like a loving mother, is ever trying to keep land and sea, mountain and valley, each in its place, to hush the angry winds and waves, balance the extremes of heat and cold, of rain and drought, that peace, harmony, and beauty may reign supreme. There is a striking analogy between matter and mind, and the present disorganization of society warns us that in the dethronement of woman we have let loose the elements of violence and ruin that she only has the power to curb. If the civilization of the age calls for an extension of the suffrage, surely a government of the most virtuous educated men and women would better represent the whole and protect the interests of all than could the representation of either sex alone.

Notes

1. *Amendment XIX.* Why do you think women were not granted the right to vote until the amendment of the United States Constitution in 1920? Was the failure to amend before that date a sad commentary on U.S. democracy? Or can the delay be explained in more neutral terms? In our present society, are there categories of the situationally deprived that may now or later be viewed as a sad commentary on U.S. democracy?

2. *Difference Feminism.* Stanton's address reflects some of the common assumptions of the "separate spheres" gender philosophy that most scholars trace to the late eighteenth century. Traces of this discourse remain in today's "difference feminism," which holds that there are fundamental differences (sometimes argued to be biologically determined) between men and women. Stanton clarifies that by "the male element," she does not refer to all individual men. *Cf.* MARILYN FRENCH, BEYOND POWER (1985) (contrasting "patriarchal" with "matriarchal" values). Is Stanton's distinction between the "male" and "female" elements valid in any sense?

3. *You've Come a Long Way, Baby.* Women in the United States have now had the suffrage for over eighty years. What has been the result? If Stanton were the keynote speaker at the next convention of the National Organization of Women, what would she say?

* * *

Joan of Arc (Fr. Jeanne d'Arc) (1412–1431) was a deeply religious girl from the rural village of Dorémy. At age thirteen she began having visions in which she identified the voices of St. Michael, St. Catherine, and St. Margaret. Joan became convinced that God had chosen her to repulse the English, who at that time largely controlled France. She attracted followers, and in 1429 led her troops to numerous victories over the English. In that year she conducted the Dauphin to Reims, where he was crowned King Charles VII. Despite his indebtedness to her, Charles did not offer her sufficient support, and her military campaigns began to fail. She was taken prisoner in May of 1430 by the Burgundians, who sold her to their English allies six months later.

She was turned over to the French ecclesiastical courts and tried on charges of sorcery, wantonness in cutting her hair and wearing men's clothing, and blasphemy for considering herself directly responsible to God rather than to the Church. Worn out by her trial and condemned to the stake, she finally signed a recantation of her alleged sins, and her sentence was commuted to life imprisonment. But after a few days she repudiated her recantation and resumed her male attire. She was turned over to a secular English court and was burned at the stake on May 30, 1431.

In 1456 the Church declared Joan innocent. In 1920 she was canonized as a saint.

More than anyone else, Joan was responsible for rejuvenating the national pride of the French and enabling them to throw off the English yoke. The following are excerpts from her trial before the bishop and 41 assessors at the Castle of Rouen on March 3, 1431.

EXAMINATION BEFORE THE BISHOP
Joan of Arc

... We required the said Jeanne simply and absolutely to swear to speak the truth on what should be asked of her. She replied: "I am ready to swear as I have already done." And thus did she swear, her hands on the Holy Gospels.

Afterwards, because she had said, in previous inquiries, that Saint Michael had wings, but had said nothing of the body and members of Saint Catherine and Saint Margaret, We asked her what she wished to say thereon.

"I have told you what I know; I will answer you nothing more. I saw Saint Michael and these two Saints so well that I know they are Saints of Paradise."

"Did you see anything else of them but the face?"

"I have told you what I know; but to tell you all I know, I would rather that you made me cut my throat. All that I know touching the Trial I will tell you willingly."

"Do you think that Saint Michael and Saint Gabriel have human heads?"

"I saw them with my eyes; and I believe it was they as firmly as I believe there is a God."

"Do you think that God made them in the form and fashion that you saw?"

"Yes."

"Do you think that God did from the first create them in this form and fashion?"

"You will have no more at present than what I have answered."

"Do you know by revelation if you will escape?"

"That does not touch on your Case. Do you wish me to speak against myself?"

"Have your Voices told you anything?"

"That is not in your Case. I refer me to the Case. If all concerned you, I would tell you all. By my faith, I know neither the day nor the hour that I shall escape!"

"Have your Voices told you anything in a general way?"

"Yes, truly, they have told me that I shall be delivered, but I know neither the day nor the hour. They said to me: 'Be of good courage and keep a cheerful countenance.' "

"When you first came to the King, did he ask you if you had any revelation about your change of dress?"

"I have answered you about that. I do not remember if I was asked. It is written at Poitiers."

"Do you not remember if the Masters who questioned you in the other Consistory, some during a month, others during three weeks, questioned you about your change of dress?"

"I do not remember. But they asked me where I had assumed this man's dress; and I told them it was at Vaucouleurs."

"Did the aforesaid Masters ask you if it were by order of your Voice that you took this dress?"

"I do not remember."

"Did not your Queen [*Mary of Anjou, wife of King Charles VII*] ask you, the first time you went to visit her?"

"I do not remember."

"Did not your King, your Queen, or some of your party, tell you to take off this man's dress?"

"That is not in your Case."

"Were you not so told at the Castle of Beaurevoir?"

"Yes, truly; and I answered that I would not take it off without leave from God. The Demoiselle de Luxembourg and the Lady de Beaurevoir [*two ladies who visited Joan during her captivity*] offered me a woman's dress, or cloth to make one, telling me to wear it. I answered them that I had not leave from Our Lord, and that it was not yet time."

"Did Messier Jean de Pressy [*a Burgundian present when she was captured*] and others at Arras never offer you a woman's dress?"

"He and many others have oftentimes offered it to me."

"Do you think that you would have done wrong or committed mortal sin by taking a woman's dress?"

"I did better to obey and serve my Sovereign Lord, who is God. Had I dared to do it, I would sooner have done it at the request of these ladies than of any other ladies in France, excepting my Queen."

"When God revealed it to you that you should change your dress, was it by the voice of Saint Michael, Saint Catherine, or Saint Margaret?"

"You shall not have anything more at present."

"When your King first set you to work, and when you had your banner made, did not the men-at-arms and others have their pennons made in the style of yours?"

"It is well to know that the Lords retained their own arms. Some of my companions-in-arms had them made at their pleasure, others not."

"Of what material did they have them made? Of linen or of cloth?"

"It was of white satin; and on some there were fleur-de-lys. In my company I had only two or three lances. But my companions-in-arms now and then had them made like mine. They only did this to know their men from others."

"Did they often renew these pennons?"

"I do not know. When the lances were broken, they had new ones made."

"Have you sometimes said that the pennons which resembled yours would be fortunate?"

"I sometimes said to my followers: 'Go in boldly among the English!' and I myself did likewise."

"Did you tell them to carry themselves boldly, and they would be fortunate?"

"I have certainly told them what has happened and what will yet happen."

"Did you put, or did you ever cause to be put, Holy Water on the pennons when they were carried for the first time?"

"I know nothing of it; and if that were done, it was not by my order."

"Did you never see any sprinkled?"

"That is not in your Case. If I ever did see any sprinkled, I am advised not to answer about it."

"Did your companions-in-arms never put on their pennons 'Jhesus Maria'?"

"By my faith! I do not know."

"Have you not yourself carried cloth, or caused it to be carried, in procession round an altar or a church, and afterwards employed this cloth for pennons?"

"No; and I never saw it done."

"When you were before Jargeau, what did you bear at the back of your helmet? Was it not something round?" [*This question may refer to a popular belief that a halo sometimes appeared on Joan's head.*]

"By my faith! there was nothing."

"Did you ever know Brother Richard?" [*A popular preacher, who prophesied that strange things would happen in 1430*]

"I had not seen him when I came before Troyes."

"What countenance did Brother Richard give you?"

"I suppose after the fashion of the town of Troyes who sent him to me, saying that they feared Jeanne was not a thing that came to them from God. When he approached me, Brother Richard made the sign of the Cross and sprinkled Holy Water; and I said to him: 'Approach boldly, I shall not fly away!' "

"Have you never seen, nor had made, any images or picture of yourself and in your likeness?"

"I saw at Arras a painting in the hands of a Scot: it was like me. I was represented fully armed, presenting a letter to my King, one knee on the ground. I have never seen, nor had made, any other image or painting in my likeness."

"In the house of your host at Orleans, was there not a picture in which was painted three women, with these words: 'Justice, Peace, Union'?"

"I know nothing about it."

"Do you not know that the people of your party had services, masses, and prayers offered for you?"

"I know nothing of it; if they had any service, it was not by my order; but if they prayed for me, my opinion is they did not do ill."

"Did those of your party firmly believe that you were sent from God?"

"I do not know if they believed it, and in this I refer to their own feeling in this matter. But even though they do not believe, yet am I sent from God."

"Do you not think they have a good belief, if they believe this?"

"If they think that I am sent from God, they will not be deceived."

"In what spirit did the people of your party kiss your hands and your garments?"

"Many came to see me willingly, but they kissed my hands as little as I could help. The poor folk came to me readily, because I never did them any unkindness: on the contrary, I loved to help them."

"What honor did the people of Troyes do you on your entry?"

"None at all. Brother Richard, so far as I remember, entered at the same time as I and our people; I do not remember seeing him at the entry."

"Did he not preach a sermon on your arrival in the town?"

"I did not stop there at all, and did not even sleep there: I know nothing of his sermon."

"Were you many days at Reims?"

"We were there, I believe, five or six days."

"Did you not act there as Godmother?" ["*lever d'enfant*"]

"At Troyes I did, to one child. At Reims, I do not remember it, nor at Chateau–Thierry. I was Godmother twice at Saint–Denis, in France. Usually, I gave to the boys the name of Charles, in honor of my King; and to the girls, Jeanne. At other times, I gave such names as pleased the mothers."

"Did not the good women of the town touch with their rings one that you wore on your finger?"

"Many women touched my hands and my rings; but I know nothing of their feelings nor their intention."

"Who of your people, before Chateau–Thierry, caught butterflies in your standard?"

"My people never did such a thing: it is your side who have invented it."

"What did you do at Reims with the gloves with which your King was consecrated?"

"There were favors of gloves for the knights and nobles at Reims. There was one who lost his gloves; I did not say he would find them again. My standard has been in the Church of Reims; and it seems to me it was near the altar."

"When you were going through the country, did you often receive the Sacraments of Penance and the Eucharist in the good towns?"

"Yes, from time to time."

"Did you receive the said Sacraments in man's dress?"

"Yes; but I do not remember ever to have received them armed."

"Why did you take the horse of the Bishop of Senlis?"

"It was bought for 200 saluts. If he received these 200 saluts, I do not know. There was a place fixed at which they were to be paid. I wrote to him that he might have his horse back if he wished; as for me, I did not wish it, because it was worth nothing for weight-carrying."

"How old was the child you visited at Lagny?"

"The child was three days old. It was brought before the image of Our Lady. They told me that the young girls of the village were before this image, and that I might wish to go also and pray God and Our Lady to give life to this infant. I went and prayed with them. At last, life returned to the child, who yawned three times, and was then baptized; soon after, it died, and was buried in consecrated ground. It was three days, they said, since life had departed from the child; it was as black as my coat; when it yawned, the color began to return to it. I was with the other young girls, praying and kneeling before Our Lady."

"Did they not say in the village that it was done through you, and at your prayer?"

"I did not inquire about it."

"Have you ever seen or known Catherine de La Rochelle?"

"Yes, at Jargeau and at Montfaucon in Berry."

"Did not Catherine show you a lady, robed in white, who, she said, sometimes appeared to her?"

"No."

"What did this Catherine say to you?"

"That a white lady came to her, dressed in cloth-of-gold, who told her to go through the good cities with heralds and trumpets which the King would give to her, and proclaim that any one who had gold, silver, or any concealed treasure should bring it immediately: that those who did not do so, and who had anything hidden, she would know, and would be able to discover the treasure. With these treasures, she told me, she would pay my men-at-arms. I told Catherine that she should return to her husband, look after her home, and bring up her children. And in order to have some certainty as to her mission, I spoke of it, either to Saint Catherine or to Saint Margaret, who told me that the mission of this Catherine was mere folly and nothing else. I wrote to the King as to what he should do about it; and, when I afterwards went to him, I told him that this mission of Catherine was only folly and nothing more. Nevertheless, Brother Richard wished to set her to work; therefore were they both displeased with me,—Brother Richard and she."

"Did you never speak with the said Catherine on the project of going to La Charite-sur-Loire?"

"She did not advise me to go there: it was too cold, and she would not go. She told me she wished to visit the Duke of Burgundy in order to make peace. I told her it seemed to me that peace would be found only at the end of the lance. I asked her if this white lady who appeared to her came to her every night? and I said that, to see her, I would sleep one night with her in the same bed. I went to bed; I watched till mid-night; I saw nothing, and then went to sleep. When morning came, I asked her if the White Lady had come. 'Yes, Jeanne,' she answered me, 'while you were asleep she came; and I could not awaken you.' Then I asked her if she would come again the following night. 'Yes,' she told me. For this reason I slept by day that I might be able to watch the night following. I went to bed with Catherine; watched all the night following: but saw nothing, although I asked her often, 'Will she never come?' and she always answered me, 'Yes, in a moment.' "

"What did you do in the trenches of La Charite?"

"I made an assault there; but I neither threw, nor caused to be thrown, Holy Water by way of aspersion."

"Why did you not enter La Charite, if you had command from God to do so?"

"Who told you I had God's command for it?"

"Did you not have counsel of your Voice?"

"I wished to go into France. The men-at-arms told me it was better to go first to La Charite."

"Were you a long time in the Tower at Beaurevoir?"

"About four months. When I knew that the English were come to take me, I was very angry; nevertheless, my Voices forbade me many times to leap. In the end, for fear of the English, I leaped, and commended myself to God and Our Lady. I was wounded. When I had leaped, the Voice of Saint Catherine said to me I was to be of good cheer, for those at Compiegne would have succor. I prayed always for those at Compiegne, with my Counsel."

"What did you say when you had leaped?"

"Some said I was dead. As soon as the Burgundians saw I was alive, they reproached me with having leapt."

"Did you not say then, that you would rather die than be in the hands of the English?"

"I said I would rather give up my soul to God than be in the hands of the English."

"Were you not then very angry, to the extent of blaspheming the Name of God?"

"Never have I cursed any of the Saints; and it is not my habit to swear."

"On the subject of Soissons and the Captain who surrendered the town, did you not blaspheme God, and say, if you got hold of this Captain you would have him cut in quarters?"

"I have never blasphemed any of the Saints; those who say so have misunderstood."

Notes

1. *Joan's Strategies.* We can only imagine the dramatic scene of Joan's interrogation, although several recent movies have attempted to depict it. See *Joan of Arc* (1999) (television miniseries starring Leelee Sobieski) and *Messenger: The Story of Joan of Arc* (1999) (motion picture starring Milla Jovovich). What were Joan's characteristic strategies in answering the questions put to her? In what sense were these strategies successful?

2. *The Inquisition.* Compare the cross-examination of Joan of Arc with that of Christ by the Grand Inquisitor in Dostoevsky's THE BROTHERS KARAMAZOV (1879–80). In that novel Christ comes to Spain during the height of the Spanish Inquisition in the fifteenth century. After performing a couple of miracles, Christ is arrested by the Grand Inquisitor and condemned to death. The Inquisitor condemns Christ for attempting to give mankind freedom of choice. Says the Inquisitor to Christ:

Instead of taking men's freedom from them, Thou didst make it greater than ever! Didst Thou forget that man prefers peace, and even death, to freedom of choice in the knowledge of good and evil? Nothing is more seductive for man than his freedom of conscience, but nothing is a greater cause of suffering. And behold, instead of giving a firm foundation for setting the conscience of man at rest forever, Thou didst choose all that is exceptional, vague and enigmatic; Thou didst choose what was utterly beyond the strength of men, acting as though Thou didst not love them at all—Thou who didst come to give Thy life for them! Instead of taking possession of men's freedom, Thou didst increase it, and burdened the spiritual kingdom of mankind with its sufferings forever.

How would John Milton respond to the Grand Inquisitor? How would Joan of Arc respond? In the novel, Christ makes no response whatsoever.

* * *

Oscar Wilde (1854–1900), playwright, novelist, and poet, was known to Victorian society as a man of letters and witty conversationalist who espoused the aesthetic theory of art championed by Walter Pater. In 1891 he met Lord Alfred Douglas, son of the Marquess of Queensberry. Queensberry vehemently disapproved of his son's friendship with Wilde and engaged in a series of confrontations with Wilde in an attempt to end the friendship. In 1895 Queensberry appeared at Wilde's London club and handed the porter his card, on which he had written, "To Oscar Wilde, posing as a somdomite [sic]." Egged on by Lord Alfred Douglas, Wilde sued Queenberry for libel.

Then, as now, truth is a complete defense. When Wilde took the stand, Lord Queensberry's counsel, Sir Edward Carson, sought to prove that Wilde did in fact pose as a sodomite. Carson began by questioning him about *The Priest and the Acolyte*, a story, not authored by Wilde, about a priest who sodomized an acolyte. The story had appeared in an Oxford University student magazine, *The Chameleon,* along with some "Phrases and Philosophies for the Use of the Young" submitted by Wilde.

TESTIMONY IN THE TRIAL OF THE MARQUESS OF QUEENSBERRY FOR LIBEL
Oscar Wilde

Q. You read *The Priest and the Acolyte*?

A. Yes.

Q. You have no doubt whatever that that was an improper story?

A. From the literary point of view it was highly improper. It is impossible for a man of literature to judge it otherwise; by literature, meaning treatment, selection of subject, and the like. I thought the treatment rotten and the subject rotten.

Q. You are of opinion, I believe, that there is no such thing as an immoral book?

A. Yes.

Q. May I take it that you think *The Priest and the Acolyte* was not immoral?

A. It was worse—it was badly written.

. . . .

Q. Do you think the story blasphemous?

A. I think it violated every artistic canon of beauty.

. . . .

Q. I wish to know whether you thought the story blasphemous.

A. The story filled me with disgust. The end was wrong.

Q. Answer the question, sir. Did you or did you not consider the story blasphemous?

A. I thought it disgusting.

Q. You know that when the priest in the story administers poison to the boy, he uses the words of the sacrament of the Church of England?

A. That I entirely forgot.

Q. Do you consider that blasphemous?

A. I think it is horrible. "Blasphemous" is not a word of mine.

[Carson then read the passage in question.]

Q. Do you approve of those words?

A. I think them disgusting, perfect twaddle.... I strongly objected to the whole story. I took no steps to express disapproval of *The Chameleon* because I think it would have been beneath my dignity as a man of letters to associate myself with an Oxford undergraduate's productions. I am aware that the magazine may have been circulated among the undergraduates of Oxford. I do not believe that any book or work of art ever had any effect whatever on morality.

Q. Am I right in saying that you do not consider the effect in creating morality or immorality?

A. Certainly, I do not.

Q. So far as your works are concerned, you pose as not being concerned about morality or immorality?

A. I do not know whether you use the word "pose" in any particular sense.

Q. Is it a favourite word of your own?

A. Is it? I have no pose in this matter. In writing a play or a book, I am concerned entirely with literature—that is, with art. I aim not at doing good or evil, but in trying to make a thing that will have some quality of beauty.

Q. Listen, sir, here is one of the "Phrases and Philosophies for the Use of the Young" which you contributed: "Wickedness is a myth invented by good people to account for the curious attractiveness of others." You think that true?

A. I rarely think that anything I write is true.

Q. Did you say "rarely"?

A. I said "rarely." I might have said "never"—not true in the actual sense of the word.

Q. "Religions die when they are proved to be true." Is that true?

A. Yes. I hold that. It is a suggestion towards a philosophy of the absorption of religions by science, but it is too big a question to go into now.

Q. Do you think that was a safe axiom to put forward for the philosophy of the young?

A. Most stimulating.

Q. "If one tells the truth, one is sure, sooner or later, to be found out."?

A. That is a pleasing paradox, but I do not set very high store by it as an axiom.

Q. Is it good for the young?

A. Anything is good that stimulates thought at whatever age.

Q. Whether moral or immoral?

A. There is no such thing as morality or immorality in thought. There is immoral emotion.

Q. "Pleasure is the only thing one should live for."?

A. I think that the realization of oneself is the prime aim of life, and to realize oneself through pleasure is finer than to do so through pain. I am, on that point, entirely on the side of the ancients—the Greeks. It is a pagan idea.

Q. "A truth ceases to be true when more than one person believes in it."?

A. Perfectly. That would be my metaphysical definition of truth: something so personal that the same truth could never be appreciated by two minds.

Q. "The condition of perfection is idleness; the aim of perfection is youth."?

A. Oh, yes, I think so. Half of it is true. The life of contemplation is the highest life, and so recognized by the philosopher.

Q. "There is something tragic about the enormous number of young men there are in England at the present moment who start life with perfect profiles, and end by adopting some useful profession."?

A. I should think that the young have enough sense of humor.

Q. You think that is humorous?

A. I think it is an amusing paradox, an amusing play on words. . . .

Q. This is in your introduction to *Dorian Gray*: "There is no such thing as a moral or an immoral book. Books are well written, or badly written." That expresses your view?

A. My view on art, yes.

Q. Then I take it that no matter how immoral a book may be, if it is well written, it is, in your opinion, a good book?

A. Yes, if it were well written so as to produce a sense of beauty, which is the highest sense of which a human being can be capable. If it were badly written, it would produce a sense of disgust.

Q. Then a well-written book putting forward perverted moral views may be a good book?

A. No work of art ever puts forward views. Views belong to people who are not artists.

Q. A perverted novel might be a good book?

A. I do not know what you mean by a "perverted" novel.

Q. Then I will suggest *Dorian Gray* as open to the interpretation of being such a novel.

A. That could only be to brutes and illiterates. The views of Philistines on art are incalculably stupid.

Q. An illiterate person reading *Dorian Gray* might consider it such a novel?

A. The views of illiterates on art are unaccountable. I am concerned only with my own view of art. I do not care twopence what other people think of it.

Q. The majority of persons would come under your definition of Philistines and illiterates?

A. I have found wonderful exceptions.

Q. Do you think that the majority of people live up to the position you are giving us?

A. I am afraid they are not cultivated enough.

Q. Not cultivated enough to draw the distinction between a good book and a bad book?

A. Certainly not.

Q. The affection and love of the artist of *Dorian Gray* might lead an ordinary individual to believe that it might have a certain tendency?

A. I have no knowledge of the views of ordinary individuals.

Q. You did not prevent the ordinary individual from buying your book?

A. I have never discouraged him!

[Carson next read a long passage from *The Picture of Dorian Gray*, including Basil Hallward's description of his early relationship with Dorian Gray.]

Q. Now, I ask you, Mr. Wilde, do you consider that that description of the feeling of one man towards a youth just grown up was a proper or an improper feeling?

A. I think it is the most perfect description of what an artist would feel on meeting a beautiful personality that was in some way necessary to his art and life.

Q. You think that is a feeling a young man should have towards another?

A. Yes, as an artist.

[Carson read another passage from the novel in which Hallward tells Dorian of his feelings.]

Q. Do you mean to say that that passage describes the natural feeling of one man towards another?

A. It would be the influence produced by a beautiful personality.

Q. A beautiful person?

A. I said a "beautiful personality." You can describe it as you like. Dorian Gray's was a most remarkable personality.

Q. May I take it that you, as an artist, have never known the feeling described here?

A. I have never allowed any personality to dominate my art.

Q. Then you have never known the feeling you described?

A. No. It is a work of fiction.

Q. So far as you are concerned you have no experience as to its being a natural feeling?

A. I think it is perfectly natural for any artist to admire intensely and love a young man. It is an incident in the life of almost every artist.

Q. But let us go over it phrase by phrase. "I quite admit that I adored you madly." What do you say to that? Have you ever adored a young man madly?

A. No, not madly. I prefer love—that is a higher form.

Q. Never mind about that. Let us keep down to the level we are at now.

A. I have never given adoration to anybody except myself. [Loud laughter in the courtroom]

Q. I suppose you think that a very smart thing?

A. Not at all.

Q. Then you have never had that feeling?

A. No. The whole idea was borrowed from Shakespeare, I regret to say. Yes, from Shakespeare's sonnets.

Q. I believe you have written an article to show that Shakespeare's sonnets were suggestive of unnatural vice?

A. On the contrary, I have written an article to show that they are not. I objected to such a perversion being put upon Shakespeare.

. . . .

Q. "I wanted to have you all to myself." Did you ever have that feeling?

A. No. I should consider it an intense nuisance, an intense bore.

Q. "I grew afraid that the world would know of my idolatry." Why should he grow afraid that the world should know of it?

A. Because there are people in the world who cannot understand the intense devotion, affection, and admiration that an artist can feel for a wonderful and beautiful personality. These are the conditions under which we live. I regret them.

Q. These unfortunate people, that have not the high understanding that you have, might put it down to something wrong?

A. Undoubtedly, to any point they chose. I am not concerned with the ignorance of others....

[Carson read another exchange between Hallward and Dorian, ending with Hallward's exclamation, "Dorian, Dorian, your reputation is infamous."]

Q. Does not this passage suggest a charge of unnatural vice?

A. It describes Dorian Gray as a man of very corrupt influence, though there is no statement as to the nature of the influence. But as a matter of fact I do not think that one person influences another, nor do I think there is any bad influence in the world.

Q. A man never corrupts a youth?

A. I think not.

Q. Nothing could corrupt him?

A. If you are talking of separate ages.

Q. No, sir, I am talking common sense.

A. I do not think one person influences another.

Q. You don't think that flattering a young man, making love to him, in fact, would be likely to corrupt him?

A. No.

[Carson then turned to compromising letters from Wilde to Lord Alfred that came to light when Douglas's overcoat was donated to charity and the letters were found in the pockets.]

Q. Why should a man of your age address a boy nearly twenty years younger as "My own Boy"?

A. I was fond of him, I have always been fond of him.

Q. Do you adore him?

A. No, but I have always liked him. I think it is a beautiful letter. It is a poem. I was not writing an ordinary letter. You might as well cross-examine me as to whether *King Lear* or a sonnet of Shakespeare was proper.

Q. Apart from art, Mr Wilde.

A.   I cannot answer apart from art.

Q.   Suppose a man who was not an artist had written this letter, would you say it was a proper letter?

A.   A man who was not an artist could not have written that letter.

Q.   Why?

A.   Because nobody but an artist could write it. He certainly could not write the language unless he were a man of letters.

Q.   I can suggest, for the sake of your reputation, that there is nothing very wonderful in this "red rose-leaf lips of yours"?

A.   A great deal depends on the way it is read.

Q.   "Your slim gilt soul walks between passion and poetry." Is that a beautiful phrase?

A.   Not as you read it, Mr Carson. You read it very badly.

Q.   I do not profess to be an artist, and when I hear you give evidence, I am glad I am not.

[Here, Sir Edward Clarke, Wilde's counsel, leapt to his feet: "I don't think my learned friend should talk like that," and to Wilde, "Pray do not criticize my learned friend's reading again."]

After questioning Wilde about literary matters, Carson turned to questions regarding a number of boys who had apparently been showered with hospitality and expensive gifts by Wilde. Despite Wilde's denial of any improper conduct or relationships, the trial ended with a verdict in favor of Queensberry. Unfortunately for Wilde, the evidence during the trial left him open to criminal charges, and shortly after the libel trial, he was arrested and charged with "committing acts of gross indecency with various male persons." Charles Gill prosecuted Wilde, who was again represented by Sir Edward Clarke.

Gill examined Wilde regarding several poems by Lord Alfred Douglas that had been published in a magazine:

Q.   ... The next poem is one described as "Two Loves." It contains these lines:

"Sweet youth,
Tell me why, sad and sighing, dost thou rove
These pleasant realms? I pray thee tell me sooth,
What is thy name?" He said, "My name is Love,"
Then straight the first did turn himself to me,
And cried, "He lieth, for his name is Shame.
But I am Love, and I was wont to be
Alone in this fair garden, till he came
Unasked by night; I am true Love, I fill
The hearts of boy and girl with mutual flame."
Then sighing said the other, "Have thy will,
I am the Love that dare not speak its name."
Was that poem explained to you?

A. I think that is clear.

Q. There is no question as to what it means?

A. Most certainly not.

Q. Is it not clear that the love described relates to natural love and unnatural love?

A. No.

Q. What is the "Love that dare not speak its name"?

A. "The love that dare not speak its name" in this century is such a great affection of an elder for a younger man as there was between David and Jonathan, such as Plato made the very basis of his philosophy, and such as you find in the sonnets of Michelangelo and Shakespeare. It is that deep, spiritual affection that is as pure as it is perfect. It dictates and pervades great works of art like those of Shakespeare and Michelangelo, and those two letters of mine, such as they are. It is in this century misunderstood, so much misunderstood that it may be described as the "Love that dare not speak its name," and on account of it I am placed where I am now. It is beautiful, it is fine, it is the noblest form of affection. There is nothing unnatural about it. It is intellectual, and it repeatedly exists between an elder and a younger man, when the elder has intellect, and the younger man has all the joy, hope, and glamour of life before him. That it should be so, the world does not understand. The world mocks at it and sometimes puts one in the pillory for it. [Loud applause, mingled with hisses, in the courtroom.]

The criminal trial resulted in a hung jury, but the Government immediately determined to retry him. Professor Douglas Linder notes speculation that the prosecutor was pressured by the Prime Minister, Lord Rosebery. Rosebery was suspected of having a homosexual affair with another of Queensberry's sons, Francis, who had recently died under circumstances suggesting suicide. Letters from Queensberry to the Prime Minister suggest that Queensberry was prepared to expose the affair if Wilde were not prosecuted. At his second criminal trial, Wilde was convicted and sentenced to two years hard labor. An outstanding source of information about Wilde's trials is Professor Douglas Linder's famous trials web site, <*http://www.law.umkc.edu/faculty/projects/ftrials/wilde*>(visited January 25, 2003).

During Wilde's imprisonment, Queensberry succeeded in having him declared a bankrupt, and all his possessions, including priceless first editions, scrapbooks, and memorabilia, were auctioned off. His wife, Constance Lloyd Wilde, moved to Switzerland with their two sons, Cyril and Vivian, and changed their surname to Holland. While in prison, Wilde completed *De Profundis*, excerpted in the next chapter. After his release from prison, he published "The Ballad of Reading Gaol" and travelled widely in Europe. He is buried in Paris.

Notes

1. *Fascination with Wilde.* Oscar Wilde is a fascinating figure for scholars. He has been the subject of a recent motion picture, *Oscar Wilde* (1997), starring Stephen Fry, and a Pulitzer Prize-winning biography by Richard Ellmann, *Oscar Wilde* (1987).

2. *Wit.* Wilde's exchanges with his interrogators were widely reported in the press at the time and have become justly famous for their wit. Was Wilde's wit appropriate? Useful? To what extent do you agree with his views on art? Does his wit make these views more or less attractive?

3. *The Influence of Literature.* Wilde was questioned about a number of literary works, some not even written by him. How were these works relevant to the cases? Should Wilde's counsel have objected to this line of questioning? In recent years, in a number of contexts, litigants have alleged that harmful conduct was caused by works of art. In these cases, the courts have divided over the relationship between art and reality. *Compare James v. Meow Media, Inc.,* 90 F.Supp.2d 798 (W.D.Ky.2000) (no liability for murder allegedly inspired by, inter alia, movie *The Basketball Diaries*); *Davidson v. Time Warner, Inc.,* 1997 WL 405907 (S.D.Tex.1997) (no liability for murder allegedly caused by Tupac Shukur recording "2Pacalypse Now"); *McCollum v. CBS, Inc.,* 202 Cal.App.3d 989, 249 Cal.Rptr. 187 (1988) (no liability for suicide allegedly caused by Ozzy Osbourne songs, including "Suicide Solution") *with Byers v. Edmondson,* 712 So.2d 681 (La.Ct.App. 1998) (liability possible for shooting allegedly inspired by movie *Natural Born Killers*); *Rice v. Paladin Enterprises, Inc.,* 128 F.3d 233 (4th Cir.1997) (liability possible for murder allegedly committed according to instructions in novel *Hit Man*).

Chapter 2

ESSAYS AND OTHER TRIALS

A. INTRODUCTION

In this chapter we present reflective essays, Bible verses, literary criticism, satire, judicial opinions, letters, autobiography, jokes, and legal instruments. As you read, ask yourself what are the peculiar characteristics of each genre, and what characteristics do all the works share.

An essay is an analytic, interpretive, and speculative composition, usually dealing with a theme or subject from a personal point of view. The verb "essay," or "assay," means to try or attempt. The word derives from the Latin *exagium,* a weighing, and *exigere,* to examine, test, or literally to drive out. In a sense all the materials in this chapter are essays, or trials.

It is instructive that the essay is the form of composition widely used to test the knowledge and abilities of the liberal arts student, including the law student. It is the form that most appropriately describes court opinions.

B. SOUL-SEARCHING

During his imprisonment, Oscar Wilde wrote a long letter to Lord Alfred Douglas. Wilde delivered the letter to a mutual friend, who copied it before giving it to Douglas. The letter was published as an essay. Wilde's own title for the work was *Epistola: In Carcere et Vinculis.* However, his literary executor entitled the work *De Profundis* for publication. The title is evidently drawn from the great Psalm 130, given here from both the Vulgate and the King James Bible:

PSALMUS 130

[1] *Canticum ascensionum.*

De profundis clamavi ad te, Domine;

[2] Domine exaudi vocem meam.

Fiant aures tuae intendentes in vocem deprecationis meae.

[3] Si iniquitate observaveris, Domine, Domine, quis sustinebit?

[4] Quia apud te propitiatio est, ut timeamus te.

[5] Sustinui te, Domine, sustinuit anima mea in verbo eius; speravit

[6] anima mea in Domino

magis quam custodes auroram.

Magis quam custodes aruroram

[7] speret Israel in Domino, quia apud Dominum misericordia, et copiosa apud eum redemptio.

[8] Et ipse redimet Israel ex omnibus iniquitatibus eius.

PSALM 130

A Song of degrees

OUT of the depths have I cried unto thee, O Lord.

[2] Lord, hear my voice: let thine ears be attentive to the voice of my supplications.

[3] If thou, Lord, shouldest mark iniquities, O Lord, who shall stand?

[4] But there is forgiveness with thee, that thou mayest be feared.

[5] I wait for the Lord, my soul doth wait, and in his word do I hope.

[6] My soul waiteth for the Lord more than they that watch for the morning; I say, more than they that watch for the morning.

[7] Let Israel hope in the Lord: for with the Lord there is mercy, and with him is plenteous redemption.

[8] And he shall redeem Israel from all his iniquities.

DE PROFUNDIS
Oscar Wilde

H.M. Prison,

Reading.

Dear Bosie,—After long and fruitless waiting I have determined to write to you myself, as much for your sake as for mine, as I would not like to think that I had passed through two long years of imprisonment without ever having received a single line from you, or any news or message even, except such as gave me pain.

Our ill-fated and most lamentable friendship has ended in ruin and public infamy for me, yet the memory of our ancient affection is often with me, and the thought that loathing, bitterness and contempt should for ever take the place in my heart once held by love is very sad to me: and you yourself will, I think, feel in your heart that to write to me as I lie in the loneliness of prison life is better than to publish my letters without my permission or to dedicate poems to me unasked, though the world will know nothing of whatever words of grief or passion, of remorse or indifference you may choose to send as your answer or your appeal.

I have no doubt that in this letter which I have to write of your life and of mine, of the past and of the future, of sweet things changed to bitterness and of bitter things that may be turned into joy, there will be much that will wound your vanity to the quick. If it prove so, read the letter over and over again till it kills your vanity. If you find in it something of which you feel that you are unjustly accused, remember that one should be thankful that there is any fault of which one can be unjustly accused. If there be in it one single passage that brings tears to your eyes, weep as we weep in prison where the day no less than the night is set apart for tears. It is the only thing that can save you....

I will begin by telling you that I blame myself terribly. As I sit here in this dark cell in convict clothes, a disgraced and ruined man, I blame myself. In the perturbed and fitful nights of anguish, in the long monotonous days of pain, it is myself I blame. I blame myself for allowing an unintellectual friendship, a friendship whose primary aim was not the creation and contemplation of beautiful things, entirely to dominate my life. From the very first there was too wide a gap between us. . . . Whether at Torquay, Goring, London, Florence, or elsewhere, my life, as long as you were by my side, was entirely sterile and uncreative. And with but few intervals you were, I regret to say, by my side always.

. . . .

But most of all I blame myself for the entire ethical degradation I allowed you to bring on me. The basis of character is will power, and my will power became absolutely subject to yours. It sounds a grotesque thing to say, but it is none the less true. Those incessant scenes that seemed to be almost physically necessary to you and in which your mind and body grew distorted and you became a thing as terrible to look at as to listen to: that dreadful mania you inherit from your father, the mania for writing revolting and loathsome letters: your entire lack of any control over your emotions, as displayed in your long resentful moods of sullen silence, no less than in your sudden fits of almost epileptic rage: . . . —these, I say, were the origin and causes of my fatal yielding to you in your daily increasing demands. You wore me out. It was the triumph of the smaller over the bigger nature. It was the case of that tyranny of the weak over the strong which somewhere in one of my plays I describe as being "the only tyranny that lasts."

. . . .

Of course, I should have got rid of you. I should have shaken you out of my life as a man shakes from his raiment a thing that has stung him. In the most wonderful of all his plays, Aeschylus tells us of the great lord who brings up in his house the lion cub and loves it because it comes bright-eyed to his call and fawns on him for its food; and the thing grows up and shows the nature of its race and destroys the lord and his house and all that he possesses. I feel that I was such a one as he. But my fault was, not that I did not part from you, but that I parted from you far too often. As far as I can make out I ended my friendship with you every three months regularly. And each time that I did so you managed by means of entreaties, telegrams, letters, the interposition of your friends, the interposition of mine, and the like to induce me to allow you back. . . . In one of the violent letters you wrote to me, . . . you said you were under "no intellectual obligation of any kind" to me. I remember that when I read that statement I felt that it was really the one true thing you had written to me in the whole course of our friendship. I saw that a less cultivated nature would really have suited you much better. I am not saying this in bitterness at all, but simply as a fact of companionship. Ultimately the bond of all companionship, whether in marriage or in friendship, is conversation, and conversation must have a common basis, and between two people of widely different culture the only common basis possible is the lowest level. The trivial in thought and action is charming. I had made it the keystone of a very brilliant philosophy expressed in plays and paradoxes. But the froth and folly of our life grew often very wearisome to me: it was only in the mire that we met: and fascinating, terribly fascinating though the one topic round which your talk invariably centred was, still at the end it became quite monotonous to me. I was often bored to death by it, and accepted it, as I accepted your passion for going to music halls, or your mania for absurd extravagances in eating and drinking, or any other of your to me less attractive characteristics, as a thing, that is to say, that one simply had to put up with, a part of the high price one had to pay for knowing you. . . .

. . . .

You send me a very nice poem of the undergraduate school of verse for my approval: I reply by a letter of fantastic literary conceits: I compare you to Hylas, or Hyacinth, Jonquil or Narcisse or some one whom the great God of Poetry favoured, and honoured with his love. The letter is like a passage from one of Shakespeare's sonnets transposed to a minor key. It can be understood only by those who had read the *Symposium* of Plato, or caught the spirit of a certain grave mood made beautiful for us in Greek marbles. It was, let me say frankly, the sort of letter I would, in a happy if wilful moment, have written to any graceful young man of either University who had sent me a poem of his own making, certain that he would have sufficient wit, or culture, to interpret rightly its fantastic phrases. Look at the history of that letter! It passes from you into the hands of a loathsome companion: from him to a gang of blackmailers: copies of it are sent about London to my friends, and to the manager of the theatre where my work is being performed: every construction but the right one is put on it: Society is thrilled with the absurd rumours that I have had to pay a huge sum of money for having written an infamous letter to you: this forms the basis of your father's worst attack: I produce the original letter myself in Court to show what it really is: it is denounced by your father's Counsel as a revolting and insidious attempt to corrupt innocence: ultimately it forms part of a criminal charge: the Crown takes it up: the Judge sums up on it with little learning and much morality: I go to prison for it at last. That is the result of writing you a charming letter.

. . . .

But, indeed, I need not go on further into more instances of the strange doom you seem to have brought on me in all things big or little. It makes me feel sometimes as if you yourself had been merely a puppet worked by some secret and unseen hand to bring terrible events to a terrible issue. But puppets themselves have passions. They will bring a new plot into what they are presenting, and twist the ordered issue of vicissitude to suit some whim or appetite of their own. To be entirely free, and at the same time entirely dominated by law, is the eternal paradox of human life that we realise at every moment: and this, I often think, is the only explanation possible of your nature, if indeed for the profound and terrible mystery of a human soul there is any explanation at all, except one that makes the mystery all the more marvellous still.

. . . .

You thought again that in attacking your own father with dreadful letters, abusive telegrams, and insulting postcards, you were really fighting your mother's battles, coming forward as her champion, and avenging the no doubt terrible wrongs and sufferings of her married life. It was quite an illusion on your part, one of your worst indeed. The way for you to have avenged your mother's wrongs on your father, if you considered it part of a son's duty to do so, was by being a better son to your mother than you had been: by not making her afraid to speak to you on serious things: by not signing bills the payment of which devolved on her: by being gentler to her, and not bringing sorrow into her days. . . . You were wrong even in fancying that it would have been an absolute delight and joy to your mother if you had managed through me to get your father put into prison. I feel sure you were wrong. And if you want to know what a woman really feels when her husband and the father of her children is in prison dress, in a prison cell, write to my wife and ask her. She will tell you. *I* also had my illusions. I thought life was going to be a brilliant comedy, and that you were to be one of the graceful figures in it. I found it to be a revolting and repellent tragedy, and that the sinister occasion of the great catastrophe, sinister in its concentration of aim and intensity of narrowed will power, was yourself, stripped of that mask of joy and pleasure by which you, no less than I, had been deceived and led astray.

You can now understand—can you not?—a little of what I am suffering. Some paper, the *Pall Mall Gazette*, I think, describing the dress rehearsal of one of my plays, spoke of you as following me about like my shadow: the memory of our friendship is the shadow that walks with me here: that seems never to leave me: that wakes me up at night to tell me the same story over and over till its wearisome iteration makes all sleep abandon me till dawn: at dawn it begins again: it follows me into the prison yard and makes me talk to myself as I tramp round: each detail that accompanied each dreadful moment I am forced to recall: there is nothing that happened in those ill-starred years that I cannot recreate in that chamber of the brain which is set apart for grief or for despair: every strained note of your voice, every twitch and gesture of your nervous hands, every bitter word, every poisonous phrase comes back to me: I remember the street or river down which we passed: the wall or woodland that surrounded us, at what figure on the dial stood the hands of the clock, which way went the wings of the wind, the shape and colour of the moon.

There is, I know, one answer to all that I have said to you, and that is that you loved me: that all through those two and a half years during which the fates were weaving into one scarlet pattern the threads of our divided lives you really loved me. Yes, I know you did. No matter what your conduct to me was, I always felt, that at heart you really did love me. Though I saw quite clearly that my position in the world of Art, the interest that my personality had always excited, my money, the luxury in which I lived, the thousand and one things that went to make up a life so charmingly and so wonderfully improbable as mine was, were, each and all of them, elements that fascinated you and made you cling to me: yet besides all this there was something more, some strange attraction for you: you loved me far better than you loved anyone else. But you, like myself, have had a terrible tragedy in your life, though one of an entirely opposite character to mine. Do you want to learn what it was? It was this. In you hate was always stronger than love. Your hatred of your father was of such stature that it entirely outstripped, overthrew, and overshadowed your love of me. There was no struggle between them at all, or but little; of such dimensions was your hatred and of such monstrous growth. You did not realize that there was no room for both passions in the same soul. They cannot live together in that fair carven house. Love is fed by the imagination, by which we become wiser than we know, better than we feel, nobler than we are: by which we can see life as a whole: by which and by which alone we can understand others in their real as in their ideal relation. Only what is fine, and finely conceived, can feed love. But anything will feed hate. There was not a glass of champagne that you drank, not a rich dish that you ate of in all those years, that did not feed your hate and make it fat. So to gratify it you gambled with my life, as you gambled with my money, carelessly, recklessly, indifferent to the consequence. If you lost, the loss would not, you fancied, be yours. If you won, yours, you knew, would be the exultation and the advantages of victory.

Hate blinds people. You were not aware of that. Love can read the writing on the remotest star; but hate so blinded you that you could see no further than the narrow, walled-in and already lust-withered garden of your common desires. Your terrible lack of imagination, the one really fatal defect of your character, was entirely the result of the hate that lived in you. Subtly, silently, and in secret, hate gnawed at your nature, as the lichen bites at the root of some sallow plant, till you grew to see nothing but the most meagre interests and the most petty aims. That faculty in you which love would have fostered, hate poisoned and paralysed. When your father first began to attack me it was as your private friend, and in a private letter to you.... From pert telegrams to priggish lawyers' letters was a natural progress, and the result of your lawyers' letters to your father was, of course, to urge him on still further. You left him no option but to go on. You forced it on him as a point of honour, or of dishonour rather, that your appeal should have the more effect. So the next time he attacks me no longer in a private letter and as your private friend, but in public and as a public man. I have to expel him from my house. He goes from restaurant to restaurant looking for me, in order to insult me before the whole world, and in such manner that if I retaliated I would be ruined, and if I did not retaliate I would be ruined also.... Having assailed me as a private gentleman and in private, as a public man and in public, he ultimately determines to make his final and great attack on me as an artist, and in the place where my art is being represented. He secures by fraud a seat for the first night of one of my plays, and contrives a plot to interrupt the performance, to make a foul speech about me to the audience, to insult my actors, to throw offensive or indecent missiles at me when I am called before the curtain at the close, utterly in some hideous way to ruin me through my work. By the merest chance, in the brief and accidental sincerity of a more than usually intoxicated mood, he boasts of his intention before others. Information is given to the police, and he is kept out of the theatre. You had your chance then. Then was your opportunity. Don't you realize now that you should have seen it, and come forward and said that you would not have my art, at any rate, ruined for your sake? You knew what my art was to me, the great primal note by which I had revealed, first myself to myself, and then myself to the world; the great passion of my life; the love to which all other loves were as marsh water to red wine; or the glowworm of the marsh to the magic mirror of the moon. Don't your understand now that your lack of imagination was the only really fatal defect of your character? What you had to do was quite simple and quite clear before you, but hate blinded you, and you could see nothing....

The key of the situation rested entirely with yourself. It was the one great opportunity you had of making some slight return to me for all the love and affection and kindness and generosity and care I had shown you. Had you appreciated me even at a tenth of my value as an artist you would have done so. But hate blinded you. The faculty "by which and by which alone we can understand others in their real, as in their ideal relations" was dead in you. You thought simply of how to get your father into prison. To see him "in the dock," as you used to say: that was your one idea. The phrase became one of the many *scies* of your daily conversation. One heard it at every meal. Well, you had your desire gratified. Hate granted you every single thing you wished for. It was an indulgent master to you. It is so, indeed, to all who serve it. For two days you sat on a high seat with the Sheriffs, and feasted your eyes with the spectacle of your father standing in the dock of the Central Criminal Court. And on the third day I took his place. What had occurred? In your hideous game of hate together, you had both thrown dice for my soul and you happened to have lost. That was all.

You see that I have to write your life to you and you have to realize it. We have known each other now for more than four years. Half of the time we have been together: the other half I have had to spend in prison as the result of our friendship.... You are surrounded, if not with all the useless luxury you had with me, at any rate with everything that is pleasurable to eye, ear and taste. Life is quite lovely to you. And yet, if you are wise, and wish to find life much lovelier still, and in a different manner, you will let the reading of this terrible letter—for such I know it is—prove to you as important a crisis and turning-point of your life as the writing of it is to me. Your pale face used to flush easily with wine or pleasure. If, as you read what is here written, it from time to time becomes scorched as though by a furnace blast, with shame, it will be all the better for you. The supreme vice is shallowness. Whatever is realized is right.

... Everything must come to one out of one's own nature. There is no use telling a person a thing that he does not feel and can't understand. . . .

I remember again, when an execution was put into my house and my books and furniture were seized and advertised to be sold, and bankruptcy was impending, I naturally wrote to tell you about it. I did not mention that it was to pay for some gifts of mine to you that the bailiffs had entered the house where you had so often dined. I thought, rightly or wrongly, that such news might pain you a little. I merely told you the bare facts. I thought it proper that you should know them. You wrote back from Boulogne in a strain of almost lyrical exultation. You said that you knew your father was "hard up for money" and had been obliged to raise £1,500 for the expenses of the trial and that my going bankrupt was really a "splendid score" off him as he would not then be able to get any of his costs out of me! Do you realize now what hate blinding a person is? Do you recognize now that when I described it as an atrophy destructive of everything but itself, I was scientifically describing a real psychological fact? That all my charming things were to be sold: my Burne-Jones drawings: my Whistler drawings: my Monticelli, my Simeon Solomons: my china: my library with its collection of presentation volumes from almost every poet of my time, from Hugo to Whitman, from Swinburne to Mallarmé, from Morris to Verlaine: with its beautifully bound editions of my father's and mother's works, its wonderful array of college and school prizes: its *éditions de luxe*, and the like: was absolutely nothing to you. You said it was a great bore: that was all. . . . Had your father had no claim for his costs on me, you, I know perfectly well, would, as far as words go, at any rate have been most sympathetic about the entire loss of my library, a loss irreparable to a man of letters, the one of all my material losses the most distressing to me. You might even, remembering the sums of money I had lavishly spent on you and how you had lived on me for years, have taken the trouble to buy in some of my books for me. The best all went for less than £150: about as much as I would spend on you in an ordinary week. But the mean, small pleasure of thinking that your father was going to be a few pence out of pocket made you forget all about trying to make me a little return, so slight, so easy, so inexpensive, so obvious, and so enormously welcome to me, had you brought it about. Am I right in saying that hate blinds people? Do you see it now? If you don't, try to see it.

How clearly I saw it then, as now, I need not tell you. But I said to myself: "At all costs, I must keep love in my heart. If I go into prison without love what will become of my soul?" ... Sins of the flesh are nothing. They are maladies for physicians to cure, if they should be cured. Sins of the soul are shameful.... But do you really think that you were worthy of the love I was showing you then, or that for a single moment I thought you were? Do you really think that at any period in our friendship you were worthy of the love I showed you, or that for a single moment I thought you were? I knew you were not. But love does not traffic in a market place, nor use a huckster's scales. Its joy, like the joy of the intellect, is to feel alive. The aim of love is to love: no more, and no less.... For my own sake there was nothing for me to do but to love you. I knew that if I allowed myself to hate you that in the dry desert of existence over which I had to travel, and am travelling still, every rock would lose its shadow, every palm tree be withered, every well of water prove poisoned at its source....

After my terrible sentence, when the prison dress was on me, and the prison house closed, I sat amidst the ruins of my wonderful life, crushed by anguish, bewildered with terror, dazed through pain. But I would not hate you. Every day I said to myself: "I must keep love in my heart to-day, else how shall I live through the day?" I reminded myself that you meant no evil, to me at any rate: I set myself to think that you had but drawn a bow at a venture, and that the arrow had pierced a king between the joints of his harness. To have weighed you against the smallest of my sorrows, the meanest of my losses, would have been, I felt, unfair. I determined I would regard you as one suffering too. I forced myself to believe that at last the scales had fallen from your long-blinded eyes. I used to fancy and with pain what your horror must have been when you contemplated your terrible handiwork. There were times, even in those dark days, the darkest of all my life, when I actually longed to console you, so sure was I that at last you had realized what you had done.

It did not occur to me then that you could have the supreme vice, shallowness. Indeed it was a real grief to me when I had to let you know that. I was obliged to reserve for my family business my first opportunity of receiving a letter: but my brother-in-law had written to me to say that if I would only write once to my wife she would, for my own sake and for our children's sake, take no action for divorce. I felt my duty was to do so. Setting aside other reasons, I could not bear the idea of being separated from Cyril, that beautiful, loving, lovable child of mine, my friend of all friends, my companion beyond all companions, one single hair of whose little golden head should have been dearer and more valuable to me than, I will not say you from top to toe, but the entire chrysolite of the whole world: was so indeed to me always, though I failed to understand it till too late.

        . . . .

    ... Remember how and why I am here at this very moment. Do you think I am here on account of my relations with the witnesses on my trial? My relations, real or supposed, with people of that kind were matters of no interest either to the Government or to Society. They knew nothing of them and cared less. I am here for having tried to put your father into prison. My attempt failed, of course. My own Counsel threw up their briefs. Your father completely turned the tables on me, and had me in prison, has me there still. That is why there is contempt felt for me. That is why people despise me. That is why I have to serve out every day, every hour, every minute of my dreadful imprisonment. That is why my petitions have been refused.

You were the only person who, and without in any way exposing yourself to scorn or danger or blame, could have given another colour to the whole affair, have put the matter in a different light, have shown to a certain degree how things really stood. I would not, of course, have expected, nor indeed wished you to have stated how and for what purpose you had sought my assistance in your trouble at Oxford: of how, and for what purpose, if you had a purpose at all, you had practically never left my side for nearly three years. My incessant attempts to break off a friendship that was so ruinous to me as an artist, as a man of position, as a member of Society even, need not have been chronicled with the accuracy with which they have been set down here. Nor would I have desired you to have described the scenes you used to make with such almost monotonous recurrence: nor to have reprinted your wonderful series of telegrams to me with their strange mixture of romance and finance: nor to have quoted from letters the more revolting or heartless passages as I have been forced to do. Still, I thought it would have been good, as well for you as for me, if you had made some protest against your father's version of our friendship, one no less grotesque than venomous and as absurd in its inference to you as it was dishonouring in its reference to me. That version has now actually passed into serious history: it is quoted, believed, and chronicled: the preacher has taken it for his text, and the moralist for his barren theme: and I who appealed to all the ages have had to accept my verdict from one who is an ape and a buffoon. I have said, and with some bitterness, I admit, in this letter that such was the irony of things that your father would live to be the hero of a Sunday school tract: that you would rank with the infant Samuel: and that my place would be between Gilles de Retz and the Marquis de Sade. I dare say it is best so. I have no desire to complain. One of the many lessons that one learns in prison is, that things are what they are and will be what they will be. Nor have I any doubt that the leper of medievalism and the author of *Justine* will prove better company than Sandford and Merton.

    . . . .

. . . Suffering is one very long moment. We cannot divide it by seasons. We can only record its moods, and chronicle their return. With us time itself does not progress. It revolves. It seems to circle round one centre of pain. The paralysing immobility of a life every circumstance of which is regulated after an unchangeable pattern, so that we eat and drink and lie down and pray, or kneel at least for prayer, according to the inflexible laws of an iron formula: this immobile quality, that makes each dreadful day in the very minutest detail like its brother, seems to communicate itself to those external forces the very essence of whose existence is ceaseless change. Of seed-time or harvest, of the reapers bending over the corn, or the grape gatherers threading through the vines, of the grass in the orchard made white with broken blossoms or strewn with fallen fruit: of these we know nothing and can know nothing.

For us there is only one season, the season of sorrow. The very sun and moon seem taken from us. Outside, the day may be blue and gold, but the light that creeps down through the thickly-muffled glass of the small iron-barred window beneath which one sits is grey and niggard. It is always twilight in one's cell, as it is always twilight in one's heart. And in the sphere of thought, no less than in the sphere of time, motion is no more. The thing that you personally have long ago forgotten, or can easily forget, is happening to me now, and will happen to me again to-morrow. Remember this, and you will be able to understand a little of why I am writing, and in this manner writing. . . .

A week later, I am transferred here. Three more months go over and my mother dies. No one knew how deeply I loved and honoured her. Her death was terrible to me; but I, once a lord of language, have no words in which to express my anguish and my shame. She and my father had bequeathed me a name they had made noble and honoured, not merely in literature, art, archaeology, and science, but in the public history of my own country, in its evolution as a nation. I had disgraced that name eternally. I had made it a low by-word among low people. I had dragged it through the very mire. I had given it to brutes that they might make it brutal, and to fools that they might turn it into a synonym for folly. What I suffered then, and still suffer, is not for pen to write or paper to record. My wife, always kind and gentle to me, rather than that I should hear the news from indifferent lips, travelled, ill as she was, all the way from Genoa to England to break to me herself the tidings of so irreparable, so irremediable, a loss. Messages of sympathy reached me from all who had still affection for me. Even people who had not known me personally, hearing that a new sorrow had broken into my life, wrote to ask that some expression of their condolence should be conveyed to me. . . .

Three months go over. The calendar of my daily conduct and labour that hangs on the outside of my cell door, with my name and sentence written upon it, tells me that it is May.

My friends come to see me again. I enquire, as I always do, after you. I am told that you are in your villa at Naples, and are bringing out a volume of poems. At the close of the interview it is mentioned casually that you are dedicating them to me. The tidings seemed to give me a sort of nausea of life. I said nothing, but silently went back to my cell with contempt and scorn in my heart. How could you dream of dedicating a volume of poems to me without first asking my permission? Dream, do I say? How could you dare do such a thing? Will you give as your answer that in the days of my greatness and fame I had consented to receive the dedication of your early work? Certainly I did so: just as I would have accepted the homage of any other young men beginning the difficult and beautiful art of literature. All homage is delightful to an artist and doubly sweet when youth brings it. Laurel and bay leaf wither when aged hands pluck them. Only youth has a right to crown an artist. That is the real privilege of being young if youth only knew it. But the days of abasement and infamy are different from those of greatness and fame. You had yet to learn that.

Prosperity, pleasure and success, may be rough of grain and common in fibre, but sorrow is the most sensitive of all created things. There is nothing that stirs in the whole world of thought to which sorrow does not vibrate in terrible and exquisite pulsation. The thin beaten-out leaf of tremulous gold that chronicles the direction of forces the eye cannot see is in comparison coarse. It is a wound that bleeds when any hand but that of love touches it, and even then must bleed again, though not in pain.

     . . . .

Where there is sorrow there is holy ground. Some day people will realise what that means. They will know nothing of life till they do. . . . When I was brought down from my prison to the Court of Bankruptcy, between two policemen, Robbie [Robert Ross] waited in the long dreary corridor that, before the whole crowd, whom an action so sweet and simple hushed into silence, he might gravely raise his hat to me, as, handcuffed and with bowed head, I passed him by. Men have gone to heaven for smaller things than that. It was in this spirit, and with this mode of love, that the saints knelt down to wash the feet of the poor, or stooped to kiss the leper on the cheek. I have never said one single word to him about what he did. I do not know to the present moment whether he is aware that I was even conscious of his action. It is not a thing for which one can render formal thanks in formal words. I store it in the treasure-house of my heart. I keep it there as a secret debt that I am glad to think I can never possibly repay. It is embalmed and kept sweet by the myrrh and cassia of many tears. When wisdom has been profitless to me, philosophy barren, and the proverbs and phrases of those who have sought to give me consolation as dust and ashes in my mouth, the memory of that little, lovely, silent act of love has unsealed for me all the wells of pity: made the desert blossom like a rose, and brought me out of the bitterness of lonely exile into harmony with the wounded, broken, and great heart of the world. When people are able to understand, not merely how beautiful Robbie's action was, but why it meant so much to me, and always will mean so much, then, perhaps, they will realize how and in what spirit they should approach me. . . .

. . .Modern life is complex and relative; those are its two distinguishing notes; to render the first we require atmosphere with its subtlety of *nuances*, of suggestion, of strange perspectives; as for the second we require background. That is why sculpture has ceased to be a representative art and why music is a representative art and why literature is, and has been and always will remain the supreme representative art.

. . . .

Other miserable men when they are thrown into prison, if they are robbed of the beauty of the world, are at least safe in some measure from the world's most deadly slings, most awful arrows. They can hide in the darkness of their cells and of their very disgrace make a mode of sanctuary. The world having had its will goes its way, and they are left to suffer undisturbed. With me it has been different. Sorrow after sorrow has come beating at the prison doors in search of me; they have opened the gates wide and let them in. Hardly if at all have my friends been suffered to see me. But my enemies have had full access to me always; twice in my public appearances in the Bankruptcy Court; twice again in my public transferences from one prison to another have I been shown under conditions of unspeakable humiliation to the gaze and mockery of men. The messenger of Death had brought me his tidings and gone his way; and in entire solitude and isolated from all that could give me comfort or suggest relief I have had to bear the intolerable burden of misery and remorse, which the memory of my mother placed upon me and places on me still. Hardly has that wound been dulled, not healed, by time, when violent and bitter and harsh letters come to me from my wife's solicitors. I am at once tainted and threatened with poverty. That I can bear. I can school myself to worse than that; but my two children are taken from me by legal procedure. That is, and always will remain to me a source of infinite distress, or infinite pain, of grief without end or limit. That the law should decide and take upon itself to decide that I am one unfit to be with my own children is something quite horrible to me. The disgrace of prison is as nothing compared with it. I envy the other men who tread the yard along with me. I am sure that their children wait for them, look for their coming, will be sweet to them.

The poor are wiser, more charitable, more kind, more sensitive than we are. In their eyes prison is a tragedy in a man's life, a misfortune, a casualty, something that calls for sympathy in others. They speak of one who is in prison as of one who is "in trouble" simply. It is the phrase they always use, and the expression has the perfect wisdom of love in it. With people of our own rank it is different.

With us, prison makes a man a pariah. I, and such as I am, have hardly any right to air and sun. Our presence taints the pleasures of others. We are unwelcome when we reappear. To revisit the glimpses of the moon is not for us. Our very children are taken away. Those lovely links with humanity are broken. We are doomed to be solitary, while our sons still live. We are denied the one thing that might heal us and keep us, that might bring balm to the bruised heart, and peace to the soul in pain.

. . . .

And the end of it all is that I have got to forgive you. I must do so. I don't write this letter to put bitterness into your heart, but to pluck it out of mine. For my own sake I must forgive you. One cannot always keep an adder in one's breast to feed on one, nor rise up every night to sow thorns in the garden of one's soul. . . .

I must say to myself that I ruined myself, and that nobody great or small can be ruined except by his own hand. I am quite ready to say so. I am trying to say so, though they may not think it at the present moment. This pitiless indictment I bring without pity against myself. Terrible as was what the world did to me, what I did to myself was far more terrible still.

I was a man who stood in symbolic relations to the art and culture of my age. I had realised this for myself at the very dawn of my manhood, and had forced my age to realise it afterwards. Few men hold such a position in their own lifetime, and have it so acknowledged. It is usually discerned, if discerned at all, by the historian, or the critic, long after both the man and his age have passed away. With me it was different. I felt it myself, and made others feel it. Byron was a symbolic figure, but his relations were to the passion of his age and its weariness of passion. Mine were to something more noble, more permanent, of more vital issue, of larger scope.

The gods had given me almost everything. I had genius, a distinguished name, high social position, brilliancy, intellectual daring; I made art a philosophy and philosophy an art; I altered the minds of men and the colours of things; there was nothing I said or did that did not make people wonder. I took the drama, the most objective form known to art, and made it as personal a mode of expression as the lyric or sonnet; at the same time I widened its range and enriched its characterization. Drama, novel, poem in prose, poem in rhyme, subtle or fantastic dialogue, whatever I touched, I made beautiful in a new mode of beauty: to truth itself I gave what is false no less than what is true as its rightful province, and showed that the false and the true are merely forms of intellectual existence. I treated art as the supreme reality and life as a mere mode of fiction. I awoke the imagination of my century so that it created myth and legend around me. I summed up all systems in a phrase and all existence in an epigram. . . . But I let myself be lured into long spells of senseless and sensual ease. I amused myself with being a *flâneur*, a dandy, a man of fashion. I surrounded myself with the smaller natures and the meaner minds. I became the spendthrift of my own genius, and to waste an eternal youth gave me a curious joy. Tired of being on the heights, I deliberately went to the depths in the search for new sensation. What the paradox was to me in the sphere of thought, perversity became to me in the sphere of passion. Desire, at the end, was a malady, or a madness, or both. I grew careless of the lives of others. I took pleasure where it pleased me, and passed on. I forgot that every little action of the common day makes or unmakes character, and that therefore what one has done in the secret chamber one has some day to cry aloud on the housetop. I ceased to be lord over myself. I was no longer the captain of my soul, and did not know it. I allowed pleasure to dominate me. I ended in horrible disgrace. There is only one thing for me now, absolute humility.

I have lain in prison for nearly two years. Out of my nature has come wild despair; an abandonment to grief that was piteous even to look at; terrible and impotent rage; bitterness and scorn; anguish that wept aloud; misery that could find no voice; sorrow that was dumb. I have passed through every possible mood of suffering. Better than Wordsworth himself I know what Wordsworth meant when he said—

Suffering is permanent, obscure, and dark,
And has the nature of infinity.

But while there were times when I rejoiced in the idea that my sufferings were to be endless, I could not bear them to be without meaning. Now I find hidden somewhere away in my nature something that tells me that nothing in the whole world is meaningless, and suffering least of all. That something hidden away in my nature, like a treasure in a field, is Humility.

It is the last thing left in me, and the best: the ultimate discovery at which I have arrived, the starting-point for a fresh development. It has come to me right out of myself, so I know that it has come at the proper time. It could not have come before, nor later. Had any one told me of it, I would have rejected it. Had it been brought to me, I would have refused it. As I found it, I want to keep it. I must do so. It is the one thing that has in it the elements of life, of a new life, a *Vita Nuova* for me. Of all things it is the strangest. One cannot acquire it, except by surrendering everything that one has. It is only when one has lost all things, that one knows that one possesses it.

. . . .

I am completely penniless, and absolutely homeless. Yet there are worse things in the world than that. I am quite candid when I say that rather than go out from this prison with bitterness in my heart against the world, I would gladly and readily beg my bread from door to door. If I got nothing from the house of the rich I would get something at the house of the poor. Those who have much are often greedy; those who have little always share. I would not a bit mind sleeping in the cool grass in summer, and when winter came on sheltering myself by the warm close-thatched rick, or under the penthouse of a great barn, provided I had love in my heart. The external things of life seem to me now of no importance at all. You can see to what intensity of individualism I have arrived—or am arriving rather, for the journey is long, and "where I walk there are thorns."

. . . .

Morality does not help me. I am a born antinomian. I am one of those who are made for exceptions, not for laws. But while I see that there is nothing wrong in what one does, I see that there is something wrong in what one becomes. It is well to have learned that.

Religion does not help me. The faith that others give to what is unseen, I give to what one can touch, and look at. My gods dwell in temples made with hands; and within the circle of actual experience is my creed made perfect and complete: too complete, it may be, for like many or all of those who have placed their heaven in this earth, I have found in it not merely the beauty of heaven, but the horror of hell also. When I think about religion at all, I feel as if I would like to found an order for those who CANNOT believe: the Confraternity of the Faithless, one might call it, where on an altar, on which no taper burned, a priest, in whose heart peace had no dwelling, might celebrate with unblessed bread and a chalice empty of wine. Every thing to be true must become a religion. And agnosticism should have its ritual no less than faith. It has sown its martyrs, it should reap its saints, and praise God daily for having hidden Himself from man. But whether it be faith or agnosticism, it must be nothing external to me. Its symbols must be of my own creating. Only that is spiritual which makes its own form. If I may not find its secret within myself, I shall never find it: if I have not got it already, it will never come to me.

Reason does not help me. It tells me that the laws under which I am convicted are wrong and unjust laws, and the system under which I have suffered a wrong and unjust system. But, somehow, I have got to make both of these things just and right to me. And exactly as in Art one is only concerned with what a particular thing is at a particular moment to oneself, so it is also in the ethical evolution of one's character. I have got to make everything that has happened to me good for me. The plank bed, the loathsome food, the hard ropes shredded into oakum till one's finger-tips grow dull with pain, the menial offices with which each day begins and finishes, the harsh orders that routine seems to necessitate, the dreadful dress that makes sorrow grotesque to look at, the silence, the solitude, the shame—each and all of these things I have to transform into a spiritual experience. There is not a single degradation of the body which I must not try and make into a spiritualising of the soul.

I want to get to the point when I shall be able to say quite simply, and without affectation that the two great turning-points in my life were when my father sent me to Oxford, and when society sent me to prison. I will not say that prison is the best thing that could have happened to me: for that phrase would savour of too great bitterness towards myself. I would sooner say, or hear it said of me, that I was so typical a child of my age, that in my perversity, and for that perversity's sake, I turned the good things of my life to evil, and the evil things of my life to good.

What is said, however, by myself or by others, matters little. The important thing, the thing that lies before me, the thing that I have to do, if the brief remainder of my days is not to be maimed, marred, and incomplete, is to absorb into my nature all that has been done to me, to make it part of me, to accept it without complaint, fear, or reluctance. The supreme vice is shallowness. Whatever is realised is right.

When first I was put into prison some people advised me to try and forget who I was. It was ruinous advice. It is only by realising what I am that I have found comfort of any kind. Now I am advised by others to try on my release to forget that I have ever been in a prison at all. I know that would be equally fatal. It would mean that I would always be haunted by an intolerable sense of disgrace, and that those things that are meant for me as much as for anybody else—the beauty of the sun and moon, the pageant of the seasons, the music of daybreak and the silence of great nights, the rain falling through the leaves, or the dew creeping over the grass and making it silver—would all be tainted for me, and lose their healing power, and their power of communicating joy. To regret one's own experiences is to arrest one's own development. To deny one's own experiences is to put a lie into the lips of one's own life. It is no less than a denial of the soul.

For just as the body absorbs things of all kinds, things common and unclean no less than those that the priest or a vision has cleansed, and converts them into swiftness or strength, into the play of beautiful muscles and the moulding of fair flesh, into the curves and colours of the hair, the lips, the eye; so the soul in its turn has its nutritive functions also, and can transform into noble moods of thought and passions of high import what in itself is base, cruel and degrading; nay, more, may find in these its most august modes of assertion, and can often reveal itself most perfectly through what was intended to desecrate or destroy.

The fact of my having been the common prisoner of a common gaol I must frankly accept, and, curious as it may seem, one of the things I shall have to teach myself is not to be ashamed of it. I must accept it as a punishment, and if one is ashamed of having been punished, one might just as well never have been punished at all. Of course there are many things of which I was convicted that I had not done, but then there are many things of which I was convicted that I had done, and a still greater number of things in my life for which I was never indicted at all. And as the gods are strange, and punish us for what is good and humane in us as much as for what is evil and perverse, I must accept the fact that one is punished for the good as well as for the evil that one does. I have no doubt that it is quite right one should be. It helps one, or should help one, to realise both, and not to be too conceited about either. And if I then am not ashamed of my punishment, as I hope not to be, I shall be able to think, and walk, and live with freedom.

Many men on their release carry their prison about with them into the air, and hide it as a secret disgrace in their hearts, and at length, like poor poisoned things, creep into some hole and die. It is wretched that they should have to do so, and it is wrong, terribly wrong, of society that it should force them to do so. Society takes upon itself the right to inflict appalling punishment on the individual, but it also has the supreme vice of shallowness, and fails to realise what it has done. When the man's punishment is over, it leaves him to himself; that is to say, it abandons him at the very moment when its highest duty towards him begins. It is really ashamed of its own actions, and shuns those whom it has punished, as people shun a creditor whose debt they cannot pay, or one on whom they have inflicted an irreparable, an irremediable wrong. I can claim on my side that if I realise what I have suffered, society should realise what it has inflicted on me; and that there should be no bitterness or hate on either side.

Of course I know that from one point of view things will be made different for me than for others; must indeed, by the very nature of the case, be made so. The poor thieves and outcasts who are imprisoned here with me are in many respects more fortunate than I am. The little way in grey city or green field that saw their sin is small; to find those who know nothing of what they have done they need go no further than a bird might fly between the twilight and the dawn; but for me the world is shrivelled to a handsbreadth, and everywhere I turn my name is written on the rocks in lead. For I have come, not from obscurity into the momentary notoriety of crime, but from a sort of eternity of fame to a sort of eternity of infamy, and sometimes seem to myself to have shown, if indeed it required showing, that between the famous and the infamous there is but one step, if as much as one.

Still, in the very fact that people will recognise me wherever I go, and know all about my life, as far as its follies go, I can discern something good for me. It will force on me the necessity of again asserting myself as an artist, and as soon as I possibly can. If I can produce only one beautiful work of art I shall be able to rob malice of its venom, and cowardice of its sneer, and to pluck out the tongue of scorn by the roots.

And if life be, as it surely is, a problem to me, I am no less a problem to life. People must adopt some attitude towards me, and so pass judgment, both on themselves and me. I need not say I am not talking of particular individuals. The only people I would care to be with now are artists and people who have suffered: those who know what beauty is, and those who know what sorrow is: nobody else interests me. Nor am I making any demands on life. In all that I have said I am simply concerned with my own mental attitude towards life as a whole; and I feel that not to be ashamed of having been punished is one of the first points I must attain to, for the sake of my own perfection, and because I am so imperfect.

Then I must learn how to be happy. Once I knew it, or thought I knew it, by instinct. It was always springtime once in my heart. My temperament was akin to joy. I filled my life to the very brim with pleasure, as one might fill a cup to the very brim with wine. Now I am approaching life from a completely new standpoint, and even to conceive happiness is often extremely difficult for me. I remember during my first term at Oxford reading in Pater's *Renaissance*—that book which has had such strange influence over my life—how Dante places low in the Inferno those who wilfully live in sadness; and going to the college library and turning to the passage in the *Divine Comedy* where beneath the dreary marsh lie those who were "sullen in the sweet air," saying for ever and ever through their sighs—

Tristi fummo

Nell' aere dolce che dal sol s'allegra.[1]

I knew the church condemned *accidia*,[2] but the whole idea seemed to me quite fantastic, just the sort of sin, I fancied, a priest who knew nothing about real life would invent. Nor could I understand how Dante, who says that "sorrow remarries us to God," could have been so harsh to those who were enamoured of melancholy, if any such there really were. I had no idea that some day this would become to me one of the greatest temptations of my life.

While I was in Wandsworth prison I longed to die. It was my one desire. When after two months in the infirmary I was transferred here, and found myself growing gradually better in physical health, I was filled with rage. I determined to commit suicide on the very day on which I left prison. After a time that evil mood passed away, and I made up my mind to live, but to wear gloom as a king wears purple: never to smile again: to turn whatever house I entered into a house of mourning: to make my friends walk slowly in sadness with me: to teach them that melancholy is the true secret of life: to maim them with an alien sorrow: to mar them with my own pain. Now I feel quite differently. I see it would be both ungrateful and unkind of me to pull so long a face that when my friends came to see me they would have to make their faces still longer in order to show their sympathy; or, if I desired to entertain them, to invite them to sit down silently to bitter herbs and funeral baked meats. I must learn how to be cheerful and happy.

The last two occasions on which I was allowed to see my friends here, I tried to be as cheerful as possible, and to show my cheerfulness, in order to make them some slight return for their trouble in coming all the way from town to see me. It is only a slight return, I know, but it is the one, I feel certain, that pleases them most. I saw R– for an hour on Saturday week, and I tried to give the fullest possible expression of the delight I really felt at our meeting. And that, in the views and ideas I am here shaping for myself, I am quite right is shown to me by the fact that now for the first time since my imprisonment I have a real desire for life.

There is before me so much to do, that I would regard it as a terrible tragedy if I died before I was allowed to complete at any rate a little of it. I see new developments in art and life, each one of which is a fresh mode of perfection. I long to live so that I can explore what is no less than a new world to me. Do you want to know what this new world is? I think you can guess what it is. It is the world in which I have been living. Sorrow, then, and all that it teaches one, is my new world.

I used to live entirely for pleasure. I shunned suffering and sorrow of every kind. I hated both. I resolved to ignore them as far as possible: to treat them, that is to say, as modes of imperfection. They were not

---

1. Canto VII, ll.121–22: "We were sullen in the sweet air that is gladdened by the sun." [Eds.]   **2.** Ennui, sloth. [Eds.]

part of my scheme of life. They had no place in my philosophy. My mother, who knew life as a whole, used often to quote to me Goethe's lines—written by Carlyle in a book he had given her years ago, and translated by him, I fancy, also:—

> Who never ate his bread in sorrow,
> > Who never spent the midnight hours
> Weeping and waiting for the morrow,—
> > He knows you not, ye heavenly powers.

They were the lines which that noble Queen of Prussia, whom Napoleon treated with such coarse brutality, used to quote in her humiliation and exile; they were the lines my mother often quoted in the troubles of her later life. I absolutely declined to accept or admit the enormous truth hidden in them. I could not understand it. I remember quite well how I used to tell her that I did not want to eat my bread in sorrow, or to pass any night weeping and watching for a more bitter dawn.

I had no idea that it was one of the special things that the Fates had in store for me: that for a whole year of my life, indeed, I was to do little else. But so has my portion been meted out to me; and during the last few months I have, after terrible difficulties and struggles, been able to comprehend some of the lessons hidden in the heart of pain. Clergymen and people who use phrases without wisdom sometimes talk of suffering as a mystery. It is really a revelation. One discerns things one never discerned before. One approaches the whole of history from a different standpoint. What one had felt dimly, through instinct, about art, is intellectually and emotionally realised with perfect clearness of vision and absolute intensity of apprehension.

I now see that sorrow, being the supreme emotion of which man is capable, is at once the type and test of all great art. What the artist is always looking for is the mode of existence in which soul and body are one and indivisible: in which the outward is expressive of the inward: in which form reveals. Of such modes of existence there are not a few: youth and the arts preoccupied with youth may serve as a model for us at one moment: at another we may like to think that, in its subtlety and sensitiveness of impression, its suggestion of a spirit dwelling in external things and making its raiment of earth and air, of mist and city alike, and in its morbid sympathy of its moods, and tones, and colours, modern landscape art is realising for us pictorially what was realised in such plastic perfection by the Greeks. Music, in which all subject is absorbed in expression and cannot be separated from it, is a complex example, and a flower or a child a simple example, of what I mean; but sorrow is the ultimate type both in life and art.

. . . .

I remember talking once on this subject to one of the most beautiful personalities I have ever known: a woman, whose sympathy and noble kindness to me, both before and since the tragedy of my imprisonment, have been beyond power and description; one who has really assisted me, though she does not know it, to bear the burden of my troubles more than any one else in the whole world has, and all through the mere fact of her existence, through her being what she is—partly an ideal and partly an influence: a suggestion of what one might become as well as a real help towards becoming it; a soul that renders the common air sweet, and makes what is spiritual seem as simple and natural as sunlight or the sea: one for whom beauty and sorrow walk hand in hand, and have the same message. On the occasion of which I am thinking I recall distinctly how I said to her that there was enough suffering in one narrow London lane to show that God did not love man, and that wherever there was any sorrow, though but that of a child, in some little garden weeping over a fault that it had or had not committed, the whole face of creation was completely marred. I was entirely wrong. She told me so, but I could not believe her. I was not in the sphere in which such belief was to be attained to. Now it seems to me that love of some kind is the only possible explanation of the extraordinary amount of suffering that there is in the world. I cannot conceive of any other explanation. I am convinced that there is no other, and that if the world has indeed, as I have said, been built of sorrow, it has been built by the hands of love, because in no other way could the soul of man, for whom the world was made, reach the full stature of its perfection. Pleasure for the beautiful body, but pain for the beautiful soul.

When I say that I am convinced of these things I speak with too much pride. Far off, like a perfect pearl, one can see the city of God. It is so wonderful that it seems as if a child could reach it in a summer's day. And so a child could. But with me and such as me it is different. One can realise a thing in a single moment, but one loses it in the long hours that follow with leaden feet. It is so difficult to keep "heights that the soul is competent to gain." We think in eternity, but we move slowly through time; and how slowly time goes with us who lie in prison I need not tell again, nor of the weariness and despair that creep back into one's cell, and into the cell of one's heart, with such strange insistence that one has, as it were, to garnish and sweep one's house for their coming, as for an unwelcome guest, or a bitter master, or a slave whose slave it is one's chance or choice to be.

. . . .

I don't regret for a single moment having lived for pleasure. I did it to the full, as one should do everything that one does. There was no pleasure I did not experience. I threw the pearl of my soul into a cup of wine. I went down the primrose path to the sound of flutes. I lived on honeycomb. But to have continued the same life would have been wrong because it would have been limiting. I had to pass on . . . .

. . . .

I see a far more intimate and immediate connection between the true life of Christ and the true life of the artist; and I take a keen pleasure in the reflection that long before sorrow had made my days her own and bound me to her wheel I had written in *The Soul of Man* that he who would lead a Christ-like life must be entirely and absolutely himself, and had taken as my types not merely the shepherd on the hillside and the prisoner in his cell, but also the painter to whom the world is a pageant and the poet for whom the world is a song. I remember saying once to André Gide, as we sat together in some Paris café, that while meta-physics had but little real interest for me, and morality absolutely none, there was nothing that either Plato or Christ had said that could not be transferred immediately into the sphere of Art and there find its complete fulfilment.

Nor is it merely that we can discern in Christ that close union of personality with perfection which forms the real distinction between the classical and romantic movement in life, but the very basis of his nature was the same as that of the nature of the artist—an intense and flamelike imagination. He realised in the entire sphere of human relations that imaginative sympathy which in the sphere of Art is the sole secret of creation. He understood the leprosy of the leper, the darkness of the blind, the fierce misery of those who live for pleasure, the strange poverty of the rich. You once wrote to me in trouble, "When you are not on your pedestal you are not interesting." How remote were you from what Matthew Arnold calls "the Secret of Jesus." Either would have taught you that whatever happens to another happens to oneself, and if you want an inscription to read at dawn and at night-time, and for pleasure or for pain, write up on the walls of your house in letters for the sun to gild and the moon to silver, "Whatever happens to oneself happens to another."

Christ's place indeed is with the poets. His whole conception of Humanity sprang right out of the imagination and can only be realised by it. What God was to the pantheist, man was to Him. He was the first to conceive the divided races as a unity. Before his time there had been gods and men, and, feeling through the mysticism of sympathy that in himself each had been made incarnate, he calls himself the Son of the one or the Son of the other, according to his mood. More than any one else in history he wakes in us that temper of wonder to which romance always appeals. There is still something to me almost incredible in the idea of a young Galilean peasant imagining that he could bear on his own shoulders the burden of the entire world; all that had already been done and suffered, and all that was yet to be done and suffered: the sins of Nero, of Caesar Borgia, of Alexander VI, and of him who was Emperor of Rome and Priest of the Sun: the sufferings of those whose names are legion and whose dwelling is among the tombs: oppressed nationalities, factory children, thieves, people in prison, outcasts, those who are dumb under oppression and whose silence is heard only of God; and not merely imagining this but actually achieving it, so that at the present moment all who come in contact with his personality, even though they may neither bow to his altar nor kneel before his priest, in some way find that the ugliness of their sin is taken away and the beauty of their sorrow revealed to them.

I had said of Christ that he ranks with the poets. That is true. Shelley and Sophocles are of his company. But his entire life also is the most wonderful of poems. For "pity and terror" there is nothing in the entire cycle of Greek tragedy to touch it. The absolute purity of the protagonist raises the entire scheme to a height of romantic art from which the sufferings of Thebes and Pelops' line are by their very horror excluded, and shows how wrong Aristotle was when he said in his treatise on the drama that it would be impossible to bear the spectacle of one blameless in pain. Nor in Aeschylus nor Dante, those stern masters of tenderness, in Shakespeare, the most purely human of all the great artists, in the whole of Celtic myth and legend, where the loveliness of the world is shown through a mist of tears, and the life of a man is no more than the life of a flower, is there anything that, for sheer simplicity of pathos wedded and made one with sublimity of tragic effect, can be said to equal or even approach the last act of Christ's passion. The little supper with his companions, one of whom has already sold him for a price; the anguish in the quiet moon-lit garden; the false friend coming close to him so as to betray him with a kiss; the friend who still believed in him, and on whom as on a rock he had hoped to build a house of refuge for Man, denying him as the bird cried to the dawn; his own utter loneliness, his submission, his acceptance of everything; and along with it all such scenes as the high priest of orthodoxy rending his raiment in wrath, and the magistrate of civil justice calling for water in the vain hope of cleansing himself of that stain of innocent blood that makes him the scarlet figure of history; the coronation ceremony of sorrow, one of the most wonderful things in the whole of recorded time; the crucifixion of the Innocent One before the eyes of his mother and of the disciple whom he loved; the soldiers gambling and throwing dice for his clothes; the terrible death by which he gave the world its most eternal symbol; and his final burial in the tomb of the rich man, his body swathed in Egyptian linen with costly spices and perfumes as though he had been a king's son. When one contemplates all this from the point of view of art alone one cannot but be grateful that the supreme office of the Church should be the playing of the tragedy without the shedding of blood: the mystical presentation, by means of dialogue and costume and gesture even, of the Passion of her Lord; and it is always a source of pleasure and awe to me to remember that the ultimate survival of the Greek chorus, lost elsewhere to art, is to be found in the servitor answering the priest at Mass.

Yet the whole life of Christ—so entirely may sorrow and beauty be made one in their meaning and manifestation—is really an idyll, though it ends with the veil of the temple being rent, and the darkness coming over the face of the earth, and the stone rolled to the door of the sepulchre. One always thinks of him as a young bridegroom with his companions, as indeed he somewhere describes himself; as a shepherd straying through a valley with his sheep in search of green meadow or cool stream; as a singer trying to build out of the music the walls of the City of God; or as a lover for whose love the whole world was too small.

His miracles seem to me to be as exquisite as the coming of spring, and quite as natural. I see no difficulty at all in believing that such was the charm of his personality that his mere presence could bring peace to souls in anguish, and that those who touched his garments or his hands forgot their pain; or that as he passed by on the highway of life people who had seen nothing of life's mystery, saw it clearly, and others who had been deaf to every voice but that of pleasure heard for the first time the voice of love and found it as "musical as Apollo's lute"; or that evil passions fled at his approach, and men whose dull unimaginative lives had been but a mode of death rose as it were from the grave when he called them; or that when he taught on the hillside the multitude forgot their hunger and thirst and the cares of this world, and that to his friends who listened to him as he sat at meat the coarse food seemed delicate, and the water had the taste of good wine, and the whole house became full of the odour and sweetness of nard.

Renan in his *Vie de Jésus*—that gracious fifth gospel, the gospel according to St. Thomas, one might call it—says somewhere that Christ's great achievement was that he made himself as much loved after his death as he had been during his lifetime. And certainly, if his place is among the poets, he is the leader of all the lovers. He saw that love was the first secret of the world for which the wise men had been looking, and that it was only through love that one could approach either the heart of the leper or the feet of God.

And above all, Christ is the most supreme of individualists. Humility, like the artistic, acceptance of all experiences, is merely a mode of manifestation. It is man's soul that Christ is always looking for. He calls it "God's Kingdom," and finds it in every one. He compares it to little things, to a tiny seed, to a handful of leaven, to a pearl. That is because one realises one's soul only by getting rid of all alien passions, all acquired culture, and all external possessions, be they good or evil.

I bore up against everything with some stubbornness of will and much rebellion of nature, till I had absolutely nothing left in the world but one thing. I had lost my name, my position, my happiness, my freedom, my wealth. I was a prisoner and a pauper. But I still had my children left. Suddenly they were taken away from me by the law. It was a blow so appalling that I did not know what to do, so I flung myself on my knees, and bowed my head, and wept, and said, "The body of a child is as the body of the Lord: I am not worthy of either." That moment seemed to save me. I saw then that the only thing for me was to accept everything. Since then—curious as it will no doubt sound—I have been happier. It was of course my soul in its ultimate essence that I had reached. In many ways I had been its enemy, but I found it waiting for me as a friend. When one comes in contact with the soul it makes one simple as a child, as Christ said one should be.

It is tragic how few people ever "possess their souls" before they die. "Nothing is more rare in any man," says Emerson, "than an act of his own." It is quite true. Most people are other people. Their thoughts are some one else's opinions, their lives a mimicry, their passions a quotation. Christ was not merely the supreme individualist, but he was the first individualist in history. People have tried to make him out an ordinary philanthropist, or ranked him as an altruist with the scientific and sentimental. But he was really neither one nor the other. Pity he has, of course, for the poor, for those who are shut up in prisons, for the lowly, for the wretched; but he has far more pity for the rich, for the hard hedonists, for those who waste their freedom in becoming slaves to things, for those who wear soft raiment and live in kings' houses. Riches and pleasure seemed to him to be really greater tragedies than poverty or sorrow. And as for altruism, who knew better than he that it is vocation not volition that determines us, and that one cannot gather grapes of thorns or figs from thistles?

To live for others as a definite self-conscious aim was not his creed. It was not the basis of his creed. When he says, "Forgive your enemies," it is not for the sake of the enemy, but for one's own sake that he says so, and because love is more beautiful than hate. In his own entreaty to the young man, "Sell all that thou hast and give to the poor," it is not of the state of the poor that he is thinking but of the soul of the young man, the soul that wealth was marring. In his view of life he is one with the artist who knows that by the inevitable law of self-perfection, the poet must sing, and the sculptor think in bronze, and the painter make the world a mirror for his moods, as surely and as certainly as the hawthorn must blossom in spring, and the corn turn to gold at harvest-time, and the moon in her ordered wanderings change from shield to sickle, and from sickle to shield.

But while Christ did not say to men, "Live for others," he pointed out that there was no difference at all between the lives of others and one's own life. By this means he gave to man an extended, a Titan personality. Since his coming the history of each separate individual is, or can be made, the history of the world. Of course, culture has intensified the personality of man. Art has made us myriad-minded. Those who have the artistic temperament go into exile with Dante and learn how salt is the bread of others, and how steep their stairs; they catch for a moment the serenity and calm of Goethe, and yet know but too well that Baudelaire cried to God—

> O Seigneur, donnez-moi la force et le courage
> De contempler mon corps et mon coeur sans dégoût.[3]

Out of Shakespeare's sonnets they draw, to their own hurt it may be, the secret of his love and make it their own; they look with new eyes on modern life, because they have listened to one of Chopin's nocturnes, or handled Greek things, or read the story of the passion of some dead man for some dead woman whose hair was like threads of fine gold, and whose mouth was as a pomegranate. But the sympathy of the artistic

---

3. O Lord, give me strength and courage   shame. [Eds.]
to contemplate myself and my soul without

temperament is necessarily with what has found expression. In words or in colours, in music or in marble, behind the painted masks of an Aeschylean play, or through some Sicilian shepherds' pierced and jointed reeds, the man and his message must have been revealed.

To the artist, expression is the only mode under which he can conceive life at all. To him what is dumb is dead. But to Christ it was not so. With a width and wonder of imagination that fills one almost with awe, he took the entire world of the inarticulate, the voiceless world of pain, as his kingdom, and made of himself its eternal mouthpiece. Those of whom I have spoken, who are dumb under oppression, and "whose silence is heard only of God," he chose as his brothers. He sought to become eyes to the blind, ears to the deaf, and a cry in the lips of those whose tongues had been tied. His desire was to be to the myriads who had found no utterance a very trumpet through which they might call to heaven. And feeling, with the artistic nature of one to whom suffering and sorrow were modes through which he could realise his conception of the beautiful, that an idea is of no value till it becomes incarnate and is made an image, he made of himself the image of the Man of Sorrows, and as such has fascinated and dominated art as no Greek god ever succeeded in doing.

. . . .

But Life itself from its lowliest and most humble sphere produced one far more marvellous than the mother of Proserpina or the son of Semele. Out of the Carpenter's shop at Nazareth had come a personality infinitely greater than any made by myth and legend, and one, strangely enough, destined to reveal to the world the mystical meaning of wine and the real beauties of the lilies of the field as none, either on Cithaeron or at Enna, had ever done.

The song of Isaiah, "He is despised and rejected of men, a man of sorrows and acquainted with grief: and we hid as it were our faces from him," had seemed to him to prefigure himself, and in him the prophecy was fulfilled. We must not be afraid of such a phrase. Every single work of art is the fulfilment of a prophecy: for every work of art is the conversion of an idea into an image. Every single human being should be the fulfilment of a prophecy: for every human being should be the realisation of some ideal, either in the mind of God or in the mind of man. Christ found the type and fixed it, and the dream of a Virgilian poet, either at Jerusalem or at Babylon, became in the long progress of the centuries incarnate in him for whom the world was waiting.

To me one of the things in history the most to be regretted is that the Christ's own renaissance, which has produced the Cathedral at Chartres, the Arthurian cycle of legends, the life of St. Francis of Assisi, the art of Giotto, and Dante's *Divine Comedy*, was not allowed to develop on its own lines, but was interrupted and spoiled by the dreary classical Renaissance that gave us Petrarch, and Raphael's frescoes, and Palladian architecture, and formal French tragedy, and St. Paul's Cathedral, and Pope's poetry, and everything that is made from without and by dead rules, and does not spring from within through some spirit informing it. But wherever there is a romantic movement in art there somehow, and under some form, is Christ, or the soul of Christ. He is in *Romeo and Juliet*, in the *Winter's Tale*, in Provençal poetry, in the *Ancient Mariner*, in *La Belle Dame sans merci*, and in Chatterton's *Ballad of Charity*.

. . . .

It is the imaginative quality of Christ's own nature that makes him this palpitating centre of romance. The strange figures of poetic drama and ballad are made by the imagination of others, but out of his own imagination entirely did Jesus of Nazareth create himself. The cry of Isaiah had really no more to do with his coming than the song of the nightingale has to do with the rising of the moon—no more, though perhaps no less. He was the denial as well as the affirmation of prophecy. For every expectation that he fulfilled there was another that he destroyed. "In all beauty," says Bacon, "there is some strangeness of proportion," and of those who are born of the spirit—of those, that is to say, who like himself are dynamic forces—Christ says that they are like the wind that "bloweth where it listeth, and no man can tell whence it cometh and whither it goeth." That is why he is so fascinating to artists. He has all the colour elements of life: mystery, strangeness, pathos, suggestion, ecstasy, love. He appeals to the temper of wonder, and creates that mood in which alone he can be understood.

And to me it is a joy to remember that if he is "of imagination all compact," the world itself is of the same substance. I said in *Dorian Gray* that the great sins of the world take place in the brain: but it is in the brain that everything takes place. We know now that we do not see with the eyes or hear with the ears. They are really channels for the transmission, adequate or inadequate, of sense impressions. It is in the brain that the poppy is red, that the apple is odorous, that the skylark sings.

Of late I have been studying with diligence the four prose poems about Christ. At Christmas I managed to get hold of a Greek Testament, and every morning, after I had cleaned my cell and polished my tins, I read a little of the Gospels, a dozen verses taken by chance anywhere. It is a delightful way of opening the day. Every one, even in a turbulent, ill-disciplined life, should do the same. Endless repetition, in and out of season, has spoiled for us the freshness, the naiveté, the simple romantic charm of the Gospels. We hear them read far too often and far too badly, and all repetition is anti-spiritual. When one returns to the Greek it is like going into a garden of lilies out of some narrow and dark house.

. . . .

While in reading the Gospels—particularly that of St. John himself, or whatever early Gnostic took his name and mantle—I see the continual assertion of the imagination as the basis of all spiritual and material life, I see also that to Christ imagination was simply a form of love, and that to him love was lord in the fullest meaning of the phrase. Some six weeks ago I was allowed by the doctor to have white bread to eat instead of the coarse black or brown bread of ordinary prison fare. It is a great delicacy. It will sound strange that dry bread could possibly be a delicacy to any one. To me it is so much so that at the close of each meal I carefully eat whatever crumbs may be left on my tin plate, or have fallen on the rough towel that one uses as a cloth so as not to soil one's table; and I do so not from hunger—I get now quite sufficient food—but simply in order that nothing should be wasted of what is given to me. So one should look on love.

Christ, like all fascinating personalities, had the power of not merely saying beautiful things himself, but of making other people say beautiful things to him; and I love the story St. Mark tells us about the Greek woman, who, when as a trial of her faith he said to her that he could not give her the bread of the children of Israel, answered him that the little dogs . . . who are under the table eat of the crumbs that the children let fall. Most people live for love and admiration. But it is by love and admiration that we should live. If any love is shown us we should recognise that we are quite unworthy of it. Nobody is worthy to be loved. The fact that God loves man shows us that in the divine order of ideal things it is written that eternal love is to be given to what is eternally unworthy. Or if that phrase seems to be a bitter one to bear, let us say that every one is worthy of love, except him who thinks that he is. Love is a sacrament that should be taken kneeling, and *Domine, non sum dignus* should be on the lips and in the hearts of those who receive it.

. . . .

His morality is all sympathy, just what morality should be. If the only thing that he ever said had been, "Her sins are forgiven her because she loved much," it would have been worth while dying to have said it. His justice is all poetical justice, exactly what justice should be. The beggar goes to heaven because he has been unhappy. I cannot conceive a better reason for his being sent there. The people who work for an hour in the vineyard in the cool of the evening receive just as much reward as those who have toiled there all day long in the hot sun. Why shouldn't they? Probably no one deserved anything. Or perhaps they were a different kind of people. Christ had no patience with the dull lifeless mechanical systems that treat people as if they were things, and so treat everybody alike: for him there were no laws: there were exceptions merely, as if anybody, or anything, for that matter, was like aught else in the world!

That which is the very keynote of romantic art was to him the proper basis of natural life. He saw no other basis. And when they brought him one, taken in the very act of sin and showed him her sentence written in the law, and asked him what was to be done, he wrote with his finger on the ground as though he did not hear them, and finally, when they pressed him again, looked up and said, "Let him of you who has never sinned be the first to throw the stone at her." It was worthwhile living to have said that.

Like all poetical natures he loved ignorant people. He knew that in the soul of one who is ignorant there is always room for a great idea. But he could not stand stupid people, especially those who are made stupid by education: people who are full of opinions not one of which they even understand, a peculiarly modern type, summed up by Christ when he describes it as the type of one who has the key of knowledge, cannot use it himself, and does not allow other people to use it, though it may be made to open the gate of God's Kingdom. His chief war was against the Philistines. That is the war every child of light has to wage. Philistinism was the note of the age and community in which he lived. In their heavy inaccessibility to ideas, their dull respectability, their tedious orthodoxy, their worship of vulgar success, their entire preoccupation with the gross materialistic side of life, and their ridiculous estimate of themselves and their importance, the Jews of Jerusalem in Christ's day were the exact counterpart of the British Philistine of our own. Christ mocked at the "whited sepulchre" of respectability, and fixed that phrase for ever. He treated worldly success as a thing absolutely to be despised. He saw nothing in it at all. He looked on wealth as an encumbrance to a man. He would not hear of life being sacrificed to any system of thought or morals. He pointed out that forms and ceremonies were made for man, not man for forms and ceremonies. He took sabbatarianism as a type of the things that should be set at nought. The cold philanthropies, the ostentatious public charities, the tedious formalisms so dear to the middle-class mind, he exposed with utter and relentless scorn. To us, what is termed orthodoxy is merely a facile unintelligent acquiescence; but to them, and in their hands, it was a terrible and paralysing tyranny. Christ swept it aside. He showed that the spirit alone was of value. He took a keen pleasure in pointing out to them that though they were always reading the law and the prophets, they had not really the smallest idea of what either of them meant. In opposition to their tithing of each separate day into the fixed routine of prescribed duties, as they tithe mint and rue, he preached the enormous importance of living completely for the moment.

Those whom he saved from their sins are saved simply for beautiful moments in their lives. Mary Magdalen, when she sees Christ, breaks the rich vase of alabaster that one of her seven lovers had given her, and spills the odorous spices over his tired dusty feet, and for that one moment's sake sits for ever with Ruth and Beatrice in the tresses of the snow-white rose of Paradise. All that Christ says to us by the way of a little warning is that every moment should be beautiful, that the soul should always be ready for the coming of the bridegroom, always waiting for the voice of the lover, Philistinism being simply that side of man's nature that is not illumined by the imagination. He sees all the lovely influences of life as modes of light: the imagination itself is the world of light. The world is made by it, and yet the world cannot understand it: that is because the imagination is simply a manifestation of love, and it is love and the capacity for it that distinguishes one human being from another.

But it is when he deals with a sinner that Christ is most romantic, in the sense of most real. The world had always loved the saint as being the nearest possible approach to the perfection of God. Christ, through some divine instinct in him, seems to have always loved the sinner as being the nearest possible approach to the perfection of man. His primary desire was not to reform people, any more than his primary desire was to relieve suffering. To turn an interesting thief into a tedious honest man was not his aim. He would have thought little of the Prisoners' Aid Society and other modern movements of the kind. The conversion of a publican into a Pharisee would not have seemed to him a great achievement. But in a manner not yet understood of the world he regarded sin and suffering as being in themselves beautiful holy things and modes of perfection.

It seems a very dangerous idea. It is—all great ideas are dangerous. That it was Christ's creed admits of no doubt. That it is the true creed I don't doubt myself.

Of course the sinner must repent. But why? Simply because otherwise he would be unable to realise what he had done. The moment of repentance is the moment of initiation. More than that: it is the means by which one alters one's past. The Greeks thought that impossible. They often say in their Gnomic aphorisms, "Even the Gods cannot alter the past." Christ showed that the commonest sinner could do it, that it was the one thing he could do. Christ, had he been asked, would have said—I feel quite certain about it—that the moment the prodigal son fell on his knees and wept, he made his having wasted his substance with harlots, his swine-herding and hungering for the husks they ate, beautiful and holy moments in his life. It is difficult for most people to grasp the idea. I dare say one has to go to prison to understand it. If so, it may be worth while going to prison.

. . . .

Indeed, that is the charm about Christ, when all is said: he is just like a work of art. He does not really teach one anything, but by being brought into his presence one becomes something. And everybody is predestined to his presence. Once at least in his life each man walks with Christ to Emmaus.

. . . .

You may realise it when I say that had I been released last May, as I tried to be, I would have left this place loathing it and every official in it with a bitterness of hatred that would have poisoned my life. I have had a year longer of imprisonment, but humanity has been in the prison along with us all, and now when I go out I shall always remember great kindnesses that I have received here from almost everybody, and on the day of my release I shall give many thanks to many people, and ask to be remembered by them in turn.

The prison style is absolutely and entirely wrong. I would give anything to be able to alter it when I go out. I intend to try. But there is nothing in the world so wrong but that the spirit of humanity, which is the spirit of love, the spirit of the Christ who is not in churches, may make it, if not right, at least possible to be borne without too much bitterness of heart.

I know also that much is waiting for me outside that is very delightful, from what St. Francis of Assisi calls "my brother the wind, and my sister the rain," lovely things both of them, down to the shop-windows and sunsets of great cities. If I made a list of all that still remains to me, I don't know where I should stop: for, indeed, God made the world just as much for me as for any one else. Perhaps I may go out with something that I had not got before. I need not tell you that to me reformations in morals are as meaningless and vulgar as Reformations in theology. But while to propose to be a better man is a piece of unscientific cant, to have become a deeper man is the privilege of those who have suffered. And such I think I have become.

If after I am free a friend of mine gave a feast, and did not invite me to it, I should not mind a bit. I can be perfectly happy by myself. With freedom, flowers, books, and the moon, who could not be perfectly happy? Besides, feasts are not for me any more. I have given too many to care about them. That side of life is over for me, very fortunately, I dare say. But if after I am free a friend of mine had a sorrow and refused to allow me to share it, I should feel it most bitterly. If he shut the doors of the house of mourning against me, I would come back again and again and beg to be admitted, so that I might share in what I was entitled to share in. If he thought me unworthy, unfit to weep with him, I should feel it as the most poignant humiliation, as the most terrible mode in which disgrace could be inflicted on me. But that could not be. I have a right to share in sorrow, and he who can look at the loveliness of the world and share its sorrow, and realise something of the wonder of both, is in immediate contact with divine things, and has got as near to God's secret as any one can get.

. . . .

To each of us different fates are meted out. My lot has been one of public infamy, of long imprisonment, of misery, of ruin, of disgrace, but I am not worthy of it—not yet, at any rate. I remember that I used to say that I thought I could bear a real tragedy if it came to me with purple pall and a mask of noble sorrow, but that the dreadful thing about modernity was that it put tragedy into the raiment of comedy, so that the great realities seemed commonplace or grotesque or lacking in style. It is quite true about modernity. It has probably always been true about actual life. It is said that all martyrdoms seemed mean to the looker on. The nineteenth century is no exception to the rule.

Everything about my tragedy has been hideous, mean, repellent, lacking in style; our very dress makes us grotesque. We are the zanies of sorrow. We are clowns whose hearts are broken. We are specially designed to appeal to the sense of humour. On November 13th, 1895, I was brought down here from London. From two o'clock till half-past two on that day I had to stand on the centre platform of Clapham Junction in convict dress, and handcuffed, for the world to look at. I had been taken out of the hospital ward without a moment's notice being given to me. Of all possible objects I was the most grotesque. When people saw me they laughed. Each train as it came up swelled the audience. Nothing could exceed their amusement. That was, of course, before they knew who I was. As soon as they had been informed they laughed still more. For half an hour I stood there in the grey November rain surrounded by a jeering mob.

For a year after that was done to me I wept every day at the same hour and for the same space of time. That is not such a tragic thing as possibly it sounds to you. To those who are in prison tears are a part of every day's experience. A day in prison on which one does not weep is a day on which one's heart is hard, not a day on which one's heart is happy.

Well, now I am really beginning to feel more regret for the people who laughed than for myself. Of course when they saw me I was not on my pedestal, I was in the pillory. But it is a very unimaginative nature that only cares for people on their pedestals. A pedestal may be a very unreal thing. A pillory is a terrific reality. They should have known also how to interpret sorrow better. I have said that behind sorrow there is always sorrow. It were wiser still to say that behind sorrow there is always a soul. And to mock at a soul in pain is a dreadful thing. In the strangely simple economy of the world people only get what they give, and to those who have not enough imagination to penetrate the mere outward of things, and feel pity, what pity can be given save that of scorn?

I write this account of the mode of my being transferred here simply that it should be realised how hard it has been for me to get anything out of my punishment but bitterness and despair. I have, however, to do it, and now and then I have moments of submission and acceptance. All the spring may be hidden in the single bud, and the low ground nest of the lark may hold the joy that is to herald the feet of many rose-red dawns. So perhaps whatever beauty of life still remains to me is contained in some moment of surrender, abasement, and humiliation. I can, at any rate, merely proceed on the lines of my own development, and, accepting all that has happened to me, make myself worthy of it.

People used to say of me that I was too individualistic. I must be far more of an individualist than ever I was. I must get far more out of myself than ever I got, and ask far less of the world than ever I asked. Indeed, my ruin came not from too great individualism of life, but from too little. The one disgraceful, unpardonable, and to all time contemptible action of my life was to allow myself to appeal to society for help and protection. To have made such an appeal would have been from the individualist point of view bad enough, but what excuse can there ever be put forward for having made it? Of course once I had put into motion the forces of society, society turned on me and said, "Have you been living all this time in defiance of my laws, and do you now appeal to those laws for protection? You shall have those laws exercised to the full. You shall abide by what you have appealed to." The result is I am in gaol. Certainly no man ever fell so ignobly, and by such ignoble instruments, as I did. . . .

The Philistine element in life is not the failure to understand art. Charming people, such as fishermen, shepherds, ploughboys, peasants and the like, know nothing about art, and are the very salt of the earth. He is the Philistine who upholds and aids the heavy, cumbrous, blind, mechanical forces of society, and who does not recognise dynamic force when he meets it either in a man or a movement.

. . . .

And the curious thing to me is that you should have tried to imitate your father in his chief characteristics. I cannot understand why he was to you an exemplar, where he should have been a warning, except that whenever there is hatred between two people there is bond or brotherhood of some kind. I suppose that, by some strange law of the antipathy of similars, you loathed each other, not because in so many points you were so different but because in some you were so like. In June 1893, when you left Oxford, without a degree and with debts, petty in themselves, but considerable to a man of your father's income, your father wrote you a very vulgar, violent and abusive letter. The letter you sent him in reply was in every way worse, and of course far less excusable, and consequently you were extremely proud of it. I remember quite well your saying to me with your most conceited air that you could beat your father "at his own trade." Quite true. But what a trade! What a competition! You used to laugh and sneer at your father for retiring from your cousin's house where he was living in order to write filthy letters to him from a neighbouring hotel. You used to do just the same to me. You constantly lunched with me at some public restaurant, sulked or made a scene during luncheon, and then retired to White's Club and wrote me a letter of the very foulest character. The only difference between you and your father was that after you had dispatched your letter to me by special messenger, you would arrive yourself at my room some hours later not to apologize, but to know if I had ordered dinner at the Savoy, and if not, why not. . . .

. . . .

Does it ever occur to you what an awful position I would have been in if for the last two years, during my appalling sentence, I had been dependent on you as a friend? Do you ever think of that? Do you ever feel any gratitude to those who by kindness without stint, devotion without limit, cheerfulness and joy in giving have lightened my black burden for me, have visited me again and again, have written to me beautiful and sympathetic letters, have managed my affairs for me, arranged my future life, and stood by me in the teeth of obloquy, taunt and open sneer, or insult even? I owe everything to them. . . . I am not ashamed of taking a thing that is given in love and affection; I am proud of it.... I think of every single person who has been kind to me in my prison life down to the warder who gives me a "Good-morning" and a "Good-night" (not one of his prescribed duties) down to the common policemen who, in their homely, rough way strove to comfort me on my journeys to and from the Bankruptcy Court under conditions of terrible mental distress—down to the poor thief who recognising me as we tramped round the yard at Wandsworth, whispered to me in the hoarse prison voice men get from long and compulsory silence: "I am sorry for you; it is harder for the likes of you than it is for the likes of us." I suppose that has never dawned on you. And yet—if you had any imagination in you—you would know that there is not one, not one of them all, I say, the very mire from whose shoes you should not be proud to kneel down and clean.

. . . .

... Your one idea of life, your one philosophy, if you are to be credited with a philosophy, was that whatever you did was to be paid for by someone else: I don't mean merely in the financial sense—that was simply the practical application of your philosophy to everyday life—but in the broadest, fullest sense of transferred responsibility. You made that your creed. It was very successful as far as it went. You forced me into taking action because you knew that your father would not attack your life or yourself in any way and that I would defend both to the utmost, and take on my own shoulders whatever would be thrust on me. You were quite right. Your father and I, each from different motives, of course, did exactly as you counted on our doing. But somehow, in spite of everything, you have not really escaped. The "infant Samuel theory," as for brevity's sake one may term it, is all very well as far as the general world knows. It may be a good deal scorned in London, and a little sneered at in Oxford, but that is merely because there are a few people who know you in each place, and because in each place you left traces of your passage. Outside of a small set in those two cities, the world looks on you as the good man who was very nearly tempted into wrongdoing by the wicked and immoral artist, but was rescued just in time by his kind and loving father. It sounds all right. And yet, you know you have not escaped. I am not referring to a silly question asked by a silly juryman which was, of course, treated with contempt by the Crown and Judge. No one cared about that. I am referring perhaps principally to yourself. In your own eyes, and some day, you will have to think of your conduct; you are not, cannot be, quite satisfied at the way in which things have turned out. Secretly you must think of yourself with a good deal of shame. A brazen face is a capital thing to show to the world, but now and then when you are alone, and have no audience, you have, I suppose, to take the mask off for breathing purposes. Else, indeed, you would be stifled.

. . . .

A great friend of mine—a friend of ten years' standing—came to see me some time ago, and told me that he did not believe a single word of what was said against me, and wished me to know that he considered me quite innocent, and the victim of a hideous plot. I burst into tears at what he said, and told him that while there was much amongst the definite charges that was quite untrue and transferred to me by revolting malice, still that my life had been full of perverse pleasures, and that unless he accepted that as a fact about me and realised it to the full I could not possibly be friends with him any more, or ever be in his company. It was a terrible shock to him, but we are friends, and I have not got his friendship on false pretences. I have said to you to speak the truth is a painful thing. To be forced to tell lies is much worse.

. . . .

I have now written, and at great length, to you in order that you should realize what you were to me before my imprisonment, during those three years' fatal friendship; what you have been to me during my imprisonment, already within two moons of its completion almost; and what I hope to be to myself and to others when my imprisonment is over. I cannot reconstruct my letter or rewrite it. You must take it as it stands, blotted in many places with tears, in some with the signs of passion or pain, and make it out as best you can, blots, corrections, and all. . . . As it stands, at any rate, my letter has its definite meaning behind every phrase. There is in it nothing of rhetoric. Whenever there is erasion or substitution, however slight, however elaborate, it is because I am seeking to render my real impression, to find for my mood its exact equivalent. . . .

. . . We think we can have our emotions for nothing. We cannot. Even the finest and the most self-sacrificing emotions have to be paid for. Strangely enough, that is what makes them fine. The intellectual and emotional life of ordinary people is a very contemptible affair. Just as they borrow their ideas from a sort of circulating library of thought— the *Zeitgeist* of an age that has no soul and send them back soiled at the end of each week—so they always try to get their emotions on credit, or refuse to pay the bill when it comes in. We must pass out of that conception of life; as soon as we have to pay for an emotion we shall know its quality and be the better for such knowledge. Remember that the sentimentalist is always a cynic at heart. Indeed sentimentality is merely the bankholiday of cynicism. And delightful as cynicism is from its intellectual side, now that it has left the tub for the club, it never can be more than the perfect philosophy for a man who has no soul. It has its social value; and to an artist all modes of expression are interesting, but in itself it is a poor affair, for to the true cynic nothing is ever revealed.

I know of nothing in all drama more incomparable from the point of view of art, nothing more suggestive in its subtlety of observation, than Shakespeare's drawing of Rosencrantz and Guildenstern. They are Hamlet's college friends. They have been his companions. They bring with them memories of pleasant days together. At the moment when they come across him in the play he is staggering under the weight of a burden intolerable to one of his temperament. The dead have come armed out of the grave to impose on him a mission at once too great and too mean for him. He is a dreamer, and he is called upon to act. He has the nature of the poet, and he is asked to grapple with the common complexity of cause and effect, with life in its practical realisation, of which he knows nothing, not with life in its ideal essence, of which he knows so much. He has no conception of what to do, and his folly is to feign folly. Brutus used madness as a cloak to conceal the sword of his purpose, the dagger of his will, but the Hamlet madness is a mere mask for the hiding of weakness. In the making of fancies and jests he sees a chance of delay. He keeps playing with action as an artist plays with a theory. He makes himself the spy of his proper actions, and listening to his own words knows them to be but "words, words, words." Instead of trying to be the hero of his own history, he seeks to be the spectator of his own tragedy. He disbelieves in everything, including himself, and yet his doubt helps him not, as it comes not from scepticism but from a divided will.

Of all this Guildenstern and Rosencrantz realise nothing. They bow and smirk and smile, and what the one says the other echoes with sickliest intonation. When, at last, by means of the play within the play, and the puppets in their dalliance, Hamlet "catches the conscience" of the King, and drives the wretched man in terror from his throne, Guildenstern and Rosencrantz see no more in his conduct than a rather painful breach of Court etiquette. That is as far as they can attain to in "the contemplation of the spectacle of life with appropriate emotions." They are close to his very secret and know nothing of it. Nor would there be any use in telling them. They are the little cups that can hold so much and no more. Towards the close it is suggested that, caught in a cunning spring set for another, they have met, or may meet, with a violent and sudden death. But a tragic ending of this kind, though touched by Hamlet's humour with something of the surprise and justice of comedy, is really not for such as they. They never die. Horatio, who in order to "report Hamlet and his cause aright to the unsatisfied,"

> Absents him from felicity a while,
> And in this harsh world draws his breath in pain,

dies, but Guildenstern and Rosencrantz are as immortal as Angelo and Tartuffe, and should rank with them. They are what modern life has contributed to the antique ideal of friendship....

There are some few things more about which I must write to you. The first is about my bankruptcy. I heard some days ago, with great disappointment I admit, that it is too late now for your family to pay your father off, that it would be illegal, and that I must remain in my present painful position for some considerable time to come. It is bitter to me because I am assured on legal authority that I cannot even publish a book without the permission of the Receiver, to whom all the accounts must be submitted. I cannot enter into a contract with the manager of a theatre, or produce a play without the receipts passing to your father and my few other creditors. I think that even you will admit now that the scheme of ''scoring off'' your father by allowing him to make me a bankrupt has not really been the brilliant all-round success you imagined it was going to turn out to be.

. . . .

I am told by More Adey in his letter that last summer you really did express on more than one occasion your desire to repay me ''a little of what I spent'' on you. As I said to him in my answer, unfortunately I spent on you my art, my life, my name, my place in history: and if your family had all the marvellous things in the world at their command, or what the world holds as marvellous, genius, beauty, wealth, high position and the like, and laid them all at my feet, it would not repay me for one tithe of the smallest things that have been taken from me, or one tear of the least tears that I have shed. However, of course, everything one does has to be paid for. Even to the bankrupt it is so.

. . . .

And what is true of a bankrupt is true of everyone else in life. For every single thing that is done someone has to pay. Even you yourself— with all your desire for absolute freedom from all duties, your insistence on having everything supplied to you by others, your attempts to reject any claim on your affection, or regard, or gratitude—even you will have some day to reflect seriously on what you have done, and try, however unavailingly, to make some attempt at atonement. The fact that you will not be able really to do so will be part of your punishment. . . . I have had to look at my past face to face. Look at your past face to face. Sit down quietly and consider it. The supreme vice is shallowness. Whatever is realised is right. . . .

. . . .

Of course to one so modern as I am, *enfant de mon siècle*, merely to look at the world will be always lovely. I tremble with pleasure when I think that on the very day of my leaving prison both the laburnum and the lilac will be blooming in the gardens, and that I shall see the wind stir into restless beauty the swaying gold of the one, and make the other toss the pale purple of its plumes so that all the air shall be Arabia for me. . . . There is not a single colour hidden away in the chalice of a flower, or the curve of a shell, to which, by some subtle sympathy with the very soul of things, my nature does not answer. . . .

Still, I am conscious now that behind all this beauty, satisfying though it may be, there is some spirit hidden of which the painted forms and shapes are but modes of manifestation, and it is with this spirit that I desire to become in harmony. I have grown tired of the articulate utterances of men and things. The Mystical in Art, the Mystical in Life, the Mystical in Nature—this is what I am looking for. It is absolutely necessary for me to find it somewhere.

I have a strange longing for the great simple primeval things, such as the sea, to me no less of a mother than the Earth. It seems to me that we all look at Nature too much, and live with her too little. I discern great sanity in the Greek attitude. They never chattered about sunsets, or discussed whether the shadows on the grass were really mauve or not. But they saw that the sea was for the swimmer, and the sand for the feet of the runner. They loved the trees for the shadow that they cast, and the forest for its silence at noon. The vineyard-dresser wreathed his hair with ivy that he might keep off the rays of the sun as he stooped over the young shoots, and for the artist and the athlete, the two types that Greece gave us, they plaited with garlands the leaves of the bitter laurel and of the wild parsley, which else had been of no service to men.

We call ours a utilitarian age, and we do not know the uses of any single thing. We have forgotten that water can cleanse, and fire purify, and that the Earth is mother to us all. As a consequence our art is of the moon and plays with shadows, while Greek art is of the sun and deals directly with things. I feel sure that in elemental forces there is purification, and I want to go back to them and live in their presence.

All trials are trials for one's life, just as all sentences are sentences of death; and three times have I been tried. The first time I left the box to be arrested, the second time to be led back to the house of detention, the third time to pass into a prison for two years. Society, as we have constituted it, will have no place for me, has none to offer; but Nature, whose sweet rains fall on unjust and just alike, will have clefts in the rocks where I may hide, and secret valleys in whose silence I may weep undisturbed. She will hang the night with stars so that I may walk abroad in the darkness without stumbling, and send the wind over my footprints so that none may track me to my hurt: she will cleanse me in great waters, and with bitter herbs make me whole.

. . . .

I hope that our meeting will be what a meeting between you and me should be, after everything that has occurred. In old days there was always a wide chasm between us, the chasm of achieved art and acquired culture; there is a still wider chasm between us now, the chasm of sorrow: but to humility there is nothing that is impossible, and to love all things are easy.

. . . .

I waited month after month to hear from you. Even if I had not been waiting but had shut the doors against you, you should have remembered that no one can possibly shut the doors against love for ever. The unjust judge in the Gospels rises up at length to give a just decision because justice comes knocking daily at his door; and at night time the friend in whose heart there is no real friendship yields at length to his friend ''because of his importunity.'' There is no prison in any world into which love cannot force an entrance. If you did not understand that, you did not understand anything about love at all.

. . . .

Remember also that I have yet to know you. Perhaps we have yet to know each other. For yourself, I have but this last thing to say. Do not be afraid of the past. If people tell you that it is irrevocable, do not believe them. The past, the present and the future are but one moment in the sight of God, in whose sight we should try to live. Time and space, succession and extension, are merely accidental conditions of thought. The imagination can transcend them, and more in a free sphere of ideal existence. Things, also, are in their essence what we choose to make them.... What lies before me is my past. I have got to make myself look on that with different eyes, to make the world look on it with different eyes, to make God look on it with different eyes. This I cannot do by ignoring it, or slighting it, or praising it, or denying it. It is only to be done fully by accepting it as an inevitable part of the evolution of my life and character: by bowing my head to everything that I have suffered. How far I am away from the true temper of soul, this letter in its changing uncertain moods, it scorn and bitterness, its aspirations and its failures to realize those aspirations, shows you quite clearly. But do not forget in what a terrible school I am sitting at my task. And incomplete, imperfect, as I am, yet from me you may have still much to gain. You came to me to learn the pleasure of life and the pleasure of art. Perhaps I am chosen to teach you something much more wonderful—the meaning of sorrow and its beauty.

> Your affectionate friend,
> Oscar Wilde

Notes

1. *Love?* If Wilde thinks Lord Alfred Douglas ("Bosie") is so "shallow," why does he bother to write him this long letter? (Bosie tore it up on receipt, but luckily the carrier preserved a copy.)

2. *Hubris?* How do you reconcile Wilde's claimed abasement with his assertions of grandeur?

3. *Religion?* Wilde disclaims any religious conviction, yet paints an enduring picture of the life of Christ. Are these positions reconcilable?

4. *Epigrams?* Wilde's novels and plays are filled with witty epigrams. Even in this soul-searching letter, he produces a number of pithy sentences, two of which form a refrain: "The supreme vice is shallowness. Whatever is realised is right." Identify some of the other epigrams here and explain in what sense they are true, or appropriate, or effective.

5. *Genre.* What is the genre of *De Profundis*? It seems to embody aspects of a letter, a deeply reflective meditation, a philosophical tract, and perhaps, a work of public vindication. How does our decision on the genre of the work affect its meaning?

6. *A Room of His Own.* This work has an interesting composition history. Wilde was given one sheet of pale blue prison stationery at a time; when that sheet was filled, it was removed, and he was given a second sheet. Wilde was not allowed to see the complete product until his release from prison, when it was handed to him and he, in turn, handed it to his friend and literary executor, Robert Ross, who delivered it to Bosie. After Douglas

destroyed the copy Ross gave him, Ross became so concerned about the preservation of the manuscript that he donated it to the British Museum, to be kept under seal until 1969. However, Ross had made a typescript from the original, and several versions of *De Profundis* were published in the early 1900's. Does this composition history add anything to the meaning of the work?

ECCLESIASTES
Or the Preacher
King James Bible

[1] The words of the Preacher, the son of David, king in Jerusalem.

[2] Vanity of vanities, saith the Preacher, vanity of vanities; all is vanity.

[3] What profit hath a man of all his labour which he taketh under the sun?

[4] One generation passeth away, and another generation cometh: but the earth abideth for ever.

[5] The sun also ariseth, and the sun goeth down, and hasteth to his place where he arose.

[6] The wind goeth toward the south, and turneth about unto the north; it whirleth about continually, and the wind returneth again according to his circuits.

[7] All the rivers run into the sea; yet the sea is not full; unto the place from whence the rivers come, thither they return again.

[8] All things are full of labour; man cannot utter it: the eye is not satisfied with seeing, nor the ear filled with hearing.

[9] The thing that hath been, it is that which shall be; and that which is done is that which shall be done: and there is no new thing under the sun.

[10] Is there any thing whereof it may be said, See, this is new? it hath been already of old time, which was before us.

[11] There is no remembrance of former things; neither shall there be any remembrance of things that are to come with those that shall come after.

[12] I the Preacher was king over Israel in Jerusalem.

[13] And I gave my heart to seek and search out by wisdom concerning all things that are done under heaven: this sore travail hath God given to the sons of man to be exercised therewith.

[14] I have seen all the works that are done under the sun; and, behold, all is vanity and vexation of spirit.

[15] That which is crooked cannot be made straight: and that which is wanting cannot be numbered.

[16] I communed with mine own heart, saying, Lo, I am come to great estate, and have gotten more wisdom than all they that have been before me in Jerusalem: yea, my heart had great experience of wisdom and knowledge.

[17] And I gave my heart to know wisdom, and to know madness and folly: I perceived that this also is vexation of spirit.

[18] For in much wisdom is much grief: and he that increaseth knowledge increaseth sorrow.

Chapter 2

[1] I said in mine heart, Go to now, I will prove thee with mirth, therefore enjoy pleasure: and, behold, this also is vanity.

[2] I said of laughter, It is mad: and of mirth, What doeth it?

[3] I sought in mine heart to give myself unto wine, yet acquainting mine heart with wisdom; and to lay hold on folly, till I might see what was that good for the sons of men, which

they should do under the heaven all the days of their life.

⁴ I made me great works; I builded me houses; I planted me vineyards:

⁵ I made me gardens and orchards, and I planted trees in them of all kind of fruits:

⁶ I made me pools of water, to water therewith the wood that bringeth forth trees:

⁷ I got me servants and maidens, and had servants born in my house; also I had great possessions of great and small cattle above all that were in Jerusalem before me:

⁸ I gathered me also silver and gold, and the peculiar treasure of kings and of the provinces: I gat me men singers and women singers, and the delights of the sons of men, as musical instruments, and that of all sorts.

⁹ So I was great, and increased more than all that were before me in Jerusalem: also my wisdom remained with me.

¹⁰ And whatsoever mine eyes desired I kept not from them, I withheld not my heart from any joy; for my heart rejoiced in all my labour: and this was my portion of all my labour.

¹¹ Then I looked on all the works that my hands had wrought, and on the labour that I had laboured to do: and, behold, all was vanity and vexation of spirit, and there was no profit under the sun.

¹² And I turned myself to behold wisdom, and madness, and folly: for what can the man do that cometh after the king? even that which hath been already done.

¹³ Then I saw that wisdom excelleth folly, as far as light excelleth darkness.

¹⁴ The wise man's eyes are in his head; but the fool walketh in darkness: and I myself perceived also that one event happeneth to them all.

¹⁵ Then said I in my heart, As it happeneth to the fool, so it happeneth even to me; and why was I then more

wise? Then I said in my heart, that this also is vanity.

¹⁶ For there is no remembrance of the wise more than of the fool for ever; seeing that which now is in the days to come shall all be forgotten. And how dieth the wise man? as the fool.

¹⁷ Therefore I hated life; because the work that is wrought under the sun is grievous unto me: for all is vanity and vexation of spirit.

¹⁸ Yea, I hated all my labour which I had taken under the sun: because I should leave it unto the man that shall be after me.

¹⁹ And who knoweth whether he shall be a wise man or a fool? yet shall he have rule over all my labour wherein I have laboured, and wherein I have shewed myself wise under the sun. This is also vanity.

²⁰ Therefore I went about to cause my heart to despair of all the labour which I took under the sun.

* * *

Chapter 3

¹ To every thing there is a season, and a time to every purpose under the heaven:

² A time to be born, and a time to die; a time to plant, and a time to pluck up that which is planted;

³ A time to kill, and a time to heal; a time to break down, and a time to build up;

⁴ A time to weep, and a time to laugh; a time to mourn, and a time to dance;

⁵ A time to cast away stones, and a time to gather stones together; a time to embrace, and a time to refrain from embracing;

⁶ A time to get, and a time to lose; a time to keep, and a time to cast away;

⁷ A time to rend, and a time to sew; a time to keep silence, and a time to speak;

8 A time to love, and a time to hate; a time of war, and a time of peace.

9 What profit hath he that worketh in that wherein he laboureth?

10 I have seen the travail, which God hath given to the sons of men to be exercised in it.

11 He hath made every thing beautiful in his time: also he hath set the world in their heart, so that no man can find out the work that God maketh from the beginning to the end.

12 I know that there is no good in them, but for a man to rejoice, and to do good in his life.

13 And also that every man should eat and drink, and enjoy the good of all his labour, it is the gift of God.

14 I know that, whatsoever God doeth, it shall be for ever: nothing can be put to it, nor any thing taken from it: and God doeth it, that men should fear before him.

15 That which hath been is now; and that which is to be hath already been; and God requireth that which is past.

16 And moreover I saw under the sun the place of judgment, that wickedness was there; and the place of righteousness, that iniquity was there.

17 I said in mine heart, God shall judge the righteous and the wicked: for there is a time there for every purpose and for every work.

18 I said in mine heart concerning the estate of the sons of men, that God might manifest them, and that they might see that they themselves are beasts.

19 For that which befalleth the sons of men befalleth beasts; even one thing befalleth them: as the one dieth, so dieth the other; yea, they have all one breath; so that a man hath no preeminence above a beast: for all is vanity.

20 All go unto one place; all are of the dust, and all turn to dust again.

21 Who knoweth the spirit of man that goeth upward, and the spirit of the beast that goeth downward to the earth?

22 Wherefore I perceive that there is nothing better, than that a man should rejoice in his own works; for that is his portion: for who shall bring him to see what shall be after him?

* * *

Chapter 5

* * *

15 As he came forth of his mother's womb, naked shall he return to go as he came, and shall take nothing of his labour, which he may carry away in his hand.

16 And this also is a sore evil, that in all points as he came, so shall he go: and what profit hath he that hath laboured for the wind?

17 All his days also he eateth in darkness, and he hath much sorrow and wrath with his sickness.

* * *

Chapter 7

1 A good name is better than precious ointment; and the day of death than the day of one's birth.

2 It is better to go to the house of mourning, than to go to the house of feasting: for that is the end of all men; and the living will lay it to his heart.

3 Sorrow is better than laughter: for by the sadness of the countenance the heart is made better.

4 The heart of the wise is in the house of mourning; but the heart of fools is in the house of mirth.

5 It is better to hear the rebuke of the wise, than for a man to hear the song of fools.

6 For as the crackling of thorns under a pot, so is the laughter of the fool: this also is vanity.

7 Surely oppression maketh a wise man mad; and a gift destroyeth the heart.

8 Better is the end of a thing than the beginning thereof: and the patient

in spirit is better than the proud in spirit.

9 Be not hasty in thy spirit to be angry: for anger resteth in the bosom of fools.

10 Say not thou, What is the cause that the former days were better than these? for thou dost not inquire wisely concerning this.

11 Wisdom is good with an inheritance: and by it there is profit to them that see the sun.

12 For wisdom is a defence, and money is a defence: but the excellency of knowledge is, that wisdom giveth life to them that have it.

13 Consider the work of God: for who can make that straight, which he hath made crooked?

14 In the day of prosperity be joyful, but in the day of adversity consider: God also hath set the one over against the other, to the end that man should find nothing after him.

15 All things have I seen in the days of my vanity: there is a just man that perisheth in his righteousness, and there is a wicked man that prolongeth his life in his wickedness.

16 Be not righteous over much; neither make thyself over wise: why shouldest thou destroy thyself?

17 Be not over much wicked, neither be thou foolish: why shouldest thou die before thy time?

18 It is good that thou shouldest take hold of this; yea, also from this withdraw not thine hand: for he that feareth God shall come forth of them all.

19 Wisdom strengtheneth the wise more than ten mighty men which are in the city.

20 For there is not a just man upon earth, that doeth good, and sinneth not.

21 Also take no heed unto all words that are spoken; lest thou hear thy servant curse thee:

22 For oftentimes also thine own heart knoweth that thou thyself likewise hast cursed others.

23 All this have I proved by wisdom: I said, I will be wise; but it was far from me.

24 That which is far off, and exceeding deep, who can find it out?

* * *

Chapter 9

1 For all this I considered in my heart even to declare all this, that the righteous, and the wise, and their works, are in the hand of God: no man knoweth either love or hatred by all that is before them.

2 All things come alike to all: there is one event to the righteous, and to the wicked; to the good and to the clean, and to the unclean; to him that sacrificeth, and to him that sacrificeth not: as is the good, so is the sinner; and he that sweareth, as he that feareth an oath.

3 This is an evil among all things that are done under the sun, that there is one event unto all: yea, also the heart of the sons of men is full of evil, and madness is in their heart while they live, and after that they go to the dead.

4 For to him that is joined to all the living there is hope: for a living dog is better than a dead lion.

5 For the living know that they shall die: but the dead know not any thing, neither have they any more a reward; for the memory of them is forgotten.

6 Also their love, and their hatred, and their envy, is now perished; neither have they any more a portion for ever in any thing that is done under the sun.

7 Go thy way, eat thy bread with joy, and drink thy wine with a merry heart; for God now accepteth thy works.

8 Let thy garments be always white; and let thy head lack no ointment.

⁹ Live joyfully with the wife whom thou lovest all the days of the life of thy vanity, which he hath given thee under the sun, all the days of thy vanity: for that is thy portion in this life, and in thy labour which thou takest under the sun.

¹⁰ Whatsoever thy hand findeth to do, do it with thy might; for there is no work, nor device, nor knowledge, nor wisdom, in the grave, whither thou goest.

¹¹ I returned, and saw under the sun, that the race is not to the swift, nor the battle to the strong, neither yet bread to the wise, nor yet riches to men of understanding, nor yet favour to men of skill; but time and chance happeneth to them all.

¹² For man also knoweth not his time: as the fishes that are taken in an evil net, and as the birds that are caught in the snare; so are the sons of men snared in an evil time, when it falleth suddenly upon them.

¹³ This wisdom have I seen also under the sun, and it seemed great unto me:

¹⁴ There was a little city, and few men within it; and there came a great king against it, and besieged it, and built great bulwarks against it:

¹⁵ Now there was found in it a poor wise man, and he by his wisdom delivered the city; yet no man remembered that same poor man.

¹⁶ Then said I, Wisdom is better than strength: nevertheless the poor man's wisdom is despised, and his words are not heard.

¹⁷ The words of wise men are heard in quiet more than the cry of him that ruleth among fools.

¹⁸ Wisdom is better than weapons of war: but one sinner destroyeth much good.

Chapter 10

* * *

⁸ He that diggeth a pit shall fall into it; and whoso breaketh an hedge, a serpent shall bite him.

⁹ Whoso removeth stones shall be hurt therewith; and he that cleaveth wood shall be endangered thereby.

¹⁰ If the iron be blunt, and he do not whet the edge, then must he put to more strength: but wisdom is profitable to direct.

¹¹ Surely the serpent will bite without enchantment; and a babbler is no better.

¹² The words of a wise man's mouth are gracious; but the lips of a fool will swallow up himself.

¹³ The beginning of the words of his mouth is foolishness: and the end of his talk is mischievous madness.

¹⁴ A fool also is full of words: a man cannot tell what shall be; and what shall be after him, who can tell him?

* * *

Chapter 11

¹ Cast thy bread upon the waters: for thou shalt find it after many days.

² Give a portion to seven, and also to eight; for thou knowest not what evil shall be upon the earth.

³ If the clouds be full of rain, they empty themselves upon the earth: and if the tree fall toward the south, or toward the north, in the place where the tree falleth, there it shall be.

⁴ He that observeth the wind shall not sow; and he that regardeth the clouds shall not reap.

⁵ As thou knowest not what is the way of the spirit, nor how the bones do grow in the womb of her that is with child: even so thou knowest not the works of God who maketh all.

⁶ In the morning sow thy seed, and in the evening withhold not thine hand: for thou knowest not whether shall prosper, either this or that, or whether they both shall be alike good.

⁷ Truly the light is sweet, and a pleasant thing it is for the eyes to behold the sun:

⁸ But if a man live many years, and rejoice in them all; yet let him remember the days of darkness; for they shall be many. All that cometh is vanity.

* * *

Chapter 12

¹ Remember now thy Creator in the days of thy youth, while the evil days come not, nor the years draw nigh, when thou shalt say, I have no pleasure in them;

² While the sun, or the light, or the moon, or the stars, be not darkened, nor the clouds return after the rain:

³ In the day when the keepers of the house shall tremble, and the strong men shall bow themselves, and the grinders cease because they are few, and those that look out of the windows be darkened,

⁴ And the doors shall be shut in the streets, when the sound of the grinding is low, and he shall rise up at the voice of the bird, and all the daughters of musick shall be brought low;

⁵ Also when they shall be afraid of that which is high, and fears shall be in the way, and the almond tree shall flourish, and the grasshopper shall be a burden, and desire shall fail: because man goeth to his long home, and the mourners go about the streets:

⁶ Or ever the silver cord be loosed, or the golden bowl be broken, or the pitcher be broken at the fountain, or the wheel broken at the cistern.

⁷ Then shall the dust return to the earth as it was: and the spirit shall return unto God who gave it.

⁸ Vanity of vanities, saith the preacher; all is vanity.

* * *

¹² And further, by these, my son, be admonished: of making many books there is no end; and much study is a weariness of the flesh.

¹³ Let us hear the conclusion of the whole matter: Fear God, and keep his commandments: for this is the whole duty of man.

¹⁴ For God shall bring every work into judgment, with every secret thing, whether it be good, or whether it be evil.

Notes

1. *Morality vs. Philosophy.* The *Book of Ecclesiastes,* taken here from the King James Bible, is one of the most baffling books in the entire Bible—matched only by the *Book of Job* (King James), given next. The philosophy of *Ecclesiastes* seems to reflect that of Candide at the conclusion of Voltaire's *L'Optimisme:* "Il fault cultiver notre jardin." The view seems to be either that work is more profitable than speculation, or that at least it is a remedy to salve man's unhappy lot. Compare this view with that of MacLeish's *J.B.,* discussed in the notes following *Job* below.

2. *Justice.* The author of *Ecclesiastes* calls into question the existence of justice—at least in this world. If the race is not to the swift, nor the battle to the strong, then this world's rewards must be based on something other than merit. Does your experience bear out this conclusion?

3. *A Time For All Things.* What does the Preacher mean in his famous poem (chp 3 verses 1–8), "To every thing there is a season"?

4. *Casting Bread. Ecclesiastes* 11:1–2 can be read both literally and figuratively. Work out a number of figurative readings for these verses.

THE BOOK OF JOB
King James Bible

Chapter 1

¹ There was a man in the land of Uz, whose name was Job; and that man was perfect and upright, and one that feared God, and eschewed evil.

² And there were born unto him seven sons and three daughters.

³ His substance also was seven thousand sheep, and three thousand camels, and five hundred yoke of oxen, and five hundred she asses, and a very great household; so that this man was the greatest of all the men of the east.

⁴ And his sons went and feasted in their houses, every one his day; and sent and called for their three sisters to eat and to drink with them.

⁵ And it was so, when the days of their feasting were gone about, that Job sent and sanctified them, and rose up early in the morning, and offered burnt offerings according to the number of them all: for Job said, It may be that my sons have sinned, and cursed God in their hearts. Thus did Job continually.

⁶ Now there was a day when the sons of God came to present themselves before the LORD, and Satan came also among them.

⁷ And the LORD said unto Satan, Whence comest thou? Then Satan answered the LORD, and said, From going to and fro in the earth, and from walking up and down in it.

⁸ And the LORD said unto Satan, Hast thou considered my servant Job, that there is none like him in the earth, a perfect and an upright man, one that feareth God, and escheweth evil?

⁹ Then Satan answered the LORD, and said, Doth Job fear God for nought?

¹⁰ Hast not thou made an hedge about him, and about his house, and about all that he hath on every side?

thou hast blessed the work of his hands, and his substance is increased in the land.

¹¹ But put forth thine hand now, and touch all that he hath, and he will curse thee to thy face.

¹² And the LORD said unto Satan, Behold, all that he hath is in thy power; only upon himself put not forth thine hand. So Satan went forth from the presence of the LORD.

¹³ And there was a day when his sons and his daughters were eating and drinking wine in their eldest brother's house:

¹⁴ And there came a messenger unto Job, and said, The oxen were plowing, and the asses feeding beside them:

¹⁵ And the Sabeans fell upon them, and took them away; yea, they have slain the servants with the edge of the sword; and I only am escaped alone to tell thee.

¹⁶ While he was yet speaking, there came also another, and said, The fire of God is fallen from heaven, and hath burned up the sheep, and the servants, and consumed them; and I only am escaped alone to tell thee.

¹⁷ While he was yet speaking, there came also another, and said, The Chaldeans made out three bands, and fell upon the camels, and have carried them away, yea, and slain the servants with the edge of the sword; and I only am escaped alone to tell thee.

¹⁸ While he was yet speaking, there came also another, and said, Thy sons and thy daughters were eating and drinking wine in their eldest brother's house:

¹⁹ And, behold, there came a great wind from the wilderness, and smote the four corners of the house, and it fell upon the young men, and they are

dead; and I only am escaped alone to tell thee.

20 Then Job arose, and rent his mantle, and shaved his head, and fell down upon the ground, and worshipped,

21 And said, Naked came I out of my mother's womb, and naked shall I return thither: the LORD gave, and the LORD hath taken away; blessed be the name of the LORD.

22 In all this Job sinned not, nor charged God foolishly.

Chapter 2

1 Again there was a day when the sons of God came to present themselves before the LORD, and Satan came also among them to present himself before the LORD.

2 And the LORD said unto Satan, From whence comest thou? And Satan answered the LORD, and said, From going to and fro in the earth, and from walking up and down in it.

3 And the LORD said unto Satan, Hast thou considered my servant Job, that there is none like him in the earth, a perfect and an upright man, one that feareth God, and escheweth evil? and still he holdeth fast his integrity, although thou movedst me against him, to destroy him without cause.

4 And Satan answered the LORD, and said, Skin for skin, yea, all that a man hath will he give for his life.

5 But put forth thine hand now, and touch his bone and his flesh, and he will curse thee to thy face.

6 And the LORD said unto Satan, Behold, he is in thine hand; but save his life.

7 So went Satan forth from the presence of the LORD, and smote Job with sore boils from the sole of his foot unto his crown.

8 And he took him a potsherd to scrape himself withal; and he sat down among the ashes.

9 Then said his wife unto him, Dost thou still retain thine integrity? curse God, and die.

10 But he said unto her, Thou speakest as one of the foolish women speaketh. What? shall we receive good at the hand of God, and shall we not receive evil? In all this did not Job sin with his lips.

11 Now when Job's three friends heard of all this evil that was come upon him, they came every one from his own place; Eliphaz the Temanite, and Bildad the Shuhite, and Zophar the Naamathite: for they had made an appointment together to come to mourn with him and to comfort him.

12 And when they lifted up their eyes afar off, and knew him not, they lifted up their voice, and wept; and they rent every one his mantle, and sprinkled dust upon their heads toward heaven.

13 So they sat down with him upon the ground seven days and seven nights, and none spake a word unto him: for they saw that his grief was very great.

Chapter 3

1 After this opened Job his mouth, and cursed his day.

2 And Job spake, and said,

3 Let the day perish wherein I was born, and the night in which it was said, There is a man child conceived.

4 Let that day be darkness; let not God regard it from above, neither let the light shine upon it.

5 Let darkness and the shadow of death stain it; let a cloud dwell upon it; let the blackness of the day terrify it.

6 As for that night, let darkness seize upon it; let it not be joined unto the days of the year, let it not come into the number of the months.

7 Lo, let that night be solitary, let no joyful voice come therein.

⁸ Let them curse it that curse the day, who are ready to raise up their mourning.

⁹ Let the stars of the twilight thereof be dark; let it look for light, but have none; neither let it see the dawning of the day:

¹⁰ Because it shut not up the doors of my mother's womb, nor hid sorrow from mine eyes.

¹¹ Why died I not from the womb? why did I not give up the ghost when I came out of the belly?

¹² Why did the knees prevent me? or why the breasts that I should suck?

¹³ For now should I have lain still and been quiet, I should have slept: then had I been at rest,

¹⁴ With kings and counsellors of the earth, which built desolate places for themselves;

¹⁵ Or with princes that had gold, who filled their houses with silver:

¹⁶ Or as an hidden untimely birth I had not been; as infants which never saw light.

¹⁷ There the wicked cease from troubling; and there the weary be at rest.

¹⁸ There the prisoners rest together; they hear not the voice of the oppressor.

¹⁹ The small and great are there; and the servant is free from his master.

²⁰ Wherefore is light given to him that is in misery, and life unto the bitter in soul;

²¹ Which long for death, but it cometh not; and dig for it more than for hid treasures;

²² Which rejoice exceedingly, and are glad, when they can find the grave?

²³ Why is light given to a man whose way is hid, and whom God hath hedged in?

²⁴ For my sighing cometh before I eat, and my roarings are poured out like the waters.

²⁵ For the thing which I greatly feared is come upon me, and that which I was afraid of is come unto me.

²⁶ I was not in safety, neither had I rest, neither was I quiet; yet trouble came.

Chapter 4

¹ Then Eliphaz the Temanite answered and said,

² If we assay to commune with thee, wilt thou be grieved? but who can withhold himself from speaking?

³ Behold, thou hast instructed many, and thou hast strengthened the weak hands.

⁴ Thy words have upholden him that was falling, and thou hast strengthened the feeble knees.

⁵ But now it is come upon thee, and thou faintest; it toucheth thee, and thou art troubled.

⁶ Is not this thy fear, thy confidence, thy hope, and the uprightness of thy ways?

⁷ Remember, I pray thee, who ever perished, being innocent? or where were the righteous cut off?

⁸ Even as I have seen, they that plow iniquity, and sow wickedness, reap the same.

⁹ By the blast of God they perish, and by the breath of his nostrils are they consumed.

¹⁰ The roaring of the lion, and the voice of the fierce lion, and the teeth of the young lions, are broken.

¹¹ The old lion perisheth for lack of prey, and the stout lion's whelps are scattered abroad.

¹² Now a thing was secretly brought to me, and mine ear received a little thereof.

¹³ In thoughts from the visions of the night, when deep sleep falleth on men,

¹⁴ Fear came upon me, and trembling, which made all my bones to shake.

¹⁵ Then a spirit passed before my face; the hair of my flesh stood up:

¹⁶ It stood still, but I could not discern the form thereof: an image was before mine eyes, there was silence, and I heard a voice, saying,

¹⁷ Shall mortal man be more just than God? shall a man be more pure than his maker?

¹⁸ Behold, he put no trust in his servants; and his angels he charged with folly:

¹⁹ How much less in them that dwell in houses of clay, whose foundation is in the dust, which are crushed before the moth?

²⁰ They are destroyed from morning to evening: they perish for ever without any regarding it.

²¹ Doth not their excellency which is in them go away? they die, even without wisdom.

Chapter 5

¹ Call now, if there be any that will answer thee; and to which of the saints wilt thou turn?

² For wrath killeth the foolish man, and envy slayeth the silly one.

³ I have seen the foolish taking root: but suddenly I cursed his habitation.

⁴ His children are far from safety, and they are crushed in the gate, neither is there any to deliver them.

⁵ Whose harvest the hungry eateth up, and taketh it even out of the thorns, and the robber swalloweth up their substance.

⁶ Although affliction cometh not forth of the dust, neither doth trouble spring out of the ground;

⁷ Yet man is born unto trouble, as the sparks fly upward.

⁸ I would seek unto God, and unto God would I commit my cause:

⁹ Which doeth great things and unsearchable; marvellous things without number:

¹⁰ Who giveth rain upon the earth, and sendeth waters upon the fields:

¹¹ To set up on high those that be low; that those which mourn may be exalted to safety.

¹² He disappointeth the devices of the crafty, so that their hands cannot perform their enterprise.

¹³ He taketh the wise in their own craftiness: and the counsel of the froward is carried headlong.

¹⁴ They meet with darkness in the daytime, and grope in the noonday as in the night.

¹⁵ But he saveth the poor from the sword, from their mouth, and from the hand of the mighty.

¹⁶ So the poor hath hope, and iniquity stoppeth her mouth.

¹⁷ Behold, happy is the man whom God correcteth: therefore despise not thou the chastening of the Almighty:

¹⁸ For he maketh sore, and bindeth up: he woundeth, and his hands make whole.

¹⁹ He shall deliver thee in six troubles: yea, in seven there shall no evil touch thee.

²⁰ In famine he shall redeem thee from death: and in war from the power of the sword.

²¹ Thou shalt be hid from the scourge of the tongue: neither shalt thou be afraid of destruction when it cometh.

²² At destruction and famine thou shalt laugh: neither shalt thou be afraid of the beasts of the earth.

²³ For thou shalt be in league with the stones of the field: and the beasts of the field shall be at peace with thee.

²⁴ And thou shalt know that thy tabernacle shall be in peace; and thou shalt visit thy habitation, and shalt not sin.

²⁵ Thou shalt know also that thy seed shall be great, and thine offspring as the grass of the earth.

²⁶ Thou shalt come to thy grave in a full age, like as a shock of corn cometh in in his season.

²⁷ Lo this, we have searched it, so it is; hear it, and know thou it for thy good.

Chapter 6

¹ But Job answered and said,

² Oh that my grief were throughly weighed, and my calamity laid in the balances together!

³ For now it would be heavier than the sand of the sea: therefore my words are swallowed up.

⁴ For the arrows of the Almighty are within me, the poison whereof drinketh up my spirit: the terrors of God do set themselves in array against me.

⁵ Doth the wild ass bray when he hath grass? or loweth the ox over his fodder?

⁶ Can that which is unsavoury be eaten without salt? or is there any taste in the white of an egg?

⁷ The things that my soul refused to touch are as my sorrowful meat.

⁸ Oh that I might have my request; and that God would grant me the thing that I long for!

⁹ Even that it would please God to destroy me; that he would let loose his hand, and cut me off!

¹⁰ Then should I yet have comfort; yea, I would harden myself in sorrow: let him not spare; for I have not concealed the words of the Holy One.

¹¹ What is my strength, that I should hope? and what is mine end, that I should prolong my life?

¹² Is my strength the strength of stones? or is my flesh of brass?

¹³ Is not my help in me? and is wisdom driven quite from me?

¹⁴ To him that is afflicted pity should be shewed from his friend; but he forsaketh the fear of the Almighty.

¹⁵ My brethren have dealt deceitfully as a brook, and as the stream of brooks they pass away;

¹⁶ Which are blackish by reason of the ice, and wherein the snow is hid:

¹⁷ What time they wax warm, they vanish: when it is hot, they are consumed out of their place.

¹⁸ The paths of their way are turned aside; they go to nothing, and perish.

¹⁹ The troops of Tema looked, the companies of Sheba waited for them.

²⁰ They were confounded because they had hoped; they came thither, and were ashamed.

²¹ For now ye are nothing; ye see my casting down, and are afraid.

²² Did I say, Bring unto me? or, Give a reward for me of your substance?

²³ Or, Deliver me from the enemy's hand? or, Redeem me from the hand of the mighty?

²⁴ Teach me, and I will hold my tongue: and cause me to understand wherein I have erred.

²⁵ How forcible are right words! but what doth your arguing reprove?

²⁶ Do ye imagine to reprove words, and the speeches of one that is desperate, which are as wind?

²⁷ Yea, ye overwhelm the fatherless, and ye dig a pit for your friend.

²⁸ Now therefore be content, look upon me; for it is evident unto you if I lie.

²⁹ Return, I pray you, let it not be iniquity; yea, return again, my righteousness is in it.

³⁰ Is there iniquity in my tongue? cannot my taste discern perverse things?

Chapter 7

¹ Is there not an appointed time to man upon earth? are not his days also like the days of an hireling?

² As a servant earnestly desireth the shadow, and as an hireling looketh for the reward of his work:

[3] So am I made to possess months of vanity, and wearisome nights are appointed to me.

[4] When I lie down, I say, When shall I arise, and the night be gone? and I am full of tossings to and fro unto the dawning of the day.

[5] My flesh is clothed with worms and clods of dust; my skin is broken, and become loathsome.

[6] My days are swifter than a weaver's shuttle, and are spent without hope.

[7] O remember that my life is wind: mine eye shall no more see good.

[8] The eye of him that hath seen me shall see me no more: thine eyes are upon me, and I am not.

[9] As the cloud is consumed and vanisheth away: so he that goeth down to the grave shall come up no more.

[10] He shall return no more to his house, neither shall his place know him any more.

[11] Therefore I will not refrain my mouth; I will speak in the anguish of my spirit; I will complain in the bitterness of my soul.

[12] Am I a sea, or a whale, that thou settest a watch over me?

[13] When I say, My bed shall comfort me, my couch shall ease my complaint;

[14] Then thou scarest me with dreams, and terrifiest me through visions:

[15] So that my soul chooseth strangling, and death rather than my life.

[16] I loathe it; I would not live alway: let me alone; for my days are vanity.

[17] What is man, that thou shouldest magnify him? and that thou shouldest set thine heart upon him?

[18] And that thou shouldest visit him every morning, and try him every moment?

[19] How long wilt thou not depart from me, nor let me alone till I swallow down my spittle?

[20] I have sinned; what shall I do unto thee, O thou preserver of men? why hast thou set me as a mark against thee, so that I am a burden to myself?

[21] And why dost thou not pardon my transgression, and take away mine iniquity? for now shall I sleep in the dust; and thou shalt seek me in the morning, but I shall not be.

Chapter 8

[1] Then answered Bildad the Shuhite, and said,

[2] How long wilt thou speak these things? and how long shall the words of thy mouth be like a strong wind?

[3] Doth God pervert judgment? or doth the Almighty pervert justice?

[4] If thy children have sinned against him, and he have cast them away for their transgression;

[5] If thou wouldest seek unto God betimes, and make thy supplication to the Almighty;

[6] If thou wert pure and upright; surely now he would awake for thee, and make the habitation of thy righteousness prosperous.

[7] Though thy beginning was small, yet thy latter end should greatly increase.

[8] For inquire, I pray thee, of the former age, and prepare thyself to the search of their fathers:

[9] (For we are but of yesterday, and know nothing, because our days upon earth are a shadow:)

[10] Shall not they teach thee, and tell thee, and utter words out of their heart?

[11] Can the rush grow up without mire? can the flag grow without water?

[12] Whilst it is yet in his greenness, and not cut down, it withereth before any other herb.

[13] So are the paths of all that forget God; and the hypocrite's hope shall perish:

¹⁴ Whose hope shall be cut off, and whose trust shall be a spider's web.

¹⁵ He shall lean upon his house, but it shall not stand: he shall hold it fast, but it shall not endure.

¹⁶ He is green before the sun, and his branch shooteth forth in his garden.

¹⁷ His roots are wrapped about the heap, and seeth the place of stones.

¹⁸ If he destroy him from his place, then it shall deny him, saying, I have not seen thee.

¹⁹ Behold, this is the joy of his way, and out of the earth shall others grow.

²⁰ Behold, God will not cast away a perfect man, neither will he help the evil doers:

²¹ Till he fill thy mouth with laughing, and thy lips with rejoicing.

²² They that hate thee shall be clothed with shame; and the dwelling place of the wicked shall come to nought.

Chapter 9

¹ Then Job answered and said,

² I know it is so of a truth: but how should man be just with God?

³ If he will contend with him, he cannot answer him one of a thousand.

⁴ He is wise in heart, and mighty in strength: who hath hardened himself against him, and hath prospered?

⁵ Which removeth the mountains, and they know not: which overturneth them in his anger.

⁶ Which shaketh the earth out of her place, and the pillars thereof tremble.

⁷ Which commandeth the sun, and it riseth not; and sealeth up the stars.

⁸ Which alone spreadeth out the heavens, and treadeth upon the waves of the sea.

⁹ Which maketh Arcturus, Orion, and Pleiades, and the chambers of the south.

¹⁰ Which doeth great things past finding out; yea, and wonders without number.

¹¹ Lo, he goeth by me, and I see him not: he passeth on also, but I perceive him not.

¹² Behold, he taketh away, who can hinder him? who will say unto him, What doest thou?

¹³ If God will not withdraw his anger, the proud helpers do stoop under him.

¹⁴ How much less shall I answer him, and choose out my words to reason with him?

¹⁵ Whom, though I were righteous, yet would I not answer, but I would make supplication to my judge.

¹⁶ If I had called, and he had answered me; yet would I not believe that he had hearkened unto my voice.

¹⁷ For he breaketh me with a tempest, and multiplieth my wounds without cause.

¹⁸ He will not suffer me to take my breath, but filleth me with bitterness.

¹⁹ If I speak of strength, lo, he is strong: and if of judgment, who shall set me a time to plead?

²⁰ If I justify myself, mine own mouth shall condemn me: if I say, I am perfect, it shall also prove me perverse.

²¹ Though I were perfect, yet would I not know my soul: I would despise my life.

²² This is one thing, therefore I said it, He destroyeth the perfect and the wicked.

²³ If the scourge slay suddenly, he will laugh at the trial of the innocent.

²⁴ The earth is given into the hand of the wicked: he covereth the faces of the judges thereof; if not, where, and who is he?

²⁵ Now my days are swifter than a post: they flee away, they see no good.

²⁶ They are passed away as the swift ships: as the eagle that hasteth to the prey.

[27] If I say, I will forget my complaint, I will leave off my heaviness, and comfort myself:

[28] I am afraid of all my sorrows, I know that thou wilt not hold me innocent.

[29] If I be wicked, why then labour I in vain?

[30] If I wash myself with snow water, and make my hands never so clean;

[31] Yet shalt thou plunge me in the ditch, and mine own clothes shall abhor me.

[32] For he is not a man, as I am, that I should answer him, and we should come together in judgment.

[33] Neither is there any daysman betwixt us, that might lay his hand upon us both.

[34] Let him take his rod away from me, and let not his fear terrify me:

[35] Then would I speak, and not fear him; but it is not so with me.

Chapter 10

[1] My soul is weary of my life; I will leave my complaint upon myself; I will speak in the bitterness of my soul.

[2] I will say unto God, Do not condemn me; shew me wherefore thou contendest with me.

[3] Is it good unto thee that thou shouldest oppress, that thou shouldest despise the work of thine hands, and shine upon the counsel of the wicked?

[4] Hast thou eyes of flesh? or seest thou as man seeth?

[5] Are thy days as the days of man? are thy years as man's days,

[6] That thou inquirest after mine iniquity, and searchest after my sin?

[7] Thou knowest that I am not wicked; and there is none that can deliver out of thine hand.

[8] Thine hands have made me and fashioned me together round about; yet thou dost destroy me.

[9] Remember, I beseech thee, that thou hast made me as the clay; and wilt thou bring me into dust again?

[10] Hast thou not poured me out as milk, and curdled me like cheese?

[11] Thou hast clothed me with skin and flesh, and hast fenced me with bones and sinews.

[12] Thou hast granted me life and favour, and thy visitation hath preserved my spirit.

[13] And these things hast thou hid in thine heart: I know that this is with thee.

[14] If I sin, then thou markest me, and thou wilt not acquit me from mine iniquity.

[15] If I be wicked, woe unto me; and if I be righteous, yet will I not lift up my head. I am full of confusion; therefore see thou mine affliction;

[16] For it increaseth. Thou huntest me as a fierce lion: and again thou shewest thyself marvellous upon me.

[17] Thou renewest thy witnesses against me, and increasest thine indignation upon me; changes and war are against me.

[18] Wherefore then hast thou brought me forth out of the womb? Oh that I had given up the ghost, and no eye had seen me!

[19] I should have been as though I had not been; I should have been carried from the womb to the grave.

[20] Are not my days few? cease then, and let me alone, that I may take comfort a little,

[21] Before I go whence I shall not return, even to the land of darkness and the shadow of death;

[22] A land of darkness, as darkness itself; and of the shadow of death, without any order, and where the light is as darkness.

Chapter 11

[1] Then answered Zophar the Naamathite, and said,

2 Should not the multitude of words be answered? and should a man full of talk be justified?

3 Should thy lies make men hold their peace? and when thou mockest, shall no man make thee ashamed?

4 For thou hast said, My doctrine is pure, and I am clean in thine eyes.

5 But oh that God would speak, and open his lips against thee;

6 And that he would shew thee the secrets of wisdom, that they are double to that which is! Know therefore that God exacteth of thee less than thine iniquity deserveth.

7 Canst thou by searching find out God? canst thou find out the Almighty unto perfection?

8 It is as high as heaven; what canst thou do? deeper than hell; what canst thou know?

9 The measure thereof is longer than the earth, and broader than the sea.

10 If he cut off, and shut up, or gather together, then who can hinder him?

11 For he knoweth vain men: he seeth wickedness also; will he not then consider it?

12 For vain man would be wise, though man be born like a wild ass's colt.

13 If thou prepare thine heart, and stretch out thine hands toward him;

14 If iniquity be in thine hand, put it far away, and let not wickedness dwell in thy tabernacles.

15 For then shalt thou lift up thy face without spot; yea, thou shalt be stedfast, and shalt not fear:

16 Because thou shalt forget thy misery, and remember it as waters that pass away:

17 And thine age shall be clearer than the noonday; thou shalt shine forth, thou shalt be as the morning.

18 And thou shalt be secure, because there is hope; yea, thou shalt dig about thee, and thou shalt take thy rest in safety.

19 Also thou shalt lie down, and none shall make thee afraid; yea, many shall make suit unto thee.

20 But the eyes of the wicked shall fail, and they shall not escape, and their hope shall be as the giving up of the ghost.

Chapter 12

1 And Job answered and said,

2 No doubt but ye are the people, and wisdom shall die with you.

3 But I have understanding as well as you; I am not inferior to you: yea, who knoweth not such things as these?

4 I am as one mocked of his neighbour, who calleth upon God, and he answereth him: the just upright man is laughed to scorn.

5 He that is ready to slip with his feet is as a lamp despised in the thought of him that is at ease.

6 The tabernacles of robbers prosper, and they that provoke God are secure; into whose hand God bringeth abundantly.

7 But ask now the beasts, and they shall teach thee; and the fowls of the air, and they shall tell thee:

8 Or speak to the earth, and it shall teach thee: and the fishes of the sea shall declare unto thee.

9 Who knoweth not in all these that the hand of the LORD hath wrought this?

10 In whose hand is the soul of every living thing, and the breath of all mankind.

11 Doth not the ear try words? and the mouth taste his meat?

12 With the ancient is wisdom; and in length of days understanding.

13 With him is wisdom and strength, he hath counsel and understanding.

14 Behold, he breaketh down, and it cannot be built again: he shutteth up a man, and there can be no opening.

¹⁵ Behold, he withholdeth the waters, and they dry up: also he sendeth them out, and they overturn the earth.

¹⁶ With him is strength and wisdom: the deceived and the deceiver are his.

¹⁷ He leadeth counsellors away spoiled, and maketh the judges fools.

¹⁸ He looseth the bond of kings, and girdeth their loins with a girdle.

¹⁹ He leadeth princes away spoiled, and overthroweth the mighty.

²⁰ He removeth away the speech of the trusty, and taketh away the understanding of the aged.

²¹ He poureth contempt upon princes, and weakeneth the strength of the mighty.

²² He discovereth deep things out of darkness, and bringeth out to light the shadow of death.

²³ He increaseth the nations, and destroyeth them: he enlargeth the nations, and straiteneth them again.

²⁴ He taketh away the heart of the chief of the people of the earth, and causeth them to wander in a wilderness where there is no way.

²⁵ They grope in the dark without light, and he maketh them to stagger like a drunken man.

Chapter 13

¹ Lo, mine eye hath seen all this, mine ear hath heard and understood it.

² What ye know, the same do I know also: I am not inferior unto you.

³ Surely I would speak to the Almighty, and I desire to reason with God.

⁴ But ye are forgers of lies, ye are all physicians of no value.

⁵ O that ye would altogether hold your peace! and it should be your wisdom.

⁶ Hear now my reasoning, and hearken to the pleadings of my lips.

⁷ Will ye speak wickedly for God? and talk deceitfully for him?

⁸ Will ye accept his person? will ye contend for God?

⁹ Is it good that he should search you out? or as one man mocketh another, do ye so mock him?

¹⁰ He will surely reprove you, if ye do secretly accept persons.

¹¹ Shall not his excellency make you afraid? and his dread fall upon you?

¹² Your remembrances are like unto ashes, your bodies to bodies of clay.

¹³ Hold your peace, let me alone, that I may speak, and let come on me what will.

¹⁴ Wherefore do I take my flesh in my teeth, and put my life in mine hand?

¹⁵ Though he slay me, yet will I trust in him: but I will maintain mine own ways before him.

¹⁶ He also shall be my salvation: for an hypocrite shall not come before him.

¹⁷ Hear diligently my speech, and my declaration with your ears.

¹⁸ Behold now, I have ordered my cause; I know that I shall be justified.

¹⁹ Who is he that will plead with me? for now, if I hold my tongue, I shall give up the ghost.

²⁰ Only do not two things unto me: then will I not hide myself from thee.

²¹ Withdraw thine hand far from me: and let not thy dread make me afraid.

²² Then call thou, and I will answer: or let me speak, and answer thou me.

²³ How many are mine iniquities and sins? make me to know my transgression and my sin.

²⁴ Wherefore hidest thou thy face, and holdest me for thine enemy?

²⁵ Wilt thou break a leaf driven to and fro? and wilt thou pursue the dry stubble?

²⁶ For thou writest bitter things against me, and makest me to possess the iniquities of my youth.

²⁷ Thou puttest my feet also in the stocks, and lookest narrowly unto all my paths; thou settest a print upon the heels of my feet.

²⁸ And he, as a rotten thing, consumeth, as a garment that is moth eaten.

Chapter 14

¹ Man that is born of a woman is of few days, and full of trouble.

² He cometh forth like a flower, and is cut down: he fleeth also as a shadow, and continueth not.

³ And dost thou open thine eyes upon such an one, and bringest me into judgment with thee?

⁴ Who can bring a clean thing out of an unclean? not one.

⁵ Seeing his days are determined, the number of his months are with thee, thou hast appointed his bounds that he cannot pass;

⁶ Turn from him, that he may rest, till he shall accomplish, as an hireling, his day.

⁷ For there is hope of a tree, if it be cut down, that it will sprout again, and that the tender branch thereof will not cease.

⁸ Though the root thereof wax old in the earth, and the stock thereof die in the ground;

⁹ Yet through the scent of water it will bud, and bring forth boughs like a plant.

¹⁰ But man dieth, and wasteth away: yea, man giveth up the ghost, and where is he?

¹¹ As the waters fail from the sea, and the flood decayeth and drieth up:

¹² So man lieth down, and riseth not: till the heavens be no more, they shall not awake, nor be raised out of their sleep.

¹³ O that thou wouldest hide me in the grave, that thou wouldest keep me secret, until thy wrath be past, that thou wouldest appoint me a set time, and remember me!

¹⁴ If a man die, shall he live again? all the days of my appointed time will I wait, till my change come.

¹⁵ Thou shalt call, and I will answer thee: thou wilt have a desire to the work of thine hands.

¹⁶ For now thou numberest my steps: dost thou not watch over my sin?

¹⁷ My transgression is sealed up in a bag, and thou sewest up mine iniquity.

¹⁸ And surely the mountain falling cometh to nought, and the rock is removed out of his place.

¹⁹ The waters wear the stones: thou washest away the things which grow out of the dust of the earth; and thou destroyest the hope of man.

²⁰ Thou prevailest for ever against him, and he passeth: thou changest his countenance, and sendest him away.

²¹ His sons come to honour, and he knoweth it not; and they are brought low, but he perceiveth it not of them.

²² But his flesh upon him shall have pain, and his soul within him shall mourn.

* * *

Chapter 23

* * *

² Even to-day is my complaint bitter: my stroke is heavier than my groaning.

³ Oh that I knew where I might find him! that I might come even to his seat!

⁴ I would order my cause before him, and fill my mouth with arguments.

⁵ I would know the words which he would answer me, and understand what he would say unto me.

⁶ Will he plead against me with his great power? No; but he would put strength in me.

⁷ There the righteous might dispute with him; so should I be delivered forever from my judge.

⁸ Behold, I go forward, but he is not there; and backward, but I cannot perceive him:

⁹ On the left hand, where he doth work, but I cannot behold him: he hideth himself on the right hand, that I cannot see him:

¹⁰ But he knoweth the way that I take: when he hath tried me, I shall come forth as gold.

¹¹ My foot hath held his steps, his way have I kept, and not declined.

¹² Neither have I gone back from the commandment of his lips; I have esteemed the words of his mouth more than my necessary food.

¹³ But he is in one mind, and who can turn him? and what his soul desireth, even that he doeth.

¹⁴ For he performeth the thing that is appointed for me: and many such things are with him.

¹⁵ Therefore am I troubled at his presence: when I consider, I am afraid of him.

¹⁶ For God maketh my heart soft, and the Almighty troubleth me:

¹⁷ Because I was not cut off before the darkness, neither hath he covered the darkness from my face.

* * *

Chapter 26

* * *

⁶ Hell is naked before him, and destruction hath no covering.

⁷ He stretcheth out the north over the empty place, and hangeth the earth upon nothing.

⁸ He bindeth up the waters in his thick clouds; and the cloud is not rent under them.

⁹ He holdeth back the face of his throne, and spreadeth his cloud upon it.

¹⁰ He hath compassed the waters with bounds, until the day and night come to an end.

¹¹ The pillars of heaven tremble and are astonished at his reproof.

¹² He divideth the sea with his power, and by his understanding he smiteth through the proud.

¹³ By his spirit he hath garnished the heavens; his hand hath formed the crooked serpent.

¹⁴ Lo, these are parts of his ways: but how little a portion is heard of him? but the thunder of his power who can understand?

Chapter 27

¹ Moreover Job continued his parable, and said,

² As God liveth, who hath taken away my judgment; and the Almighty, who hath vexed my soul;

³ All the while my breath is in me, and the spirit of God is in my nostrils;

⁴ My lips shall not speak wickedness, nor my tongue utter deceit.

⁵ God forbid that I should justify you: till I die I will not remove mine integrity from me.

⁶ My righteousness I hold fast, and will not let it go: my heart shall not reproach me so long as I live.

* * *

Chapter 31

* * *

⁴ Doth not he see my ways, and count all my steps?

⁵ If I have walked with vanity, or if my foot hath hasted to deceit;

⁶ Let me be weighed in an even balance, that God may know mine integrity.

⁷ If my step hath turned out of the way, and mine heart walked after mine eyes, and if any blot hath cleaved to mine hands;

⁸ Then let me sow, and let another eat; yea, let my offspring be rooted out.

⁹ If mine heart have been deceived by a woman, or if I have laid wait at my neighbour's door;

[10] Then let my wife grind unto another, and let others bow down upon her.

[11] For this is an heinous crime; yea, it is an iniquity to be punished by the judges.

[12] For it is a fire that consumeth to destruction, and would root out all mine increase.

[13] If I did despise the cause of my manservant or of my maidservant, when they contended with me;

[14] What then shall I do when God riseth up? and when he visiteth, what shall I answer him?

[15] Did not he that made me in the womb make him? and did not one fashion us in the womb?

[16] If I have withheld the poor from their desire, or have caused the eyes of the widow to fail;

[17] Or have eaten my morsel myself alone, and the fatherless hath not eaten thereof;

[18] (For from my youth he was brought up with me, as with a father, and I have guided her from my mother's womb;)

[19] If I have seen any perish for want of clothing, or any poor without covering;

[20] If his loins have not blessed me, and if he were not warmed with the fleece of my sheep;

[21] If I have lifted up my hand against the fatherless, when I saw my help in the gate:

[22] Then let mine arm fall from my shoulder blade, and mine arm be broken from the bone.

[23] For destruction from God was a terror to me, and by reason of his highness I could not endure.

[24] If I have made gold my hope, or have said to the fine gold, Thou art my confidence;

[25] If I rejoiced because my wealth was great, and because mine hand had gotten much;

[26] If I beheld the sun when it shined, or the moon walking in brightness;

[27] And my heart hath been secretly enticed, or my mouth hath kissed my hand:

[28] This also were an iniquity to be punished by the judge: for I should have denied the God that is above.

[29] If I rejoiced at the destruction of him that hated me, or lifted up myself when evil found him:

[30] Neither have I suffered my mouth to sin by wishing a curse to his soul.

[31] If the men of my tabernacle said not, Oh that we had of his flesh! we cannot be satisfied.

[32] The stranger did not lodge in the street: but I opened my doors to the traveller.

[33] If I covered my transgressions as Adam, by hiding mine iniquity in my bosom:

[34] Did I fear a great multitude, or did the contempt of families terrify me, that I kept silence, and went not out of the door?

[35] Oh that one would hear me! behold, my desire is, that the Almighty would answer me, and that mine adversary had written a book.

[36] Surely I would take it upon my shoulder, and bind it as a crown to me.

[37] I would declare unto him the number of my steps; as a prince would I go near unto him.

[38] If my land cry against me, or that the furrows likewise thereof complain;

[39] If I have eaten the fruits thereof without money, or have caused the owners thereof to lose their life:

[40] Let thistles grow instead of wheat, and cockle instead of barley. The words of Job are ended.

Chapter 32

[1] So these three men ceased to answer Job, because he was righteous in his own eyes.

* * *

Chapter 38

¹ Then the LORD answered Job out of the whirlwind, and said,

² Who is this that darkeneth counsel by words without knowledge?

³ Gird up now thy loins like a man; for I will demand of thee, and answer thou me.

⁴ Where wast thou when I laid the foundations of the earth? declare, if thou hast understanding.

⁵ Who hath laid the measures thereof, if thou knowest? or who hath stretched the line upon it?

⁶ Whereupon are the foundations thereof fastened? or who laid the corner stone thereof;

⁷ When the morning stars sang together, and all the sons of God shouted for joy?

* * *

Chapter 39

¹ Knowest thou the time when the wild goats of the rock bring forth? or canst thou mark when the hinds do calve?

² Canst thou number the months that they fulfil? or knowest thou the time when they bring forth?

³ They bow themselves, they bring forth their young ones, they cast out their sorrows.

⁴ Their young ones are in good liking, they grow up with corn; they go forth, and return not unto them.

⁵ Who hath sent out the wild ass free? or who hath loosed the bands of the wild ass?

⁶ Whose house I have made the wilderness, and the barren land his dwellings.

⁷ He scorneth the multitude of the city, neither regardeth he the crying of the driver.

⁸ The range of the mountains is his pasture, and he searcheth after every green thing.

⁹ Will the unicorn be willing to serve thee, or abide by thy crib?

¹⁰ Canst thou bind the unicorn with his band in the furrow? or will he harrow the valleys after thee?

¹¹ Wilt thou trust him, because his strength is great? or wilt thou leave thy labour to him?

¹² Wilt thou believe him, that he will bring home thy seed, and gather it into thy barn?

¹³ Gavest thou the goodly wings unto the peacocks? or wings and feathers unto the ostrich?

¹⁴ Which leaveth her eggs in the earth, and warmeth them in dust,

¹⁵ And forgetteth that the foot may crush them, or that the wild beast may break them.

¹⁶ She is hardened against her young ones, as though they were not hers: her labour is in vain without fear;

¹⁷ Because God hath deprived her of wisdom, neither hath he imparted to her understanding.

¹⁸ What time she lifteth up herself on high, she scorneth the horse and his rider.

¹⁹ Hast thou given the horse strength? hast thou clothed his neck with thunder?

²⁰ Canst thou make him afraid as a grasshopper? the glory of his nostrils is terrible.

²¹ He paweth in the valley, and rejoiceth in his strength: he goeth on to meet the armed men.

²² He mocketh at fear, and is not affrighted; neither turneth he back from the sword.

²³ The quiver rattleth against him, the glittering spear and the shield.

²⁴ He swalloweth the ground with fierceness and rage: neither believeth he that it is the sound of the trumpet.

²⁵ He saith among the trumpets, Ha, ha; and he smelleth the battle afar off, the thunder of the captains, and the shouting.

26 Doth the hawk fly by thy wisdom, and stretch her wings toward the south?

27 Doth the eagle mount up at thy command, and make her nest on high?

28 She dwelleth and abideth on the rock, upon the crag of the rock, and the strong place.

29 From thence she seeketh the prey, and her eyes behold afar off.

30 Her young ones also suck up blood: and where the slain are, there is she.

Chapter 40

1 Moreover the LORD answered Job, and said,

2 Shall he that contendeth with the Almighty instruct him? he that reproveth God, let him answer it.

3 Then Job answered the LORD, and said,

4 Behold, I am vile; what shall I answer thee? I will lay mine hand upon my mouth.

5 Once have I spoken; but I will not answer: yea, twice; but I will proceed no further.

6 Then answered the LORD unto Job out of the whirlwind, and said,

7 Gird up thy loins now like a man: I will demand of thee, and declare thou unto me.

8 Wilt thou also disannul my judgment? wilt thou condemn me, that thou mayest be righteous?

9 Hast thou an arm like God? or canst thou thunder with a voice like him?

10 Deck thyself now with majesty and excellency; and array thyself with glory and beauty.

11 Cast abroad the rage of thy wrath: and behold every one that is proud, and abase him.

12 Look on every one that is proud, and bring him low; and tread down the wicked in their place.

13 Hide them in the dust together; and bind their faces in secret.

14 Then will I also confess unto thee that thine own right hand can save thee.

15 Behold now behemoth, which I made with thee; he eateth grass as an ox.

16 Lo now, his strength is in his loins, and his force is in the navel of his belly.

17 He moveth his tail like a cedar: the sinews of his stones are wrapped together.

18 His bones are as strong pieces of brass; his bones are like bars of iron.

19 He is the chief of the ways of God: he that made him can make his sword to approach unto him.

20 Surely the mountains bring him forth food, where all the beasts of the field play.

21 He lieth under the shady trees, in the covert of the reed, and fens.

22 The shady trees cover him with their shadow; the willows of the brook compass him about.

23 Behold, he drinketh up a river, and hasteth not: he trusteth that he can draw up Jordan into his mouth.

24 He taketh it with his eyes: his nose pierceth through snares.

Chapter 41

1 Canst thou draw out leviathan with an hook? or his tongue with a cord which thou lettest down?

2 Canst thou put an hook into his nose? or bore his jaw through with a thorn?

3 Will he make many supplications unto thee? will he speak soft words unto thee?

4 Will he make a covenant with thee? wilt thou take him for a servant for ever?

5 Wilt thou play with him as with a bird? or wilt thou bind him for thy maidens?

⁶ Shall the companions make a banquet of him? shall they part him among the merchants?

⁷ Canst thou fill his skin with barbed iron? or his head with fish spears?

⁸ Lay thine hand upon him, remember the battle, do no more.

⁹ Behold, the hope of him is in vain: shall not one be cast down even at the sight of him?

¹⁰ None is so fierce that dare stir him up: who then is able to stand before me?

¹¹ Who hath prevented me, that I should repay him? whatsoever is under the whole heaven is mine.

¹² I will not conceal his parts, nor his power, nor his comely proportion.

¹³ Who can discover the face of his garment? or who can come to him with his double bridle?

¹⁴ Who can open the doors of his face? his teeth are terrible round about.

¹⁵ His scales are his pride, shut up together as with a close seal.

¹⁶ One is so near to another, that no air can come between them.

¹⁷ They are joined one to another, they stick together, that they cannot be sundered.

¹⁸ By his neesings a light doth shine, and his eyes are like the eyelids of the morning.

¹⁹ Out of his mouth go burning lamps, and sparks of fire leap out.

²⁰ Out of his nostrils goeth smoke, as out of a seething pot or caldron.

²¹ His breath kindleth coals, and a flame goeth out of his mouth.

²² In his neck remaineth strength, and sorrow is turned into joy before him.

²³ The flakes of his flesh are joined together: they are firm in themselves; they cannot be moved.

²⁴ His heart is as firm as a stone; yea, as hard as a piece of the nether millstone.

²⁵ When he raiseth up himself, the mighty are afraid: by reason of breakings they purify themselves.

²⁶ The sword of him that layeth at him cannot hold: the spear, the dart, nor the habergeon.

²⁷ He esteemeth iron as straw, and brass as rotten wood.

²⁸ The arrow cannot make him flee: slingstones are turned with him into stubble.

²⁹ Darts are counted as stubble: he laugheth at the shaking of a spear.

³⁰ Sharp stones are under him: he spreadeth sharp pointed things upon the mire.

³¹ He maketh the deep to boil like a pot: he maketh the sea like a pot of ointment.

³² He maketh a path to shine after him; one would think the deep to be hoary.

³³ Upon earth there is not his like, who is made without fear.

³⁴ He beholdeth all high things: he is a king over all the children of pride.

Chapter 42

¹ Then Job answered the LORD, and said,

² I know that thou canst do every thing, and that no thought can be withholden from thee.

³ Who is he that hideth counsel without knowledge? therefore have I uttered that I understood not; things too wonderful for me, which I knew not.

⁴ Hear, I beseech thee, and I will speak: I will demand of thee, and declare thou unto me.

⁵ I have heard of thee by the hearing of the ear: but now mine eye seeth thee.

⁶ Wherefore I abhor myself, and repent in dust and ashes.

⁷ And it was so, that after the LORD had spoken these words unto Job, the LORD said to Eliphaz the Temanite, My wrath is kindled against thee, and against thy two friends: for ye have not spoken of me the thing that is right, as my servant Job hath.

⁸ Therefore take unto you now seven bullocks and seven rams, and go to my servant Job, and offer up for yourselves a burnt offering; and my servant Job shall pray for you: for him will I accept: lest I deal with you after your folly, in that ye have not spoken of me the thing which is right, like my servant Job.

⁹ So Eliphaz the Temanite and Bildad the Shuhite and Zophar the Naamathite went, and did according as the LORD commanded them: the LORD also accepted Job.

¹⁰ And the LORD turned the captivity of Job, when he prayed for his friends: also the LORD gave Job twice as much as he had before.

¹¹ Then came there unto him all his brethren, and all his sisters, and all they that had been of his acquaintance before, and did eat bread with him in his house: and they bemoaned him, and comforted him over all the evil that the LORD had brought upon him: every man also gave him a piece of money, and every one an earring of gold.

¹² So the LORD blessed the latter end of Job more than his beginning: for he had fourteen thousand sheep, and six thousand camels, and a thousand yoke of oxen, and a thousand she asses.

¹³ He had also seven sons and three daughters.

¹⁴ And he called the name of the first, Jemima; and the name of the second, Kezia; and the name of the third, Keren-happuch.

¹⁵ And in all the land were no women found so fair as the daughters of Job: and their father gave them inheritance among their brethren.

¹⁶ After this lived Job an hundred and forty years, and saw his sons, and his sons' sons, even four generations.

¹⁷ So Job died, being old and full of days.

Notes

1. *The Mysteries of Job.* Why did God enter into a wager with Satan (chapters 1–2)? Why was God so angry with Job (chapters 38–41)? What if the *Book of Job* had ended with chapter 42 verse 6?

In what sense may it be said that *Job* is nonfiction prose? May it be equally well categorized as fiction? As poetry?

2. *Analytical Psychology.* C.G. Jung, in his book *Answer to Job* (1954), places a very unorthodox interpretation on the *Book of Job.* He views God and Satan as essentially the same entity. At the end, after Job placates God, God begins his ascent back to heaven and then suddenly realizes that Job has tricked him by his extravagant protestations of humility and shame. ("Wherefore I abhor myself, and repent in dust and ashes," 42:6). Job's ingratiating remarks might be compared to the approach of a manipulative lawyer. It is at this point, according to Jung, that God realizes he does not understand the mind of the creature he has created—man. The only way he can ever do so is to become a man himself, in the form of his son Jesus Christ. God decides on an immaculate conception, to avoid the intervention of a male, who may be associated with the satanical side of God.

3. *J.B.* Archibald MacLeish, who was primarily a poet, in 1958 wrote his powerful verse drama, *J.B.,* which won him his third Pulitzer Prize.

There, two second-rate actors are singled out to play God and Satan in a reenactment of the story of the *Book of Job.* While the conversation throughout the play is generally informal and breezy, it takes on a spine-chilling seriousness whenever the two two-bit actors raise their masks to their faces to recite the words of God and Satan, as given in the *Book of Job.*

J.B. (Job) is a hale-fellow-well-met, George Babbitt sort of person. His wife is ever fearful of their good fortune. When the family's downfall comes, she leaves Job because she can't bear to witness his misery. At the end, she returns, and they decide to start all over again.

4. *The King James Bible.* The King James Bible (1611), largely based on an earlier English translation by William Tyndale (1492–1536), is widely recognized as one of the greatest works of literature in the English language. Alister McGrath, in his book IN THE BEGINNING (2001), notes at page 310 that the purpose of the King James translators was to produce a book that was simply written so as to "be understood even of the very vulgar," to the end that they might discover "the doorway to salvation." In the process, they accidentally produced a "classic work of English literature.... Sadly, we shall never see its equal—or even its like—again."

What verses from *Ecclesiastes* or *Job* do you find beautiful? Why? What features of the verses make then beautiful to you?

McGrath also asserts that the King James translators deliberately used a number of words and phrases that were archaic even in 1611. An example is the distinction between "thee" and "you," which was even then dying out. Which aspects of the verses from *Ecclesiastes* and *Job* are archaic to the modern reader? Do these archaic aspects enhance or obstruct your enjoyment of the verses? Why?

XVII. MEDITATION
John Donne

PERCHANCE hee for whom this Bell tolls, may be so ill, as that he knowes not it tolls for him; And perchance I may thinke my selfe so much better than I am, as that they who are about mee, and see my state, may have caused it to toll for mee, and I know not that. The *Church* is *Catholike, universall*, so are all her *Actions*; *All* that she does, belongs to *all*. When she *baptizes a child,* that action concernes mee; for that child is thereby connected to that *Head* which is my Head too, and engraffed into that body, whereof I am a *member*. And when she *buries* a *Man*, that action concernes me: All *mankinde* is of one *Author*, and is one *volume*; when one Man dies, one *Chapter* is not torne out of the *booke*, but *translated* into a better *language*; and every *Chapter* must be so *translated*; God emploies several *translators*; some peeces are translated by *age*, some by *sicknesse*, some by *warre*, some by *justice*; but *Gods* hand is in every *translation*; and his hand shall binde up all our scattered leaves againe, for that *Librarie* where every *booke* shall lie open to one another: As therefore the *Bell* that rings to a *Sermon*, calls not upon the *Preacher* onely, but upon the *Congregation* to come; so this *Bell* calls us all: but how much more mee, who am brought so neere the *doore* by this *sicknesse*. There was a *contention* as farre as a *suite*, (in which both *pietie* and *dignitie*, *religion*, and *estimation*, were mingled) which of the religious *Orders* should ring to *praiers* first in the *Morning*; and it was *determined* that *they should ring first that rose earliest*. If we understand aright the *dignitie* of this *Belle* that tolls for our *evening prayer*, wee would bee glad to make it ours, by rising early, in that *application*, that it might bee ours, as wel as his, whose indeed it is. The Bell doth toll for him that *thinkes* it doth; and though it intermit againe, yet from that *minute*, that that occasion wrought upon him, hee is united to *God*. Who casts not up his *Eye* to the *Sunne* when it rises? but who takes off his *Eye* from a *Comet* when that breakes out? Who bends not his *eare* to any *bell*, which upon any occasion rings? but who can remove it from that bell, which is passing a *peece of himselfe* out of this *world*? No man is an *Iland*, intire of it selfe; every man is a peece of the *Continent*, a part of the *maine*; if a Clod bee washed away by the *Sea*, *Europe* is the lesse, as well as if a *Promontorie* were, as well as if a *Mannor* of thy *friends* or of *thine owne* were; any mans *death* diminishes *me*, because I am involved in *Mankinde*; And therefore never send to know for whom the *bell* tolls; It tolls for *thee*. Neither can we call this a *begging* of *Miserie* or a *borrowing* of *Miserie*, as though we were not miserable enough of our selves, but must fetch in more from the next house, in taking upon us the *Miserie* of our *Neighbours*. Truly it were an excusable *covetousnesse* if wee did; for *affliction* is a treasure, and scarce any man hath enough of it. No man hath *affliction* enough that is not matured, and ripened by it, and made fit for God by that affliction. If a man carry *treasure* in bullion, or in a *wedge of gold*, and have none coined into *currant Monies*, his *treasure* will not defray him as he travells. *Tribulation* is *Treasure* in the *nature* of it, but it is not *currant money* in the *use* of it, except wee get nearer and nearer our *home*, *Heaven*, by it. Another man may be sicke too, and sick to *death*, and this *affliction* may lie in his *bowels*, as *gold* in a *Mine*, and be of no use to him; but this *bell*, that tells me of his *affliction*, digs out, and applies that *gold* to *mee*: if by this consideration of anothers danger, I take mine owne into contemplation, and so secure my selfe, by making my recourse to my *God*, who is our onely securitie.

Note

1. *Famous Quotes.* This Meditation by John Donne contains two familiar quotations: "No man is an island" and "Ask not for whom the bell tolls—it tolls for thee." How is your understanding of these quotes affected by reading them in their original literary context?

* * *

Twylah Nitsch was born on the Cattaraugus Indian Reservation, home of the Seneca Tribe in upstate New York. She was a spiritual teacher of the Seneca Wolf Clan from her youth. She attended high school, but dropped out of college during the Great Depression. She has traveled widely as a lecturer in the United States and Europe. She is the author of four books on the mythologies and philosophies of Native Americans. The following is an essay on her philosophy of life.

SHE WHOSE VOICE RIDES ON THE WIND
Twylah Nitsch

We should never say *try*. We should say *trust*. Trust means that whatever work you are aspiring toward will be done well, with power and conviction and *energy* behind it. If you are standing in the middle of the river, "trying" is like placing a big boulder in the middle of the river; it stops the energy flow in midstream. Only *trust* will keep the energy going forward.

When I was a child, I was told by my elders, my two grandparents who raised me, that the most important thing was to recognize my own truth. As long as I knew what the truth was, my dignity, my integrity, and my stability would always be assured. When I was little, I was a handful, always getting into things, but nobody ever hit me. *Ever*. The first thing the elders would say was, "Are you happy?" And I would stop and think and listen to my truth within. If I said yes, they would say, "Maybe you should think again. Maybe you can't see ahead to how you might get hurt." Getting hurt meant that there could be some kind of pain, the pain I could cause myself by not knowing my truth. So I was warned: If I continued, I would be solely responsible for the consequences—the pain—that would follow. That is how I learned the difference between right and wrong: Right is comfort, wrong is pain.

In Native culture, children are regarded as teachers, because they have not yet had any experience of having their truth and their trust chipped away by people who want to control them. Elders are also honored as teachers, because they have already performed their duties of learning and working and raising families, and what they have learned it is their responsibility and honor to teach. But when I was five years old, the government said that it was time for me to go to school, away from the reservation and into the home of a white family. That was my first look at the discrepancies between the two cultures.

In the home of the first family I lived with, there was a little girl my own age who was constantly being spanked by her mother. This mother was *huge*, and she was always hitting her child for something that was not very important, or for something that was the mother's own fault. There was very little discipline and almost no consistency in the house, so that it was hard to know what was acceptable and what would be punished. One day, she grabbed her daughter by the ear, yanked her down over her knee, and started hitting her. I went right up to her and said, "Stop! You're hurting your little girl!" At first, I couldn't understand why there was always so much yelling and screaming going on in that house. Afterward, I understood that this mother had no balance, no self-direction, because she didn't know what she wanted from one minute to the next. And it seemed to me that the reason was that she was not centered, she did not have an inner truth that she could depend on.

I also learned about competitiveness and jealousy from living in that house. The little girl disliked me from the beginning, because she was forced to share her bed with me. I knew immediately that I was in her space, and that it would be natural for her to resent me. I tried to stay as quiet as I could, so she wouldn't have any reason to resent me. Her parents forced her to take piano lessons, which she absolutely hated with a passion. I would listen to her practice, and taught myself how to play by ear. One day, her parents asked us both to play for their guests. I tried to refuse, but they insisted. And because the little girl hated the piano, she played badly, and because I love it, I played from my heart. After that day, she never liked me. I tried to make her my friend. I told her I would never again play the piano and that she was doing a good job, and anyway, if we were friends it wouldn't matter so much. But she rejected my apologies and refused to ever walk to school with me again or be my friend. I saw that there would never be any possibility of friendship between us, because there was no *wholeness* in that culture, everyone being in competition with each other, rather than in *cooperation,* as I had been taught. So the culture was not compatible to either of us.

At school, I was different from all the other children. I didn't talk like them, didn't gossip, didn't giggle, didn't chatter; I never said anything unless I had something to say. I felt that some of the teachers were only interested in getting their paychecks at the end of the week, that they were not committed to teaching, but just to putting in their time. They would promise us many things, like a trip to the zoo, then not keep their word. I was very puzzled by that. Where I came from, people never made a promise they couldn't keep.

The second family I lived with loved me and accepted me as if I were their own daughter. The four boys in the family were just like the brothers I never had—kind, gentle, and sensitive. I saw them hurt and misused at various times—being lied to, promised a reward for work they had done that never materialized, being stood up by a friend—and that hurt *me,* too. Native people are taught that male energy is protective and female energy is nourishing and that we have both male and female capacities within ourselves. When the boys were hurt, I saw that males were just as susceptible to getting their feelings hurt as girls. The lesson there was, again, the value of truth: Dignity and self-esteem suffer when children are lied to. And because I loved them, I took on their suffering just as if it were my own.

Every summer, I would go back home and relearn the lessons of my elders: respect, self-respect, truth. Many people talk about how much they love their children, but few know what love really is. This society is bent on destroying self-esteem within its children. Children are deprived of the love and comfort they need when they're told they don't know anything, they're stupid, they're unworthy of being treated with respect.

That can make them doubt their own truth. All children are born knowing what their truth is, but that can be compromised when people are constantly lying to you. It can change that posture of trust that we were born to have toward life. Trust is the thought, love is the action, and truth is the source.

Living in the homes of white families during the school year was a huge culture shock to me. The lesson was that not all people live alike, not everyone thinks alike. I knew I would be rubbing elbows with all kinds of people all through my life and that I had to learn to get along with even incompatible people and look for the truth within each person. If I saw examples of meanness, lying, disrespect, lack of integrity, I realized that they were not living their truth, and therefore had all kinds of lessons to learn. Whenever I encountered such people, I used to write a tiny mark on the steps of their house that nobody could see except me. If I made a mark in orange crayon, it meant that they didn't keep promises. A pencil mark meant that they had poor judgment and lacked integrity. Pink meant they lacked compassion. A circle meant that they were whole, complete, but a straight line meant they had a long way to go. I was learning about all these other people, deciding whether or not I wanted to be their friend. I decided that it was up to me to be available if they wanted to be friends but that it didn't affect *my* truth in any way if they didn't. Later, I was ashamed that I had defaced the entrances of their homes and went around and rubbed them off.

In Native culture, children are given names before they are born. When my mother was pregnant with me, my mother was told by her father that she would have a little girl, that the girl would be fragile, and that her name would be Yehwehnod, which means "She Whose Voice Rides on the Wind." It would be my destiny, grandfather said, to live that name.

There is an ancient story that was handed down through the generations to my elders. There were four people of wisdom—one deaf, one sightless, one crippled, and one forgetful—who used to sit together all the time. One day, there was a total eclipse of the sun, the world became dark, and the people were very frightened. A hand appeared in the sky, and a voice thundered down, saying, "See this hand, four fingers and a thumb, when the hand is closed, all fingers become united, the hand becomes one." When the four people of wisdom heard the message, they came as teachers to our people to teach this lesson of unity—that the necessity for growth sometimes requires going deaf before we can hear, blind before we can remember. So before I was born, my destiny was given to me: I knew that my physical body was fragile and that I would have to learn my lessons through the frailty of my body. My grandfather said that before my voice could be heard in the world, I had to experience the loss of my senses and then regain them in order to see, hear, and move in the right direction.

When I was still in high school, I lost my hearing for eight months. Because I couldn't hear anything, I wasn't distracted by noise or chatter.

I began to write poetry, because I wasn't only *listening* to my inner truth, I was able to *hear* it much better. My deafness introduced me to my spirit teachers, who speak in poetry form. Spirit teachers need this sort of communication to make a connection with human beings on earth. Each teacher expresses a particular rhythm; thus the need for rhyming. Years later—I can't remember exactly how many years because time loses its meaning when you can't see the clock—I went blind. It was wonderful being blind. It gave me a measure of awareness into the dimensions of time, space, distance, the shape and weight of the world, that I wouldn't have had otherwise. The lesson in blindness is that you have to *see*, not just look. When you're blind, all of your other senses are heightened and magnified, which increases your sensitivity to the living world, to its beauty and perfection. Anyone can do it, we can all get into that dimension, if we choose. All we have to do is close our eyes and focus on our truth within.

I'm having trouble with my eyes now, but I have no fear of blindness, because I've been there. I'm grateful that I have seen trees, I have seen my family, my friends, the mountains, the sun and the moon—I've seen everything. I don't have to feel that I am being deprived of seeing nature. Everyone has to go through some darkness sometime, but if you've already experienced blindness, it holds no unexpected terror, the terror of the unknown. Eyesight is a bonus.

I learned very, very young, even before I went to live with white people, about the cycles that women go through—from childhood to procreation to old age to death—and that this cycle was natural, and therefore sacred. There is only one time in life set aside for producing children, and only one mate for that purpose. I knew that sex was sacred, because it's part of a natural function of bodies, and you don't play around with anything that's natural. I had a reputation in high school of being untouchable—the boys used to say I had a cement wall around me. I loved to go out, have fun, and dance, but sex was sacred and limited to one true mate, and I hadn't found him yet. When I did find him, I married him right away. We went to live in my ancestral home, in the same house my mother and I were born in. He was a wonderful person of Dutch descent, and his mother put him, her only child, out of her life because he had married an "Indian." He often said that my mother and dad were more parents to him than his own. We had four children, two girls and two boys, and right after my last child was born, I became a cripple.

The doctors had given me a spinal block for anesthesia during the delivery, and there was some kind of injury to my spinal cord. I went completely numb in my legs and feet. For three years, I couldn't walk. I had to find alternate ways to move—a wheelchair, crawling on the floor, pulling my body behind me like a frog.... Because it was my destiny to teach people how to heal themselves, and my students would be people with multiple disabilities, and I needed to understand where they were coming from. I felt, in my own body, what it was like to be crippled, and was grateful for the opportunity to become more aware, more sensitive, and more compassionate toward other cripples. That was the lesson I was supposed to learn. Every time I lost something, I never asked, "Why is this happening to me?" I asked, "What can I learn from this?" My grandfather had told my mother that I would overcome all these handicaps, so I *trusted* that I would. And I did.

I was raised both in my own culture's religion and in Christianity, and I have no quarrel with any religion one chooses to embrace. I had fun with all the churches I went to, and as far as Jesus Christ is concerned, I think he was a good man who got a lousy deal, being hung up on the cross like that. The main drawback I saw to Christianity was that every time, as a Christian, you summon up the image of God, it is always a male image, and my culture raises us to understand that the Supreme Being contains both male and female energy. The worst thing that happens to humankind is when the *truth within* is taken away and put out on a cloud somewhere *out there*. Then people who are looking for God start looking in the wrong place, because God is and always was and forever will be within. *Separation* rather than unity, and *control* rather than freedom, became the way the word of God was disseminated. Western cultures seem to want to divide everything into light and dark, good and evil, the right way and the wrong way. They do not realize that everything is light, we are all beings of light. We have no darkness within us, we have *lessons* within us. Blackness is listening and thinking, harmony; there is nothing more harmonious than black. When the Western cultures accuse somebody of being evil, they are blinder than I was when I lost my vision. Turn *evil* around and it spells *live*.

My husband and I raised four children and were very happy together for fifty years. Just before he died in my arms, I said to him, "Oh, please don't go yet, Bob," and then I remembered something that had happened when I was seven years old. I was home for summer, and one morning I was awakened by a huge bump, as if something heavy had been dropped on my bed. I opened my eyes and saw a gigantic rat staring at me. The rat looked into my eyes and I looked into his eyes, and something happened to both of us in that moment. It sounds ridiculous, but I saw the truth of his being in the eyes of that rat, and he saw the truth in mine. *Love* was exchanged between us. Then the cat jumped up onto the bed and started mauling the rat. The two of them were fighting, screeching, making horrible noises. I ran downstairs to call my grandparents, and when we all got back upstairs, the cat and the rat lay dead on the floor in a pool of blood. I was horrified. We buried them together in one box, in a deep hole in the backyard. My grandmother said, "This is good, burying their bodies together. They have finished their work and learned their lessons, and now they're going back to earth where they came from." After that, I was never again afraid of death. I saw the very, very thin line that separates life and death, that they are two parts of the same whole, the vital energy that can never and will never be lost. So when Bob was dying and I begged him not to go, I said, "No, I can't say that to you. You've finished your work, and that's wonderful! You certainly can go, and we'll talk later on." I rejoiced that I had the chance to know him, to be with him for fifty years, and felt the peace that comes from acceptance and gratitude for being allowed to take this earthwalk with him, even though his life was now coming to an end. And that gave me so much comfort, knowing that everything was exactly as it was supposed to be, that life and death are exactly as they are supposed to be. So I wasn't miserable that he was gone, but happy that his work was done. I didn't emphasize the horror of his dying; I emphasized the release, the learning. Because death is an experience that we all have to learn. And I knew I would see him again when my earthwalk was over. There is no death, just a change into a different dimension.

Before he died, my grandfather, reminding me of my destiny, said to me, "You will continue where I leave off. Your voice will appear in the world." He said it was time to start writing down the teachings so that they wouldn't get lost. I vaguely recall making a promise to him that I would do what he asked. Then, just before my mother died, she sat down next to me in the kitchen and said, "I'm getting tired. I've taught you everything I know, and now it's time for you to carry on." She walked to the sink and threw her blood pressure pills down the drain. We spent the next twelve days talking, and then on the twelfth day, she took the hearing aids out of her ears, and died a few hours later, at the age of eighty-five. I was living within the white society and had forgotten the teachings. I was very busy, working as a teacher and raising my children with my husband and constantly running around all the time. I had decided, years ago, that I didn't want my voice to be heard in the world. I felt that no one was really listening, anyway. It seemed to me that most people thought they knew everything already, and therefore their eyes and ears were closed to the truth. And so I began to feel that what I had to say wasn't important.

As a child living within the white society, I was considered slightly abnormal, because I was always foretelling things that made people uncomfortable. I was constantly told to be quiet, not to talk about "stuff like that." When I was alone in my room, in silence and in stillness, I would hear voices talking to me in poetry. I knew that these voices were not *mine,* not consciously, but they matched the deep truth within that I recognized as my own. Although I felt these images powerfully, I never wrote them down, except during that one period in high school when I lost my hearing. Later, I shut the voices out completely, feeling that my ability to discern the difference between lies and truth might be misused. I was fighting my destiny; I needed to be writing, but I didn't want to write. So when I was already in my seventies, the first thing that happened was that my dear old friend who I hadn't seen in years came to visit me, and when I saw his face, I was so happy to see him that I hugged him, and he hugged me so hard, he broke two of my ribs. Everyone in the room heard the noise of my ribs cracking. Then a week later, I fell and fractured my kneecap. Before that, I was still running around doing things, not writing, but when I broke my knee, my destiny spoke out, saying, "You have not been responsible, you have not been disciplined, you must now sit down and do nothing but write." So I was forced to stay in the house and begin writing down the teachings. I don't really care anymore whether it sounds good or is acceptable to people; I'm just writing because it's my responsibility to do so. And I think that it's not just my own destiny but the destiny of everyone, somehow, some way, to make their voice, their inner truth, heard in the world.

A lot of people running around these days calling themselves healers, but no one is a healer. How can anyone feel someone else's pain? Only the sick person knows what his inner truth is. Healing is attracting truth, and truth can only move through silence. So when someone is sick, we teach them to be silent, to listen to their truth within. If they don't know their own inner truth, there are guidelines to help them heal themselves, to awaken their awareness of what they can do for themselves. People sometimes call me a healer, but that is not an accurate description of what I do. I teach people to give thanks. Not to pray, because prayer is asking for a favor. In giving thanks, we ask for nothing for ourselves, because everything we need is already here, provided by Mother Earth. The trees are growing, the rivers are flowing. . . . Everything is as it should be. Healing means gratitude—gratitude for being allowed to perform this earthwalk, to be given the gifts of Mother Earth, knowing they're walking *with* the earth, not *on* her. Healing is being grateful for being allowed to survive. In one's own nature is the clue, the key to healing, and that key is gratitude, the source of which is truth.

* * *

Gao Xingjian, novelist, playwright, critic, and painter, was born in 1940 in Ganzhou, Jiangxi province, in southeastern China. During several years of forced labor during the Cultural Revolution, he burned all his existing manuscripts. He was finally permitted to publish his writings in 1979 and became recognized for his essays, fiction, and experimental plays. Facing increased official harassment during the 1980's, he emigrated to France in 1987 and became a French citizen. Thereafter his works were banned in China. Perhaps his best-known works in the West are his novels *Soul Mountain* and *One Man's Bible*.

The following is his speech accepting the Nobel Prize in Literature at Stockholm, Sweden in 2000.

THE CASE FOR LITERATURE
Gao Xingjian[1]

I have no way of knowing whether it was fate that has pushed me onto this dais but as various lucky coincidences have created this opportunity I may as well call it fate. Putting aside discussion of the existence or non-existence of God, I would like to say that despite my being an atheist I have always shown reverence for the unknowable.

A person cannot be God, certainly not replace God, and rule the world as a Superman; he will only succeed in creating more chaos and

1. Translated by Mabel Lee; translation provided by the Nobel Foundation.

make a greater mess of the world. In the century after Nietzsche man-made disasters left the blackest records in the history of mankind. Supermen of all types called leader of the people, head of the nation and commander of the race did not baulk at resorting to various violent means in perpetrating crimes that in no way resemble the ravings of a very egotistic philosopher. However, I do not wish to waste this talk on literature by saying too much about politics and history, what I want to do is to use this opportunity to speak as one writer in the voice of an individual.

A writer is an ordinary person, perhaps he is more sensitive but people who are highly sensitive are often more frail. A writer does not speak as the spokesperson of the people or as the embodiment of righteousness. His voice is inevitably weak but it is precisely this voice of the individual that is more authentic.

What I want to say here is that literature can only be the voice of the individual and this has always been so. Once literature is contrived as the hymn of the nation, the flag of the race, the mouthpiece of a political party or the voice of a class or a group, it can be employed as a mighty and all-engulfing tool of propaganda. However, such literature loses what is inherent in literature, ceases to be literature, and becomes a substitute for power and profit.

In the century just ended literature confronted precisely this misfortune and was more deeply scarred by politics and power than in any previous period, and the writer too was subjected to unprecedented oppression.

In order that literature safeguard the reason for its own existence and not become the tool of politics it must return to the voice of the individual, for literature is primarily derived from the feelings of the individual and is the result of feelings. This is not to say that literature must therefore be divorced from politics or that it must necessarily be involved in politics. Controversies about literary trends or a writer's political inclinations were serious afflictions that tormented literature during the past century. Ideology wreaked havoc by turning related controversies over tradition and reform into controversies over what was conservative or revolutionary and thus changed literary issues into a struggle over what was progressive or reactionary. If ideology unites with power and is transformed into a real force then both literature and the individual will be destroyed.

Chinese literature in the twentieth century time and again was worn out and indeed almost suffocated because politics dictated literature: both the revolution in literature and revolutionary literature alike passed death sentences on literature and the individual. The attack on Chinese traditional culture in the name of the revolution resulted in the public prohibition and burning of books. Countless writers were shot, imprisoned, exiled or punished with hard labour in the course of the past one hundred years. This was more extreme than in any imperial dynastic period of China's history, creating enormous difficulties for writings in the Chinese language and even more for any discussion of creative freedom.

If the writer sought to win intellectual freedom the choice was either to fall silent or to flee. However the writer relies on language and not to speak for a prolonged period is the same as suicide. The writer who sought to avoid suicide or being silenced and furthermore to express his own voice had no option but to go into exile. Surveying the history of literature in the East and the West this has always been so: from Qu Yuan to Dante, Joyce, Thomas Mann, Solzhenitsyn, and to the large numbers of Chinese intellectuals who went into exile after the Tiananmen massacre in 1989. This is the inevitable fate of the poet and the writer who continues to seek to preserve his own voice.

During the years when Mao Zedong implemented total dictatorship even fleeing was not an option. The monasteries on far away mountains that provided refuge for scholars in feudal times were totally ravaged and to write even in secret was to risk one's life. To maintain one's intellectual autonomy one could only talk to oneself, and it had to be in utmost secrecy. I should mention that it was only in this period when it was utterly impossible for literature that I came to comprehend why it was so essential: literature allows a person to preserve a human consciousness.

It can be said that talking to oneself is the starting point of literature and that using language to communicate is secondary. A person pours his feelings and thoughts into language that, written as words, becomes literature. At the time there is no thought of utility or that some day it might be published yet there is the compulsion to write because there is recompense and consolation in the pleasure of writing. I began writing my novel *Soul Mountain* to dispel my inner loneliness at the very time when works I had written with rigorous self-censorship had been banned. *Soul Mountain* was written for myself and without the hope that it would be published.

From my experience in writing, I can say that literature is inherently man's affirmation of the value of his own self and that this is validated during the writing, literature is born primarily of the writer's need for self-fulfillment. Whether it has any impact on society comes after the completion of a work and that impact certainly is not determined by the wishes of the writer.

In the history of literature there are many great enduring works which were not published in the lifetimes of the authors. If the authors had not achieved self-affirmation while writing, how could they have continued to write? As in the case of Shakespeare, even now it is difficult to ascertain the details of the lives of the four geniuses who wrote China's greatest novels, *Journey to the West, Water Margin, Jin Ping Mei* and *Dream of Red Mansions*. All that remains is an autobiographical essay by Shi Naian and had he not as he said consoled himself by writing, how else could he have devoted the rest of his life to that huge work for which he received no recompense during life? And was this not also the case with Kafka who pioneered modern fiction and with Fernando Pessoa the most profound poet of the twentieth century? Their turning to language was not in order to reform the world and while profoundly aware of the helplessness of the individual they still spoke out, for such is the magic of language.

Language is the ultimate crystallization of human civilization. It is intricate, incisive and difficult to grasp and yet it is pervasive, penetrates human perceptions and links man, the perceiving subject, to his own understanding of the world. The written word is also magical for it allows communication between separate individuals, even if they are from different races and times. It is also in this way that the shared present time in the writing and reading of literature is connected to its eternal spiritual value.

In my view, for a writer of the present to strive to emphasise a national culture is problematical. Because of where I was born and the language I use, the cultural traditions of China naturally reside within me. Culture and language are always closely related and thus characteristic and relatively stable modes of perception, thought and articulation are formed. However a writer's creativity begins precisely with what has already been articulated in his language and addresses what has not been adequately articulated in that language. As the creator of linguistic art there is no need to stick on oneself a stock national label that can be easily recognised.

Literature transcends national boundaries—through translations it transcends languages and then specific social customs and inter-human relationships created by geographical location and history—to make profound revelations about the universality of human nature. Furthermore, the writer today receives multicultural influences outside the culture of his own race so, unless it is to promote tourism, emphasising the cultural features of a people is inevitably suspect.

Literature transcends ideology, national boundaries and racial consciousness in the same way as the individual's existence basically transcends this or that-ism. This is because man's existential condition is superior to any theories or speculations about life. Literature is a universal observation on the dilemmas of human existence and nothing is taboo. Restrictions on literature are always externally imposed: politics, society, ethics and customs set out to tailor literature into decorations for their various frameworks.

However, literature is neither an embellishment for authority or a socially fashionable item, it has its own criterion of merit: its aesthetic quality. An aesthetic intricately related to the human emotions is the only indispensable criterion for literary works. Indeed, such judgements differ from person to person because the emotions are invariably that of different individuals. However such subjective aesthetic judgements do have universally recognised standards. The capacity for critical appreciation nurtured by literature allows the reader to also experience the poetic feeling and the beauty, the sublime and the ridiculous, the sorrow and the absurdity, and the humour and the irony that the author has infused into his work.

Poetic feeling does not derive simply from the expression of the emotions nevertheless unbridled egotism, a form of infantilism, is difficult to avoid in the early stages of writing. Also, there are numerous levels of emotional expression and to reach higher levels requires cold detachment. Poetry is concealed in the distanced gaze. Furthermore, if this gaze also examines the person of the author and overarches both the characters of the book and the author to become the author's third eye, one that is as neutral as possible, the disasters and the refuse of the human world will all be worthy of scrutiny. Then as feelings of pain, hatred and abhorrence are aroused so too are feelings of concern and love for life.

An aesthetic based on human emotions does not become outdated even with the perennial changing of fashions in literature and in art. However literary evaluations that fluctuate like fashions are premised on what is the latest: that is, whatever is new is good. This is a mechanism in general market movements and the book market is not exempted, but if the writer's aesthetic judgement follows market movements it will mean the suicide of literature. Especially in the so-called consumerist society of the present, I think one must resort to cold literature.

Ten years ago, after concluding *Soul Mountain* which I had written over seven years, I wrote a short essay proposing this type of literature:

> Literature is not concerned with politics but is purely a matter of the individual. It is the gratification of the intellect together with an observation, a review of what has been experienced, reminiscences and feelings or the portrayal of a state of mind.

> The so-called writer is nothing more than someone speaking or writing and whether he is listened to or read is for others to choose. The writer is not a hero acting on orders from the people nor is he worthy of worship as an idol, and certainly he is not a criminal or enemy of the people. He is at times victimised along with his writings simply because of others' needs. When the authorities need to manufacture a few enemies to divert people's attention, writers become sacrifices and worse still writers who have been duped actually think it is a great honour to be sacrificed.

> In fact the relationship of the author and the reader is always one of spiritual communication and there is no need to meet or to socially interact, it is a communication simply through the work. Literature remains an indispensable form of human activity in which both the reader and the writer are engaged of their own volition. Hence, literature has no duty to the masses.

> This sort of literature that has recovered its innate character can be called cold literature. It exists simply because humankind seeks a purely spiritual activity beyond the gratification of material desires. This sort of literature of course did not come into being

today. However, whereas in the past it mainly had to fight oppressive political forces and social customs, today it has to do battle with the subversive commercial values of consumerist society. For it to exist depends on a willingness to endure the loneliness.

If a writer devotes himself to this sort of writing he will find it difficult to make a living. Hence the writing of this sort of literature must be considered a luxury, a form of pure spiritual gratification. If this sort of literature has the good fortune of being published and circulated it is due to the efforts of the writer and his friends, Cao Xueqin and Kafka are such examples. During their lifetimes, their works were unpublished so they were not able to create literary movements or to become celebrities. These writers lived at the margins and seams of society, devoting themselves to this sort of spiritual activity for which at the time they did not hope for any recompense. They did not seek social approval but simply derived pleasure from writing.

Cold literature is literature that will flee in order to survive, it is literature that refuses to be strangled by society in its quest for spiritual salvation. If a race cannot accommodate this sort of non-utilitarian literature it is not merely a misfortune for the writer but a tragedy for the race.

It is my good fortune to be receiving, during my lifetime, this great honour from the Swedish Academy, and in this I have been helped by many friends from all over the world. For years without thought of reward and not shirking difficulties they have translated, published, performed and evaluated my writings. However I will not thank them one by one for it is a very long list of names.

I should also thank France for accepting me. In France where literature and art are revered I have won the conditions to write with freedom and I also have readers and audiences. Fortunately I am not lonely although writing, to which I have committed myself, is a solitary affair.

What I would also like to say here is that life is not a celebration and that the rest of the world is not peaceful as in Sweden where for one hundred and eighty years there has been no war. This new century will not be immune to catastrophes simply because there were so many in the past century, because memories are not transmitted like genes. Humans have minds but are not intelligent enough to learn from the past and when malevolence flares up in the human mind it can endanger human survival itself.

The human species does not necessarily move in stages from progress to progress, and here I make reference to the history of human civilisation. History and civilisation do not advance in tandem. From the stagnation of Medieval Europe to the decline and chaos in recent times on the mainland of Asia and to the catastrophes of two world wars in the twentieth century, the methods of killing people became increasingly sophisticated. Scientific and technological progress certainly does not imply that humankind as a result becomes more civilised.

Using some scientific-ism to explain history or interpreting it with a historical perspective based on pseudo-dialectics have failed to clarify human behaviour. Now that the utopian fervour and continuing revolution of the past century have crumbled to dust, there is unavoidably a feeling of bitterness amongst those who have survived.

The denial of a denial does not necessarily result in an affirmation. Revolution did not merely bring in new things because the new utopian world was premised on the destruction of the old. This theory of social revolution was similarly applied to literature and turned what had once been a realm of creativity into a battlefield in which earlier people were overthrown and cultural traditions were trampled upon. Everything had to start from zero, modernisation was good, and the history of literature too was interpreted as a continuing upheaval.

The writer cannot fill the role of the Creator so there is no need for him to inflate his ego by thinking that he is God. This will not only bring about psychological dysfunction and turn him into a madman but will also transform the world into a hallucination in which everything external to his own body is purgatory and naturally he cannot go on living. Others are clearly hell: presumably it is like this when the self loses control. Needless to say he will turn himself into a sacrifice for the future and also demand that others follow suit in sacrificing themselves.

There is no need to rush to complete the history of the twentieth century. If the world again sinks into the ruins of some ideological framework this history will have been written in vain and later people will revise it for themselves.

The writer is also not a prophet. What is important is to live in the present, to stop being hoodwinked, to cast off delusions, to look clearly at this moment of time and at the same time to scrutinise the self. This self too is total chaos and while questioning the world and others one may as well look back at one's self. Disaster and oppression do usually come from another but man's cowardice and anxiety can often intensify the suffering and furthermore create misfortune for others.

Such is the inexplicable nature of humankind's behaviour, and man's knowledge of his self is even harder to comprehend. Literature is simply man focusing his gaze on his self and while he does a thread of consciousness which sheds light on this self begins to grow.

To subvert is not the aim of literature, its value lies in discovering and revealing what is rarely known, little known, thought to be known but in fact not very well known of the truth of the human world. It would seem that truth is the unassailable and most basic quality of literature.

The new century has already arrived. I will not bother about whether or not it is in fact new but it would seem that the revolution in literature and revolutionary literature, and even ideology, may have all come to an end. The illusion of a social utopia that enshrouded more than a century has vanished and when literature throws off the fetters of this and that-ism it will still have to return to the dilemmas of human existence. However the dilemmas of human existence have changed very little and will continue to be the eternal topic of literature.

This is an age without prophecies and promises and I think it is a good thing. The writer playing prophet and judge should also cease since the many prophecies of the past century have all turned out to be frauds. And there is no need to manufacture new superstitions about the future, it is much better to wait and see. It would be best also for the writer to revert to the role of witness and strive to present the truth.

This is not to say that literature is the same as a document. Actually there are few facts in documented testimonies and the reasons and motives behind incidents are often concealed. However, when literature deals with the truth the whole process from a person's inner mind to the incident can be exposed without leaving anything out. This power is inherent in literature as long as the writer sets out to portray the true circumstances of human existence and is not just making up nonsense.

It is a writer's insights in grasping truth that determine the quality of a work and word games or writing techniques cannot serve as substitutes. Indeed, there are numerous definitions of truth and how it is dealt with varies from person to person but it can be seen at a glance whether a writer is embellishing human phenomena or making a full and honest portrayal. The literary criticism of a certain ideology turned truth and untruth into semantic analysis, but such principles and tenets are of little relevance in literary creation.

However whether or not the writer confronts truth is not just an issue of creative methodology, it is closely linked to his attitude towards writing. Truth when the pen is taken up at the same time implies that one is sincere after one puts down the pen. Here truth is not simply an evaluation of literature but at the same time has ethical connotations. It is not the writer's duty to preach morality and while striving to portray various people in the world he also unscrupulously exposes in his self, even the secrets of his inner mind. For the writer truth in literature approximates ethics, it is the ultimate ethics of literature.

In the hand of a writer with a serious attitude to writing even literary fabrications are premised on the portrayal of the truth of human life, and this has been the vital life force of works that have endured from ancient times to the present. It is precisely for this reason that Greek tragedy and Shakespeare will never become outdated.

Literature does not simply make a replica of reality but penetrates the surface layers and reaches deep into the inner workings of reality; it removes false illusions, look down from great heights at ordinary happenings, and with a broad perspective reveals happenings in their entirety.

Of course literature also relies on the imagination but this sort of journey in the mind is not just putting together a whole lot of rubbish. Imagination that is divorced from true feelings and fabrications that are divorced from the basis of life experiences can only end up insipid and weak, and works that fail to convince the author himself will not be able to move readers. Indeed, literature does not only rely on the experiences of ordinary life nor is the writer bound by what he has personally experienced. It is possible for the things heard and seen through a language carrier and the things related in the literary works of earlier writers all to be transformed into one's own feelings. This too is the magic of the language of literature.

As with a curse or a blessing language has the power to stir body and mind. The art of language lies in the presenter being able to convey his feelings to others, it is not some sign system or semantic structure requiring nothing more than grammatical structures. If the living person behind language is forgotten, semantic expositions easily turn into games of the intellect.

Language is not merely concepts and the carrier of concepts, it simultaneously activates the feelings and the senses and this is why signs and signals cannot replace the language of living people. The will, motives, tone and emotions behind what someone says cannot be fully expressed by semantics and rhetoric alone. The connotations of the language of literature must be voiced, spoken by living people, to be fully expressed. So as well as serving as a carrier of thought literature must also appeal to the auditory senses. The human need for language is not simply for the transmission of meaning, it is at the same time listening to and affirming a person's existence.

Borrowing from Descartes, it could be said of the writer: I say and therefore I am. However, the I of the writer can be the writer himself, can be equated to the narrator, or become the characters of a work. As the narrator-subject can also be he and you, it is tripartite. The fixing of a key speaker pronoun is the starting point for portraying perceptions and from this various narrative patterns take shape. It is during the process of searching for his own narrative method that the writer gives concrete form to his perceptions.

In my fiction I use pronouns instead of the usual characters and also use the pronouns I, you, and he to tell about or to focus on the protagonist. The portrayal of the one character by using different pro-nouns creates a sense of distance. As this also provides actors on the stage with a broader psychological space I have also introduced the changing of pronouns into my drama.

The writing of fiction or drama has not and will not come to an end and there is no substance to flippant announcements of the death of certain genres of literature or art.

Born at the start of human civilisation, like life, language is full of wonders and its expressive capacity is limitless. It is the work of the writer to discover and develop the latent potential inherent in language.

The writer is not the Creator and he cannot eradicate the world even if it is too old. He also cannot establish some new ideal world even if the present world is absurd and beyond human comprehension. However he can certainly make innovative statements either by adding to what earlier people have said or else starting where earlier people stopped.

To subvert literature was Cultural Revolution rhetoric. Literature did not die and writers were not destroyed. Every writer has his place on the bookshelf and he has life as long as he has readers. There is no greater consolation for a writer than to be able to leave a book in humankind's vast treasury of literature that will continue to be read in future times.

Literature is only actualised and of interest at that moment in time when the writer writes it and the reader reads it. Unless it is pretence, to write for the future only deludes oneself and others as well. Literature is for the living and moreover affirms the present of the living. It is this eternal present and this confirmation of individual life that is the absolute reason why literature is literature, if one insists on seeking a reason for this huge thing that exists of itself.

When writing is not a livelihood or when one is so engrossed in writing that one forgets why one is writing and for whom one is writing it becomes a necessity and one will write compulsively and give birth to literature. It is this non-utilitarian aspect of literature that is fundamental to literature. That the writing of literature has become a profession is an ugly outcome of the division of labour in modern society and a very bitter fruit for the writer.

This is especially the case in the present age where the market economy has become pervasive and books have also become commodities. Everywhere there are huge undiscriminating markets and not just individual writers but even the societies and movements of past literary schools have all gone. If the writer does not bend to the pressures of the market and refuses to stoop to manufacturing cultural products by writing to satisfy the tastes of fashions and trends, he must make a living by some other means. Literature is not a best-selling book or a book on a ranked list and authors promoted on television are engaged in advertising rather than in writing. Freedom in writing is not conferred and cannot be purchased but comes from an inner need in the writer himself.

Instead of saying that Buddha is in the heart it would be better to say that freedom is in the heart and it simply depends on whether one makes use of it. If one exchanges freedom for something else then the bird that is freedom will fly off, for this is the cost of freedom.

The writer writes what he wants without concern for recompense not only to affirm his self but also to challenge society. This challenge is not pretence and the writer has no need to inflate his ego by becoming a hero or a fighter. Heroes and fighters struggle to achieve some great work or to establish some meritorious deed and these lie beyond the scope of literary works. If the writer wants to challenge society it must be through language and he must rely on the characters and incidents of his works, otherwise he can only harm literature. Literature is not angry shouting and furthermore cannot turn an individual's indignation into accusations. It is only when the feelings of the writer as an individual are dispersed in a work that his feelings will withstand the ravages of time and live on for a long time.

Therefore it is actually not the challenge of the writer to society but rather the challenge of his works. An enduring work is of course a powerful response to the times and society of the writer. The clamour of the writer and his actions may have vanished but as long as there are readers his voice in his writings continues to reverberate.

Indeed such a challenge cannot transform society. It is merely an individual aspiring to transcend the limitations of the social ecology and taking a very inconspicuous stance. However this is by no means an ordinary stance for it is one that takes pride in being human. It would be said if human history is only manipulated by the unknowable laws and moves blindly with the current so that the different voices of individuals cannot be heard. It is in this sense that literature fills in the gaps of history. When the great laws of history are not used to explain human-kind it will be possible for people to leave behind their own voices. History is not all that humankind possesses, there is also the legacy of literature. In literature the people are inventions but they retain an essential belief in their own self-worth.

Honourable members of the Academy, I thank you for awarding this Nobel Prize to literature, to literature that is unwavering in its independence, that avoids neither human suffering nor political oppression and that furthermore does not serve politics. I thank all of you for awarding this most prestigious prize for works that are far removed from the writings of the market, works that have aroused little attention but are actually worth reading. At the same time, I also thank the Swedish Academy for allowing me to ascend this dais to speak before the eyes of the world. A frail individual's weak voice that is hardly worth listening to and that normally would not be heard in the public media has been allowed to address the world. However I believe that this is precisely the meaning of the Nobel Prize and I thank everyone for this opportunity to speak.

Notes

1. *Literature.* Compare the views of literature expressed by Wilde, Nitsch, and Gao. How do they differ in their views of the course of literature and its function, and the relationship among author, literary work, and reader?

2. *Culture vs. the Individual.* Do you agree with Gao that humankind's existential condition transcends culture and that "emphasising the cultural features of a people is inevitably suspect"? Isn't an individual's identity or self—which Gao insists is the source of true literature—inevitably molded by

the culture within which he or she lives? In what ways do the selections from Wilde, Nitsch, and Gao himself support or challenge his assertion about the individual vs. culture?

3. *Timeless, Universal Truths.* Do you agree with Gao that "Greek tragedy and Shakespeare will never become outdated"? You will read both in this volume. When was the last time you read either for pleasure?

4. *Cold Literature.* In what sense does lawyers' writing constitute "cold literature" as defined by Gao?

C. CRITICISM

Cleanth Brooks (1906–1994) was one of the most influential American literary critics of the twentieth century. Born in Kentucky, he was a Rhodes Scholar at Oxford and taught literature at Yale. He was a leader in the development of the New Criticism. This school emphasized close stylistic analysis, stressing paradox, irony, and symbolism. His collection of essays, *The Well-Wrought Urn*, is the classic example of New Criticism. The following essay on Donne's *The Canonization* first appeared as Chapter One of that collection.

THE CANONIZATION
John Donne

For Gods sake hold your tongue, and let me love,
Or chide my palsy, or my gout,
My five grey haires, or ruin'd Fortune flout,
With wealth your state, your minde with arts improve,
Take you a course, get you a place,
Observe his Honour, or his Grace,
Or the Kings reall, or his stamped face
Contemplate, what you will, approve,
So you will let me love.

Alas, alas, who's injur'd by my love?
What merchants ships have my sighs drown'd?
Who saies my tears have overflow'd his ground?
When did my colds a forward spring remove?
When did the heats which my veines fill
Adde one more to the plagie bill?
Soldiers finde warres, and Lawyers finde out still
Litigeous men, which quarrels move,
Though she and I do love.

Call us what you will, wee are made such by love;
Call her one, mee another flye,
We'are Tapers too, and at our owne cost die,
And wee in us finde the'Eagle and the Dove.
The phoenix riddle hath more wit
By us, we two being one, are it.
So to one neutrale thing both sexes fit,

Wee dye and rise the same, and prove
Mysterious by this love.

Wee can dye by it, if not live by love,
And if unfit for tombes and hearse
Our legend bee, it will be fit for verse;
And if no peece of Chronicle wee prove,
We'll build in sonnets pretty roomes;
As well a well-wrought urne becomes
The greatest ashes, as half-acre tombes,
And by these hymnes all shall approve
Us Canoniz'd for Love;

And thus invoke us: "You, whom reverend love
Made one anothers hermitage;
You, to whom love was peace, that now is rage;
Who did the whole worlds soule contract, and drove
Into the glasses of your eyes
(So made such mirrors, and such spies,
That they did all to you epitomize,)
Countries, Townes, Courtes: Beg from above
A patterne of your love!"

THE LANGUAGE OF PARADOX
Cleanth Brooks

Few of us are prepared to accept the statement that the language of
poetry is the language of paradox. Paradox is the language of sophistry,
hard, bright, witty; it is hardly the language of the soul. We are willing
to allow that paradox is a permissible weapon which a Chesterton may
on occasion exploit. We may permit it in epigram, a special subvariety of
poetry; and in satire. which though useful, we are hardly willing to allow
to be poetry at all. Our prejudices force us to regard paradox as
intellectual rather than emotional, clever rather than profound, rational
rather than divinely irrational.

Yet there is a sense in which paradox is the language appropriate
and inevitable to poetry. It is the scientist whose truth requires a
language purged of every trace of paradox; apparently the truth which
the poet utters can be approached only in terms of paradox. I overstate
the case, to be sure; it is possible that the title of this chapter is itself to
be treated as merely a paradox. But there are reasons for thinking that
the overstatement which I propose may light up some elements in the
nature of poetry which tend to be overlooked.

. . . .

We may approach the problem in this way: the poet has to work by
analogies. All of the subtler states of emotion, as I.A. Richards has
pointed out, necessarily demand metaphor for their expression. The poet
must work by analogies, but the metaphors do not lie in the same plane
or fit neatly edge to edge. There is a continual tilting of the planes;

necessary overlappings, discrepancies, contradictions. Even the most direct and simple poet is forced into paradoxes far more often than we think, if we are sufficiently alive to what he is doing.

But in dilating on the difficulties of the poet's task, I do not want to leave the impression that it is a task which necessarily defeats him, or even that with his method he may not win to a fine precision. To use Shakespeare's figure, he can

> *with assays of bias*
> *By indirections find directions out.*

Shakespeare had in mind the game of lawnbowls in which the bowl is distorted, a distortion which allows the skillful player to bowl a curve. To elaborate the figure, science makes use of the perfect sphere and its attack can be direct. The method of art can, I believe, never be direct—is always indirect. But that does not mean that the master of the game cannot place the bowl where he wants it. The serious difficulties will only occur when he confuses his game with that of science and mistakes the nature of his appropriate instrument. Mr. Stuart Chase a few years ago, with a touching naïveté, urged us to take the distortion out of the bowl—to treat language like notation.

I have said that even the apparently simple and straightforward poet is forced into paradoxes by the nature of his instrument. Seeing this, we should not be surprised to find poets who consciously employ it to gain a compression and precision otherwise unobtainable. Such a method, like any other, carries with it its own perils. But the dangers are not overpowering; the poem is not predetermined to a shallow and glittering sophistry. The method is an extension of the normal language of poetry, not a perversion of it.

I should like to refer the reader to a concrete case. Donne's *Canonization* ought to provide a sufficiently extreme instance. The basic metaphor which underlies the poem (and which is reflected in the title) involves a sort of paradox. For the poet daringly treats profane love as if it were divine love. The canonization is not that of a pair of holy anchorites who have renounced the world and the flesh. The hermitage of each is the other's body; but they do renounce the world, and so their title to sainthood is cunningly argued. The poem then is a parody of Christian sainthood; but it is an intensely serious parody of a sort that modern man, habituated as he is to an easy yes or no, can hardly understand. He refuses to accept the paradox as a serious rhetorical device; and since he is able to accept it only as a cheap trick, he is forced into this dilemma. Either: Donne does not take love seriously; here he is merely sharpening his wit as a sort of mechanical exercise. Or: Donne does not take sainthood seriously; here he is merely indulging in a cynical and bawdy parody.

Neither account is true; a reading of the poem will show that Donne takes both love and religion seriously; it will show, further, that the paradox is here his inevitable instrument. But to see this plainly will require a closer reading than most of us give to poetry.

The poem opens dramatically on a note of exasperation. The "you" whom the speaker addresses is not identified. We can imagine that it is a person, perhaps a friend, who is objecting to the speaker's love affair. At any rate, the person represents the practical world which regards love as a silly affectation. To use the metaphor on which the poem is built, the friend represents the secular world which the lovers have renounced.

Donne begins to suggest this metaphor in the first stanza by the contemptuous alternatives which he suggests to the friend:

> *. . . chide my palsie, or my gout,*
> *My five gray haires, or ruin'd Fortune flout. . . .*

The implications are: (1) All right, consider my love as an infirmity, as a disease, if you will, but confine yourself to my other infirmities, my palsy, my approaching old age, my ruined fortune. You stand a better chance of curing those; in chiding me for this one, you are simply wasting your time as well as mine. (2) Why don't you pay attention to your own welfare—go on and get wealth and honor for yourself. What should you care if I do give these up in pursuing my love.

The two main categories of secular success are neatly and contemptuously epitomized in the line

> *Or the Kings reall, or his stamped face. . . .*

Cultivate the court and gaze at the king's face there or, if you prefer, get into business and look at his face stamped on coins. But let me alone.

This conflict between the "real" world and the lover absorbed in the world of love runs through the poem; it dominates the second stanza in which the torments of love, so vivid to the lover, affect the real world not at all—

> *What merchants ships have my sighs drown'd?*

It is touched on in the fourth stanza in the contrast between the word "Chronicle" which suggests secular history with its pomp and magnificence, the history of kings and princes, and the word "sonnets" with its suggestions of trivial and precious intricacy. The conflict appears again in the last stanza, only to be resolved when the unworldly lovers, love's saints who have given up the world, paradoxically achieve a more intense world. But here the paradox is still contained in, and supported by, the dominant metaphor: so does the holy anchorite win a better world by giving up this one.

But before going on to discuss this development of the theme, it is important to see what else the second stanza does. For it is in this second stanza and the third, that the poet shifts the tone of the poem, modulating from the note of irritation with which the poem opens into the quite different tone with which it closes.

Donne accomplishes the modulation of tone by what may be called an analysis of love-metaphor. Here, as in many of his poems, he shows that he is thoroughly self-conscious about what he is doing. This second stanza, he fills with the conventionalized figures of the Petrarchan tradition: the wind of lovers' sighs, the floods of lovers' tears, etc.—extravagant figures with which the contemptuous secular friend might be expected to tease the lover. The implication is that the poet himself recognizes the absurdity of the Petrarchan love metaphors. But what of it? The very absurdity of the jargon which lovers are expected to talk makes for his argument: their love, however absurd it may appear to the world, does no harm to the world. The practical friend need have no fears: there will still be wars to fight and lawsuits to argue.

The opening of the third stanza suggests that this vein of irony is to be maintained. The poet points out to his friend the infinite fund of such absurdities which can be applied to lovers:

> *Call her one, mee another flye,*
> *We'are Tapers too, and at our owne cost die....*

For that matter, the lovers can conjure up for themselves plenty of such fantastic comparisons: they know what the world thinks of them. But these figures of the third stanza are no longer the threadbare Petrarchan conventionalities; they have sharpness and bite. The last one, the likening of the lovers to the phoenix, is fully serious, and with it, the tone has shifted from ironic banter into a defiant but controlled tenderness.

The effect of the poet's implied awareness of the lovers' apparent madness is to cleanse and revivify metaphor; to indicate the sense in which the poet accepts it, and thus to prepare us for accepting seriously the fine and seriously intended metaphors which dominate the last two stanzas of the poem.

The opening line of the fourth stanza,

> *Wee can dye by it, if not live by love,*

achieves an effect of tenderness and deliberate resolution. The lovers are ready to die to the world, they are committed; they are not callow but confident. (The basic metaphor of the saint, one notices, is being carried on; the lovers in their renunciation of the world have something of the confident resolution of the saint. By the bye, the word "legend"—

> *... if unfit for tombes and hearse*
> *Our legend bee—*

in Donne's time meant "the life of a saint.") The lovers are willing to forego [*sic*] the ponderous and stately chronicle and to accept the trifling and insubstantial "sonnet" instead; but then if the urn be well wrought it provides a finer memorial for one's ashes than does the pompous and grotesque monument. With the finely contemptuous, yet quiet phrase, "halfe-acre tombes," the world which the lovers reject expands into something gross and vulgar. But the figure works further; the pretty sonnets will not merely hold their ashes as a decent earthly memorial. Their legend, their story, will gain them canonization; and approved as love's saints, other lovers will invoke them.

In this last stanza, the theme receives a final complication. The lovers in rejecting life actually win to the most intense life. This paradox has been hinted at earlier in the phoenix metaphor. Here it receives a powerful dramatization. The lovers in becoming hermits, find that they have not lost the world, but have gained the world in each other, now a more intense, more meaningful world. Donne is not content to treat the lovers' discovery as something which comes to them passively, but rather as something which they actively achieve. They are like the saint, God's athlete:

> *Who did the whole worlds soule* contract, *and* drove
> *Into the glasses of your eyes . . . .*

The image is that of a violent squeezing as of a powerful hand. And what do the lovers "drive" into each other's eyes? The "Countries, Townes," and "Courtes," which they renounced in the first stanza of the poem. The unworldly lovers thus become the most "worldly" of all.

The tone with which the poem closes is one of triumphant achievement, but the tone is a development contributed to by various earlier elements. One of the more important elements which works toward our acceptance of the final paradox is the figure of the phoenix, which will bear a little further analysis.

The comparison of the lovers to the phoenix is very skillfully related to the two earlier comparisons, that in which the lovers are like burning tapers, and that in which they are like the eagle and the dove. The phoenix comparison gathers up both: the phoenix is a bird, and like the tapers, it burns. We have a selected series of items: the phoenix figure seems to come in a natural stream of association. "Call us what you will," the lover says, and rattles off in his desperation the first comparisons that occur to him. The comparison to the phoenix seems thus merely another outlandish one, the most outrageous of all. But it is this most fantastic one, stumbled over apparently in his haste, that the poet goes on to develop. It really describes the lovers best and justifies their renunciation. For the phoenix is not two but one, "we two being one, are it"; and it burns, not like the taper at its own cost, but to live again. Its death is life: "Wee dye and rise the same . . ." The poet literally justifies the fantastic assertion. In the sixteenth and seventeenth centuries to "die" means to experience the consummation of the act of love. The lovers after the act are the same. Their love is not exhausted in mere lust. This is their title to canonization. Their love is like the phoenix.

I hope that I do not seem to juggle the meaning of *die*. The meaning that I have cited can be abundantly justified in the literature of the period; Shakespeare uses "die" in this sense; so does Dryden. Moreover, I do not think that I give it undue emphasis. The word is in a crucial position. On it is pivoted the transition to the next stanza,

> *Wee can dye by it, if not live by love,*
> *And if unfit for tombes . . .*

Most important of all, the sexual submeaning of "die" does not contradict the other meanings: the poet is saying: "Our death is really a more intense life"; "We can afford to trade life (the world) for death (love), for that death is the consummation of life"; "After all one does not expect to live *by* love, one expects, and wants, to die *by* it." But in the total passage he is also saying: "Because our love is not mundane, we can give up the world"; "Because our love is not merely lust, we can give up the other lusts, the lust for wealth and power"; "because," and this is said with an inflection of irony as by one who knows the world too well, "because our love can outlast its consummation, we are a minor miracle, we are love's saints." This passage with its ironical tenderness and its realism feeds and supports the brilliant paradox with which the poem closes.

There is one more factor in developing and sustaining the final effect. The poem is an instance of the doctrine which it asserts; it is both the assertion and the realization of the assertion. The poet has actually before our eyes built within the song the "pretty room" with which he says the lovers can be content. The poem itself is the well-wrought urn which can hold the lovers' ashes and which will not suffer in comparison with the prince's "halfe-acre tomb."

And how necessary are the paradoxes? Donne might have said directly, "Love in a cottage is enough." "The Canonization" contains this admirable thesis; but it contains a great deal more. He might have been as forthright as a later lyricist who wrote, "We'll build a sweet little nest,/ Somewhere out in the West,/ And let the rest of the world go by." He might even have imitated that more metaphysical lyric, which maintains, "You're the cream in my coffee." "The Canonization" touches on all these observations, but it goes beyond them, not merely in dignity, but in precision.

I submit that the only way by which the poet could say what "The Canonization" says is by paradox. More direct methods may be tempting, but all of them enfeeble and distort what is to be said. This statement may seem the less surprising when we reflect on how many of the important things which the poet has to say have to be said by means of paradox: most of the language of lovers is such—"The Canonization" is a good example; so is most of the language of religion—"He who would save his life, must lose it"; "The last shall be first." Indeed, almost any insight important enough to warrant a great poem apparently has to be stated in such terms. Deprived of the character of paradox with its twin concomitants of irony and wonder, the matter of Donne's poem unravels into "facts," biological, sociological, and economic. What happens to Donne's lovers if we consider them "scientifically," without benefit of the supernaturalism which the poet confers upon them? Well, what happens to Shakespeare's lovers, for Shakespeare uses the basic metaphor of "The Canonization" in his *Romeo and Juliet*? In their first conversation, the lovers play with the analogy between the lover and the pilgrim to the Holy Land. Juliet says:

For saints have hands that pilgrims' hands do touch

And palm to palm is holy palmers' kiss.

Considered scientifically, the lovers become Mr. Aldous Huxley's animals, "quietly sweating, palm to palm."

 . . . .

Notes

1. *The Preacher-Poet.* John Donne (circa 1572–1631) was the foremost of the metaphysical poets. Born a Roman Catholic, in his youth he loved the good life and beautiful women. In 1614 he was converted to Anglicanism, and in 1621 he was appointed to the exalted position of dean of St. Paul's Cathedral in London.

Donne's early poems were ironic and erotic, his later ones religious. While his writings were well regarded in the latter part of the seventeenth century, he was hardly noted in the 1700's and 1800's. In the twentieth century he was rediscovered by the New Critics, and today he is considered one of the greatest of the English poets.

2. *The Lawyer as Critic.* If one method of literary criticism is close reading of the text, then lawyers surely are literary critics. What is the goal of literary criticism? Do legal and nonlegal literary critics share the same goals?

* * *

Randall Jarrell (1914–1965) was an American poet, novelist, critic, and English professor. His post-World War II war poems express his bitterness about war, and his poetry in general deals with the loneliness of everyday life. His literary criticism was collected in POETRY AND THE AGE (1953). The following excerpts are from an essay in that collection, *The Obscurity of the Poet.*

THE OBSCURITY OF THE POET
Randall Jarrell

 . . . .

Anyone who has spent much time finding out what people do when they read a poem, what poems actually mean for them, will have discovered that a surprising part of the difficulty they have comes from their almost systematic unreceptiveness, their queer unwillingness to pay attention even to the reference of pronouns, the meaning of the punctuation, which subject goes with which verb, and so on; "after all," they seem to feel, "I'm not reading *prose.*" You need to read good poetry with an attitude that is a mixture of sharp intelligence and of willing emotional empathy, at once penetrating and generous. . . .

 . . . .

. . . And this reminds one that, today, many of the readers a poet would value most have hardly learned to read any poetry; and many of those who regularly read his poems have values so different from his that he is troubled by their praise, and vexed but reassured by their blame.

Tomorrow morning some poet may, like Byron, wake up to find himself famous—for having written a novel, for having killed his wife; it will not be for having written a poem. That is still logically, but no longer socially, possible. Let me illustrate with a story. I once met on a boat, travelling to Europe with his wife and daughter, a man with whom I played pingpong. Having learned from a friend that I wrote poetry, he asked one day with uninterested politeness, "Who are the American poets you like best?" I said, "Oh, T.S. Eliot, Robert Frost." Then this man—this father who every night danced with his daughter with the well-taught, dated, decorous attractiveness of the hero of an old *Saturday Evening Post* serial by E. Phillips Oppenheim; who had had the best professional in Los Angeles teach his wife and daughter the tennis strokes he himself talked of with wearying authority; who never in his life had gone through a doorway before anyone over the age of seven—this well-dressed, well-mannered, travelled, urbane, educated gentleman said placidly: "I don't believe I've heard of them." For so far as literature, the arts, philosophy, and science were concerned, he might better have been the policeman on the corner. But he was perfectly correct in thinking—not that he had ever thought about it—that a knowledge of these things is not an essential requirement of the society of which he is a part. We belong to a culture whose old hierarchy of values—which demanded that a girl read Pope just as it demanded that she go to church and play the pianoforte—has virtually disappeared....

. . . .

... The poet lives in a world whose newspapers and magazines and books and motion pictures and radio stations and television stations have destroyed, in a great many people, even the capacity for understanding real poetry, real art of any kind. The man who monthly reads, with vacant relish, the carefully predigested sentences which the *Reader's Digest* feeds to him as a mother pigeon feeds her squabs—this man *cannot* read the *Divine Comedy,* even if it should ever occur to him to try: it is too obscure. Yet one sort of clearness shows a complete contempt for the reader, just as one sort of obscurity shows a complete respect. Which patronizes and degrades the reader, the *Divine Comedy* with its four levels of meaning, or the *Reader's Digest* with its one level so low that it seems not a level but an abyss into which the reader consents to sink? The writer's real dishonesty is to give an easy paraphrase of the hard truth....

. . . .

Art matters not merely because it is the most magnificent ornament and the most nearly unfailing occupation of our lives, but because it is life itself. From Christ to Freud we have believed that, if we know the truth, the truth will set us free: art is indispensable because so much of this truth can be learned through works of art and through works of art alone—for which of us could have learned for himself what Proust and Chekhov, Hardy and Yeats and Rilke, Shakespeare and Homer learned for us? And in what other way could they have made us see the truths which they themselves saw, those differing and contradictory truths which seem nevertheless, to the mind which contains them, in some sense a single truth? And all these things, by their very nature, demand to be shared; if we are satisfied to know these things ourselves, and to look with superiority or indifference at those who do not have that knowledge, we have made a refusal that corrupts us as surely as anything can. If while most of our people (the descendants of those who, ordinarily, listened to Grimm's Tales and the ballads and the Bible; who, exceptionally, listened to Aeschylus and Shakespeare) listen not to simple or naive art, but to an elaborate and sophisticated substitute for art, an immediate and infallible synthetic as effective and terrifying as advertisements or the speeches of Hitler—if, knowing all this, we say: *Art has always been a matter of a few,* we are using truism to hide a disaster. One of the oldest, deepest, and most nearly conclusive attractions of democracy is manifested in our feeling that through it not only material but also spiritual goods can be shared: that in a democracy bread and justice, education and art, will be accessible to everybody. If a democracy should offer its citizens a show of education, a sham art, a literacy more dangerous than their old illiteracy, then we should have to say that it is not a democracy at all, but one more variant of those "People's Democracies" which share with any true democracy little more than the name....

... Human life without some form of poetry is not human life but animal existence.... But what will happen to the public—to that portion of it divorced from any real art even of the simplest kind—I do not know....

Notes

1. *Wilde and Jarrell.* Compare the attitudes of Oscar Wilde and Randall Jarrell towards art.

2. *Truth and Art.* Is Jarrell right that some truth can be learned "through works of art alone"? If so, can law make any claim to such truth?

3. *Democracy and Art.* Do you agree that there is a literacy more dangerous than illiteracy? If so, how would you describe it? How would you change it?

* * *

Virginia Woolf (1882–1941) was a pioneer in modern fiction. She was inspired by Doestoevsky, and developed her own stream-of-consciousness style in such novels as to The Lighthouse, Mrs. Dalloway, and The Waves. She was also a superb essayist. She was attracted by the mental freedom of the essay, and wrote admiringly of the great essayists Montaigne, Hazlitt, and Addison. She suffered from lifelong melancholia and periods of mental illness. She was fascinated with the relation between life and death. Her essay, *The Death of the Moth,* is a study of that relation. In 1941, she killed herself by filling her pockets with stones and walking into a river near her home.

THE DEATH OF THE MOTH
Virginia Woolf

Moths that fly by day are not properly to be called moths; they do not excite that pleasant sense of dark autumn nights and ivy-blossom which the commonest yellow-underwing asleep in the shadow of the curtain never fails to rouse in us. They are hybrid creatures, neither gay like butterflies nor somber like their own species. Nevertheless the present specimen, with his narrow hay-coloured wings, fringed with a tassel of the same colour, seemed to be content with life. It was a pleasant morning, mid-September, mild, benignant, yet with a keener breath than that of the summer months. The plough was already scoring the field opposite the window, and where the share had been, the earth was pressed flat and gleamed with moisture. Such vigour came rolling in from the fields and the down beyond that it was difficult to keep the eyes strictly turned upon the book. The rooks too were keeping one of their annual festivities; soaring round the tree tops until it looked as if a vast net with thousands of black knots in it had been cast up into the air; which, after a few moments sank slowly down upon the trees until every twig seemed to have a knot at the end of it. Then, suddenly, the net would be thrown into the air again in a wider circle this time, with the utmost clamour and vociferation, as though to be thrown into the air and settle slowly down upon the tree tops were a tremendously exciting experience.

The same energy which inspired the rooks, the ploughmen, the horses, and even, it seemed, the lean bare-backed downs, sent the moth fluttering from side to side of his square of the window-pane. One could not help watching him. One was, indeed, conscious of a queer feeling of pity for him. The possibilities of pleasure seemed that morning so enormous and so various that to have only a moth's part in life, and a day moth's at that, appeared a hard fate, and his zest in enjoying his meager opportunities to the full, pathetic. He flew vigorously to one corner of his compartment, and, after waiting there a second, flew across to another. What remained for him but to fly to a third corner and then to a fourth? That was all he could do, in spite of the size of the downs, the width of the sky, the far-off smoke of houses, and the romantic voice, now and then, of a steamer out at sea. What he could do he did. Watching him, it seemed as if a fibre, very thin but pure, of the enormous energy of the world had been thrust into his frail and diminutive body. As often as he crossed the pane, I could fancy that a thread of vital light became visible. He was little or nothing but life.

Yet, because he was so small, and so simple a form of the energy that was rolling in at the open window and driving its way through so many narrow and intricate corridors in my own brain and in those of other human beings, there was something marvelous as well as pathetic about him. It was as if someone had taken a tiny bead of pure life and decking it as lightly as possible with down and feathers, had set it dancing and zigzagging to show us the true nature of life. Thus displayed one could not get over the strangeness of it. One is apt to forget all about life, seeing it humped and bossed and garnished and cumbered so that it has to move with the greatest circumspection and dignity. Again, the thought of all that life might have been had he been born in any other shape caused one to view his simple activities with a kind of pity.

After a time, tired by his dancing apparently, he settled on the window ledge in the sun, and, the queer spectacle being at an end, I forgot about him. Then, looking up, my eye was caught by him. He was trying to resume his dancing, but seemed either so stiff or so awkward that he could only flutter to the bottom of windowpane; and when he tried to fly across it he failed. Being intent on other matters I watched these futile attempts for a time without thinking, unconsciously waiting for him to resume his flight, as one waits for a machine, that has stopped momentarily, to start again without considering the reason of its failure. After perhaps a seventh attempt he slipped from the wooden ledge and fell, fluttering his wings, on to his back on the window sill. The helplessness of his attitude roused me. It flashed upon me that he was in difficulties; he could no longer raise himself; his legs struggled vainly. But, as I stretched out a pencil, meaning to help him to right himself, it came over me that the failure and awkwardness were the approach of death. I laid the pencil down again.

The legs agitated themselves once more. I looked as if for the enemy against which he struggled. I looked out of doors. What had happened there? Presumably it was midday, and work in the fields had stopped. Stillness and quiet had replaced the previous animation. The birds had taken themselves off to feed in the brooks. The horses stood still. Yet the power was there all the same, massed outside, indifferent, impersonal, not attending to anything in particular. Somehow it was opposed to the little hay-colored moth. It was useless to try to do anything. One could only watch the extraordinary efforts made by those tiny legs against an oncoming doom which could, had it chosen, have submerged an entire city, not merely a city, but masses of human beings; nothing, I knew, had any chance against death. Nevertheless after a pause of exhaustion the legs fluttered again. It was superb this last protest, and so frantic that he succeeded at last in righting himself. One's sympathies, of course, were all on the side of life. Also, when there was nobody to care or to know, this gigantic effort on the part of an insignificant little moth, against a power of such magnitude, to retain what no one else valued or desired to keep, moved one strangely. Again, somehow, one saw life, a pure bead. I lifted the pencil again, useless though I knew it to be. But even as I did so, the unmistakable tokens of death showed themselves. The body relaxed, and instantly grew stiff. The struggle was over. The insignificant little creature now knew death. As I looked at the dead moth, this minute wayside triumph of so great a force over so mean an antagonist filled me with wonder. Just as life had been strange a few minutes before, so death was now as strange. The moth having righted himself now lay most decently and uncomplainingly composed. O yes, he seemed to say, death is stronger than I am.

Notes

1. *Who's Afraid?* If Virginia Woolf's essay may be considered criticism, what is the subject of her criticism?

2. *Symbolism.* What does the moth in Woolf's essay symbolize, if anything?

D. HUMOR

When one thinks of satire, one thinks of Jonathan Swift (1667–1745). His scathing attacks on all forms of pretense made him a fearful foe for his enemies. A devout clergyman, he attacked the pretensions of organized religion in the following essay, which is as biting today as when it was written in 1708.

AN ARGUMENT AGAINST ABOLISHING CHRISTIANITY
Jonathan Swift

I am very sensible what Weakness and Presumption it is, to reason against the general Humour and Disposition of the World. I remember it was with great Justice, and a due regard to the freedom both of the Publick and the Press, forbidden upon severe Penalties to Write, or Discourse, or lay Wagers against the Union, even before it was confirmed by Parliament, because that was look'd upon as a Design, to oppose the Current of the People, which besides the Folly of it, is a manifest Breach of the Fundamental Law that makes this Majority of Opinion the Voice of God. In like manner, and for the very same Reasons, it may perhaps be neither safe nor prudent to argue against the abolishing of Christianity: at a Juncture when all Parties seem so unanimously determined upon the Point, as we cannot but allow from their Actions, their Discourses, and their Writings. However, I know not how, whether from the Affectation of Singularity, or the Perverseness of Human Nature, but so it unhappily falls out, that I cannot be entirely of this Opinion. Nay, although I were sure, an Order were issued out for my immediate Prosecution by the Attorney General, I should still confess that in the present Posture of our Affairs at home or abroad, I do not yet see the absolute Necessity of extirpating the Christian Religion from among us.

This perhaps may appear too great a Paradox even for our wise and paradoxical Age to endure; therefore I shall handle it with all Tenderness, and with the utmost Deference to that great and profound Majority which is of another Sentiment.

And yet the Curious may please to observe, how much the Genius of a Nation is liable to alter in half an Age. I have heard it affirmed for certain by some very old People, that the contrary Opinion was even in their Memories as much in Vogue as the other is now; And, that a

Project for the abolishing Christianity would then have appeared as singular, and been thought as absurd, as it would be at this time to write or discourse in its Defence.

Therefore I freely own that all Appearances are against me. The System of the Gospel after the Fate of other Systems is generally antiquated and exploded; and the Mass or Body of the common People, among whom it seems to have had its latest Credit, are now grown as much ashamed of it as their Betters: Opinions like Fashions always descending from those of Quality to the middle sort, and thence to the Vulgar, where at length they are dropp'd and vanish.

But here I would not be mistaken, and must therefore be so bold as to borrow a Distinction from the Writers on the other side, when they make a Difference between Nominal and Real Trinitarians. I hope no Reader imagines me so weak to stand up in the Defence of real Christianity, such as used in primitive Times (if we may believe the Authors of those Ages) to have an Influence upon Men's Belief and Actions: To offer at the restoring of That would indeed be a wild Project, It would be to dig up Foundations, to destroy at one Blow all the Wit, and half the Learning of the Kingdom; to break the entire Frame and Constitution of Things, to ruin Trade, extinguish Arts and Sciences with the Professors of them; in short, to turn our Courts, Exchanges, and shops into Deserts; and would be full as absurd as the Proposal of Horace, where he advises the Romans, all in a Body to leave their City, and seek a new Seat in some remote Part of the World, by way of a Cure for the Corruption of their Manners.

Therefore I think this Caution was in itself altogether unnecessary (which I have inserted only to prevent all Possibility of Caviling) since every candid Reader will easily understand my Discourse to be intended only in Defence of nominal Christianity, the other having been for some time wholly laid aside by general Consent, as utterly inconsistent with all our present Schemes of Wealth and Power.

But why we should therefore cast off the Name and Title of Christians, although the general Opinion and Resolution be so violent for it, I confess I cannot (with Submission) apprehend the Consequence necessary. However, since the Undertakers propose such wonderful Advantages to the Nation by this Project, and advance many plausible Objections against the System of Christianity, I shall briefly consider the Strength of both, fairly allow them their greatest Weight, and offer such Answers as I think most reasonable. After which I will beg leave to shew what Inconveniencies may possibly happen by such an Innovation, in the present Posture of our Affairs.

First, One great Advantage proposed by the abolishing of Christianity is, That it would very much enlarge and establish Liberty of Conscience, that great Bulwark of our Nation, and of the Protestant Religion, which is still too much limited by Priest-craft, notwithstanding all the good Intentions of the Legislature, as we have lately found by a severe Instance. For it is confidently reported, that two Young Gentlemen of great Hopes, bright Wit, and profound Judgment, who upon a thorough Examination of Causes and Effects, and by the mere Force of natural Abilities, without the least Tincture of Learning, having made a Discovery, that there was no God, and generously communicating their Thoughts for the good of the Publick; were some time ago by an unparalleled Severity, and upon I know not what obsolete Law, broke only for Blasphemy. And as it hath been wisely observed, if Persecution once begins no Man alive knows how far it may reach, or where it will end.

In answer to all which, with deference to wiser Judgments, I think this rather shews the Necessity of a nominal Religion among us. Great Wits love to be free with the highest Objects, and if they cannot be allowed a God to revile or renounce; they will speak Evil of Dignities, abuse the Government, and reflect upon the Ministry, which I am sure few will deny to be of much more pernicious Consequence, according to the saying of *Tiberius, Deorum Offensa Diis curae.* As to the particular Fact related, I think it is not fair to argue from one Instance, perhaps another cannot be produced, yet (to the Comfort of all those who may be apprehensive of Persecution) Blasphemy we know is freely spoke a Million of times in every Coffee-House and Tavern, or wherever else good Company meet. It must be allowed indeed that to break an English Free-born Officer only for Blasphemy, was, to speak the gentlest of such an Action, a very high strain of absolute Power. Little can be said in Excuse for the General; Perhaps he was afraid it might give Offence to the Allies, among whom, for ought I know, it may be the Custom of the Country to believe a God. But if he argued, as some have done, upon a mistaken Principle, that an Officer who is guilty of speaking Blasphemy, may sometime or other proceed so far as to raise a Mutiny, the Consequence is by no means to be admitted: For, surely the Commander of an English Army is like to be but ill obey'd, whose Soldiers fear and reverence him as little as they do a Deity.

It is further objected against the Gospel System, that it obliges men to the Belief of Things too difficult for free Thinkers, and such who have shook off the Prejudices that usually cling to a confin'd Education. To which I answer, that Men should be cautious how they raise Objections which reflect upon the Wisdom of the Nation. Is not every body freely allowed to believe whatever he pleaseth, and to publish his Belief to the World whenever he thinks fit, especially if it serve to strengthen the Party which is in the Right? Would any indifferent Foreigner, who should read the Trumpery lately written by Asgil, Tindall, Toland, Coward, and Forty more, imagine the Gospel to be our Rule of Faith, and to be confirmed by Parliaments? Does any Man either believe, or say he believes, or desire to have it thought that he says he believes one Syllable of the Matter, and is any Man worse received upon that Score, or does he find his want of nominal Faith a disadvantage to him in the Pursuit of any Civil or Military Employment? What if there be an old dormant Statute or two against him, are they not now obsolete, to a degree, that Empson and Dudley themselves, if they were now alive, would find it impossible to put them in Execution?

. . . .

Another advantage proposed by the abolishing of Christianity, is the clear Gain of one Day in seven, which is now entirely lost, and consequently the Kingdom one seventh less considerable in Trade, Business, and Pleasure; beside the Loss to the Publick of so many stately Structures now in the Hands of the Clergy, which might be converted into Play-houses, Exchanges, Market-houses, common Dormitories, and other publick Edifices.

I hope I shall be forgiven a hard Word if I call this a perfect Cavil. I readily own there hath been an old Custom time out of mind, for People to assemble in the Churches every Sunday, and that shops are still frequently shut, in order as it is conceived, to preserve the Memory of that ancient Practice, but how this can prove a hindrance to Business or Pleasure, is hard to imagine. What if the Men of Pleasure are forced one Day in the Week to game at Home instead of the Chocolate-House? Are not the Taverns and Coffee-Houses open? Can there be a more convenient Season for taking a Dose of Physick? Are fewer Claps got upon Sundays than other Days? Is not that the chief Day for Traders to sum up the Accounts of the Week, and for Lawyers to prepare their Briefs? But I would fain know how it can be pretended that the Churches are misapplied. Where are more Appointments and Rendezvouzes of Gallantry? Where more Care to appear in the foremost Box with greater Advantage of Dress? Where more Meetings for Business? Where more Bargains driven of all Sorts? And where so many Conveniences or Incitements to Sleep?

. . . .

It is again objected as a very absurd ridiculous Custom, that a Set of Men should be suffered, much less employed and hired, to bawl one Day in Seven against the Lawfulness of those Methods most in use towards the Pursuit of Greatness, Riches and Pleasure, which are the constant Practice of all Men alive on the other Six. But this Objection is I think, a little unworthy so refined an Age as ours. Let us argue this Matter calmly; I appeal to the Breast of any polite Free-Thinker, whether in the Pursuit of gratifying a predominant Passion, he hath not always felt a wonderful Incitement, by reflecting it was a Thing forbidden: And therefore we see, in order to cultivate this Taste, the Wisdom of the Nation hath taken special Care, that the Ladies should be furnished with Prohibited Silks, and the Men with Prohibited Wine; And indeed it were to be wisht, that some other Prohibitions were promoted, in order to improve the Pleasures of the Town, which for want of such Expedients, begin already, as I am told, to flag and grow languid, giving way daily to cruel Inroads from the Spleen.

It is likewise proposed as a great Advantage to the Publick, that if we once discard the System of the Gospel, all Religion will of course be banished for ever, and consequently along with it, those grievous Prejudices of Education, which under the Names of Virtue, Conscience, Honour, Justice, and the like, are so apt to disturb the Peace of human Minds, and the Notions whereof are so hard to be eradicated by Right Reason or Free Thinking, sometimes during the whole Course of our Lives

. . . .

To all this I answer, that there is one darling Inclination of Man-kind, which usually affects to be a Retainer to Religion, though she be neither its Parent, its Godmother, or its Friend; I mean the Spirit of Opposition, that lived long before Christianity, and can easily subsist without it. . . .

Having thus consider'd the most important Objections against Christianity, and the chief Advantages proposed by the Abolishing there-of; I shall now with equal Deference and Submission to wiser Judgments as before, proceed to mention a few Inconveniencies that may happen, if the Gospel should be repealed; which perhaps the Projectors may not have sufficiently considered.

And first, I am very sensible how much the Gentlemen of Wit and Pleasure are apt to murmur, and be shocked at the sight of so many daggled-tail Parsons, that happen to fall in their way, and offend their Eyes; but at the same Time these wise Reformers do not consider what an Advantage and Felicity it is, for great Wits to be always provided with Objects of Scorn and Contempt, in order to exercise and improve their Talents, and divert their Spleen from falling on each other or on themselves, especially when all this may be done without the least imaginable Danger to their Persons.

And to urge another Argument of a parallel Nature. If Christianity were once abolished, how could the Free Thinkers, the Strong Reason-ers, and the Men of profound Learning, be able to find another Subject so calculated in all Points whereon to display their Abilities. What wonderful Productions of Wit should we be deprived of, from those whose Genius by continual Practice hath been wholly turn'd upon Railery and Invectives against Religion, and would therefore never be able to shine or distinguish themselves upon any other Subject. We are daily complaining of the great decline of Wit among us, and would we take away the greatest, perhaps the only Topick we have left? Who would ever have suspected Asgil for a Wit, or Toland for a Philosopher, if the inexhaustible Stock of Christianity had not been at hand to provide them with Materials? What other Subject through all Art or Nature could have produced Tindall for a profound Author, or furnished him with Readers? It is the wise Choice of the Subject that alone adorns and distinguishes the Writer. For, had a Hundred such Pens as these been employed on the side of Religion, they would have immediately sunk into Silence and Oblivion.

Upon the whole, if it shall still be thought for the Benefit of Church and State, that Christianity be abolished, I conceive however, it may be more convenient to defer the Execution to a Time of Peace, and not venture in this Conjuncture to disoblige our Allies, who as it falls out, are all Christians, and many of them, by the Prejudices of their Education, so bigotted, as to place a sort of Pride in the Appellation. If upon being rejected by them, we are to trust to an Alliance with the Turk, we shall find our selves much deceived: For, as he is too remote, and generally engaged in War with the Persian Emperor, so his People would be more scandalized at our Infidelity, than our Christian Neighbours. Because the Turks are not only strict Observers of religious Worship; but what is worse, believe a God; which is more than is required of us, even while we preserve the Name of Christians.

To conclude, Whatever some may think of the great Advantages to Trade by this favourite Scheme, I do very much apprehend, that in Six Months time after the Act is past for the Extirpation of the Gospel, the Bank, and East–India Stock, may fall at least One per Cent. And since that is Fifty times more than ever the Wisdom of our Age thought fit to venture for the Preservation of Christianity, there is no Reason we should be at so great a Loss, merely for the sake of destroying it.

Notes

1. *Satire.* Can one properly describe a satire as humorous? Satire is often topical and, therefore, sometimes does not survive its own cultural context. Did you find *An Argument Against Abolishing Christianity* funny? Were any of the references lost on you? If so, how did this affect your appreciation of the work? Compare the television program *Saturday Night Live.* How long will the satiric skits on that show continue to be humorous (if they ever were)? Is it possible to write a non-topical satire, one that is universal in its appeal?

2. *Humor.* What makes a work of literature funny? We have on occasion assigned Mark Twain's story, *The Jumping Frog of Calaveras County* (reprinted in Chapter Three), in our Law and Literature class. Some don't find the story funny at all. We have also assigned Eudora Welty's *The Ponder Heart,* and some don't find that funny either.

There must be a close connection between laughter and sorrow, since Shakespeare wrote both comedies and tragedies, and the Greeks of the fifth century B.C. performed both comedies and tragedies in their annual theater festival honoring Dionysus. The greatest American humorist, Mark Twain, at heart was a pessimist. Euripides wrote both the delightful comedy *Alcestis*, (reprinted in Chapter Four) and the blood-curdling tragedy *Medea.*

* * *

Ted Cohen is a professional student of humor. His little book, JOKES (1999), is well worth reading. Prof. Cohen thinks that humor is a way of striking back at those more powerful than oneself. It is a way at getting back at the senselessness of life. It is a way of bonding with those who appreciate your sense of humor. Yet he recognizes that humor may also be cruel, and tasteless.

The following are a couple of jokes from Cohen's JOKES.

JOKES

I

Cruising on Fifth Avenue one day, a taxi is hailed by a man standing on the corner. Entering the cab, the man says, "Take me to the Palmer House."

"The Palmer House?" says the cabbie. "That's in Chicago."

"I know," says his fare. "That's where I want to go."

"I'll drive you to Kennedy," says the cabbie. "You can fly."

"I'm afraid of flying."

"Then I'll drive you over to Grand Central and you can take the train."

"No, the train takes too long and besides, then I'd have to get from Union Station to the Palmer House."

"If I drove you all the way to Chicago it would cost a fortune. Twice a fortune, because you'd have to pay for me to deadhead back to New York."

"That's OK, I can afford it. Here's a few hundred dollars now. I'll pay the rest when we get there."

With no further argument to make, the cabbie drives out of Manhattan into New Jersey and then connects with the Pennsylvania Turnpike, thence to the Ohio Turnpike, the Indiana Turnpike, and finally the Skyway into Chicago. He takes Stony Island to 57th Street, where he turns onto Lake Shore Drive. He drives north as far as Congress, cuts over to Michigan Avenue, goes north again until he can pull over to Wabash, drives back one block south, and screeches to a stop in front of the Wabash entrance to the Palmer House—after two days and one night of non-stop driving.

The passenger peers at the meter, gives the cabbie several hundred dollars to cover the fare and a decent tip, and then opens the door to step onto the sidewalk.

Before anyone can close the door, two women who have been standing at the curb slide into the back seat. Before the startled cabbie can speak, one of the women says, "We want to go to an address on Flatbush Avenue."

"Uh-uh, lady," says the cabbie. "I don't go to Brooklyn."

II

Around the turn of the century a Polish nobleman cultivated his interest in theology. He heard of a certain Jesuit theologian reputed to be the best debating scholar in all of European Christendom, and by various inducements succeeded in bringing this learned man to his estates. Near the center of the nobleman's vast holdings was a small

Jewish village. The prince sent word to the village that there was to be a debate, a learned quarrel concerning theological matters, whose contending participants were to be the newly arrived Jesuit and some Jew from the village. The village was instructed to choose a champion and send him to the castle at the appropriate time.

This instruction was something of nuisance for the village, but, as always, they thought it best to placate their Polish landholder, and so they set about deciding whom to send. While they were making this decision, another message came from the prince explaining the format of the debate.

The debate would be held, said the prince through his messenger, in the traditional manner, with each participant asking a question of the other until one debater was unable to answer. This would end the debate with the asker of the question declared winner and the one who was unable to answer declared loser. Furthermore, said the messenger, the loss would be emphasized, again in the traditional manner, by the prince's axman, who would decapitate the loser.

The villagers apprehended this new message with considerable alarm. Preferring not to risk the head of any villager, even with the possible reward of a decapitated Jesuit, they sent the prince a reply. They conceded the debate, they said: the Jesuit should be declared winner without even a contest.

Soon the prince's messenger reappeared in the village. The prince was determined that there should be a theological spectacular wherein was exhibited the superiority of Christianity to Judaism, and if there could be no civilized debate, then the prince would have to send various emissaries into the village with the purpose of carrying out a slight theological pogrom.

The village was in a hopeless quandary. The elders realized at once that unless someone was sent to debate the Jesuit, they would have more to fear than a single decapitation. But that single decapitation was a certainty: there were no men of learning in the village, no scholars, certainly no theological debaters. But someone would have to go—never to return. The elders set about casting lots among themselves to choose a martyr, but before they finished they were approached by Berl, a poor, ignorant villager who earned his small livelihood mostly through the charity of the village. "I will go," he said.

The elders were astonished, for, as one of them said, "You, Berl, who did not complete even two years of elementary Hebrew school? How could you possibly debate this Jesuit champion?"

"Yes, I know," replied the usually excessively humble but now surprisingly confident Berl, "I did not finish the second year of *cheder*, but I feel that I can do this."

The elders had a new quandary, another real moral problem. To accept Berl's self-nomination would be to send him to his death. But if not Berl, then who? No one from the village had a chance to prevail in any scholarly debate, and certainly not against such a fierce warrior-scholar as the priest promised to be. And if they sent no one, then the prince's minions would descend upon them all. Finally, after much discussion and even more weeping, they drew upon what little knowledge they had of Jewish law and the greater knowledge they took from fatalistic common sense and agreed that Berl would go. He assumed the task with modest pride.

On the appointed day the entire village went with Berl to the palace of the prince. There they discovered that the formal apparatus of the debate was already in place. At the head of the large hall stood a great wooden chair in which sat the prince. Ahead of him and to his right was a small table, and behind the table sat the Jesuit theologian. Ahead of the prince and to his left was another table with a chair behind it meant for Berl. Between the two debaters' tables stood a giant man, the prince's chief huntsman, and he leaned upon his immense ax.

The sight terrified the villagers and they set up a hushed wailing as they took their positions, standing, at the rear of the hall. Berl went to the chair behind his table.

The prince ordered the debate to begin. Customarily these debates begin with the flipping of a zloty coin, or some similar lot-casting, in order to decide who will ask the first question; but the priest saw at once that his opponent was a thoroughly unlearned man who could not possibly know any serious theology, and even so, the priest believed so firmly in the intellectual triumph of Christianity that he was sure he would prevail over any Jew who debated him, and so he said that he would give to the Jew the chance to ask the first question.

Berl looked into the steely eyes of his opponent and in a small, barely audible voice said, "What does this mean?—'Ani lo yodea'?"

Perhaps you do not know what this means, but the Jesuit priest was a master of biblical languages and many other languages as well, and of course he knew that his Hebrew sentence means "I do not know," and he said at once, "I do not know."

Alas for the priest, the axman knew no Hebrew, and when he heard "I do not know," he enforced the penalty for not knowing the answer to a question, and in a flash the head of the finest Christian theologian in all that part of Europe lay at the feet of the prince.

The prince was aghast. The assembled people, Jews and Christians, were stunned. When the Jews had recovered they ran to the front of the room, hoisted Berl to their shoulders, and made their way home to their village as fast as they could.

Once at home they went directly to the synagogue and offered countless prayers, including one improvised for the occasion, "Words of thanksgiving from those recently delivered from Jesuit theology." Afterward they repaired to the largest room in the village, in the study house, where they drank a little and sang and danced and congratulated Berl endlessly, always complimenting him on the immense subtlety of his question.

At last one of the villagers had celebrated long enough for his curiosity and courage to rise, and he approached Berl, saying, "Berl, you are a great man and your name will live forever; but I would like to ask you, master of the theological interrogation: how did you, a man who never passed through even the second year of *cheder*, how did you think of such a magnificent question?"

"It is true," said Berl, "that I completed but one year of *cheder*, but it was in *cheder* I learned that which saved us today. During that first year, one day the *cheder* was visited by a very famous man. It was Rabbi Weinstein, from Berlin, who was making a visit to our village to see an old aunt of his. The famous Rabbi Weinstein, the greatest scholar and teacher in Berlin, paid a brief visit to the *cheder*. When he stopped by me I was trying to read my Hebrew text. There was a sentence I could not translate, and so I said to the great scholar, "Rabbi Weinstein, please, what does this mean—'*Ani lo yodea*'? And he said, 'I do not know.' Today I thought, if even Rabbi Weinstein didn't know, then surely this Jesuit priest does not know."

* * *

In order to provide a balanced perspective, we present you some jokes from Southern Appalachia.

III

One day a man died and arrived at the Pearly Gates. St. Peter welcomed him and told him that all new arrivals get a grand tour of Heaven. As they walked over Heaven, the man saw many beautiful sights: the streets of gold, the angels playing lovely melodies on their harps, beautiful mansions made of fine jewels.

But over in a corner, the man spotted a group of ragged, unshaven, muttering folks, all tied up together. St. Peter hurried by them, but the man stopped him and said, "Hey, who are those people over there, and why are they all tied up together?"

"Oh," said St. Peter, embarrassed, "those are the hillbillies. We have to tie them up or they go home on the weekends."

IV

There was an old farmer up in the hills who raised hogs. He didn't really feed them, just let them roam around in the woods, eating acorns and whatever else they could find. One day the county agent came by and offered him some free advice. "You ought to feed them hogs on corn," he said. "That way you'll save a lot of time."

The farmer thought about that for a minute, and finally asked, "What's time to a hog?"

V

One day this city fellow was driving down the interstate behind a man in an old pickup truck. All of a sudden, the truck started backfiring and smoking, and the man pulled over on the shoulder and stopped. The city fellow pulled over also, to see if he could help. As he was getting out of his car, he saw the driver of the pickup truck run up the bank beside the road. He picked two bunches of wild daisies and ran back to the truck. He took two empty milk jugs out of the back, stuck the daisies in them, and put one milk jug in front of the truck and one behind.

The city fellow was puzzled as all get out by this behavior, so he asked the truck driver what he was doing.

"Well," said the man, "that's simple. If you break down on the highway, you have to put flares out."

Notes

1. *Common Denominator?* Do all these jokes have anything in common?

2. *Cultural Context.* Do these jokes, like satire, depend for their effect on the reader's knowledge of the cultural context within which they originated? Did you "get" all the jokes? If you didn't "get" any of them, why not? Is there such a thing as universal humor?

3. *Lawyer Jokes.* Is the law funny? We have all heard lawyer jokes. The popularity of these jokes is often cited as symptomatic of declining public confidence in the legal profession. Do you agree? Do you laugh at lawyer jokes? What's your favorite lawyer joke?

E. OPINIONS

TEXAS v. JOHNSON

491 U.S. 397, 109 S.Ct. 2533, 105 L.Ed.2d 342 (1989).

Justice BRENNAN delivered the opinion of the Court.

After publicly burning an American flag as a means of political protest, Gregory Lee Johnson was convicted of desecrating a flag in violation of Texas law. This case presents the question whether his conviction is consistent with the First Amendment. We hold that it is not.

I

While the Republican National Convention was taking place in Dallas in 1984, respondent Johnson participated in a political demonstration dubbed the "Republican War Chest Tour." As explained in literature distributed by the demonstrators and in speeches made by them, the purpose of this event was to protest the policies of the Reagan administration and of certain Dallas-based corporations. The demonstrators marched through the Dallas streets, chanting political slogans and stopping at several corporate locations to stage "die-ins" intended to dramatize the consequences of nuclear war. On several occasions they spray-painted the walls of buildings and overturned potted plants, but Johnson himself took no part in such activities. He did, however, accept an American flag handed to him by a fellow protestor who had taken it from a flagpole outside one of the targeted buildings.

The demonstration ended in front of Dallas City Hall, where Johnson unfurled the American flag, doused it with kerosene, and set it on fire. While the flag burned, the protestors chanted: "America, the red, white, and blue, we spit on you." After the demonstrators dispersed, a witness to the flag burning collected the flag's remains and buried them in his backyard. No one was physically injured or threatened with injury, though several witnesses testified that they had been seriously offended by the flag burning.

Of the approximately 100 demonstrators, Johnson alone was charged with a crime. The only criminal offense with which he was charged was the desecration of a venerated object in violation of Tex. Penal Code Ann. § 42.09(a)(3) (1989).[1] After a trial, he was convicted, sentenced to one year in prison, and fined $2,000. The Court of Appeals for the Fifth District of Texas at Dallas affirmed Johnson's conviction, 706 S.W.2d 120 (1986), but the Texas Court of Criminal Appeals reversed, 755 S.W.2d 92 (1988), holding that the State could not, consistent with the First Amendment, punish Johnson for burning the flag in these circumstances.

The Court of Criminal Appeals began by recognizing that Johnson's conduct was symbolic speech protected by the First Amendment: "Given the context of an organized demonstration, speeches, slogans, and the distribution of literature, anyone who observed appellant's act would have understood the message that appellant intended to convey. The act for which appellant was convicted was clearly 'speech' contemplated by the First Amendment." *Id.,* at 95. To justify Johnson's conviction for engaging in symbolic speech, the State asserted two interests: preserving the flag as a symbol of national unity and preventing breaches of the peace. The Court of Criminal Appeals held that neither interest supported his conviction.

Acknowledging that this Court had not yet decided whether the Government may criminally sanction flag desecration in order to preserve the flag's symbolic value, the Texas court nevertheless concluded

---

1. Texas Penal Code Ann. § 42.09 (1989) provides in full:

"§ 42.09. Desecration of Venerated Object

"(a) A person commits an offense if he intentionally or knowingly desecrates:

"(1) a public monument;

"(2) a place of worship or burial; or

"(3) a state or national flag.

"(b) For purposes of this section, 'desecrate' means deface, damage, or otherwise physically mistreat in a way that the actor knows will seriously offend one or more persons likely to observe or discover his action.

"(c) An offense under this section is a Class A misdemeanor."

that our decision in *West Virginia Board of Education v. Barnette,* 319 U.S. 624, 63 S.Ct. 1178, 87 L.Ed. 1628 (1943), suggested that furthering this interest by curtailing speech was impermissible. "Recognizing that the right to differ is the centerpiece of our First Amendment freedoms," the court explained, "a government cannot mandate by fiat a feeling of unity in its citizens. Therefore, that very same government cannot carve out a symbol of unity and prescribe a set of approved messages to be associated with that symbol when it cannot mandate the status or feeling the symbol purports to represent." 755 S.W.2d, at 97. Noting that the State had not shown that the flag was in "grave and immediate danger," *Barnette, supra,* at 639, 63 S.Ct., at 1186, of being stripped of its symbolic value, the Texas court also decided that the flag's special status was not endangered by Johnson's conduct.

As to the State's goal of preventing breaches of the peace, the court concluded that the flag-desecration statute was not drawn narrowly enough to encompass only those flag burnings that were likely to result in a serious disturbance of the peace. And in fact, the court emphasized, the flag burning in this particular case did not threaten such a reaction. " 'Serious offense' occurred," the court admitted, "but there was no breach of peace nor does the record reflect that the situation was potentially explosive. One cannot equate 'serious offense' with incitement to breach the peace." *Id.,* at 96. The court also stressed that another Texas statute, Tex. Penal Code Ann. § 42.01 (1989), prohibited breaches of the peace. Citing *Boos v. Barry,* 485 U.S. 312, 108 S.Ct. 1157, 99 L.Ed.2d 333 (1988), the court decided that § 42.01 demonstrated Texas' ability to prevent disturbances of the peace without punishing this flag desecration. 755 S.W.2d, at 96.

Because it reversed Johnson's conviction on the ground that § 42.09 was unconstitutional as applied to him, the state court did not address Johnson's argument that the statute was, on its face, unconstitutionally vague and overbroad. We granted certiorari, 488 U.S. 907, 109 S.Ct. 257, 102 L.Ed.2d 245 (1988), and now affirm.

II

Johnson was convicted of flag desecration for burning the flag rather than for uttering insulting words. This fact somewhat complicates our consideration of his conviction under the First Amendment. We must first determine whether Johnson's burning of the flag constituted expressive conduct, permitting him to invoke the First Amendment in challenging his conviction. See, *e.g., Spence v. Washington,* 418 U.S. 405, 409–411, 94 S.Ct. 2727, 2729–31, 41 L.Ed.2d 842 (1974). If his conduct was expressive, we next decide whether the State's regulation is related to the suppression of free expression. If the State's regulation is not related to expression, then the less stringent standard we announced in *United States v. O'Brien* for regulations of noncommunicative conduct controls. If it is, then we are outside of *O'Brien's* test, and we must ask whether this interest justifies Johnson's conviction under a more demanding standard.[2] A third possibility is that the State's asserted interest is simply not implicated on these facts, and in that event the interest drops out of the picture.

The First Amendment literally forbids the abridgment only of "speech," but we have long recognized that its protection does not end at the spoken or written word. While we have rejected "the view that an apparently limitless variety of conduct can be labeled 'speech' whenever the person engaging in the conduct intends thereby to express an idea," *United States v. O'Brien, supra,* at 376, 88 S.Ct., at 1678, we have acknowledged that conduct may be "sufficiently imbued with elements of communication to fall within the scope of the First and Fourteenth Amendments," *Spence, supra,* at 409, 94 S.Ct., at 2730.

In deciding whether particular conduct possesses sufficient communicative elements to bring the First Amendment into play, we have asked whether "[a]n intent to convey a particularized message was present, and [whether] the likelihood was great that the message would be understood by those who viewed it." 418 U.S., at 410–411, 94 S.Ct., at 2730. Hence, we have recognized the expressive nature of students' wearing of black armbands to protest American military involvement in Vietnam, *Tinker v. Des Moines Independent Community School Dist.,* 393 U.S. 503, 505, 89 S.Ct. 733, 735, 21 L.Ed.2d 731 (1969); of a sit-in by blacks in a "whites only" area to protest segregation, *Brown v. Louisiana,* 383 U.S. 131, 141–142, 86 S.Ct. 719, 723–24, 15 L.Ed.2d 637 (1966); of the wearing of American military uniforms in a dramatic presentation criticizing American involvement in Vietnam, *Schacht v. United States,* 398 U.S. 58, 90 S.Ct. 1555, 26 L.Ed.2d 44 (1970); and of picketing about a wide variety of causes, see, *e.g., Food Employees v. Logan Valley Plaza, Inc.,* 391 U.S. 308, 313–314, 88 S.Ct. 1601, 1605–06, 20 L.Ed.2d 603 (1968); *United States v. Grace,* 461 U.S. 171, 176, 103 S.Ct. 1702, 1706, 75 L.Ed.2d 736 (1983).

Especially pertinent to this case are our decisions recognizing the communicative nature of conduct relating to flags. Attaching a peace sign to the flag, *Spence, supra,* at 409–410, 94 S.Ct., at 2729–30; refusing to salute the flag, *Barnette,* 319 U.S., at 632, 63 S.Ct., at 1182; and displaying a red flag, *Stromberg v. California,* 283 U.S. 359, 368–369, 51 S.Ct. 532, 535–36, 75 L.Ed. 1117 (1931), we have held, all may find shelter under the First Amendment. See also *Smith v. Goguen,* 415 U.S. 566, 588, 94 S.Ct. 1242, 1254, 39 L.Ed.2d 605 (1974) (WHITE, J., concurring in judgment) (treating flag "contemptuously" by wearing pants with small flag sewn into their seat is expressive conduct). That we have had little difficulty identifying an expressive element in conduct

---

2. A tired person might, for example, drag a flag through the mud, knowing that this conduct is likely to offend others, and yet have no thought of expressing any idea; neither the language nor the Texas courts' interpretations of the statute precludes the possibility that such a person would be prosecuted for flag desecration. Because the prosecution of a person who had not engaged in expressive conduct would pose a different case, and because this case may be disposed of on narrower grounds, we address only Johnson's claim that § 42.09 as applied to political expression like his violates the First Amendment.

relating to flags should not be surprising. The very purpose of a national flag is to serve as a symbol of our country; it is, one might say, "the one visible manifestation of two hundred years of nationhood." *Id.,* at 603, 94 S.Ct., at 1262 (REHNQUIST, J., dissenting). Thus, we have observed:

> "[T]he flag salute is a form of utterance. Symbolism is a primitive but effective way of communicating ideas. The use of an emblem or flag to symbolize some system, idea, institution, or personality, is a short cut from mind to mind. Causes and nations, political parties, lodges and ecclesiastical groups seek to knit the loyalty of their followings to a flag or banner, a color or design." *Barnette, supra,* at 632, 63 S.Ct., at 1182.

Pregnant with expressive content, the flag as readily signifies this Nation as does the combination of letters found in "America."

We have not automatically concluded, however, that any action taken with respect to our flag is expressive. Instead, in characterizing such action for First Amendment purposes, we have considered the context in which it occurred. In *Spence,* for example, we emphasized that Spence's taping of a peace sign to his flag was "roughly simultaneous with and concededly triggered by the Cambodian incursion and the Kent State tragedy." 418 U.S., at 410, 94 S.Ct., at 2730. The State of Washington had conceded, in fact, that Spence's conduct was a form of communication, and we stated that "the State's concession is inevitable on this record." *Id.,* at 409.

The State of Texas conceded for purposes of its oral argument in this case that Johnson's conduct was expressive conduct, and this concession seems to us as prudent as was Washington's in *Spence.* Johnson burned an American flag as part—indeed, as the culmination— of a political demonstration that coincided with the convening of the Republican Party and its renomination of Ronald Reagan for President. The expressive, overtly political nature of this conduct was both intentional and overwhelmingly apparent. At his trial, Johnson explained his reasons for burning the flag as follows: "The American Flag was burned as Ronald Reagan was being renominated as President. And a more powerful statement of symbolic speech, whether you agree with it or not, couldn't have been made at that time. It's quite a just position [juxtaposition]. We had new patriotism and no patriotism." 5 Record 656. In these circumstances, Johnson's burning of the flag was conduct "sufficiently imbued with elements of communication," *Spence,* 418 U.S., at 409, 94 S.Ct., at 2730, to implicate the First Amendment.

III

The government generally has a freer hand in restricting expressive conduct than it has in restricting the written or spoken word. It may not, however, proscribe particular conduct *because* it has expressive elements. "[W]hat might be termed the more generalized guarantee of freedom of expression makes the communicative nature of conduct an inadequate *basis* for singling out that conduct for proscription. A law *directed at* the communicative nature of conduct must, like a law directed at speech itself, be justified by the substantial showing of need that the First Amendment requires." *Community for Creative Non-Violence v. Watt,* 227 U.S.App.D.C. 19, 55–56, 703 F.2d 586, 622–623 (1983) (Scalia, J., dissenting) (emphasis in original), rev'd *sub nom. Clark v. Community for Creative Non-Violence, supra.* It is, in short, not simply the verbal or nonverbal nature of the expression, but the governmental interest at stake, that helps to determine whether a restriction on that expression is valid.

Thus, although we have recognized that where " 'speech' and 'nonspeech' elements are combined in the same course of conduct, a sufficiently important governmental interest in regulating the nonspeech element can justify incidental limitations on First Amendment freedoms," *O'Brien, supra,* at 376, 88 S.Ct., at 1678, we have limited the applicability of *O'Brien*'s relatively lenient standard to those cases in which "the governmental interest is unrelated to the suppression of free expression." *Id.,* at 377, 88 S.Ct., at 1679; see also *Spence, supra,* at 414, n. 8, 94 S.Ct., at 2732, n. 8. In stating, moreover, that *O'Brien*'s test "in the last analysis is little, if any, different from the standard applied to time, place, or manner restrictions," *Clark, supra,* at 298, 104 S.Ct., at 3071, we have highlighted the requirement that the governmental interest in question be unconnected to expression in order to come under *O'Brien*'s less demanding rule.

In order to decide whether *O'Brien*'s test applies here, therefore, we must decide whether Texas has asserted an interest in support of Johnson's conviction that is unrelated to the suppression of expression. If we find that an interest asserted by the State is simply not implicated on the facts before us, we need not ask whether *O'Brien*'s test applies. The State offers two separate interests to justify this conviction: preventing breaches of the peace and preserving the flag as a symbol of nationhood and national unity. We hold that the first interest is not implicated on this record and that the second is related to the suppression of expression.

A

Texas claims that its interest in preventing breaches of the peace justifies Johnson's conviction for flag desecration. However, no disturbance of the peace actually occurred or threatened to occur because of Johnson's burning of the flag. Although the State stresses the disruptive behavior of the protestors during their march toward City Hall, Brief for Petitioner 34–36, it admits that "no actual breach of the peace occurred at the time of the flag burning or in response to the flag burning." *Id.,* at 34. The State's emphasis on the protestors' disorderly actions prior to arriving at City Hall is not only somewhat surprising given that no charges were brought on the basis of this conduct, but it also fails to show that a disturbance of the peace was a likely reaction to Johnson's conduct. The only evidence offered by the State at trial to show the reaction to Johnson's actions was the testimony of several persons who had been seriously offended by the flag burning.

The State's position, therefore, amounts to a claim that an audience that takes serious offense at particular expression is necessarily likely to disturb the peace and that the expression may be prohibited on this basis. Our precedents do not countenance such a presumption. On the contrary, they recognize that a principal "function of free speech under our system of government is to invite dispute. It may indeed best serve its high purpose when it induces a condition of unrest, creates dissatisfaction with conditions as they are, or even stirs people to anger." *Terminiello v. Chicago,* 337 U.S. 1, 4, 69 S.Ct. 894, 896, 93 L.Ed. 1131 (1949). It would be odd indeed to conclude *both* that "if it is the speaker's opinion that gives offense, that consequence is a reason for according it constitutional protection," *FCC v. Pacifica Foundation,* 438 U.S. 726, 745, 98 S.Ct. 3026, 3038, 57 L.Ed.2d 1073 (1978) (opinion of STEVENS, J.), *and* that the government may ban the expression of certain disagreeable ideas on the unsupported presumption that their very disagreeableness will provoke violence.

Thus, we have not permitted the government to assume that every expression of a provocative idea will incite a riot, but have instead required careful consideration of the actual circumstances surrounding such expression, asking whether the expression "is directed to inciting or producing imminent lawless action and is likely to incite or produce such action." *Brandenburg v. Ohio,* 395 U.S. 444, 447, 89 S.Ct. 1827, 1829, 23 L.Ed.2d 430 (1969) (reviewing circumstances surrounding rally and speeches by Ku Klux Klan). To accept Texas' arguments that it need only demonstrate "the potential for a breach of the peace," Brief for Petitioner 37, and that every flag burning necessarily possesses that potential, would be to eviscerate our holding in *Brandenburg.* This we decline to do.

Nor does Johnson's expressive conduct fall within that small class of "fighting words" that are "likely to provoke the average person to retaliation, and thereby cause a breach of the peace." *Chaplinsky v. New Hampshire,* 315 U.S. 568, 574, 62 S.Ct. 766, 770, 86 L.Ed. 1031 (1942). No reasonable onlooker would have regarded Johnson's generalized expression of dissatisfaction with the policies of the Federal Government as a direct personal insult or an invitation to exchange fisticuffs....

We thus conclude that the State's interest in maintaining order is not implicated on these facts. The State need not worry that our holding will disable it from preserving the peace. We do not suggest that the First Amendment forbids a State to prevent "imminent lawless action." *Brandenburg, supra,* at 447, 89 S.Ct., at 1829. And, in fact, Texas already has a statute specifically prohibiting breaches of the peace, Tex. Penal Code Ann. § 42.01 (1989), which tends to confirm that Texas need not punish this flag desecration in order to keep the peace. See *Boos v. Barry,* 485 U.S., at 327–329, 108 S.Ct., at 1167–1168.

B

The State also asserts an interest in preserving the flag as a symbol of nationhood and national unity. In *Spence,* we acknowledged that the government's interest in preserving the flag's special symbolic value "is directly related to expression in the context of activity" such as affixing a peace symbol to a flag. 418 U.S., at 414, n. 8, 94 S.Ct., at 2732, n. 8. We are equally persuaded that this interest is related to expression in the case of Johnson's burning of the flag. The State, apparently, is concerned that such conduct will lead people to believe either that the flag does not stand for nationhood and national unity, but instead reflects other, less positive concepts, or that the concepts reflected in the flag do not in fact exist, that is, that we do not enjoy unity as a Nation. These concerns blossom only when a person's treatment of the flag communicates some message, and thus are related "to the suppression of free expression" within the meaning of *O'Brien.* We are thus outside of *O'Brien*'s test altogether.

IV

It remains to consider whether the State's interest in preserving the flag as a symbol of nationhood and national unity justifies Johnson's conviction.

As in *Spence,* "[w]e are confronted with a case of prosecution for the expression of an idea through activity," and "[a]ccordingly, we must examine with particular care the interests advanced by [petitioner] to support its prosecution." 418 U.S., at 411, 94 S.Ct., at 2730. Johnson was not, we add, prosecuted for the expression of just any idea; he was prosecuted for his expression of dissatisfaction with the policies of this country, expression situated at the core of our First Amendment values.

Moreover, Johnson was prosecuted because he knew that his politically charged expression would cause "serious offense." If he had burned the flag as a means of disposing of it because it was dirty or torn, he would not have been convicted of flag desecration under this Texas law: federal law designates burning as the preferred means of disposing of a flag "when it is in such condition that it is no longer a fitting emblem for display," 36 U.S.C. § 176(k), and Texas has no quarrel with this means of disposal. Brief for Petitioner 45. The Texas law is thus not aimed at protecting the physical integrity of the flag in all circumstances, but is designed instead to protect it only against impairments that would cause serious offense to others. Texas concedes as much: "Section 42.09(b) reaches only those severe acts of physical abuse of the flag carried out in a way likely to be offensive. The statute mandates intentional or knowing abuse, that is, the kind of mistreatment that is not innocent, but rather is intentionally designed to seriously offend other individuals." *Id.,* at 44.

Whether Johnson's treatment of the flag violated Texas law thus depended on the likely communicative impact of his expressive conduct. Our decision in *Boos v. Barry, supra,* tells us that this restriction on

Johnson's expression is content based. In *Boos,* we considered the constitutionality of a law prohibiting "the display of any sign within 500 feet of a foreign embassy if that sign tends to bring that foreign government into 'public odium' or 'public disrepute.' " *Id.,* at 315, 108 S.Ct., at 1160. Rejecting the argument that the law was content neutral because it was justified by "our international law obligation to shield diplomats from speech that offends their dignity," *id.,* at 320, 108 S.Ct., at 1163, we held that "[t]he emotive impact of speech on its audience is not a 'secondary effect' " unrelated to the content of the expression itself. *Id.,* at 321, 108 S.Ct., at 1164 (plurality opinion); see also *id.,* at 334, 108 S.Ct., at 1171 (Brennan, J., concurring in part and concurring in judgment).

According to the principles announced in *Boos,* Johnson's political expression was restricted because of the content of the message he conveyed. We must therefore subject the State's asserted interest in preserving the special symbolic character of the flag to "the most exacting scrutiny." *Boos v. Barry, supra,* 485 U.S., at 321, 108 S.Ct., at 1164.[3]

Texas argues that its interest in preserving the flag as a symbol of nationhood and national unity survives this close analysis. Quoting extensively from the writings of this Court chronicling the flag's historic and symbolic role in our society, the State emphasizes the " 'special place' " reserved for the flag in our Nation. Brief for Petitioner 22, quoting *Smith v. Goguen,* 415 U.S., at 601, 94 S.Ct., at 1261 (REHNQUIST, J., dissenting). The State's argument is not that it has an interest simply in maintaining the flag as a symbol of *something,* no matter what it symbolizes; indeed, if that were the State's position, it would be difficult to see how that interest is endangered by highly symbolic conduct such as Johnson's. Rather, the State's claim is that it has an interest in preserving the flag as a symbol of *nationhood* and *national unity,* a symbol with a determinate range of meanings. According to Texas, if one physically treats the flag in a way that would tend to cast doubt on either the idea that nationhood and national unity are the flag's referents or that national unity actually exists, the message conveyed thereby is a harmful one and therefore may be prohibited.[4]

3. Our inquiry is, of course, bounded by the particular facts of this case and by the statute under which Johnson was convicted. There was no evidence that Johnson himself stole the flag he burned, Tr. of Oral Arg. 17, nor did the prosecution or the arguments urged in support of it depend on the theory that the flag was stolen. *Ibid.* Thus, our analysis does not rely on the way in which the flag was acquired, and nothing in our opinion should be taken to suggest that one is free to steal a flag so long as one later uses it to communicate an idea. We also emphasize that Johnson was prosecuted *only* for flag desecration—not for trespass, disorderly conduct, or arson.

4. Texas claims that "Texas is not endorsing, protecting, avowing or prohibiting any particular philosophy." Brief for Petitioner 29. If Texas means to suggest that its asserted interest does not prefer Democrats over Socialists, or Republicans over Democrats, for example, then it is beside the point, for Johnson does not rely on such an argument. He argues instead that the State's desire to maintain the flag as a symbol of nationhood and national unity assumes that there is only one proper view of the flag. Thus, if Texas means to argue that its interest does not prefer *any* viewpoint over another, it is mistaken; surely

If there is a bedrock principle underlying the First Amendment, it is that the government may not prohibit the expression of an idea simply because society finds the idea itself offensive or disagreeable. . . .

We have not recognized an exception to this principle even where our flag has been involved. In *Street v. New York,* 394 U.S. 576, 89 S.Ct. 1354, 22 L.Ed.2d 572 (1969), we held that a State may not criminally punish a person for uttering words critical of the flag. Rejecting the argument that the conviction could be sustained on the ground that Street had "failed to show the respect for our national symbol which may properly be demanded of every citizen," we concluded that "the constitutionally guaranteed 'freedom to be intellectually . . . diverse or even contrary,' and the 'right to differ as to things that touch the heart of the existing order,' encompass the freedom to express publicly one's opinions about our flag, including those opinions which are defiant or contemptuous." *Id.,* at 593, 89 S.Ct., at 1366, quoting *Barnette,* 319 U.S., at 642, 63 S.Ct., at 1187. Nor may the government, we have held, compel conduct that would evince respect for the flag. "To sustain the compulsory flag salute we are required to say that a Bill of Rights which guards the individual's right to speak his own mind, left it open to public authorities to compel him to utter what is not in his mind." *Id.,* at 634, 63 S.Ct., at 1183.

In holding in *Barnette* that the Constitution did not leave this course open to the government, Justice Jackson described one of our society's defining principles in words deserving of their frequent repetition: "If there is any fixed star in our constitutional constellation, it is that no official, high or petty, can prescribe what shall be orthodox in politics, nationalism, religion, or other matters of opinion or force citizens to confess by word or act their faith therein." *Id.,* at 642, 63 S.Ct., at 1187. In *Spence,* we held that the same interest asserted by Texas here was insufficient to support a criminal conviction under a flag-misuse statute for the taping of a peace sign to an American flag. "Given the protected character of [Spence's] expression and in light of the fact that no interest the State may have in preserving the physical integrity of a privately owned flag was significantly impaired on these facts," we held, "the conviction must be invalidated." 418 U.S., at 415, 94 S.Ct., at 2732. See also *Goguen, supra,* 415 U.S., at 588, 94 S.Ct., at 1254 (WHITE, J., concurring in judgment) (to convict person who had sewn a flag onto the seat of his pants for "contemptuous" treatment of the flag would be "[t]o convict not to protect the physical integrity or to protect against acts interfering with the proper use of the flag, but to punish for communicating ideas unacceptable to the controlling majority in the legislature").

In short, nothing in our precedents suggests that a State may foster its own view of the flag by prohibiting expressive conduct relating to it.[5]

one's attitude toward the flag and its referents is a viewpoint.

5. Our decision in *Halter v. Nebraska,* 205 U.S. 34, 27 S.Ct. 419, 51 L.Ed. 696 (1907), addressing the validity of a state law

To bring its argument outside our precedents, Texas attempts to convince us that even if its interest in preserving the flag's symbolic role does not allow it to prohibit words or some expressive conduct critical of the flag, it does permit it to forbid the outright destruction of the flag. The State's argument cannot depend here on the distinction between written or spoken words and nonverbal conduct. That distinction, we have shown, is of no moment where the nonverbal conduct is expressive, as it is here, and where the regulation of that conduct is related to expression, as it is here. See *supra,* at 2538–2539. In addition, both *Barnette* and *Spence* involved expressive conduct, not only verbal communication, and both found that conduct protected.

Texas' focus on the precise nature of Johnson's expression, moreover, misses the point of our prior decisions: their enduring lesson, that the government may not prohibit expression simply because it disagrees with its message, is not dependent on the particular mode in which one chooses to express an idea.[6] If we were to hold that a State may forbid flag burning wherever it is likely to endanger the flag's symbolic role, but allow it wherever burning a flag promotes that role—as where, for example, a person ceremoniously burns a dirty flag—we would be saying that when it comes to impairing the flag's physical integrity, the flag itself may be used as a symbol—as a substitute for the written or spoken word or a "short cut from mind to mind"—only in one direction. We would be permitting a State to "prescribe what shall be orthodox" by saying that one may burn the flag to convey one's attitude toward it and its referents only if one does not endanger the flag's representation of nationhood and national unity.

We never before have held that the Government may ensure that a symbol be used to express only one view of that symbol or its referents. Indeed, in *Schacht v. United States,* we invalidated a federal statute permitting an actor portraying a member of one of our Armed Forces to

prohibiting certain commercial uses of the flag, is not to the contrary. That case was decided "nearly 20 years before the Court concluded that the First Amendment applies to the States by virtue of the Fourteenth Amendment." *Spence v. Washington,* 418 U.S. 405, 413, n. 7, 94 S.Ct. 2727, 2731, n. 7, 41 L.Ed.2d 842 (1974). More important, as we continually emphasized in *Halter* itself, that case involved purely commercial rather than political speech. 205 U.S., at 38, 41, 42, 45, 27 S.Ct., at 420, 421, 422, 423.

Nor does *San Francisco Arts & Athletics, Inc. v. United States Olympic Committee,* 483 U.S. 522, 524, 107 S.Ct. 2971, 2975, 97 L.Ed.2d 427 (1987), addressing the validity of Congress' decision to "authoriz[e] the United States Olympic Committee to prohibit certain commercial and promotional uses of the word 'Olympic,'" relied upon by THE CHIEF JUSTICE's dissent, *post,* at 2552,

even begin to tell us whether the government may criminally punish physical conduct towards the flag engaged in as a means of political protest.

6. THE CHIEF JUSTICE's dissent appears to believe that Johnson's conduct may be prohibited and, indeed, criminally sanctioned, because "his act ... conveyed nothing that could not have been conveyed and was not conveyed just as forcefully in a dozen different ways." *Post,* at 2553. Not only does this assertion sit uneasily next to the dissent's quite correct reminder that the flag occupies a unique position in our society—which demonstrates that messages conveyed without use of the flag are not "just as forcefu[l]" as those conveyed with it—but it also ignores the fact that, in *Spence, supra,* we "rejected summarily" this very claim. See 418 U.S., at 411, n. 4, 94 S.Ct., at 2731.

" 'wear the uniform of that armed force if the portrayal does not tend to discredit that armed force.' " 398 U.S., at 60, 90 S.Ct., at 1557, quoting 10 U.S.C. § 772(f). This proviso, we held, "which leaves Americans free to praise the war in Vietnam but can send persons like Schacht to prison for opposing it, cannot survive in a country which has the First Amendment." *Id.*, at 63, 90 S.Ct., at 1559.

We perceive no basis on which to hold that the principle underlying our decision in *Schacht* does not apply to this case. To conclude that the government may permit designated symbols to be used to communicate only a limited set of messages would be to enter territory having no discernible or defensible boundaries. Could the government, on this theory, prohibit the burning of state flags? Of copies of the Presidential seal? Of the Constitution? In evaluating these choices under the First Amendment, how would we decide which symbols were sufficiently special to warrant this unique status? To do so, we would be forced to consult our own political preferences, and impose them on the citizenry, in the very way that the First Amendment forbids us to do.

There is, moreover, no indication—either in the text of the Constitution or in our cases interpreting it—that a separate juridical category exists for the American flag alone. Indeed, we would not be surprised to learn that the persons who framed our Constitution and wrote the Amendment that we now construe were not known for their reverence for the Union Jack. The First Amendment does not guarantee that other concepts virtually sacred to our Nation as a whole—such as the principle that discrimination on the basis of race is odious and destructive—will go unquestioned in the marketplace of ideas. We decline, therefore, to create for the flag an exception to the joust of principles protected by the First Amendment.

It is not the State's ends, but its means, to which we object. It cannot be gainsaid that there is a special place reserved for the flag in this Nation, and thus we do not doubt that the government has a legitimate interest in making efforts to "preserv[e] the national flag as an unalloyed symbol of our country." *Spence*, 418 U.S., at 412, 94 S.Ct., at 2731. We reject the suggestion, urged at oral argument by counsel for Johnson, that the government lacks "any state interest whatsoever" in regulating the manner in which the flag may be displayed. Congress has, for example, enacted precatory regulations describing the proper treatment of the flag, see 36 U.S.C. §§ 173–177, and we cast no doubt on the legitimacy of its interest in making such recommendations. To say that the government has an interest in encouraging proper treatment of the flag, however, is not to say that it may criminally punish a person for burning a flag as a means of political protest. "National unity as an end which officials may foster by persuasion and example is not in question. The problem is whether under our Constitution compulsion as here employed is a permissible means for its achievement." *Barnette,* 319 U.S., at 640, 63 S.Ct., at 1186.

We are fortified in today's conclusion by our conviction that forbidding criminal punishment for conduct such as Johnson's will not endanger the special role played by our flag or the feelings it inspires. To paraphrase Justice Holmes, we submit that nobody can suppose that this one gesture of an unknown man will change our Nation's attitude towards its flag. See *Abrams v. United States*, 250 U.S. 616, 628, 40 S.Ct. 17, 21, 63 L.Ed. 1173 (1919) (Holmes, J., dissenting). Indeed, Texas' argument that the burning of an American flag " 'is an act having a high likelihood to cause a breach of the peace,' " Brief for Petitioner 31, and its statute's implicit assumption that physical mistreatment of the flag will lead to "serious offense," tend to confirm that the flag's special role is not in danger; if it were, no one would riot or take offense because a flag had been burned.

We are tempted to say, in fact, that the flag's deservedly cherished place in our community will be strengthened, not weakened, by our holding today. Our decision is a reaffirmation of the principles of freedom and inclusiveness that the flag best reflects, and of the conviction that our toleration of criticism such as Johnson's is a sign and source of our strength. Indeed, one of the proudest images of our flag, the one immortalized in our own national anthem, is of the bombardment it survived at Fort McHenry. It is the Nation's resilience, not its rigidity, that Texas sees reflected in the flag—and it is that resilience that we reassert today.

The way to preserve the flag's special role is not to punish those who feel differently about these matters. It is to persuade them that they are wrong. . . . We can imagine no more appropriate response to burning a flag than waving one's own, no better way to counter a flag burner's message than by saluting the flag that burns, no surer means of preserving the dignity even of the flag that burned than by—as one witness here did—according its remains a respectful burial. We do not consecrate the flag by punishing its desecration, for in doing so we dilute the freedom that this cherished emblem represents.

V

Johnson was convicted for engaging in expressive conduct. The State's interest in preventing breaches of the peace does not support his conviction because Johnson's conduct did not threaten to disturb the peace. Nor does the State's interest in preserving the flag as a symbol of nationhood and national unity justify his criminal conviction for engaging in political expression. The judgment of the Texas Court of Criminal Appeals is therefore

Affirmed.

[Justice KENNEDY's concurring opinion is omitted.]

Chief Justice REHNQUIST, with whom Justice WHITE and Justice O'CONNOR join, dissenting.

In holding this Texas statute unconstitutional, the Court ignores Justice Holmes' familiar aphorism that "a page of history is worth a volume of logic." *New York Trust Co. v. Eisner,* 256 U.S. 345, 349, 41 S.Ct. 506, 507, 65 L.Ed. 963 (1921). For more than 200 years, the American flag has occupied a unique position as the symbol of our Nation, a uniqueness that justifies a governmental prohibition against flag burning in the way respondent Johnson did here.

At the time of the American Revolution, the flag served to unify the Thirteen Colonies at home, while obtaining recognition of national sovereignty abroad. Ralph Waldo Emerson's "Concord Hymn" describes the first skirmishes of the Revolutionary War in these lines:

> "By the rude bridge that arched the flood
>   Their flag to April's breeze unfurled,
> Here once the embattled farmers stood
>   And fired the shot heard round the world."

During that time, there were many colonial and regimental flags, adorned with such symbols as pine trees, beavers, anchors, and rattle-snakes, bearing slogans such as "Liberty or Death," "Hope," "An Appeal to Heaven," and "Don't Tread on Me." The first distinctive flag of the Colonies was the "Grand Union Flag"—with 13 stripes and a British flag in the left corner—which was flown for the first time on January 2, 1776, by troops of the Continental Army around Boston. By June 14, 1777, after we declared our independence from England, the Continental Congress resolved:

> "That the flag of the thirteen United States be thirteen stripes, alternate red and white: that the union be thirteen stars, white in a blue field, representing a new constellation." 8 Journal of the Continental Congress 1774–1789, p. 464 (W. Ford ed. 1907).

One immediate result of the flag's adoption was that American vessels harassing British shipping sailed under an authorized national flag. Without such a flag, the British could treat captured seamen as pirates and hang them summarily; with a national flag, such seamen were treated as prisoners of war.

During the War of 1812, British naval forces sailed up Chesapeake Bay and marched overland to sack and burn the city of Washington. They then sailed up the Patapsco River to invest the city of Baltimore, but to do so it was first necessary to reduce Fort McHenry in Baltimore Harbor. Francis Scott Key, a Washington lawyer, had been granted permission by the British to board one of their warships to negotiate the release of an American who had been taken prisoner. That night, waiting anxiously on the British ship, Key watched the British fleet firing on Fort McHenry. Finally, at daybreak, he saw the fort's American flag still flying; the British attack had failed. Intensely moved, he began to scribble on the back of an envelope the poem that became our national anthem:

> "O say can you see by the dawn's early light,

What so proudly we hail'd at the twilight's last gleaming,
Whose broad stripes & bright stars, thro' the perilous fight
O'er the ramparts we watch'd were so gallantly streaming?
And the rocket's red glare, the bomb bursting in air,
Gave proof through the night that our flag was still there,
O say does that star-spangled banner yet wave
O'er the land of the free & the home of the brave?''

The American flag played a central role in our Nation's most tragic conflict, when the North fought against the South. The lowering of the American flag at Fort Sumter was viewed as the start of the war. G. Preble, History of the Flag of the United States of America 453 (1880). The Southern States, to formalize their separation from the Union, adopted the ''Stars and Bars'' of the Confederacy. The Union troops marched to the sound of ''Yes We'll Rally Round The Flag Boys, We'll Rally Once Again.'' President Abraham Lincoln refused proposals to remove from the American flag the stars representing the rebel States, because he considered the conflict not a war between two nations but an attack by 11 States against the National Government. *Id.*, at 411. By war's end, the American flag again flew over ''an indestructible union, composed of indestructible states.'' *Texas v. White,* 74 U.S. (7 Wall.) 700, 725, 19 L.Ed. 227 (1869).

One of the great stories of the Civil War is told in John Greenleaf Whittier's poem, ''Barbara Frietchie'':

''Up from the meadows rich with corn,
Clear in the cool September morn,

The clustered spires of Frederick stand
Green-walled by the hills of Maryland.

Round about them orchards sweep,
Apple- and peach-tree fruited deep,

Fair as a garden of the Lord
To the eyes of the famished rebel horde,

On that pleasant morn of the early fall
When Lee marched over the mountain wall,—

Over the mountains winding down,
Horse and foot, into Frederick town.

Forty flags with their silver stars,
Forty flags with their crimson bars,

Flapped in the morning wind: the sun
Of noon looked down, and saw not one.

Up rose old Barbara Frietchie then,
Bowed with her fourscore years and ten;

Bravest of all in Frederick town,
She took up the flag the men hauled down;

In her attic-window the staff she set,

To show that one heart was loyal yet.

Up the street came the rebel tread,
Stonewall Jackson riding ahead.

Under his slouched hat left and right
He glanced: the old flag met his sight.

"Halt!"—the dust-brown ranks stood fast.
"Fire!"—out blazed the rifle-blast.

It shivered the window, pane and sash;
It rent the banner with seam and gash.

Quick, as it fell, from the broken staff
Dame Barbara snatched the silken scarf;

She leaned far out on the window-sill,
And shook it forth with a royal will.

"Shoot, if you must, this old gray head,
But spare your country's flag," she said.

A shade of sadness, a blush of shame,
Over the face of the leader came;

The nobler nature within him stirred
To life at that woman's deed and word;

"Who touches a hair of yon gray head
Dies like a dog! March on!" he said.

All day long through Frederick street
Sounded the tread of marching feet:

All day long that free flag tost
Over the heads of the rebel host.

Ever its torn folds rose and fell
On the loyal winds that loved it well;

And through the hill-gaps sunset light
Shone over it with a warm good-night.

Barbara Frietchie's work is o'er,
And the Rebel rides on his raids no more.

Honor to her! and let a tear
Fall, for her sake, on Stonewall's bier.

Over Barbara Frietchie's grave,
Flag of Freedom and Union, wave!

Peace and order and beauty draw
Round thy symbol of light and law;

And ever the stars above look down
On thy stars below in Frederick town!

In the First and Second World Wars, thousands of our countrymen
died on foreign soil fighting for the American cause. At Iwo Jima in the
Second World War, United States Marines fought hand to hand against

thousands of Japanese. By the time the Marines reached the top of Mount Suribachi, they raised a piece of pipe upright and from one end fluttered a flag. That ascent had cost nearly 6,000 American lives. The Iwo Jima Memorial in Arlington National Cemetery memorializes that event. President Franklin Roosevelt authorized the use of the flag on labels, packages, cartons, and containers intended for export as lend-lease aid, in order to inform people in other countries of the United States' assistance. Presidential Proclamation No. 2605, 58 Stat. 1126.

During the Korean war, the successful amphibious landing of American troops at Inchon was marked by the raising of an American flag within an hour of the event. Impetus for the enactment of the Federal Flag Desecration Statute in 1967 came from the impact of flag burnings in the United States on troop morale in Vietnam. Representative L. Mendel Rivers, then Chairman of the House Armed Services Committee, testified that "[t]he burning of the flag ... has caused my mail to increase 100 percent from the boys in Vietnam, writing me and asking me what is going on in America." Desecration of the Flag, Hearings on H.R. 271 before Subcommittee No. 4 of the House Committee on the Judiciary, 90th Cong., 1st Sess., 189 (1967). Representative Charles Wiggins stated: "The public act of desecration of our flag tends to undermine the morale of American troops. That this finding is true can be attested by many Members who have received correspondence from servicemen expressing their shock and disgust of such conduct." 113 Cong.Rec. 16459 (1967).

The flag symbolizes the Nation in peace as well as in war. It signifies our national presence on battleships, airplanes, military installations, and public buildings from the United States Capitol to the thousands of county courthouses and city halls throughout the country. Two flags are prominently placed in our courtroom. Countless flags are placed by the graves of loved ones each year on what was first called Decoration Day, and is now called Memorial Day. The flag is traditionally placed on the casket of deceased members of the Armed Forces, and it is later given to the deceased's family. 10 U.S.C. §§ 1481, 1482. Congress has provided that the flag be flown at half-staff upon the death of the President, Vice President, and other government officials "as a mark of respect to their memory." 36 U.S.C. § 175(m). The flag identifies United States merchant ships, 22 U.S.C. § 454, and "[t]he laws of the Union protect our commerce wherever the flag of the country may float." *United States v. Guthrie,* 58 U.S. (17 How.) 284, 309, 15 L.Ed. 102 (1855).

No other American symbol has been as universally honored as the flag. In 1931, Congress declared "The Star-Spangled Banner" to be our national anthem. 36 U.S.C. § 170. In 1949, Congress declared June 14th to be Flag Day. § 157. In 1987, John Philip Sousa's "The Stars and Stripes Forever" was designated as the national march. Pub. L. 101–186, 101 Stat. 1286. Congress has also established "The Pledge of Allegiance to the Flag" and the manner of its deliverance. 36 U.S.C. § 172. The flag has appeared as the principal symbol on approximately 33 United States postal stamps and in the design of at least 43 more, more times than any other symbol. United States Postal Service, Definitive Mint Set 15 (1988).

Both Congress and the States have enacted numerous laws regulating misuse of the American flag. Until 1967, Congress left the regulation of misuse of the flag up to the States. Now, however, 18 U.S.C. § 700(a) provides that:

> "Whoever knowingly casts contempt upon any flag of the United States by publicly mutilating, defacing, defiling, burning, or trampling upon it shall be fined not more than $1,000 or imprisoned for not more than one year, or both."

Congress has also prescribed, *inter alia,* detailed rules for the design of the flag, 4 U.S.C. § 1, the time and occasion of flag's display, 36 U.S.C. § 174, the position and manner of its display, § 175, respect for the flag, § 176, and conduct during hoisting, lowering, and passing of the flag, § 177. With the exception of Alaska and Wyoming, all of the States now have statutes prohibiting the burning of the flag. Most of the state statutes are patterned after the Uniform Flag Act of 1917, which in § 3 provides: "No person shall publicly mutilate, deface, defile, defy, trample upon, or by word or act cast contempt upon any such flag, standard, color, ensign or shield." Proceedings of National Conference of Commissioners on Uniform State Laws 323–324 (1917). Most were passed by the States at about the time of World War I. Rosenblatt, Flag Desecration Statutes: History and Analysis, 1972 Wash.U.L.Q. 193, 197.

The American flag, then, throughout more than 200 years of our history, has come to be the visible symbol embodying our Nation. It does not represent the views of any particular political party, and it does not represent any particular political philosophy. The flag is not simply another "idea" or "point of view" competing for recognition in the marketplace of ideas. Millions and millions of Americans regard it with an almost mystical reverence regardless of what sort of social, political, or philosophical beliefs they may have. I cannot agree that the First Amendment invalidates the Act of Congress, and the laws of 48 of the 50 States, which make criminal the public burning of the flag.

More than 80 years ago in *Halter v. Nebraska,* 205 U.S. 34, 27 S.Ct. 419, 51 L.Ed. 696 (1907), this Court upheld the constitutionality of a Nebraska statute that forbade the use of representations of the American flag for advertising purposes upon articles of merchandise. The Court there said:

> "For that flag every true American has not simply an appreciation but a deep affection.... Hence, it has often occurred that insults to a flag have been the cause of war, and indignities put upon it, in the presence of those who revere it, have often been resented and sometimes punished on the spot." *Id.,* at 41, 27 S.Ct., at 421.

Only two Terms ago, in *San Francisco Arts & Athletics, Inc. v. United States Olympic Committee,* 483 U.S. 522, 107 S.Ct. 2971, 97

L.Ed.2d 427 (1987), the Court held that Congress could grant exclusive use of the word "Olympic" to the United States Olympic Committee. The Court thought that this "restrictio[n] on expressive speech properly [was] characterized as incidental to the primary congressional purpose of encouraging and rewarding the USOC's activities." *Id.,* at 536, 107 S.Ct., at 2981. As the Court stated, "when a word [or symbol] acquires value 'as the result of organization and the expenditure of labor, skill, and money' by an entity, that entity constitutionally may obtain a limited property right in the word [or symbol]." *Id.,* at 532, 107 S.Ct., at 2974, quoting *International News Service v. Associated Press,* 248 U.S. 215, 239, 39 S.Ct. 68, 72, 63 L.Ed. 211 (1918). Surely Congress or the States may recognize a similar interest in the flag.

But the Court insists that the Texas statute prohibiting the public burning of the American flag infringes on respondent Johnson's freedom of expression. Such freedom, of course, is not absolute. See *Schenck v. United States,* 249 U.S. 47, 39 S.Ct. 247, 63 L.Ed. 470 (1919). In *Chaplinsky v. New Hampshire,* 315 U.S. 568, 62 S.Ct. 766, 86 L.Ed. 1031 (1942), a unanimous Court said:

> "Allowing the broadest scope to the language and purpose of the Fourteenth Amendment, it is well understood that the right of free speech is not absolute at all times and under all circumstances. There are certain well-defined and narrowly limited classes of speech, the prevention and punishment of which have never been thought to raise any Constitutional problem. These include the lewd and obscene, the profane, the libelous, and the insulting or 'fighting' words—those which by their very utterance inflict injury or tend to incite an immediate breach of the peace. It has been well observed that such utterances are no essential part of any exposition of ideas, and are of such slight social value as a step to truth that any benefit that may be derived from them is clearly outweighed by the social interest in order and morality." *Id.,* at 571–572 (footnotes omitted).

The Court upheld Chaplinsky's conviction under a state statute that made it unlawful to "address any offensive, derisive or annoying word to any person who is lawfully in any street or other public place." *Id.,* at 569, 62 S.Ct., at 768. Chaplinsky had told a local marshal, " ' "You are a God damned racketeer" and a "damned Fascist and the whole government of Rochester are Fascists or agents of Fascists." ' " *Ibid.*

Here it may equally well be said that the public burning of the American flag by Johnson was no essential part of any exposition of ideas, and at the same time it had a tendency to incite a breach of the peace. Johnson was free to make any verbal denunciation of the flag that he wished; indeed, he was free to burn the flag in private. He could publicly burn other symbols of the Government or effigies of political leaders. He did lead a march through the streets of Dallas, and conducted a rally in front of the Dallas City Hall. He engaged in a "die-in" to protest nuclear weapons. He shouted out various slogans during the march, including: "Reagan, Mondale which will it be? Either one means

World War III''; ''Ronald Reagan, killer of the hour, Perfect example of U.S. power''; and ''red, white and blue, we spit on you, you stand for plunder, you will go under.'' Brief for Respondent 3. For none of these acts was he arrested or prosecuted; it was only when he proceeded to burn publicly an American flag stolen from its rightful owner that he violated the Texas statute.

The Court could not, and did not, say that Chaplinsky's utterances were not expressive phrases—they clearly and succinctly conveyed an extremely low opinion of the addressee. The same may be said of Johnson's public burning of the flag in this case; it obviously did convey Johnson's bitter dislike of his country. But his act, like Chaplinsky's provocative words, conveyed nothing that could not have been conveyed and was not conveyed just as forcefully in a dozen different ways. As with ''fighting words,'' so with flag burning, for purposes of the First Amendment: It is ''no essential part of any exposition of ideas, and [is] of such slight social value as a step to truth that any benefit that may be derived from [it] is clearly outweighed'' by the public interest in avoiding a probable breach of the peace. The highest courts of several States have upheld state statutes prohibiting the public burning of the flag on the grounds that it is so inherently inflammatory that it may cause a breach of public order. See, *e.g., State v. Royal,* 113 N.H. 224, 229, 305 A.2d 676, 680 (1973); *State v. Waterman,* 190 N.W.2d 809, 811–812 (Iowa 1971); see also *State v. Mitchell,* 32 Ohio App.2d 16, 30, 288 N.E.2d 216, 226 (1972).

The result of the Texas statute is obviously to deny one in Johnson's frame of mind one of many means of ''symbolic speech.'' Far from being a case of ''one picture being worth a thousand words,'' flag burning is the equivalent of an inarticulate grunt or roar that, it seems fair to say, is most likely to be indulged in not to express any particular idea, but to antagonize others. Only five years ago we said in *City Council of Los Angeles v. Taxpayers for Vincent,* 466 U.S. 789, 812, 104 S.Ct. 2118, 2132, 80 L.Ed.2d 772 (1984), that ''the First Amendment does not guarantee the right to employ every conceivable method of communication at all times and in all places.'' The Texas statute deprived Johnson of only one rather inarticulate symbolic form of protest—a form of protest that was profoundly offensive to many—and left him with a full panoply of other symbols and every conceivable form of verbal expression to express his deep disapproval of national policy. Thus, in no way can it be said that Texas is punishing him because his hearers—or any other group of people—were profoundly opposed to the message that he sought to convey. Such opposition is no proper basis for restricting speech or expression under the First Amendment. It was Johnson's use of this particular symbol, and not the idea that he sought to convey by it or by his many other expressions, for which he was punished.

. . . .

The Court concludes its opinion with a regrettably patronizing civics lecture, presumably addressed to the Members of both Houses of Congress, the members of the 48 state legislatures that enacted prohibitions against flag burning, and the troops fighting under that flag in Vietnam who objected to its being burned: "The way to preserve the flag's special role is not to punish those who feel differently about these matters. It is to persuade them that they are wrong." *Ante,* at 2547. The Court's role as the final expositor of the Constitution is well established, but its role as a Platonic guardian admonishing those responsible to public opinion as if they were truant school-children has no similar place in our system of government. The cry of "no taxation without representation" animated those who revolted against the English Crown to found our Nation—the idea that those who submitted to government should have some say as to what kind of laws would be passed. Surely one of the high purposes of a democratic society is to legislate against conduct that is regarded as evil and profoundly offensive to the majority of people—whether it be murder, embezzlement, pollution, or flag burning.

Our constitution wisely places limits on powers of legislative majorities to act, but the declaration of such limits by this court "is, at all times, a question of much delicacy, which ought seldom, if ever, to be decided in the affirmative, in a doubtful case." *Fletcher v. Peck,* 10 U.S. (6 Cranch) 87, 128, 3 L.Ed. 162 (1810) (Marshall, C.J.). Uncritical extension of constitutional protection to the burning of the flag risks the frustration of the very purpose for which organized governments are instituted. The court decides that the American flag is just another symbol, about which not only must opinions pro and con be tolerated, but for which the most minimal public respect may not be enjoined. The government may conscript men into the armed forces where they must fight and perhaps die for the flag, but the government may not prohibit the public burning of the banner under which they fight. I would uphold the Texas statute as applied in this case.

Justice STEVENS, dissenting.

As the Court analyzes this case, it presents the question whether the State of Texas, or indeed the Federal Government, has the power to prohibit the public desecration of the American flag. The question is unique. In my judgment rules that apply to a host of other symbols, such as state flags, armbands, or various privately promoted emblems of political or commercial identity, are not necessarily controlling. Even if flag burning could be considered just another species of symbolic speech under the logical application of the rules that the Court has developed in its interpretation of the First Amendment in other contexts, this case has an intangible dimension that makes those rules inapplicable.

A country's flag is a symbol of more than "nationhood and national unity." *Ante,* at 2541, 2542, 2544, and n. 9, 2546, 2548. It also signifies the ideas that characterize the society that has chosen that emblem as well as the special history that has animated the growth and power of those ideas. The fleurs-de-lis and the tricolor both symbolized "nationhood and national unity," but they had vastly different meanings. The message conveyed by some flags—the swastika, for example—may survive long after it has outlived its usefulness as a symbol of regimented unity in a particular nation.

So it is with the American flag. It is more than a proud symbol of the courage, the determination, and the gifts of nature that transformed 13 fledgling Colonies into a world power. It is a symbol of freedom, of equal opportunity, of religious tolerance, and of good will for other peoples who share our aspirations. The symbol carries its message to dissidents both at home and abroad who may have no interest at all in our national unity or survival.

The value of the flag as a symbol cannot be measured. Even so, I have no doubt that the interest in preserving that value for the future is both significant and legitimate. Conceivably that value will be enhanced by the Court's conclusion that our national commitment to free expression is so strong that even the United States as ultimate guarantor of that freedom is without power to prohibit the desecration of its unique symbol. But I am unpersuaded. . . .

     . . . .

The ideas of liberty and equality have been an irresistible force in motivating leaders like Patrick Henry, Susan B. Anthony, and Abraham Lincoln, schoolteachers like Nathan Hale and Booker T. Washington, the Philippine Scouts who fought at Bataan, and the soldiers who scaled the bluff at Omaha Beach. If those ideas are worth fighting for—and our history demonstrates that they are—it cannot be true that the flag that uniquely symbolizes their power is not itself worthy of protection from unnecessary desecration.

I respectfully dissent.

HOLY TRINITY CHURCH v. UNITED STATES

143 U.S. 457, 12 S.Ct. 511, 36 L.Ed. 226 (1892).

In error to the circuit court of the United States for the southern district of New York. Reversed.

Mr. Justice BREWER delivered the opinion of the court.

Plaintiff in error is a corporation duly organized and incorporated as a religious society under the laws of the state of New York. E. Walpole Warren was, prior to September, 1887, an alien residing in England. In that month the plaintiff in error made a contract with him, by which he was to remove to the city of New York, and enter into its service as rector and pastor; and, in pursuance of such contract, Warren did so remove and enter upon such service. It is claimed by the United States that this contract on the part of the plaintiff in error was forbidden by chapter 164, 23 St. p. 332; and an action was commenced to recover the penalty prescribed by that act. The circuit court held that the contract was within the prohibition of the statute, and rendered judgment accordingly, 36 Fed. Rep. 303, and the single question presented for our determination is whether it erred in that conclusion.

The first section describes the act forbidden, and is in these words:

Be it enacted by the senate and house of representatives of the United States of America, in congress assembled, that from and after the passage of this act it shall be unlawful for any person, company, partnership, or corporation, in any manner whatsoever, to prepay the transportation, or in any way assist or encourage the importation or migration, of any alien or aliens, any foreigner or foreigners, into the United States, its territories, or the District of Columbia, under contract or agreement, parol or special, express or implied, made previous to the importation or migration of such alien or aliens, foreigner or foreigners, to perform labor or service of any kind in the United States, its territories, or the District of Columbia.

It must be conceded that the act of the corporation is within the letter of this section, for the relation of rector to his church is one of service, and implies labor on the one side with compensation on the other. Not only are the general words "labor" and "service" both used, but also, as it were to guard against any narrow interpretation and emphasize a breadth of meaning, to them is added "of any kind"; and, further, as noticed by the circuit judge in his opinion, the fifth section, which makes specific exceptions, among them professional actors, artists, lecturers, singers, and domestic servants, strengthens the idea that every other kind of labor and service was intended to be reached by the first section. While there is great force to this reasoning, we cannot think Congress intended to denounce with penalties a transaction like that in the present case. It is a familiar rule that a thing may be within the letter of the statute and yet not within the statute, because not within its spirit nor within the intention of its makers. This has been often asserted, and the Reports are full of cases illustrating its application. This is not the substitution of the will of the judge for that of the legislator; for frequently words of general meaning are used in a statute, words broad enough to include an act in question, and yet a consideration of the whole legislation, or of the circumstances surrounding its enactment, or of the absurd results which follow from giving such broad meaning to the words, makes it unreasonable to believe that the legislator intended to include the particular act. . . .

. . . .

Among other things which may be considered in determining the intent of the legislature is the title of the act. We do not mean that it may be used to add to or take from the body of the statute, Hadden v. Collector, 5 Wall. 107, but it may help to interpret its meaning. In the case of U. S. v. Fisher, 2 Cranch, 358, 386, Chief Justice Marshall said: "On the influence which the title ought to have in construing the enacting clauses, much has been said, and yet it is not easy to discern the point of difference between the opposing counsel in this respect. Neither party contends that the title of an act can control plain words in the body of the statute; and neither denies that, taken with other parts, it may assist in removing ambiguities. Where the intent is plain, nothing is left to construction. Where the mind labors to discover the design of the legislature, it seizes everything from which aid can be derived; and in such case the title claims a degree of notice, and will have its due share of consideration." . . .

It will be seen that words as general as those used in the first section of this act were by that decision limited, and the intent of Congress with respect to the act was gathered partially, at least, from its title. Now, the title of this act is, "An act to prohibit the importation and migration of foreigners and aliens under contract or agreement to perform labor in the United States, its territories, and the District of Columbia." Obviously the thought expressed in this reaches only to the work of the manual laborer, as distinguished from that of the professional man. No one reading such a title would suppose that Congress had in its mind any purpose of staying the coming into this country of ministers of the gospel, or, indeed, of any class whose toil is that of the brain. The common understanding of the terms "labor" and "laborers" does not include preaching and preachers, and it is to be assumed that words and phrases are used in their ordinary meaning. So whatever of light is thrown upon the statute by the language of the title indicates an exclusion from its penal provisions of all contracts for the employment of ministers, rectors, and pastors.

Again, another guide to the meaning of a statute is found in the evil which it is designed to remedy; and for this the court properly looks at contemporaneous events, the situation as it existed, and as it was pressed upon the attention of the legislative body. U. S. v. Railroad Co., 91 U. S. 72, 79. The situation which called for this statute was briefly but fully stated by Mr. Justice Brown when, as district judge, he decided the case of U. S. v. Craig, 28 Fed. Rep. 795, 798:

> The motives and history of the act are matters of common knowledge. It had become the practice for large capitalists in this country to contract with their agents abroad for the shipment of great numbers of an ignorant and servile class of foreign laborers, under contracts by which the employer agreed, upon the one hand, to prepay their passage, while, upon the other hand, the laborers agreed to work after their arrival for a certain time at a low rate of wages. The effect of this was to break down the labor market, and to reduce other laborers engaged in like occupations to the level of the assisted immigrant. The evil finally became so flagrant that an appeal was made to congress for relief by the passage of the act in question, the design of which was to raise the standard of foreign immigrants, and to discountenance the migration of those who had not sufficient means in their own hands, or those of their friends, to pay their passage.

It appears, also, from the petitions, and in the testimony presented before the committees of Congress, that it was this cheap, unskilled labor which was making the trouble, and the influx of which Congress sought to prevent. It was never suggested that we had in this country a surplus of brain toilers, and, least of all, that the market for the services of Christian ministers was depressed by foreign competition. Those were matters to which the attention of congress, or of the people, was not directed. So far, then, as the evil which was sought to be remedied interprets the statute, it also guides to an exclusion of this contract from the penalties of the act.

A singular circumstance, throwing light upon the intent of Congress, is found in this extract from the report of the Senate committee on education and labor, recommending the passage of the bill:

> The general facts and considerations which induce the committee to recommend the passage of this bill are set forth in the report of the committee of the house. The committee report the bill back without amendment, although there are certain features thereof which might well be changed or modified, in the hope that the bill may not fail of passage during the present session. Especially would the committee have otherwise recommended amendments, substituting for the expression, "labor and service," whenever it occurs in the body of the bill, the words "manual labor" or "manual service," as sufficiently broad to accomplish the purposes of the bill, and that such amendments would remove objections which a sharp and perhaps unfriendly criticism may urge to the proposed legislation. The committee, however, believing that the bill in its present form will be construed as including only those whose labor or service is manual in character, and being very desirous that the bill become a law before the adjournment, have reported the bill without change.

Page 6059, Congressional Record, 48th Cong. And, referring back to the report of the committee of the house, there appears this language:

> It seeks to restrain and prohibit the immigration or importation of laborers who would have never seen our shores but for the inducements and allurements of men whose only object is to obtain labor at the lowest possible rate, regardless of the social and material well-being of our own citizens, and regardless of the evil consequences which result to American laborers from such immigration. This class of immigrants care nothing about our institutions, and in many instances never even heard of them. They are men whose passage is paid by the importers. They come here under contract to labor for a certain number of years. They are ignorant of our social condition, and, that they may remain so, they are isolated and prevented from coming into contact with Americans. They are generally from the lowest social stratum, and live upon the coarsest food, and in hovels of a character before unknown to American workmen. They, as a rule, do not become citizens, and are certainly not a desirable acquisition to the body politic. The inevitable tendency of their presence among us is to degrade American labor, and to reduce it to the level of the imported pauper labor.

Page 5359, Congressional Record, 48th Cong.

We find, therefore, that the title of the act, the evil which was intended to be remedied, the circumstances surrounding the appeal to Congress, the reports of the committee of each house, all concur in affirming that the intent of congress was simply to stay the influx of this cheap, unskilled labor.

But, beyond all these matters, no purpose of action against religion can be imputed to any legislation, state or national, because this is a religious people. This is historically true. From the discovery of this continent to the present hour, there is a single voice making this affirmation. The commission to Christopher Columbus, prior to his sail westward, is from "Ferdinand and Isabella, by the grace of God, king and queen of Castile," etc., and recites that "it is hoped that by God's assistance some of the continents and islands in the ocean will be discovered," etc. The first colonial grant, that made to Sir Walter Raleigh in 1584, was from "Elizabeth, by the grace of God, of England, Fraunce and Ireland, queene, defender of the faith," etc.; and the grant authorizing him to enact statutes of the government of the proposed colony provided that "they be not against the true Christian faith nowe professed in the Church of England." . . .

Coming nearer to the present time, the Declaration of Independence recognizes the presence of the Divine in human affairs in these words: "We hold these truths to be self-evident, that all men are created equal, that they are endowed by their Creator with certain unalienable Rights, that among these are Life, Liberty, and the pursuit of Happiness." "We, therefore, the Representatives of the united States of America, in General Congress, Assembled, appealing to the Supreme Judge of the world for the rectitude of our intentions, do, in the Name and by Authority of the good People of these Colonies, solemnly publish and declare," etc.; "And for the support of this Declaration, with a firm reliance on the Protection of Divine Providence, we mutually pledge to each other our Lives, our Fortunes, and our sacred Honor." . . .

Even the Constitution of the United States, which is supposed to have little touch upon the private life of the individual, contains in the first amendment a declaration common to the constitutions of all the states, as follows: "Congress shall make no law respecting an establishment of religion, or prohibiting the free exercise thereof," etc.,—and also provides in article 1, § 7, (a provision common to many constitutions,) that the executive shall have 10 days (Sundays excepted) within which to determine whether he will approve or veto a bill.

There is no dissonance in these declarations. There is a universal language pervading them all, having one meaning. They affirm and reaffirm that this is a religious nation. These are not individual sayings, declarations of private persons. They are organic utterances. They speak the voice of the entire people. . . .

If we pass beyond these shall it be believed that a Congress of the United States intended to make it a misdemeanor for a church of this country to contract for the services of a Christian minister residing in another nation?

Suppose, in the congress that passed this act, some member had offered a bill which in terms declared that, if any Roman Catholic church in this country should contract with Cardinal Manning to come to this country, and enter into its service as pastor and priest, or any Episcopal church should enter into a like contract with Canon Farrar, or any Baptist church should make similar arrangements with Rev. Mr. Spurgeon, or any Jewish synagogue with some eminent rabbi, such contract should be adjudged unlawful and void, and the church making it be subject to prosecution and punishment. Can it be believed that it would have received a minute of approving thought or a single vote? Yet it is contended that such was, in effect, the meaning of this statute. The construction invoked cannot be accepted as correct. It is a case where there was presented a definite evil, in view of which the legislature used general terms with the purpose of reaching all phases of that evil; and thereafter, unexpectedly, it is developed that the general language thus employed is broad enough to reach cases and acts which the whole history and life of the country affirm could not have been intentionally legislated against. It is the duty of the courts, under those circumstances, to say that, however broad the language of the statute may be, the act, although within the letter, is not within the intention of the legislature, and therefore cannot be within the statute.

The judgment will be reversed, and the case remanded for further proceedings in accordance with this opinion.

Notes

1. *Wholly.* Is *Holy Trinity* humorous? Is the flag-burning case humorous? Was the attitude of the male-dominated society humorous in denying women the right to vote until 1920 (see chapter 1)?

Jack Balkin and Sanford Levinson, in *The Constitutional Revolution,* 87 VA. L. REV. 1045 (2001) thought it was a "howler" when the Court in *Bush v. Gore,* 531 U.S. 98, 121 S.Ct. 525, 148 L.Ed.2d 388 (2000), said:

> None are more conscious of the vital limits on judicial authority than are the members of this Court, and none stand more in admiration of the Constitution's design to leave the selection of the President to the people, through their legislatures, and to the political sphere. When contending parties invoke the process of the courts, however, it becomes our unsought responsibility to resolve the federal and constitutional issues the judicial system has been forced to confront.

2. *Analysis.* The Court in the flag-burning case employs both conceptual analysis (*e.g.,* did the United States have an ownership interest in the American flag? Was desecratory flag-burning speech or conduct?) and policy analysis (will freedom of thought and of diversity be promoted, or national unity be irreparably damaged, by allowing desecratory flag-burning to go unpunished?). But are not both types of analysis conceptual? Is a policy reading of a statute (*Holy Trinity*) any less conceptual than a literal reading?

3. *Judicial Notice.* Both Chief Justice Rehnquist in *Johnson* and the Court in *Holy Trinity Church* quote materials outside the record to support their analyses. Is this interpretive strategy legitimate? Should the Court take more account of popular culture than it typically does?

4. *Civics Lesson.* In *Johnson* Chief Justice Rehnquist accuses the majority of indulging in "a regrettably patronizing civics lecture." Isn't every judicial opinion a civics lecture? Do you agree that the majority's discourse is "patronizing"? How does the majority's opinion support or challenge Hand's definition of "The Spirit of Liberty"? How would Hand have voted in *Johnson*?

F. LETTERS

Typically, the letter is an informal genre, addressed by one individual to another. In terms of genre, it occupies the polar opposite position from speeches, which are typically formal and addressed to a group. The greater informality and intimacy of a letter typically produces corresponding changes in tone, vocabulary, and self-revelation. As Dr. Samuel Johnson said, "In a man's letters, you know, madam, his soul lies naked." And Sir Walter Scott: "The chief interest of a study of the great letter writers is that it introduces us not to literary works, but to persons."

The twentieth century saw a remarkable explosion in means of communication—telephone, telegraph, radio, television, fax, and the ubiquitous email. Will email render the letter passé, just as the computer has outmoded the typewriter? Will such a change be desirable?

* * *

Benjamin Franklin was one of the most stellar figures in American history. A consummate politician, a striking inventor, and a considerable writer, he was a legend in his own time. Aphorisms from his POOR RICHARD'S ALMANACK are known to all school children. His AUTOBIOGRAPHY is considered one of the classics of the genre.

He went to France in 1776 to attend to American interests during the American Revolutionary War. Franklin, who had lost his beloved wife in 1744, became enamored of Madame Helvétius, a neighbor and the widow of a distinguished financier, philosopher, and wit. In 1780, when he was 72 and she 61, he proposed marriage to her, but she graciously declined. They remained true friends. The following letter is a renewal of his proposal to Madame Helvétius.

BEN FRANKLIN TO MADAME HELVÉTIUS
written from Passy, France, January 1780

CHAGRINED at your resolution, pronounced so decidedly last evening, to remain single for life, in honour of your dear husband, I went home, fell upon my bed, thought myself dead, and found myself in the Elysian fields.

They asked me if I had any desire to see any persons in particular. "Lead me to the philosophers." "There are two that reside here in this garden. They are very good neighbours and very friendly to each other." "Who are they?" "Socrates and Helvétius." "I esteem them both prodigiously; but let me see Helvétius first, because I understand a little French and not a word of Greek." [Helvétius] viewed me with much courtesy, having known me, he said, by reputation for some time. He asked me a thousand things about the war, and the present state of religion, liberty and government in France. "You ask me nothing, then, respecting your friend Madame Helvétius, and yet she loves you still excessively; it is but an hour since I was at her house." "Ah!" said he, "you make me recollect my former felicity; but I ought to forget it to be happy here. For many years I thought of nothing but her. At last I am consoled. I have taken another wife, the most like her that I could find. She is not, it is true, quite so handsome; but she has as much good sense and wit, and loves me infinitely. Her continued study is to please me; she is at present gone to look for the best nectar and ambrosia to regale me this evening; stay with me and you will see her."

"I perceive," said I, "that your old friend is more faithful than you; for many good matches have been offered her, all of which she has refused. I confess to you that I love her myself to excess; but she was severe to me, and has absolutely refused me, for love of you." "I commiserate you," said he, "for your misfortune; for indeed she is a good woman, and very amiable. But the Abbé de la Roche and the Abbé Morellet, are they not still sometimes at her house?" "Yes, indeed, for she has not lost a single one of your friends." "If you had gained over the Abbé Morellet with coffee and cream to speak for you, perhaps you would have succeeded, for he is as subtle a reasoner as Scotus or St. Thomas, and puts his arguments in such good order that they become almost irresistible: or if you had secured the Abbé de la Roche, by giving him some fine edition of an old classic, to speak against you, that would have been better; for I have always observed that when he advises anything, she has a very strong inclination to do the reverse."

At these words the new Madame Helvétius entered with the nectar; I reclaimed her, but she said to me coldly, "I have been your good wife forty-nine years and four months; almost half a century; be content with that." Dissatisfied with this refusal of my Eurydice I immediately resolved to quit those ungrateful shades and to return to this good world to see again the sun and you. Here I am. Let us avenge ourselves.

* * *

Near the end of the bitter year of 1864, Governor Andrew of Massachusetts wrote President Lincoln about Mrs. Lydia Bixby, a widow living at 15 Dover Street, Boston. According to the Governor, she had sent five sons to fight for the Union, and all had been killed in action. After the presidential election of 1864, Lincoln wrote the following consolatory letter to Mrs. Bixby.

ABRAHAM LINCOLN TO MRS. LYDIA BIXBY

Executive Mansion
Washington, Nov. 21, 1864

TO MRS. BIXBY, Boston, Mass.

Dear Madam,

I have been shown in the files of the War Department a statement of the Adjutant General of Massachusetts that you are the mother of five sons who have died gloriously on the field of battle. I feel how weak and fruitless must be any word of mine which should attempt to beguile you from the grief of a loss so overwhelming. But I cannot refrain from tendering you the consolation that may be found in the thanks of the republic they died to save. I pray that our Heavenly Father may assuage the anguish of your bereavement, and leave you only the cherished memory of the loved and lost, and the solemn pride that must be yours to have laid so costly a sacrifice upon the altar of freedom.

Yours very sincerely and respectfully,

A.   Lincoln

* * *

In 1862, when she was 32, Emily Dickinson began her correspondence with Colonel Thomas Wentworth Higginson, a man of letters. This correspondence continued for 24 years. The following is one of the letters she wrote to him.

EMILY DICKINSON TO COL. HIGGINSON

August 1870

TRUTH is such a rare thing, it is delightful to tell it.

I find ecstacy in living; the mere sense of living is joy enough. How do most people live without any thoughts? There are many people in the world,—you must have noticed them in the street,—how do they live? How do they get strength to put on their clothes in the morning?

If I read a book and it makes my whole body so cold no fire can ever warm me, I know that is poetry. If I feel physically as if the top of my head were taken off, I know that is poetry. These are the only ways I know it. Is there any other way?

* * *

Harry S. Truman (1884–1972), thirty-third president of the United States (1945–1953), was born and raised as a poor farmer in northwestern Missouri. He had aspirations of being a concert pianist, but that didn't work out. He served with distinction in the First World War. Unable to finish college because of his father's financial difficulties, he returned home to work on the farm.

He saw Elizabeth Virginia (Bess) Wallace, a neighbor, at Sunday school when he was 6, and she 5. He said he fell in love with her on sight, and after that he "never really liked another girl." ROBERT H. FERRELL, DEAR BESS—THE LETTERS FROM HARRY TO BESS TRUMAN, 1910–1959, at 3 (1983).

Harry courted Bess for years, writing her letters regularly. In 1911, at age 27, he proposed to her, but she turned him down. He was of a lower social class—or so Bess's mother thought—so Bess declined under maternal pressure. But Harry persisted, and finally won her hand.

The following two excerpts are from the letter containing his first marriage proposal and the letter responding to her rejection of that proposal.

HARRY TRUMAN TO BESS WALLACE

Grandview, Mo.
June 22, 1911

Dear Bessie:

From all appearances I am not such a very pious person am I? The elements evidently mistook one of my wishes for dry instead of wet. I guess we'll all have to go to drinking whiskey if it doesn't rain very soon. Water and potatoes will soon be as much of a luxury as pineapples and diamonds.

Speaking of diamonds, would you wear a solitaire on your left hand should I get it? Now that is a rather personal or pointed question provided you take it for all it means. You know, were I an Italian or a poet I would commence and use all the luscious language of two continents. I am not either but only a kind of good-for-nothing American farmer. I've always had a sneakin' notion that some day maybe I'd amount to something. I doubt it now though like everything. It is a family failing of ours to be poor financiers. I am blest that way. Still that doesn't keep me from having always thought that you were all that a girl could be possibly and impossibly. You may not have guessed it but I've been crazy about you ever since we went to Sunday school together. But I never had the nerve to think you'd even look at me. I don't think so now but I can't keep from telling you what I think of you....

Grandview, Mo.
July 12, 1911

Dear Bessie:

You know that you turned me down so easy that I am almost happy anyway. I never was fool enough to think that a girl like you could ever care for a fellow like me but I couldn't help telling you how I felt. I have always wanted you to have some fine, rich, good-looking man, but I knew that if ever I got the chance I'd tell you how I felt even if I didn't even get to say another word to you. What makes me feel real good is that you were good enough to answer me seriously and not make fun of me anyway. You know when a fellow tells a girl all his heart and she makes a joke of it I suppose it would be the awfulest feeling in the world. You see I never had any desire to say such things to anyone else. All my girl friends think I am a cheerful idiot and a confirmed old bach. They really don't know the reason nor ever will. I have been so afraid you were not even going to let me be your good friend. To be even in that class is something.

You may think I'll get over it as all boys do. I guess I am something of a freak myself. I really never had any desire to make love to a girl just for the fun of it, and you have always been the reason. I have never met a girl in my life that you were not the first to be compared with her, to see wherein she was lacking and she always was.

Please don't think I am talking nonsense or bosh, for if ever I told the truth I am telling it now and I'll never tell such things to anyone else or bother you with them again. I have always been more idealist than practical anyway, so I really never expected any reward for loving you. I shall always hope though.

As I said before I am more than glad to be your good friend for that is more than I expected. So when I come down there Saturday (which I'll do if I don't hear from you) I'll not put on any hangdog airs but will try to be the same *old Harry*.

You need not be afraid of bumping the proprieties with me. You couldn't. So send your package along. My new book has come and it is a dandy. A Hindu myth and really fine I think. I sent you *Mollie Make-Believe* by Nellie this time. I hope you got it.

I was at the stockyards yesterday and a fellow offered to buy a bank down here in the south part of the county if I'd run it. I don't know if I could be a banker or not. You know a man has to be real stingy and save every one-cent stamp he can. Then sometimes he has to take advantage of adverse conditions and sell a good man out. That is one reason I like being a farmer....

Still if this man makes the call loud enough, as the preacher said, I may take it. I can stay at home and help run the farm anyway.

Don't you know of some way to make it rain? We need it so badly that if it does not come it will be a real calamity. They say it rains on the just and the unjust alike but it is certainly passing some of us this year. Twenty miles south they have had plenty.

I hope you will continue your good letters as I really enjoy them and will try to answer them to the best of my ability, and although I may sometimes remind you of how I feel toward you I'll try and not bore you to death with it.

> Very sincerely,
> Harry

Notes

1. *Love Letters.* Would your heart be bowled over by love letters such as these? Would you have a "sneakin' notion," based on these letters, that someday the writer might "amount to something"?

2. *Authorship.* There is debate about whether Abraham Lincoln actually wrote the letter to Mrs. Bixby. Some authorities, including Michael Burlingame, author of THE COMPLETE CIVIL WAR DIARY OF JOHN HAY, believe that his secretary, John Hay, was actually the author. Assuming that Lincoln actually wrote the Gettysburg Address and the Second Inaugural Address, reprinted in Chapter One, can you compare the style of the speeches and the letter to determine whether Lincoln actually wrote the letter?

3. *Authenticity.* The original of the Bixby letter has been lost. The letter was reprinted in *The Boston Evening Transcript* of November 25, 1864, and instantly became famous. It recently resurfaced when it was read in the Steven Spielberg movie, *Saving Private Ryan* (1998). It appears on several websites devoted to a patriotic theme. Unfortunately, it turns out that only two of Mrs. Bixby's sons actually died in the Civil War. According to the National Park Service, administrator of the Lincoln Home in Springfield, Illinois, "Another son was honorably discharged, one was dishonorably discharged, and one either deserted or died in a prison camp." *<http://www.nps.gov/liho/souvenir.htm>* (visited March 22, 2003). How do these facts affect our reaction to the letter?

G.   LEGAL INSTRUMENTS

The performative, or word act, has long fascinated linguists. J.L. Austin defines a performative essentially as a word that performs an action. Performatives are contrasted with constatives, which are words that describe past action, or utterances that are capable of being judged true or false. Performatives do not state a provable fact; they are simply acts. The American Declaration of Independence and Lincoln's Emancipation Proclamation are word acts. Through the Declaration, America severed its political ties with England. Through the Proclamation, President Lincoln gave freedom to Southern slaves.

Divine acts in the Bible are preeminently performatives. God said let there be light, and there was light. Jesus said take up your bed and walk, and the cripple did just that. "In the beginning was the Word, and the Word was with God, and the Word was God." *John* 1:1.

The law has in many respects had an uncomfortable affair with the relation between words and acts. If the actor intends by her acts to speak, the weakling hearsay rule may be involved; but if she intends simply to act, rather than to make an assertion of truth, or fact, there is no hearsay problem, but only a bold act—or so the rule says. But can one ever act without an intention, conscious or unconscious, to say something? For purposes of free speech protection, the same sort of brittle dichotomy between speech and act exits. *See, e.g., Johnson, supra.* But here, curiously, the meaning-full act is treated as speech.

Austin suggests that there may be no real distinction between constatives and performatives. The concepts merge and overlap. But insofar as there is a distinction, what is it?

The essence of the word act is that of power. Performatives are actions, not puny words.

The materials in this book concern themselves with the power of words. Laws are supposed to be performatives, and literature fragile words. But Baron Lytton told us that the pen is mightier than the sword. The power of the law as the sword is enthralled by the word.

The following anonymous piece illustrates the point:

> My colleague suggested that the law requiring witnesses to take an oath, as a condition to establishing perjury, be dispensed with. One who testifies before a judicial tribunal can be supposed impliedly to agree to tell the truth, on penalty of perjury for willful failure to speak truly. The oath is an unnecessary formality to achieve this end.
>
> In *United States v. Looper*, 419 F.2d 1405 (4th Cir.1969), the court held that the defendant could not be compelled against his religious convictions to swear or affirm in God's name or to raise his right hand, as a condition to testifying. "The district court could qualify defendant to testify in any form which stated or symbolized that defendant would tell the truth and which, under defendant's religious beliefs, purported to impress on him the necessity of doing so." In *United States v. Fowler*, 605 F.2d 181 (5th Cir.1979), the court apparently went so far as to say that it would be sufficient, as a condition to testifying, for the defendant simply to say, "I state that I will tell the truth in my testimony." This he refused to do, however.
>
> Sir Thomas More refused to take the oath affirming the legitimacy of Henry VIII's divorce, and for this he lost his head. Sir Thomas, of course, was a Catholic who feared for his soul. Today presumably almost anyone could take an oath without batting an eye, and without its affecting her or his conscience one way or the other. So why adhere to an outworn formality? For a small number, the oath may be religiously offensive; for the vast majority, it is meaningless; and the Thomas Mores are practically extinct. Shall we keep the oath merely as homage to the Mores that once were?
>
> That way away from the oath leads, however, to the French Revolution and the Reign of Terror. If I were to cast about to discard all the outworn formalities in our society, I might well end up naked, shorn of history, tradition, and meaning. Oyez, oyez, oyez, this honorable Court is now open pursuant to adjournment. Do you take this woman to be your lawful wedded wife? May it please the Court. With this ring I do thee wed. Good morning. Hello. Congratulations. And pardon me.

* * *

Are all legal documents performatives, or word acts? Why, or why not?

* * *

The Declaration of Independence is among the most sacred documents in American history. Adopted by the Continental Congress in 1776, it—unlike the 1788 Constitution—states unequivocally that all men are created equal, and that they are endowed with certain inalienable rights, including life, liberty, and the pursuit of happiness. Although few Americans have ever read the Declaration in its entirety, the date of its adoption, July 4, has become a national holiday that rivals Christmas and Easter.

THE AMERICAN DECLARATION OF INDEPENDENCE

IN CONGRESS, July 4, 1776.

The unanimous Declaration of the thirteen united States of America,

When in the Course of human events, it becomes necessary for one people to dissolve the political bands which have connected them with another, and to assume among the powers of the earth, the separate and equal station to which the Laws of Nature and of Nature's God entitle them, a decent respect to the opinions of mankind requires that they should declare the causes which impel them to the separation.—We hold these truths to be self-evident, that all men are created equal, that they are endowed by their Creator with certain unalienable Rights, that among these are Life, Liberty and the pursuit of Happiness. That to secure these rights, Governments are instituted among Men, deriving their just Powers from the consent of the governed,—That whenever any Form of Government becomes destructive of these ends, it is the Right of the People to alter or to abolish it, and to institute new Government, laying its foundation on such principles and organizing its powers in such form, as to them shall seem most likely to effect their Safety and Happiness. Prudence, indeed, will dictate that Governments long established should not be changed for light and transient causes; and accordingly all experience hath shewn, that mankind are more disposed to suffer, while evils are sufferable, than to right themselves by abolishing the forms to which they are accustomed. But when a long train of abuses and usurpations, pursuing invariably the same Object evinces a design to reduce them under absolute Despotism, it is their right, it is their duty, to throw off such Government, and to provide new guards for their future security—Such has been the patient sufferance of these Colonies; and such is now the necessity which constrains them to alter their former Systems of Government.—The history of the present King of Great Britain is a history of repeated injuries and usurpations, all having in direct object the establishment of an absolute Tyranny over these States. To prove this, let facts be submitted to a candid world.—He has refused his Assent to Laws, the most wholesome and necessary for the public good.—He has forbidden his Governors to pass Laws of immediate and pressing importance, unless suspended in their operation till his Assent should be obtained; and when so suspended, he has utterly neglected to attend to them. He has refused to pass other Laws for the accommodation of large districts of people, unless those people would relinquish the right of Representation in the Legislature, a right inestimable to them and formidable to tyrants only.—He has called together legislative bodies at places unusual, uncomfortable, and distant from the depository of their Public Records, for the sole purpose of fatiguing them into compliance with his measures.—He has dissolved Representative Houses repeatedly, for opposing with manly firmness his invasions on the rights of the people.—He has refused for a long time, after such dissolutions, to cause others to be elected; whereby the Legislative Powers, incapable of Annihilation, have returned to the People at large for their exercise; the State remaining in the mean time exposed to all the dangers of invasion from without, and convulsions within.—He has endeavoured to prevent the population of these States; for that purpose obstructing the Laws for Naturalization of Foreigners; refusing to pass others to encourage their migrations hither, and raising the conditions of new Appropriations of Lands.—He has obstructed the Administration of Justice, by refusing his Assent to Laws for establishing Judiciary Powers.—He has made Judges dependent on his Will alone, for the tenure of their offices, and the amount and payment of their salaries.—He has erected a multitude of New Offices, and sent hither swarms of Officers to harrass our People, and eat out their substance.—He has kept among us, in times of peace, Standing Armies without the Consent of our legislatures.—He has affected to render the Military independent of and superior to the Civil Power.—He has combined with others to subject us to a jurisdiction foreign to our constitution, and unacknowledged by our laws; giving his Assent to their Acts of pretended Legislation:—For Quartering large bodies of armed troops among us: For protecting them, by a mock Trial, from Punishment for any Murders which they should commit on the Inhabitants of these States:—For cutting off our Trade with all parts of the world:—For imposing Taxes on us without our Consent:—For depriving us in many cases, of the benefits of Trial by Jury:—For transporting us beyond seas to be tried for pretended offences:—For abolishing the free system of English Laws in a neighbouring Province, establishing therein an Arbitrary government, and enlarging its Boundaries so as to render it at once an example and fit instrument for introducing the same absolute rule into these Colonies:—For taking away our Charters, abolishing our most valuable Laws, and altering fundamentally the forms of our Governments:—For suspending our own Legislature, and declaring themselves invested with power to legislate for us in all cases whatsoever.—He has abdicated Government here, by declaring us out of his Protection and waging War against us.—He has plundered our seas, ravaged our Coasts, burnt our towns, and destroyed the lives of our people.—He is at this time transporting large Armies of foreign Mercenaries to compleat the works of death, desolation and tyranny, already begun with circumstances of Cruelty and perfidy scarcely paralleled in the most barbarous ages, and totally unworthy the Head of a civilized nation.—He has constrained our fellow Citizens taken Captive on the high Seas to bear Arms against their Country, to become the executioners of their friends and Brethren, or to fall themselves by their Hands.—He has excited domestic insurrections amongst us, and has endeavoured to bring on the inhabitants of our frontiers, the merciless Indian Savages, whose known rule of warfare, is an undistinguished destruction of all ages, sexes and conditions.—In every stage of these Oppressions we have Petitioned for Redress in the most humble terms: Our repeated Petitions have been answered only by repeated injury. A Prince, whose character is thus marked by every act which may define a Tyrant, is unfit to be the ruler of a free people.—Nor have we been wanting in attention to our Brittish brethren. We have warned them from time to time of attempts by their legislature to extend an unwarrantable jurisdiction over us. We have reminded them of the circumstances of our emigration and settlement here. We have appealed to their native justice and magnanimity, and we have conjured them by the ties of our common kindred to disavow these usurpations, which, would inevitably interrupt our connections and correspondence. They too have been deaf to the voice of justice and of consanguinity. We must, therefore, acquiesce in the necessity, which denounces our Separation, and hold them, as we hold the rest of mankind, Enemies in War, in Peace Friends.—

We, therefore, the Representatives of the united States of America, in General Congress, Assembled, appealing to the Supreme Judge of the world for the rectitude of our intentions, do, in the Name, and by Authority of the good People of these Colonies, solemnly publish and declare, That these United Colonies are, and of Right ought to be Free and Independent States; that they are absolved from all Allegiance to the British Crown, and that all political connection between them and the State of Great Britain, is and ought to be totally dissolved; and that as Free and Independent States, they have full Power to levy War, conclude Peace, contract Alliances, establish Commerce, and to do all other Acts and Things which Independent States may of right do.—And for the support of this Declaration, with a firm reliance on the protection of Divine Providence, we mutually pledge to each other our Lives, our Fortunes and our sacred Honor.

Button Gwinnett	John Hancock	William Floyd
Lyman Hall	Robert Morris	Philip Livingston
George Walton	Benjamin Rush	Francis Lewis
William Hooper	Benjamin Franklin	Lewis Morris
Joseph Hewes	John Morton	Richard Stockton
John Penn	George Clymer	John Witherspoon
Edward Rutledge	James Smith	Francis Hopkinson
Thomas Heyward, Jr.	George Taylor	John Hart
Thomas Lynch, Jr.	James Wilson	Abraham Clark
Arthur Middleton	George Ross	Josiah Bartlett
Samuel Chase	Ceasar Rodney	William Whipple

William Paca   George Read   Samuel Adams
Thomas Stone   Thomas McKean   John Adams
Charles Carroll of Carrollton   Robert Treat Paine
George Wythe   Elbridge Gerry
Richard Henry Lee   Stephen Hopkins
Thomas Jefferson   William Ellery
Benjamin Harrison   Roger Sherman
Thomas Nelson, Jr.   Samuel Huntington
Francis Lightfoot Lee   William Williams
Carter Braxton   Oliver Wolcott
                                               Matthew Thornton

THE EMANCIPATION PROCLAMATION
January 1, 1863

Whereas, on the twenty-second day of September, in the year of our Lord one thousand eight hundred and sixty-two, a proclamation was issued by the President of the United States, containing, among other things, the following, to wit:

"That on the first day of January, in the year of our Lord one thousand eight hundred and sixty-three, all persons held as slaves within any State or designated part of a State, the people whereof shall then be in rebellion against the United States, shall be then, thenceforward, and forever free; and the Executive Government of the United States, including the military and naval authority thereof, will recognize and maintain the freedom of such persons, and will do no act or acts to repress such persons, or any of them, in any efforts they may make for their actual freedom.

"That the Executive will, on the first day of January aforesaid, by proclamation, designate the States and parts of States, if any, in which the people thereof, respectively, shall then be in rebellion against the United States; and the fact that any State, or the people thereof, shall on that day be, in good faith, represented in the Congress of the United States by members chosen thereto at elections wherein a majority of the qualified voters of such State shall have participated, shall, in the absence of strong countervailing testimony, be deemed conclusive evidence that such State, and the people thereof, are not then in rebellion against the United States."

Now, therefore I, Abraham Lincoln, President of the United States, by virtue of the power in me vested as Commander-in-Chief, of the Army and Navy of the United States in time of actual armed rebellion against the authority and government of the United States, and as a fit and necessary war measure for suppressing said rebellion, do, on this first day of January, in the year of our Lord one thousand eight hundred and sixty-three, and in accordance with my purpose so to do publicly proclaimed for the full period of one hundred days, from the day first above mentioned, order and designate as the States and parts of States wherein the people thereof respectively, are this day in rebellion against the United States, the following, to wit:

Arkansas, Texas, Louisiana, (except the Parishes of St. Bernard, Plaquemines, Jefferson, St. John, St. Charles, St. James Ascension, Assumption, Terrebonne, Lafourche, St. Mary, St. Martin, and Orleans, including the City of New Orleans) Mississippi, Alabama, Florida, Georgia, South Carolina, North Carolina, and Virginia, (except the forty-eight counties designated as West Virginia, and also the counties of Berkley, Accomac, Northampton, Elizabeth City, York, Princess Ann, and Norfolk, including the cities of Norfolk and Portsmouth, and which excepted parts, are for the present, left precisely as if this proclamation were not issued).

And by virtue of the power, and for the purpose aforesaid, I do order and declare that all persons held as slaves within said designated States, and parts of States, are, and henceforward shall be free; and that the Executive government of the United States, including the military and naval authorities thereof, will recognize and maintain the freedom of said persons.

And I hereby enjoin upon the people so declared to be free to abstain from all violence, unless in necessary self-defence; and I recommend to them that, in all cases when allowed, they labor faithfully for reasonable wages.

And I further declare and make known, that such persons of suitable condition, will be received into the armed service of the United States to garrison forts, positions, stations, and other places, and to man vessels of all sorts in said service.

And upon this act, sincerely believed to be an act of justice, warranted by the Constitution, upon military necessity, I invoke the considerate judgment of mankind, and the gracious favor of Almighty God.

Notes

1. *The Scope of the Proclamation.* Note that the proclamation of September 22, 1862, did not declare emancipation, but adumbrated it. If the formal instrument had not been issued on January 1, 1863, would the slaves nevertheless have been freed on the latter date?

The Emancipation Proclamation was issued pursuant to the President's power as commander-in-chief of the armed forces of the United States. Why, then, was the Thirteenth Amendment to the constitution, abolishing slavery, adopted in 1865?

2. *The Declaration.* Had you ever read the complete Declaration of Independence before? Is it worth reading? Modern anthologizers usually omit the portion of the Declaration cataloging the transgressions of King George III. Does this catalogue add anything to a modern reader's understanding of the Declaration? Should the Declaration be required reading for American law students?

Chapter 3

STORIES

A. INTRODUCTION

A great deal has been written about the relevance of stories both to literature and to law. Although stories are not the be-all and end-all for law and literature, stories are central to both. At the heart of most litigation is a story, a narrative. Most legal cases center around a narrative, or sequence of events. The stories in *Texas v. Johnson* and *Holy Trinity Church v. United States,* given in the previous chapter, are short but central to the opinions of the Court. In other cases, as for example in a criminal case, the story may be long, detailed, and complicated, with much depending on the ascertainment and interpretation of the precise facts involved. A question on a law school exam is often built around a story, whose facts must be carefully weighed and interpreted by the examinee.

In literature, stories occupy a very prominent place. Today the novel is the most popular literary genre. Both the Old and the New Testaments of the Bible are filled with riveting stories. Poems often tell a story. Plays almost always do. Why is the story so essential to both law and literature? Perhaps because stories enable us to come to grips with what we believe to be reality, in a way that few other experiences can. A story has a beginning, a middle, and an end. That sequence mirrors the experience of life.

People often equate law with truth, and literature with fiction. Both are deeply misleading equations. Few trial lawyers would claim that they get at—or even want to get at—what the true facts of a situation may be. Instead, they want to construct a persuasive story for the benefit of their clients. Many, if not most, judicial opinions are based on broad, a priori, and largely unverifiable premises. History is built on large myths, stories that mold our behavior because we believe them to be true.

One of the fascinations of literature is that it makes no attempt to distinguish between fact and fiction, or between reality and myth. All the world is a stage, as Shakespeare said, and we but actors thereon. We are attracted to literature, and especially to poetry, because in many ways it seems more real than life itself. "The republic is a dream," wrote Carl

Sandburg: "Nothing happens unless first a dream." Joseph in the Book of Genesis was a dreamer. Martin Luther King had a dream, which should be a bedrock of our national hopes and aspirations.

Students tend to approach law literally, and literature figuratively. Students often believe that the law has a certain meaning—if only we could figure it out. Conversely, students usually do not expect a literary work to have one correct meaning, finding it easy to believe that literature has layers of meaning.

Law students early learn to recognize the ambiguity of language. Then they move from law to literature, to accept the multiple layers of meaning in both. The ambiguity in either will never be resolved.

B. SHORT STORIES AND NOVELLAS

The name "O. Henry"—the pen name of William Sydney Porter (1862–1910)—is virtually synonymous with the term "short story." Born in North Carolina in 1862, he moved to Texas as a young man and became a teller in a bank. Accused of embezzling funds from the bank, he fled to Central America but returned and served three years in a federal penitentiary on the embezzlement charge. His guilt has been hotly contested. He liked to write about modest people, and that penchant was greatly enhanced by his term in prison. O. Henry perfected the surprise ending, a device especially effective in the short story.

THE FURNISHED ROOM
O. Henry

Restless, shifting, fugacious as time itself is a certain vast bulk of the population of the red brick district of the lower West Side. Homeless, they have a hundred homes. They flit from furnished room to furnished room, transients forever—transients in abode, transients in heart and mind. They sing "Home, Sweet Home" in ragtime; they carry their *lares et penates* in a bandbox; their vine is entwined about a picture hat; a rubber plant is their fig tree.

Hence the houses of this district, having had a thousand dwellers, should have a thousand tales to tell, mostly dull ones, no doubt; but it would be strange if there could not be found a ghost or two in the wake of all these vagrant guests.

One evening after dark a young man prowled among these crumbling red mansions, ringing their bells. At the twelfth he rested his lean handbaggage upon the step and wiped the dust from his hatband and forehead. The bell sounded faint and far away in some remote, hollow depths.

To the door of this, the twelfth house whose bell he had rung, came a housekeeper who made him think of an unwholesome, surfeited worm that had eaten its nut to a hollow shell and now sought to fill the vacancy with edible lodgers.

He asked if there was a room to let.

"Come in," said the housekeeper. Her voice came from her throat; her throat seemed lined with fur. "I have the third floor back, vacant since a week back. Should you wish to look at it?"

The young man followed her up the stairs. A faint light from no particular source mitigated the shadows of the halls. They trod noiselessly upon a stair carpet that its own loom would have forsworn. It seemed to have become vegetable; to have degenerated in that rank, sunless air to lush lichen or spreading moss that grew in patches to the staircase and was viscid under the foot like organic matter. At each turn of the stairs were vacant niches in the wall. Perhaps plants had once been set within them. If so they had died in that foul and tainted air. It may be that statues of the saints had stood there, but it was not difficult to conceive that imps and devils had dragged them forth in the darkness and down to the unholy depths of some furnished pit below.

"This is the room," said the housekeeper, from her furry throat. "It's a nice room. It ain't often vacant. I had some most elegant people in it last summer—no trouble at all, and paid in advance to the minute. The water's at the end of the hall. Sprowls and Mooney kept it three months. They done a vaudeville sketch. Miss B'retta Sprowls—you may have heard of her—Oh, that was just the stage names—right there over the dresser is where the marriage certificate hung, framed. The gas is here, and you see there is plenty of closet room. It's a room everybody likes. It never stays idle long."

"Do you have many theatrical people rooming here?" asked the young man.

"They comes and goes. A good proportion of my lodgers is connected with the theatres. Yes, sir, this is the theatrical district. Actor people never stays long anywhere. I get my share. Yes, they comes and they goes."

He engaged the room, paying for a week in advance. He was tired, he said, and would take possession at once. He counted out the money. The room had been made ready, she said, even to towels and water. As the housekeeper moved away he put, for the thousandth time, the question that he carried at the end of his tongue.

"A young girl—Miss Vashner—Miss Eloise Vashner—do you remember such a one among your lodgers? She would be singing on the stage, most likely. A fair girl, of medium height and slender, with reddish, gold hair and a dark mole near her left eyebrow."

"No, I don't remember the name. Them stage people has names they change as often as their rooms. They comes and they goes. No, I don't call that one to mind."

No. Always no. Five months of ceaseless interrogation and the inevitable negative. So much time spent by day in questioning managers, agents, schools and choruses; by night among the audiences of theatres from all-star casts down to music halls so low that he dreaded to find what he most hoped for. He who had loved her best had tried to find her. He was sure that since her disappearance from home this great, water-girt city held her somewhere, but it was like a monstrous quicksand, shifting its particles constantly, with no foundation, its upper granules of today buried tomorrow in ooze and slime.

The furnished room received its latest guest with a first glow of pseudo-hospitality, a hectic, haggard, perfunctory welcome like the specious smile of a demirep. The sophistical comfort came in reflected gleams from the decayed furniture, the ragged brocade upholstery of a couch and two chairs, a footwide cheap pier glass between the two windows, from one or two gilt picture frames and a brass bedstead in a corner.

The guest reclined, inert, upon a chair, while the room, confused in speech as though it were an apartment in Babel, tried to discourse to him of its divers tenantry.

A polychromatic rug like some brilliant-flowered rectangular, tropical islet lay surrounded by a billowy sea of soiled matting. Upon the gay-papered wall were those pictures that pursue the homeless one from house to house—The Huguenot Lovers, The First Quarrel, The Wedding Breakfast, Psyche at the Fountain. The mantel's chastely severe outline was ingloriously veiled behind some pert drapery drawn rakishly askew like the sashes of the Amazonian ballet. Upon it was some desolate flotsam cast aside by the room's marooned when a lucky sail had borne them to a fresh port—a trifling vase or two, pictures of actresses, a medicine bottle, some stray cards out of a deck.

One by one, as the characters of a cryptograph become explicit, the little signs left by the furnished room's procession of guests developed a significance. The threadbare space in the rug in front of the dresser told that lovely women had marched in the throng. Tiny finger prints on the wall spoke of little prisoners trying to feel their way to sun and air. A splattered stain, raying like the shadow of a bursting bomb, witnessed where a hurled glass or bottle had splintered with its contents against the wall. Across the pier glass had been scrawled with a diamond in staggering letters the name "Marie." It seemed that the succession of dwellers in the furnished room had turned in fury—perhaps tempted beyond forbearance by its garish coldness—and wreaked upon it their passions. The furniture was chipped and bruised; the couch, distorted by bursting springs, seemed a horrible monster that had been slain during the stress of some grotesque convulsion. Some more potent upheaval had cloven a great slice from the marble mantel. Each plank in the floor owned its particular cant and shriek as from a separate and individual agony. It seemed incredible that all this malice and injury had been wrought upon the room by those who had called it for a time their home; and yet it may have been the cheated home instinct surviving blindly, the resentful rage at false household gods that had kindled their wrath. A hut that is our own we can sweep and adorn and cherish.

The young tenant in the chair allowed these thoughts to file, softshod, through his mind, while there drifted into the room furnished sounds and furnished scents. He heard in one room a tittering and incontinent, slack laughter; in others the monologue of a scold, the rattling of dice, a lullaby, and one crying dully; above him a banjo tinkled with spirit. Doors banged somewhere; the elevated trains roared intermittently; a cat yowled miserably upon a back fence. And he breathed the breath of the house—a dank savour rather than a smell—a cold, musty effluvium as from underground vaults mingled with the reeking exhalations of linoleum and mildewed and rotten woodwork.

Then, suddenly, as he rested there, the room was filled with the strong, sweet odour of mignonette. It came as upon a single buffet of wind with such sureness and fragrance and emphasis that it almost seemed a living visitant. And the man cried aloud: "What, dear?" as if he had been called, and sprang up and faced about. The rich odour clung to him and wrapped him around. He reached out his arms for it, all his senses for the time confused and commingled. How could one be peremptorily called by an odour? Surely it must have been a sound. But, was it not the sound that had touched, that had caressed him?

"She has been in this room," he cried, and he sprang to wrest from it a token, for he knew he would recognize the smallest thing that had belonged to her or that she had touched. This enveloping scent of mignonette, the odour that she had loved and made her own—whence came it?

The room had been but carelessly set in order. Scattered upon the flimsy dresser scarf were half a dozen hairpins—those discreet, indistinguishable friends of womankind, feminine of gender, infinite of mood and uncommunicative of tense. These he ignored, conscious of their triumphant lack of identity. Ransacking the drawers of the dresser he came upon a discarded, tiny, ragged handkerchief. He pressed it to his face. It was racy and insolent with heliotrope; he hurled it to the floor. In another drawer he found odd buttons, a theatre programme, a pawnbroker's card, two lost marshmallows, a book on the divination of dreams. In the last was a woman's black satin hair bow, which halted him, poised between ice and fire. But the black satin hairbow also is femininity's demure, impersonal, common ornament, and tells no tales.

And then he traversed the room like a hound on the scent, skimming the walls, considering the corners of the bulging matting on his hands and knees, rummaging mantel and tables, the curtains and hangings, the drunken cabinet in the corner, for a visible sign, unable to perceive that she was there beside, around, against, within, above him, clinging to him, wooing him, calling him so poignantly through the finer senses that even his grosser ones became cognizant of the call. Once again he answered loudly: "Yes, dear!" and turned, wild-eyed, to gaze on vacancy, for he could not yet discern form and colour and love and outstretched arms in the odour of mignonette. Oh, God! whence that odour, and since when have odours had a voice to call? Thus he groped.

He burrowed in crevices and corners, and found corks and cigarettes. These he passed in passive contempt. But once he found in a fold of the matting a half-smoked cigar, and this he ground beneath his heel with a green and trenchant oath. He sifted the room from end to end. He found dreary and ignoble small records of many a peripatetic tenant; but of her whom he sought, and who may have lodged there, and whose spirit seemed to hover there, he found no trace.

And then he thought of the housekeeper.

He ran from the haunted room downstairs and to a door that showed a crack of light. She came out to his knock. He smothered his excitement as best he could.

"Will you tell me, madam," he besought her, "who occupied the room I have before I came?"

"Yes, sir. I can tell you again. 'Twas Sprowls and Mooney, as I said. Miss B'retta Sprowls it was in the theatres, but Missis Mooney she was. My house is well known for respectability. The marriage certificate hung, framed, on a nail over—"

"What kind of a lady was Miss Sprowls—in looks, I mean?"

"Why, black-haired, sir, short, and stout, with a comical face. They left a week ago Tuesday."

"And before they occupied it?"

"Why, there was a single gentleman connected with the draying business. He left owing me a week. Before him was Missis Crowder and her two children, that stayed four months; and back of them was old Mr. Doyle, whose sons paid for him. He kept the room six months. That goes back a year, sir, and further I do not remember."

He thanked her and crept back to his room. The room was dead. The essence that had vivified it was gone. The perfume of mignonette had departed. In its place was the old, stale odour of mouldy house furniture, of atmosphere in storage.

The ebbing of his hope drained his faith. He sat staring at the yellow, singing gaslight. Soon he walked to the bed and began to tear the sheets into strips. With the blade of his knife he drove them tightly into every crevice around windows and door. When all was snug and taut he turned out the light, turned the gas full on again and laid himself gratefully upon the bed.

It was Mrs. McCool's night to go with the can for beer. So she fetched it and sat with Mrs. Purdy in one of those subterranean retreats where housekeepers foregather and the worm dieth seldom.

"I rented out my third floor, back, this evening," said Mrs. Purdy, across a fine circle of foam. "A young man took it. He went up to bed two hours ago."

"Now, did ye, Mrs. Purdy, ma'am?" said Mrs. McCool, with intense admiration. "You do be a wonder for rentin' rooms of that kind. And did ye tell him, then?" she concluded in a husky whisper, laden with mystery.

"Rooms," said Mrs. Purdy, in her furriest tones, "are furnished for to rent. I did not tell him, Mrs. McCool."

" 'Tis right ye are, ma'am; 'tis by renting rooms we kape alive. Ye have the rale sense for business, ma'am. There be many people will rayjict the rentin' of a room if they be tould a suicide has been after dyin' in the bed of it."

"As you say, we has our living to be making," remarked Mrs. Purdy.

"Yis, ma'am; 'tis true. 'Tis just one wake ago this day I helped ye lay out the third floor, back. A pretty slip of a colleen she was to be killin' herself wid the gas—a swate little face she had, Mrs. Purdy, ma'am."

"She'd a-been called handsome, as you say," said Mrs. Purdy, assenting but critical, "but for that mole she had a-growin' by her left eyebrow. Do fill up your glass again, Mrs. McCool."

Notes

1. *Vocabulary.* This story contains two notable uses of language: the arcane vocabulary of the protagonist, and the eye dialect used to depict Mrs. McCool's words. How do these two devices function in the story?

2. *Moral.* Does this story have a moral? If so, what is it?

* * *

"Quoth the Raven, 'Nevermore!' " What American schoolchild has not heard Edgar Allen Poe's sonorous poem, *The Raven*?

Poe's was a short, unhappy life. Born in 1809 and orphaned at the age of two, in 1836 he married his thirteen-year-old cousin, who died eleven years later. He addressed his poem *Annabel Lee* to her. Poe was addicted to alcohol, and went on drinking bouts that left him debilitated. He died at forty, penniless. Today he has an almost cult following; each year on the anniversary of his death in Baltimore, Maryland, a masked figure appears at his grave to leave roses and a bottle of cognac.

One of Poe's specialities was the horror story, exemplified by *The Pit and the Pendulum* and *The Tell-Tale Heart*. Most scholars credit him with the invention of the modern detective story, in *The Murders in the Rue Morgue*. The story that follows is another of Poe's detective master-pieces. As you read it, note the lawyerly qualities displayed by M. Dupin.

THE PURLOINED LETTER
Edgar Allan Poe

Nil sapientiae odiosius acumine nimio.—Seneca[1]

At Paris, just after dark one gusty evening in the autumn of 18—, I was enjoying the twofold luxury of meditation and a meerschaum, in

---

1. ["Nothing is more hateful to wisdom than excessive acuity." The authors are grateful to Elizabeth Sutherland for this translation. Eds.]

company with my friend, C. Auguste Dupin, in his little back library, or book-closet, *au troisième*, No. 33 *Rue Dunôt, Faubourg St. Germain*. For one hour at least we had maintained a profound silence; while each, to any casual observer, might have seemed intently and exclusively occupied with the curling eddies of smoke that oppressed the atmosphere of the chamber. For myself, however, I was mentally discussing certain topics which had formed matter for conversation between us at an earlier period of the evening; I mean the affair of the Rue Morgue, and the mystery attending the murder of Marie Rogêt. I looked upon it, therefore, as something of a coincidence, when the door of our apartment was thrown open and admitted our old acquaintance, Monsieur G—the Prefect of the Parisian police.

We gave him a hearty welcome; for there was nearly half as much of the entertaining as of the contemptible about the man, and we had not seen him for several years. We had been sitting in the dark, and Dupin now arose for the purpose of lighting a lamp, but sat down again, without doing so, upon G.'s saying that he had called to consult us, or rather to ask the opinion of my friend, about some official business which had occasioned a great deal of trouble.

"If it is any point requiring reflection," observed Dupin, as he forbore to enkindle the wick, "we shall examine it to better purpose in the dark."

"That is another one of your odd notions," said the Prefect, who had the fashion of calling everything "odd" that was beyond his comprehension, and thus lived amid an absolute legion of "oddities."

"Very true," said Dupin, as he supplied his visitor with a pipe, and rolled toward him a comfortable chair.

"And what is the difficulty now?" I asked. "Nothing more in the assassination way, I hope?"

"Oh, no; nothing of that nature. The fact is, the business is very simple indeed, and I make no doubt that we can manage it sufficiently well ourselves; but then I thought Dupin would like to hear the details of it because it is so excessively *odd*."

"Simple and odd," said Dupin.

"Why, yes; and not exactly that either. The fact is, we have all been a good deal puzzled because the affair is so simple, and yet baffles us altogether."

"Perhaps it is the very simplicity of the thing which puts you at fault," said my friend.

"What nonsense you *do* talk!" replied the Prefect, laughing heartily.

"Perhaps the mystery is a little *too* plain," said Dupin.

"Oh, good heavens! who ever heard of such an idea?"

"A little *too* self-evident."

"Ha! ha! ha!—ha! ha! ha!—ho! ho! ho!" roared our visitor, profoundly amused, "oh, Dupin, you will be the death of me yet!"

"And what, after all, *is* the matter on hand?" I asked.

"Why, I will tell you," replied the Prefect, as he gave a long, steady, and contemplative puff, and settled himself in his chair. "I will tell you in a few words; but, before I begin, let me caution you that this is an affair demanding the greatest secrecy, and that I should most probably lose the position I now hold, were it known that I confided it to any one."

"Proceed," said I.

"Or not," said Dupin.

"Well, then; I have received personal information, from a very high quarter, that a certain document of the last importance has been purloined from the royal apartments. The individual who purloined it is known; that beyond a doubt; he was seen to take it. It is known, also, that it still remains in his possession."

"How is this known?" asked Dupin.

"It is clearly inferred," replied the Prefect, "from the nature of the document, and from the non-appearance of certain results which would at once arise from its passing *out* of the robber's possession;—that is to say, from his employing it as he must design in the end to employ it."

"Be a little more explicit," I said.

"Well, I may venture so far as to say that the paper gives its holder a certain power in a certain quarter where such power is immensely valuable." The Prefect was fond of the cant of diplomacy.

"Still I do not quite understand," said Dupin.

"No? Well; the disclosure of the document to a third person, who shall be nameless, would bring in question the honor of a personage of most exalted station; and this fact gives the holder of the document an ascendancy over the illustrious personage whose honor and peace are so jeopardized."

"But this ascendancy," I interposed, "would depend upon the robber's knowledge of the loser's knowledge of the robber. Who would dare—"

"The thief," said G., "is the Minister D——, who dares all things, those unbecoming as well as those becoming a man. The method of the theft was not less ingenious than bold. The document in question—a letter, to be frank—had been received by the personage robbed while alone in the royal *boudoir*. During its perusal she was suddenly interrupted by the entrance of the other exalted personage from whom especially it was her wish to conceal it. After a hurried and vain endeavor to thrust it in a drawer, she was forced to place it, open as it was, upon a table. The address, however, was uppermost, and, the contents thus unexposed, the letter escaped notice. At this juncture enters the Minister D——. His lynx eye immediately perceives the paper, recognizes the handwriting of the address, observes the confusion of the personage addressed, and fathoms her secret. After some business transactions, hurried through in his ordinary manner, he produces a letter somewhat similar to the one in question, opens it, pretends to read it, and then places it in close juxtaposition to the other. Again he converses, for some fifteen minutes, upon the public affairs. At length, in taking leave, he takes also from the table the letter to which he has no claim. Its rightful owner saw, but, of course, dared not call attention to the act, in the presence of the third person who stood at her elbow. The minister decamped; leaving his own letter—one of no importance—upon the table."

"Here, then," said Dupin to me, "you have precisely what you demand to make the ascendancy complete—the robber's knowledge of the loser's knowledge of the robber."

"Yes," replied the Prefect; "and the power thus attained has, for some months past, been wielded, for political purposes, to a very dangerous extent. The personage robbed is more thoroughly convinced, every day, of the necessity of reclaiming her letter. But this, of course, cannot be done openly. In fine, driven to despair, she has committed the matter to me."

"Than whom," said Dupin, amid a perfect whirlwind of smoke, "no more sagacious agent could, I suppose, be desired, or even imagined."

"You flatter me," replied the Prefect; "but it is possible that some such opinion may have been entertained."

"It is clear," said I, "as you observe, that the letter is still in the possession of the minister; since it is this possession, and not any employment of the letter, which bestows the power. With the employment the power departs."

"True," said G.; "and upon this conviction I proceeded. My first care was to make a thorough search of the minister's hotel; and here my chief embarrassment lay in the necessity of searching without his knowledge. Beyond all things, I have been warned of the danger which would result from giving him reason to suspect our design."

"But," said I, "you are quite *au fait* in these investigations. The Parisian police have done this thing often before."

"Oh, yes; and for this reason I did not despair. The habits of the minister gave me, too, a great advantage. He is frequently absent from home all night. His servants are no means numerous. They sleep at a distance from their master's apartment, and, being chiefly Neapolitans, are readily made drunk. I have keys, as you know, with which I can open any chamber or cabinet in Paris. For three months a night has not passed, during the greater part of which I have not been engaged, personally, in ransacking the D—— Hotel. My honor is interested, and, to mention a great secret, the reward is enormous. So I did not abandon the search until I had become fully satisfied that the thief is a more astute man than myself. I fancy that I have investigated every nook and corner of the premises in which it is possible that the paper can be concealed.''

"But is it not possible," I suggested, "that although the letter may be in possession of the minister, as it unquestionably is, he may have concealed it elsewhere than upon his own premises?''

"This is barely possible," said Dupin. "The present peculiar condition of affairs at court, and especially of those intrigues in which D—— is known to be involved, would render the instant availability of the document—its susceptibility of being produced at a moment's notice—a point of nearly equal importance with its possession.''

"Its susceptibility of being produced?" said I.

"That is to say, of being *destroyed*," said Dupin.

"True," I observed; "the paper is clearly then upon the premises. As for its being upon the person of the minister, we may consider that as out of the question.''

"Entirely," said the Prefect. "He has been twice waylaid, as if by footpads, and his person rigidly searched for my own inspection.''

"You might have spared yourself this trouble," said Dupin. "D—, I presume, is not altogether a fool, and, if not, must have anticipated these waylayings, as a matter of course.''

"Not *altogether* a fool," said G., "but then he is a poet, which I take to be only one remove from a fool.''

"True," said Dupin, after a long and thoughtful whiff from his meerschaum, "although I have been guilty of certain doggerel myself.''

"Suppose you detail," said I, "the particulars of your search.''

"Why, the fact is, we took our time, and we searched *everywhere*. I have had long experience in these affairs. I took the entire building, room by room; devoting the nights of a whole week to each. We examined, first the furniture of each apartment. We opened every possible drawer; and I presume you know that, to a properly trained police agent, such a thing as a 'secret' drawer is impossible. Any man is a dolt who permits a 'secret' drawer to escape him in a search of this kind. The thing is *so* plain. There is a certain amount of bulk—of space—to be accounted for in every cabinet. Then we have accurate rules. The fiftieth part of a line could not escape us. After the cabinets we took the chairs. The cushions we probed with the fine ling needles you have seen me employ. From the tables we removed the tops.''

"Why so?''

"Sometimes the top of a table, or other similarly arranged piece of furniture, is removed by the person wishing to conceal an article; then the leg is excavated, the article deposited within the cavity, and the top replaced. The bottoms and tops of bedposts are employed in the same way.''

"But could not the cavity be detected by sounding?" I asked.

"By no means, if, when the article is deposited, a sufficient wadding of cotton be placed around it. Besides, in our case, we were obliged to proceed without noise."

"But you could not have removed—you could not have taken to pieces *all* articles of furniture in which it would have been possible to make a deposit in the manner you mention. A letter may be compressed into a thin spiral roll, not differing much in shape or bulk from a large knitting-needle, and in this form it might be inserted into the rung of a chair, for example. You did not take to pieces all the chairs?"

"Certainly not; but we did better—we examined the rungs of every chair in the hotel, and, indeed, the jointings of every description of furniture, by the aid of a most powerful microscope. Had there been any traces of recent disturbance we should not have failed to detect it instantly. A single grain of gimlet-dust, for example, would have been as obvious as an apple. Any disorder in the gluing—any unusual gap in the joints—would have sufficed to insure detection."

"I presume you looked to the mirrors, between the boards and the plates, and you probed the beds and the bedclothes, as well as the curtains and carpets."

"That of course; and when we had absolutely completed every particle of the furniture in this way, then we examined the house itself. We divided its entire surface into compartments, which we numbered, so that none might be missed; then we scrutinized each individual square inch throughout the premises, including the two houses immediately adjoining, with the microscope, as before."

"The two houses adjoining!" I exclaimed; "you must have had a great deal of trouble."

"We had; but the reward offered is prodigious."

"You included the *grounds* about the houses?"

"All the grounds are paved with brick. They gave us comparatively little trouble. We examined the moss between the bricks, and found it undisturbed."

"You looked among D——'s papers, of course, and into the books of the library?"

"Certainly; we opened every package and parcel; we not only opened every book, but we turned over every leaf in each volume, not contenting ourselves with a mere shake, according to the fashion of some of our police officers. We also measured the thickness of every book-cover, with the most accurate admeasurement, and applied to each the most jealous scrutiny of the microscope. Had any of the bindings been recently meddled with, it would have been utterly impossible that the fact should have escaped observation. Some five or six volumes, just from the hands of the binder, we carefully probed, longitudinally, with the needles."

"You explored the floors beneath the carpets?"

"Beyond doubt. We removed every carpet, and examined the boards with the microscope."

"And the paper on the walls?"

"Yes."

"You looked into the cellars?"

"We did."

"Then," I said, "you have been making a miscalculation, and the letter is not upon the premises, as you suppose."

"I fear you are right there," said the Prefect. "And now, Dupin, what would you advise me to do?"

"To make a thorough research of the premises."

"That is absolutely needless," replied G——. "I am not more sure that I breathe than I am that the letter is not at the hotel."

"I have no better advice to give you," said Dupin. "You have, of course, an accurate description of the letter?"

"Oh, yes!"—And here the Prefect, producing a memorandum-book, proceeded to read aloud a minute account of the internal, and especially of the external, appearance of the missing document. Soon after finishing the perusal of this description, he took his departure, more entirely depressed in spirits than I have ever known the good gentleman before.

In about a month afterward he paid another visit, and found us occupied very nearly as before. He took a pipe and a chair and entered into some ordinary conversation. At length I said:

"Well, but G., what of the purloined letter? I presume you have at last made up your mind that there is no such thing as overreaching the Minister?"

"Confound him, say I—yes; I made the re-examination, however, as Dupin suggested—but it was all labor lost, as I knew it would be."

"How much was the reward offered, did you say?" asked Dupin.

"Why, a very great deal—a *very* liberal reward—I don't like to say how much precisely; but one thing I *will* say, that I wouldn't mind giving my individual check for fifty thousand francs to any one who could obtain me that letter. The fact is, it is becoming of more and more importance every day; and the reward has been lately doubled. If it were trebled, however, I could do no more than I have done."

"Why, yes," said Dupin, drawlingly, between the whiffs of his meerschaum, "I really—think, G., you have not exerted yourself—to the utmost in the matter. You might—do a little more, I think, eh?"

"How?—in what way?"

"Why—puff, puff—you might—puff, puff—employ counsel in the matter, eh?—puff, puff, puff. Do you remember the story they tell of Abernethy?"

"No; hang Abernethy!"

"To be sure! hang him and welcome. But, once upon a time, a certain rich miser conceived the design of spunging upon this Abernethy for a medical opinion. Getting up, for this purpose, an ordinary conversation in a private company, he insinuated his case to the physician, as that of an imaginary individual.

" 'We will suppose,' said the miser, 'that his symptoms are such and such; now, doctor, what would *you* have directed him to take?'

" 'Take!' said Abernethy, 'why, take *advice*, to be sure.' "

"But," said the Prefect, a little discomposed, "*I* am *perfectly* willing to take advice, and to pay for it. I would *really* give fifty thousand francs to any one who would aid me in the matter."

"In that case," replied Dupin, opening a drawer, and producing a check-book, "you may as well fill me up a check for the amount mentioned. When you have signed it, I will hand you the letter."

I was astonished. The Prefect appeared absolutely thunder-stricken. For some minutes he remained speechless and motionless, looking incredulously at my friend with open mouth, and eyes that seemed startling from their sockets; then apparently recovering himself in some measure, he seized a pen, and after several pauses and vacant stares, finally filled up and signed a check for fifty thousand francs, and handed it across the table to Dupin. The latter examined it carefully and deposited it in his pocket-book; then, unlocking an *escritoire*, took thence a letter and gave it to the Prefect. This functionary grasped it in a perfect agony of joy, opened it with a trembling hand, cast a rapid glance at its contents, and then, scrambling and struggling to the door, rushed at length unceremoniously from the room and from the house, without having uttered a syllable since Dupin had requested him to fill up the check.

When he had gone, my friend entered into some explanations.

"The Parisian police," he said, "are exceedingly able in their way. They are persevering, ingenious, cunning, and thoroughly versed in the knowledge which their duties seem chiefly to demand. Thus, when G—— detailed to us his mode of searching the premises at the Hotel D——, I felt entire confidence in his having made a satisfactory investigation—so far as his labors extended."

"So far as his labors extended?" said I.

"Yes," said Dupin. "The measures adopted were not only the best of their kind, but carried out to absolute perfection. Had the letter been deposited within the range of their search, these fellows would, beyond a question, have found it."

I merely laughed—but he seemed quite serious in all that he said.

"The measures, then," he continued, "were good in their kind, and well executed; their defect lay in their being inapplicable to the case and to the man. A certain set of highly ingenious resources are, with the

Prefect, a sort of Procrustean bed, to which he forcibly adapts his designs. But he perpetually errs by being too deep or too shallow for the matter in hand; and many a school-boy is a better reasoner than he. I knew one about eight years of age, whose success at guessing in the game of 'even and odd' attracted universal admiration. This game is simple, and is played with marbles. One player holds in his hand a number of these toys, and demands of another whether that number is even or odd. If the guess is right, the guesser wins one; if wrong, he loses one. The boy to whom I allude won all the marbles of the school. Of course he had some principle of guessing; and this lay in mere observation and admeasurement of the astuteness of his opponents. For example, an arrant simpleton is his opponent, and, holding up his closed hand, asks, 'Are they even or odd?' Our schoolboy replies, 'Odd,' and loses; but upon the second trial he wins, for he then says to himself: 'The simpleton had them even upon the first trial, and his amount of cunning is just sufficient to make him have them odd upon the second; I will therefore guess odd';—he guesses odd and wins. Now, with a simpleton a degree above the first, he would have reasoned thus: 'This fellow finds that in the first instance I guessed odd, and, in the second, he will propose to himself, upon the first impulse, a simple variation from even to odd, as did the first simpleton; but then a second thought will suggest that this is too simple a variation, and finally he will decide upon putting it even as before. I will therefore guess even';—he guesses even, and wins. Now this mode of reasoning in the schoolboy, whom his fellows termed 'lucky,'—what, in its last analysis, is it?"

"It is merely," I said, "an identification of the reasoner's intellect with that of his opponent."

"It is," said Dupin; "and, upon inquiring of the boy by what means he effected the *thorough* identification in which his success consisted, I received answer as follows: 'When I wish to find out how wise, or how stupid, or how good, or how wicked is any one, or what are his thoughts at the moment, I fashion the expression of my face, as accurately as possible, in accordance with the expression of his, and then wait to see what thoughts or sentiments arise in my mind or heart, as if to match or correspond with the expression.' This response of the school-boy lies at the bottom of all the spurious profundity which has been attributed to Rochefoucault, to La Bougive, to Machiavelli, and to Campanella."

"And the identification," I said, "of the reasoner's intellect with that of his opponent, depends, if I understand you aright, upon the accuracy with which the opponent's intellect is admeasured."

"For its practical value it depends upon this," replied Dupin; "and the Prefect and his cohort fail so frequently, first, by default of this identification, and, secondly, by ill-admeasurement, or rather through non-admeasurement, of the intellect with which they are engaged. They consider only their *own* ideas of ingenuity; and, in searching for any thing hidden, advert only to the modes in which *they* would have hidden it. They are right in this much—that their own ingenuity is a faithful representative of that of *the mass*; but when the cunning of the individual felon is diverse in character from their own, the felon foils them, of course. This always happens when it is above their own, and very usually when it is below. They have no variation of principle in their investigations; at best, when urged by some unusual emergency—by some extraordinary reward—they extend or exaggerate their old modes of *practice*, without touching their principles. What, for example, in this case of D——, has been done to vary the principle of action? What is all this boring, and probing, and sounding, and scrutinizing with the microscope, and dividing the surface of the building into registered square inches—what is it all but an exaggeration of the application of the one principle or set of principles of search, which are based upon the one set of notions regarding human ingenuity, to which the Prefect, in the long routine of his duty, has been accustomed? Do you not see he has taken it for granted that *all* men proceed to conceal a letter, not exactly in a gimlet-hole bored in a chair-leg, but, at least, in *some* out-of-the-way hole or corner suggested by the same tenor of thought which would urge a man to secrete a letter in a gimlet-hole bored in a chair-leg? And do you not see also, that such *recherchés* nooks for concealment are adapted only for ordinary occasions, and would be adopted by ordinary intellects; for, in all cases of concealment, a disposal of the article concealed—a disposal in this *recherché* manner,—is, in the very first instance, presumable and presumed; and thus its discovery depends, not at all upon the acumen, but altogether upon the mere care, patience, and determination of the seekers; and where the case is of importance—or, what amounts to the same thing in the political eyes, when the reward is of magnitude,—the qualities in question have *never* been known to fail. You will now understand what I mean in suggesting that, had the purloined letter been hidden anywhere within the limits of the Prefect's examination—in other words, had the principle of its concealment been comprehended within the principles of the Prefect—its discovery would have been a matter altogether beyond question. This functionary, however, has been thoroughly mystified; and the remote source of his defeat lies in the supposition that the Minister is a fool, because he has acquired renown as a poet. All fools are poets; this the Prefect feels; and he is merely guilty of a *non distributio medii* in thence inferring that all poets are fools."

"But is this really the poet?" I asked. "There are two brothers, I know; and both have attained reputation in letters. The minister I believe has written learnedly on the Differential Calculus. He is a mathematician, and no poet."

"You are mistaken; I know him well; he is both. As poet *and* mathematician, he would reason well; as a mere mathematician, he could not have reasoned at all, and thus would have been at the mercy of the Prefect."

"You surprise me," I said, "by these opinions, which have been contradicted by the voice of the world. You do not mean to set at naught the well-digested ideas of centuries. The mathematical reason has long been regarded as *the* reason *par excellence*."

" '*Il y a à parièr,*' " replied Dupin, quoting from Chamfort, " '*que toute idée publique, toute convention reçue, est une sottise, car elle a convenue au plus grand nombre.*'[2] The mathematicians, I grant you, have done their best to promulgate the popular error to which you allude, and which is none the less an error for its promulgation as truth. With an art worthy a better cause, for example, they have insinuated the term 'analysis' into application to algebra. The French are the originators of this particular deception; but if a term is of any importance—if words derive any value from applicability—then 'analysis' conveys 'algebra' about as much as, in Latin, '*ambitus*' implies 'ambition,' '*religio*' 'religion,' or '*homines honesti*' a set of *honorable* men."

"You have a quarrel on hand, I see," said I, "with some of the algebraists of Paris; but proceed."

"I dispute the availability, and thus the value, of that reason which is cultivated in any especial form other than the abstractly logical. I dispute, in particular, the reason educed by mathematical study. The mathematics are the science of form and quantity; mathematical reasoning is merely logic applied to observation upon form and quantity. The great error lies in supposing that even the truths of what is called *pure* algebra are abstract or general truths. And this error is so egregious that I am confounded at the universality with which it has been received. Mathematical axioms are *not* axioms of general truth. What is true of *relation*—of form and quantity—is often grossly false in regard to morals, for example. In this latter science it is very usually *un*true that the aggregated parts are equal to the whole. In chemistry also the axiom fails. In the consideration of motive it fails; for two motives, each of a given value, have not, necessarily, a value when united, equal to the sum of their values apart. There are numerous other mathematical truths which are only truths within the limits of *relation*. But the mathematician argues from his finite truths, through habit, as if they were of an absolutely general applicability—as the world indeed imagines them to be. Bryant, in his very learned 'Mythology,' mentions an analogous source of error, when he says that 'although the Pagan fables are not believed, yet we forget ourselves continually, and make inferences from them as existing realities.' With the algebraists, however, who are Pagans themselves, the 'Pagan fables' *are* believed, and the inferences are made, not so much through lapse of memory as through an unaccountable addling of the brains. In short, I never yet encountered the mere mathematician who would be trusted out of equal roots, or one who did not clandestinely hold it as a point of his faith that $x^2 + px$ was absolutely and unconditionally equal to q. Say to one of these gentlemen, by way of experiment, if you please, that you believe occasions may occur when $x^2 + px$ is not altogether equal to q, and, having made him

2. ["It's a safe bet that every publicly held belief, every accepted convention, is an idiocy, precisely because it suits the largest number of people." The authors are grateful to Jennifer Coffin for this translation. Eds.]

understand what you mean, get out of his reach as speedily as convenient, for beyond doubt, he will endeavor to knock you down.

"I mean to say," continued Dupin, while I merely laughed at his last observations, "that if the Minister had been no more than a mathematician, the Prefect would have been under no necessity of giving me this check. I knew him, however, as both mathematician and poet, and my measures were adapted to his capacity, with reference to the circumstances by which he was surrounded. I knew him as a courtier, too, and as a bold *intriguant*. Such a man, I considered, could not fail to be aware of the ordinary political modes of action. He could not fail to be anticipate—and events have proved he did not fail to anticipate—the waylayings to which he was subjected. He must have foreseen, I reflected, the secret investigations of his premises. His frequent absences from home at night, which were hailed by the Prefect as certain aids to his success, I regarded only as *ruses*, to afford opportunity for thorough search to the police, and thus sooner to impress them with the conviction to which G——, in fact, did finally arrive—the conviction that the letter was not upon the premises. I felt, also, that the whole train of thought, which I was at some pains in detailing to you just now, concerning the invariable principle of political action in searches for articles concealed— I felt that this whole train of thought would necessarily pass through the mind of the minister. It would imperatively lead him to despise all the ordinary *nooks* of concealment. *He* could not, I reflected, be so weak as not to see that the most intricate and remote recess of his hotel would be as open as his commonest closets to the eyes, to the probes, to the gimlets, and to the microscopes of the Prefect. I saw, in fine, that he would be driven, as a matter of course, to *simplicity*, if not deliberately induced to it as a matter of choice. You will remember, perhaps, how desperately the Prefect laughed when I suggested, upon our first interview, that it was just possible this mystery troubled him so much on account of its being so *very* self-evident."

"Yes," said I, "I remember his merriment well. I really thought he would have fallen into convulsions."

. . . .

"But the more I reflected upon the daring, dashing, and discriminating ingenuity of D——; upon the fact that the document must always have been *at hand*, if he intended to use it to good purpose; and upon the decisive evidence, obtained by the Prefect, that it was not hidden within the limits of that dignitary's ordinary search—the more satisfied I became that, to conceal this letter, the minister had resorted to the comprehensive and sagacious expedient of not attempting to conceal it at all.

"Full of these ideas, I prepared myself with a pair of green spectacles, and called one fine morning, quite by accident, at the Ministerial hotel. I found D—— at home, yawning, lounging, and dawdling, as usual, and pretending to be in the last extremity of *ennui*. He is, perhaps, the most really energetic human being now alive—but that is only when nobody sees him.

"To be even with him, I complained of my weak eyes, and lamented the necessity of the spectacles, under cover of which I cautiously and thoroughly surveyed the whole apartment, while seemingly intent only upon the conversation of my host.

"I paid especial attention to a large writing-table near where he sat, and upon which lay confusedly, some miscellaneous letters and other papers, with one or two musical instruments and a few books. Here, however, after a long and very deliberate scrutiny, I saw nothing to excite particular suspicion.

"At length my eyes, in going the circuit of the room, fell upon a trumpery filigree card-rack of pasteboard, that hung dangling by a dirty blue ribbon, from a little brass knob just beneath the middle of the mantelpiece. In this rack, which had three or four compartments, were five or six visiting cards and a solitary letter. The last was much soiled and crumpled. It was torn nearly in two, across the middle—as if a design, in the first instance, to tear it entirely up as worthless, had been altered, or stayed, in the second. It had a large black seal, bearing the D—— cipher *very* conspicuously, and was addressed, in a diminutive female hand, to D——, the minister, himself. It was thrust carelessly, and even, as it seemed, contemptuously, into one of the uppermost divisions of the rack.

"No sooner had I glanced at this letter than I concluded it to be that of which I was in search. To be sure, it was, to all appearance, radically different from the one of which the Prefect had read to us so minute a description. Here the seal was large and black, with the D—— cipher; there it was small and red, with the ducal arms of the S—— family. Here, the address, to the minister, was diminutive and feminine; there the superscription, to a certain royal personage, was markedly bold and decided; the size alone formed a point of correspondence. But, then, the *radicalness* of these differences, which was excessive; the dirt; the soiled and torn condition of the paper, so inconsistent with the *true* methodical habits of D——, and so suggestive of a design to delude the beholder into an idea of the worthlessness of the document;—these things, together with the hyperobtrusive situation of this document, full in the view of every visitor, and thus exactly in accordance with the conclusions to which I had previously arrived; these things, I say, were strongly corroborative of suspicion, in one who came with the intention to suspect.

"I protracted my visit as long as possible, and, while I maintained a most animated discussion with the minister, upon a topic which I knew well had never failed to interest and excite him, I kept my attention really riveted upon the letter. In examination, I committed to memory its external appearance and arrangement in the rack; and also fell, at length, upon a discovery which set at rest whatever trivial doubt I might have entertained. In scrutinizing the edges of the paper, I observed them to be more *chafed* than seemed necessary. They presented the *broken* appearance which is manifested when a stiff paper, having been once folded and pressed with a folder, is refolded in a reversed direction, in the same creases or edges which had formed the original fold. This discovery was sufficient. It was clear to me that the letter had been turned, as a glove, inside out, re-directed and re-sealed. I bade the minister good-morning, and took my departure at once, leaving a gold snuff-box upon the table.

"The next morning I called for the snuff-box, when we resumed, quite eagerly, the conversation of the preceding day. While thus engaged, however, a large report, as if of a pistol, was heard immediately beneath the windows of the hotel, and was succeeded by a series of fearful screams, and the shoutings of a terrified mob. D—— rushed to a casement, threw it open, and looked out. In the meantime I stepped to the card-rack, took the letter, put it in my pocket, and replaced it by a *fac-simile*, (so far as regards externals) which I had carefully prepared at my lodgings—imitating the D—— cipher, very readily, by means of a seal formed of bread.

"The disturbance in the street had been occasioned by the frantic behavior of a man with a musket. He had fired it among a crowd of women and children. It proved, however, to have been without ball, and the fellow was suffered to go his way as a lunatic or a drunkard. When he had gone, D—— came from the window, whither I had followed him immediately upon securing the object in view. Soon afterward I bade him farewell. The pretended lunatic was a man in my own pay."

"But what purpose had you," I asked, "in replacing the letter by a *fac-simile*? Would it not have been better, at the first visit, to have seized it openly, and departed?"

"D——," replied Dupin, "is a desperate man, and a man of nerve. His hotel, too, is not without attendants devoted to his interests. Had I made the wild attempt you suggest, I might never have left the Ministerial presence alive. The good people of Paris might have heard of me no more. But I had an object apart from these considerations. You know my political prepossessions. In this matter, I act as a partisan of the lady concerned. For eighteen months the Minister has had her in his power. She has now him in hers—since, being unaware that the letter is not in his possession, he will proceed with his exactions as if it was. Thus will he inevitably commit himself, at once, to his political destruction. His downfall, too, will not be more precipitate than awkward. It is all very well to talk about the *facilis descensus Averni*; but in all kinds of climbing, as Catalani said of singing, it is far more easy to get up than to come down. In the present instance I have no sympathy—at least no pity—for him who descends. He is that *monstrum horrendum*, an unprincipled man of genius. I confess, however, that I should like very well to know the precise character of his thoughts, when, being defied by her whom the Prefect terms 'a certain personage,' he is reduced to opening the letter which I left for him in the card-rack."

"How? did you put any thing particular in it?"

"Why—it did not seem altogether right to leave the interior blank—that would have been insulting. D——, at Vienna once, did me an evil turn, which I told him, quite good-humoredly, that I should remember. So, as I knew he would feel some curiosity in regard to the identity of the person who had outwitted him, I thought it a pity not to give him a clew. He is well acquainted with my MS., and I just copied into the middle of the blank sheet the words—

          " '———— Un dessein si funeste,
S'il n'est digne d'Atrée, est digne de Thyeste.'

They are to be found in Crébillon's *Atrée*."[3]

Notes

1. *The Poet.* We are led by Dupin to believe that Minister D—— is a despicable person. Why, then, does Poe characterize D—— as a poet?

2. *The Mystery.* Why is the reader not told the contents of the purloined letter?

3. *Mathematics.* What is the rhetorical, or artistic, purpose of Dupin's disquisition on mathematics?

* * *

Susan Glaspell (1876–1948) was born in Davenport, Iowa. Known primarily as a playwright, she was a founder of the Provincetown Players on Cape Cod, a group that included Eugene O'Neill and Edna St. Vincent Millay. She established a reputation as a feminist writer and won the Pulitzer Prize in 1931 for *Alison's House*, a play based on the life of Emily Dickinson. The following story was originally written as a play, *Trifles*, in 1915. It is based on a true story that Glaspell reported while working as a journalist at the *Des Moines Daily News*. As you read it, ask yourself whether it still bears traces of its dramatic origins.

A JURY OF HER PEERS
Susan Glaspell

When Martha Hale opened the storm-door and got a cut of the north wind, she ran back for her big woolen scarf. As she hurriedly wound that round her head her eye made a scandalized sweep of her kitchen. It was no ordinary thing that called her away—it was probably further from ordinary than anything that had ever happened in Dickson County. But

---

3. ["So infamous a scheme,/If unworthy of Atreus, is worthy of Thyestes." The reference is to Thyestes, who seduced Atreus's wife. From that union came a son, whom Atreus raised as his own, not realizing that Thyestes was the child's father. Years later, when Atreus learned the truth, he served Thyestes his own son for dinner. Atreus justified himself by thinking, "It may not be worthy of me, but Thyestes deserves it." Because D—— had done Dupin an evil turn at Vienna once, Dupin could not resist the temptation to let him know that he (Dupin) had repaid the turn. The authors are grateful to Chris Lord for this material. Eds.]

what her eye took in was that her kitchen was in no shape for leaving: her bread all ready for mixing, half the flour sifted and half unsifted.

She hated to see things half done; but she had been at that when the team from town stopped to get Mr. Hale, and then the sheriff came running in to say his wife wished Mrs. Hale would come too—adding, with a grin, that he guessed she was getting scary and wanted another woman along. So she had dropped everything right where it was.

"Martha!" now came her husband's impatient voice. "Don't keep folks waiting out here in the cold."

She again opened the storm-door, and this time joined the three men and the one woman waiting for her in the big two-seated buggy.

After she had the robes tucked around her she took another look at the woman who sat beside her on the back seat. She had met Mrs. Peters the year before at the county fair, and the thing she remembered about her was that she didn't seem like a sheriff's wife. She was small and thin and didn't have a strong voice. Mrs. Gorman, sheriff's wife before Gorman went out and Peters came in, had a voice that somehow seemed to be backing up the law with every word. But if Mrs. Peters didn't look like a sheriff's wife, Peters made it up in looking like a sheriff. He was to a dot the kind of man who could get himself elected sheriff—a heavy man with a big voice, who was particularly genial with the law-abiding, as if to make it plain that he knew the difference between criminals and non-criminals. And right there it came into Mrs. Hale's mind, with a stab, that this man who was so pleasant and lively with all of them was going to the Wrights' now as a sheriff.

"The country's not very pleasant this time of year," Mrs. Peters at last ventured, as if she felt they ought to be talking as well as the men.

Mrs. Hale scarcely finished her reply, for they had gone up a little hill and could see the Wright place now, and seeing it did not make her feel like talking. It looked very lonesome this cold March morning. It had always been a lonesome-looking place. It was down in a hollow, and the poplar trees around it were lonesome-looking trees. The men were looking at it and talking about what had happened. The county attorney was bending to one side of the buggy, and kept looking steadily at the place as they drew up to it.

"I'm glad you came with me," Mrs. Peters said nervously, as the two women were about to follow the men in through the kitchen door.

Even after she had her foot on the door-step, her hand on the knob, Martha Hale had a moment of feeling she could not cross that threshold. And the reason it seemed she couldn't cross it now was simply because she hadn't crossed it before. Time and time again it had been in her mind, "I ought to go over and see Minnie Foster"—she still thought of her as Minnie Foster, though for twenty years she had been Mrs. Wright. And then there was always something to do and Minnie Foster would go from her mind. But *now* she could come.

The men went over to the stove. The women stood close together by the door. Young Henderson, the county attorney, turned around and said, "Come up to the fire, ladies."

Mrs. Peters took a step forward, then stopped. "I'm not—cold," she said.

And so the two women stood by the door, at first not even so much as looking around the kitchen.

The men talked for a minute about what a good thing it was the sheriff had sent his deputy out that morning to make a fire for them, and then Sheriff Peters stepped back from the stove, unbuttoned his outer coat, and leaned his hands on the kitchen table in a way that seemed to mark the beginning of official business. "Now, Mr. Hale," he said in a sort of semi-official voice, "before we move things about, you tell Mr. Henderson just what it was you saw when you came here yesterday morning."

The county attorney was looking around the kitchen.

"By the way," he said, "has anything been moved?" He turned to the sheriff. "Are things just as you left them yesterday?"

Peters looked from cupboard to sink; from that to a small worn rocker a little to one side of the kitchen table.

"It's just the same."

"Somebody should have been left here yesterday," said the county attorney.

"Oh—yesterday," returned the sheriff, with a little gesture as of yesterday having been more than he could bear to think of. "When I had to send Frank to Morris Center for that man who went crazy—let me tell you. I had my hands full yesterday. I knew you could get back from Omaha by today, George, and as long as I went over everything here myself—"

"Well, Mr. Hale," said the county attorney, in a way of letting what was past and gone go, "tell just what happened when you came here yesterday morning."

Mrs. Hale, still leaning against the door, had that sinking feeling of the mother whose child is about to speak a piece. Lewis often wandered along and got things mixed up in a story. She hoped he would tell this straight and plain, and not say unnecessary things that would just make things harder for Minnie Foster. He didn't begin at once, and she noticed that he looked queer—as if standing in that kitchen and having to tell what he had seen there yesterday morning made him almost sick.

"Yes, Mr. Hale?" the county attorney reminded.

"Harry and I had started to town with a load of potatoes," Mrs. Hale's husband began.

Harry was Mrs. Hale's oldest boy. He wasn't with them now, for the very good reason that those potatoes never got to town yesterday and he was taking them this morning, so he hadn't been home when the sheriff stopped to say he wanted Mr. Hale to come over to the Wright place and tell the county attorney his story there, where he could point it all out. With all Mrs. Hale's other emotions came the fear now that maybe Harry wasn't dressed warm enough—they hadn't any of them realized how that north wind did bite.

"We come along this road," Hale was going on, with a motion of his hand to the road over which they had just come, "and as we got in sight of the house I says to Harry, 'I'm goin' to see if I can't get John Wright to take a telephone.' You see," he explained to Henderson, "unless I can get somebody to go in with me they won't come out this branch road except for a price *I* can't pay. I'd spoke to Wright about it once before; but he put me off, saying folks talked too much anyway, and all he asked was peace and quiet—guess you know about how much he talked himself. But I thought maybe if I went to the house and talked about it before his wife, and said all the women-folks liked the telephones, and that in this lonesome stretch of road it would be a good thing—well, I said to Harry that that was what I was going to say—though I said at the same time that I didn't know as what his wife wanted made much difference to John—"

Now there he was!—saying things he didn't need to say. Mrs. Hale tried to catch her husband's eye, but fortunately the county attorney interrupted with:

"Let's talk about that a little later, Mr. Hale. I do want to talk about that but, I'm anxious now to get along to just what happened when you got here."

When he began this time, it was very deliberately and carefully:

"I didn't see or hear anything. I knocked at the door. And still it was all quiet inside. I knew they must be up—it was past eight o'clock. So I knocked again, louder, and I thought I heard somebody say, 'Come in.' I wasn't sure—I'm not sure yet. But I opened the door—this door," jerking a hand toward the door by which the two women stood. "and there, in that rocker"—pointing to it—"sat Mrs. Wright."

Everyone in the kitchen looked at the rocker. It came into Mrs. Hale's mind that that rocker didn't look in the least like Minnie Foster—the Minnie Foster of twenty years before. It was a dingy red, with wooden rungs up the back, and the middle rung was gone, and the chair sagged to one side.

"How did she—look?" the county attorney was inquiring.

"Well," said Hale, "she looked—queer."

"How do you mean—queer?"

As he asked it he took out a note-book and pencil. Mrs. Hale did not like the sight of that pencil. She kept her eye fixed on her husband, as if to keep him from saying unnecessary things that would go into that note-book and make trouble.

Hale did speak guardedly, as if the pencil had affected him too.

"Well, as if she didn't know what she was going to do next. And kind of—done up."

"How did she seem to feel about your coming?"

"Why, I don't think she minded—one way or other. She didn't pay much attention. I said, 'Ho' do, Mrs. Wright? It's cold, ain't it?' And she said. 'Is it?'—and went on pleatin' at her apron.

"Well, I was surprised. She didn't ask me to come up to the stove, or to sit down, but just set there, not even lookin' at me. And so I said: 'I want to see John.'

"And then she—laughed. I guess you would call it a laugh.

"I thought of Harry and the team outside, so I said, a little sharp, 'Can I see John?' 'No,' says she—kind of dull like. 'Ain't he home?' says I. Then she looked at me. 'Yes,' says she, 'he's home.' 'Then why can't I see him?' I asked her, out of patience with her now. 'Cause he's dead' says she, just as quiet and dull—and fell to pleatin' her apron. 'Dead?' says I, like you do when you can't take in what you've heard.

"She just nodded her head, not getting a bit excited, but rockin' back and forth.

" 'Why—where is he?' says I, not knowing *what* to say.

"She just pointed upstairs—like this"—pointing to the room above.

"I got up, with the idea of going up there myself. By this time I—didn't know what to do. I walked from there to here; then I says: 'Why, what did he die of?'

" 'He died of a rope around his neck,' says she; and just went on pleatin' at her apron."

Hale stopped speaking, and stood staring at the rocker, as if he were still seeing the woman who had sat there the morning before. Nobody spoke; it was as if every one were seeing the woman who had sat there the morning before.

"And what did you do then?" the county attorney at last broke the silence.

"I went out and called Harry. I thought I might—need help. I got Harry in, and we went upstairs." His voice fell almost to a whisper. "There he was—lying over the—"

"I think I'd rather have you go into that upstairs," the county attorney interrupted, "where you can point it all out. Just go on now with the rest of the story."

"Well, my first thought was to get that rope off. It looked—"

He stopped, his face twitching.

"But Harry, he went up to him, and he said. 'No, he's dead all right, and we'd better not touch anything.' So we went downstairs.

"She was still sitting that same way. 'Has anybody been notified?' I asked. 'No,' says she, unconcerned.

" 'Who did this, Mrs. Wright?' said Harry. He said it businesslike, and she stopped pleatin' at her apron. 'I don't know,' she says. 'You don't *know*?' says Harry. 'Weren't you sleepin' in the bed with him?' 'Yes,' says she, 'but I was on the inside.' 'Somebody slipped a rope round his neck and strangled him, and you didn't wake up?' says Harry. 'I didn't wake up,' she said after him.

"We may have looked as if we didn't see how that could be, for after a minute she said, 'I sleep sound.'

"Harry was going to ask her more questions, but I said maybe that weren't our business; maybe we ought to let her tell her story first to the coroner or the sheriff. So Harry went fast as he could over to High Road—the Rivers' place, where there's a telephone."

"And what did she do when she knew you had gone for the coroner?" The attorney got his pencil in his hand all ready for writing.

"She moved from that chair to this one over here"—Hale pointed to a small chair in the corner—"and just sat there with her hands held together and lookin' down. I got a feeling that I ought to make some conversation, so I said I had come in to see if John wanted to put in a telephone; and at that she started to laugh, and then she stopped and looked at me—scared."

At the sound of a moving pencil the man who was telling the story looked up.

"I dunno—maybe it wasn't scared," he hastened: "I wouldn't like to say it was. Soon Harry got back, and then Dr. Lloyd came, and you, Mr. Peters, and so I guess that's all I know that you don't."

He said that last with relief, and moved a little, as if relaxing. Everyone moved a little. The county attorney walked toward the stair door.

"I guess we'll go upstairs first—then out to the barn and around there."

He paused and looked around the kitchen.

"You're convinced there was nothing important here?" he asked the sheriff. "Nothing that would—point to any motive?"

The sheriff too looked all around, as if to re-convince himself.

"Nothing here but kitchen things," he said, with a little laugh for the insignificance of kitchen things.

The county attorney was looking at the cupboard—a peculiar, ungainly structure, half closet and half cupboard, the upper part of it being built in the wall, and the lower part just the old-fashioned kitchen cupboard. As if its queerness attracted him, he got a chair and opened the upper part and looked in. After a moment he drew his hand away sticky.

"Here's a nice mess," he said resentfully.

The two women had drawn nearer, and now the sheriff's wife spoke.

"Oh—her fruit," she said, looking to Mrs. Hale for sympathetic understanding.

She turned back to the county attorney and explained: "She worried about that when it turned so cold last night. She said the fire would go out and her jars might burst."

Mrs. Peters' husband broke into a laugh.

"Well, can you beat the women! Held for murder, and worrying about her preserves!"

The young attorney set his lips.

"I guess before we're through with her she may have something more serious than preserves to worry about."

"Oh, well," said Mrs. Hale's husband, with good-natured superiority, "women are used to worrying over trifles."

The two women moved a little closer together. Neither of them spoke. The county attorney seemed suddenly to remember his manners—and think of his future.

"And yet," said he, with the gallantry of a young politician. "for all their worries, what would we do without the ladies?"

The women did not speak, did not unbend. He went to the sink and began washing his hands. He turned to wipe them on the roller towel—whirled it for a cleaner place.

"Dirty towels! Not much of a housekeeper, would you say, ladies?"

He kicked his foot against some dirty pans under the sink.

"There's a great deal of work to be done on a farm," said Mrs. Hale stiffly.

"To be sure. And yet"—with a little bow to her—"I know there are some Dickson County farm-houses that do not have such roller towels." He gave it a pull to expose its full length again.

"Those towels get dirty awful quick. Men's hands aren't always as clean as they might be."

"Ah, loyal to your sex, I see," he laughed. He stopped and gave her a keen look, "But you and Mrs. Wright were neighbors. I suppose you were friends, too."

Martha Hale shook her head.

"I've seen little enough of her of late years. I've not been in this house—it's more than a year."

"And why was that? You didn't like her?"

"I liked her well enough," she replied with spirit. "Farmers' wives have their hands full, Mr. Henderson. And then—" She looked around the kitchen.

"Yes?" he encouraged.

"It never seemed a very cheerful place," said she, more to herself than to him.

"No," he agreed; "I don't think anyone would call it cheerful. I shouldn't say she had the home-making instinct."

"Well, I don't know as Wright had, either," she muttered.

"You mean they didn't get on very well?" he was quick to ask.

"No; I don't mean anything," she answered, with decision. As she turned a little away from him, she added: "But I don't think a place would be any the cheerfuller for John Wright's bein' in it."

"I'd like to talk to you about that a little later, Mrs. Hale," he said. "I'm anxious to get the lay of things upstairs now."

He moved toward the stair door, followed by the two men.

"I suppose anything Mrs. Peters does'll be all right?" the sheriff inquired. "She was to take in some clothes for her, you know—and a few little things. We left in such a hurry yesterday."

The county attorney looked at the two women they were leaving alone there among the kitchen things.

"Yes—Mrs. Peters," he said, his glance resting on the woman who was not Mrs. Peters, the big farmer woman who stood behind the sheriff's wife. "Of course Mrs. Peters is one of us," he said, in a manner of entrusting responsibility. "And keep your eye out, Mrs. Peters, for anything that might be of use. No telling; you women might come upon a clue to the motive—and that's the thing we need."

Mr. Hale rubbed his face after the fashion of a showman getting ready for a pleasantry.

"But would the women know a clue if they did come upon it?" he said; and, having delivered himself of this, he followed the others through the stair door.

The women stood motionless and silent, listening to the footsteps, first upon the stairs, then in the room above them.

Then, as if releasing herself from something strange, Mrs. Hale began to arrange the dirty pans under the sink, which the county attorney's disdainful push of the foot had deranged.

"I'd hate to have men comin' into my kitchen," she said testily— "snoopin' round and criticizin'."

"Of course it's no more than their duty," said the sheriff's wife, in her manner of timid acquiescence.

"Duty's all right," replied Mrs. Hale bluffly; "but I guess that deputy sheriff that come out to make the fire might have got a little of this on." She gave the roller towel a pull. "Wish I'd thought of that sooner! Seems mean to talk about her for not having things slicked up, when she had to come away in such a hurry."

She looked around the kitchen. Certainly it was not "slicked up." Her eye was held by a bucket of sugar on a low shelf. The cover was off the wooden bucket, and beside it was a paper bag—half full.

Mrs. Hale moved toward it.

"She was putting this in there," she said to herself—slowly.

She thought of the flour in her kitchen at home—half sifted, half not sifted. She had been interrupted, and had left things half done. What had interrupted Minnie Foster? Why had that work been left half done? She made a move as if to finish it,—unfinished things always bothered her,—and then she glanced around and saw that Mrs. Peters was watching her—and she didn't want Mrs. Peters to get that feeling she had got of work begun and then—for some reason—not finished.

"It's a shame about her fruit," she said, and walked toward the cupboard that the county attorney had opened, and got on the chair, murmuring: "I wonder if it's all gone."

It was a sorry enough looking sight, but "Here's one that's all right," she said at last. She held it toward the light. "This is cherries, too." She looked again. "I declare I believe that's the only one."

With a sigh, she got down from the chair, went to the sink, and wiped off the bottle.

"She'll feel awful bad, after all her hard work in the hot weather. I remember the afternoon I put up my cherries last summer."

She set the bottle on the table, and, with another sigh, started to sit down in the rocker. But she did not sit down. Something kept her from sitting down in that chair. She straightened—stepped back, and, half turned away, stood looking at it, seeing the woman who had sat there "pleatin' at her apron."

The thin voice of the sheriff's wife broke in upon her: "I must be getting those things from the front-room closet." She opened the door into the other room, started in, stepped back. "You coming with me, Mrs. Hale?" she asked nervously. "You—you could help me get them."

They were soon back—the stark coldness of that shut-up room was not a thing to linger in.

"My!" said Mrs. Peters, dropping the things on the table and hurrying to the stove.

Mrs. Hale stood examining the clothes the woman who was being detained in town had said she wanted.

"Wright was close!" she exclaimed, holding up a shabby black skirt that bore the marks of much making over. "I think maybe that's why she kept so much to herself. I s'pose she felt she couldn't do her part; and then, you don't enjoy things when you feel shabby. She used to wear pretty clothes and be lively—when she was Minnie Foster, one of the town girls, singing in the choir. But that—oh, that was twenty years ago."

With a carefulness in which there was something tender, she folded the shabby clothes and piled them at one corner of the table. She looked up at Mrs. Peters, and there was something in the other woman's look that irritated her.

"She don't care," she said to herself. "Much difference it makes to her whether Minnie Foster had pretty clothes when she was a girl."

Then she looked again, and she wasn't so sure; in fact, she hadn't at any time been perfectly sure about Mrs. Peters. She had that shrinking manner, and yet her eyes looked as if they could see a long way into things.

"This all you was to take in?" asked Mrs. Hale.

"No," said the sheriff's wife; "she said she wanted an apron. Funny thing to want," she ventured in her nervous little way, "for there's not much to get you dirty in jail, goodness knows. But I suppose just to make her feel more natural. If you're used to wearing an apron—. She said they were in the bottom drawer of this cupboard. Yes—here they are. And then her little shawl that always hung on the stair door."

She took the small gray shawl from behind the door leading up-stairs, and stood a minute looking at it.

Suddenly Mrs. Hale took a quick step toward the other woman, "Mrs. Peters!"

"Yes, Mrs. Hale?"

"Do you think she—did it?"

A frightened look blurred the other thing in Mrs. Peters' eyes.

"Oh, I don't know," she said, in a voice that seemed to shrink away from the subject.

"Well, I don't think she did," affirmed Mrs. Hale stoutly. "Asking for an apron, and her little shawl. Worryin' about her fruit."

"Mr. Peters says—." Footsteps were heard in the room above; she stopped, looked up, then went on in a lowered voice: "Mr. Peters says—it looks bad for her. Mr. Henderson is awful sarcastic in a speech, and he's going to make fun of her saying she didn't—wake up."

For a moment Mrs. Hale had no answer. Then, "Well, I guess John Wright didn't wake up—when they was slippin' that rope under his neck," she muttered.

"No, it's *strange,*" breathed Mrs. Peters. "They think it was such a—funny way to kill a man."

She began to laugh; at the sound of the laugh, she abruptly stopped.

"That's just what Mr. Hale said," said Mrs. Hale, in a resolutely natural voice. "There was a gun in the house. He says that's what he can't understand."

"Mr. Henderson said, coming out, that what was needed for the case was a motive. Something to show anger—or sudden feeling."

"Well, I don't see any signs of anger around here," said Mrs. Hale, "I don't—" She stopped. It was as if her mind tripped on something. Her eye was caught by a dish-towel in the middle of the kitchen table. Slowly she moved toward the table. One half of it was wiped clean, the other half messy. Her eyes made a slow, almost unwilling turn to the bucket of sugar and the half empty bag beside it. Things begun—and not finished.

After a moment she stepped back, and said, in that manner of releasing herself:

"Wonder how they're finding things upstairs? I hope she had it a little more red up there. You know,"—she paused, and feeling gathered,—"it seems kind of *sneaking:* locking her up in town and coming out here to get her own house to turn against her!"

"But, Mrs. Hale," said the sheriff's wife, "the law is the law."

"I s'pose 'tis," answered Mrs. Hale shortly.

She turned to the stove, saying something about that fire not being much to brag of. She worked with it a minute, and when she straightened up she said aggressively:

"The law is the law—and a bad stove is a bad stove. How'd you like to cook on this?"—pointing with the poker to the broken lining. She opened the oven door and started to express her opinion of the oven; but she was swept into her own thoughts, thinking of what it would mean, year after year, to have that stove to wrestle with. The thought of Minnie Foster trying to bake in that oven—and the thought of her never going over to see Minnie Foster—.

She was startled by hearing Mrs. Peters say: "A person gets discouraged—and loses heart."

The sheriff's wife had looked from the stove to the sink—to the pail of water which had been carried in from outside. The two women stood there silent, above them the footsteps of the men who were looking for evidence against the woman who had worked in that kitchen. That look of seeing into things, of seeing through a thing to something else, was in the eyes of the sheriff's wife now. When Mrs. Hale next spoke to her, it was gently:

"Better loosen up your things, Mrs. Peters. We'll not feel them when we go out."

Mrs. Peters went to the back of the room to hang up the fur tippet she was wearing. A moment later she exclaimed, "Why, she was piecing a quilt," and held up a large sewing basket piled high with quilt pieces.

Mrs. Hale spread some of the blocks on the table.

"It's log-cabin pattern," she said, putting several of them together, "Pretty, isn't it?"

They were so engaged with the quilt that they did not hear the footsteps on the stairs. Just as the stair door opened Mrs. Hale was saying:

"Do you suppose she was going to quilt it or just knot it?"

The sheriff threw up his hands.

"They wonder whether she was going to quilt it or just knot it!"

There was a laugh for the ways of women, a warming of hands over the stove, and then the county attorney said briskly:

"Well, let's go right out to the barn and get that cleared up."

"I don't see as there's anything so strange," Mrs. Hale said resentfully, after the outside door had closed on the three men—"our taking up our time with little things while we're waiting for them to get the evidence. I don't see as it's anything to laugh about."

"Of course they've got awful important things on their minds," said the sheriff's wife apologetically.

They returned to an inspection of the block for the quilt. Mrs. Hale was looking at the fine, even sewing, and preoccupied with thoughts of the woman who had done that sewing, when she heard the sheriff's wife say, in a queer tone:

"Why, look at this one."

She turned to take the block held out to her.

"The sewing," said Mrs. Peters, in a troubled way, "All the rest of them have been so nice and even—but—this one. Why, it looks as if she didn't know what she was about!"

Their eyes met—something flashed to life, passed between them; then, as if with an effort, they seemed to pull away from each other. A moment Mrs. Hale sat there, her hands folded over that sewing which was so unlike all the rest of the sewing. Then she had pulled a knot and drawn the threads.

"Oh, what are you doing, Mrs. Hale?" asked the sheriff's wife, startled.

"Just pulling out a stitch or two that's not sewed very good," said Mrs. Hale mildly.

"I don't think we ought to touch things," Mrs. Peters said, a little helplessly.

"I'll just finish up this end," answered Mrs. Hale, still in that mild, matter-of-fact fashion.

She threaded a needle and started to replace bad sewing with good. For a little while she sewed in silence. Then, in that thin, timid voice, she heard:

"Mrs. Hale!"

"Yes, Mrs. Peters?"

"What do you suppose she was so—nervous about?"

"Oh, *I* don't know," said Mrs. Hale, as if dismissing a thing not important enough to spend much time on. "I don't know as she was— nervous. I sew awful queer sometimes when I'm just tired."

She cut a thread, and out of the corner of her eye looked up at Mrs. Peters. The small, lean face of the sheriff's wife seemed to have tightened up. Her eyes had that look of peering into something. But the next moment she moved, and said in her thin, indecisive way:

"Well, I must get those clothes wrapped. They may be through sooner than we think. I wonder where I could find a piece of paper—and string."

"In that cupboard, maybe," suggested to Mrs. Hale, after a glance around.

One piece of the crazy sewing remained unripped. Mrs. Peter's back turned, Martha Hale now scrutinized that piece, compared it with the dainty, accurate sewing of the other blocks. The difference was startling. Holding this block made her feel queer, as if the distracted thoughts of the woman who had perhaps turned to it to try and quiet herself were communicating themselves to her.

Mrs. Peters' voice roused her.

"Here's a bird-cage," she said. "Did she have a bird, Mrs. Hale?"

"Why, I don't know whether she did or not." She turned to look at the cage Mrs. Peters was holding up. "I've not been here in so long." She sighed. "There was a man round last year selling canaries cheap— but I don't know as she took one. Maybe she did. She used to sing real pretty herself."

Mrs. Peters looked around the kitchen.

"Seems kind of funny to think of a bird here." She half laughed—an attempt to put up a barrier. "But she must have had one—or why would she have a cage? I wonder what happened to it."

"I suppose maybe the cat got it," suggested Mrs. Hale, resuming her sewing.

"No; she didn't have a cat. She's got that feeling some people have about cats—being afraid of them. When they brought her to our house yesterday, my cat got in the room, and she was real upset and asked me to take it out."

"My sister Bessie was like that," laughed Mrs. Hale.

The sheriff's wife did not reply. The silence made Mrs. Hale turn round. Mrs. Peters was examining the bird-cage.

"Look at this door," she said slowly. "It's broke. One hinge has been pulled apart."

Mrs. Hale came nearer.

"Looks as if someone must have been—rough with it."

Again their eyes met—startled, questioning, apprehensive. For a moment neither spoke nor stirred. Then Mrs. Hale, turning away, said brusquely:

"If they're going to find any evidence, I wish they'd be about it. I don't like this place."

"But I'm awful glad you came with me, Mrs. Hale." Mrs. Peters put the bird-cage on the table and sat down. "It would be lonesome for me—sitting here alone."

"Yes, it would, wouldn't it?" agreed Mrs. Hale, a certain determined naturalness in her voice. She had picked up the sewing, but now it dropped in her lap, and she murmured in a different voice: "But I tell you what I *do* wish, Mrs. Peters. I wish I had come over sometimes when she was here. I wish—I had."

"But of course you were awful busy, Mrs. Hale. Your house—and your children."

"I could've come," retorted Mrs. Hale shortly. "I stayed away because it weren't cheerful—and that's why I ought to have come. I"—she looked around—"I've never liked this place. Maybe because it's down in a hollow and you don't see the road. I don't know what it is, but it's a lonesome place, and always was. I wish I had come over to see Minnie Foster sometimes. I can see now—" She did not put it into words.

"Well, you mustn't reproach yourself," counseled Mrs. Peters. "Somehow, we just don't see how it is with other folks till—something comes up."

"Not having children makes less work," mused Mrs. Hale, after a silence, "but it makes a quiet house—and Wright out to work all day—and no company when he did come in. Did you know John Wright, Mrs. Peters?"

"Not to know him. I've seen him in town. They say he was a good man."

"Yes—good," conceded John Wright's neighbor grimly. "He didn't drink, and kept his word as well as most, I guess, and paid his debts. But he was a hard man, Mrs. Peters. Just to pass the time of day with him—." She stopped, shivered a little. "Like a raw wind that gets to the bone." Her eye fell upon the cage on the table before her, and she added, almost bitterly: "I should think she would've wanted a bird!"

Suddenly she leaned forward, looking intently at the cage. "But what do you s'pose went wrong with it?"

"I don't know," returned Mrs. Peters; "unless it got sick and died."

But after she said it she reached over and swung the broken door. Both women watched it as if somehow held by it.

"You didn't know—her?" Mrs. Hale asked, a gentler note in her voice.

"Not till they brought her yesterday," said the sheriff's wife.

"She—come to think of it, she was kind of like a bird herself. Real sweet and pretty, but kind of timid and—fluttery. How—she—did—change."

That held her for a long time. Finally, as if struck with a happy thought and relieved to get back to everyday things, she exclaimed:

"Tell you what, Mrs. Peters, why don't you take the quilt in with you? It might take up her mind."

"Why, I think that's a real nice idea, Mrs. Hale," agreed the sheriff's wife, as if she too were glad to come into the atmosphere of a simple kindness. "There couldn't possibly be any objection to that, could there? Now, just what will I take? I wonder if her patches are in here—and her things?"

They turned to the sewing basket.

"Here's some red," said Mrs. Hale, bringing out a roll of cloth. Underneath that was a box. "Here, maybe her scissors are in here—and her things." She held it up. "What a pretty box! I'll warrant that was something she had a long time ago—when she was a girl."

She held it in her hand a moment; then, with a little sigh, opened it.

Instantly her hand went to her nose.

"Why—!"

Mrs. Peters drew nearer—then turned away.

"There's something wrapped up in this piece of silk," faltered Mrs. Hale.

"This isn't her scissors," said Mrs. Peters, in a shrinking voice.

Her hand not steady, Mrs. Hale raised the piece of silk. "Oh, Mrs. Peters!" she cried. "It's—"

Mrs. Peters bent closer.

"It's the bird," she whispered.

"But, Mrs. Peters!" cried Mrs. Hale. "*Look* at it! Its *neck*—look at its neck! It's all—other side *to*."

She held the box away from her.

The sheriff's wife again bent closer.

"Somebody wrung its neck," said she, in a voice that was slow and deep.

And then again the eyes of the two women met—this time clung together in a look of dawning comprehension, of growing horror. Mrs. Peters looked from the dead bird to the broken door of the cage. Again their eyes met. And just then there was a sound at the outside door. Mrs. Hale slipped the box under the quilt pieces in the basket, and sank into the chair before it. Mrs. Peters stood holding to the table. The county attorney and the sheriff came in from outside.

"Well, ladies," said the county attorney, as one turning from serious things to little pleasantries, "have you decided whether she was going to quilt it or knot it?"

"We think," began the sheriff's wife in a flurried voice, "that she was going to—knot it."

He was too preoccupied to notice the change that came in her voice on that last.

"Well, that's very interesting, I'm sure," he said tolerantly. He caught sight of the bird-cage.

"Has the bird flown?"

"We think the cat got it," said Mrs. Hale in a voice curiously even.

He was walking up and down, as if thinking something out.

"Is there a cat?" he asked absently.

Mrs. Hale shot a look up at the sheriff's wife.

"Well, not *now,*" said Mrs. Peters. "They're superstitious, you know; they leave."

She sank into her chair.

The county attorney did not heed her. "No sign at all of anyone having come in from the outside," he said to Peters, in the manner of continuing an interrupted conversation. "Their own rope. Now let's go upstairs again and go over it, piece by piece. It would have to have been someone who knew just the—"

The stair door closed behind them and their voices were lost.

The two women sat motionless, not looking at each other, but as if peering into something and at the same time holding back. When they spoke now it was as if they were afraid of what they were saying, but as if they could not help saying it.

"She liked the bird," said Martha Hale, low and slowly. "She was going to bury it in that pretty box."

"When I was a girl," said Mrs. Peters, under her breath, "my kitten—there was a boy took a hatchet, and before my eyes—before I could get there—" She covered her face an instant. "If they hadn't held me back I would have"—she caught herself, looked upstairs where footsteps were heard, and finished weakly— "hurt him."

Then they sat without speaking or moving.

"I wonder how it would seem," Mrs. Hale at last began, as if feeling her way over strange ground—"never to have had any children around?" Her eyes made a slow sweep of the kitchen, as if seeing what that kitchen had meant through all the years "No, Wright wouldn't like the bird," she said after that—"a thing that sang. She used to sing. He killed that too." Her voice tightened.

Mrs. Peters moved uneasily.

"Of course we don't know who killed the bird."

"I knew John Wright," was Mrs. Hale's answer.

"It was an awful thing was done in this house that night, Mrs. Hale," said the sheriff's wife. "Killing a man while he slept—slipping a thing round his neck that choked the life out of him."

Mrs. Hale's hand went out to the bird cage.

"We don't *know* who killed him," whispered Mrs. Peters wildly. "We don't *know*."

Mrs. Hale had not moved. "If there had been years and years of—nothing, then a bird to sing to you, it would be awful—still—after the bird was still."

It was as if something within her not herself had spoken, and it found in Mrs. Peters something she did not know as herself.

"I know what stillness is," she said, in a queer, monotonous voice. "When we homesteaded in Dakota, and my first baby died—after he was two years old—and me with no other then—"

Mrs. Hale stirred.

"How soon do you suppose they'll be through looking for the evidence?"

"I know what stillness is," repeated Mrs. Peters, in just that same way. Then she too pulled back. "The law has got to punish crime, Mrs. Hale," she said in her tight little way.

"I wish you'd seen Minnie Foster," was the answer, "when she wore a white dress with blue ribbons, and stood up there in the choir and sang."

The picture of that girl, the fact that she had lived neighbor to that girl for twenty years, and had let her die for lack of life, was suddenly more than she could bear.

"Oh, I *wish* I'd come over here once in a while!" she cried. "That was a crime! Who's going to punish that?"

"We mustn't take on," said Mrs. Peters, with a frightened look toward the stairs.

"I might 'a' *known* she needed help! I tell you, it's *queer*, Mrs. Peters. We live close together, and we live far apart. We all go through the same things—it's all just a different kind of the same thing! If it weren't—why do you and I *understand*? Why do we *know*—what we know this minute?"

She dashed her hand across her eyes. Then, seeing the jar of fruit on the table she reached for it and choked out:

"If I was you I wouldn't *tell* her her fruit was gone! Tell her it *ain't*. Tell her it's all right—all of it. Here—take this in to prove it to her! She—she may never know whether it was broke or not."

She turned away.

Mrs. Peters reached out for the bottle of fruit as if she were glad to take it—as if touching a familiar thing, having something to do, could keep her from something else. She got up, looked about for something to wrap the fruit in, took a petticoat from the pile of clothes she had brought from the front room, and nervously started winding that round the bottle.

"My!" she began, in a high, false voice, "it's a good thing the men couldn't hear us! Getting all stirred up over a little thing like a—dead canary." She hurried over that. "As if that could have anything to do with—with—My, wouldn't they *laugh*?"

Footsteps were heard on the stairs.

"Maybe they would," muttered Mrs. Hale—"maybe they wouldn't."

"No, Peters," said the county attorney incisively; "it's all perfectly clear, except the reason for doing it. But you know juries when it comes to women. If there was some definite thing—something to show. Something to make a story about. A thing that would connect up with this clumsy way of doing it."

In a covert way Mrs. Hale looked at Mrs. Peters. Mrs. Peters was looking at her. Quickly they looked away from each other. The outer door opened and Mr. Hale came in.

"I've got the team round now," he said. "Pretty cold out there."

"I'm going to stay here awhile by myself," the county attorney suddenly announced. "You can send Frank out for me, can't you?" he asked the sheriff. "I want to go over everything. I'm not satisfied we can't do better."

Again, for one brief moment, the two women's eyes found one another.

The sheriff came up to the table.

"Did you want to see what Mrs. Peters was going to take in?"

The county attorney picked up the apron. He laughed.

"Oh, I guess they're not very dangerous things the ladies have picked out."

Mrs. Hale's hand was on the sewing basket in which the box was concealed. She felt that she ought to take her hand off the basket. She did not seem able to. He picked up one of the quilt blocks which she had piled on to cover the box. Her eyes felt like fire. She had a feeling that if he took up the basket she would snatch it from him.

But he did not take it up. With another little laugh, he turned away, saying:

"No; Mrs. Peters doesn't need supervising. For that matter, a sheriff's wife is married to the law. Ever think of it that way, Mrs. Peters?"

Mrs. Peters was standing beside the table. Mrs. Hale shot a look up at her; but she could not see her face. Mrs. Peters had turned away. When she spoke, her voice was muffled.

"Not—just that way," she said.

"Married to the law!" chuckled Mrs. Peters' husband. He moved toward the door into the front room, and said to the county attorney:

"I just want you to come in here a minute, George. We ought to take a look at these windows."

"Oh—windows," said the county attorney scoffingly.

"We'll be right out, Mr. Hale," said the sheriff to the farmer, who was still waiting by the door.

Hale went to look after the horses. The sheriff followed the county attorney into the other room. Again—for one final moment—the two women were alone in that kitchen.

Martha Hale sprang up, her hands tight together, looking at that other woman, with whom it rested. At first she could not see her eyes, for the sheriff's wife had not turned back since she turned away at that suggestion of being married to the law. But now Mrs. Hale made her turn back. Her eyes made her turn back. Slowly, unwillingly, Mrs. Peters turned her head until her eyes met the eyes of the other woman. There was a moment when they held each other in a steady, burning look in which there was no evasion or flinching. Then Martha Hale's eyes pointed the way to the basket in which was hidden the thing that would make certain the conviction of the other woman—that woman who was not there and yet who had been there with them all through that hour.

For a moment Mrs. Peters did not move. And then she did it. With a rush forward, she threw back the quilt pieces, got the box, tried to put it in her handbag. It was too big. Desperately she opened it, started to take the bird out. But there she broke—she could not touch the bird. She stood there helpless, foolish.

There was the sound of a knob turning in the inner door. Martha Hale snatched the box from the sheriff's wife, and got it in the pocket of her big coat just as the sheriff and the county attorney came back into the kitchen.

"Well, Henry," said the county attorney facetiously, "at least we found out that she was not going to quilt it. She was going to—what is it you call it, ladies?"

Mrs. Hale's hand was against the pocket of her coat.

"We call it—knot it, Mr. Henderson."

Notes

1. *Titles.* Explore the implications of the two titles borne by this work, "Trifles," and "A Jury of Her Peers." What dichotomies do these titles suggest? How does Glaspell establish these dichotomies in the story?

2. *Alternative Moralities*. Are the two women justified in their actions? Explain the principles on which they act. How are those principles related to the idea of the jury? In recent years, the jury system has been portrayed as the villain in stories of large monetary awards in products liability and other tort cases. In the John Grisham novel, THE RUNAWAY JURY, an individual juror becomes a powerful actor within the system. After the verdict in the O.J. Simpson murder trial, many commentators excoriated the jury in that case as unduly swayed by Simpson's celebrity status. How does Glaspell's story fit into these more recent portrayals of the jury?

* * *

Herman Melville (1819–1891) is best known for his novel, MOBY DICK. After initial success with his first two books, TYPEE and OMOO, Melville's fortunes as a writer faltered. His magnum opus, MOBY DICK, written with the encouragement of Nathaniel Hawthorne, was not appreciated until after his death. Although he wrote many stories, including the following one, purely for money, he became financially dependent upon his father-in-law, Lemuel Shaw, who served as Chief Justice of Massachusetts. It has been suggested that the following story reflects Melville's relationship with him.

BARTLEBY THE SCRIVENER
A STORY OF WALL STREET
Herman Melville

I am a rather elderly man. The nature of my avocations for the last thirty years has brought me into more than ordinary contact with what would seem an interesting and somewhat singular set of men of whom as yet nothing that I know of has ever been written:—I mean the law-copyists or scriveners. I have known very many of them, professionally and privately, and if I pleased, could relate divers histories, at which good-natured gentlemen might smile, and sentimental souls might weep. But I waive the biographies of all other scriveners for a few passages in the life of Bartleby, who was a scrivener the strangest I ever saw or heard of. While of other law-copyists I might write the complete life, of Bartleby nothing of that sort can be done. I believe that no materials exist for a full and satisfactory biography of this man. It is an irreparable loss to literature. Bartleby was one of those beings of whom nothing is ascertainable, except from the original sources, and in his case those are very small. What my own astonished eyes saw of Bartleby, *that* is all I know of him, except, indeed, one vague report which will appear in the sequel.

Ere introducing the scrivener, as he first appeared to me, it is fit I make some mention of myself, my *employés*, my business, my chambers, and general surroundings; because some such description is indispensable to an adequate understanding of the chief character about to be presented. *Imprimis*: I am a man who, from his youth upwards, has been filled with a profound conviction that the easiest way of life is the best. Hence, though I belong to a profession proverbially energetic and nervous, even to turbulence, at times, yet nothing of that sort have I ever suffered to invade my peace. I am one of those unambitious lawyers who never addresses a jury, or in any way draws down public applause; but in the cool tranquillity of a snug retreat, do a snug business among rich men's bonds and mortgages and title-deeds. The late John Jacob Astor, a personage little given to poetic enthusiasm, had no hesitation in pronouncing my first grand point to be prudence; my next, method. I do not speak it in vanity, but simply record the fact, that I was not unemployed in my profession by the late John Jacob Astor; a name which, I admit, I love to repeat, for it hath a rounded and orbicular sound to it, and rings like unto bullion. I will freely add, that I was not insensible to the late John Jacob Astor's good opinion.

Some time prior to the period at which this little history begins, my avocations had been largely increased. The good old office, now extinct in the State of New York, of a Master in Chancery, had been conferred upon me. It was not a very arduous office, but very pleasantly remunerative. I seldom lose my temper; much more seldom indulge in dangerous indignation at wrongs and outrages; but I must be permitted to be rash here and declare, that I consider the sudden and violent abrogation of the office of Master of Chancery, by the new Constitution, as a— premature act; inasmuch as I had counted upon a life-lease of the profits, whereas I only received those of a few short years. But this is by the way.

My chambers were up stairs at No.__ Wall-street. At one end they looked upon the white wall of the interior of a spacious sky-light shaft, penetrating the building from top to bottom. This view might have been considered rather tame than otherwise, deficient in what landscape painters call "life." But if so, the view from the other end of my chambers offered, at least, a contrast, if nothing more. In that direction my windows commanded an unobstructed view of a lofty brick wall, black by age and everlasting shade; which wall required no spy-glass to bring out its lurking beauties, but for the benefit of all near-sighted spectators, was pushed up to within ten feet of my window panes. Owing to the great height of the surrounding buildings, and my chambers being on the second floor, the interval between this wall and mine not a little resembled a huge square cistern.

At the period just preceding the advent of Bartleby, I had two persons as copyists in my employment, and a promising lad as an office-boy. First, Turkey; second, Nippers; third, Ginger Nut. These may seem names, the like of which are not usually found in the Directory. In truth they were nicknames, mutually conferred upon each other by my three clerks, and were deemed expressive of their respective persons or characters. Turkey was a short, pursy Englishman of about my own age, that is, somewhere not far from sixty. In the morning, one might say, his face was of a fine florid hue, but after twelve o'clock, meridian—his dinner hour—it blazed like a grate full of Christmas coals; and continued blazing—but, as it were, with a gradual wane—till 6 o'clock, P.M. or thereabouts, after which I saw no more of the proprietor of the face, which gaining its meridian with the sun, seemed to set with it, to rise, culminate, and decline the following day, with the like regularity and undiminished glory. There are many singular coincidences I have known in the course of my life, not the least among which was the fact that exactly when Turkey displayed his fullest beams from his red and radiant countenance, just then, too, at the critical moment, began the daily period when I considered his business capacities as seriously disturbed for the remainder of the twenty-four hours. Not that he was absolutely idle, or averse to business then; far from it. The difficulty was, he was apt to be altogether too energetic. There was a strange, inflamed, flurried, flighty recklessness of activity about him. He would be incautious in dipping his pen into his inkstand. All his blots upon my documents, were dropped there after twelve o'clock, meridian. Indeed, not only would he be reckless and sadly given to making blots in the afternoon, but some days he went further, and was rather noisy. At such times, too, his face flamed with augmented blazonry, as if cannel coal had been heaped on anthracite. He made an unpleasant racket with his chair; spilled his sand-box; in mending his pens, impatiently split them all to pieces, and threw them on the floor in a sudden passion; stood up and leaned over his table, boxing his papers about in a most indecorous manner, very sad to behold in an elderly man like him. Nevertheless, as he was in many ways a most valuable person to me, and all the time before twelve o'clock, meridian, was the quickest, steadiest creature too, accomplishing a great deal of work in a style not easy to be matched—for these reasons, I was willing to overlook his eccentricities, though indeed, occasionally, I remonstrated with him. I did this very gently, however, because, though the civilest, nay, the blandest and most reverential of men in the morning, yet in the afternoon he was disposed, upon provocation, to be slightly rash with his tongue, in fact, insolent. Now, valuing his morning services as I did, and resolved not to lose them; yet, at the same time made uncomfortable by his inflamed ways after twelve o'clock; and being a man of peace, unwilling by my admonitions to call forth unseemly retorts from him; I took upon me, one Saturday noon (he was always worse on Saturdays), to hint to him, very kindly, that perhaps now that he was growing old, it might be well to abridge his labors; in short, he need not come to my chambers after twelve o'clock, but, dinner over, had best go home to his lodgings and rest himself till tea-time. But no; he insisted upon his afternoon devotions. His countenance became intolerably fervid, as he oratorically assured me—gesticulating with a long ruler at the other end of the room—that if his services in the morning were useful, how indispensible, then, in the afternoon?

"With submission, sir," said Turkey on this occasion, "I consider myself your right-hand man. In the morning I but marshal and deploy my columns; but in the afternoon I put myself at their head, and gallantly charge the foe, thus!"—and he made a violent thrust with the ruler.

"But the blots, Turkey," intimated I.

"True,—but, with submission, sir, behold these hairs! I am getting old. Surely, sir, a blot or two of a warm afternoon is not to be severely urged against gray hairs. Old age—even if it blot the page—is honorable. With submission, sir, we *both* are getting old."

This appeal to my fellow-feeling was hardly to be resisted. At all events, I saw that go he would not. So I made up my mind to let him stay, resolving, nevertheless, to see to it, that during the afternoon he had to do with my less important papers.

Nippers, the second on my list, was a whiskered, sallow, and, upon the whole, rather piratical-looking young man of about five and twenty. I always deemed him the victim of two evil powers—ambition and indigestion. The ambition was evinced by a certain impatience of the duties of a mere copyist, an unwarrantable usurpation of strictly professional affairs, such as the original drawing up of legal documents. The indigestion seemed betokened in an occasional nervous testiness and grinning irritability, causing the teeth to audibly grind together over mistakes committed in copying; unnecessary maledictions, hissed, rather than spoken, in the heat of business; and especially by a continual discontent with the height of the table where he worked. Though of a very ingenious mechanical turn, Nippers could never get this table to suit him. He put chips under it, blocks of various sorts, bits of pasteboard, and at last went so far as to attempt an exquisite adjustment by final pieces of folded blotting-paper. But no invention would answer. If, for the sake of easing his back, he brought the table lid at a sharp angle well up towards his chin, and wrote there like a man using the steep roof of a Dutch house for his desk:—then he declared that it stopped the circulation in his arms. If now he lowered the table to his waistbands, and stooped over it in writing, then there was a sore aching in his back. In short, the truth of the matter was, Nippers knew not what he wanted. Or, if he wanted anything, it was to be rid of a scrivener's table altogether. Among the manifestations of his diseased ambition was a fondness he had for receiving visits from certain ambiguous-looking fellows in seedy coats, whom he called his clients. Indeed I was aware that not only was he, at times, considerable of a ward-politician, but he occasionally did a little business at the Justices' courts, and was not unknown on the steps of the Tombs. I have good reason to believe, however, that one individual who called upon him at my chambers, and who, with a grand air, he insisted was his client, was no other than a dun, and the alleged title-deed, a bill. But with all his failings, and the annoyances he caused me, Nippers, like his compatriot Turkey, was a very useful man to me; wrote a neat, swift hand; and, when he chose, was not deficient in a gentlemanly sort of deportment. Added to this, he always dressed in a gentlemanly sort of way; and so, incidentally, reflected credit upon my chambers. Whereas with respect to Turkey, I had much ado to keep him from being a reproach to me. His clothes were apt to look oily and smell of eating-houses. He wore his pantaloons very loose and baggy in summer. His coats were execrable; his hat not to be handled. But while the hat was a thing of indifference to me, inasmuch as his natural civility and deference, as a dependent Englishman, always led him to doff it the moment he entered the room, yet his coat was another matter. Concerning his coats, I reasoned with him; but with no effect. The truth was, I suppose, that a man with so small an income, could not afford to sport such a lustrous face and a lustrous coat at one and the same time. As Nippers once observed, Turkey's money went chiefly for red ink. One winter day I presented Turkey with a highly-respectable looking coat of my own, a padded gray coat, of a most comfortable warmth, and which buttoned straight up from the knee to the neck. I thought Turkey would appreciate the favor, and abate his rashness and obstreperousness of afternoons. But no. I verily believe that buttoning himself up in so downy and blanket-like a coat had a pernicious effect upon him; upon the same principle that too much oats are bad for horses. In fact, precisely as a rash, restive horse is said to feel his oats, so Turkey felt his coat. It made him insolent. He was a man whom prosperity harmed.

Though, concerning the self-indulgent habits of Turkey, I had my own private surmises, yet touching Nippers I was well persuaded that whatever might be his faults in other respects, he was, at least, a temperate young man. But indeed, nature herself seemed to have been his vintner, and at his birth charged him so thoroughly with an irritable, brandy-like disposition, that all subsequent potations were needless. When I consider how, amid the stillness of my chambers, Nippers would sometimes impatiently rise from his seat, and stooping over his table, spread his arms wide apart, seize the whole desk, and move it, and jerk it, with a grim, grinding motion on the floor, as if the table were a perverse voluntary agent, intent on thwarting and vexing him; I plainly perceive that for Nippers, brandy and water were altogether superfluous.

It was fortunate for me that, owing to its course—indigestion—the irritability and consequent nervousness of Nippers, were mainly observable in the morning, while in the afternoon he was comparatively mild. So that Turkey's paroxysms only coming on about twelve o'clock, I never had to do with their eccentricities at one time. Their fits relieved each other like guards. When Nippers' was on, Turkey's was off, and *vice versa*. This was a good natural arrangement under the circumstances.

Ginger Nut, the third on my list, was a lad some twelve years old. His father was a carman, ambitious of seeing his son on the bench instead of a cart, before he died. So he sent him to my office as a student at law, errand-boy, and cleaner and sweeper, at the rate of one dollar a week. He had a little desk to himself, but he did not use it much. Upon inspection, the drawer exhibited a great array of the shells of various sorts of nuts. Indeed, to this quick-witted youth the whole noble science of the law was contained in a nut-shell. Not the least among the employments of Ginger Nut, as well as one which he discharged with the most alacrity, was his duty as cake and apple purveyor for Turkey and Nippers. Copying law-papers being proverbially a dry, husky sort of business, my two scriveners were fain to moisten their mouths very often with Spitzenbergs to be had at the numerous stalls nigh the Custom House and Post Office. Also, they sent Ginger Nut very frequently for that peculiar cake—small, flat, round, and very spicy—after which he had been named by them. Of a cold morning when business was but dull, Turkey would gobble up scores of these cakes, as if they were mere wafers—indeed they sell them at the rate of six or eight for a penny—the scrape of his pen blending with the crunching of the crisp particles in his mouth. Of all the fiery afternoon blunders and flurried rashnesses of Turkey, was his once moistening a ginger-cake between his lips, and clapping it on to a mortgage, for a seal. I came within an ace of dismissing him then. But he mollified me by making an oriental bow, and saying—

"With submission, sir, it was generous of me to find you in stationery on my own account."

Now my original business—that of a conveyancer and title hunter, and drawer-up of recondite documents of all sorts—was considerably increased by receiving the master's office. There was now great work for scriveners. Not only must I push the clerks already with me, but I must have additional help. In answer to my advertisement, a motionless young man one morning stood upon my office threshold, the door being open, for it was summer. I can see that figure now—pallidly neat, pitiably respectable, incurably forlorn! It was Bartleby.

After a few words touching his qualifications, I engaged him, glad to have among my corps of copyists a man of so singularly sedate an aspect, which I thought might operate beneficially upon the flighty temper of Turkey, and the fiery one of Nippers.

I should have stated before that ground-glass folding-doors divided my premises into two parts, one of which was occupied by my scriveners, the other by myself. According to my humor I threw open these doors, or closed them. I resolved to assign Bartleby a corner by the folding-doors, but on my side of them, so as to have this quiet man within easy call, in case any trifling thing was to be done. I placed his desk close up to a small sidewindow in that part of the room, a window which originally had afforded a lateral view of certain grimy back-yards and bricks, but which, owing to subsequent erections, commanded at present no view at all, though it gave some light. Within three feet of the panes was a wall, and the light came down from far above, between two lofty buildings, as from a very small opening in a dome. Still further to a satisfactory arrangement, I procured a high green folding screen, which might entirely isolate Bartleby from my sight, though not remove him from my voice. And thus, in a manner, privacy and society were conjoined.

At first, Bartleby did an extraordinary quantity of writing. As if long famishing for something to copy, he seemed to gorge himself on my documents. There was no pause for digestion. He ran a day and night line, copying by sun-light and by candle-light. I should have been quite delighted with his application, had he been cheerfully industrious. But he wrote on silently, palely, mechanically.

It is, of course, an indispensable part of a scrivener's business to verify the accuracy of his copy, word by word. Where there are two or more scriveners in an office, they assist each other in this examination, one reading from the copy, the other holding the original. It is a very dull, wearisome, and lethargic affair. I can readily imagine that to some sanguine temperaments it would be altogether intolerable. For example, I cannot credit that the mettlesome poet Byron would have contentedly sat down with Bartleby to examine a law document of, say five hundred pages, closely written in a crimpy hand.

Now and then, in the haste of business, it had been my habit to assist in comparing some brief document myself, calling Turkey or Nippers for this purpose. One object I had in placing Bartleby so handy to me behind the screen, was to avail myself of his services on such trivial occasions. It was on the third day, I think, of his being with me, and before any necessity had arisen for having his own writing examined, that, being much hurried to complete a small affair I had in hand, I abruptly called to Bartleby. In my haste and natural expectancy of instant compliance, I sat with my head bent over the original on my desk, and my right hand sideways, and somewhat nervously extended with the copy, so that immediately upon emerging from his retreat, Bartleby might snatch it and proceed to business without the least delay.

In this very attitude did I sit when I called to him, rapidly stating what it was I wanted him to do—namely, to examine a small paper with me. Imagine my surprise, nay, my consternation, when without moving from his privacy, Bartleby, in a singularly mild, firm voice, replied, "I would prefer not to."

I sat awhile in perfect silence, rallying my stunned faculties. Immediately it occurred to me that my ears had deceived me, or Bartleby had entirely misunderstood my meaning. I repeated my request in the clearest tone I could assume. But in quite as clear a one came the previous reply, "I would prefer not to."

"Prefer not to," echoed I, rising in high excitement, and crossing the room with a stride, "What do you mean? Are you moon-struck? I want you to help me compare this sheet here—take it," and I thrust it towards him.

"I would prefer not to," said he.

I looked at him steadfastly. His face was leanly composed; his gray eye dimly calm. Not a wrinkle of agitation rippled him. Had there been the least uneasiness, anger, impatience or impertinence in his manner; in other words, had there been anything ordinarily human about him, doubtless I should have violently dismissed him from the premises. But as it was, I should have as soon thought of turning my pale plaster-of-paris bust of Cicero out of doors. I stood gazing at him awhile, as he went on with his own writing, and then reseated myself at my desk. This is very strange, thought I. What had one best do? But my business hurried me. I concluded to forget the matter for the present, reserving it for my future leisure. So calling Nippers from the other room, the paper was speedily examined.

A few days after this, Bartleby concluded four lengthy documents, being quadruplicates of a week's testimony taken before me in my High Court of Chancery. It became necessary to examine them. It was an important suit, and great accuracy was imperative. Having all things arranged I called Turkey, Nippers and Ginger Nut from the next room, meaning to place the four copies in the hands of my four clerks, while I should read from the original. Accordingly Turkey, Nippers and Ginger Nut had taken their seats in a row, each with his document in hand, when I called to Bartleby to join this interesting group.

"Bartleby! quick, I am waiting."

I heard a low scrape of his chair legs on the unscraped floor, and soon he appeared standing at the entrance of his hermitage.

"What is wanted?" said he mildly.

"The copies, the copies," said I hurriedly. "We are going to examine them. There"—and I held towards him the fourth quadruplicate.

"I would prefer not to," he said, and gently disappeared behind the screen.

For a few moments I was turned into a pillar of salt, standing at the head of my seated column of clerks. Recovering myself, I advanced towards the screen, and demanded the reason for such extraordinary conduct.

"*Why* do you refuse?"

"I would prefer not to."

With any other man I should have flown outright into a dreadful passion, scorned all further words, and thrust him ignominiously from my presence. But there was something about Bartleby that not only strangely disarmed me, but in a wonderful manner touched and disconcerted me. I began to reason with him.

"These are your own copies we are about to examine. It is labor saving to you, because one examination will answer for your four papers. It is common usage. Every copyist is bound to help examine his copy. Is it not so? Will you not speak? Answer!"

"I prefer not to," he replied in a flute-like tone. It seemed to me that while I had been addressing him, he carefully revolved every statement that I made; fully comprehended the meaning; could not gainsay the irresistible conclusion; but, at the same time, some paramount consideration prevailed with him to reply as he did.

"You are decided, then, not to comply with my request—a request made according to common usage and common sense?"

He briefly gave me to understand that on that point my judgment was sound. Yes: his decision was irreversible.

It is not seldom the case that when a man is browbeaten in some unprecedented and violently unreasonable way, he begins to stagger in his own plainest faith. He begins, as it were, vaguely to surmise that, wonderful as it may be, all the justice and all the reason is on the other side. Accordingly, if any disinterested persons are present, he turns to them for some reinforcement for his own faltering mind.

"Turkey," said I, "what do you think of this? Am I not right?"

"With submission, sir," said Turkey, with his blandest tone, "I think that you are."

"Nippers," said I, "what do *you* think of it?"

"I think I should kick him out of the office."

(The reader of nice perceptions will here perceive that, it being morning, Turkey's answer is couched in polite and tranquil terms, but Nippers replies in ill-tempered ones. Or, to repeat a previous sentence, Nipper's ugly mood was on duty, and Turkey's off.)

"Ginger Nut," said I, willing to enlist the smallest suffrage in my behalf, "what do *you* think of it?"

"I think, sir, he's a little *luny*," replied Ginger Nut, with a grin.

"You hear what they say," said I, turning towards the screen, "come forth and do your duty."

But he vouchsafed no reply. I pondered a moment in sore perplexity. But once more business hurried me. I determined again to postpone the consideration of this dilemma to my future leisure. With a little trouble we made out to examine the papers without Bartleby, though at every page or two, Turkey deferentially dropped his opinion that this proceeding was quite out of the common; while Nippers, twitching in his chair with a dyspeptic nervousness, ground out between his set teeth occasional hissing maledictions against the stubborn oaf behind the screen. And for his (Nipper's) part, this was the first and the last time he would do another man's business without pay.

Meanwhile Bartleby sat in his hermitage, oblivious to everything but his own peculiar business there.

Some days passed, the scrivener being employed upon another lengthy work. His late remarkable conduct led me to regard his way narrowly. I observed that he never went to dinner; indeed that he never went any where. As yet I had never of my personal knowledge known him to be outside of my office. He was a perpetual sentry in the corner. At about eleven o'clock though, in the morning, I noticed that Ginger Nut would advance toward the opening in Bartleby's screen, as if silently beckoned thither by a gesture invisible to me where I sat. That boy would then leave the office jingling a few pence, and reappear with a handful of ginger-nuts which he delivered in the hermitage, receiving two of the cakes for his trouble.

He lives, then, on ginger-nuts, thought I; never eats a dinner, properly speaking; he must be a vegetarian then, but no; he never eats even vegetables, he eats nothing but ginger-nuts. My mind then ran on in reveries concerning the probable effects upon the human constitution of living entirely on ginger-nuts. Ginger-nuts are so called because they contain ginger as one of their peculiar constituents, and the final flavoring one. Now what was ginger? A hot, spicy thing. Was Bartleby hot and spicy? Not at all. Ginger, then, had no effect upon Bartleby. Probably he preferred it should have none.

Nothing so aggravates an earnest person as a passive resistance. If the individual so resisted be of a not inhumane temper, and the resisting one perfectly harmless in his passivity; then, in the better moods of the former, he will endeavor charitably to construe to his imagination what proves impossible to be solved by his judgment. Even so, for the most part, I regarded Bartleby and his ways. Poor fellow! thought I, he means no mischief; it is plain he intends no insolence; his aspect sufficiently evinces that his eccentricities are involuntary. He is useful to me. I can get along with him. If I turn him away, the chances are he will fall in with some less indulgent employer, and then he will be rudely treated, and perhaps driven forth miserably to starve. Yes. Here I can cheaply purchase a delicious self-approval. To befriend Bartleby; to humor him in his strange willfulness, will cost me little or nothing, while I lay up in my soul what will eventually prove a sweet morsel for my conscience. But this mood was not invariable with me. The passiveness of Bartleby sometimes irritated me. I felt strangely goaded on to encounter him in new opposition, to elicit some angry spark from him answerable to my own. But indeed I might as well have essayed to strike fire with my knuckles against a bit of Windsor soap. But one afternoon the evil impulse in me mastered me, and the following little scene ensued:

"Bartleby," said I, "when those papers are all copied, I will compare them with you."

"I would prefer not to."

"How? Surely you do not mean to persist in that mulish vagary?"

No answer.

I threw open the folding-doors near by, and turning upon Turkey and Nippers, exclaimed in an excited manner—

"He says, a second time, he won't examine his papers. What do you think of it, Turkey?"

It was afternoon, be it remembered. Turkey sat glowing like a brass boiler, his bald head steaming, his hands reeling among his blotted papers.

"Think of it?" roared Turkey; "I think I'll just step behind his screen, and black his eyes for him!"

So saying, Turkey rose to his feet and threw his arms into a pugilistic position. He was hurrying away to make good his promise, when I detained him, alarmed at the effect of incautiously rousing Turkey's combativeness after dinner.

"Sit down, Turkey," said I, "and hear what Nippers has to say. What do you think of it, Nippers? Would I not be justified in immediately dismissing Bartleby?"

"Excuse me, that is for you to decide, sir. I think his conduct quite unusual, and indeed unjust, as regards Turkey and myself. But it may only be a passing whim."

"Ah," exclaimed I, "you have strangely changed your mind then—you speak very gently of him now."

"All beer," cried Turkey; "gentleness is effects of beer—Nippers and I dined together today. You see how gentle *I* am, sir. Shall I go and black his eyes?"

"You refer to Bartleby, I suppose. No, not today, Turkey," I replied; "pray, put up your fists."

I closed the doors, and again advanced towards Bartleby. I felt additional incentives tempting me to my fate. I burned to be rebelled against again. I remembered that Bartleby never left the office.

"Bartleby," said I, "Ginger Nut is away; just step round to the Post Office, won't you? (it was but a three minutes' walk,) and see if there is anything for me."

"I would prefer not to."

"You *will* not?"

"I *prefer* not."

I staggered to my desk, and sat there in a deep study. My blind inveteracy returned. Was there any other thing in which I could procure myself to be ignominiously repulsed by this lean, penniless wight?—my hired clerk? What added thing is there, perfectly reasonable, that he will be sure to refuse to do?

"Bartleby!"

No answer.

"Bartleby," in a louder tone.

No answer.

"Bartleby," I roared.

Like a very ghost, agreeably to the laws of magical invocation, at the third summons, he appeared at the entrance of his hermitage.

"Go to the next room, and tell Nippers to come to me."

"I prefer not to," he respectfully and slowly said, and mildly disappeared.

"Very good, Bartleby," said I, in a quiet sort of serenely severe self-possessed tone, intimating the unalterable purpose of some terrible retribution very close at hand. At the moment I half intended something of the kind. But upon the whole, as it was drawing towards my dinner hour, I thought it best to put on my hat and walk home for the day, suffering much from perplexity and distress of mind.

Shall I acknowledge it? The conclusion of this whole business was that it soon became a fixed fact of my chambers, that a pale young scrivener, by the name of Bartleby, had a desk there; that he copied for me at the usual rate of four cents a folio (one hundred words); but he was permanently exempt from examining the work done by him, that duty being transferred to Turkey and Nippers, one of compliment doubtless to their superior acuteness; moreover, said Bartleby was never on any account to be dispatched on the most trivial errand of any sort; and that even if entreated to take upon him such a matter, it was generally understood that he would prefer not to—in other words, that he would refuse point-blank.

As days passed on, I became considerably reconciled to Bartleby. His steadiness, his freedom from all dissipation, his incessant industry (except when he chose to throw himself into a standing revery behind his screen), his great stillness, his unalterableness of demeanor under all circumstances, made him a valuable acquisition. One prime thing was this,—*he was always there*—first in the morning, continually through the day, and the last at night. I had a singular confidence in his honesty. I felt my most precious papers perfectly safe in his hands. Sometimes to be sure I could not, for the very soul of me, avoid falling into sudden spasmodic passions with him. For it was exceeding difficult to bear in mind all the time those strange peculiarities, privileges, and unheard of exemptions, forming the tacit stipulations on Bartleby's part under which he remained in my office. Now and then, in the eagerness of dispatching pressing business, I would inadvertently summon Bartleby, in a short, rapid tone, to put his finger, say, on the incipient tie of a bit of red tape with which I was about compressing some papers. Of course, from behind the screen the usual answer, "I prefer not to," was sure to come; and then, how could a human creature with the common infirmities of our nature, refrain from bitterly exclaiming upon such perverseness—such unreasonableness? However, every added repulse of this sort which I received only tended to lessen the probability of my repeating the inadvertence.

Here it must be said, that according to the custom of most legal gentlemen occupying chambers in densely-populated law buildings, there were several keys to my door. One was kept by a woman residing in the attic, which person weekly scrubbed and daily swept and dusted my apartments. Another was kept by Turkey for convenience sake. The third I sometimes carried in my own pocket. The fourth I knew not who had.

Now, one Sunday morning I happened to go to Trinity Church, to hear a celebrated preacher, and finding myself rather early on the ground, I thought I would walk round to my chambers for a while. Luckily I had my key with me; but upon applying it to the lock, I found it resisted by something inserted from the inside. Quite surprised, I called out; when to my consternation a key was turned from within; and thrusting his lean visage at me, and holding the door ajar, the apparition of Bartleby appeared, in his shirt sleeves, and otherwise in a strangely tattered dishabille, saying quietly that he was sorry, but he was deeply engaged just then, and—preferred not admitting me at present. In a brief word or two, he moreover added, that perhaps I had better walk round the block two or three times, and by that time he would probably have concluded his affairs.

Now, the utterly unsurmised appearance of Bartleby, tenanting my law chambers of a Sunday morning, with his cadaverously gentlemanly *nonchalance*, yet withal firm and self-possessed, had such a strange effect upon me, that incontinently I slunk away from my own door, and did as desired. But not without sundry twinges of impotent rebellion against the mild effrontery of this unaccountable scrivener. Indeed, it was his wonderful mildness chiefly, which not only disarmed me, but unmanned me, as it were. For I consider that one, for the time, is a sort of unmanned when he tranquilly permits his hired clerk to dictate to him, and order him away from his own premises. Furthermore, I was full of uneasiness as to what Bartleby could possibly be doing in my office in his shirt sleeves, and in an otherwise dismantled condition of a Sunday morning. Was anything amiss going on? Nay, that was out of the question. It was not to be thought of for a moment that Bartleby was an immoral person. But what could he be doing there?—copying? Nay again, whatever might be his eccentricities, Bartleby was an eminently decorous person. He would be the last man to sit down to his desk in any state approaching to nudity. Besides, it was Sunday; and there was something about Bartleby that forbade the supposition that he would by any secular occupation violate the proprieties of the day.

Nevertheless, my mind was not pacified; and full of a restless curiosity, at last I returned to the door. Without hindrance I inserted my key, opened it, and entered. Bartleby was not to be seen. I looked round anxiously, peeped behind his screen; but it was very plain that he was gone. Upon more closely examining the place, I surmised that for an indefinite period Bartleby must have eaten, dressed, and slept in my office, and that too without plate, mirror, or bed. The cushioned seat of a ricketty old sofa in one corner bore the faint impress of a lean, reclining form. Rolled away under his desk, I found a blanket; under the empty grate, a blacking box and brush; on a chair, a tin basin, with soap and a ragged towel; in a newspaper a few crumbs of ginger-nuts and a morsel of cheese. Yet, thought I, it is evident enough that Bartleby has been making his home here, keeping bachelor's hall all by himself. Immediately then the thought came sweeping across me, What miserable friendlessness and loneliness are here revealed! His poverty is great; but his solitude, how horrible! Think of it. Of a Sunday, Wall-street is deserted as Petra; and every night of every day it is an emptiness. This building too, which of week-days hums with industry and life, at nightfall echoes with sheer vacancy, and all through Sunday is forlorn. And here Bartleby makes his home; sole spectator of a solitude which he has seen all populous—a sort of innocent and transformed Marius brooding among the ruins of Carthage!

For the first time in my life a feeling of overpowering stinging melancholy seized me. Before, I had never experienced aught but a notunpleasing sadness. The bond of a common humanity now drew me irresistibly to gloom. A fraternal melancholy! For both I and Bartleby were sons of Adam. I remembered the bright silks and sparkling faces I had seen that day in gala trim, swan-like sailing down the Mississippi of Broadway; and I contrasted them with the pallid copyist, and thought to myself, Ah, happiness courts the light, so we deem the world is gay; but misery hides aloof, so we deem that misery there is none. These sad fancyings—chimeras, doubtless, of a sick and silly brain—led on to other and more special thoughts, concerning the eccentricities of Bartleby. Presentiments of strange discoveries hovered round me. The scrivener's pale form appeared to me laid out, among uncaring strangers, in its shivering winding sheet.

Suddenly I was attracted by Bartleby's closed desk, the key in open sight left in the lock.

I mean no mischief, seek the gratification of no heartless curiosity, thought I; besides, the desk is mine, and its contents too, so I will make bold to look within. Everything was methodically arranged, the papers smoothly placed. The pigeon holes were deep, and removing the files of documents, I groped into their recesses. Presently I felt something there, and dragged it out. It was an old bandanna handkerchief, heavy and knotted. I opened it, and saw it was a savings bank.

I now recalled all the quiet mysteries which I had noted in the man. I remembered that he never spoke but to answer; that though at intervals he had considerable time to himself, yet I had never seen him reading—no, not even a newspaper; that for long periods he would stand looking out, at his pale window behind the screen, upon the dead brick wall; I was quite sure he never visited any refectory or eating house; while his pale face clearly indicated that he never drank beer like Turkey, or tea and coffee even, like other men; that he never went anywhere in particular that I could learn; never went out for a walk, unless indeed that was the case at present; that he had declined telling who he was, or whence he came, or whether he had any relatives in the world; that though so thin and pale, he never complained of ill health. And more than all, I remembered a certain unconscious air of pallid—how shall I call it?—of pallid haughtiness, say, or rather an austere reserve about him, which had positively awed me into my tame compliance with his eccentricities, when I had feared to ask him to do the slightest incidental thing for me, even though I might know, from his long-continued motionlessness, that behind his screen he must be standing in one of those dead-wall reveries of his.

Revolving all these things, and coupling them with the recently discovered fact that he made my office his constant abiding place and home, and not forgetful of his morbid moodiness; revolving all these things, a prudential feeling began to steal over me. My first emotions had been those of pure melancholy and sincerest pity; but just in proportion as the forlornness of Bartleby grew and grew to my imagination, did that same melancholy merge into fear, that pity into repulsion. So true it is, and so terrible too, that up to a certain point the thought or sight of misery enlists our best affections; but, in certain special cases, beyond that point it does not. They err who would assert that invariably this is owing to the inherent selfishness of the human heart. It rather proceeds from a certain hopelessness of remedying excessive and organic ill. To a sensitive being, pity is not seldom pain. And when at last it is perceived that such pity cannot lead to effectual succor, common sense bids the soul be rid of it. What I saw that morning persuaded me that the scrivener was the victim of innate and incurable disorder. I might give alms to his body; but his body did not pain him; it was his soul that suffered, and his soul I could not reach.

I did not accomplish the purpose of going to Trinity Church that morning. Somehow, the things I had seen disqualified me for the time from church-going. I walked homeward, thinking what I would do with Bartleby. Finally, I resolved upon this;—I would put certain calm questions to him the next morning, touching his history, etc., and if he declined to answer then openly and unreservedly (and I supposed he would prefer not), then to give him a twenty dollar bill over and above whatever I might owe him, and tell him his services were no longer required; but that if in any other way I could assist him, I would be happy to do so, especially if he desired to return to his native place, wherever that might be, I would willingly help to defray the expenses. Moreover, if after reaching home, he found himself at any time in want of aid, a letter from him would be sure of a reply.

The next morning came.

"Bartleby," said I, gently calling to him behind the screen.

No reply.

"Bartleby," said I, in a still gentler tone, "come here; I am not going to ask you to do anything you would prefer not to do—I simply wish to speak to you."

Upon this he noiselessly slid into view.

"Will you tell me, Bartleby, where you were born?"

"I would prefer not to."

"Will you tell me *anything* about yourself?"

"I would prefer not to."

"But what reasonable objection can you have to speak to me? I feel friendly towards you."

He did not look at me while I spoke, but kept his glance fixed upon my bust of Cicero, which as I then sat, was directly behind me, some six inches above my head.

"What is your answer, Bartleby?" said I, after waiting a considerable time for a reply, during which his countenance remained immovable, only there was the faintest conceivable tremor of the white attenuated mouth.

"At present I prefer to give no answer," he said, and retired into his hermitage.

It was rather weak in me I confess, but his manner on this occasion nettled me. Not only did there seem to lurk in it a certain disdain, but his perverseness seemed ungrateful, considering the undeniable good usage and indulgence he had received from me.

Again I sat ruminating what I should do. Mortified as I was at his behavior, and resolved as I had been to dismiss him when I entered my office, nevertheless I strangely felt something superstitious knocking at my heart, and forbidding me to carry out my purpose, and denouncing me for a villain if I dared to breathe one bitter word against this forlornest of mankind. At last, familiarly drawing my chair behind his screen, I sat down and said: "Bartleby, never mind then about revealing your history; but let me entreat you, as a friend, to comply as far as may be with the usages of this office. Say now you will help to examine papers tomorrow or next day: in short, say now that in a day or two you will begin to be a little reasonable:—say so, Bartleby."

"At present I would prefer not to be a little reasonable," was his mildly cadaverous reply.

Just then the folding-doors opened, and Nippers approached. He seemed suffering from an unusually bad night's rest, induced by severer indigestion than common. He overheard those final words of Bartleby.

"*Prefer not*, eh?" gritted Nippers—"I'd *prefer* him, if I were you, sir," addressing me—"I'd *prefer* him; I'd give him preferences, the stubborn mule! What is it, sir, pray, that he *prefers* not to do now?"

Bartleby moved not a limb.

"Mr. Nippers," said I, "I'd prefer that you would withdraw for the present."

Somehow, of late I had got into the way of involuntary using this word "prefer" upon all sorts of not exactly suitable occasions. And I trembled to think that my contact with the scrivener had already and seriously affected me in a mental way. And what further and deeper aberration might it not yet produce? This apprehension had not been without efficacy in determining me to summary means.

As Nippers, looking very sour and sulky, was departing, Turkey blandly and deferentially approached.

"With submission, sir," said he, "yesterday I was thinking about Bartleby here, and I think that if he would but prefer to take a quart of good ale every day, it would do much towards mending him, and enabling him to assist in examining his papers."

"So you have got the word too," said I, slightly excited.

"With submission, what word, sir," asked Turkey, respectfully crowding himself into the contracted space behind the screen, and by so doing, making me jostle the scrivener. "What word, sir?"

"I would prefer to be left alone here," said Bartleby, as if offended at being mobbed in his privacy.

"*That's* the word, Turkey," said I—"*that's* it."

"Oh, *prefer*? oh yes—queer word. I never use it myself. But, sir as I was saying, if he would but prefer—"

"Turkey," interrupted I, "you will please withdraw."

"Oh, certainly, sir, if you prefer that I should."

As he opened the folding-door to retire, Nippers at his desk caught a glimpse of me, and asked whether I would prefer to have a certain paper copied on blue paper or white. He did not in the least roguishly accent the word prefer. It was plain that it involuntarily rolled from his tongue. I thought to myself, surely I must get rid of a demented man, who already has in some degree turned the tongues, if not the heads of myself and clerks. But I thought it prudent not to break the dismission at once.

The next day I noticed that Bartleby did nothing but stand at his window in his dead-wall revery. Upon asking him why he did not write, he said that he had decided upon doing no more writing.

"Why, how now? what next?" exclaimed I, "do no more writing?"

"No more."

"And what is the reason?"

"Do you not see the reason for yourself," he indifferently replied.

I looked steadfastly at him, and perceived that his eyes looked dull and glazed. Instantly it occurred to me, that his unexampled diligence in copying by his dim window for the first few weeks of his stay with me might have temporarily impaired his vision.

I was touched. I said something in condolence with him. I hinted that of course he did wisely in abstaining from writing for a while; and urged him to embrace that opportunity of taking wholesome exercise in the open air. This, however, he did not do. A few days after this, my other clerks being absent, and being in a great hurry to dispatch certain letters by the mail, I thought that, having nothing else earthly to do, Bartleby would surely be less inflexible than usual, and carry these letters to the post-office. But he blankly declined. So, much to my inconvenience, I went myself.

Still added days went by. Whether Bartleby's eyes improved or not, I could not say. To all appearance, I thought they did. But when I asked him if they did, he vouchsafed no answer. At all events, he would do no copying. At last, in reply to my urgings, he informed me that he had permanently given up copying.

"What!" exclaimed I; "suppose your eyes should get entirely well— better than ever before—would you not copy then?"

"I have given up copying," he answered, and slid aside.

He remained as ever, a fixture in my chamber. Nay—if that were possible—he became still more of a fixture than before. What was to be done? He would do nothing in the office: why should he stay there? In plain fact, he had now become a millstone to me, not only useless as a necklace, but afflictive to bear. Yet I was sorry for him. I speak less than truth when I say that, on his own account, he occasioned me uneasiness. If he would but have named a single relative or friend, I would instantly have written, and urged their taking the poor fellow away to some convenient retreat. But he seemed alone, absolutely alone in the universe. A bit of wreck in the mid Atlantic. At length, necessities connected with my business tyrannized over all other considerations. Decently as I could, I told Bartleby that in six days' time he must unconditionally leave the office. I warned him to take measures, in the interval, for procuring some other abode. I offered to assist him in this endeavor, if he himself would but take the first step towards a removal. "And when you finally quit me, Bartleby," added I, "I shall see that you go not away entirely unprovided. Six days from this hour, remember."

At the expiration of that period, I peeped behind the screen, and lo! Bartleby was there.

I buttoned up my coat, balanced myself; advanced slowly towards him, touched his shoulder, and said, "The time has come; you must quit this place; I am sorry for you; here is money; but you must go."

"I would prefer not," he replied, with his back still towards me.

"You *must*."

He remained silent.

Now I had an unbounded confidence in this man's common honesty. He had frequently restored to me six pences and shillings carelessly dropped upon the floor, for I am apt to be very reckless in such shirt button affairs. The proceeding then which followed will not be deemed extraordinary.

"Bartleby," said I, "I owe you twelve dollars on account; here are thirty-two; the odd twenty are yours.—Will you take it?" and I handed the bills towards him.

But he made no motion.

"I will leave them here then," putting them under a weight on the table. Then taking my hat and cane and going to the door I tranquilly turned and added—"After you have removed your things from these offices, Bartleby, you will of course lock the door—since every one is now gone for the day but you—and if you please, slip your key underneath the mat, so that I may have it in the morning. I shall not see you again; so good-bye to you. If hereafter in your new place of abode I can be of any service to you, do not fail to advise me by letter. Good-bye, Bartleby, and fare you well."

But he answered not a word; like the last column of some ruined temple, he remained standing mute and solitary in the middle of the otherwise deserted room.

As I walked home in a pensive mood, my vanity got the better of my pity. I could not but highly plume myself on my masterly management in getting rid of Bartleby. Masterly I call it, and such it must appear to any dispassionate thinker. The beauty of my procedure seemed to consist in its perfect quietness. There was no vulgar bullying, no bravado of any sort, no choleric hectoring and striding to and fro across the apartment, jerking out vehement commands for Bartleby to bundle himself off with his beggarly traps. Nothing of the kind. Without loudly bidding Bartleby depart—as an inferior genius might have done—I assumed the ground that depart he must; and upon the assumption built all I had to say. The more I thought over my procedure, the more I was charmed with it. Nevertheless, next morning, upon awakening, I had my doubts,—I had somehow slept off the fumes of vanity. One of the coolest and wisest hours a man has, is just after he awakes in the morning. My procedure seemed as sagacious as ever,—but only in theory. How it would prove in practice—there was the rub. It was truly a beautiful thought to have assumed Bartleby's departure; but, after all, that assumption was simply my own, and none of Bartleby's. The great point was, not whether I had assumed that he would quit me, but whether he would prefer so to do. He was more a man of preferences than assumptions.

After breakfast, I walked down town, arguing the probabilities *pro* and *con*. One moment I thought it would prove a miserable failure, and Bartleby would be found all alive at my office as usual; the next moment it seemed certain that I should see his chair empty. And so I kept veering about. At the corner of Broadway and Canal street, I saw quite an excited group of people standing in earnest conversation.

"I'll take odds he doesn't," said a voice as I passed.

"Doesn't go?—done!" said I, "put up your money."

I was instinctively putting my hand in my pocket to produce my own, when I remembered that this was an election day. The words I had overheard bore no reference to Bartleby, but to the success or nonsuccess of some candidate for the mayoralty. In my intent frame of mind, I had, as it were, imagined that all Broadway shared in my excitement, and were debating the same question with me. I passed on, very thankful that the uproar of the street screened my momentary absent-mindedness.

As I had intended, I was earlier than usual at my office door. I stood listening for a moment. All was still. He must be gone. I tried the knob. The door was locked. Yes, my procedure had worked to a charm; he indeed must be vanished. Yet a certain melancholy mixed with this: I was almost sorry for my brilliant success. I was fumbling under the door mat for the key, which Bartleby was to have left there for me, when accidentally my knee knocked against a panel, producing a summoning sound, and in response a voice came to me from within—"Not yet; I am occupied."

It was Bartleby.

I was thunderstruck. For an instant I stood like the man who, pipe in mouth, was killed one cloudless afternoon long ago in Virginia, by summer lightning; at his own warm open window he was killed, and remained leaning out there upon the dreamy afternoon, till some one touched him, when he fell.

"Not gone!" I murmured at last. But again obeying that wondrous ascendancy which the inscrutable scrivener had over me, and from which ascendancy, for all my chafing, I could not completely escape, I slowly went down stairs and out into the street, and while walking round the block, considered what I should next do in this unheard-of perplexity. Turn the man out by an actual thrusting I could not; to drive him away by calling him hard names would not do; calling in the police was an unpleasant idea; and yet, permit him to enjoy his cadaverous triumph over me,—this too I could not think of. What was to be done? or, if nothing could be done, was there anything further that I could assume in the matter? Yes, as before I had prospectively assumed that Bartleby would depart, so now I might retrospectively assume that departed he was. In the legitimate carrying out of this assumption, I might enter my office in a great hurry, and pretending not to see Bartleby at all, walk straight against him as if he were air. Such a proceeding would in a singular degree have the appearance of a home-thrust. It was hardly possible that Bartleby could withstand such an application of the doctrine of assumptions. But upon second thoughts the success of the plan seemed rather dubious. I resolved to argue the matter over with him again.

"Bartleby," said I, entering the office, with a quietly severe expression. "I am seriously displeased. I am pained, Bartleby. I had thought better of you. I had imagined you of such a gentlemanly organization, that in any delicate dilemma a slight hint would suffice—in short, an assumption. But it appears I am deceived. Why," I added, unaffectedly starting, "you have not even touched the money yet," pointing to it, just where I had left it the evening previous.

He answered nothing.

"Will you, or will you not, quit me?" I now demanded in a sudden passion, advancing close to him.

"I would prefer *not* to quit you," he replied, gently emphasizing the *not*.

"What earthly right have you to stay here? Do you pay any rent? Do you pay my taxes? Or is this property yours?"

He answered nothing.

"Are you ready to go on and write now? Are your eyes recovered? Could you copy a small paper for me this morning? or help examine a few lines? or step round to the post-office? In a word, will you do anything at all, to give a coloring to your refusal to depart the premises?"

He silently retired into his hermitage.

I was now in such a state of nervous resentment that I thought it but prudent to check myself at present from further demonstrations. Bartleby and I were alone. I remembered the tragedy of the unfortunate Adams and the still more unfortunate Colt in the solitary office of the latter; and how poor Colt, being dreadfully incensed by Adams, and imprudently permitting himself to get wildly excited, was at unawares hurried into his fatal act—an act which certainly no man could possibly deplore more than the actor himself. Often it had occurred to me in my ponderings upon the subject, that had that altercation taken place in the public street, or at a private residence, it would not have terminated as it did. It was the circumstance of being alone in a solitary office, upstairs, of a building entirely unhallowed by humanizing domestic associations— an uncarpeted office, doubtless of a dusty, haggard sort of appearance;— this it must have been, which greatly helped to enhance the irritable desperation of the hapless Colt.

But when this old Adam of resentment rose in me and tempted me concerning Bartleby, I grappled him and threw him. How? Why, simply by recalling the divine injunction: "A new commandment give I unto you, that ye love one another." Yes, this it was that saved me. Aside from higher considerations, charity often operates as a vastly wise and prudent principle—a great safeguard to its possessor. Men have committed murder for jealousy's sake, and anger's sake, and hatred's sake, and selfishness' sake, and spiritual pride's sake; but no man that ever I heard of, ever committed a diabolical murder for sweet charity's sake. Mere self-interest, then, if no better motive can be enlisted, should, especially with high-tempered men, prompt all beings to charity and philanthropy. At any rate, upon the occasion in question, I strove to drown my exasperated feelings towards the scrivener by benevolently construing his conduct. Poor fellow, poor fellow! thought I, he don't mean anything; and besides, he has seen hard times, and ought to be indulged.

I endeavored also immediately to occupy myself, and at the same time to comfort my despondency. I tried to fancy that in the course of the morning, at such time as might prove agreeable to him, Bartleby, of his own free accord, would emerge from his hermitage, and take up some decided line of march in the direction of the door. But no. Half-past twelve o'clock came; Turkey began to glow in the face, overturn his inkstand, and become generally obstreperous; Nippers abated down into quietude and courtesy; Ginger Nut munched his noon apple; and Bartleby remained standing at his window in one of his profoundest deadwall reveries. Will it be credited? Ought I to acknowledge it? That afternoon I left the office without saying one further word to him.

Some days now passed, during which, at leisure intervals I looked a little into "Edwards on the Will," and "Priestly on Necessity." Under the circumstances, those books induced a salutary feeling. Gradually I slid into the persuasion that these troubles of mine touching the scrivener, had been all predestinated from eternity, and Bartleby was billeted upon me for some mysterious purpose of an all-wise Providence, which it was not for a mere mortal like me to fathom. Yes, Bartleby, stay there behind your screen, thought I; I shall persecute you no more; you are harmless and noiseless as any of these old chairs; in short, I never feel so private as when I know you are here. At least I see it, I feel it; I penetrate to the predestinated purpose of my life. I am content. Others may have loftier parts to enact; but my mission in this world, Bartleby, is to furnish you with office-room for such period as you may see fit to remain.

I believe that this wise and blessed frame of mind would have continued with me, had it not been for the unsolicited and uncharitable remarks obtruded upon me by my professional friends who visited the rooms. But thus it often is, that the constant friction of illiberal minds wears out at last the best resolves of the more generous. Though to be sure, when I reflected upon it, it was not strange that people entering my office should be struck by the peculiar aspect of the unaccountable Bartleby, and so be tempted to throw out some sinister observations concerning him. Sometimes an attorney having business with me, and calling at my office, and finding no one but the scrivener there, would undertake to obtain some sort of precise information from him touching my whereabouts; but without heeding his idle talk, Bartleby would remain standing immovable in the middle of the room. So after contemplating him in that position for a time, the attorney would depart, no wiser than he came.

Also, when a Reference was going on, and the room full of lawyers and witnesses and business was driving fast; some deeply occupied legal gentleman present, seeing Bartleby wholly unemployed, would request him to run round to his (the legal gentleman's) office and fetch some papers for him. Thereupon, Bartleby would tranquilly decline, and remain idle as before. Then the lawyer would give a great stare, and turn to me. And what could I say? At last I was made aware that all through the circle of my professional acquaintance, a whisper of wonder was running round, having reference to the strange creature I kept at my office. This worried me very much. And as the idea came upon me of his possibly turning out a long-lived man, and keep occupying my chambers, and denying my authority; and perplexing my visitors; and scandalizing my professional reputation; and casting a general gloom over the premises; keeping soul and body together to the last upon his savings (for doubtless he spent but half a dime a day), and in the end perhaps outlive me, and claim possession of my office by right of his perpetual occupancy: as all these dark anticipations crowded upon me more and more, and my friends continually intruded their relentless remarks upon the apparition in my room; a great change was wrought in me. I resolved to gather all my faculties together, and forever rid me of this intolerable incubus.

Ere revolving any complicated project, however, adapted to this end, I first simply suggested to Bartleby the propriety of his permanent departure. In a calm and serious tone, I commended the idea to his careful and mature consideration. But having taken three days to meditate upon it, he apprised me that his original determination remained the same; in short, that he still preferred to abide with me.

What shall I do? I now said to myself, buttoning up my coat to the last button. What shall I do? what ought I to do? what does conscience say I *should* do with this man, or rather ghost. Rid myself of him, I must; go, he shall. But how? You will not thrust him, the poor, pale, passive mortal,—you will not thrust such a helpless creature out of your door? you will not dishonor yourself by such cruelty? No, I will not, I cannot do that. Rather would I let him live and die here, and then mason up his remains in the wall. What then will you do? For all your coaxing, he will not budge. Bribes he leaves under your own paperweight on your table; in short, it is quite plain that he prefers to cling to you.

Then something severe, something unusual must be done. What! surely you will not have him collared by a constable, and commit his innocent pallor to the common jail? And upon what ground could you procure such a thing to be done?—a vagrant, is he? What! he a vagrant, a wanderer, who refuses to budge? It is because he will not be a vagrant, then, that you seek to count him as a vagrant. That is too absurd. No visible means of support: there I have him. Wrong again: for indubitably he *does* support himself, and that is the only unanswerable proof that any man can show of his possessing the means so to do. No more then. Since he will not quit me, I must quit him. I will change my offices; I will move elsewhere; and give him fair notice, that if I find him on my new premises I will then proceed against him as a common trespasser.

Acting accordingly, next day I thus addressed him: "I find these chambers too far from the City Hall; the air is unwholesome. In a word, I propose to remove my offices next week, and shall no longer require your services. I tell you this now, in order that you may seek another place."

He made no reply, and nothing more was said.

On the appointed day I engaged carts and men, proceeded to my chambers, and having but little furniture, everything was removed in a few hours. Throughout, the scrivener remained standing behind the screen, which I directed to be removed the last thing. It was withdrawn; and being folded up like a huge folio, left him the motionless occupant of a naked room. I stood in the entry watching him a moment, while something from within me upbraided me.

I re-entered, with my hand in my pocket—and—and my heart in my mouth.

"Good-bye, Bartleby; I am going—good-bye, and God some way bless you; and take that," slipping something in his hand. But it dropped to the floor, and then,—strange to say—I tore myself from him whom I had so longed to be rid of.

Established in my new quarters, for a day or two I kept the door locked, and started at every footfall in the passages. When I returned to my rooms after any little absence, I would pause at the threshold for an instant, and attentively listen, ere applying my key. But these fears were needless. Bartleby never came nigh me.

I thought all was going well, when a perturbed looking stranger visited me, inquiring whether I was the person who had recently occupied rooms at No.__ Wall-street.

Full of forebodings, I replied that I was.

"Then, sir," said the stranger, who proved a lawyer, "you are responsible for the man you left there. He refuses to do any copying; he refuses to do anything; he says he prefers not to; and he refuses to quit the premises."

"I am very sorry, sir," said I, with assumed tranquillity, but an inward tremor, "but, really, the man you allude to is nothing to me—he is no relation or apprentice of mine, that you should hold me responsible for him."

"In mercy's name, who is he?"

"I certainly cannot inform you. I know nothing about him. Formerly I employed him as a copyist; but he has done nothing for me now for some time past."

"I shall settle him then,—good morning, sir."

Several days passed, and I heard nothing more; and though I often felt a charitable prompting to call at the place and see poor Bartleby, yet a certain squeamishness of I know not what withheld me.

All is over with him, by this time, thought I at last, when through another week no further intelligence reached me. But coming to my room the day after, I found several persons waiting at my door in a high state of nervous excitement.

"That's the man—here he comes," cried the foremost one, whom I recognized as the lawyer who had previously called upon me alone.

"You must take him away, sir, at once," cried a portly person among them, advancing upon me, and whom I knew to be the landlord of No.__ Wall-street. "These gentlemen, my tenants, cannot stand it any longer; Mr. B——" pointing to the lawyer, "has turned him out of his room, and he now persists in haunting the building generally, sitting upon the banisters of the stairs by day, and sleeping in the entry by night. Every body is concerned; clients are leaving the offices; some fears are entertained of a mob; something you must do, and that without delay."

Aghast at this torment, I fell back before it, and would fain have locked myself in my new quarters. In vain I persisted that Bartleby was nothing to me—no more than to any one else. In vain:—I was the last person known to have anything to do with him, and they held me to the terrible account. Fearful then of being exposed in the papers (as one person present obscurely threatened) I considered the matter, and at length said, that if the lawyer would give me a confidential interview with the scrivener, in his (the lawyer's) own room, I would that afternoon strive my best to rid them of the nuisance they complained of.

Going up stairs to my old haunt, there was Bartleby silently sitting upon the banister at the landing.

"What are you doing here, Bartleby?" said I.

"Sitting upon the banister," he mildly replied.

I motioned him into the lawyer's room, who then left us.

"Bartleby," said I, "are you aware that you are the cause of great tribulation to me, by persisting in occupying the entry after being dismissed from the office?"

No answer.

"Now one of two things must take place. Either you must do something or something must be done to you. Now what sort of business would you like to engage in? Would you like to re-engage in copying for some one?"

"No; I would prefer not to make any change."

"Would you like a clerkship in a dry-goods store?"

"There is too much confinement about that. No, I would not like a clerkship; but I am not particular."

"Too much confinement," I cried, "why you keep yourself confined all the time!"

"I would prefer not to take a clerkship," he rejoined, as if to settle that little item at once.

"How would a bartender's business suit you? There is no trying of the eyesight in that."

"I would not like it at all; though, as I said before, I am not particular."

His unwonted wordiness inspirited me. I returned to the charge.

"Well then, would you like to travel through the country collecting bills for the merchants? That would improve your health."

"No, I would prefer to be doing something else."

"How then would going as a companion to Europe, to entertain some young gentleman with your conversation,—how would that suit you?"

"Not at all. It does not strike me that there is anything definite about that. I like to be stationary. But I am not particular."

"Stationary you shall be then," I cried, now losing all patience, and for the first time in all my exasperating connection with him fairly flying into a passion. "If you do not go away from these premises before night, I shall feel bound—indeed I *am* bound—to—to—to quit the premises myself!" I rather absurdly concluded, knowing not with what possible threat to try to frighten his immobility into compliance. Despairing of all further efforts, I was precipitately leaving him, when a final thought occurred to me—one which had not been wholly unindulged before.

"Bartleby," said I, in the kindest tone I could assume under such exciting circumstances, "will you go home with me now—not to my office, but my dwelling—and remain there till we can conclude upon some convenient arrangement for you at our leisure? Come, let us start now, right away."

"No: at present I would prefer not to make any change at all."

I answered nothing; but effectually dodging every one by the suddenness and rapidity of my flight, rushed from the building, ran up Wall Street towards Broadway, and jumping into the first omnibus was soon removed from pursuit. As soon as tranquility returned I distinctly perceived that I had now done all that I possibly could, both in respect to the demands of the landlord and his tenants, and with regard to my own desire and sense of duty, to benefit Bartleby, and shield him from rude persecution. I now strove to be entirely carefree and quiescent; and my conscience justified me in the attempt; though indeed it was not so successful as I could have wished. So fearful was I of being again hunted out by the incensed landlord and his exasperated tenants, that, surrendering my business to Nippers, for a few days I drove about the upper part of the town and through the suburbs, in my rockaway; crossed over to Jersey City and Hoboken, and paid fugitive visits to Manhattanville and Astoria. In fact I almost lived in my rockaway for the time.

When again I entered my office, lo, a note from the landlord lay upon the desk. I opened it with trembling hands. It informed me that the writer had sent to the police, and had Bartleby removed to the Tombs as a vagrant. Moreover, since I knew more about him than any one else, he wished me to appear at that place, and make a suitable statement of the facts. These tidings had a conflicting effect upon me. At first I was indignant; but at last almost approved. The landlord's energetic, summary disposition had led him to adopt a procedure which I do not think I would have decided upon myself; and yet as a last resort, under such peculiar circumstances, it seemed the only plan.

As I afterwards learned, the poor scrivener, when told that he must be conducted to the Tombs, offered not the slightest obstacle, but in his pale unmoving way, silently acquiesced.

Some of the compassionate and curious bystanders joined the party; and headed by one of the constables arm in arm with Bartleby, the silent procession filed its way through all the noise, and heat, and joy of the roaring thoroughfares at noon.

The same day I received the note I went to the Tombs, or to speak more properly, the Halls of Justice. Seeking the right officer, I stated the purpose of my call, and was informed that the individual I described was indeed within. I then assured the functionary that Bartleby was a perfectly honest man, and greatly to be compassionated, however unaccountably eccentric. I narrated all I knew, and closed by suggesting the idea of letting him remain in as indulgent confinement as possible till something less harsh might be done—though indeed I hardly knew what. At all events, if nothing else could be decided upon, the almshouse must receive him. I then begged to have an interview.

Being under no disgraceful charge, and quite serene and harmless in all his ways, they had permitted him freely to wander about the prison, and especially in the inclosed grass-platted yards thereof. And so I found him there, standing all alone in the quietest of the yards, his face towards a high wall, while all around, from the narrow slits of the jail windows, I thought I saw peering out upon him the eyes of murderers and thieves.

"Bartleby!"

"I know you," he said, without looking round,—"and I want nothing to say to you."

"It was not I that brought you here, Bartleby," said I, keenly pained at his implied suspicion. "And to you, this should not be so vile a place. Nothing reproachful attaches to you by being here. And see, it is not so sad a place as one might think. Look, there is the sky, and here is the grass."

"I know where I am," he replied, but would say nothing more, and so I left him.

As I entered the corridor again, a broad meat-like man, in an apron, accosted me, and jerking his thumb over his shoulder said—"Is that your friend?"

"Yes."

"Does he want to starve? If he does, let him live on the prison fare, that's all."

"Who are you?" asked I, not knowing what to make of such an unofficially speaking person in such a place.

"I am the grub-man. Such gentlemen as have friends here, hire me to provide them with something good to eat."

"Is this so?" said I, turning to the turnkey.

He said it was.

"Well then," said I, slipping some silver into the grub-man's hands (for so they called him), "I want you to give particular attention to my friend there; let him have the best dinner you can get. And you must be as polite to him as possible."

"Introduce me, will you?" said the grub-man, looking at me with an expression which seemed to say he was all impatience for an opportunity to give a specimen of his breeding.

Thinking it would prove of benefit to the scrivener, I acquiesced; and asking the grub-man his name, went up with him to Bartleby.

"Bartleby, this is Mr. Cutlets; you will find him very useful to you."

"Your sarvant, sir, your sarvant," said the grub-man, making a low salutation behind his apron. "Hope you find it pleasant here, sir;—spacious grounds—cool apartments, sir—hope you'll stay with us some time—try to make it agreeable. What will you have for dinner today?"

"I prefer not to dine to-day," said Bartleby, turning away. "It would disagree with me; I am unused to dinners." So saying he slowly moved to the other side of the inclosure, and took up a position fronting the dead-wall.

"How's this?" said the grub-man, addressing me with a stare of astonishment. "He's odd, ain't he?"

"I think he is a little deranged," said I, sadly.

"Deranged? deranged is it? Well now, upon my word, I thought that friend of yourn was a gentleman forger; they are always pale and genteel-like, them forgers. I can't help pity 'em—can't help it, sir. Did you know Monroe Edwards?" he added touchingly, and paused. Then, laying his hand pityingly on my shoulder, sighed, "he died of consumption at Sing–Sing. So you weren't acquainted with Monroe?"

"No, I was never socially acquainted with any forgers. But I cannot stop longer. Look to my friend yonder. You will not lose by it. I will see you again."

Some few days after this, I again obtained admission to the Tombs, and went through the corridors in quest of Bartleby; but without finding him.

"I saw him coming from his cell not long ago," said a turnkey, "may be he's gone to loiter in the yards."

So I went in that direction.

"Are you looking for the silent man?" said another turnkey passing me. "Yonder he lies—sleeping in the yard there. 'Tis not twenty minutes since I saw him lie down."

The yard was entirely quiet. It was not accessible to the common prisoners. The surrounding walls, of amazing thickness, kept off all sound behind them. The Egyptian character of the masonry weighed upon me with its gloom. But a soft imprisoned turf grew under foot. The heart of the eternal pyramids, it seemed, wherein, by some strange magic, through the clefts, grass-seed, dropped by birds, had sprung.

Strangely huddled at the base of the wall, his knees drawn up, and lying on his side, his head touching the cold stones, I saw the wasted Bartleby. But nothing stirred. I paused; then went close up to him; stooped over, and saw that his dim eyes were open; otherwise he seemed profoundly sleeping. Something prompted me to touch him. I felt his hand, when a tingling shiver ran up my arm and down my spine to my feet.

The round face of the grub-man peered upon me now. "His dinner is ready. Won't he dine today, either? Or does he live without dining?"

"Lives without dining," said I, and closed the eyes.

"Eh!—He's asleep, ain't he?"

"With kings and counsellors," murmured I.

* * *

There would seem little need for proceeding further in this history. Imagination will readily supply the meagre recital of poor Bartleby's interment. But ere parting with the reader, let me say, that if this little narrative has sufficiently interested him, to awaken curiosity as to who Bartleby was, and what manner of life he led prior to the present narrator's making his acquaintance, I can only reply, that in such curiosity I fully share, but am wholly unable to gratify it. Yet here I hardly know whether I should divulge one little item of rumor, which came to my ear a few months after the scrivener's decease. Upon what basis it rested, I could never ascertain; and hence how true it is I cannot now tell. But inasmuch as this vague report has not been without a certain strange suggestive interest to me, however said, it may prove the same with some others; and so I will briefly mention it. The report was this: that Bartleby had been a subordinate clerk in the Dead Letter Office at Washington, from which he had been suddenly removed by a change in the administration. When I think over this rumor, I cannot adequately express the emotions which seize me. Dead letters! does it not sound like dead men? Conceive a man by nature and misfortune prone to a pallid hopelessness, can any business seem more fitted to heighten it than that of continually handling these dead letters and assorting them for the flames? For by the cart-load they are annually burned. Sometimes from out the folded paper the pale clerk takes a ring:—the bank-note sent in swiftest charity:—he whom it would relieve, nor eats nor hungers any more; pardon for those who died despairing; hope for those who died unhoping; good tidings for those who died stifled by unrelieved calamities. On errands of life, these letters speed to death.

Ah Bartleby! Ah humanity!

Notes

1. *Characters.* Who is the protagonist of the story? What is the theme of the story? Could the story have been set somewhere other than a scrivener's office?

2. *Innocents.* The innocent Bartleby should be compared with *Billy Budd, Sailor*, written by Melville near the end of his life. Billy, the handsome, beloved sailor, ran afoul of Claggart, the evil master-at-arms, whom Billy reflexively struck and killed when Billy was falsely accused before Captain Vere of plotting mutiny. The captain, who witnessed the unfortu-

nate event and who was fond of Billy, nevertheless summoned a drumhead court and had Billy condemned to death by hanging. The incident occurred during time of war, and Vere feared the very real danger of mutiny if harsh justice were not meted out.

Billy accepted his sentence meekly—almost cheerfully. As he walked the plank he called out, "God Bless Captain Vere!" When he walked into the noose, rather than being jerked, he ascended, taking "the full rose of the dawn . . . [N]o motion was apparent."

Various rumors later circulated about Billy, and as to the nature and cause of his death.

Ah, Bartleby! Ah, Billy! Ah, humanity!

C. NOVELS AND STORIES

Franz Kafka is one of the writers whose very name has infiltrated the minds of Western society, to describe a genre of writing—Kafkaesque. The dictionary defines "Kafkaesque" as writing having a nightmarishly complex, bizarre, or illogical quality. His short story *Metamorphosis* is the epitome of the style. His novel, THE TRIAL, from which the following excerpts are taken, also illustrate that quality. In THE TRIAL Joseph K. is arrested on a charge of which he is never apprised. He spends the rest of his life trying to find the basis of the charge, but he is overcome with bureaucratic red tape. Finally one evening he is taken and, without explanation, executed.

THE TRIAL
Franz Kafka

CHAPTER ONE

The Arrest

Someone must have been telling lies about Joseph K., for without having done anything wrong he was arrested one fine morning. His landlady's cook, who always brought him his breakfast at eight o'clock, failed to appear on this occasion. That had never happened before. K. waited for a little while longer, watching from his pillow the old lady opposite, who seemed to be peering at him with a curiosity unusual even for her, but then, feeling both put out and hungry, he rang the bell. At once there was a knock at the door and a man entered whom he had never seen before in the house. He was slim and yet well knit, he wore a closely fitting black suit furnished with all sorts of pleats, pockets, buckles, and buttons, as well as a belt, like a tourist's outfit, and in consequence looked eminently practical, though one could not quite tell what actual purpose it served. "Who are you?" asked K., half raising himself in bed. But the man ignored the question, as though his appearance needed no explanation, and merely said: "Did you ring?" "Anna is to bring me my breakfast," said K., and then studied the fellow, silently and carefully, trying to make out who he could be. The man did not submit to this scrutiny for very long, but turned to the door and opened it slightly so as to report to someone who was evidently standing just behind it: "He says Anna is to bring him his breakfast." A short guffaw from the next room came in answer; and it rather sounded as if several people had joined in. Although the strange man could not have learned anything from it that he did not know already, he now said to K., as if passing on a statement: "It can't be done." "This is news indeed," cried K., springing out of bed and quickly pulling on his trousers. "I must see what people these are next door, and how Frau Grubach can account to me for such behavior." Yet it occurred to him at once that he should not have said this aloud and that by doing so he had in a way admitted the stranger's right to superintend his actions; still, that did not seem important to him at the moment. The stranger, however, took his words in some such sense, for he asked: "Hadn't you better stay here?" "I shall neither stay here nor let you address me until you have introduced yourself." "I meant well enough," said the stranger, and then of his own accord threw the door open. In the next room, which K. entered more slowly than he had intended, everything looked at first glance almost as it had the evening before. It was Frau Grubach's living room; perhaps among all the furniture, rugs, china, and photographs with which it was crammed there was a little more free space than usual, yet one did not perceive that at first, especially as the main change consisted in the presence of a man who was sitting at the open window reading a book, from which he now glanced up. "You should have stayed in your room! Didn't Franz tell you that?" "Yes, but what are you doing here?" asked K., looking from his new acquaintance to the man called Franz, who was still standing by the door, and then back again. Through the open window he had another glimpse of the old woman, who with truly senile inquisitiveness had moved along to the window exactly opposite, in order to go on seeing all that could be seen. "I'd better get Frau Grubach—" said K., as if wrenching himself away from the two men (though they were standing at quite a distance from him) and making as if to go out. "No," said the man at the window, flinging the book down on the table and getting up. "You can't go out, you are arrested." "So it seems," said K. "But what for?" he added. "We are not authorized to tell you that. Go to your room and wait there. Proceedings have been instituted against you, and you will be informed of everything in due course. I am exceeding my instructions in speaking freely to you like this. But I hope nobody hears me except Franz, and he himself has been too free with you, against his express instructions. If you continue to have as good luck as you have had in the choice of your warders, then you can be confident of the final result." K. felt he must sit down, but now he saw that there was no seat in the whole room except the chair beside the window. "You'll soon discover that we're telling you the truth," said Franz, advancing toward him simultaneously with the other man. The latter overtopped K. enormously and kept clapping him on the shoulder. They both examined his nightshirt and said that he would have to wear a less fancy shirt now, but that they would take charge of this one and the rest of his underwear and, if his case turned out well, restore them to him later. "Much better give these things to us than hand them over to the depot," they said, "for in the depot there's lots of thieving, and besides they sell everything there after a certain length of time, no matter whether your case is settled or not. And you never know how long these cases will last, especially these days. Of course you would get the money out of the depot in the long run, but in the first place the prices they pay you are always wretched, for they sell your things to the best briber, not the best bidder, and anyhow it's well known that money dwindles a lot if it passes from hand to hand from one year to another." K. paid hardly any attention to this advice. Any right to dispose of his own things which he might possess he did not prize very highly; far more important to him was the necessity to understand his situation clearly; but with these people beside him he could not even think. The belly of the second warder—for they could only be warders—kept butting against him in an almost friendly way, yet if he looked up he caught sight of a face which did not in the least suit that fat body, a dry, bony face with a great nose, twisted to one side, which seemed to be consulting over his head with the other warder. Who could these men be? What were they talking about? What authority could they represent? K. lived in a country with a legal constitution, there was universal peace, all the laws were in force; who dared seize him in his own dwelling? He had always been inclined to take things easily, to believe in the worst only when the worst happened, to take no care for the morrow even when the outlook was threatening. But that struck him as not being the right policy here, one could certainly regard the whole thing as a joke, a rude joke which his colleagues in the Bank had concocted for some unknown reason, perhaps because this was his thirtieth birthday, that was of course possible, perhaps he had only to laugh knowingly in these men's faces and they would laugh with him, perhaps they were merely porters from the street corner—they looked very like it—nevertheless his very first glance at the man Franz had decided him for the time being not to give away any advantage that he might possess over these people. There was a slight risk that later on his friends might possibly say he could not take a joke, but he had in mind—though it was not usual with him to learn from experience—several occasions, of no importance in themselves, when against all his friends' advice he had behaved with deliberate recklessness and without the slightest regard for possible consequences, and had had in the end to pay dearly for it. That must not happen again, at least not this time; if this was a comedy he would insist on playing it to the end.

. . . .

Chapter 10

The End

On the evening before K.'s thirty-first birthday—it was about nine o'clock, the time when a hush falls on the streets—two men came to his lodging. In frock coats, pallid and plump, with top hats that were apparently irremovable. After some exchange of formalities regarding precedence at the front door, they repeated the same ceremony more elaborately before K.'s door. Without having been informed of their visit, K. was sitting also dressed in black in an armchair near the door, slowly pulling on a pair of new gloves that fitted tightly over the fingers, looking as if he were expecting guests. He stood up at once and scrutinized the gentlemen with curiosity. "So you are meant for me?" he asked. The gentlemen bowed, each indicating the other with the hand that held the top hat. K. admitted to himself that he had been expecting different visitors. He went to the window and took another look at the dark street. Nearly all the windows at the other side of the street were also in darkness; in many of them the curtains were drawn. At one lighted tenement window some babies were playing behind bars, reaching with their little hands toward each other although not able to move themselves from the spot. "Tenth-rate old actors they send for me," said K. to himself, glancing round again to confirm the impression. "They want to finish me off cheaply." He turned abruptly toward the men and asked: "What theater are you playing at?" "Theater?" said one, the corners of his mouth twitching as he looked for advice to the other, who acted as if he were a dumb man struggling to overcome a stubborn disability. "They're not prepared to answer questions," said K. to himself and went to fetch his hat.

While still on the stairs the two of them tried to take K. by the arms, and he said: "Wait till we're in the street, I'm not an invalid." But just outside the street door they fastened on him in a fashion he had never before experienced. They kept their shoulders close behind his and instead of crooking their elbows, wound their arms round his at full length, holding his hands in a methodical, practiced, irresistible grip. K. walked rigidly between them, the three of them were interlocked in a unity which would have brought all three down together had one of them been knocked over. It was a unity such as can hardly be formed except by lifeless matter.

Under the street lamps K. attempted time and time again, difficult though it was at such very close quarters, to see his companions more clearly than had been possible in the dusk of his room. Perhaps they are tenors, he thought, as he studied their fat double chins. He was repelled by the painful cleanliness of their faces. One could literally see that the cleansing hand had been at work in the corners of the eyes, rubbing the upper lip, scrubbing out the furrows at the chin.

When that occurred to K. he halted, and in consequence the others halted too; they stood on the verge of an open, deserted square adorned with flower beds. "Why did they send you, of all people!" he said; it was more a cry than a question. The gentlemen obviously had no answer to make, they stood waiting with their free arms hanging, like sickroom attendants waiting while their patient takes a rest. "I won't go any farther," said K. experimentally. No answer was needed to that, it was sufficient that the two men did not loosen their grip and tried to propel K. from the spot; but he resisted them. I shan't need my strength much longer, I'll expend all the strength I have, he thought. Into his mind came a recollection of flies struggling away from the flypaper till their little legs were torn off. The gentlemen won't find it easy.

And then before them Fräulein Bürstner appeared, mounting a small flight of steps leading into the square from a low-lying side-street. It was not quite certain that it was she, but the resemblance was close enough. Whether it were really Fräulein Bürstner or not, however, did not matter to K.; the important thing was that he suddenly realized the futility of resistance. There would be nothing heroic in it were he to resist, to make difficulties for his companions, to snatch at the last appearance of life by struggling. He set himself in motion, and the relief his warders felt was transmitted to some extent even to himself. They suffered him now to lead the way, and he followed the direction taken by the girl ahead of him, not that he wanted to overtake her or to keep her in sight as long as possible, but only that he might not forget the lesson she had brought into his mind. "The only thing I can do now," he told himself, and the regular correspondence between his steps and the steps of the other two confirmed his thought, "the only thing for me to go on doing is to keep my intelligence calm and analytical to the end. I always wanted to snatch at the world with twenty hands, and not for a very laudable motive, either. That was wrong, and am I to show now that not even a year's trial has taught me anything? Am I to leave this world as a man who has no common sense? Are people to say of me after I am gone that at the beginning of my case I wanted to finish it, and at the end of it I wanted to begin it again? I don't want that to be said. I am grateful for the fact that these half-dumb, senseless creatures have been sent to accompany me on this journey, and that I have been left to say to myself all that is needed."

Fräulein Bürstner meanwhile had gone round the bend into a side street, but by this time K. could do without her and submitted himself to the guidance of his escort. In complete harmony all three now made their way across a bridge in the moonlight, the two men readily yielded to K.'s slightest movement, and when he turned slightly toward the parapet they turned, too, in a solid front. The water, glittering and trembling in the moonlight, divided on either side of a small island, on which the foliage of trees and bushes rose in thick masses, as if bunched together. Beneath the trees ran gravel paths, now invisible, with convenient benches on which K. had stretched himself at ease many a summer. "I didn't mean to stop," he said to his companions, shamed by their obliging compliance. Behind K.'s back the one seemed to reproach the other gently for the mistaken stop they had made, and then all three went on again.

They passed through several steeply rising streets, in which policemen stood or patrolled at intervals; sometimes a good way off, sometimes quite near. One with a bushy mustache, his hand on the hilt of his saber, came up as of set purpose close to the not quite harmless-looking group. The two gentlemen halted, the policeman seemed to be already opening his mouth, but K. forcibly pulled his companions forward. He kept looking round cautiously to see if the policeman were following; as soon as he had put a corner between himself and the policeman he started to run, and his two companions, scant of breath as they were, had to run beside him.

So they came quickly out of the town, which at this point merged almost without transition into the open fields. A small stone quarry, deserted and desolate, lay quite near to a still completely urban house. Here the two men came to a standstill, whether because this place had been their goal from the very beginning or because they were too exhausted to go farther. Now they loosened their hold of K., who stood waiting dumbly, took off the top hats and wiped the sweat from their brows with pocket handkerchiefs, meanwhile surveying the quarry. The moon shone down on everything with that simplicity and serenity which no other light possesses.

After an exchange of courteous formalities regarding which of them was to take precedence in the next task—these emissaries seemed to have been given no specific assignments in the charge laid jointly upon them—one of them came up to K. and removed his coat, his waistcoat, and finally his shirt. K. shivered involuntarily, whereupon the man gave him a light, reassuring pat on the back. Then he folded the clothes carefully together, as if they were likely to be used again at some time, although perhaps not immediately. Not to leave K. standing motionless, exposed to the night breeze, which was rather chilly, he took him by the arm and walked him up and down a little, while his partner investigated the quarry to find a suitable spot. When he had found it he beckoned, and K.'s companion led him over there. It was a spot near the cliffside where a loose boulder was lying. The two of them laid K. down on the ground, propped him against the boulder, and settled his head upon it. But in spite of the pains they took and all the willingness K. showed, his posture remained contorted and unnatural-looking. So one of the men begged the other to let him dispose K. all by himself, yet even that did not improve matters. Finally they left K. in a position which was not even the best of the positions they had already tried out. Then one of them opened his frock coat and out of a sheath that hung from a belt girt round his waistcoat drew a long, thin, double-edged butcher's knife, held it up, and tested the cutting edges in the moonlight. Once more the odious courtesies began, the first handed the knife across K. to the second, who handed it across K. back again to the first. K. now perceived clearly that he was supposed to seize the knife himself, as it traveled from hand to hand above him, and plunge it into his own breast. But he did not do so, he merely turned his head, which was still free to move, and gazed around him. He could not completely rise to the occasion, he could not relieve the officials of all their tasks; the responsibility for this last failure of his lay with him who had not left him the remnant of strength necessary for the deed. His glance fell on the top story of the house adjoining the quarry. With a flicker as of a light going up, the casements of a window there suddenly flew open; a human figure, faint and insubstantial at that distance and that height, leaned abruptly far forward and stretched both arms still farther. Who was it? A friend? A good man? Someone who sympathized? Someone who wanted to help? Was it one person only? Or was it mankind? Was help at hand? Were there arguments in his favor that had been overlooked? Of course there must be. Logic is doubtless unshakable, but it cannot withstand a man who wants to go on living. Where was the Judge whom he had never seen? Where was the High Court, to which he had never penetrated? He raised his hands and spread out all his fingers.

But the hands of one of the partners were already at K.'s throat, while the other thrust the knife deep into his heart and turned it there twice. With failing eyes K. could still see the two of them immediately before him, cheek leaning against cheek, watching the final act. "Like a dog!" he said; it was as if the shame of it must outlive him.

* * *

Flann O'Brien (1911–1966) (pen name of Brian O'Nolan) was an Irish essayist, novelist and playwright. He spoke nothing but Gaelic until the age of six, and the lilt of Gaelic shines transparently through his English prose. He secured a place in the Irish Civil Service after receiving his University degree, and his first novel, AT SWIM-TWO-BIRDS (1939), was a critical success. However, his second novel, THE THIRD POLICEMAN, was rejected even by his own publisher. Embittered by this rejection, he devoted the rest of his career primarily to producing brilliant columns for the *Irish Times*, under the pen name of Myles na Gopaleen. He drank himself to death. His second novel was published posthumously, in 1967.

In THE THIRD POLICEMAN the narrator, a murderer, has been killed and gone to hell. The surreal world of hell is Kafkaesque, but with an Irish lilt and sense of craziness.

THE THIRD POLICEMAN
Flann O'Brien

V

The long and unprecedented conversation I had with Policeman MacCruiskeen after I went in to him on my mission with the cigarette brought to my mind afterwards several of the more delicate speculations of de Selby, notably his investigation of the nature of time and eternity by a system of mirrors. His theory as I understand it is as follows.

If a man stands before a mirror and sees in it his reflection, what he sees is not a true reproduction of himself but a picture of himself when he was a younger man. De Selby's explanation of this phenomenon is quite simple. Light, as he points out truly enough, has an ascertained and finite rate of travel. Hence before the reflection of any object in a mirror can be said to be accomplished, it is necessary that rays of light should first strike the object and subsequently impinge on the glass, to be thrown back again to the object—to the eyes of a man, for instance. There is therefore an appreciable and calculable interval of time between the throwing by a man of a glance at his own face in a mirror and the registration of the reflected image in his eye.

So far, one may say, so good. Whether this idea is right or wrong, the amount of time involved is so negligible that few reasonable people would argue the point. But de Selby ever loath to leave well enough alone, insists on reflecting the first reflection in a further mirror and professing to detect minute changes in this second image. Ultimately he constructed the familiar arrangement of parallel mirrors, each reflecting diminishing images of an interposed object indefinitely. The interposed object in this case was de Selby's own face and this he claims to have studied backwards through an infinity of reflections by means of "a powerful glass." What he states to have seen through his glass is astonishing. He claims to have noticed a growing youthfulness, in the reflections of his face according as they receded, the most distant of them—too tiny to be visible to the naked eye—being the face of a beardless boy of twelve, and, to use his own words, "a countenance of singular beauty and nobility." He did not succeed in pursuing the matter back to the cradle "owing to the curvature of the earth and the limitations of the telescope."

So much for de Selby. I found MacCruiskeen with a red face at the kitchen table panting quietly from all the food he had hidden in his belly. In exchange for the cigarette he gave me searching looks. "Well, now," he said.

He lit the cigarette and sucked at it and smiled covertly at me.

"Well, now," he said again. He had his little lamp beside him on the table and he played his fingers on it.

"That is a fine day," I said. "What are you doing with a lamp in the white morning?"

"I can give you a question as good as that," he responded. "Can you notify me of the meaning of a bulbul?"

"A bulbul?"

"What would you say a bulbul is?"

This conundrum did not interest me but I pretended to rack my brains and screwed my face in perplexity until I felt it half the size it should be.

"Not one of those ladies who take money?" I said.

"No."

"Not the brass knobs on a German steam organ?"

"Not the knobs."

"Nothing to do with the independence of America or such-like?"

"No."

"A mechanical engine for winding clocks?"

"No."

"A tumour, or the lather in a cow's mouth, or those elastic articles that ladies wear?"

"Not them by a long chalk."

"Not an eastern musical instrument played by Arabs?"

He clapped his hands.

"Not that but very near it," he smiled, "something next door to it. You are a cordial intelligible man. A bulbul is a Persian nightingale. What do you think of that now?"

"It is seldom I am far out," I said dryly.

He looked at me in admiration and the two of us sat in silence for a while as if each was very pleased with himself and with the other and had good reason to be.

"You are a B.A. with little doubt?" he questioned.

I gave no direct answer but tried to look big and learned and far from simple in my little chair.

"I think you are a sempiternal man," he said slowly.

He sat for a while giving the floor a strict examination and then put his dark jaw over to me and began questioning me about my arrival in the parish.

"I do not want to be insidious," he said, "but would you inform me about your arrival in the parish? Surely you had a three-speed gear for the hills?"

"I had no three-speed gear," I responded rather sharply, "and no two-speed gear and it is also true that I had no bicycle and little or no pump and if I had a lamp itself it would not be necessary if I had no bicycle and there would be no bracket to hang it on."

"That may be," said MacCruiskeen, "but likely you were laughed at on the tricycle?"

"I had neither bicycle nor tricycle and I am not a dentist," I said with severe categorical thoroughness, "and I do not believe in the penny-farthing or the scooter, the velocipede or the tandem-tourer."

MacCruiskeen got white and shaky and gripped my arm and looked at me intensely.

"In my natural puff," he said at last, in a strained voice, "I have never encountered a more fantastic epilogue or a queerer story. Surely you are a queer far-fetched man. To my dying night I will not forget this today morning. Do not tell me that you are taking a hand at me?"

"No," I said.

"Well Great Crikes!"

He got up and brushed his hair with a flat hand back along his skull and looked out of the window for a long interval, his eyes popping and dancing and his face like an empty bag with no blood in it.

Then he walked around to put back the circulation and took a little spear from a place he had on the shelf.

"Put your hand out," he said.

I put it out idly enough and he held the spear at it. He kept putting it near me and nearer and when he had the bright point of it about half a foot away, I felt a prick and gave a short cry. There was a little bead of my red blood in the middle of my palm.

"Thank you very much," I said. I felt too surprised to be annoyed with him.

"That will make you think," he remarked in triumph, "unless I am an old Dutchman by profession and nationality."

He put his little spear back on the shelf and looked at me crookedly from a sidewise angle with a certain quantity of what may be called *rois'amuse*.

"Maybe you can explain that?" he said.

"That is the limit," I said wonderingly.

"It will take some analysis," he said, "intellectually."

"Why did your spear sting when the point was half a foot away from where it made me bleed?"

"That spear," he answered quietly, "is one of the first things I ever manufactured in my spare time. I think only a little of it now but the year I made it I was proud enough and would not get up in the morning for any sergeant. There is no other spear like it in the length and breadth of Ireland and there is only one thing like it in Amurikey but I have not heard what it is. But I cannot get over the no-bicycle. Great Crikes!"

"But the spear," I insisted, "give me the gist of it like a good man and I will tell no one."

"I will tell you because you are a confidential man," he said, "and a man that said something about bicycles that I never heard before. What you think is the point is not the point at all but only the beginning of the sharpness."

"Very wonderful," I said, "but I do not understand you."

"The point is seven inches long and it is so sharp and thin that you cannot see it with the old eye. The first half of the sharpness is thick and strong but you cannot see it either because the real sharpness runs into it and if you saw the one you could see the other or maybe you would notice the joint."

"I suppose it is far thinner than a match?" I asked.

"There *is* a difference," he said. "Now the proper sharp part is so thin that nobody could see it no matter what light is on it or what eye is looking. About an inch from the end it is so sharp that sometimes—late at night or on a soft bad day especially—you cannot think of it or try to make it the subject of a little idea because you will hurt your box with the excruciation of it."

I gave a frown and tried to make myself look like a wise person who was trying to comprehend something that called for all his wisdom.

"You cannot have fire without bricks," I said, nodding.

"Wisely said," MacCruiskeen answered.

"It was sharp sure enough," I conceded, "it drew a little bulb of the red blood but I did not feel the pricking hardly at all. It must be very sharp to work like that."

MacCruiskeen gave a laugh and sat down again at the table and started putting on his belt.

"You have not got the whole gist of it at all," he smiled. "Because what gave you the prick and brought the blood was not the point at all; it was the place I am talking about that is a good inch from the reputed point of the article under our discussion."

"And what is this inch that is left?" I asked. "What in heaven's name would you call that?"

"That is the real point," said MacCruiskeen, "but it is so thin that it could go into your hand and out in the other extremity externally and you would not feel a bit of it and you would see nothing and hear nothing. It is so thin that maybe it does not exist at all and you could spend half an hour trying to think about it and you could put no thought around it in the end. The beginning part of the inch is thicker than the last part and is nearly there for a fact but I don't think it is if it is my private opinion that you are anxious to enlist."

I fastened my fingers around my jaw and started to think with great concentration, calling into play parts of my brain that I rarely used. Nevertheless I made no progress at all as regards the question of the points. MacCruiskeen had been at the dresser a second time and was back at the table with a little black article like a leprechaun's piano with diminutive keys of white and black and brass pipes and circular revolving cogs like parts of a steam engine or the business end of a thrashing-mill. His white hands were moving all over it and feeling it as if they were trying to discover some tiny lump on it, and his face was looking up in the air in a spiritual attitude and he was paying no attention to my personal existence at all. There was an overpowering tremendous silence as if the roof of the room had come down half-way to the floor, he at his queer occupation with the instrument and myself still trying to comprehend the sharpness of the points and to get the accurate understanding of them.

After ten minutes he got up and put the thing away. He wrote for a time in his notebook and then lit his pipe.

"Well now," he remarked expansively.

"Those points," I said.

"Did I happen to ask you what a bulbul is?"

"You did," I responded, "but the question of those points is what takes me to the fair."

"It is not today or yesterday I started pointing spears," he said, "but maybe you would like to see something else that is a medium fair example of supreme art?"

"I would indeed," I answered.

"But I cannot get over what you confided in me privately *sub-rosa* about the no-bicycle, that is a story that would make your golden fortune if you wrote down in a book where people could pursue it literally."

He walked back to the dresser, opened the lower part of it, and took out a little chest till he put it on the table for my inspection. Never in my life did I inspect anything more ornamental and well-made. It was a brown chest like those owned by seafaring men or lascars from Singapore, but it was diminutive in a very perfect way as if you were looking at a full-size one through the wrong end of a spy-glass. It was about a foot in height, perfect in its proportions and without fault in workmanship. There were indents and carving and fanciful excoriations and designs on every side of it and there was a bend on the lid that gave the article great distinction. At every corner there was a shiny brass corner-piece and on the lid there were brass corner-pieces beautifully wrought and curved impeccably against the wood. The whole thing had the dignity and the satisfying quality of true art.

"There now," said MacCruiskeen.

"It is nearly too nice," I said at last, "to talk about it."

"I spent two years manufacturing it when I was a lad," said MacCruiskeen, "and it still takes me to the fair."

"It is unmentionable," I said.

"Very nearly," said MacCruiskeen.

The two of us then started looking at it and we looked at it for five minutes so hard that it seemed to dance on the table and look even smaller than it might be.

"I do not often look at boxes or chests," I said, simply, "but this is the most beautiful box I have ever seen and I will always remember it. There might be something inside it?"

"There might be," said MacCruiskeen.

He went to the table and put his hands around the article in a fawning way as if he were caressing a sheepdog and he opened the lid with a little key but shut it down again before I could inspect the inside of it.

"I will tell you a story and give you a synopsis of the ramification of the little plot," he said. "When I had the chest made and finished, I tried to think what I would keep in it and what I would use it for at all. First I thought of them letters from Bridie, the ones on the blue paper with the strong smell but I did not think it would be anything but a sacrilege in the end because there was hot bits in them letters. Do you comprehend the trend of my observations?"

"I do," I answered.

"Then there was my studs and the enamel badge and my presentation iron-pencil with a screw on the end of it to push the point out, an intricate article full of machinery and a Present from Southport. All these things are what are called Examples of the Machine Age."

"They would be contrary to the spirit of the chest," I said.

"They would be indeed. Then there was my razor and the spare plate in case I was presented with an accidental bash on the gob in the execution of me duty ..."

"But not them."

"Not them. Then there was my certificates and me cash and the picture of Peter the Hermit and the brass thing with straps that I found on the road one night near Matthew O'Carahan's. But not them either."

"It is a hard conundrum," I said.

"In the end I found there was only one thing to do to put myself right with my private conscience."

"It is a great thing that you found the right answer at all," I countered.

"I decided to myself," said MacCruiskeen, "that the only sole correct thing to contain in the chest was another chest of the same make but littler in cubic dimension."

"That was very competent masterwork," I said, endeavouring to speak his own language.

He went to the little chest and opened it up again and put his hands down sideways like flat plates or like the fins on a fish and took out of it a smaller chest but one resembling its mother-chest in every particular of appearance and dimension. It almost interfered with my breathing, it was so delightfully unmistakable. I went over and felt it and covered it with my hand, to see how big its smallness was. Its brasswork had a shine like the sun on the sea and the colour of the wood was a rich deep richness like a colour deepened and toned only by the years. I got slightly weak from looking at it and sat down on a chair and for the purpose of pretending that I was not disturbed I whistled *The Old Man Twangs His Braces*.

MacCruiskeen gave me a smooth inhuman smile.

"You may have come on no bicycle," he said, "but that does not say that you know everything."

"Those chests," I said, "are so like one another that I do not believe they are there at all because that is a simpler thing to believe than the contrary. Nevertheless the two of them are the most wonderful two things I have ever seen."

"I was two years manufacturing it," MacCruiskeen said.

"What is in the little one?" I asked.

"What would you think now?"

"I am completely half afraid to think," I said, speaking truly enough.

"Wait now till I show you," said MacCruiskeen, "and give you an exhibition and a personal inspection individually."

He got two thin butter-spades from the shelf and put them down into the little chest and pulled out something that seemed to me remarkably like another chest. I went over to it and gave it a close examination with my hand, feeling the same identical wrinkles, the same proportions and the same completely perfect brasswork on a smaller scale. It was so faultless and delightful that it reminded me forcibly, strange and foolish as it may seem, of something I did not understand and had never even heard of.

"Say nothing," I said quickly to MacCruiskeen, "but go ahead with what you are doing and I will watch here and I will take care to be sitting down."

He gave me a nod in exchange for my remark and got two straight-handled teaspoons and put the handles into his last chest. What came out may well be guessed at. He opened this one and took another one out with the assistance of two knives. He worked knives, small knives and smaller knives, till he had twelve little chests on the table, the last of them an article half the size of a matchbox. It was so tiny that you would not quite see the brasswork at all only for the glitter of it in the light. I did not see whether it had the same identical carvings upon it because I was content to take a swift look at it and then turn away. But I knew in my soul that it was exactly the same as the others. I said no word at all because my mind was brimming with wonder at the skill of the police-man.

"That last one," said MacCruiskeen, putting away the knives, "took me three years to make and it took me another year to believe that I had made it. Have you got the convenience of a pin?"

I gave him my pin in silence. He opened the smallest of them all with a key like a piece of hair and worked with the pin till he had another little chest on the table, thirteen in all arranged in a row upon the table. Queerly enough they looked to me as if they were all the same size but invested with some crazy perspective. This idea surprised me so much that I got my voice back and said:

"These are the most surprising thirteen things I have ever seen together."

"Wait now, man," MacCruiskeen said.

All my senses were now strained so tensely watching the police-man's movements that I could almost hear my brain rattling in my head when I gave a shake as if it was drying up into a wrinkled pea. He was manipulating and prodding with his pin till he had twenty-eight little chests on the table and the last of them so small that it looked like a bug or a tiny piece of dirt except that there was a glitter from it. When I looked at it again I saw another thing beside it like something you would take out of a red eye on a windy dry day and I knew then that the strict computation was then twenty-nine.

"Here is your pin," said MacCruiskeen.

He put it into my stupid hand and went back to the table thoughtfully. He took a something from his pocket that was too small for me to see and started working with the tiny black thing on the table beside the bigger thing which was itself too small to be described.

At this point I became afraid. What he was doing was no longer wonderful but terrible. I shut my eyes and prayed that he would stop while still doing things that were at least possible for a man to do. When I looked again I was happy that there was nothing to see and that he had put no more of the chests prominently on the table but he was working to the left with the invisible thing in his hand on a bit of the table itself. When he felt my look he came over to me and gave me an enormous magnifying-glass which looked like a basin fixed to a handle. I felt the muscles around my heart tightening painfully as I took the instrument.

"Come over here to the table," he said, "and look there till you see what you see infra-ocularly."

When I saw the table it was bare only for the twenty-nine chest articles but through the agency of the glass I was in a position to report that he had two more out beside the last ones, the smallest of all being nearly half a size smaller than ordinary invisibility. I gave him back the glass instrument and took to the chair without a word. In order to reassure myself and make a loud human noise I whistled the *Corncrake Plays the Bagpipes*.

"There now," said MacCruiskeen.

He took two wrinkled cigarettes from his fob and lit the two at the same time and handed me one of them.

"Number Twenty-Two," he said, "I manufactured fifteen years ago and I have made another different one every year since with any amount of nightwork and overtime and piecework and time-and-a-half incidentally."

"I understand you clearly," I said.

"Six years ago they began to get invisible, glass or no glass. Nobody has ever seen the last five I made because no glass is strong enough to make them big enough to be regarded truly as the smallest things ever made. Nobody can see me making them because my little tools are invisible into the same bargain. The one I am making now is nearly as small as nothing. Number One would hold a million of them at the same time and there would be room left for a pair of woman's horse-breeches

if they were rolled up. The dear knows where it will stop and termi-
nate.''

"Such work must be very hard on the eyes," I said, determined to
pretend that everybody was an ordinary person like myself.

"Some of these days," he answered, "I will have to buy spectacles
with gold ear-claws. My eyes are crippled with the small print in the
newspapers and in the offeecial forms."

"Before I go back to the day-room," I said, "would it be right to ask
you what you were performing with that little small piano-instrument,
the article with the knobs, and the brass pins?"

"That is my personal musical instrument," said MacCruiskeen,
"and I was playing my own tunes on it in order to extract private
satisfaction from the sweetness of them."

"I was listening," I answered, "but I did not succeed in hearing
you."

"That does not surprise me intuitively," said MacCruiskeen, "because it is an indigenous patent of my own. The vibrations of the true
notes are so high in their fine frequencies that they cannot be appreciated by the human earcup. Only myself has the secret of the thing and the
intimate way of it, the confidential knack of circumventing it. Now what
do you think of that?"

I climbed up to my legs to go back to the day-room, passing a hand
weakly about my brow.

"I think it is extremely acatalectic," I answered.

VI

. . . .

"There is one puzzle," I remarked, "that is hurting the back of my
head and causing me a lot of curiosity. It is about the bicycle. I have
never heard of detective-work as good as that being done before. Not
only did you find the lost bicycle but you found all the clues as well. I
find it is a great strain for me to believe what I see, and I am becoming
afraid occasionally to look at some things in case they would have to be
believed. What is the secret of your constabulary virtuosity?"

He laughed at my earnest inquiries and shook his head with great
indulgence at my simplicity.

"It was an easy thing," he said.

"How easy?"

"Even without the clues I could have succeeded in ultimately finding
the bicycle."

"It seems a very difficult sort of easiness," I answered. "Did you
know where the bicycle was?

"I did."

"How?"

"Because I put it there."

"You stole the bicycle yourself ?"

"Certainly."

"And the pump and the other clues?"

"I put them where they were finally discovered also."

"And why?"

He did not answer in words for a moment but kept on walking strongly beside me looking as far ahead as possible.

"The County Council is the culprit," he said at last.

I said nothing, knowing that he would blame the County Council at greater length if I waited till he had the blame thought out properly. It was not long till he turned in my direction to talk to me again. His face was grave.

"Did you ever discover or hear tell of the Atomic Theory?" he inquired.

"No," I answered.

He leaned his mouth confidentially over to my ear.

"Would it surprise you to be told," he said darkly, "that the Atomic Theory is at work in this parish?"

"It would indeed."

"It is doing untold destruction," he continued, "the half of the people are suffering from it, it is worse than the smallpox."

I thought it better to say *something*.

"Would it be advisable," I said, "that it should be taken in hand by the Dispensary Doctor or by the National Teachers or do you think it is a matter for the head of the family?"

"The lock stock and barrel of it all," said the Sergeant, "is the County Council."

He walked on looking worried and preoccupied as if what he was examining in his head was unpleasant in a very intricate way.

"The Atomic Theory," I sallied, "is a thing that is not clear to me at all."

"Michael Gilhaney," said the Sergeant, "is an example of a man that is nearly banjaxed from the principle of the Atomic Theory. Would it astonish you to hear that he is nearly half a bicycle?"

"It would surprise me unconditionally," I said.

"Michael Gilhaney," said the Sergeant, "is nearly sixty years of age by plain computation and if he is itself, he has spent no less than thirty-five years riding his bicycle over the rocky roadsteads and up and down the hills and into the deep ditches when the road goes astray in the strain of the winter. He is always going to a particular destination or other on his bicycle at every hour of the day or coming back from there at every other hour. If it wasn't that his bicycle was stolen every Monday he would be sure to be more than half-way now."

"Half-way to where?"

"Half-way to being a bicycle himself," said the Sergeant.

"Your talk," I said, "is surely the handiwork of wisdom because not one word of it do I understand."

"Did you never study atomics when you were a lad?" asked the Sergeant, giving me a look of great inquiry and surprise.

"No," I answered.

"That is a very serious defalcation," he said, "but all the same I will tell you the size of it. Everything is composed of small particles of itself and they are flying around in concentric circles and arcs and segments and innumerable other geometrical figures too numerous to mention collectively, never standing still or resting but spinning away and darting hither and thither and back again, all the time on the go. These diminutive gentlemen are called atoms. Do you follow me intelligently?"

"Yes."

"They are lively as twenty leprechauns doing a jig on top of a tombstone."

"*A very pretty figure*," Joe murmured.[1]

"Now take a sheep," the Sergeant said. "What is a sheep only millions of little bits of sheepness whirling around and doing intricate convolutions inside the sheep? What else is it but that?"

"That would be bound to make the beast dizzy," I observed, "especially if the whirling was going on inside the head as well."

The Sergeant gave me a look which I am sure he himself would describe as one of *non-possum* and *noli-me-tangere*.

"That remark is what may well be called buncombe," he said sharply, "because the nerve-strings and the sheep's head itself are whirling into the same bargain and you can cancel out one whirl against the other and there you are—like simplifying a division sum when you have fives above and below the bar."

"To say the truth I did not think of that," I said.

"Atomics is a very intricate theorem and can be worked out with algebra but you would want to take it by degrees because you might spend the whole night proving a bit of it with rulers and cosines and similar other instruments and then at the wind-up not believe what you had proved at all. If that happened you would have to go back over it till you got a place where you could believe your own facts and figures as delineated from Hall and Knight's Algebra and then go on again from

1.   [Joe is our protagonist's spirit. Eds.]

that particular place till you had the whole thing properly believed and not have bits of it half-believed or a doubt in your head hurting you like when you lose the stud of your shirt in bed."

"Very true," I said.

"Consecutively and consequentially," he continued, "you can safely infer that you are made of atoms yourself and so is your fob pocket and the tail of your shirt and the instrument you use for taking the leavings out of the crook of your hollow tooth. Do you happen to know what takes place when you strike a bar of iron with a good coal hammer or with a blunt instrument?"

"What?"

"When the wallop falls, the atoms are bashed away down to the bottom of the bar and compressed and crowded there like eggs under a good clucker. After a while in the course of time they swim around and get back at last to where they were. But if you keep hitting the bar long enough and hard enough they do not get a chance to do this and what happens then?"

"That is a hard question."

"Ask a blacksmith for the true answer and he will tell you that the bar will dissipate itself away by degrees if you persevere with the hard wallops. Some of the atoms of the bar will go into the hammer and the other half into the table or the stone or the particular article that is underneath the bottom of the bar."

"That is well-known," I agreed.

"The gross and net result of it is that people who spent most of their natural lives riding iron bicycles over the rocky roadsteads of this parish get their personalities mixed up with the personalities of their bicycle as a result of the interchanging of the atoms of each of them and you would be surprised at the number of people in these parts who nearly are half people and half bicycles."

I let go a gasp of astonishment that made a sound in the air like a bad puncture.

"And you would be flabbergasted at the number of bicycles that are half-human almost half-man, half-partaking of humanity."

Apparently there is no limit, Joe remarked. *Anything can be said in this place and it will be true and will have to be believed.*

I would not mind being working this minute on a steamer in the middle of the sea, I said, coiling ropes and doing the hard manual work. I would like to be far away from here.

I looked carefully around me. Brown bogs and black bogs were arranged neatly on each side of the road with rectangular boxes carved out of them here and there, each with a filling of yellow-brown brown-yellow water. Far away near the sky tiny people were stooped at their turfwork, cutting out precisely-shaped sods with their patent spades and building them into a tall memorial twice the height of a horse and cart. Sounds came from them to the Sergeant and myself, delivered to our ears without charge by the west wind, sounds of laughing and whistling and bits of verses from the old bog-songs. Nearer, a house stood attended by three trees and surrounded by the happiness of a coterie of fowls, all of them picking and rooting and disputating loudly in the unrelenting manufacture of their eggs. The house was quiet in itself and silent but a canopy of lazy smoke had been erected over the chimney to indicate that people were within engaged on tasks. Ahead of us went the road, running swiftly across the flat land and pausing slightly to climb slowly up a hill that was waiting for it in a place where there was tall grass, grey boulders and rank stunted trees. The whole overhead was occupied by the sky, serene, impenetrable, ineffable and incomparable, with a fine island of clouds anchored in the calm two yards to the right of Mr. Jarvis's outhouse.

The scene was real and incontrovertible and at variance with the talk of the Sergeant, but I knew that the Sergeant was talking the truth and if it was a question of taking my choice, it was possible that I would have to forego the reality of all the simple things my eyes were looking at.

I took a sideways view of him. He was striding on with signs of anger against the County Council on his coloured face.

"Are you certain about the humanity of the bicycle?" I inquired of him. "Is the Atomic Theory as dangerous as you say?"

"It is between twice and three times as dangerous as it might be," he replied gloomily. "Early in the morning I often think it is four times, and what is more, if you lived here for a few days and gave full play to your observation and inspection, you would know how certain the sureness of certainty is."

"Gilhaney did not look like a bicycle," I said. "He had no back wheel on him and I did not think he had a front wheel either, although I did not give much attention to his front."

The Sergeant looked at me with some commiseration.

"You cannot expect him to grow handlebars out of his neck but I have seen him do more indescribable things than that. Did you ever notice the queer behaviour of bicycles in these parts?"

"I am not long in this district."

Thanks be, said Joe.

"Then watch the bicycles if you think it is pleasant to be surprised continuously," he said. "When a man lets things go so far that he is half or more than half a bicycle, you will not see so much because he spends a lot of his time leaning with one elbow on walls or standing propped by one foot at kerbstones. Of course there are other things connected with ladies and ladies' bicycles that I will mention to you separately some time. But the man-charged bicycle is a phenomenon of great charm and intensity and a very dangerous article.''

. . . .

VII

. . . .

''Inspector O'Corky!'' he said.

''What is the meaning of the vacuity of the station in routine hours?'' barked the Inspector.

The sound his voice made was rough like coarse cardboard rubbed on sandpaper and it was clear that he was not pleased with himself or with other people.

''I was out myself,'' the Sergeant replied respectfully, ''on emergency duty and policework of the highest gravity.''

''Did you know that a man called Mathers was found in the crotch of a ditch up the road two hours ago with his belly opened up with a knife or sharp instrument?''

To say that this was a surprise which interfered seriously with my heart-valves would be the same as saying that a red-hot poker would heat your face if somebody decided to let you have it there. I stared from the Sergeant to the Inspector and back again with my whole inside fluttering in consternation.

It seems that our mutual friend Finnucane is in the environs, Joe said.

''Certainly I did,'' said the Sergeant.

Very strange. How could he if he has been out with us after the bicycle for the last four hours?

''And what steps have you taken and how many steps?'' barked the Inspector.

''Long steps and steps in the right direction,'' replied the Sergeant evenly. ''I know who the murderer is.''

''Then why is he not arrested into custody?''

''He is,'' said the Sergeant pleasantly.

''Where?''

''Here.''

This was the second thunderbolt. After I had glanced fearfully to my rear without seeing a murderer it became clear to me that I myself was the subject of the private conversation of the two Policemen. I made no protest because my voice was gone and my mouth was bone-dry.

Inspector O'Corky was too angry to be pleased at anything so surprising as what the Sergeant said.

"Then why is he not confined under a two-way key and padlock in the cell?" he roared.

For the first time the Sergeant looked a bit crestfallen and shame-faced. His face got a little redder than it was and he put his eyes on the stone floor.

"To tell you the truth," he said at last, "I keep my bicycle there!"

"I see," said the Inspector.

He stooped quickly and rammed black clips on the extremities of his trousers and stamped on the floor. For the first time I saw that he had been leaning by one elbow on the counter.

"See that you regularise your irregularity instantaneously," he called as his good-bye, "and set right your irrectitude and put the murderer in the cage before he rips the bag out of the whole country-side."

After that he was gone. Sounds came to us of coarse scraping on the gravel, a sign that the Inspector favoured the old-fashioned method of mounting from the back-step.

"Well, now," the Sergeant said.

He took off his cap and went over to a chair and sat on it, easing himself on his broad pneumatic seat. He took a red cloth from his fob and decanted the globes of perspiration from his expansive countenance and opened the buttons of his tunic as if to let out on wing the trouble that was imprisoned there. He then took to carrying out a scientifically precise examination of the soles and the toes of his constabulary boots, a sign that he was wrestling with some great problem.

"What is your worry?" I inquired, very anxious by now that what had happened should be discussed.

"The bicycle," he said.

"The bicycle?"

"How can I put it out of the cell?" he asked.

"I have always kept it in solitary confinement when I am not riding it to make sure it is not leading a personal life inimical to my own inimitability. I cannot be too careful. I have to ride long rides on my constabulary ridings."

"Do you mean that I should be locked in the cell and kept there and hidden from the world?"

"You surely heard the instructions of the Inspector?"

Ask is it all a joke? Joe said.

"Is this all a joke for entertainment purposes?"

"If you take it that way I will be indefinitely beholden to you," said the Sergeant earnestly, "and I will remember you with real emotion. It would be a noble gesture and an unutterable piece of supreme excellence on the part of the deceased."

"What!" I cried.

"You must recollect that to turn everything to your own advantage is one of the regulations of true wisdom as I informed you privately. It is the following of this rule on my part that makes you a murderer this today evening.

"The Inspector required a captured prisoner as the least tiniest minimum for his inferior *bonhomie* and *mal d'esprit*. It was your personal misfortune to be present adjacently at the time but it was likewise my personal good fortune and good luck. There is no option but to stretch you for the serious offence."

"Stretch me?"

"Hang you by the windpipe before high breakfast time."

"That is most unfair," I stuttered, "it is unjust ... rotten ... fiendish." My voice rose to a thin tremolo of fear.

"It is the way we work in this part of the country," explained the Sergeant.

"I will resist," I shouted, "and will resist to the death and fight for my existence even if I lose my life in the attempt."

The Sergeant made a soothing gesture in deprecation. He took out an enormous pipe and when he stuck it in his face it looked like a great hatchet.

"About the bicycle," he said when he had it in commission.

"What bicycle?"

"My own one. Would it inconvenience you if I neglected to bar you into the inside of the cell? I do not desire to be selfish but I have to think carefully about my bicycle. The wall of this day-room is no place for it."

"I do not mind," I said quietly.

"You can remain in the environs on parole and ticket of leave till we have time to build the high scaffold in the backyard."

"How do you know I will not make excellent my escape?" I asked, thinking that it would be better to discover all the thoughts and intentions of the Sergeant so that my escape would in fact be certain.

He smiled at me as much as the weight of the pipe would let him.

"You will not do that," he said. "It would not be honourable but even if it was we would easily follow the track of your rear tyre and besides the rest of everything Policeman Fox would be sure to apprehend you single-handed on the outskirts. There would be no necessity for a warrant."

Both of us sat silent for a while occupied with our thoughts, he thinking about his bicycle and I about my death.

By the bye, Joe remarked, *I seem to remember our friend saying that the law could not lay a finger on us on account of your congenital anonymity.*

"Quite right," I said. "I forgot that."

As things are I fancy it would not be much more than a debating point.

"It is worth mentioning," I said.

O Lord, yes.

"By the way," I said to the Sergeant, "did you recover my American watch for me?"

"The matter is under consideration and is receiving attention," he said officially.

"Do you recall that you told me that I was not here at all because I had no name and that my personality was invisible to the law?"

"I said that."

"Then how can I be hanged for a murder, even if I did commit it and there is no trial or preliminary proceedings, no caution administered and no hearing before a Commissioner of the Public Peace?"

Watching the Sergeant, I saw him take the hatchet from his jaws in surprise and knot his brows into considerable corrugations. I could see that he was severely troubled with my inquiry. He looked darkly at me and then doubled his look, giving me a compressed stare along the line of his first vision.

"Well great cripes!" he said.

For three minutes he sat giving my representations his undivided attention. He was frowning so heavily with wrinkles which were so deep that the blood was driven from his face leaving it black and forbidding.

Then he spoke.

"Are you completely doubtless that you are nameless?" he asked.

"Positively certain."

"Would it be Mick Barry?"

"No."

"Charlemange O'Keeffe?"

"No."

"Sir Justin Spens?"

"Not that."

"Kimberley?"

"No."

"Bernard Fann?"

"No."

"Joseph Poe or Nolan?"

"No."

"One of the Garvins or the Moynihans?"

"Not them."

"Rosencranz O'Dowd?"

"No."

"Would it be O'Benson?"

"Not O'Benson."

"The Quigleys, The Mulrooneys, or the Hounimen?"

"No."

"The Hardimen or the Merrimen?"

"Not them."

"Peter Dundy?"

"No."

"Scrutch?"

"No."

"Lord Brad?"

"Not him."

"The O'Growneys, the O'Roartys or the Finnehys?"

"No."

"That is an amazing piece of denial and denunciation," he said.

He passed the red cloth over his face again to reduce the moisture.

"An astonishing parade of nullity," he added.

"My name is not Jenkins either," I vouchsafed.

"Roger MacHugh?"

"Not Roger."

"Sitric Hogan?"

"No."

"Not Conroy?"

"No."

"Not O'Conroy?"

"Not O'Conroy."

"There are very few more names that you could have, then," he said. "Because only a black man could have a name different to the ones I have recited. Or a red man. Not Byrne?"

"No."

"Then it is a nice pancake," he said gloomily. He bent double to give full scope to the extra brains he had at the rear of his head.

"Holy suffering senators," he muttered.

I think we have won the day.

We are not home and dried yet, I answered.

Nevertheless I think we can relax. Evidently he has never heard of Signor Bari, the golden-throated budgerigar of Milano.

I don't think this is the time for pleasantries.

Or J. Courtney Wain, private investigator and member of the inner bar. Eighteen thousand guineas marked on the brief. The singular case of the red-headed men.

"By Scot!" said the Sergeant suddenly. He got up to pace the flooring.

"I think the case can be satisfactorily met," he said pleasantly, "and ratified unconditionally."

I did not like his smile and asked him for his explanation.

"It is true," he said, "that you cannot commit a crime and that the right arm of the law cannot lay its finger on you irrespective of the degree of your criminality. Anything you do is a lie and nothing that happens to you is true."

I nodded my agreement comfortably.

"For that reason alone," said the Sergeant, "we can take you and hang the life out of you and you are not hanged at all and there is no entry to be made in the death papers. The particular death you die is not even a death (which is an inferior phenomenon at the best) only an insanitary abstraction in the backyard, a piece of negative nullity neutralised and rendered void by asphyxiation and the fracture of the spinal string. If it is not a lie to say that you have been given the final hammer behind the barrack, equally it is true to say that nothing has happened to you."

"You mean that because I have no name I cannot die and that you cannot be held answerable for death even if you kill me?"

"That is about the size of it," said the Sergeant.

. . . .

MacCruiskeen sighed and went again to the dresser, taking something from the drawer. When he sat down at the table again, he started to move his hands together, performing intricate loops and convolutions with his fingers as if they were knitting something but there were no needles in them at all, nothing to be seen except his naked hands.

"Are you working again at the little chest?" I asked.

"I am," he said.

. . . .

The door was flung open and in came Gilhaney, his red face puffed from the rough road. He did not quite stop or sit down but kept moving restlessly about the day-room, paying no attention to me at all. MacCruiskeen had reached a meticulous point in his work and had his head nearly on the table to make sure that his fingers were working correctly and making no serious mistakes. When he had passed the difficulty he looked up somewhat at Gilhaney.

"Is it about a bicycle?" he asked casually.

"Only about timber," said Gilhaney.

"And what is your timber news?"

"The prices have been put up by a Dutch ring, the cost of a good scaffold would cost a fortune."

"Trust the Dutchmen," MacCruiskeen said in a tone that meant that he knew the timber trade inside out.

"A three-man scaffold with a good trap and satisfactory steps would set you back ten pounds without rope or labour," Gilhaney said.

"Ten pounds is a lot of money for a hanger," said MacCruiskeen.

"But a two-man scaffold with a push-off instead of the mechanical trap and a ladder for the steps would cost the best majority of six pound, rope extra."

"And dear at the same price," said MacCruiskeen.

"But the ten-pound scaffold is a better job, there is more class about it," said Gilhaney. "There is a charm about a scaffold if it is well-made and satisfactory."

What occurred next I did not see properly because I was listening to this pitiless talk even with my eyes. But something astonishing happened again. Gilhaney had gone near MacCruiskeen to talk down at him seriously and I think he made the mistake of stopping dead completely instead of keeping on the move to preserve his perpendicular balance. The outcome was that he crashed down, half on bent MacCruiskeen and half on the table, bringing the two of them with him into a heap of shouts and legs and confusion on the floor. The policeman's face when I saw it was a frightening sight. It was the colour of a dark plum with passion, but his eyes burned like bonfires in the forehead and there were frothy discharges at his mouth. He said no words for a while, only sounds of jungle anger, wild grunts and clicks of demoniacal hostility. Gilhaney had cowered to the wall and raised himself with the help of it and then retreated to the door. When MacCruiskeen found his tongue again he used the most unclean language ever spoken and invented dirtier words than the dirtiest ever spoken anywhere. He put names on Gilhaney too impossible and revolting to be written with known letters. He was temporarily insane with anger because he rushed ultimately to the dresser where he kept his properties and pulled out a patent pistol and swept it round the room to threaten the two of us and every breakable article in the house.

"Get down on your four knees, the two of you, on the floor," he roared, "and don't stop searching for that chest you have knocked down till you find it!"

Gilhaney slipped down to his knees at once and I did the same thing without troubling to look at the Policeman's face because I could remember distinctly what it looked like the last time I had eyed it. We crawled feebly about the floor, peering and feeling for something that could not be felt or seen and that was really too small to be lost at all.

This is amusing. You are going to be hung for murdering a man you did not murder and now you will be shot for not finding a tiny thing that probably does not exist at all and which in any event you did not lose.

I deserve it all, I answered, for not being here at all, to quote the words of the Sergeant.

How long we remained at our peculiar task, Gilhaney and I, it is not easy to remember. Ten minutes or ten years, perhaps, with MacCruiskeen seated near us, fingering the iron and glaring savagely at our bent forms. Then I caught Gilhaney showing his face to me sideways and giving me a broad private wink. Soon he closed his fingers, got up erect with the assistance of the door-handle and advanced to where MacCruiskeen was, smiling his gappy smile.

"Here you are and here it is," he said with his closed hand outstretched.

"Put it on the table," MacCruiskeen said evenly.

Gilhaney put his hand on the table and opened it.

"You can now go away and take your departure," MacCruiskeen told him, "and leave the premises for the purpose of attending to the timber."

When Gilhaney was gone I saw that most of the passion had ebbed from the Policeman's face. He sat silent for a time, then gave his customary sigh and got up.

"I have more to do tonight," he said to me civilly, "so I will show you where you are to sleep for the dark night-time."

He lit a queer light that had wires to it and a diminutive box full of minor noises, and led me into a room where there were two white beds and nothing else.

"Gilhaney thinks he is a clever one and a master mind," he said.

"He might be or maybe not," I muttered.

"He does not take much account of coincidental chances."

"He does not look like a man that would care much."

"When he said he had the chest he thought he was making me into a prize pup and blinding me by putting his thumb in my eye."

"That is what it looked like."

"But by a rare chance he *did* accidentally close his hand on the chest and it was the chest and nothing else that he replaced in due course on the table."

There was some silence here.

"Which bed?" I asked.

"This one," said MacCruiskeen.

Notes

1. *Theme.* We might fairly say that the theme of both THE TRIAL and THE THIRD POLICEMAN is the arbitrariness of the law. How do Kafka and O'Brien, respectively, depict this theme? What distinguishes an arbitrary legal system from a fair one?

2. *Language.* Even though the two works share a common theme, the two differ widely in terms of language. How would you describe this difference? Does the contrast in language affect your overall impression of the works? Flann O'Brien writes in a rich Irish tradition that includes James Joyce and W.B. Yeats. Writers in this tradition emphasize luxuriant vocabulary, surprising word play, and nontraditional syntax. Which writing style, Kafka's or O'Brien's, would be most useful to the legal writer? Why?

* * *

Born Chloe Anthony Wofford in Lorain, Ohio, Toni Morrison is one of the leading American novelists of our time. Her precise, musical language, combined with supernatural and mythological elements, creates a rich fabric. Her novels often focus on the hardships of black American women. Her novel BELOVED won the Pulitzer Prize in 1987, and in 1993 she became the first African-American woman to be awarded the Nobel Prize in literature.

Her novel SULA (1973) is a close study of a particularly talented woman and the community in which she comes of age, known as "the Bottom." The following is an excerpt recounting the death and funeral of one of the community's children, Chicken Little.

SULA
Toni Morrison

Then summer came. A summer limp with the weight of blossomed things. Heavy sunflowers weeping over fences; iris curling and browning at the edges far away from their purple hearts; ears of corn letting their auburn hair wind down to their stalks. And the boys. The beautiful, beautiful boys who dotted the landscape like jewels, split the air with their shouts in the field, and thickened the river with their shining wet backs. Even their footsteps left a smell of smoke behind.

It was in that summer, the summer of their twelfth year, the summer of the beautiful black boys, that they became skittish, frightened and bold—all at the same time.

In that mercury mood in July, Sula and Nel wandered about the Bottom barefoot looking for mischief. They decided to go down by the river where the boys sometimes swam. Nel waited on the porch of 7 Carpenter's Road while Sula ran into the house to go to the toilet. On the way up the stairs, she passed the kitchen where Hannah sat with two friends, Patsy and Valentine. The two women were fanning themselves and watching Hannah put down some dough, all talking casually about one thing and another, and had gotten around, when Sula passed by, to the problems of child rearing.

"They a pain."

"Yeh. Wish I'd listened to mamma. She told me not to have 'em too soon."

"Any time atall is too soon for me."

"Oh, I don't know. My Rudy minds his daddy. He just wild with me. Be glad when he growed and gone."

Hannah smiled and said, "Shut your mouth. You love the ground he pee on."

"Sure I do. But he still a pain. Can't help loving your own child. No matter what they do."

"Well, Hester grown now and I can't say love is exactly what I feel."

"Sure you do. You love her, like I love Sula. I just don't like her. That's the difference."

"Guess so. Likin' them is another thing."

"Sure. They different people, you know ..."

She only heard Hannah's words, and the pronouncement sent her flying up the stairs. In bewilderment, she stood at the window fingering the curtain edge, aware of a sting in her eye. Nel's call floated up and into the window, pulling her away from dark thoughts back into the bright, hot daylight.

They ran most of the way.

Heading toward the wide part of the river where trees grouped themselves in families darkening the earth below. They passed some boys swimming and clowning in the water, shrouding their words in laughter.

They ran in the sunlight, creating their own breeze, which pressed their dresses into their damp skin. Reaching a kind of square of four leaf-locked trees which promised cooling, they flung themselves into the four-cornered shade to taste their lip sweat and contemplate the wildness that had come upon them so suddenly. They lay in the grass, their foreheads almost touching, their bodies stretched away from each other at a 180–degree angle. Sula's head rested on her arm, an undone braid coiled around her wrist. Nel leaned on her elbows and worried long blades of grass with her fingers. Underneath their dresses flesh tightened and shivered in the high coolness, their small breasts just now beginning to create some pleasant discomfort when they were lying on their stomachs.

Sula lifted her head and joined Nel in the grass play. In concert, without ever meeting each other's eyes, they stroked the blades up and down, up and down. Nel found a thick twig and, with her thumbnail, pulled away its bark until it was stripped to a smooth, creamy innocence. Sula looked about and found one too. When both twigs were undressed Nel moved easily to the next stage and began tearing up rooted grass to make a bare spot of earth. When a generous clearing was made, Sula traced intricate patterns in it with her twig. At first Nel was content to do the same. But soon she grew impatient and poked her twig rhythmically and intensely into the earth, making a small neat hole that grew deeper and wider with the least manipulation of her twig. Sula copied her, and soon each had a hole the size of a cup. Nel began a more strenuous digging and, rising to her knee, was careful to scoop out the dirt as she made her hole deeper. Together they worked until the two holes were one and the same. When the depression was the size of a small dishpan, Nel's twig broke. With a gesture of disgust she threw the pieces into the hole they had made. Sula threw hers in too. Nel saw a bottle cap and tossed it in as well. Each then looked around for more debris to throw into the hole: paper, bits of glass, butts of cigarettes, until all of the small defiling things they could find were collected there. Carefully they replaced the soil and covered the entire grave with uprooted grass.

Neither one had spoken a word.

They stood up, stretched, then gazed out over the swift dull water as an unspeakable restlessness and agitation held them. At the same instant each girl heard footsteps in the grass. A little boy in too big knickers was coming up from the lower bank of the river. He stopped when he saw them and picked his nose.

"Your mamma tole you to stop eatin' snot, Chicken," Nel hollered at him through cupped hands.

"Shut up," he said, still picking. "Come up here and say that."

"Leave him 'lone, Nel. Come here, Chicken. Lemme show you something."

"Naw."

"You scared we gone take your bugger away?"

"Leave him 'lone, I said. Come on, Chicken. Look. I'll help you climb a tree."

Chicken looked at the tree Sula was pointing to—a big double beech with low branches and lots of bends for sitting.

He moved slowly toward her.

"Come on, Chicken, I'll help you up."

Still picking his nose, his eyes wide, he came to where they were standing. Sula took him by the hand and coaxed him along. When they reached the base of the beech, she lifted him to the first branch, saying, "Go on. Go on. I got you." She followed the boy, steadying him, when he needed it, with her hand and her reassuring voice. When they were as high as they could go, Sula pointed to the far side of the river.

"See? Bet you never saw that far before, did you?"

"Uh uh."

"Now look down there." They both leaned a little and peered through the leaves at Nel standing below, squinting up at them. From their height she looked small and foreshortened.

Chicken Little laughed.

"Y'all better come on down before you break your neck," Nel hollered.

"I ain't never coming down," the boy hollered back.

"Yeah. We better. Come on, Chicken."

"Naw. Lemme go."

"Yeah, Chicken. Come on, now." Sula pulled his leg gently.

"OK, I'm leavin' you." She started on.

"Wait!" he screamed.

Sula stopped and together they slowly worked their way down.

Chicken was still elated. "I was way up there, wasn't I? Wasn't I? I'm a tell my brovver."

Sula and Nel began to mimic him: "I'm a tell my brovver; I'm a tell my brovver."

Sula picked him up by his hands and swung him outward then around and around. His knickers ballooned and his shrieks of frightened joy startled the birds and the fat grasshoppers. When he slipped from her hands and sailed away out over the water they could still hear his bubbly laughter.

The water darkened and closed quickly over the place where Chicken Little sank. The pressure of his hard and tight little fingers was still in Sula's palms as she stood looking at the closed place in the water. They expected him to come back up, laughing. Both girls stared at the water.

Nel spoke first. "Somebody saw." A figure appeared briefly on the opposite shore.

The only house over there was Shadrack's. Sula glanced at Nel. Terror widened her nostrils. Had he seen?

The water was so peaceful now. There was nothing but the baking sun and something newly missing. Sula cupped her face for an instant, then turned and ran up to the little plank bridge that crossed the river to Shadrack's house. There was no path. It was as though neither Shadrack nor anyone else ever came this way.

Her running was swift and determined, but when she was close to the three little steps that led to his porch, fear crawled into her stomach and only the something newly missing back there in the river made it possible for her to walk up the three steps and knock at the door.

No one answered. She started back, but thought again of the peace of the river. Shadrack would be inside, just behind the door ready to pounce on her. Still she could not go back. Ever so gently she pushed the door with the tips of her fingers and heard only the hinges weep. More. And then she was inside. Alone. The neatness, the order startled her, but more surprising was the restfulness. Everything was so tiny, so common, so unthreatening. Perhaps this was not the house of the Shad. The terrible Shad who walked about with his penis out, who peed in front of ladies and girl-children, the only black who could curse white people and get away with it, who drank in the road from the mouth of the bottle, who shouted and shook in the streets. This cottage? This sweet old cottage? With its made-up bed? With its rag rug and wooden table? Sula stood in the middle of the little room and in her wonder forgot what she had come for until a sound at the door made her jump. He was there in the doorway looking at her. She had not heard his coming and now he was looking at her.

More in embarrassment than terror she averted her glance. When she called up enough courage to look back at him, she saw his hand resting upon the door frame. His fingers, barely touching the wood, were arranged in a graceful arc. Relieved and encouraged (no one with hands like that, no one with fingers that curved around wood so tenderly, could kill her), she walked past him out of the door, feeling his gaze turning, turning with her.

At the edge of the porch, gathering the wisps of courage that were fast leaving her, she turned once more to look at him, to ask him . . . had he . . .?

He was smiling, a great smile, heavy with lust and time to come. He nodded his head as though answering a question, and said, in a pleasant conversational tone, a tone of cooled butter, "Always."

Sula fled down the steps, and shot through the greenness and the baking sun back to Nel and the dark closed place in the water. There she collapsed in tears.

Nel quieted her. "Sh, sh. Don't, don't. You didn't mean it. It ain't your fault. Sh. Sh. Come on, le's go, Sula. Come on, now. Was he there? Did he see? Where's the belt to your dress?"

Sula shook her head while she searched her waist for the belt.

Finally she stood up and allowed Nel to lead her away "He said, 'Always. Always.' "

"What?"

Sula covered her mouth as they walked down the hill. Always. He had answered a question she had not asked, and its promise licked at her feet.

A bargeman, poling away from the shore, found Chicken late that afternoon stuck in some rocks and weeds, his knickers ballooning about his legs. He would have left him there but noticed that it was a child, not an old black man, as it first appeared, and he prodded the body loose, netted it and hauled it aboard. He shook his head in disgust at the kind of parents who would drown their own children. When, he wondered, will those people ever be anything but animals, fit for nothing but substitutes for mules, only mules didn't kill each other the way niggers did. He dumped Chicken Little into a burlap sack and tossed him next to some egg crates and boxes of wool cloth. Later, sitting down to smoke on an empty lard tin, still bemused by God's curse and the terrible burden his own kind had of elevating Ham's sons, he suddenly became alarmed by the thought that the corpse in this heat would have a terrible odor, which might get into the fabric of his woolen cloth. He dragged the sack away and hooked it over the side, so that the Chicken's body was half in and half out of the water.

Wiping the sweat from his neck, he reported his find to the sheriff at Porter's Landing, who said they didn't have no niggers in their county, but that some lived in those hills "cross the river, up above Medallion. The bargeman said he couldn't go all the way back there, it was every bit of two miles. The sheriff said whyn't he throw it on back into the water. The bargeman said he never shoulda taken it out in the first place. Finally they got the man who ran the ferry twice a day to agree to take it over in the morning."

That was why Chicken Little was missing for three days and didn't get to the embalmer's until the fourth day, by which time he was unrecognizable to almost everybody who once knew him, and even his mother wasn't deep down sure, except that it just had to be him since nobody could find him. When she saw his clothes lying on the table in the basement of the mortuary, her mouth snapped shut, and when she saw his body her mouth flew wide open again and it was seven hours before she was able to close it and make the first sound.

So the coffin was closed.

The Junior Choir, dressed in white, sang "Nearer My God to Thee" and "Precious Memories," their eyes fastened on the songbooks they did not need, for this was the first time their voices had presided at a real-life event.

Nel and Sula did not touch hands or look at each other during the funeral. There was a space, a separateness, between them. Nel's legs had turned to granite and she expected the sheriff or Reverend Deal's pointing finger at any moment. Although she knew she had "done nothing," she felt convicted and hanged right there in the pew—two rows down from her parents in the children's section.

Sula simply cried. Soundlessly and with no heaving and gasping for breath, she let the tears roll into her mouth and slide down her chin to dot the front of her dress.

As Reverend Deal moved into his sermon, the hands of the women unfolded like pairs of raven's wings and flew high above their hats in the air. They did not hear all of what he said; they heard the one word, or phrase, or inflection that was for them the connection between the event and themselves. For some it was the term "Sweet Jesus." And they saw the Lamb's eye and the truly innocent victim: themselves. They acknowledged the innocent child hiding in the corner of their hearts, holding a sugar-and-butter sandwich. That one. The one who lodged deep in their fat, thin, old, young skin, and was the one the world had hurt. Or they thought of their son newly killed and remembered his legs in short pants and wondered where the bullet went in. Or they remembered how dirty the room looked when their father left home and wondered if that is the way the slim, young Jew felt, he who for them was both son and lover and in whose downy face they could see the sugar-and-butter sandwiches and feel the oldest and most devastating pain there is: not the pain of childhood, but the remembrance of it.

Then they left their pews. For with some emotions one has to stand. They spoke, for they were full and needed to say. They swayed, for the rivulets of grief or of ecstasy must be rocked. And when they thought of all that life and death locked into that little closed coffin they danced and screamed, not to protest God's will but to acknowledge it and confirm once more their conviction that the only way to avoid the Hand of God is to get in it.

In the colored part of the cemetery, they sank Chicken Little in between his grandfather and an aunt. Butterflies flew in and out of the bunches of field flowers now loosened from the top of the bier and lying in a small heap at the edge of the grave. The heat had gone, but there was still no breeze to lift the hair of the willows.

Nel and Sula stood some distance away from the grave, the space that had sat between them in the pews had dissolved. They held hands and knew that only the coffin would lie in the earth; the bubbly laughter and the press of fingers in the palm would stay aboveground forever. At first, as they stood there, their hands were clenched together. They relaxed slowly until during the walk back home their fingers were laced in as gentle a clasp as that of any two young girlfriends trotting up the road on a summer day wondering what happened to butterflies in the winter.

Notes

1. *A Paradox?* What does the author mean when she says that the mourners at the funeral thought "the only way to avoid the Hand of God is to get in it?"

2. *A Crime?* Was a crime committed here? Is justice needed? If so, how can justice be obtained?

3. *Virtuoso Writing.* Toni Morrison is one of the great literary stylists of our time. Identify the characteristics of Morrison's style and explain how they contribute to the effect of her prose.

* * *

The psychological depth of Fyodor Dostoyevsky's novels is dazzling. One of his greatest novels is CRIME AND PUNISHMENT, in which the protagonist, Raskolnikov, a brilliant, poverty-stricken student, decides to commit the perfect crime by murdering an elderly female pawnbroker. Unfortunately for Rakolnikov, the old pawnbroker's kind sister enters as the crime is taking place, and he is forced to kill the sister as well.

Raskolnikov probably would have avoided detection, but he ultimately confesses out of his sense of guilt. He is sentenced to hard labor in Siberia, where he is cared for by a loving Christian female companion. The murder scene is described in the following excerpt.

CRIME AND PUNISHMENT
Fyodor Dostoyevsky

PART ONE, CHAPTER VI

. . . .

Luckily for him, everything went well again at the gates. At that very moment, as though expressly for his benefit, a huge waggon of hay had just driven in at the gate, completely screening him as he passed under the gateway, and the waggon had scarcely had time to drive through into the yard, before he had slipped in a flash to the right. On the other side of the waggon he could hear shouting and quarrelling; but no one noticed him and no one met him. Many windows looking into that huge quadrangular yard were open at that moment, but he did not raise his head—he had not the strength to. The staircase leading to the old woman's room was close by, just on the right of the gateway. He was already on the stairs. . . .

Drawing a breath, pressing his hand against his throbbing heart, and once more feeling for the axe and setting it straight, he began softly and cautiously ascending the stairs, listening every minute. But the stairs, too, were quite deserted; all the doors were shut; he met no one. One flat indeed on the first floor was wide open and painters were at work in it, but they did not glance at him. He stood still, thought a minute and went on. "Of course it would be better if they had not been here, but ... it's two storeys above them."

And here was the fourth storey, here was the door, here was the flat opposite, the empty one. The flat underneath the old woman's was apparently empty also; the visiting card nailed on the door had been torn off—they had gone away! ... He was out of breath. For one instant the thought floated through his mind: "Shall I go back?" But he made no answer and began listening at the old woman's door, a dead silence. Then he listened again on the staircase, listened long and intently ... then looked about him for the last time, pulled himself together, drew himself up, and once more tried the axe in the noose. "Am I very pale?" he wondered. "Am I not evidently agitated? She is mistrustful.... Had I better wait a little longer ... till my heart leaves off thumping?"

But his heart did not leave off. On the contrary, as though to spite him, it throbbed more and more violently. He could stand it no longer, but he slowly put out his hand to the bell and rang. Half a minute later he rang again, more loudly.

No answer. To go on ringing was useless and out of place. The old woman was, of course, at home, but she was suspicious and alone. He had some knowledge of her habits ... and once more he put his ear to the door. Either his senses were peculiarly keen (which it is difficult to suppose), or the sound was really very distinct. Anyway, he suddenly heard something like the cautious touch of a hand on the lock and the rustle of a skirt at the very door. Someone was standing stealthily close to the lock and just as he was doing on the outside was secretly listening within, and seemed to have her ear to the door.... He moved a little on purpose and muttered something aloud so that he might not have the appearance of hiding, then rang a third time, but quietly, soberly and without impatience. Recalling it afterwards, that moment stood out in his mind vividly, distinctly, forever; he could not make out how he had had such cunning, for his mind was as it were clouded at moments and he was almost unconscious of his body.... An instant later he heard the latch unfastened.

PART ONE, CHAPTER VII

The door was as before opened a tiny crack, and again two sharp and suspicious eyes stared at him out of the darkness. Then Raskolnikov lost his head and nearly made a great mistake.

Fearing the old woman would be frightened by their being alone, and not hoping that the sight of him would disarm her suspicions, he took hold of the door and drew it towards him to prevent the old woman from attempting to shut it again. Seeing this she did not pull the door back, but she did not let go the handle so that he almost dragged her out with it on to the stairs. Seeing that she was standing in the doorway not allowing him to pass, he advanced straight upon her. She stepped back in alarm, tried to say something, but seemed unable to speak and stared with open eyes at him.

"Good evening, Alyona Ivanovna," he began, trying to speak easily, but his voice would not obey him, it broke and shook. "I have come ... I have brought something ... but we'd better come in ... to the light...."

And leaving her, he passed straight into the room uninvited. The old woman ran after him; her tongue was unloosed.

"Good heavens! What is it? Who is it? What do you want?"

"Why, Alyona Ivanovna, you know me ... Raskolnikov ... here, I brought you the pledge I promised the other day...." and he held out the pledge.

The old woman glanced for a moment at the pledge, but at once stared in the eyes of her uninvited visitor. She looked intently, maliciously and mistrustfully. A minute passed; he even fancied something like a sneer in her eyes, as though she had already guessed everything. He felt that he was losing his head, that he was almost frightened, so frightened that if she were to look like that and not say a word for another half minute, he thought he would have run away from her.

"Why do you look at me as though you did not know me?" he said suddenly, also with malice. "Take it if you like, if not I'll go elsewhere, I am in a hurry."

He had not even thought of saying this, but it was suddenly said of itself. The old woman recovered herself, and her visitor's resolute tone evidently restored her confidence.

"But why, my good sir, all of a minute.... What is it?" she asked, looking at the pledge.

"The silver cigarette case; I spoke of it last time, you know."

She held out her hand.

"But how pale you are, to be sure ... and your hands are trembling too? Have you been bathing, or what?"

"Fever," he answered abruptly. "You can't help getting pale ... if you've nothing to eat," he added, with difficulty articulating the words.

His strength was failing him again. But his answer sounded like the truth; the old woman took the pledge.

"What is it?" she asked once more, scanning Raskolnikov intently and weighing the pledge in her hand.

"A thing ... cigarette case.... Silver.... Look at it."

"It does not seem somehow like silver.... How he has wrapped it up!"

Trying to untie the string and turning to the window, to the light (all her windows were shut, in spite of the stifling heat), she left him altogether for some seconds and stood with her back to him. He unbuttoned his coat and freed the axe from the noose, but did not yet take it out altogether, simply holding it in his right hand under the coat. His hands were fearfully weak, he felt them every moment growing more numb and more wooden. He was afraid he would let the axe slip and fall.... A sudden giddiness came over him.

"But what has he tied it up like this for?" the old woman cried with vexation and moved towards him.

He had not a minute more to lose. He pulled the axe quite out, swung it with both arms, scarcely conscious of himself, and almost without effort, almost mechanically, brought the blunt side down on her head. He seemed not to use his own strength in this. But as soon as he had once brought the axe down, his strength returned to him.

The old woman was as always bareheaded. Her thin, light hair, streaked with grey, thickly smeared with grease, was plaited in a rat's tail and fastened by a broken horn comb which stood out on the nape of her neck. As she was so short, the blow fell on the very top of her skull. She cried out, but very faintly, and suddenly sank all of a heap on the floor, raising her hands to her head. In one hand she still held "the pledge." Then he dealt her another and another blow with the blunt side and on the same spot. The blood gushed forth as from an overturned glass, the body fell back. He stepped back, let it fall, and at once bent over her face; she was dead. Her eyes seemed to be starting out of their sockets, the brow and the whole face were drawn and contorted convulsively.

He laid the axe on the ground near the dead body and felt at once in her pocket (trying to avoid the streaming blood)—the same right hand pocket from which she had taken the key on his last visit. He was in full possession of his faculties, free from confusion or giddiness, but his hands were still trembling. He remembered afterwards that he had been particularly collected and careful, trying all the time not to get smeared with blood.... He pulled out the keys at once, they were all, as before, in one bunch on a steel ring. He ran at once into the bedroom with them. It was a very small room with a whole shrine of holy images. Against the other wall stood a big bed, very clean and covered with a silk patchwork wadded quilt. Against a third wall was a chest of drawers. Strange to say, so soon as he began to fit the keys into the chest, so soon as he heard their jingling, a convulsive shudder passed over him. He suddenly felt tempted again to give it all up and go away. But that was only for an instant; it was too late to go back. He positively smiled at himself, when suddenly another terrifying idea occurred to his mind. He suddenly fancied that the old woman might still be alive and might recover her senses. Leaving the keys in the chest, he ran back to the body, snatched up the axe and lifted it once more over the old woman, but did not bring it down. There was no doubt that she was dead. Bending down and examining her again more closely, he saw clearly that the skull was broken and even battered in on one side. He was about to feel it with his finger, but drew back his hand and indeed it was evident without that. Meanwhile there was a perfect pool of blood. All at once he noticed a string on her neck; he tugged at it, but the string was strong and did not snap and besides, it was soaked with blood. He tried to pull it out from the front of the dress, but something held it and prevented its coming. In his impatience he raised the axe again to cut the string from above on the body, but did not dare, and with difficulty, smearing his hand and the axe in the blood, after two minutes' hurried effort, he cut the string and took it off without touching the body with the axe; he was not mistaken—it was a purse. On the string were two crosses, one of Cyprus wood and one of copper, and an image in silver filigree, and with them a small greasy chamois leather purse with a steel rim and ring. The purse was stuffed very full; Raskolnikov thrust it in his pocket without looking at it, flung the crosses on the old woman's body and rushed back into the bedroom, this time taking the axe with him.

He was in terrible haste, he snatched the keys, and began trying them again. But he was unsuccessful. They would not fit in the locks. It was not so much that his hands were shaking, but that he kept making mistakes; though he saw for instance that a key was not the right one and would not fit, still he tried to put it in. Suddenly he remembered and realised that the big key with the deep notches, which was hanging there with the small keys, could not possibly belong to the chest of drawers (on his last visit this had struck him), but to some strong box, and that everything perhaps was hidden in that box. He left the chest of drawers, and at once felt under the bedstead, knowing that old women usually keep boxes under their beds. And so it was; there was a good-sized box under the bed, at least a yard in length, with an arched lid covered with red leather and studded with steel nails. The notched key fitted at once and unlocked it. At the top, under a white sheet, was a coat of red brocade lined with hareskin; under it was a silk dress, then a shawl and it seemed as though there was nothing below but clothes. The first thing he did was to wipe his blood-stained hands on the red brocade. "It's red, and on it red blood will be less noticeable," the thought passed through his mind; then he suddenly came to himself. "Good God, am I going out of my senses?" he thought with terror.

But no sooner did he touch the clothes than a gold watch slipped from under the fur coat. He made haste to turn them all over. There turned out to be various articles made of gold among the clothes—probably all pledges, unredeemed or waiting to be redeemed—bracelets, chains, ear-rings, pins and such things. Some were in cases, others simply wrapped in newspaper, carefully and exactly folded, and tied round with tape. Without any delay, he began filling up the pockets of his trousers and overcoat without examining or undoing the parcels and cases; but he had not time to take many. . . .

He suddenly heard steps in the room where the old woman lay. He stopped short and was still as death. But all was quiet, so it must have been his fancy. All at once he heard distinctly a faint cry, as though some one had uttered a low broken moan. Then again dead silence for a minute or two. He sat squatting on his heels by the box and waited holding his breath. Suddenly he jumped up, seized the axe and ran out of the bedroom.

In the middle of the room stood Lizaveta with a big bundle in her arms. She was gazing in stupefaction at her murdered sister, white as a sheet and seeming not to have the strength to cry out. Seeing him run out of the bedroom, she began faintly quivering all over, like a leaf, a shudder ran down her face; she lifted her hand, opened her mouth, but still did not scream. She began slowly backing away from him into the corner, staring intently, persistently at him, but still uttered no sound, as though she could not get breath to scream. He rushed at her with the axe; her mouth twitched piteously, as one sees babies' mouths, when they begin to be frightened, stare intently at what frightens them and are on the point of screaming. And this hapless Lizaveta was so simple and had been so thoroughly crushed and scared that she did not even raise a hand to guard her face, though that was the most necessary and natural action at the moment, for the axe was raised over her face. She only put up her empty left hand, but not to her face, slowly holding it out before her as though motioning him away. The axe fell with the sharp edge just on the skull and split at one blow all the top of her head. She fell heavily at once. Raskolnikov completely lost his head, snatched up her bundle, dropped it again and ran into the entry.

. . . .

* * *

Charles Dickens is probably the most cherished novelist of the English language. His novels, including GREAT EXPECTATIONS, A TALE OF TWO CITIES, OLIVER TWIST, and DAVID COPPERFIELD, with their colorful, unforgettable characters, have been beloved by generations of readers. But Dickens was not just a master storyteller, he was also a sharp social commentator.

The inscription over the Gate of Hell, as Dante wrote, reads:

> Lasciate ogni speranza, voi, ch'entrate
> Abandon hope, all ye who enter here.

So it may be said of those who enter chancery court, to litigate the case of *Jarndyce and Jarndyce*. Only the lawyers ever come out of the case. But, if one believes Dickens, they probably have a special pass into and out of hell. BLEAK HOUSE takes the interminable lawsuit as its central structure, typifying all things formal and institutional. Contrasting with the lawsuit is the world of John Jarndyce and Esther Summerson, typifying all things personal and familial. For Dickens, the device of a Chancery lawsuit came naturally; he had worked both as a law clerk and as a shorthand reporter in the law courts. He knew and despised the failings of the legal system. The following excerpt—the first chapter of the novel—brilliantly characterizes the Court of Chancery.

BLEAK HOUSE
Charles Dickens

CHAPTER 1

In Chancery

LONDON. Michaelmas Term lately over, and the Lord Chancellor sitting in Lincoln's Inn Hall. Implacable November weather. As much mud in the streets as if the waters had but newly retired from the face of the earth, and it would not be wonderful to meet a Megalosaurus, forty feet long or so, waddling like an elephantine lizard up Holborn Hill. Smoke lowering down from chimney-pots, making a soft black drizzle, with flakes of soot in it as big as full-grown snow-flakes—gone into mourning, one might imagine, for the death of the sun. Dogs, undistinguishable in mire. Horses, scarcely better; splashed to their very blinkers. Foot passengers, jostling one another's umbrellas in a general infection of ill-temper, and losing their foot-hold at street-corners, where tens of thousands of other foot passengers have been slipping and sliding since the day broke (if the day ever broke), adding new deposits to the crust upon crust of mud, sticking at those points tenaciously to the pavement, and accumulating at compound interest.

Fog everywhere. Fog up the river, where it flows among green aits and meadows; fog down the river, where it rolls defiled among the tiers of shipping and the waterside pollutions of a great (and dirty) city. Fog on the Essex marshes, fog on the Kentish heights. Fog creeping into the cabooses of collier-brigs; fog lying out on the yards, and hovering in the rigging of great ships; fog drooping on the gunwales of barges and small boats. Fog in the eyes and throats of ancient Greenwich pensioners, wheezing by the firesides of their wards; fog in the stem and bowl of the afternoon pipe of the wrathful skipper, down in his close cabin; fog cruelly pinching the toes and fingers of his shivering little 'prentice boy on deck. Chance people on the bridges peeping over the parapets into a nether sky of fog, with fog all round them, as if they were up in a balloon, and hanging in the misty clouds.

Gas looming through the fog in divers places in the streets, much as the sun may, from the spongey fields, be seen to loom by husbandman and ploughboy. Most of the shops lighted two hours before their time— as the gas seems to know, for it has a haggard and unwilling look.

The raw afternoon is rawest, and the dense fog is densest, and the muddy streets are muddiest near that leaden-headed old obstruction, appropriate ornament for the threshold of a leaden-headed old corporation, Temple Bar. And hard by Temple Bar, in Lincoln's Inn Hall, at the very heart of the fog, sits the Lord High Chancellor in his High Court of Chancery.

Never can there come fog too thick, never can there come mud and mire too deep, to assort with the groping and floundering condition which this High Court of Chancery, most pestilent of hoary sinners, holds this day in the sight of heaven and earth.

On such an afternoon, if ever, the Lord High Chancellor ought to be sitting here—as here he is—with a foggy glory round his head, softly fenced in with crimson cloth and curtains, addressed by a large advocate with great whiskers, a little voice, and an interminable brief, and outwardly directing his contemplation to the lantern in the roof, where he can see nothing but fog. On such an afternoon some score of members of the High Court of Chancery bar ought to be—as here they are— mistily engaged in one of the ten thousand stages of an endless cause, tripping one another up on slippery precedents, groping knee-deep in technicalities, running their goat-hair and horse-hair warded heads against walls of words and making a pretence of equity with serious faces, as players might. On such an afternoon the various solicitors in the cause, some two or three of whom have inherited it from their fathers, who made a fortune by it, ought to be—as are they not?—ranged in a line, in a long matted well (but you might look in vain for truth at the bottom of it) between the registrar's red table and the silk gowns, with bills, cross-bills, answers, rejoinders, injunctions, affidavits, issues, references to masters, masters' reports, mountains of costly nonsense, piled before them. Well may the court be dim, with wasting candles here and there; well may the fog hang heavy in it, as if it would never get out; well may the stained-glass windows lose their colour and admit no light of day into the place; well may the uninitiated from the streets, who peep in through the glass panes in the door, be deterred from entrance by its owlish aspect and by the drawl, languidly echoing to the roof from the padded dais where the Lord High Chancellor looks into the lantern that has no light in it and where the attendant wigs are all stuck in a fog-bank! This is the Court of Chancery, which has its decaying houses and its blighted lands in every shire, which has its worn-out lunatic in every madhouse and its dead in every churchyard, which has its ruined suitor with his slipshod heels and threadbare dress borrowing and begging through the round of every man's acquaintance, which gives to monied might the means abundantly of wearying out the right; which so ex-hausts finances, patience, courage, hope, so overthrows the brain and breaks the heart, that there is not an honourable man among its practitioners who would not give—who does not often give—the warn-ing, "Suffer any wrong that can be done you rather than come here!"

Who happen to be in the Lord Chancellor's court this murky afternoon besides the Lord Chancellor, the counsel in the cause, two or three counsel who are never in any cause, and the well of solicitors before mentioned? There is the registrar below the judge, in wig and gown; and there are two or three maces, or petty-bags, or privy-purses, or whatever they may be, in legal court suits. These are all yawning, for no crumb of amusement ever falls from JARNDYCE AND JARNDYCE (the cause in hand), which was squeezed dry years upon years ago. The short-hand writers, the reporters of the court, and the reporters of the newspapers invariably decamp with the rest of the regulars when Jarndyce and Jarndyce comes on. Their places are a blank. Standing on a seat at the side of the hall, the better to peer into the curtained sanctuary, is a little mad old woman in a squeezed bonnet, who is always in court, from its sitting to its rising, and always expecting some incomprehensible judg-ment to be given in her favour. Some say she really is, or was, a party to a suit, but no one knows for certain because no one cares. She carries some small litter in a reticule which she calls her documents, principally consisting of paper matches and dry lavender. A sallow prisoner has come up, in custody, for the half-dozenth time to make a personal application "to purge himself of his contempt," which, being a solitary surviving executor who has fallen into a state of conglomeration about accounts of which it is not pretended that he had ever any knowledge, he is not at all likely ever to do. In the meantime his prospects in life are ended. Another ruined suitor, who periodically appears from Shropshire, and breaks out into efforts to address the Chancellor at the close of the day's business and who can by no means be made to understand that the Chancellor is legally ignorant of his existence after making it desolate for a quarter of a century, plants himself in a good place and keeps an eye on the judge, ready to call out "My Lord!" in a voice of sonorous complaint on the instant of his rising. A few lawyers' clerks and others who know this suitor by sight linger on the chance of his furnishing some fun and enlivening the dismal weather a little.

Jarndyce and Jarndyce drones on. This scarecrow of a suit has, in course of time, become so complicated that no man alive knows what it means. The parties to it understand it least, but it has been observed that no two Chancery lawyers can talk about it for five minutes without coming to a total disagreement as to all the premises. Innumerable children have been born into the cause; innumerable young people have married into it; innumerable old people have died out of it. Scores of persons have deliriously found themselves made parties in Jarndyce and Jarndyce without knowing how or why; whole families have inherited legendary hatreds with the suit. The little plaintiff or defendant who was promised a new rocking-horse when Jarndyce and Jarndyce should be settled has grown up, possessed himself of a real horse, and trotted away into the other world. Fair wards of court have faded into mothers and grandmothers; a long procession of Chancellors has come in and gone out; the legion of bills in the suit have been transformed into mere bills of mortality; there are not three Jarndyces left upon the earth perhaps since old Tom Jarndyce in despair blew his brains out at a coffee-house in Chancery Lane; but Jarndyce and Jarndyce still drags its dreary length before the court, perennially hopeless.

Jarndyce and Jarndyce has passed into a joke. That is the only good that has ever come of it. It has been death to many, but it is a joke in the profession. Every master in Chancery has had a reference out of it. Every Chancellor was "in it," for somebody or other, when he was counsel at the bar. Good things have been said about it by blue-nosed, bulbous-shoed old benchers in select port-wine committee after dinner in hall. Articled clerks have been in the habit of fleshing their legal wit upon it. The last Lord Chancellor handled it neatly, when, correcting Mr Blowers, the eminent silk gown who said that such a thing might happen when the sky rained potatoes, he observed, "or when we get through Jarndyce and Jarndyce, Mr Blowers"—a pleasantry that particularly tickled the maces, bags, and purses.

How many people out of the suit, Jarndyce and Jarndyce has stretched forth its unwholesome hand to spoil and corrupt, would be a very wide question. From the master upon whose impaling files reams of dusty warrants in Jarndyce and Jarndyce have grimly writhed into many shapes, down to the copying clerk in the Six Clerks' Office who has copied his tens of thousands of Chancery folio-pages under that eternal heading, no man's nature has been made better by it. In trickery, evasion, procrastination, spoliation, botheration, under false pretences of all sorts, there are influences that can never come to good. The very solicitors' boys who have kept the wretched suitors at bay, by protesting time out of mind that Mr Chizzle, Mizzle, or otherwise was particularly engaged and had appointments until dinner, may have got an extra moral twist and shuffle into themselves out of Jarndyce and Jarndyce. The receiver in the cause has acquired a goodly sum of money by it but has acquired too a distrust of his own mother and a contempt for his own kind. Chizzle, Mizzle, and otherwise have lapsed into a habit of vaguely promising themselves that they will look into that outstanding little matter and see what can be done for Drizzle—who was not well used—when Jarndyce and Jarndyce shall be got out of the office. Shirking and sharking, in all their many varieties, have been sown broadcast by the ill-fated cause; and even those who have contemplated its history from the outer-most circle of such evil have been insensibly tempted into a loose way of letting bad things alone to take their own bad course, and a loose belief that if the world go wrong it was in some off-hand manner never meant to go right.

Thus, in the midst of the mud and at the heart of the fog, sits the Lord High Chancellor in his High Court of Chancery.

"Mr Tangle," says the Lord High Chancellor, latterly something restless under the eloquence of that learned gentleman.

"Mlud," says Mr Tangle. Mr Tangle knows more of Jarndyce and Jarndyce than anybody. He is famous for it—supposed never to have read anything else since he left school.

"Have you nearly concluded your argument?"

"Mlud, no—variety of points—feel it my duty tsubmit—ludship," is the reply that slides out of Mr Tangle.

"Several members of the bar are still to be heard, I believe?" says the Chancellor with a slight smile.

Eighteen of Mr Tangle's learned friends, each armed with a little summary of eighteen hundred sheets, bob up like eighteen hammers in a pianoforte, make eighteen bows, and drop into their eighteen places of obscurity.

"We will proceed with the hearing on Wednesday fortnight," says the Chancellor. For the question at issue is only a question of costs, a mere bud on the forest tree of the parent suit, and really will come to a settlement one of these days.

The Chancellor rises; the bar rises; the prisoner is brought forward in a hurry; the man from Shropshire cries, "My lord!" Maces, bags, and purses indignantly proclaim silence and frown at the man from Shropshire.

"In reference," proceeds the Chancellor, still on Jarndyce and Jarndyce, "to the young girl—"

"Begludship's pardon—boy," says Mr Tangle prematurely.

"In reference," proceeds the Chancellor with extra distinctness, "to the young girl and boy, the two young people,"

(Mr Tangle crushed.)

"Whom I directed to be in attendance today and who are now in my private room, I will see them and satisfy myself as to the expediency of making the order for their residing with their uncle."

Mr Tangle on his legs again.

"Begludship's pardon—dead."

"With their,"—Chancellor looking through his double eye-glass at the papers on his desk, "grandfather."

"Begludship's pardon—victim of rash action—brains."

Suddenly a very little counsel with a terrific bass voice arises, fully inflated, in the back settlements of the fog, and says, "Will your lordship allow me? I appear for him. He is a cousin, several times removed. I am not at the moment prepared to inform the court in what exact remove he is a cousin, but he *is* a cousin."

Leaving this address (delivered like a sepulchral message) ringing in the rafters of the roof, the very little counsel drops, and the fog knows him no more. Everybody looks for him. Nobody can see him.

"I will speak with both the young people," says the Chancellor anew, "and satisfy myself on the subject of their residing with their cousin. I will mention the matter tomorrow morning when I take my seat."

The Chancellor is about to bow to the bar when the prisoner is presented. Nothing can possibly come of the prisoner's conglomeration but his being sent back to prison, which is soon done. The man from Shropshire ventures another remonstrative "My lord!" but the Chancellor, being aware of him, has dexterously vanished. Everybody else quickly vanishes too. A battery of blue bags is loaded with heavy charges of papers and carried off by clerks; the little mad old woman marches off with her documents; the empty court is locked up. If all the injustice it has committed and all the misery it has caused could only be locked up with it, and the whole burnt away in a great funeral pyre—why, so much the better for other parties than the parties in Jarndyce and Jarndyce!

Notes

1. *The Court of Chancery.* Dickens skewers the Court of Chancery for its delay, allegiance to technicalities, and indifference to human values. Ironically, the Court of Chancery developed from the medieval practice of

appealing to the Chancellor, a royal official, for relief from the hardships resulting from the strict application of the law. Thus, Chancery's original purpose was to ameliorate the harshness of law by consulting principles of equity. In time, however, the doctrines and procedures of Chancery became just as ossified as those of Law.

2. *Setting.* This first chapter of BLEAK HOUSE is justly famous for its atmospheric quality. Rarely has a novelist so effectively set his scene. Identify the stylistic elements of this chapter that make it so effective.

* * *

D. TALL TALES

RUMPELSTILTSKIN
Jacob Grimm and Wilhelm Grimm

Once there was a miller who was poor, but who had a beautiful daughter. Now it happened that he had to go and speak to the king, and in order to make himself appear important he said to him, "I have a daughter who can spin straw into gold."

The king said to the miller, "That is an art which pleases me well; if your daughter is as clever as you say, bring her to-morrow to my palace, and I will put her to the test."

And when the girl was brought to him he took her into a room which was quite full of straw, gave her a spinning-wheel and a reel, and said, "Now set to work, and if by to-morrow morning early you have not spun this straw into gold during the night, you must die." Thereupon he himself locked up the room, and left her in it alone. So there sat the poor miller's daughter, and for the life of her could not tell what to do, she had no idea how straw could be spun into gold, and she grew more and more frightened, until at last she began to weep.

But all at once the door opened, and in came a little man, and said, "Good evening, mistress miller, why are you crying so?"

"Alas," answered the girl, "I have to spin straw into gold, and I do not know how to do it."

"What will you give me," said the manikin, "if I do it for you?"

"My necklace," said the girl.

The little man took the necklace, seated himself in front of the wheel, and whirr, whirr, whirr, three turns, and the reel was full, then he put another on, and whirr, whirr, whirr, three times round, and the second was full too. And so it went on until the morning, when all the straw was spun, and all the reels were full of gold.

By daybreak the king was already there, and when he saw the gold he was astonished and delighted, but his heart became only more greedy. He had the miller's daughter taken into another room full of straw, which was much larger, and commanded her to spin that also in one night if she valued her life. The girl knew not how to help herself, and was crying, when the door opened again, and the little man appeared, and said, "What will you give me if I spin that straw into gold for you?"

"The ring on my finger," answered the girl.

The little man took the ring, again began to turn the wheel, and by morning had spun all the straw into glittering gold.

The king rejoiced beyond measure at the sight, but still he had not gold enough, and he had the miller's daughter taken into a still larger room full of straw, and said, "You must spin this, too, in the course of this night, but if you succeed, you shall be my wife." Even if she be a miller's daughter, thought he, I could not find a richer wife in the whole world.

When the girl was alone the manikin came again for the third time, and said, "What will you give me if I spin the straw for you this time also?"

"I have nothing left that I could give," answered the girl.

"Then promise me, if you should become queen, to give me your first child."

Who knows whether that will ever happen, thought the miller's daughter, and, not knowing how else to help herself in this strait, she promised the manikin what he wanted, and for that he once more spun the straw into gold.

And when the king came in the morning, and found all as he had wished, he took her in marriage, and the pretty miller's daughter became a queen.

A year after, she brought a beautiful child into the world, and she never gave a thought to the manikin. But suddenly he came into her room, and said, "Now give me what you promised."

The queen was horror-struck, and offered the manikin all the riches of the kingdom if he would leave her the child. But the manikin said, "No, something alive is dearer to me than all the treasures in the world."

Then the queen began to lament and cry, so that the manikin pitied her.

"I will give you three days' time," said he, "and if by that time you find out my name, then shall you keep your child."

So the queen thought the whole night of all the names that she had ever heard, and she sent a messenger over the country to inquire, far and wide, for any other names that there might be. When the manikin came the next day, she began with Caspar, Melchior, Balthazar, and said all the names she knew, one after another, but to every one the little man said, "That is not my name."

On the second day she had inquiries made in the neighborhood as to the names of the people there, and she repeated to the manikin the most uncommon and curious. Perhaps your name is Shortribs, or Sheep-shanks, or Laceleg, but he always answered, "That is not my name."

On the third day the messenger came back again, and said, "I have not been able to find a single new name, but as I came to a high mountain at the end of the forest, where the fox and the hare bid each other good night, there I saw a little house, and before the house a fire was burning, and round about the fire quite a ridiculous little man was jumping, he hopped upon one leg, and shouted—

"To-day I bake, to-morrow brew,

The next I'll have the young queen's child.

Ha! glad am I that no one knew

That Rumpelstiltskin I am styled."

You may imagine how glad the queen was when she heard the name. And when soon afterwards the little man came in, and asked, "Now, mistress queen, what is my name?"

At first she said, "Is your name Conrad?"

"No."

"Is your name Harry?"

"No."

"Perhaps your name is Rumpelstiltskin?"

"The devil has told you that! The devil has told you that!" cried the little man, and in his anger he plunged his right foot so deep into the earth that his whole leg went in, and then in rage he pulled at his left leg so hard with both hands that he tore himself in two.

Notes

1. *Rumpelstiltskin.* What moral does this story illustrate, if any? Is this story as good as *The Lord of the Rings*? *The Narnia Chronicle*? *Star Wars*? *Harry Potter*?

Why do people yearn after the supernatural in stories? Is this yearning in keeping with the scientific mind? The practical? The legal?

Compare the style of the Grimm brothers with that of Kafka.

2. *Naming.* Whatever moral, if any, this or any of the other weird Grimm children stories may have, *Rumpelstiltskin* touches on the age-old concept of naming. Just before Odysseus and his men escape the deadly grasp of the Cyclops Polyphemus, Odysseus cannot resist turning on his tormentor to reveal his true name:

> Cyclops, if any one of mortal men shall ask thee of the unsightly blinding of thine eye, say that it was Odysseus that blinded it, the waster of cities, son of Laertes, whose dwelling is in Ithaca.

"After God had created man in his own image," according to *Genesis* 2:19, "out of the ground the Lord God formed every beast of the field, and every fowl of the air; and brought them to Adam to see what he would call them: and whatever Adam called every living creature, that was the name thereof."

Mark Twain has it, in *The Bible According to Mark Twain*, that the "new creature" (Eve) does the naming, onomatopoetically. Muses Adam:

> I got no chance to name anything myself. The new creature names everything that comes along, before I can get in a protest. And always the same pretext is offered—it *looks* like the thing. There is the dodo, for instance. Says the moment one looks at it one sees at a glance that it "looks like a dodo." It will have to keep that name, no doubt. It wearies me to fret about it, and it does no good, anyway. Dodo! It looks no more like a dodo that I do.

The purist may object to describing Eve's naming as onomatopoeic. But neurologists contend that the senses interact. *See* Lila Guterman, *Do You Smell What I Hear? Neuroscientists Discover Crosstalk Among the Senses*, THE CHRONICLE OF HIGHER EDUCATION A17 (Dec. 14, 2001).

One of the most electrifying naming stories of all times appears in Chapter 32 of *Genesis*. The great schemer, Jacob, who had tricked his brother Esau, his father Isaac, and his father-in-law Laban, was returning home when he heard that his brother Esau was coming to meet him, "and four hundred men with him." Jacob was badly frightened, because Esau had threatened to slay him twenty years earlier for the deceit Jacob practiced on their father in stealing Esau's patrimonial blessing:

> [22] And he rose up that night, and took his two wives, and his two womenservants, and his eleven sons, and passed over the ford Jabbok.

> [23] And he took them, and sent them over the brook, and sent over that he had.

> [24] And Jacob was left alone; and there wrestled a man with him until the breaking of day.

> [25] And when he saw that he prevailed not against him, he touched the hollow of his thigh; and the hollow of Jacob's thigh was out of joint, as he wrestled with him.

> [26] And he said, Let me go, for the day breaketh. And he said, I will not let thee go, except thou bless me.

> [27] And he said unto him, What is thy name? And he said, Jacob.

> [28] And he said, Thy name shall be called no more Jacob, but Israel: for as a prince hast thou power with God and with men, and hast prevailed.

> [29] And Jacob asked him, and said, Tell me, I pray thee, thy name. And he said, Wherefore is it that thou dost ask after my name? And he blessed him there.

THE CELEBRATED JUMPING FROG
OF CALAVERAS COUNTY
Mark Twain

In compliance with the request of a friend of mine, who wrote me from the East, I called on good-natured, garrulous old Simon Wheeler, and inquired after my friend's friend, Leonidas W. Smiley, as requested to do, and I hereunto append the result. I have a lurking suspicion that Leonidas W. Smiley is a myth; that my friend never knew such a personage; and that he only conjectured that, if I asked old Wheeler about him, it would remind him of his infamous *Jim* Smiley, and he would go to work and bore me nearly to death with some infernal reminiscence of him as long and tedious as it should be useless to me. If that was the design, it certainly succeeded.

I found Simon Wheeler dozing comfortably by the bar-room stove of the old, dilapidated tavern in the ancient mining camp of Angel's, and I noticed that he was fat and bald-headed, and had an expression of winning gentleness and simplicity upon his tranquil countenance. He roused up and gave me good-day. I told him a friend of mine had commissioned me to make some inquiries about a cherished companion of his boyhood named Leonidas W. Smiley—Rev. Leonidas W. Smiley—a young minister of the Gospel, who he had heard was at one time a resident of Angel's Camp. I added that, if Mr. Wheeler could tell me anything about this Rev. Leonidas W. Smiley, I would feel under many obligations to him.

Simon Wheeler backed me into a corner and blockaded me there with his chair, and then sat me down and reeled off the monotonous narrative which follows this paragraph. He never smiled, he never frowned, he never changed his voice from the gentle-flowing key to which he tuned the initial sentence, he never betrayed the slightest suspicion of enthusiasm; but all through the interminable narrative there ran a vein of impressive earnestness and sincerity, which showed me plainly that, so far from his imagining that there was any thing ridiculous or funny about his story, he regarded it as a really important matter, and admired its two heroes as men of transcendent genius in *finesse.* To me, the spectacle of a man drifting serenely along through such a queer yarn without ever smiling, was exquisitely absurd. As I said before, I asked him to tell me what he knew of Rev. Leonidas W. Smiley, and he replied as follows. I let him go on in his own way, and never interrupted him once:

There was a feller here once by the name of *Jim* Smiley, in the winter of '49—, maybe it was the spring of '50—I don't recollect exactly, somehow, though what makes me think it was one or the other is because I remember the big flume wasn't finished when he first came to the camp; but anyway, he was the curiosest man about always betting on anything that turned up you ever see, if he could get any body to bet on the other side; and if he couldn't, he'd change sides. Any way that suited the other man would suit him—anyway just so's he got a bet, *he* was satisfied. But still he was lucky, uncommon lucky; he most always come out winner. He was always ready and laying for a chance; there couldn't be no solitry thing mentioned but that feller'd offer to bet on it, and take ary side you please, as I was just telling you. If there was a horse-race, you'd find him flush, or you'd find him busted at the end of it; if there was a dog-fight, he'd bet on it; if there was a cat-fight, he'd bet on it; if there was a chicken-fight, he'd bet on it; why, if there was two birds setting on a fence, he would bet you which one would fly first; or if there was a camp-meeting, he would be there reg'lar, to bet on Parson Walker, which he judged to be the best exhorter about here, and so he was, too, and a good man. If he even seen a straddle-bug start to go anywheres, he would bet you how long it would take him to get wherever he was going to, and if you took him up, he would foller that straddle-bug to Mexico but what he would find out where he was bound for and how long he was on the road. Lots of the boys here has seen that Smiley, and can tell you about him. Why, it never made no difference to *him*—he would bet on *any* thing—the dangdest feller. Parson Walker's wife laid very sick once, for a good while, and it seemed as if they warn't going to save her; but one morning he come in, and Smiley asked how she was, and he said she was considerable better—thank the Lord for his inf'nit mercy—and coming on so smart that, with the blessing of Prov'dence, she'd get well yet; and Smiley, before he thought, says, "Well, I'll risk two-and-a-half that she don't, anyway."

Thish-yer Smiley had a mare—the boys called her the fifteen-minute nag, but that was only in fun, you know, because, of course, she was faster than that—and he used to win money on that horse, for all she was so slow and always had the asthma, or the distemper, or the consumption, or something of that kind. They used to give her two or three hundred yards' start, and then pass her under way; but always at the fag-end of the race she'd get excited and desperate-like, and come cavorting and straddling up, and scattering her legs around limber, sometimes in the air, and sometimes out to one side amongst the fences, and kicking up m-o-r-e dust, and raising m-o-r-e racket with her coughing and sneezing and blowing her nose—and always fetch up at the stand just about a neck ahead, as near as you could cipher it down.

And he had a little small bull pup, that to look at him you'd think he wan't worth a cent, but to set around and look ornery, and lay for a chance to steal something. But as soon as money was up on him, he was a different dog; his under-jaw'd begin to stick out like the fo'castle of a steamboat, and his teeth would uncover, and shine savage like the furnaces. And a dog might tackle him, and bully-rag him, and bite him, and throw him over his shoulder two or three times, and Andrew Jackson—which was the name of the pup—Andrew Jackson would never let on but what *he* was satisfied, and hadn't expected nothing else—and the bets being doubled and doubled on the other side all the time, till the money was all up; and then all of a sudden he would grab that other dog jest by the j'int of his hind leg and freeze to it—not chew, you understand, but only jest grip and hang on till they throwed up the sponge, if it was a year. Smiley always come out winner on that pup, till he harnessed a dog once that didn't have no hind legs, because they'd been sawed off by a circular saw, and when the thing had gone along far enough, and the money was all up, and he come to make a snatch for his pet holt, he saw in a minute how he'd been imposed on, and how the other dog had him in the door, so to speak, and he 'peared surprised, and then he looked sorter discouraged-like, and didn't try no more to win the fight, and so he got shucked out bad. He give Smiley a look, as much as to say his heart was broke, and it was *his* fault, for putting up a dog that hadn't no hind legs for him to take holt of, which was his main dependence in a fight, and then he limped off a piece and laid down and died. It was a good pup, was that Andrew Jackson, and would have made a name for hisself if he'd lived, for the stuff was in him, and he had genius—I know it, because he hadn't had no opportunities to speak of, and it don't stand to reason that a dog could make such a fight as he could under them circumstances, if he hadn't no talent. It always makes me feel sorry when I think of that last fight of his'n, and the way it turned out.

Well, thish-yer Smiley had rat-tarriers, and chicken cocks, and tom-cats, and all them kind of things, till you couldn't rest, and you couldn't fetch nothing for him to bet on but he'd match you. He ketched a frog one day, and took him home, and said he cal'klated to edercate him; and so he never done nothing for three months but set in his back yard and learn that frog to jump. And you bet you he *did* learn him, too. He'd give him a little punch behind, and the next minute you'd see that frog whirling in the air like a doughnut—see him turn one summerset, or may be a couple, if he got a good start, and come down flat-footed and all right, like a cat. He got him up so in the matter of catching flies, and kept him in practice so constant, that he'd nail a fly everytime as far as he could see him. Smiley said all a frog wanted was education, and he could do most anything—and I believe him. Why, I've seen him set Dan'l Webster down here on this floor—Dan'l Webster was the name of the frog—and sing out, "Flies, Dan'l, flies!" and quicker'n you could wink, he'd spring straight up, and snake a fly off'n the counter there, and flop down on the floor again as solid as a gob of mud, and fall to scratching the side of his head with his hind foot as indifferent as if he hadn't no idea he'd been doin' any more'n any frog might do. You never see a frog so modest and straightfor'ard as he was, for all he was so gifted. And when it come to fair and square jumping on a dead level, he could get over more ground at one straddle than any animal of his breed you ever see. Jumping on a dead level was his strong suit, you understand; and when it come to that, Smiley would ante up money on him as long as he had a red. Smiley was monstrous proud of his frog, and well he might be, for fellers that had traveled and been everywheres, all said he laid over any frog that ever *they* see.

Well, Smiley kept the beast in a little lattice box, and he used to fetch him down town sometimes and lay for a bet. One day a feller—a stranger in the camp, he was—come across him with his box, and says:

"What might it be that you've got in the box?"

And Smiley says, sorter indifferent like, "It might be a parrot, or it might be a canary, maybe, but it an't—it's only just a frog."

And the feller took it, and looked at it careful, and turned it round this way and that, and says, "H'm—so 'tis. Well, what's *he* good for?"

"Well," Smiley says, easy and careless, "He's good enough for *one* thing, I should judge—he can outjump any frog in Calaveras county."

The feller took the box again, and took another long, particular look, and give it back to Smiley, and says, very deliberate, "Well, I don't see no p'ints about that frog that's any better'n any other frog."

"Maybe you don't," Smiley says. "Maybe you understand frogs, and maybe you don't understand 'em; maybe you've had experience, and maybe you an't only a amature, as it were. Anyways, I've got *my* opinion, and I'll risk forty dollars that he can outjump any frog in Calaveras county."

And the feller studied a minute, and then says, kinder sad like, "Well, I'm only a stranger here, and I an't got no frog; but if I had a frog, I'd bet you."

And then Smiley says, "That's all right—that's all right—if you'll hold my box a minute, I'll go and get you a frog." And so the feller took the box, and put up his forty dollars along with Smiley's, and set down to wait.

So he set there a good while thinking and thinking to hisself, and then he got the frog out and prized his mouth open and took a teaspoon and filled him full of quail shot—filled him pretty near up to his chin—and set him on the floor. Smiley he went to the swamp and slopped around in the mud for a long time, and finally he ketched a frog, and fetched him in, and give him to this feller, and says:

"Now, if you're ready, set him alongside of Dan'l, with his fore-paws just even with Dan'l, and I'll give the word." Then he says, "One—two—three—jump!" and him and the feller touched up the frogs from behind, and the new frog hopped off, but Dan'l give a heave, and hysted up his shoulders—so—like a Frenchman, but it wan't no use—he couldn't budge; he was planted as solid as an anvil, and he couldn't no more stir than if he was anchored out. Smiley was a good deal surprised, and he was disgusted too, but he didn't have no idea what the matter was, of course.

The feller took the money and started away; and when he was going out at the door, he sorter jerked his thumb over his shoulders—this way—at Dan'l, and says again, very deliberate, "Well, *I* don't see no p'ints about that frog that's any better'n any other frog."

Smiley he stood scratching his head and looking down at Dan'l a long time, and at last he says, "I do wonder what in the nation that frog throw'd off for—I wonder if there an't something the matter with him—he 'pears to look mighty baggy, somehow." And he ketched Dan'l by the nap of the neck, and lifted him up and says, "Why, blame my cats, if he don't weigh five pound!" and turned him upside down, and he belched out a double handful of shot. And then he see how it was, and he was the maddest man—he set the frog down and took out after that feller, but he never ketched him. And—

[Here Simon Wheeler heard his name called from the front yard, and got up to see what was wanted.] And turning to me as he moved away, he said: "Just set where you are, stranger, and rest easy—I an't going to be gone a second."

But, by your leave, I did not think that a continuation of the history of the enterprising vagabond *Jim* Smiley would be likely to afford me much information concerning the Rev. *Leonidas W.* Smiley, and so I started away.

At the door I met the sociable Wheeler returning, and he button-holed me and recommenced:

"Well, thish-yer Smiley had a yaller one-eyed cow that didn't have no tail, only jest a short stump like a bannanner, and—"

"Oh! hang Smiley and his afflicted cow!" I muttered, good-naturedly, and bidding the old gentleman good-day, I departed.

INTERVENING, SUPERSEDING CAUSE
Anon.

The most subtil Serpent had led Eve to the Tree of Knowledge of Good and Evil, and was now cajoling her to have a bite. "Why should God not want you to learn the difference between good and evil? It is a virtue devoutly to be desired. How could He possibly be angry at your attempts at self-improvement?"

So she did eat, or at least she started to.

Shortly before Eve's arrival at the Tree, a Bird of Paradise had flown over the spot and had had in an in-flight bowel movement, and the excrement had fallen on the very apple Eve now chose to sample.

As soon as she bit into the apple she expelled the bite violently with an execration. She flung the remainder of the apple into the forest, and the Serpent slunk away in dismay.

That same day, in the cool of the evening, God was taking a stroll in the Garden when by chance He encountered Eve.

"My dear Eve, mother of mankind," He began in his most unctuous voice, "do you know if anyone has been eating of the Tree of Forbidden Fruit?"

"Not me, my Lord," she responded sheepishly.

"I think otherwise," He pontificated.

"One of the apples is missing from the Tree, and Uriel says he distictly recalls having glimpsed you at the tree in the presence of the subtil Serpent at about noontime today."

Realizing that truth is always the best policy, particularly when you are cornered, Eve reluctantly responded:

"Well, my Lord, yes, I did take a little bite, but I spat it out because it tasted like bird shit."

"I beg your pardon?" the Lord interrupted huffily.

"Bird shit," she repeated. "Then I flung the apple away into the forest. Come, I'll show you if you like."

"That will not be necessary," He replied haughtily. "And you didn't swallow any of the apple?"

"No, my Lord, I didn't."

"Intending to sin is just as bad as sinning," the Lord announced sententiously.

"May I remind my Lord," said Eve, "that you simply told us 'Thou shalt not eat,' You never said anything about not thinking about eating."

"My God!" exclaimed God to Himself. He was taken aback, and filled with premonitions.

Note

1. *Performative Revisited.* Suppose the events as described in *Intervening, Superseding Cause* had occurred in *Genesis* 3. Would Eve be guilty of mortal sin? Is your answer that of a moralist, or of a lawyer?

MAN THREW DOG FROM BALCONY

Terrence Davies, aged 32, a labourer, of Brixton, South London, who threw a mongrel bitch to its death from his fourth-floor balcony, was sentenced to six weeks' imprisonment suspended for two years, and banned from keeping a dog for five years by Camberwell magistrates yesterday.

He admitted ill-treating the animal after it pulled down washing on his balcony.

Note

1. *Stranger Than Fiction.* This short article appeared as prominently as news may be displayed in one of the world's leading and intellectual newspapers. Therefore, it must be assumed that the item was newsworthy, or so the editors thought. A Brit said that had Mr. Davies thrown his wife over the balcony, it would have hardly merited a mention in the obituaries.

One can only speculate why on this particular occasion Mr. Davies chose to hurl his mongrel bitch to her death. Had he had a run-in with his wife, and was he throwing her over the balcony in effigy? Had the dog pulled down his washing from the balcony on former occasions, or was this the first unnerving occasion? Could the washing not be hung elsewhere, or the balcony door closed? All these and many other questions that would intrigue a Sherlock Holmes leap to the mind.

Who reported him—a neighbor, or his wife? Or did he turn himself in? Did he, or does he, feel any remorse? Once the five-year injunction has expired, will he get another dog? Or will he get a cat? Can he get a cat now?

E. PARABLES FROM THE KING JAMES BIBLE, NEW TESTAMENT

THE SOWER
Matthew 13:1–8

[1] The same day went Jesus out of the house, and sat by the sea side.

[2] And great multitudes were gathered together unto him, so that he went into a ship, and sat; and the whole multitude stood on the shore.

[3] And he spake many things unto them in parables, saying, Behold, a sower went forth to sow;

[4] And when he sowed, some seeds fell by the way side, and the fowls came and devoured them up:

[5] Some fell upon stony places, where they had not much earth: and forthwith they sprung up, because they had no deepness of earth:

[6] And when the sun was up, they were scorched; and because they had no root, they withered away.

[7] And some fell among thorns; and the thorns sprung up, and choked them:

[8] But other fell into good ground, and brought forth fruit, some an hundredfold, some sixtyfold, some thirtyfold.

THE VINEYARD KEEPER
Matthew 20:1–16

[1] For the kingdom of heaven is like unto a man that is an householder, which went out early in the morning to hire labourers into his vineyard.

[2] And when he had agreed with the labourers for a penny a day, he sent them into his vineyard.

[3] And he went out about the third hour, and saw others standing idle in the marketplace,

[4] And said unto them, Go ye also into the vineyard, and whatsoever is right I will give you. And they went their way.

[5] Again he went out about the sixth and the ninth hour, and did likewise.

[6] And about the eleventh hour he went out, and found others standing idle, and saith unto them, Why stand ye here all the day idle?

[7] They say unto him, Because no man hath hired us. He saith unto them, Go ye also into the vineyard; and whatsoever is right, that shall ye receive.

[8] So when even was come, the lord of the vineyard saith unto his steward, Call the labourers, and give them their hire, beginning from the last unto the first.

[9] And when they came that were hired about the eleventh hour, they received every man a penny.

[10] But when the first came, they supposed that they should have received more; and they likewise received every man a penny.

[11] And when they received it, they murmured against the goodman of the house,

[12] Saying, These last have wrought but one hour, and thou hast made them equal unto us, which have borne the burden and heat of the day.

[13] But he answered one of them, and said, Friend, I do thee no wrong: didst not thou agree with me for a penny?

[14] Take that thine is, and go thy way: I will give unto this last, even as unto thee.

[15] Is it not lawful for me to do what I will with mine own? Is thine eye evil, because I am good?

[16] So the last shall be first, and the first last: for many be called, but few chosen.

THE TALENTS
Matthew 25:14–30

[14] For the kingdom of heaven is as a man travelling into a far country, who called his own servants, and delivered unto them his goods.

[15] And unto one he gave five talents, to another two. and to another one; to every man according to his several ability; and straightway took to his journey.

[16] Then he that had received the five talents went and traded with the same, and made them other five talents.

[17] And likewise he that had received two, he also gained other two.

[18] But he that had received one went and digged in the earth, and hid his lord's money.

[19] After a long time the lord of those servants cometh, and reckoneth with them.

[20] And so he that had received five talents came and brought other five talents, saying, Lord, thou deliveredst unto me five talents: behold, I have gained beside them five talents more.

[21] His lord said unto him, Well done, thou good and faithful servant: thou hast been faithful over a few things, I will make thee ruler over many things; enter thou into the joy of thy lord.

[22] He also that had received two talents came and said, Lord, thou deliveredst unto me two talents: behold, I have gained two other talents beside them.

[23] His lord said unto him, Well done, good and faithful servant; thou hast been faithful over a few things, I will make thee ruler over many things; enter thou into the joy of thy lord.

[24] Then he which had received the one talent came and said, Lord, I knew thee that thou art an hard man, reaping where thou hast not sown, and gathering where thou hast not strawed:

[25] And I was afraid, and went and hid thy talent in the earth: lo, there thou hast that is thine.

[26] His lord answered and said unto him, Thou wicked and slothful servant, thou knewest that I reap where I sowed not, and gather where I have not strawed:

[27] Thou oughtest therefore to have put my money to the exchangers, and then at my coming I should have received mine own with usury.

[28] Take therefore the talent from him, and give it unto him which hath ten talents.

[29] For unto every one that hath shall be given, and he shall have abundance: but from him that hath not shall be taken away even that which he hath.

[30] And cast ye the unprofitable servant into outer darkness: there shall be weeping and gnashing of teeth.

THE GOOD SAMARITAN
Luke 10:25–37

[25] And, behold, a certain lawyer stood up and tempted him, saying, Master, what shall I do to inherit eternal life?

[26] He said unto him, what is written in the law? How readest thou?

[27] And he answering said, Thou shalt love the Lord thy God with all thy heart, and with all thy soul, and with all thy strength, and with all thy mind; and thy neighbour as thyself.

[28] And he said unto him, thou hast answered right: this do, and thou shalt live.

[29] But he, willing to justify himself, said unto Jesus, and who is my neighbour?

[30] And Jesus answering said, A certain man went down from Jerusalem to Jericho, and fell among thieves, which stripped him of his raiment, and wounded him, and departed, leaving him half dead.

³¹ And by chance there came down a certain priest that way: and when he saw him, he passed by on the other side.

³² And likewise a Levite, when he was at the place, came and looked on him, and passed by on the other side.

³³ But a certain Samaritan, as he journeyed, came where he was: and when he saw him, he had compassion on him.

³⁴ And went to him, and bound up his wounds, pouring in oil and wine, and set him on his own beast, and brought him to an inn, and took care of him.

³⁵ And on the morrow when he departed, he took out two pence, and gave them to the host, and said unto him, Take care of him; and whatsoever thou spendest more, when I come again, I will repay thee.

³⁶ Which now of these three, thinkest thou, was neighbour unto him that fell among the thieves?

³⁷ And he said, He that shewed mercy on him. Then said Jesus unto him, Go, and do thou likewise.

THE PRODIGAL SON
Luke 15:11–32

¹¹ And he said, a certain man had two sons:

¹² And the younger of them said to his father, Father, give me the portion of goods that falleth to me. And he divided unto them his living.

¹³ And not many days after the younger son gathered all together, and took his journey into a far country, and there wasted his substance with riotous living.

¹⁴ And when he had spent all, there arose a mighty famine in the land: and he began to be in want.

¹⁵ And he went and joined himself to a citizen of that country; and he sent him into his fields to feed swine.

¹⁶ And he would fain have filled his belly with the husks that the swine did eat: and no man gave unto him.

¹⁷ And when he came to himself, he said, How many hired servants of my father's have bread enough to spare, and I perish with hunger!

¹⁸ I will arise and go to my father, and will say unto him, Father, I have sinned against heaven, and before thee.

¹⁹ And am no more worthy to be called thy son: make me as one of thy hired servants.

²⁰ And he arose, and came to his father. But when he was yet a great way off, his father saw him, and had compassion, and ran, and fell on his neck, and kissed him.

²¹ And the son said unto him, Father, I have sinned against heaven, and in thy sight, and am no more worthy to be called thy son.

²² But the father said to his servants, bring forth the best robe, and put it on him: and put a ring on his hand, and shoes on his feet:

²³ And bring hither the fatted calf, and kill it; and let us eat, and be merry:

²⁴ For this my son was dead, and is alive again; he was lost, and is found. And they began to be merry.

²⁵ Now his elder son was in the field: and as he came and drew nigh to the house, he heard musick and dancing.

²⁶ And he called one of the servants, and asked what these things meant.

²⁷ And he said unto him, Thy brother is come; and thy father hath killed the fatted calf, because he hath received him safe and sound.

²⁸ And he was angry, and would not go in: therefore came his father out, and intreated him.

²⁹ And he answering said to his father, Lo, these many years do I serve thee, neither transgressed I at any time thy commandment: and yet thou never gavest me a kid, that I might make merry with my friends:

³⁰ But as soon as this thy son was come, which hath devoured thy living with harlots, thou hast killed for him the fatted calf.

³¹ And he said unto him, Son, thou art ever with me, and all that I have is thine.

³² It was meet that we should make merry, and be glad: for this thy brother was dead, and is alive again; and was lost, and is found.

THE CLEVER STEWARD
Luke 16:1–9

¹ And he said also unto his disciples, There was certain rich man, which had a steward; and the same was accused unto him that he had wasted his goods.

² And he called him, and said unto him, How is it that I hear this of thee? Give an account of thy stewardship; for thou mayest be no longer steward.

³ Then the steward said within himself, What shall I do? For my lord taketh away from me the stewardship: I cannot dig; to beg I am ashamed.

⁴ I am resolved what to do, that when I am put out of the stewardship, they may receive me into their houses.

⁵ So he called every one of his lord's debtors unto him, and said unto the first, How much owest thou unto my lord?

⁶ And he said, An hundred measures of oil. And he said unto him, Take thy bill, and sit down quickly, and write fifty.

[7] Then said he to another, And how much owest thou? And he said, An hundred measures of wheat. And he said unto him, Take thy bill, and write fourscore.

[8] And the lord commended the unjust steward, because he had done wisely: for the children of this world are in their generation wiser than the children of light.

[9] And I say unto you, Make to yourselves friends of the mammon of unrighteousness; that when ye fail, they may receive you into everlasting habitations.

Notes

1. *A Parable.* Define a parable. Write a parable of your own.

2. *Fairness.* Which, if any, of the preceding parables challenges your idea of fairness or justice? Rewrite any such parable so as to satisfy your sense of fairness or justice.

3. *Mammon.* What is the "mammon of unrighteousness"? How would one go about making friends with it?

F. OLD TESTAMENT STORIES FROM THE KING JAMES BIBLE

The Old Testament stories, like those of the New Testament, have inspired countless generations. The sparseness and vividness of the King James style are nonpareil.

One of the fascinating inquiries in studying the spoken and the written word is to ask what critical things are left out of an account, and why? This inquiry is particularly rewarding when one reads the King James Old Testament stories.

For the spoken word, the intonation of the speaker often provides as many clues to the speaker's meaning as do the words themselves. For the written word, the cadence of the language provides the same kind of insight into meaning as does the intonation of the spoken word. When reading aloud, the reader can imaginatively provide her own interpretation through the intonation of the text.

THE CREATION AND THE FALL
Genesis

Chapter 1

[1] In the beginning God created the heaven and the earth.

[2] And the earth was without form, and void; and darkness was upon the face of the deep. And the Spirit of God moved upon the face of the waters.

[3] And God said, Let there be light: and there was light.

[4] And God saw the light, that it was good: and God divided the light from the darkness.

⁵ And God called the light Day, and the darkness he called Night. And the evening and the morning were the first day.

⁶ And God said, Let there be a firmament in the midst of the waters, and let it divide the waters from the waters.

⁷ And God made the firmament, and divided the waters which were under the firmament from the waters which were above the firmament: and it was so.

⁸ And God called the firmament Heaven. And the evening and the morning were the second day.

⁹ And God said, Let the waters under the heaven be gathered together unto one place, and let the dry land appear: and it was so.

¹⁰ And God called the dry land Earth; and the gathering together of the waters called he Seas: and God saw that it was good.

¹¹ And God said, Let the earth bring forth grass, the herb yielding seed, and the fruit tree yielding fruit after his kind, whose seed is in itself, upon the earth: and it was so.

¹² And the earth brought forth grass, and herb yielding seed after his kind, and the tree yielding fruit, whose seed was in itself, after his kind: and God saw that it was good.

¹³ And the evening and the morning were the third day.

¹⁴ And God said, Let there be lights in the firmament of the heaven to divide the day from the night; and let them be for signs, and for seasons, and for days, and years:

¹⁵ And let them be for lights in the firmament of the heaven to give light upon the earth: and it was so.

¹⁶ And God made two great lights; the greater light to rule the day, and the lesser light to rule the night: he made the stars also.

¹⁷ And God set them in the firmament of the heaven to give light upon the earth,

¹⁸ And to rule over the day and over the night, and to divide the light from the darkness: and God saw that it was good.

¹⁹ And the evening and the morning were the fourth day.

²⁰ And God said, Let the waters bring forth abundantly the moving creature that hath life, and fowl that may fly above the earth in the open firmament of heaven.

²¹ And God created great whales, and every living creature that moveth, which the waters brought forth abundantly, after their kind, and every winged fowl after his kind: and God saw that it was good.

²² And God blessed them, saying, Be fruitful, and multiply, and fill the waters in the seas, and let fowl multiply in the earth.

²³ And the evening and the morning were the fifth day.

[24] And God said, Let the earth bring forth the living creature after his kind, cattle, and creeping thing, and beast of the earth after his kind: and it was so.

[25] And God made the beast of the earth after his kind, and cattle after their kind, and every thing that creepeth upon the earth after his kind: and God saw that it was good.

[26] And God said, Let us make man in our image, after our likeness: and let them have dominion over the fish of the sea, and over the fowl of the air, and over the cattle, and over all the earth, and over every creeping thing that creepeth upon the earth.

[27] So God created man in his own image, in the image of God created he him; male and female created he them.

[28] And God blessed them, and God said unto them, Be fruitful, and multiply, and replenish the earth, and subdue it: and have dominion over the fish of the sea, and over the fowl of the air, and over every living thing that moveth upon the earth.

[29] And God said, Behold, I have given you every herb bearing seed, which is upon the face of all the earth, and every tree, in the which is the fruit of a tree yielding seed; to you it shall be for meat.

[30] And to every beast of the earth, and to every fowl of the air, and to every thing that creepeth upon the earth, wherein there is life, I have given every green herb for meat: and it was so.

[31] And God saw every thing that he had made, and, behold, it was very good. And the evening and the morning were the sixth day.

Chapter 2

[1] Thus the heavens and the earth were finished, and all the host of them.

[2] And on the seventh day God ended his work which he had made; and he rested on the seventh day from all his work which he had made.

[3] And God blessed the seventh day, and sanctified it: because that in it he had rested from all his work which God created and made.

[4] These are the generations of the heavens and of the earth when they were created, in the day that the LORD God made the earth and the heavens,

[5] And every plant of the field before it was in the earth, and every herb of the field before it grew: for the LORD God had not caused it to rain upon the earth, and there was not a man to till the ground.

[6] But there went up a mist from the earth, and watered the whole face of the ground.

[7] And the LORD God formed man of the dust of the ground, and breathed into his nostrils the breath of life; and man became a living soul.

⁸ And the Lord God planted a garden eastward in Eden; and there he put the man whom he had formed.

⁹ And out of the ground made the Lord God to grow every tree that is pleasant to the sight, and good for food; the tree of life also in the midst of the garden, and the tree of knowledge of good and evil.

¹⁰ And a river went out of Eden to water the garden; and from thence it was parted, and became into four heads.

¹¹ The name of the first is Pison: that is it which compasseth the whole land of Havilah, where there is gold;

¹² And the gold of that land is good: there is bdellium and the onyx stone.

¹³ And the name of the second river is Gihon: the same is it that compasseth the whole land of Ethiopia.

¹⁴ And the name of the third river is Hiddekel: that is it which goeth toward the east of Assyria. And the fourth river is Euphrates.

¹⁵ And the Lord God took the man, and put him into the garden of Eden to dress it and to keep it.

¹⁶ And the Lord God commanded the man, saying, Of every tree of the garden thou mayest freely eat:

¹⁷ But of the tree of the knowledge of good and evil, thou shalt not eat of it: for in the day that thou eatest thereof thou shalt surely die.

¹⁸ And the Lord God said, It is not good that the man should be alone; I will make him an help meet for him.

¹⁹ And out of the ground the Lord God formed every beast of the field, and every fowl of the air; and brought them unto Adam to see what he would call them: and whatsoever Adam called every living creature, that was the name thereof.

²⁰ And Adam gave names to all cattle, and to the fowl of the air, and to every beast of the field; but for Adam there was not found an help meet for him.

²¹ And the Lord God caused a deep sleep to fall upon Adam and he slept: and he took one of his ribs, and closed up the flesh instead thereof;

²² And the rib, which the Lord God had taken from man, made he a woman, and brought her unto the man.

²³ And Adam said, This is now bone of my bones, and flesh of my flesh: she shall be called Woman, because she was taken out of Man.

²⁴ Therefore shall a man leave his father and his mother, and shall cleave unto his wife: and they shall be one flesh.

²⁵ And they were both naked, the man and his wife, and were not ashamed.

Chapter 3

[1] Now the serpent was more subtil than any beast of the field which the Lord God had made. And he said unto the woman, Yea, hath God said, Ye shall not eat of every tree of the garden?

[2] And the woman said unto the serpent, We may eat of the fruit of the trees of the garden:

[3] But of the fruit of the tree which is in the midst of the garden, God hath said, Ye shall not eat of it, neither shall ye touch it, lest ye die.

[4] And the serpent said unto the woman, Ye shall not surely die:

[5] For God doth know that in the day ye eat thereof, then your eyes shall be opened, and ye shall be as gods, knowing good and evil.

[6] And when the woman saw that the tree was good for food, and that it was pleasant to the eyes, and a tree to be desired to make one wise, she took of the fruit thereof, and did eat, and gave also unto her husband with her; and he did eat.

[7] And the eyes of them both were opened, and they knew that they were naked; and they sewed fig leaves together, and made themselves aprons.

[8] And they heard the voice of the Lord God walking in the garden in the cool of the day: and Adam and his wife hid themselves from the presence of the Lord God amongst the trees of the garden.

[9] And the Lord God called unto Adam, and said unto him, Where art thou?

[10] And he said, I heard thy voice in the garden, and I was afraid, because I was naked; and I hid myself.

[11] And he said, Who told thee that thou wast naked? Hast thou eaten of the tree, whereof I commanded thee that thou shouldest not eat?

[12] And the man said, The woman whom thou gavest to be with me, she gave me of the tree, and I did eat.

[13] And the Lord God said unto the woman, What is this that thou hast done? And the woman said, The serpent beguiled me, and I did eat.

[14] And the Lord God said unto the serpent, Because thou hast done this, thou art cursed above all cattle, and above every beast of the field; upon thy belly shalt thou go, and dust shalt thou eat all the days of thy life:

[15] And I will put enmity between thee and the woman, and between thy seed and her seed; it shall bruise thy head, and thou shalt bruise his heel.

[16] Unto the woman he said, I will greatly multiply thy sorrow and thy conception; in sorrow thou shalt bring forth children; and thy desire shall be to thy husband, and he shall rule over thee.

[17] And unto Adam he said, Because thou hast hearkened unto the voice of thy wife, and hast eaten of the tree, of which I commanded thee,

saying, Thou shalt not eat of it: cursed is the ground for thy sake; in sorrow shalt thou eat of it all the days of thy life;

[18] Thorns also and thistles shall it bring forth to thee; and thou shalt eat the herb of the field;

[19] In the sweat of thy face shalt thou eat bread, till thou return unto the ground; for out of it wast thou taken: for dust thou art, and unto dust shalt thou return.

[20] And Adam called his wife's name Eve; because she was the mother of all living.

[21] Unto Adam also and to his wife did the LORD God make coats of skins, and clothed them.

[22] And the LORD God said, Behold, the man is become as one of us, to know good and evil: and now, lest he put forth his hand, and take also of the tree of life, and eat, and live for ever:

[23] Therefore the LORD God sent him forth from the garden of Eden, to till the ground from whence he was taken.

[24] So he drove out the man; and he placed at the east of the garden of Eden Cherubims, and a flaming sword which turned every way, to keep the way of the tree of life.

Notes

1. *The Creation.* "In the beginning," *Genesis* 1:1, of what? Note that there are two accounts of the creation of mankind, *Genesis* 1:27 and *Genesis* 2:21–22. Do these two accounts conflict?

2. *Other Versions of the Fall.* In PARADISE LOST, Book 9, Milton emphasizes that the serpent tempted Eve alone. Does this interpretation conflict with *Genesis* 3:6?

Mark Twain, in his PASSAGE FROM SATAN'S DIARY, emphasizes that Adam and Eve could not have been at fault in disobeying God, because they didn't know the difference between right and wrong before eating of the forbidden fruit. Does Twain pose an antimony?

3. *Innuendos.* Do you find any sexual imagery in the Biblical account of the Fall, *i.e.*, in the serpent, tempting a naked woman, to eat of the forbidden fruit?

The first knowledge that Adam and Eve acquired after eating the forbidden fruit was that they were naked. They clothed themselves with aprons of fig leaves, Adam says, because he "was afraid." Milton says they did so because they were ashamed of their nakedness. *Cf. Genesis* 2:25.

4. *Sin and Feminism.* The account of the Fall given here forms the foundation for the Judeo–Christian concept of original sin (*i.e.*, that all humans are born sinful). How does the inherently sinful nature of humankind find expression in the Anglo–American legal system?

Interestingly, these chapters also form the foundation for most Western theories of women's subordination. Why is the story of the Creation and the Fall gendered?

SAMSON AND DELILAH
Judges

Chapter 16

[1] Then went Samson to Gaza, and saw there an harlot, and went in unto her.

[2] And it was told the Gazites, saying, Samson is come hither. And they compassed him in, and laid wait for him all night in the gate of the city, and were quiet all the night, saying, In the morning, when it is day, we shall kill him.

[3] And Samson lay till midnight, and arose at midnight, and took the doors of the gate of the city, and the two posts, and went away with them, bar and all, and put them upon his shoulders, and carried them up to the top of an hill that is before Hebron.

[4] And it came to pass afterward, that he loved a woman in the valley of Sorek, whose name was Delilah.

[5] And the lords of the Philistines came up unto her, and said unto her, Entice him, and see wherein his great strength lieth, and by what means we may prevail against him, that we may bind him to afflict him: and we will give thee every one of us eleven hundred pieces of silver.

[6] And Delilah said to Samson, Tell me, I pray thee, wherein thy great strength lieth, and wherewith thou mightest be bound to afflict thee.

[7] And Samson said unto her, If they bind me with seven green withs that were never dried, then shall I be weak, and be as another man.

[8] Then the lords of the Philistines brought up to her seven green withs which had not been dried, and she bound him with them.

[9] Now there were men lying in wait, abiding with her in the chamber. And she said unto him, The Philistines be upon thee, Samson. And he brake the withs, as a thread of tow is broken when it toucheth the fire. So his strength was not known.

[10] And Delilah said unto Samson, Behold, thou hast mocked me, and told me lies: now tell me, I pray thee, wherewith thou mightest be bound.

[11] And he said unto her, If they bind me fast with new ropes that never were occupied, then shall I be weak, and be as another man.

[12] Delilah therefore took new ropes, and bound him therewith, and said unto him, The Philistines be upon thee, Samson. And there were liers in wait abiding in the chamber. And he brake them from off his arms like a thread.

[13] And Delilah said unto Samson, Hitherto thou hast mocked me, and told me lies: tell me wherewith thou mightest be bound. And he said unto her, If thou weavest the seven locks of my head with the web.

¹⁴ And she fastened it with the pin, and said unto him, The Philistines be upon thee, Samson. And he awaked out of his sleep, and went away with the pin of the beam, and with the web.

¹⁵ And she said unto him, How canst thou say, I love thee, when thine heart is not with me? thou hast mocked me these three times, and hast not told me wherein thy great strength lieth.

¹⁶ And it came to pass, when she pressed him daily with her words, and urged him, so that his soul was vexed unto death;

¹⁷ That he told her all his heart, and said unto her, There hath not come a razor upon mine head; for I have been a Nazarite unto God from my mother's womb: if I be shaven, then my strength will go from me, and I shall become weak, and be like any other man.

¹⁸ And when Delilah saw that he had told her all his heart, she sent and called for the lords of the Philistines, saying, Come up this once, for he hath shewed me all his heart. Then the lords of the Philistines came up unto her, and brought money in their hand.

¹⁹ And she made him sleep upon her knees; and she called for a man, and she caused him to shave off the seven locks of his head; and she began to afflict him, and his strength went from him.

²⁰ And she said, The Philistines be upon thee, Samson. And he awoke out of his sleep, and said, I will go out as at other times before, and shake myself. And he wist not that the LORD was departed from him.

²¹ But the Philistines took him, and put out his eyes, and brought him down to Gaza, and bound him with fetters of brass; and he did grind in the prison house.

²² Howbeit the hair of his head began to grow again after he was shaven.

²³ Then the lords of the Philistines gathered them together for to offer a great sacrifice unto Dagon their god, and to rejoice: for they said, Our god hath delivered Samson our enemy into our hand.

²⁴ And when the people saw him, they praised their god: for they said, Our god hath delivered into our hands our enemy, and the destroyer of our country, which slew many of us.

²⁵ And it came to pass, when their hearts were merry, that they said, Call for Samson, that he may make us sport. And they called for Samson out of the prison house; and he made them sport: and they set him between the pillars.

²⁶ And Samson said unto the lad that held him by the hand, Suffer me that I may feel the pillars whereupon the house standeth, that I may lean upon them.

²⁷ Now the house was full of men and women; and all the lords of the Philistines were there; and there were upon the roof about three thousand men and women, that beheld while Samson made sport.

[28] And Samson called unto the LORD, and said, O Lord GOD, remember me, I pray thee, and strengthen me, I pray thee, only this once, O God, that I may be at once avenged of the Philistines for my two eyes.

[29] And Samson took hold of the two middle pillars upon which the house stood, and on which it was borne up, of the one with his right hand, and of the other with his left.

[30] And Samson said, Let me die with the Philistines. And he bowed himself with all his might; and the house fell upon the lords, and upon all the people that were therein. So the dead which he slew at his death were more than they which he slew in his life.

[31] Then his brethren and all the house of his father came down, and took him, and brought him up, and buried him between Zorah and Eshtaol in the burying place of Manoah his father. And he judged Israel twenty years.

Note

1.   *The Temptation.* Unless Samson was pretty dumb (which he appears not to have been), he must have caught on to what the Philistine Delilah was up to after her first failed attempt to discover the source of his great strength. Why then does he continue the charade, ultimately revealing the source of his strength to her?

Samson seems to have had a fatal attraction for Philistine women, although his parents urged him to take a wife from his own people rather than "to take a wife of the uncircumcised Philistines." (*Judges* 14:3). Why do you suppose Samson was not satisfied with the "daughters of [his] brethren," *id.*, particularly since the Philistines were such domineering enemies of the Jews?

THE TOWER OF BABEL
Genesis

Chapter 11

[1] And the whole earth was of one language, and of one speech.

[2] And it came to pass, as they journeyed from the east, that they found a plain in the land of Shinar; and they dwelt there.

[3] And they said one to another, Go to, let us make brick, and burn them throughly. And they had brick for stone, and slime had they for morter.

[4] And they said, Go to, let us build us a city and a tower, whose top may reach unto heaven; and let us make us a name, lest we be scattered abroad upon the face of the whole earth.

[5] And the LORD came down to see the city and the tower, which the children of men builded.

[6] And the LORD said, Behold, the people is one, and they have all one language; and this they begin to do: and now nothing will be restrained from them, which they have imagined to do.

⁷ Go to, let us go down, and there confound their language, that they may not understand one another's speech.

⁸ So the LORD scattered them abroad from thence upon the face of all the earth: and they left off to build the city.

⁹ Therefore is the name of it called Babel; because the LORD did there confound the language of all the earth: and from thence did the LORD scatter them abroad upon the face of the earth.

Note

1. *One language.* This myth of the origin of different languages gives unusual power to commonalty of language. Or is the story simply about hubris? Reconsider *Genesis* 3:22. Cross-reference the Pentecost, *Acts* Chapter 2. *Mark* 16:17 states that the disciples "shall speak with new tongues," but those who speak in tongues out of religious fervor are notable for their incomprehensibility.

ABRAHAM AND ISAAC
Genesis

Chapter 22

¹ And it came to pass after these things, that God did tempt Abraham, and said unto him, Abraham: and he said, Behold, here I am.

² And he said, Take now thy son, thine only son Isaac, whom thou lovest, and get thee into the land of Moriah; and offer him there for a burnt offering upon one of the mountains which I will tell thee of.

³ And Abraham rose up early in the morning, and saddled his ass, and took two of his young men with him, and Isaac his son, and clave the wood for the burnt offering, and rose up, and went unto the place of which God had told him.

⁴ Then on the third day Abraham lifted up his eyes, and saw the place afar off.

⁵ And Abraham said unto his young men, Abide ye here with the ass; and I and the lad will go yonder and worship, and come again to you.

⁶ And Abraham took the wood of the burnt offering, and laid it upon Isaac his son; and he took the fire in his hand, and a knife; and they went both of them together.

⁷ And Isaac spake unto Abraham his father, and said, My father: and he said, Here am I, my son. And he said, Behold the fire and the wood: but where is the lamb for a burnt offering?

⁸ And Abraham said, My son, God will provide himself a lamb for a burnt offering: so they went both of them together.

⁹ And they came to the place which God had told him of; and Abraham built an altar there, and laid the wood in order, and bound Isaac his son, and laid him on the altar upon the wood.

[10] And Abraham stretched forth his hand, and took the knife to slay his son.

[11] And the angel of the LORD called unto him out of heaven, and said, Abraham, Abraham: and he said, Here am I.

[12] And he said, Lay not thine hand upon the lad, neither do thou any thing unto him: for now I know that thou fearest God, seeing thou hast not withheld thy son, thine only son from me.

[13] And Abraham lifted up his eyes, and looked, and behold behind him a ram caught in a thicket by his horns: and Abraham went and took the ram, and offered him up for a burnt offering in the stead of his son.

[14] And Abraham called the name of that place Jehovah-jireh: as it is said to this day, In the mount of the LORD it shall be seen.

[15] And the angel of the LORD called unto Abraham out of heaven the second time,

[16] And said, By myself have I sworn, saith the LORD, for because thou hast done this thing, and hast not withheld thy son, thine only son:

[17] That in blessing I will bless thee, and in multiplying I will multiply thy seed as the stars of the heaven, and as the sand which is upon the sea shore; and thy seed shall possess the gate of his enemies;

[18] And in thy seed shall all the nations of the earth be blessed; because thou hast obeyed my voice.

Notes

1. *The Advocate vs. the Acquiescent Abe.* God advises Abraham, in *Genesis* Chapter 18, that He intends to destroy Sodom and Gomorrah because "their sin is very grievous." *Genesis* 18:20. Abraham tries to talk God out of his resolve: "And Abraham drew near, and said, Wilt thou also destroy the righteous with the wicked?" *Genesis* 18:23.

Peradventure, Abe says, you would spare the city if fifty righteous therein can be found? I will spare it, God said. How about forty-five? I would spare it. Would forty be enough? Yes. Thirty? Yes. Twenty? Yes.

> [32] And he said, Oh let not the Lord be angry, and I will speak yet but this once: Peradventure ten shall be found there. And he said, I will not destroy it for ten's sake.

When God directs Abraham to sacrifice his son Isaac, however, Abraham sets about to obey without a single question or objection. Why?

2. *Fear and Trembling.* The Danish theologian Søren Kierkegaard (1813–1855) was fascinated with the Abraham-Isaac story. In FEAR AND TREMBLING (1843), he wrote multiple sequels to the story. He maintained that Abraham's obedience was the ultimate expression of devoutness. Do you agree?

3. *Point of View.* Rewrite this story from Isaac's point of view. From the point of view of Sarah (Abraham's wife).

ESAU AND JACOB
Genesis

Chapter 27[1]

[1] And it came to pass, that when Isaac was old, and his eyes were dim, so that he could not see, he called Esau his eldest son, and said unto him, My son: and he said unto him, Behold, here am I.

[2] And he said, Behold now, I am old, I know not the day of my death:

[3] Now therefore take, I pray thee, thy weapons, thy quiver and thy bow, and go out to the field, and take me some venison;

[4] And make me savoury meat, such as I love, and bring it to me, that I may eat; that my soul may bless thee before I die.

[5] And Rebekah heard when Isaac spake to Esau his son. And Esau went to the field to hunt for venison, and to bring it.

[6] And Rebekah spake unto Jacob her son, saying, Behold, I heard thy father speak unto Esau thy brother, saying,

[7] Bring me venison, and make me savoury meat, that I may eat, and bless thee before the LORD before my death.

[8] Now therefore, my son, obey my voice according to that which I command thee.

[9] Go now to the flock, and fetch me from thence two good kids of the goats; and I will make them savoury meat for thy father, such as he loveth:

[10] And thou shalt bring it to thy father, that he may eat, and that he may bless thee before his death.

[11] And Jacob said to Rebekah his mother, Behold, Esau my brother is a hairy man, and I am a smooth man:

[12] My father peradventure will feel me, and I shall seem to him as a deceiver; and I shall bring a curse upon me, and not a blessing.

[13] And his mother said unto him, Upon me be thy curse, my son: only obey my voice, and go fetch me them.

[14] And he went, and fetched, and brought them to his mother: and his mother made savoury meat, such as his father loved.

[15] And Rebekah took goodly raiment of her eldest son Esau, which were with her in the house, and put them upon Jacob her younger son:

[16] And she put the skins of the kids of the goats upon his hands, and upon the smooth of his neck:

[17] And she gave the savoury meat and the bread, which she had prepared, into the hand of her son Jacob.

---

1. In this story Rebekah is Isaac's wife.
Esau and Jacob are their children.

¹⁸ And he came unto his father, and said, My father: and he said, Here am I; who art thou, my son?

¹⁹ And Jacob said unto his father, I am Esau thy firstborn; I have done according as thou badest me: arise, I pray thee, sit and eat of my venison, that thy soul may bless me.

²⁰ And Isaac said unto his son, How is it that thou hast found it so quickly, my son? And he said, Because the LORD thy God brought it to me.

²¹ And Isaac said unto Jacob, Come near, I pray thee, that I may feel thee, my son, whether thou be my very son Esau or not.

²² And Jacob went near unto Isaac his father; and he felt him, and said, The voice is Jacob's voice, but the hands are the hands of Esau.

²³ And he discerned him not, because his hands were hairy, as his brother Esau's hands: so he blessed him.

²⁴ And he said, Art thou my very son Esau? And he said, I am.

²⁵ And he said, Bring it near to me, and I will eat of my son's venison, that my soul may bless thee. And he brought it near to him, and he did eat: and he brought him wine, and he drank.

²⁶ And his father Isaac said unto him, Come near now, and kiss me, my son.

²⁷ And he came near, and kissed him: and he smelled the smell of his raiment, and blessed him, and said, See, the smell of my son is as the smell of a field which the LORD hath blessed:

²⁸ Therefore God give thee of the dew of heaven, and the fatness of the earth, and plenty of corn and wine:

²⁹ Let people serve thee, and nations bow down to thee: be lord over thy brethren, and let thy mother's sons bow down to thee: cursed be every one that curseth thee, and blessed be he that blesseth thee.

³⁰ And it came to pass, as soon as Isaac had made an end of blessing Jacob, and Jacob was yet scarce gone out from the presence of Isaac his father, that Esau his brother came in from his hunting.

³¹ And he also had made savoury meat, and brought it unto his father, and said unto his father, Let my father arise, and eat of his son's venison, that thy soul may bless me.

³² And Isaac his father said unto him, Who art thou? And he said, I am thy son, thy firstborn Esau.

³³ And Isaac trembled very exceedingly, and said, Who? where is he that hath taken venison, and brought it me, and I have eaten of all before thou camest, and have blessed him? yea, and he shall be blessed.

³⁴ And when Esau heard the words of his father, he cried with a great and exceeding bitter cry, and said unto his father, Bless me, even me also, O my father.

[35] And he said, Thy brother came with subtilty, and hath taken away thy blessing.

[36] And he said, Is not he rightly named Jacob? for he hath supplanted me these two times: he took away my birthright; and, behold, now he hath taken away my blessing. And he said, Hast thou not reserved a blessing for me?

[37] And Isaac answered and said unto Esau, Behold, I have made him thy lord, and all his brethren have I given to him for servants; and with corn and wine have I sustained him: and what shall I do now unto thee, my son?

[38] And Esau said unto his father, Hast thou but one blessing, my father? bless me, even me also, O my father. And Esau lifted up his voice, and wept.

[39] And Isaac his father answered and said unto him, Behold, thy dwelling shall be the fatness of the earth, and of the dew of heaven from above;

[40] And by thy sword shalt thou live, and shalt serve thy brother; and it shall come to pass when thou shalt have the dominion, that thou shalt break his yoke from off thy neck.

[41] And Esau hated Jacob because of the blessing wherewith his father blessed him: and Esau said in his heart, The days of mourning for my father are at hand; then will I slay my brother Jacob.

[42] And these words of Esau her elder son were told to Rebekah: and she sent and called Jacob her younger son, and said unto him, Behold, thy brother Esau, as touching thee, doth comfort himself, purposing to kill thee.

[43] Now therefore, my son, obey my voice; and arise, flee thou to Laban my brother to Haran;

[44] And tarry with him a few days, until thy brother's fury turn away;

[45] Until thy brother's anger turn away from thee, and he forget that which thou hast done to him: then I will send, and fetch thee from thence: why should I be deprived also of you both in one day?

[46] And Rebekah said to Isaac, I am weary of my life because of the daughters of Heth: if Jacob take a wife of the daughters of Heth, such as these which are of the daughters of the land, what good shall my life do me?

DAVID AND GOLIATH
I Samuel

Chapter 17

[1] Now the Philistines gathered together their armies to battle, and were gathered together at Shochoh, which belongeth to Judah, and pitched between Shochoh and Azekah, in Ephes-dammim.

² And Saul and the men of Israel were gathered together, and pitched by the valley of Elah, and set the battle in array against the Philistines.

³ And the Philistines stood on a mountain on the one side, and Israel stood on a mountain on the other side: and there was a valley between them.

⁴ And there went out a champion out of the camp of the Philistines, named Goliath, of Gath, whose height was six cubits and a span.

⁵ And he had an helmet of brass upon his head, and he was armed with a coat of mail; and the weight of the coat was five thousand shekels of brass.

⁶ And he had greaves of brass upon his legs, and a target of brass between his shoulders.

⁷ And the staff of his spear was like a weaver's beam; and his spear's head weighed six hundred shekels of iron: and one bearing a shield went before him.

⁸ And he stood and cried unto the armies of Israel, and said unto them, Why are ye come out to set your battle in array? am not I a Philistine, and ye servants to Saul? choose you a man for you, and let him come down to me.

⁹ If he be able to fight with me, and to kill me, then will we be your servants: but if I prevail against him, and kill him, then shall ye be our servants, and serve us.

¹⁰ And the Philistine said, I defy the armies of Israel this day; give me a man, that we may fight together.

¹¹ When Saul and all Israel heard those words of the Philistine, they were dismayed, and greatly afraid.

¹² Now David was the son of that Ephrathite of Bethlehemjudah, whose name was Jesse; and he had eight sons: and the man went among men for an old man in the days of Saul.

¹³ And the three eldest sons of Jesse went and followed Saul to the battle: and the names of his three sons that went to the battle were Eliab the firstborn, and next unto him Abinadab, and the third Shammah.

¹⁴ And David was the youngest: and the three eldest followed Saul.

¹⁵ But David went and returned from Saul to feed his father's sheep at Bethlehem.

¹⁶ And the Philistine drew near morning and evening, and presented himself forty days.

¹⁷ And Jesse said unto David his son, Take now for thy brethren an ephah of this parched corn, and these ten loaves, and run to the camp to thy brethren;

¹⁸ And carry these ten cheeses unto the captain of their thousand, and look how thy brethren fare, and take their pledge.

¹⁹ Now Saul, and they, and all the men of Israel, were in the valley of Elah, fighting with the Philistines.

²⁰ And David rose up early in the morning, and left the sheep with a keeper, and took, and went, as Jesse had commanded him; and he came to the trench, as the host was going forth to the fight, and shouted for the battle.

²¹ For Israel and the Philistines had put the battle in array, army against army.

²² And David left his carriage in the hand of the keeper of the carriage, and ran into the army, and came and saluted his brethren.

²³ And as he talked with them, behold, there came up the champion, the Philistine of Gath, Goliath by name, out of the armies of the Philistines, and spake according to the same words: and David heard them.

²⁴ And all the men of Israel, when they saw the man, fled from him, and were sore afraid.

²⁵ And the men of Israel said, Have ye seen this man that is come up? surely to defy Israel is he come up: and it shall be, that the man who killeth him, the king will enrich him with great riches, and will give him his daughter, and make his father's house free in Israel.

²⁶ And David spake to the men that stood by him, saying, What shall be done to the man that killeth this Philistine, and taketh away the reproach from Israel? for who is this uncircumcised Philistine, that he should defy the armies of the living God?

²⁷ And the people answered him after this manner, saying, So shall it be done to the man that killeth him.

²⁸ And Eliab his eldest brother heard when he spake unto the men; and Eliab's anger was kindled against David, and he said, Why camest thou down hither? and with whom hast thou left those few sheep in the wilderness? I know thy pride, and the naughtiness of thine heart; for thou art come down that thou mightest see the battle.

²⁹ And David said, What have I now done? Is there not a cause?

³⁰ And he turned from him toward another, and spake after the same manner: and the people answered him again after the former manner.

³¹ And when the words were heard which David spake, they rehearsed them before Saul: and he sent for him.

³² And David said to Saul, Let no man's heart fail because of him; thy servant will go and fight with this Philistine.

³³ And Saul said to David, Thou art not able to go against this Philistine to fight with him: for thou art but a youth, and he a man of war from his youth.

³⁴ And David said unto Saul, Thy servant kept his father's sheep, and there came a lion, and a bear, and took a lamb out of the flock:

³⁵ And I went out after him, and smote him, and delivered it out of his mouth: and when he arose against me, I caught him by his beard, and smote him, and slew him.

³⁶ Thy servant slew both the lion and the bear: and this uncircumcised Philistine shall be as one of them, seeing he hath defied the armies of the living God.

³⁷ David said moreover, The LORD that delivered me out of the paw of the lion, and out of the paw of the bear, he will deliver me out of the hand of this Philistine. And Saul said unto David, Go, and the LORD be with thee.

³⁸ And Saul armed David with his armour, and he put an helmet of brass upon his head; also he armed him with a coat of mail.

³⁹ And David girded his sword upon his armour, and he assayed to go; for he had not proved it. And David said unto Saul, I cannot go with these; for I have not proved them. And David put them off him.

⁴⁰ And he took his staff in his hand, and chose him five smooth stones out of the brook, and put them in a shepherd's bag which he had, even in a scrip; and his sling was in his hand: and he drew near to the Philistine.

⁴¹ And the Philistine came on and drew near unto David; and the man that bare the shield went before him.

⁴² And when the Philistine looked about, and saw David, he disdained him: for he was but a youth, and ruddy, and of a fair countenance.

⁴³ And the Philistine said unto David, Am I a dog, that thou comest to me with staves? And the Philistine cursed David by his gods.

⁴⁴ And the Philistine said to David, Come to me, and I will give thy flesh unto the fowls of the air, and to the beasts of the field.

⁴⁵ Then said David to the Philistine, Thou comest to me with a sword, and with a spear, and with a shield: but I come to thee in the name of the Lord of hosts, the God of the armies of Israel, whom thou hast defied.

⁴⁶ This day will the LORD deliver thee into mine hand; and I will smite thee, and take thine head from thee; and I will give the carcases of the host of the Philistines this day unto the fowls of the air, and to the wild beasts of the earth; that all the earth may know that there is a God in Israel.

⁴⁷ And all this assembly shall know that the LORD saveth not with sword and spear: for the battle is the LORD'S, and he will give you into our hands.

⁴⁸ And it came to pass, when the Philistine arose, and came and drew nigh to meet David, that David hasted, and ran toward the army to meet the Philistine.

⁴⁹ And David put his hand in his bag, and took thence a stone, and slang it, and smote the Philistine in his forehead, that the stone sunk into his forehead; and he fell upon his face to the earth.

⁵⁰ So David prevailed over the Philistine with a sling and with a stone, and smote the Philistine, and slew him; but there was no sword in the hand of David.

⁵¹ Therefore David ran, and stood upon the Philistine, and took his sword, and drew it out of the sheath thereof, and slew him, and cut off his head therewith. And when the Philistines saw their champion was dead, they fled.

⁵² And the men of Israel and of Judah arose, and shouted, and pursued the Philistines, until thou come to the valley, and to the gates of Ekron. And the wounded of the Philistines fell down by the way to Shaaraim, even unto Gath, and unto Ekron.

⁵³ And the children of Israel returned from chasing after the Philistines, and they spoiled their tents.

⁵⁴ And David took the head of the Philistine, and brought it to Jerusalem; but he put his armour in his tent.

⁵⁵ And when Saul saw David go forth against the Philistine, he said unto Abner, the captain of the host, Abner, whose son is this youth? And Abner said, As thy soul liveth, O king, I cannot tell.

⁵⁶ And the king said, Inquire thou whose son the stripling is.

⁵⁷ And as David returned from the slaughter of the Philistine, Abner took him, and brought him before Saul with the head of the Philistine in his hand.

⁵⁸ And Saul said to him, Whose son art thou, thou young man? And David answered, I am the son of thy servant Jesse the Bethlehemite.

Notes

1. *Five Smooth Stones.* Why *five* smooth stones (*I Samuel* 17:40). If David missed the first time, did he think he would have a second chance?

2. *The Underdog.* The story of David and Goliath has become eponymous for a battle in which the underdog is greatly outmatched. Was the battle here unequal? How? Can you think of recent legal battles, as represented in the popular media, analogous to that between David and Goliath? If so, draw out the analogy in detail.

DAVID AND BATHSHEBA
II Samuel

Chapter 11

² And it came to pass in an eveningtide, that David arose from off his bed, and walked upon the roof of the king's house: and from the roof he saw a woman washing herself; and the woman was very beautiful to look upon.

³ And David sent and inquired after the woman. And one said, Is not this Bath-sheba, the daughter of Eliam, the wife of Uriah the Hittite?

⁴ And David sent messengers, and took her; and she came in unto him, and he lay with her; for she was purified from her uncleanness: and she returned unto her house.

⁵ And the woman conceived, and sent and told David, and said, I am with child.

⁶ And David sent to Joab, saying, Send me Uriah the Hittite. And Joab sent Uriah to David.

⁷ And when Uriah was come unto him, David demanded of him how Joab did, and how the people did, and how the war prospered.

⁸ And David said to Uriah, Go down to thy house, and wash thy feet. And Uriah departed out of the king's house, and there followed him a mess of meat from the king.

⁹ But Uriah slept at the door of the king's house with all the servants of his Lord, and went not down to his house.

¹⁰ And when they had told David, saying, Uriah went not down unto his house, David said unto Uriah, Camest thou not from thy journey? why then didst thou not go down unto thine house?

¹¹ And Uriah said unto David, The ark, and Israel, and Judah, abide in tents; and my lord Joab, and the servants of my lord, are encamped in the open fields; shall I then go into mine house, to eat and to drink, and to lie with my wife? as thou livest, and as thy soul liveth, I will not do this thing.

¹² And David said to Uriah, Tarry here to day also, and to morrow I will let thee depart. So Uriah abode in Jerusalem that day, and the morrow.

¹³ And when David had called him, he did eat and drink before him; and he made him drunk: and at even he went out to lie on his bed with the servants of his lord, but went not down to his house.

¹⁴ And it came to pass in the morning, that David wrote a letter to Joab, and sent it by the hand of Uriah.

¹⁵ And he wrote in the letter, saying, Set ye Uriah in the forefront of the hottest battle, and retire ye from him, that he may be smitten, and die.

[16] And it came to pass, when Joab observed the city, that he assigned Uriah unto a place where he knew that valiant men were.

[17] And the men of the city went out, and fought with Joab: and there fell some of the people of the servants of David; and Uriah the Hittite died also.

. . . .

[26] And when the wife of Uriah heard that Uriah her husband was dead, she mourned for her husband.

[27] And when the mourning was past, David sent and fetched her to his house, and she became his wife, and bare him a son. But the thing that David had done displeased the LORD.

Chapter 12[1]

[1] And the LORD sent Nathan unto David. And he came unto him, and said unto him, There were two men in one city; the one rich, and the other poor.

[2] The rich man had exceeding many flocks and herds:

[3] But the poor man had nothing, save one little ewe lamb, which he had bought and nourished up: and it grew up together with him, and with his children; it did eat of his own meat, and drank of his own cup, and lay in his bosom, and was unto him as a daughter.

[4] And there came a traveller unto the rich man, and he spared to take of his own flock and of his own herd, to dress for the wayfaring man that was come unto him; but took the poor man's lamb, and dressed it for the man that was come to him.

[5] And David's anger was greatly kindled against the man; and he said to Nathan, As the LORD liveth, the man that hath done this thing shall surely die:

[6] And he shall restore the lamb fourfold, because he did this thing, and because he had no pity.

[7] And Nathan said to David, Thou art the man. Thus saith the LORD God of Israel, I anointed thee king over Israel, and I delivered thee out of the hand of Saul;

[8] And I gave thee thy master's house, and thy master's wives into thy bosom, and gave thee the house of Israel and of Judah; and if that had been too little, I would moreover have given unto thee such and such things.

[9] Wherefore hast thou despised the commandment of the LORD, to do evil in his sight? thou hast killed Uriah the Hittite with the sword, and hast taken his wife to be thy wife, and hast slain him with the sword of the children of Ammon.

1. In this story Nathan is a prophet.

[10] Now therefore the sword shall never depart from thine house; because thou hast despised me, and hast taken the wife of Uriah the Hittite to be thy wife.

[11] Thus saith the LORD, Behold, I will raise up evil against thee out of thine own house, and I will take thy wives before thine eyes, and give them unto thy neighbour, and he shall lie with thy wives in the sight of this sun.

[12] For thou didst it secretly: but I will do this thing before all Israel, and before the sun.

[13] And David said unto Nathan, I have sinned against the LORD. And Nathan said unto David, The LORD also hath put away thy sin; thou shalt not die.

[14] Howbeit, because by this deed thou hast given great occasion to the enemies of the LORD to blaspheme, the child also that is born unto thee shall surely die.

[15] And Nathan departed unto his house. And the LORD struck the child that Uriah's wife bare unto David, and it was very sick.

[16] David therefore besought God for the child; and David fasted, and went in, and lay all night upon the earth.

[17] And the elders of his house arose, and went to him, to raise him up from the earth: but he would not, neither did he eat bread with them.

[18] And it came to pass on the seventh day, that the child died. And the servants of David feared to tell him that the child was dead: for they said, Behold, while the child was yet alive, we spake unto him, and he would not hearken unto our voice: how will he then vex himself, if we tell him that the child is dead?

[19] But when David saw that his servants whispered, David perceived that the child was dead: therefore David said unto his servants, Is the child dead? And they said, He is dead.

[20] Then David arose from the earth, and washed, and anointed himself, and changed his apparel, and came into the house of the LORD, and worshipped: then he came to his own house; and when he required, they set bread before him, and he did eat.

[21] Then said his servants unto him, What thing is this that thou hast done? thou didst fast and weep for the child, while it was alive; but when the child was dead, thou didst rise and eat bread.

[22] And he said, While the child was yet alive, I fasted and wept: for I said, Who can tell whether GOD will be gracious to me, that the child may live?

[23] But now he is dead, wherefore should I fast? can I bring him back again? I shall go to him, but he shall not return to me.

Notes

1. *The Deceiver.* Jacob deceived his father, and later his father-in-law. And yet it was Jacob who wrestled with the Angel of the Lord and was named Israel, the father of his nation, *Genesis* 32:24–29. What are we to make of this system of rewards and punishments?

David, the "man after God's own heart," *see I Samuel* 13:14, turned out to be quite a sinner. Another strange example of rewards and punishments?

Jesus showed especial sympathy for the ne'er-do-wells and social outcasts, yet he hated the pharisees and hypocrites with a passion.

What dichotomy is being drawn by this line of examples?

2. *Prophets.* In the story of David and Bathsheba, Nathan uses a hypothetical to convict David out of his own mouth. Using a story as a trap is a standard literary device; for example, in *Hamlet* the protagonist uses the "play within a play" to discern Claudius's guilt. Is this a legitimate or ethical use of storytelling?

THE WISDOM OF SOLOMON
I Kings

Chapter 3

[5] In Gibeon the Lord appeared to Solomon in a dream by night: and God said, Ask what I shall give thee.

[6] And Solomon said, Thou hast shewed unto thy servant David my father great mercy, according as he walked before thee in truth, and in righteousness, and in uprightness of heart with thee; and thou hast kept for him this great kindness, that thou hast given him a son to sit on his throne, as it is this day.

[7] And now, O Lord my God, thou hast made thy servant king instead of David my father: and I am but a little child: I know not how to go out or come in.

[8] And thy servant is in the midst of thy people which thou hast chosen, a great people, that cannot be numbered nor counted for multitude.

[9] Give therefore thy servant an understanding heart to judge thy people, that I may discern between good and bad: for who is able to judge this thy so great a people?

[10] And the speech pleased the Lord, that Solomon had asked this thing.

[11] And God said unto him, Because thou hast asked this thing, and hast not asked for thyself long life; neither hast asked riches for thyself, nor hast asked the life of thine enemies; but hast asked for thyself understanding to discern judgment;

[12] Behold, I have done according to thy words: lo, I have given thee a wise and an understanding heart; so that there was none like thee before thee, neither after thee shall any arise like unto thee.

¹³ And I have also given thee that which thou hast not asked, both riches, and honour: so that there shall not be any among the kings like unto thee all thy days.

¹⁴ And if thou wilt walk in my ways, to keep my statutes and my commandments, as thy father David did walk, then I will lengthen thy days.

¹⁵ And Solomon awoke; and, behold, it was a dream. And he came to Jerusalem, and stood before the ark of the covenant of the LORD, and offered up burnt offerings, and offered peace offerings, and made a feast to all his servants.

¹⁶ Then came there two women, that were harlots, unto the king, and stood before him.

¹⁷ And the one woman said, O my lord, I and this woman dwell in one house; and I was delivered of a child with her in the house.

¹⁸ And it came to pass the third day after that I was delivered, that this woman was delivered also: and we were together; there was no stranger with us in the house, save we two in the house.

¹⁹ And this woman's child died in the night; because she overlaid it.

²⁰ And she arose at midnight, and took my son from beside me, while thine handmaid slept, and laid it in her bosom, and laid her dead child in my bosom.

²¹ And when I rose in the morning to give my child suck, behold, it was dead: but when I had considered it in the morning, behold, it was not my son, which I did bear.

²² And the other woman said, Nay; but the living is my son, and the dead is thy son. And this said, No; but the dead is thy son, and the living is my son. Thus they spake before the king.

²³ Then said the king, The one saith, This is my son that liveth, and thy son is the dead: and the other saith, Nay; but thy son is the dead, and my son is the living.

²⁴ And the king said, Bring me a sword. And they brought a sword before the king.

²⁵ And the king said, Divide the living child in two, and give half to the one, and half to the other.

²⁶ Then spake the woman whose the living child was unto the king, for her bowels yearned upon her son, and she said, O my lord, give her the living child, and in no wise slay it. But the other said, Let it be neither mine nor thine, but divide it.

²⁷ Then the king answered and said, Give her the living child, and in no wise slay it: she is the mother thereof.

²⁸ And all Israel heard of the judgment which the king had judged; and they feared the king: for they saw that the wisdom of God was in him, to do judgment.

Notes

1. *Judgment.* Solomon's actions in this story have been lauded as the ultimate demonstration of wise judgment. What was the basis of Solomon's judgment here? Law? Psychology? Spiritual discernment? What if the true mother had not spoken out? What would Solomon have done then?

2. *Motherhood.* What stereotypes of motherhood are embodied in this story? Are those stereotypes still present in twenty-first-century America?

RUTH

Chapter 1

[1] Now it came to pass in the days when the judges ruled, that there was a famine in the land. And a certain man of Bethlehemjudah went to sojourn in the country of Moab, he, and his wife, and his two sons.

[2] And the name of the man was Elimelech, and the name of his wife Naomi, and the name of his two sons Mahlon and Chilion, Ephrathites of Bethlehemjudah. And they came into the country of Moab, and continued there.

[3] And Elimelech Naomi's husband died; and she was left, and her two sons.

[4] And they took them wives of the women of Moab; the name of the one was Orpah, and the name of the other Ruth: and they dwelled there about ten years.

[5] And Mahlon and Chilion died also both of them; and the woman was left of her two sons and her husband.

[6] Then she arose with her daughters in law, that she might return from the country of Moab: for she had heard in the country of Moab how that the LORD had visited his people in giving them bread.

[7] Wherefore she went forth out of the place where she was, and her two daughters in law with her; and they went on the way to return unto the land of Judah.

[8] And Naomi said unto her two daughters in law, Go, return each to her mother's house: the LORD deal kindly with you, as ye have dealt with the dead, and with me.

[9] The LORD grant you that ye may find rest, each of you in the house of her husband. Then she kissed them; and they lifted up their voice, and wept.

[10] And they said unto her, Surely we will return with thee unto thy people.

[11] And Naomi said, Turn again, my daughters: why will ye go with me? are there yet any more sons in my womb, that they may be your husbands?

¹² Turn again, my daughters, go your way; for I am too old to have an husband. If I should say, I have hope, if I should have an husband also to night, and should also bear sons;

¹³ Would ye tarry for them till they were grown? would ye stay for them from having husbands? nay, my daughters; for it grieveth me much for your sakes that the hand of the LORD is gone out against me.

¹⁴ And they lifted up their voice, and wept again: and Orpah kissed her mother in law; but Ruth clave unto her.

¹⁵ And she said, Behold, thy sister in law is gone back unto her people, and unto her gods: return thou after thy sister in law.

¹⁶ And Ruth said, Intreat me not to leave thee, or to return from following after thee: for whither thou goest, I will go; and where thou lodgest, I will lodge: thy people shall be my people, and thy God my God:

¹⁷ Where thou diest, will I die, and there will I be buried: the LORD do so to me, and more also, if ought but death part thee and me.

¹⁸ When she saw that she was stedfastly minded to go with her, then she left speaking unto her.

¹⁹ So they two went until they came to Bethlehem. And it came to pass, when they were come to Bethlehem, that all the city was moved about them, and they said, Is this Naomi?

²⁰ And she said unto them, Call me not Naomi, call me Mara: for the Almighty hath dealt very bitterly with me.

²¹ I went out full, and the LORD hath brought me home again empty: why then call ye me Naomi, seeing the LORD hath testified against me, and the Almighty hath afflicted me?

²² So Naomi returned, and Ruth the Moabitess, her daughter in law, with her, which returned out of the country of Moab: and they came to Bethlehem in the beginning of barley harvest.

Chapter 2

¹ And Naomi had a kinsman of her husband's, a mighty man of wealth, of the family of Elimelech; and his name was Boaz.

² And Ruth the Moabitess said unto Naomi, Let me now go to the field, and glean ears of corn after him in whose sight I shall find grace. And she said unto her, Go, my daughter.

³ And she went, and came, and gleaned in the field after the reapers: and her hap was to light on a part of the field belonging unto Boaz, who was of the kindred of Elimelech.

⁴ And behold, Boaz came from Bethlehem, and said unto the reapers, The LORD be with you. And they answered him, The LORD bless thee.

⁵ Then said Boaz unto his servant that was set over the reapers, Whose damsel is this?

⁶ And the servant that was set over the reapers answered and said, It is the Moabitish damsel that came back with Naomi out of the country of Moab:

⁷ And she said, I pray you, let me glean and gather after the reapers among the sheaves: so she came, and hath continued even from the morning until now, that she tarried a little in the house.

⁸ Then said Boaz unto Ruth, Hearest thou not, my daughter? Go not to glean in another field, neither go from hence, but abide here fast by my maidens:

⁹ Let thine eyes be on the field that they do reap, and go thou after them: have I not charged the young men that they shall not touch thee? and when thou art athirst, go unto the vessels, and drink of that which the young men have drawn.

¹⁰ Then she fell on her face, and bowed herself to the ground, and said unto him, Why have I found grace in thine eyes, that thou shouldest take knowledge of me, seeing I am a stranger?

¹¹ And Boaz answered and said unto her, It hath fully been shewed me, all that thou hast done unto thy mother in law since the death of thine husband: and how thou hast left thy father and thy mother, and the land of thy nativity, and art come unto a people which thou knewest not heretofore.

¹² The LORD recompense thy work, and a full reward be given thee of the LORD God of Israel, under whose wings thou art come to trust.

¹³ Then she said, Let me find favour in thy sight, my lord; for that thou hast comforted me, and for that thou hast spoken friendly unto thine handmaid, though I be not like unto one of thine handmaidens.

¹⁴ And Boaz said unto her, At mealtime come thou hither, and eat of the bread, and dip thy morsel in the vinegar. And she sat beside the reapers: and he reached her parched corn, and she did eat, and was sufficed, and left.

¹⁵ And when she was risen up to glean, Boaz commanded his young men, saying, Let her glean even among the sheaves, and reproach her not:

¹⁶ And let fall also some of the handfuls of purpose for her, and leave them, that she may glean them, and rebuke her not.

¹⁷ So she gleaned in the field until even, and beat out that she had gleaned: and it was about an ephah of barley.

¹⁸ And she took it up, and went into the city: and her mother in law saw what she had gleaned: and she brought forth, and gave to her that she had reserved after she was sufficed.

¹⁹ And her mother in law said unto her, Where hast thou gleaned to day? and where wroughtest thou? blessed be he that did take knowledge of thee. And she shewed her mother in law with whom she had wrought, and said, The man's name with whom I wrought to day is Boaz.

[20] And Naomi said unto her daughter in law, Blessed be he of the LORD, who hath not left off his kindness to the living and to the dead. And Naomi said unto her, The man is near of kin unto us, one of our next kinsmen.

[21] And Ruth the Moabitess said, He said unto me also, Thou shalt keep fast by my young men, until they have ended all my harvest.

[22] And Naomi said unto Ruth her daughter in law, It is good, my daughter, that thou go out with his maidens, that they meet thee not in any other field.

[23] So she kept fast by the maidens of Boaz to glean unto the end of barley harvest and of wheat harvest; and dwelt with her mother in law.

Chapter 3

[1] Then Naomi her mother in law said unto her, My daughter, shall I not seek rest for thee, that it may be well with thee?

[2] And now is not Boaz of our kindred, with whose maidens thou wast? Behold, he winnoweth barley to night in the threshingfloor.

[3] Wash thyself therefore, and anoint thee, and put thy raiment upon thee, and get thee down to the floor: but make not thyself known unto the man, until he shall have done eating and drinking.

[4] And it shall be, when he lieth down, that thou shalt mark the place where he shall lie, and thou shalt go in, and uncover his feet, and lay thee down; and he will tell thee what thou shalt do.

[5] And she said unto her, All that thou sayest unto me I will do.

[6] And she went down unto the floor, and did according to all that her mother in law bade her.

[7] And when Boaz had eaten and drunk, and his heart was merry, he went to lie down at the end of the heap of corn: and she came softly, and uncovered his feet, and laid her down.

[8] And it came to pass at midnight, that the man was afraid, and turned himself: and, behold, a woman lay at his feet.

[9] And he said, Who art thou? And she answered, I am Ruth thine handmaid: spread therefore thy skirt over thine handmaid; for thou art a near kinsman.

[10] And he said, Blessed be thou of the LORD, my daughter: for thou hast shewed more kindness in the latter end than at the beginning, inasmuch as thou followedst not young men, whether poor or rich.

[11] And now, my daughter, fear not; I will do to thee all that thou requirest: for all the city of my people doth know that thou art a virtuous woman.

[12] And now it is true that I am thy near kinsman: howbeit there is a kinsman nearer than I.

¹³ Tarry this night, and it shall be in the morning, that if he will perform unto thee the part of a kinsman, well; let him do the kinsman's part: but if he will not do the part of a kinsman to thee, then will I do the part of a kinsman to thee, as the Lord liveth: lie down until the morning.

¹⁴ And she lay at his feet until the morning: and she rose up before one could know another. And he said, Let it not be known that a woman came into the floor.

¹⁵ Also he said, Bring the vail that thou hast upon thee, and hold it. And when she held it, he measured six measures of barley, and laid it on her: and she went into the city.

¹⁶ And when she came to her mother in law, she said, Who art thou, my daughter? And she told her all that the man had done to her.

¹⁷ And she said, These six measures of barley gave he me; for he said to me, Go not empty unto thy mother in law.

¹⁸ Then said she, Sit still, my daughter, until thou know how the matter will fall: for the man will not be in rest, until he have finished the thing this day.

Chapter 4

¹ Then went Boaz up to the gate, and sat him down there: and, behold, the kinsman of whom Boaz spake came by; unto whom he said, Ho, such a one! turn aside, sit down here. And he turned aside, and sat down.

² And he took ten men of the elders of the city, and said, Sit ye down here. And they sat down.

³ And he said unto the kinsman, Naomi, that is come again out of the country of Moab, selleth a parcel of land, which was our brother Elimelech's:

⁴ And I thought to advertise thee, saying, Buy it before the inhabitants, and before the elders of my people. If thou wilt redeem it, redeem it: but if thou wilt not redeem it, then tell me, that I may know: for there is none to redeem it beside thee; and I am after thee. And he said, I will redeem it.

⁵ Then said Boaz, What day thou buyest the field of the hand of Naomi, thou must buy it also of Ruth the Moabitess, the wife of the dead, to raise up the name of the dead upon his inheritance.

⁶ And the kinsman said, I cannot redeem it for myself, lest I mar mine own inheritance: redeem thou my right to thyself; for I cannot redeem it.

⁷ Now this was the manner in former time in Israel concerning redeeming and concerning changing, for to confirm all things; a man plucked off his shoe, and gave it to his neighbour: and this was a testimony in Israel.

[8] Therefore the kinsman said unto Boaz, Buy it for thee. So he drew off his shoe.

[9] And Boaz said unto the elders, and unto all the people, Ye are witnesses this day, that I have bought all that was Elimelech's, and all that was Chilion's and Mahlon's, of the hand of Naomi.

[10] Moreover Ruth the Moabitess, the wife of Mahlon, have I purchased to be my wife, to raise up the name of the dead upon his inheritance, that the name of the dead be not cut off from among his brethren, and from the gate of his place: ye are witnesses this day.

[11] And all the people that were in the gate, and the elders, said, We are witnesses. The LORD make the woman that is come into thine house like Rachel and like Leah, which two did build the house of Israel: and do thou worthily in Ephratah, and be famous in Bethlehem:

[12] And let thy house be like the house of Pharez, whom Tamar bare unto Judah, of the seed which the LORD shall give thee of this young woman.

[13] So Boaz took Ruth, and she was his wife: and when he went in unto her, the LORD gave her conception, and she bare a son.

[14] And the women said unto Naomi, Blessed be the LORD, which hath not left thee this day without a kinsman, that his name may be famous in Israel.

[15] And he shall be unto thee a restorer of thy life, and a nourisher of thine old age: for thy daughter in law, which loveth thee, which is better to thee than seven sons, hath born him.

[16] And Naomi took the child, and laid it in her bosom, and became nurse unto it.

[17] And the women her neighbours gave it a name, saying, There is a son born to Naomi; and they called his name Obed: he is the father of Jesse, the father of David.

[18] Now these are the generations of Pharez: Pharez begat Hezron,

[19] And Hezron begat Ram, and Ram begat Amminadab,

[20] And Amminadab begat Nahshon, and Nahshon begat Salmon,

[21] And Salmon begat Boaz, and Boaz begat Obed,

[22] And Obed begat Jesse, and Jesse begat David.

Notes

1. *Intreat me not.* When Naomi urges Ruth to return to her people, Ruth replies, "Intreat me not to leave thee, or to return from following after thee." *Ruth* 1:16. The first phrase of this famous passage ("Intreat me not to leave thee") can be read in two ways: (1) Don't ask me to leave you; or (2) Ask me not to leave you. Do you think the translators of the King James Bible intended these two meanings to be implied in the phrase? Does it matter whether they did or not? What complexity does the double meaning lend to the phrase?

Verses 16–17 of Chapter 1 of *Ruth* have been widely adapted for use as a wedding song. Does this usage strike you as odd?

2. *The Tone.* What is the moral, if any, of this story? From whose point of view is the story told and how does that affect what we learn about these characters?

3. *Women in the Bible.* Ruth and Naomi are frequently cited as examples of the Bible's depiction of strong, independent, virtuous women. How would you describe them?

JONAH

Chapter 1

[1] Now the word of the LORD came unto Jonah the son of Amittai, saying,

[2] Arise, go to Nineveh, that great city, and cry against it; for their wickedness is come up before me.

[3] But Jonah rose up to flee unto Tarshish from the presence of the LORD, and went down to Joppa; and he found a ship going to Tarshish: so he paid the fare thereof, and went down into it, to go with them unto Tarshish from the presence of the LORD.

[4] But the LORD sent out a great wind into the sea, and there was a mighty tempest in the sea, so that the ship was like to be broken.

[5] Then the mariners were afraid, and cried every man unto his god, and cast forth the wares that were in the ship into the sea, to lighten it of them. But Jonah was gone down into the sides of the ship; and he lay, and was fast asleep.

[6] So the shipmaster came to him, and said unto him, What meanest thou, O sleeper? arise, call upon thy God, if so be that God will think upon us, that we perish not.

[7] And they said every one to his fellow, Come, and let us cast lots, that we may know for whose cause this evil is upon us. So they cast lots, and the lot fell upon Jonah.

[8] Then said they unto him, Tell us, we pray thee, for whose cause this evil is upon us; What is thine occupation? and whence comest thou? what is thy country? and of what people art thou?

[9] And he said unto them, I am an Hebrew; and I fear the LORD, the God of heaven, which hath made the sea and the dry land.

[10] Then were the men exceedingly afraid, and said unto him, Why hast thou done this? For the men knew that he fled from the presence of the LORD, because he had told them.

[11] Then said they unto him, What shall we do unto thee, that the sea may be calm unto us? for the sea wrought, and was tempestuous.

¹² And he said unto them, Take me up, and cast me forth into the sea; so shall the sea be calm unto you: for I know that for my sake this great tempest is upon you.

¹³ Nevertheless the men rowed hard to bring it to the land; but they could not: for the sea wrought, and was tempestuous against them.

¹⁴ Wherefore they cried unto the LORD, and said, We beseech thee, O LORD, we beseech thee, let us not perish for this man's life, and lay not upon us innocent blood: for thou, O LORD, hast done as it pleased thee.

¹⁵ So they took up Jonah, and cast him forth into the sea: and the sea ceased from her raging.

¹⁶ Then the men feared the LORD exceedingly, and offered a sacrifice unto the LORD, and made vows.

¹⁷ Now the LORD had prepared a great fish to swallow up Jonah. And Jonah was in the belly of the fish three days and three nights.

Chapter 2

¹ Then Jonah prayed unto the LORD his God out of the fish's belly,

² And said, I cried by reason of mine affliction unto the LORD, and he heard me; out of the belly of hell cried I, and thou heardest my voice.

³ For thou hadst cast me into the deep, in the midst of the seas; and the floods compassed me about: all thy billows and thy waves passed over me.

⁴ Then I said, I am cast out of thy sight; yet I will look again toward thy holy temple.

⁵ The waters compassed me about, even to the soul: the depth closed me round about, the weeds were wrapped about my head.

⁶ I went down to the bottoms of the mountains; the earth with her bars was about me for ever: yet hast thou brought up my life from corruption, O LORD my God.

⁷ When my soul fainted within me I remembered the LORD: and my prayer came in unto thee, into thine holy temple.

⁸ They that observe lying vanities forsake their own mercy.

⁹ But I will sacrifice unto thee with the voice of thanksgiving; I will pay that that I have vowed. Salvation is of the LORD.

¹⁰ And the LORD spake unto the fish, and it vomited out Jonah upon the dry land.

Chapter 3

¹ And the word of the LORD came unto Jonah the second time, saying,

² Arise, go unto Nineveh, that great city, and preach unto it the preaching that I bid thee.

³ So Jonah arose, and went unto Nineveh, according to the word of the LORD. Now Nineveh was an exceeding great city of three days' journey.

⁴ And Jonah began to enter into the city a day's journey, and he cried, and said, Yet forty days, and Nineveh shall be overthrown.

⁵ So the people of Nineveh believed God, and proclaimed a fast, and put on sackcloth, from the greatest of them even to the least of them.

⁶ For word came unto the king of Nineveh, and he arose from his throne, and he laid his robe from him, and covered him with sackcloth, and sat in ashes.

⁷ And he caused it to be proclaimed and published through Nineveh by the decree of the king and his nobles, saying, Let neither man nor beast, herd nor flock, taste any thing: let them not feed, nor drink water:

⁸ But let man and beast be covered with sackcloth, and cry mightily unto God: yea, let them turn every one from his evil way, and from the violence that is in their hands.

⁹ Who can tell if God will turn and repent, and turn away from his fierce anger, that we perish not?

¹⁰ And God saw their works, that they turned from their evil way; and God repented of the evil, that he had said that he would do unto them; and he did it not.

Chapter 4

¹ But it displeased Jonah exceedingly, and he was very angry.

² And he prayed unto the LORD, and said, I pray thee, O LORD, was not this my saying, when I was yet in my country? Therefore I fled before unto Tarshish: for I knew that thou art a gracious God, and merciful, slow to anger, and of great kindness, and repentest thee of the evil.

³ Therefore now, O LORD, take, I beseech thee, my life from me; for it is better for me to die than to live.

⁴ Then said the LORD, Doest thou well to be angry?

⁵ So Jonah went out of the city, and sat on the east side of the city, and there made him a booth, and sat under it in the shadow, till he might see what would become of the city.

⁶ And the LORD God prepared a gourd, and made it to come up over Jonah, that it might be a shadow over his head, to deliver him from his grief. So Jonah was exceeding glad of the gourd.

⁷ But God prepared a worm when the morning rose the next day, and it smote the gourd that it withered.

⁸ And it came to pass, when the sun did arise, that God prepared a vehement east wind; and the sun beat upon the head of Jonah, that he fainted, and wished in himself to die, and said, It is better for me to die than to live.

[9] And God said to Jonah, Doest thou well to be angry for the gourd? And he said, I do well to be angry, even unto death.

[10] Then said the LORD, Thou hast had pity on the gourd, for the which thou hast not laboured, neither madest it grow; which came up in a night, and perished in a night:

[11] And should not I spare Nineveh, that great city, wherein are more than sixscore thousand persons that cannot discern between their right hand and their left hand; and also much cattle?

Notes

1. *The Great Fish.* What is the symbolic significance of the "great fish"? Of the gourd?

2. *The Genre.* Is *Jonah* a comedy? Tragedy? Morality tale? Why should we care about Jonah's pique with God?

CHAPTER 4

PLAYS

A. A STUDENT PRODUCTION

Several years ago the authors team-taught a course on law and drama. The course centered around the Scopes Trial (1925). The students read the complete transcript of the trial; visited the Rhea County (Tennessee) Courthouse, where the trial took place; saw the Clarence Brown Company production of the play, *Inherit the Wind*; and read many of the writings of Clarence Darrow and William Jennings Bryan.

As the final exam for the course, each student was required to write a one-act play on a subject of her choice. The following is one of those plays, reprinted here with the author's permission.

RUSH
Nicole C. Lally

Scene 1

A group of about seventy college-age girls are in their sorority chapter room. The girls are all Alpha Deltas, and students at a university in Mississippi. The chapter room is a very large living room, located inside a university dorm. The chapter room is freezing despite the Mississippi August heat outside, as the central air conditioning is running full blast, unregulated by a thermostat. The girls have on shorts and sweatshirts and are huddled together on the floor in groups under blankets.

The girls have just returned from their summer vacation, excited to be reunited with their friends and anticipating the week ahead—"Rush." Rush at this Mississippi university is a production. Those who wish to reform the Greek system have not yet succeeded at this University. Sorority Rush occurs before classes begin, and it lasts approximately a week. It is an event that is taken quite seriously by all involved.

A couple of chapter officers, Brooke and Ashley, are standing in the front of the room, next to the grand piano, trying to quiet the group of girls and get their attention. The officers are more than a little on edge, as Rush, and therefore the future of the chapter, rest in their hands.

BROOKE: *yelling*: All right, girls—Let's quiet down!!! I know every-one's excited to be back, but we've got a lot of work to do. If we are all quiet and pay attention, we can get out of here that much sooner.

Erin calls roll.

BROOKE: Now, Ashley is passing out a list of rushee names. We're going to go over this list and get to know these girls. Y'all, we've got some awesome girls that are coming through, and this Rush is going to be really big—so we really need to get to know all these girls before they walk through our doors in just a few days.

Maggie rushes in late with a pillow in her hand and pulling a long blanket behind her, and whispers "sorry" to Erin, who checks her off the roll.

Victoria turns on the overhead projector and puts a picture of a girl on the projector.

VICTORIA: Ok, I just want y'all to know that we don't have pictures on all these girls because they're not allowed to send them in with their rush applications. We just have them from alum recs.

This is Katy Abernathy. She is a freshman, from Milton, and she graduated from Milton High. She dances and was in the National Honor Society.

The girls scribble down notes next to Katy's name.

BROOKE: Do any of the Milton girls know her?

MISSY: I do. She's a good girl, but I'm not sure if she's an AD. Y'all will just have to get to know her.

About half the girls now put a question mark by Katy's name.

BROOKE: Ok. What's her name?

ALL *in unison*: Katy Abernathy.

BROOKE: Where's she from?

ALL: Milton.

BROOKE: What does she do?

ALL: Dances. . . . National Honor Society.

About half the group says one, and the other half says the other.

VICTORIA: OK, next, we have Beth Ackinson.

She puts the picture up on the projector and there are a few snickers from the audience. The girl pictured is heavy-set with large curly hair and heavy makeup.

BROOKE *admonishing*: Y'all be sweet!

Everyone quiets.

VICTORIA: This is Beth Ackinson. She's a junior from Jones Junior College, where she played in the band.

BROOKE: Anyone know her?

No one responds.

BROOKE: Ok, what's her name?

ALL: Beth Ack—

A fire alarm sounds. The entire group gets up moaning.

BROOKE: For the love of God ... Com'own y'all—Everyone go to the fire escape.

To Ashley Why do we live in this hell-hole? You would think they could at least fix the wiring in this place. It's freakin' 50 degrees in here! This is doing nothing for my nerves.

ASHLEY: No lie—I'll be right down.

Ashley dashes off.

Everyone files outside, chattering and complaining, all seemingly unconcerned by the extremely loud alarm.

NATALIE: Lord, does it have to be so loud? It's not like it doesn't happen once a week.

SASHA *laughing*: Yes, or Lee would sleep through it, too.

NATALIE *laughing*: So true—I hear her alarm woke up the Delta Chi's in the 8th floor last semester.

LEE: Y'all kiss my ass—I have sleep apnea.

Sasha rolls her eyes.

Natalie makes a hand like a claw and hisses like a cat.

NATALIE: Little testy this morning, aren't we—what happened, did your alarm actually wake you up this morning?

Lee chases Natalie down six flights of the fire escape.

Now the whole chapter is on the front lawn of the dorm building. The dorm is ten stories high, and each balcony has a different set of large wooden sorority letters on it. Other girls from other sororities are all filing out, some of them in bathrobes—obviously interrupted in the middle of their shower.

BROOKE *to a group of Ay Dees*: Have y'all seen Ashley?

TRACY: Holloway, Parker, Russel, or McMinn?

BROOKE: Holloway.

TRACY: No, where is she? She always takes these fire alarms a touch too seriously.

Ashley Holloway comes racing out of the dorm with a large framed document of some kind.

BROOKE: No, she did not....

TRACY: Oh my God!!!! Leave it to you, Holloway!

ASHLEY: Heck, yeah! Couldn't let the chapter charter go up in flames!

By this time the entire chapter is hysterically laughing.

TRACY: Leave it to Holloway—her family has given so much to this chapter that I swear she bleeds AD colors—green and white.

Scene 2

Later that day, after several rounds of "rushee review" have taken place, the Ay Dees have a little free time on their hands in which to eat and relax before the next scheduled event.

Sasha, Natalie, and Lee are in the sixth-floor bathroom, which is located on the same floor as the chapter room. Sasha is cranking open a window, while Lee and Natalie haul a large water hose to the window. They are all giddy and obviously up to mischief.

SASHA: Ok, y'all, here they come.

LEE *doubling over laughing*: Oh my God, this is so funny I might pee in my pants.

NATALIE: Ok, y'all tell me when to turn it on.

SASHA: Ok, now!

Voices from six floors below start screaming, while Sasha, Lee and Natalie are hysterically laughing, spraying the people below with water.

A few minutes later Brooke and Leslie come racing into the bathroom soaking wet, only to find that the perpetrators have fled.

TRACY *out of breath*: Ten bucks says this was Sasha and Maggie—I'm gonna kill them.

BROOKE: Heck with killin' em—let's soak 'em. Don't you have a water gun?

TRACY *grinning*: Yeah, that bazooka....

Loud noises erupt from outside the building.

BROOKE: What the . . .?

TRACY: Ohmigod—it's the freakin' AEB's!

BROOKE: Stop! Not a panty raid?

The fraternity boys below are yelling "Panty Raid!" and "Throw down your panties!"

BROOKE: How juvenile.

TRACY: Heh-heh—I have grannie panties for just this occasion.

BROOKE: That'll serve 'em right.

Tracy runs and gets her "grannie panties." She returns to the bathroom window and leans out the window, waving them around before she throws them down.

From an adjacent window, Sasha yells to the fraternity boys below:

SASHA: Leslie here says she'll give you her panties if you let her enter your wet T-shirt contest!!

TRACY *yelling back out the window at Sasha*: Sasha, I knew that was you with that damn hose! Watch out, because you're gonna be sleeping in a wet bed tonight!!

Sasha disappears from the window as she runs to lock her dorm room door. The scene fades.

Scene 3

Rush is moving inexorably toward closure. The entire chapter is excited, nervous, and full of adrenaline.

The scene is set in a University building, and all seventy girls are sitting in a square in one very large, and not surprisingly, very cold room.

NATALIE *sitting in her chair with her knees under her sweatshirt*: Man, it's freakin' freezing in here. Are they trying to make us all sick, or is that just a little bonus for them?

LEE: At least it's better than the dorm. I swear there are spores growing in my air filter, it hasn't been changed in so long.

BROOKE: All right, everybody, quiet down! This is our first bid session, so let's start things off right. We're going to open with a prayer, and then, Ann Doris, our rush advisor, is going to give us a few reminders about how this bid session should be run.

Everyone stands, hold hands, and bows their head.

STEPHANIE: Lord, we thank you for all of your blessings and for letting us all return this fall to share another year together. Lord, we thank you for our sisterhood, its bonds that unite us and its combined strength which is greater than any one of us could be on our own. Lord, we pray for all of the rushees, that each may find a home in a sisterhood of their own, and we pray that you will guide us tonight and help us to be kind and to make wise decisions. In Christ's name we pray.

ALL: Amen.

BROOKE: Thank you, Stephanie. Ann Doris, would you like to say a few words?

ANN DORIS: Sure, Brooke. I just want to remind all of you who have done this before about how a bid session is run, and explain a few things to those of you who are experiencing your first Rush. First, Rush is hard. It's physically exhausting and it's emotionally draining. We're going to have to work very hard the next few days in order to have a successful Rush, and y'all are going to have to make some really tough decisions. You're going to have to decide who the next Alpha Delta pledge class will be, and with that carries a huge burden. You need to listen to your sisters who know these rushees from home or who have met these rushees during Rush, and pay attention to their achievements. You may fall in love with a precious girl during Rush, but if she's not involved and an achiever, she may not be the best fit for us. And girls, no pettiness. None of this garbage about "she went out with my ex-boyfriend in high school." If you have a negative to say, it better be about matters of substance: scholarship, reputation, or group fit. Now, I'm done with my sermon, and I just want to explain one more thing. In bid session, we start out with a positive, then a negative may be said. If there are any negatives, then we have another positive. *And we always end on a positive.* And we have to cut forty-three girls tonight—Panhellenic rules.

BROOKE: Ok, thanks, Ann Doris. First we have Katy Abernathy.

Victoria places Katy's picture on the projector.

BROOKE: Do I have a positive?

Lee stands up.

LEE: I talked to her, and I thought she was very nice. Very easy to talk to. But she's from Milton, right? I'd like to hear from a Milton girl.

MISSY *standing*: I like her, but I'm not sure if she's a Ay Dee. I just wanted y'all to get to know her.

BROOKE: Any negatives? *Silence.* Ok, sounds like she's not a first day cut. Y'all get to know her. Heads down, voting cards up.

Brooke, Ann Doris, and Victoria count the number of negative votes and then confer. Victoria is flipping through a very large binder, containing information on many of the rushees.

BROOKE: Ok, she stays. Next is Beth Ackinson. Positive?

JENNIFER *standing*: I talked to her. She was nice, and she was very excited to be here.

BROOKE: Ok. Any negatives?

ROBIN *standing*: I found her hard to talk to. Plus, I don't think she's a group fit.

A few girls raise their hands in agreement.

BROOKE: Ok. Do I have another positive?

Silence.

C'mon girls.

BRITTNEY: She has a nice smile.

BROOKE: Good. Heads down, cards up.

Brooke, Victoria, and Ann Doris count again, and then confer.

BROOKE: She stays. Next we have Heather Adkins. Jennifer, since you are Heather's sister, I'm going to have to ask you to step out at this time.

Jennifer, one of the girls sitting in the square, gets up and walks outside. Everyone now seems on edge, and the tension in the room is palpable.

BROOKE: Ok, y'all. We're going to have a vote on Heather now, Jennifer's sister. Now let's remember, she is a legacy, and therefore she should get extra consideration. Can I have a positive?

PAGE *standing*: I love Heather. She is so fun. I got to know her this summer, and I think she'd be an asset to this chapter.

BROOKE: Negative?

ROBIN *slowly rising*: Ok, y'all. I hate to be the one to say it, but we all know it. Heather has a very questionable reputation. She is known to dabble in drugs and sleep around, and every Greenville girl knows it. I know her sister is in our chapter, and I love Jennifer to death, and if Heather wasn't so incredibly bad, I would just keep my mouth shut. But the truth of the matter is, if we take Heather, we can forget about getting any decent Greenville girl as long as she's in our chapter.

VICTORIA *looking at her binder from her seat at the table in the front of the room*: I have a few alum recommendations here that question Heather's reputation. Plus her grades aren't stellar. 2.97. Technically, we're supposed to cut anyone below a 3.0.

BROOKE: Ok, any positives?

PAGE: Well, I'll say it again. She's a fun girl. I'd love to call her a sister, and she sure thinks she's gonna be an Ay Dee. Not to mention it would be really shitty of us not to take her after all that Jennifer and her family have done for this chapter. What is it y'all—sisters by blood can't always be sisters in our chapter?

Page sits down.

ROBIN *standing again*: No, they can't. You're not born into our sisterhood; it's a process of mutual selection and a privilege—

BROOKE *interrupting*: Robin, you're out of order. Ok, I want to remind you that if we're going to cut a legacy, we can do it as late as tomorrow night, but not after that. If we're going to cut them, we need to do it in time for them to give another sorority a chance. We don't want them counting on a bid from us and then ending up not taking a bid from anyone. Let's vote. Heads down, cards up.

Brooke, Victoria, and Ann Doris count votes again and then confer.

Heather Adkins stays. You can bring Jennifer back in.

Jennifer comes back into the room.

JENNIFER: Geeze, that took a while. *She gives them all a funny look.*

BROOKE: Ok, next we have . . .

Scene fades.

Scene 4

The scene is the chapter room, but now the chapter room is largely unrecognizable. The sofas, chairs, and grand piano have been moved. The walls are covered from the floor to the very tall ceilings with painted drop cloths. The room has been reconstructed to suggest scenes from the Wizard of Oz. In the foyer is a painted plywood house, which has a witch's feet curled up beneath it. The chapter room has a bale of hay and cornstalks in one corner, a tinman's costume in another corner, and in the center of the room is a painted plywood Emerald Castle. White lights are strung from the ceiling, and, in the center of the room, there are rows of white wooden folding chairs. The Ay Dees are all dressed in brightly colored, solid, sleeveless, linen sundresses and sandals, with the exception of the characters, who are in costume. It is Day Three of Rush Week, the second to last day. Tensions are running very high as the mutual selection process continues: the sorority cutting some rushees, and the rushees cutting some sororities.

BROOKE: Have we seen the cut list this morning?

ASHLEY: Yes, Katy Abernathy cut us.

BROOKE: You're kidding? Oh, well, she wasn't one of our stars.

ASHLEY: How are you doing this morning? The chapter room looks awesome.

BROOKE: Thanks. It should.We were up till three. We need to make sure all of the girls are staying in the dorm this week. We'll need everyone here tonight to set up for tomorrow. God, Ashley, bid session last night killed me.

ASHLEY: It was terrible. I don't think there was a dry eye in that room.

BROOKE: Is Jennifer still here?

ASHLEY: No, she handed in her membership pin this morning. She's not taking it very well.

BROOKE: Who would? God, that was terrible. I'm so glad that I only count the votes, rather than cast them.

ASHLEY: Yea, but it needed to be done. I've put too much into this sorority to see that girl ruin our reputation.

BROOKE: Hmm. *Yelling*: Alright everybody—in your places!! Let's line up, and don't forget who your girl is!!

The chapter begins singing a song, and Brooke opens the door, and the rushees file in one by one. As the rushees enter the chapter room, they are met by an Ay Dee who is assigned to that rushee, and the Ay Dee escorts the rushee to a chair. The rushees are seated in the white chairs in the center of the room. After all of the rushees have been seated, the members cease singing and sit down in front of the rushees. After a few minutes, another Ay Dee replaces the one who has been sitting in front of a rushee, and the Ay Dee who has been relieved goes to relieve yet another Ay Dee. This process is called "rotation," and it enables many different Ay Dees to talk to many different rushees. However, no one Ay Dee talks to any one rushee for longer than ten minutes. After twenty minutes of rotation, the lights are dimmed, and a skit begins in the center of the room.

A girl dressed as Dorothy walks into the center of the room. She is wearing a rushee name tag that indicates that her name is Dorothy and that her home state is Kansas. She looks around, and says:

DOROTHY: Oh, my, Toto—where are we? I don't believe we're in Panhellenic Rush anymore.

In enters Claire, dressed as "Addie" the Good Witch. Addie is dressed in a tiara and large white ball gown with a full tulle skirt and is holding a magic wand.

CLAIRE: Don't be afraid, Dorothy. You have entered the land of Alpha Delta, a place you can call your home.

The skit continues, but the focus now turns to Brooke and Ashley, who are watching the skit intently from the back corner.

BROOKE: Ohmigod—Did our Addie just flub her line? Doesn't the home bit come a little later?

ASHLEY *chuckling*: Yeah, leave it to Claire. You can't honestly be surprised; that girl has a talent for making an entrance. You remember last year at Spring Formal she fell down in those heels and brought that potted tree down with her?

BROOKE *rolling her eyes*: Lord, give me strength. She's so beautiful, though. Makes such a great Addie. Anyway, I don't think the rushees caught on.

Dorothy continues on her way, meets the scarecrow, the tinman, and the lion, and travels to the Emerald City. Once in Emerald City, a kind and beautiful wizard, dressed in an emerald-hued gown, grants Dorothy's wish of sending her home by granting her a home in Ay Dee. Just then, a wicked witch appears, attempting to spoil the day. But the entire chapter, armed with glitter, throws the glitter on the witch, representing their bonds of sisterhood, and the wicked witch melts and disappears. The girls hold hands around the center of the room, sing a song in unison, and then go and talk to the rushees for another twenty minutes.

BROOKE *to Ashley*: I'm going to go say hello to some of the rushees. We've got to get rid of this skit next year. The cheese is unbelievable. Delta Chi's new skit is precious—so upbeat.

ASHLEY *looking worried*: I know. I'm gonna send one of our alums up there to watch it and report back.

The lights are dimmed and quick goodbyes are said. The Ay Dees rise and sing the following song as they escort the rushees to the door and send the rushees on their way to their next Rush party:

>Always think of Ay Dee when you hear this melody,
>We'll be wishing you goodnight in sleepy harmony.
>May days all be bright ones,
>May cares all be light ones,
>Tonight while moonlight beams.
>Dream tonight of Alpha Delta, we will dream of you.
>And when daylight comes again our love will still be true.
>So whisper goodnight, dear,
>In stillness may you hear
>The Alpha Delta Song of Dreams.

Brooke closes the door and places a finger over her lips.

BROOKE *whispering*: Quiet, girls. They can hear us out there. Now, go take your notes and then come back here to get the name of your next rushee.

Sasha elbows Lee.

SASHA *grinning*: Girl, you were so off key!

LEE *grinning back*: Whatever, Sasha! You're the one no one will let sing. Didn't they tell you just to mouth "watermelon, watermelon" when everyone else is singing?

Sasha grabs Addie's wand and hits Lee on the head.

NATALIE: Don't worry about it, y'all. We're not exactly known as singers. That's where Delta Chi kicks our butt.

SASHA: No lie . . .

The Delta Chis' melodies can be heard faintly in the Ay Dee chapter room. The Ay Dees scurry around, taking notes and cleaning up glitter, and the scene fades.

Scene 5

The scene is one of extreme excitement. Rush is over, and the Ay Dees have just learned the names of the girls who will comprise their next pledge class. Brooke, the rush chairman, is extremely pleased with the new pledge class and is smiling a genuine smile for the first time all week. The Ay Dees are all in their chapter room, which has been returned to more or less its original state, with the exception of some very large banners welcoming the new pledge class. The Ay Dees are all dressed in khaki shorts and the same T-shirt, a "bid-day" shirt. In the corner are about forty baskets, all containing a similar T-shirt and Ay Dee goodies for the new pledge class.

BROOKE *yelling above the excited din*: Alright, y'all! I just got a call from Greek Life—They're running over now!!

Immediately, all of the Ay Dees run out to their balcony to see all of the pledges in a full-out run to the Panhellenic dorm. Some of the pledges are headed to the Ay Dee chapter room, and the rest are headed to one of the other ten sororities. On every balcony in the Panhellenic building there are excited sorority members screaming to welcome their new pledges.

BROOKE *to herself*: Ohmigod, it's Courtney Radcliffe! I love her! I was so scared she was going Delta Chi. *Aloud*: Alright, y'all let's do "I'm an Ay!"

The Ay Dees begin clapping and chanting in unison:

> I am an Ay
> I am an Ay
> I am an A–L–P–H–A Dee–L–T–A
> And I have A–L–P–H–A Dee–L–T–A in my heart
> And I will L–O–V–E A–D F–O–R–E–V–E–R!
> I am an Ay . . .

The first of the new pledges runs into the room, and all of the Ay Dees scream. Several also hug her. The Ay Dee assigned to this new pledge brings that pledge her goodie basket, and offers her a soft drink and food. The ritual is repeated each time a new pledge runs through the door. When all of the new pledges have arrived, many group photos are taken, and in every picture, every single face is beaming. It is a time of celebration and sisterhood.

BROOKE: Alright, y'all. I just want to officially welcome you all to our chapter and say how excited we are to have you all here. All of you should have a Secret Sis, a member who picked you to show you the ropes of Ay Dee for the first few weeks. We're going to pass out a phone list, in case y'all need any of our numbers, and then we're going to head over to the pool at Becca White's house. Miss Becca is an alum of our chapter and is now an officer in National Ay Dee. So I have directions for those of you who are driving, and pledges, y'all can just ride over with your secret sis.

The Ay Dees, both new and old members, are still chatting excitedly. They start heading toward the door.

ASHLEY: Wait y'all—just one more thing! *Yelling:* HIP, HIP

ALL: Ay—DEE!

ASHLEY: HIP, HIP

ALL: Ay—DEE!

ASHLEY: HIP, HIP

ALL: AAAAAAAAY—DEEEE!!!

Everyone cheers, and then turns to leave. As the chapter room clears out, Ashley walks up to Brooke.

ASHLEY: So, Bee Dub knows to expect us?

BROOKE: Yes. And please pray to God that I don't slip up and call Becca White either Bee Dubyah or Bee Dub to her face. She might just die.

ASHLEY: Brooke, she does not have time to be offended. *Mocking Miss Becca's drawl and mannerisms*: Well, the cement business is just booming for Lawrence, so we're thinking about putting in a golf course, and I've had people out here looking at the lawn all week. Not to mention, Debbie, the Ay Dee national president, is just running me ragged, trying to prepare for this year's Ay Dee Convention.

BROOKE *laughing*: God, you've got her nailed! Did you hear about the new security gate?

ASHLEY: No!

BROOKE: Oh yes. It's this big gaudy brick and iron thing with "White" inscribed on the brick. It has a security code *and* automatic gates. It's a trip.

ASHLEY: That's hilarious! What will our poor pledges think! You comin'?

BROOKE: In a minute. You go ahead, and I'll meet you downstairs.

Brooke walks around the empty chapter room, picks up some paper off the floor, and walks out of the foyer into the stairwell shared by all of the Panhellenic dorm. Heather Adkins rushes by, smiling and wearing a Beta Phi bid shirt. Heather doesn't see Brooke at first.

BROOKE *smiling*: Hi, Heather. Congratulations on Beta Phi.

Heather just looks at Brooke, says nothing, and continues down the stairs.

Brooke's smile disappears. She sighs, closes the foyer door, and proceeds down the stairs to join her sisters.

Notes

1. *Attitude.* Does the writer approve of the sorority system? Disapprove? How can you tell?

2. *Theme.* What universal theme(s) does this play engage, if any?

B. GREEK DRAMA

Greek drama reached its zenith at Athens during the fifth century B.C. Aeschylus (525–456 B.C.), Sophocles (496–406 B.C.), and Euripides (c.480–405 B.C.) were the three greatest tragedians of the period, and indeed of any period.

The Greek chorus was an integral part of the Athenian theatre. Individual actors were a relatively late development in Greek drama. The actors wore masks that indicated their character.

Euripides, a prolific writer, was not greatly respected in his own time. Indeed, late in his career, he left Athens and moved to Macedonia, where he died. After writing *Alcestis,* which is almost a comedy, he produced some of the darkest tragedies of the Greek period, including *Medea.*

ALCESTIS
Euripides

Dramatis Personae

APOLLO
DEATH
CHORUS OF OLD MEN
A WOMAN SERVANT
ALCESTIS, the Queen, wife of ADMETUS
ADMETUS, King of Thessaly
EUMELUS, their child
HERACLES

PHERES, father of ADMETUS

At Pherae, outside the Palace of ADMETUS, King of Thessaly. The centre of the scene represents a portico with columns and a large double-door.To the left are the women's quarters, to the right the guest rooms.The centre doors of the Palace slowly open inwards, and Apollo comes out. In his left hand he carries a large unstrung golden bow. He moves slowly and majestically, turns, and raises his right hand in salutation to the Palace.

APOLLO: Dwelling of Admetus, wherein I, a God, deigned to accept the food of serfs!

The cause was Zeus. He struck Asclepius, my son, full in the breast with a bolt of thunder, and laid him dead. Then in wild rage I slew the Cyclopes who forge the fire of Zeus. To atone for this my Father forced me to labour as a hireling for a mortal man; and I came to this country, and tended oxen for my host. To this hour I have protected him and his. I, who am just, chanced on the son of Pheres, a just man, whom I have saved from Death by tricking the Fates. The Goddesses pledged me their faith Admetus should escape immediate death if, in exchange, another corpse were given to the Under-Gods.
One by one he tested all his friends, and even his father and the old mother who had brought him forth—and found none that would die for him and never more behold the light of day, save only his wife. Now, her spirit waiting to break loose, she droops upon his arm within the house; this is the day when she must die and render up her life. But I must leave this Palace's dear roof, for fear pollution soil me in the house.

See! Death, Lord of All the Dead, now comes to lead her to the house of Hades! Most punctually he comes! How well he marked the day she had to die!

(From the right comes DEATH, with a drawn sword in his hand. He moves stealthily towards the Palace; then sees APOLLO and halts abruptly. The two Deities confront each other.)

DEATH: Ha! Phoebus! You! Before this Palace! Lawlessly would you grasp, abolish the rights of the Lower Gods! Did you not beguile the Fates and snatch Admetus from the grave? Does not that suffice? Now, once again, you have armed your hand with the bow, to guard the daughter of Pelias who must die in her husband's stead!

APOLLO: Fear not! I hold for right, and proffer you just words.

DEATH: If you hold for right, why then your bow?

APOLLO: My custom is ever to carry it.

DEATH: Yes! And you use it unjustly to aid this house!

APOLLO: I grieve for a friend's woe.

DEATH: So you would rob me of a second body?

APOLLO: Not by force I won the other.

DEATH: Why, then, is he in the world and not below the ground?

APOLLO: In his stead he gives his wife—whom you have come to take.

DEATH: And shall take—to the Underworld below the earth!

APOLLO: Take her, and go! I know not if I can persuade you ...

DEATH: Not to kill her I must kill? I am appointed to that task.

APOLLO: No, no! But to delay death for those about to die.

DEATH: I hear your words and guess your wish!

APOLLO: May not Alcestis live to old age?

DEATH: No! I also prize my rights!

APOLLO: Yet at most you win one life.

DEATH: They who die young yield me a greater prize.

APOLLO: If she dies old, the burial will be richer.

DEATH: Phoebus, that argument favours the rich.

APOLLO: What! Are you witty unawares?

DEATH: The rich would gladly pay to die old.

APOLLO: So you will not grant me this favour?

DEATH: Not I! You know my nature.

APOLLO: Yes! Hateful to men and a horror to the gods!

DEATH: You cannot always have more than your due.

APOLLO: Yet you shall change, most cruel though you are! For a man comes to the dwelling of Pheres, sent by Eurystheus to fetch a horse-drawn chariot from the harsh-wintered lands of Thrace; and he shall be a guest in the house of Admetus, and by force shall he tear this woman from you. Thus shall you gain no thanks from us, and yet you shall do this thing—and my hatred be upon you.

(APOLLO goes out. DEATH gazes after him derisively.)

DEATH: Talk all you will, you get no more of me! The woman shall go down to the dwelling of Hades. Now must I go to consecrate her for the sacrifice with this sword; for when once this blade has shorn the victim's hair, then he is sacred to the Lower Gods!

(DEATH enters the Palace by the open main door. The CHORUS enters from the right. They are the Elders or Notables of the city, and, therefore move slowly, leaning upon their staffs.)

LEADER OF THE CHORUS *(chanting)*: Why is there no sound outside the Palace? Why is the dwelling of Admetus silent? Not a friend here to tell me if I must weep for a dead Queen or whether she lives and looks upon the light, Alcestis, the daughter of Pelias, whom among all women I hold the best wife to her spouse!

CHORUS *(Singing)*: Is a sob to be heard?
Or the beating of hands
In the house?

The lament for her end?
Not one,
Not one of her servants
Stands at the gate!
Ah! to roll back the wave of our woe,
O Healer,
Appear!

FIRST SEMI-CHORUS: Were she dead
They had not been silent.

SECOND SEMI-CHORUS: She is but a dead body!

FIRST SEMI-CHORUS: Yet she has not departed the house.

SECOND SEMI-CHORUS: Ah! Let me not boast!
Why do you cling to hope?

FIRST SEMI-CHORUS: Would Admetus bury her solitary,
Make a grave alone for a wife so dear?

CHORUS: At the gate I see not
The lustral water from the spring
Which stands at the gates of the dead!
No shorn tress in the portal
Laid in lament for the dead!
The young women beat not their hands!

SECOND SEMI-CHORUS: Yet to-day is the day appointed....

FIRST SEMI-CHORUS: Ah! What have you said?

SECOND SEMI-CHORUS: When she must descend under earth.

FIRST SEMI-CHORUS: You have pierced my soul!
You have pierced my mind!

SECOND SEMI-CHORUS: He that for long
Has been held in esteem
Must weep when the good are destroyed.

CHORUS: No!
There is no place on earth
To send forth a suppliant ship—
Not to Lycia,
Not to Ammon's waterless shrine—
To save her from death!
The dreadful doom is at hand.
To what laden altar of what God
Shall I turn my steps?
He alone—
If the light yet shone for his eye—
Asclepius, Phoebus's son,
Could have led her back
From the land of shadows,
From the gates of Hades,
For he raised the dead

Ere the Zeus-driven shaft
Slew him with thunder fire . . .
But now
What hope can I hold for her life?

LEADER (*chanting*): The King has fulfilled
Every rite;
The altars of all the Gods
Drip with the blood of slain beasts:
Nothing, nothing avails.

(*From the women's quarters in the left wing of the Palace comes a woman in tears. She is not a slave, but one of the personal attendants on the Queen.*)

But now from the house comes one of her women servants, all in tears. What now shall I learn?

(*To the weeping Servant*) It is well to weep when our lords are in sorrow—but tell us, we would know, is she alive, is she dead?

SERVANT: You may say she is both alive and dead.

LEADER: How can the same man be dead and yet behold the light?

SERVANT: She gasps, she is on the verge of death.

LEADER: Ah, unhappy man! For such a husband what loss is such a wife!

SERVANT: The King will not know his loss until he suffers it.

LEADER: Then there is no hope that her life may be saved?

SERVANT: The fated day constrains her.

LEADER: Are all things befitting prepared for her?

SERVANT: The robes in which her lord will bury her are ready.

LEADER: Then let her know that she dies gloriously, the best of women beneath the sun by far!

SERVANT: How should she not be the best! Who shall deny it? What should the best among women be? How better might a woman hold faith to her lord than gladly to die for him? This the whole city knows, but you will marvel when you hear what she has done within the house. When she knew that the last of her days was come she bathed her white body in river water, she took garments and gems from her rooms of cedar wood, and clad herself nobly; then, standing before the hearth-shrine, she uttered this prayer:

"O Goddess, since now I must descend beneath the earth, for the last time I make supplication to you: and entreat you to protect my motherless children. Wed my son to a fair bride, and my daughter to a noble husband. Let not my children die untimely, as I their mother am destroyed, but grant that they live out happy lives with good fortune in their own land!"

To every altar in Admetus's house she went, hung them with garlands, offered prayer, cut myrtle boughs—unweeping, unlamenting; nor did the coming doom change the bright colour of her face. Then to her marriage-room she went, flung herself down upon her bed, and wept, and said:

> "O my marriage-bed, wherein I loosed my virgin girdle to him for whom I die! Farewell! I have no hatred for you. Only me you lose. Because I held my faith to you and to my lord I must die. Another woman shall possess you, not more chaste indeed than I, more fortunate perhaps."

She fell upon her knees and kissed it, and all the bed was damp with the tide of tears which flooded to her eyes. And when she was fulfilled of many tears, drooping she rose from her bed and made as if to go, and many times she turned to go and many times turned back, and flung herself once more upon the bed. Her children clung to their mother's dress, and wept; and she clasped them in her arms and kissed them turn by turn, as a dying woman. All the servants in the house wept with compassion for their Queen, But she held out her hand to each, and there was none so base to whom she did not speak, and who did not reply again. Such is the misery in Admetus's house. If he had died, he would be nothing now; and, having escaped, he suffers an agony he will never forget.

LEADER: And does Admetus lament this woe—since he must be robbed of so noble a woman?

SERVANT: He weeps, and clasps in his arms his dear bedfellow, and cries to her not to abandon him, asking impossible things. For she pines, and is wasted by sickness. She falls away, a frail burden on his arm; and yet, though faintly, she still breathes, still strives to look upon the sunlight, which she shall never see hereafter—since now for the last time she looks upon the orb and splendour of the sun.

I go, and shall announce that you are here; for all men are not so well-minded to their lords as loyally to stand near them in misfortunes, but you for long have been a friend to both my lords.

(She goes back into the women's quarters of the Palace. The CHORUS now begins to sing.)

FIRST SEMI–CHORUS: O Zeus,
What end to these woes?
What escape from the Fate
Which oppresses our lords?

SECOND SEMI–CHORUS: Will none come forth?
Must I shear my hair?
Must we wrap ourselves
In black mourning folds?

FIRST SEMI–CHORUS: It is certain, O friends, it is certain?
But still let us cry to the Gods;
Very great is the power of the Gods.

CHORUS: O King, O Healer,
Seek out appeasement
To Admetus's agony!
Grant this, Oh, grant it!
Once before did you find it;
Now once more
Be the Releaser from death.
The Restrainer of blood-drenched Hades!

SECOND SEMI-CHORUS: Alas!
O son of Pheres.
What ills shall you suffer
Being robbed of your spouse!

FIRST SEMI-CHORUS: At sight of such woes
Shall we cut our throats?
Shall we slip
A dangling noose round our necks?

CHORUS: See! See!
She comes
From the house with her lord!
Cry out, Oh, lament.
O land of Pherae,
For the best of women
Fades away in her doom
Under the earth,
To dark Hades!

(From the central door of the Palace comes a splendid but tragical procession. Preceded by the royal guards, ADMETUS enters, supporting ALCESTIS. The two children, a boy and a girl, cling to their mother's dress. There is a train of attendants and waiting women, who bring a low throne for the fainting ALCESTIS.)

LEADER OF THE CHORUS *(chanting)*: Never shall I say that we ought to rejoice in marriage, but rather weep; this have I seen from of old and now I look upon the fate of the King, who loses the best of wives, and henceforth until the end his life shall be intolerable.

ALCESTIS *(chanting)*: Sun, and you, light of day,
Vast whirlings of swift cloud!

ADMETUS: The sun looks upon you and me, both of us miserable, who have wrought nothing against the Gods to deserve death.

ALCESTIS *(chanting)*: O Earth, O roof-tree of my home, Bridal-bed of my country, Iolcus!

ADMETUS: Rouse up, O unhappy one, and, do not leave me! Call upon the mighty Gods to pity!

ALCESTIS *(starting up and gazing wildly in terror, chanting)*: I see the two-oared boat, I see the boat on the lake! And Charon, Ferryman of the

Dead, calls to me, his hand on the oar: "Why linger? Hasten! You delay me!" Angrily he urges me.

ADMETUS: Alas! How bitter to me is that ferrying of which you speak! O my unhappy one, how we suffer!

ALCESTIS (chanting): He drags me, he drags me away—
Do you not see?—
To the House of the Dead,
The Winged One
Glaring under dark brows,
Hades!
What is it you do?
Set me free!
What a path must I travel,
O most hapless of women!

ADMETUS: O piteous to those that love you, above all to me and to these children who sorrow in this common grief!

ALCESTIS (chanting): Loose me, Oh, loose me now;
Lay me down;
All strength is gone from my feet.
(She falls back in the throne.)
Hades draws near!
Dark night falls on my eyes,
My children, my children,
Never more, Oh, never more
Shall your mother be yours!
O children, farewell,
Live happy in the light of day!

ADMETUS (chanting): Alas! I hear this unhappy speech, and for me it is worse than all death. Ah! By the Gods, do not abandon me! Ah! By our children, whom you leave motherless, take heart! If you die, I become as nothing; in you we have our life and death; we revere your love.

ALCESTIS (recovering herself): Admetus, you see the things I suffer; and now before I die I mean to tell you what I wish. To show you honour and at the cost of my life that you may still behold the light, I die; and yet I might have lived and wedded any in Thessaly I chose, and dwelt with happiness in a royal home. But, torn from you, I would not live with fatherless children, nor have I hoarded up those gifts of youth in which I found delight. Yet he who begot you, she who brought you forth, abandoned you when it had been beautiful in them to die, beautiful to die with dignity to save their son! They had no child but you, no hope if you were dead that other children might be born to them. Thus I should have lived my life out, and you too, and you would not lament as now, made solitary from your wife, that you must rear our children motherless! But these things are a God's doing and are thus.

Well! Do not forget this gift, for I shall ask—not a recompense, since nothing is more precious than life, but—only what is just, as you yourself will say, since if you have not lost your senses you must love these children no less than I. Let them be masters in my house; marry not again, and set a stepmother over them, a woman harsher than I, who in her jealousy will lift her hand against my children and yours. Ah! not this, let not this be, I entreat you! The new stepmother hates the first wife's children, the viper itself is not more cruel. The son indeed finds a strong rampart in his father—but you, my daughter, how shall you live your virgin life out in happiness? How will you fare with your father's new wife? Ah! Let her not cast evil report upon you and thus wreck your marriage in the height of your youth!

You will have no mother, O my child, to give you in marriage, to comfort you in childbed when none is tenderer than a mother! And I must die. Not to-morrow nor to-morrow's morrow comes this misfortune on me, but even now I shall be named with those that are no more. Farewell! Live happy! You, my husband, may boast you had the best of wives; and you, my children, that you lost the best of mothers!

(She falls back.)

LEADER: Take heart! I do not hesitate to speak for him. This he will do, unless he has lost his senses.

ADMETUS: It shall be so, it shall be! Have no fear! And since I held you living as my wife, so, when dead, you only shall be called my wife, and in your place no bride of Thessaly shall salute me hers; no other woman is noble enough for that, no other indeed so beautiful of face. My children shall suffice me; I pray the Gods I may enjoy them, since you we have not enjoyed. I shall wear mourning for you, O my wife, not for one year but all my days, abhorring the woman who bore me, hating my father— for they loved me in words, not deeds. But you—to save my life you give the dearest thing you have! Should I not weep then, losing such a wife as you? I shall make an end of merry drinking parties, and of flower-crowned feasts and of the music which possessed my house. Never again shall I touch the lyre, never again shall I raise my spirits to sing to the Libyan flute—for you have taken from me all my joy. Your image, carven by the skilled hands of artists, shall be laid in our marriage-bed; I shall clasp it, and my hands shall cling to it and I shall speak your name and so, not having you, shall think I have my dear wife in my arms—a cold delight, I know, but it will lighten the burden of my days. Often you will gladden me, appearing in my dreams; for sweet it is to look on those we love in dreams, however brief the night.

Ah! If I had the tongue and song of Orpheus so that I might charm Demeter's Daughter or her Lord, and snatch you back from Hades, I would go down to hell; and neither Pluto's dog nor Charon, Leader of the Dead, should hinder me until I had brought your life back to the light! At least await me there whenever I shall die, and prepare the house where you will dwell with me. I shall lay a solemn charge upon these children to stretch me in the same cedar shroud with you, and lay my side against your side; for even in death let me not be separate from you, you who alone were faithful to me!

LEADER *(to ADMETUS)*: And I also will keep this sad mourning with you, as a friend with a friend; for she is worthy of it.

ALCESTIS: O my children, you have heard your father say that never will he set another wife over you and never thus insult me.

ADMETUS: Again I say it, and will perform it too!

ALCESTIS *(placing the children's hands in his)*: Then take these children from my hand.

ADMETUS: I take them—dear gifts from a dear hand.

ALCESTIS: Now you must be the mother for me to my children.

ADMETUS: It must be so, since they are robbed of you.

ALCESTIS: O children, I should have lived my life out—and I go to the Underworld.

ADMETUS: Alas! What shall I do, left alone by you?

ALCESTIS: Time will console you. The dead are nothing.

ADMETUS: Take me with you, by the Gods! Take me to the Underworld!

ALCESTIS: It is enough that I should die—for you.

ADMETUS: O Fate, what a wife you steal from me!

ALCESTIS *(growing faint)*: My dimmed eyes are heavily oppressed.

ADMETUS: O woman, I am lost if you leave me!

ALCESTIS: You may say of me that I am nothing.

ADMETUS: Lift up your head! Do not abandon your children!

ALCESTIS: Ah! Indeed it is unwillingly—but, farewell, my children!

ADMETUS: Look at them, look....

ALCESTIS: I am nothing.

ADMETUS: What are you doing? Are you leaving me?

ALCESTIS *(falling back dead)*: Farewell.

ADMETUS *(staring at the body)*: Wretch that I am, I am lost!

LEADER: She is gone! The wife of Admetus is no more.

EUMELUS *(chanting)*: Ah! Misery!
Mother has gone,
Gone to the Underworld!
She lives no more,
O my Father,
In the sunlight.
O sad one,
You have left us
To live motherless!

See, Oh, see her eyelids
And her drooping hands!
Mother, Mother,
Hearken to me, listen,
I beseech you!
Mother!
I am calling to you,
Your little bird fallen upon your face!

ADMETUS: She hears not, she sees not. You and I are smitten by a dread calamity.

EUMELUS (*chanting*): Father, I am a child,
And I am left
Like a lonely ship
By the mother I loved.
Oh! The cruel things I suffer!
And you, little sister,
Suffer with me.
O my Father,
Vain, vain was your wedding,
You did not walk with her
To the end of old age.
She died first;
And your death, O Mother,
Destroys our house.

LEADER: Admetus, you must endure this calamity. You are not the first and will not be the last to lose a noble wife. We all are doomed to die.

ADMETUS: I know it. Not unawares did this woe swoop down on me; for long it has gnawed at me. But, since I shall ordain the funeral rites for this dead body, you must be there, and meanwhile let a threnody re-echo to the implacable God of the Underworld. And all you men of Thessaly whom I rule—I order you to share the mourning for this woman with severed hair and black-robed garb. You who yoke the four-horsed chariot and the swift single horses, cut the mane from their necks with your steel. Let there be no noise of flutes or lyre within the city until twelve moons are fulfilled. Never shall I bury another body so dear to me, never one that has loved me better. From me she deserves all honour, since she alone would die for me!

(*The body of ALCESTIS is carried solemnly into the Palace, followed by ADMETUS, with bowed head, holding one of his children by each hand. When all have entered, the great doors are quietly shut.*)

CHORUS (*singing, strophe 1*):
O Daughter of Pelias,
Hail to you in the house of Hades,
In the sunless home where you shall dwell!

Let Hades, the dark-haired God,
Let the old man, Leader of the Dead,
Who sits at the oar and helm,
Know you:
Far, far off is the best of women
Borne beyond the flood of Acheron
In the two-oared boat!

(antistrophe 1)

Often shall the Muses' servants
Sing of you to the seven-toned
Lyre-shell of the mountain-tortoise,
And praise you with mourning songs at Sparta
When the circling season
Brings back the month Carneius
Under the nightlong upraised moon,
And in bright glad Athens.
Such a theme do you leave by your death
For the music of singers!

(strophe 2)

Ah! That I had the power
To bring you back to the light
From the dark halls of Hades,
And from the waves of Cocytus
With the oar of the river of hell
Oh, you only,
O dearest of women,
You only dared give your life
For the life of your lord in Hades!
Light rest the earth above you,
O woman.
If your lord choose another bridal-bed
He shall be hateful to me
As to your own children.

(antistrophe 2)

When his mother
And the old father that begot him
Would not give their bodies to the earth
For their son's sake,
They dared not deliver him—O cruel!
Though their heads were grey.
But you,
In your lively youth,
Died for him, and are gone from the light!
Ah! might I be joined
With a wife so dear!
But in life such fortune is rare.
How happy were his days with her!

(From the left HERACLES enters.
He is black-bearded and of great physical strength; he wears a lion-skin over his shoulders and carries a large club.)

HERACLES *(with a gesture of salutation)*: Friends, dwellers in the lands of Pherae, do I find Admetus in his home?

LEADER OF THE CHORUS: The son of Pheres is in his home, O Heracles. But, tell us, what brings you to the land of Thessaly and to the city of Pherae?

HERACLES: I have a task I must achieve for Eurystheus of Tiryns.

LEADER: Where do you go? To what quest are you yoked?

HERACLES: The quest of the four-horsed chariot of Diomedes, the Thracian.

LEADER: But how will you achieve it? Do you know this stranger?

HERACLES: No, I have never been to the land of the Bistones.

LEADER: You cannot obtain the horses without a struggle.

HERACLES: I cannot renounce my labours.

LEADER: You must kill to return, or you will remain there dead.

HERACLES: It will not be the first contest I have risked.

LEADER: And if you conquer the King will you gain anything?

HERACLES: I shall bring back his foals to the lord of Tiryns.

LEADER: It is not easy to thrust the bit into their jaws.

HERACLES: Only if they breathe fire from their nostrils!

LEADER: But they tear men with their swift jaws.

HERACLES: You speak of the food of wild mountain beasts, not of horses.

LEADER: You may see their mangers foul with blood.

HERACLES: Of what father does the breeder boast himself the son?

LEADER: Of Ares, the lord of the gold-rich shield of Thrace!

HERACLES: In this task once more you remind me of my fate, which is ever upon harsh steep ways, since I must join battle with the sons of Ares—first with Lycaon, then with Cycnus, and now in this third contest I am come to match myself with these steeds and their master!

LEADER: But see, the lord of this land, Admetus himself, comes from the house!

(The central doors of the Palace have opened, and ADMETUS comes slowly on the Stage, preceded and followed by guards and attendants. The King has put off all symbols of royalty, and is dressed in black. His long hair is clipped close to his head. ADMETUS dissembles his grief throughout this scene, in obedience to the laws of hospitality, which were particularly reverenced in Thessaly.)

ADMETUS: Hail Son of Zeus and of the blood of Perseus!

HERACLES: And hail to you, Admetus, lord of the Thessalians

ADMETUS: May it be so! I know your friendship well.

HERACLES: What means this shorn hair, this mourning robe?

ADMETUS: To-day I must bury a dead body.

HERACLES: May a God avert harm from your children!

ADMETUS: The children I have begotten are alive in the house.

HERACLES: Your father was ripe for death—is it is he has gone?

ADMETUS: He lives—and she who brought me forth, O Heracles.

HERACLES: Your wife—Alcestis—she is not dead?

ADMETUS *(evasively)*: Of her I might make a double answer.

HERACLES: Do you mean that she is dead or alive?

ADMETUS *(ambiguously)*: She is and is not—and for this I grieve.

HERACLES *(perplexed)*: I am no wiser—you speak obscurely.

ADMETUS: Did you not know the fate which must befall her?

HERACLES: I know she submitted to die for you.

ADMETUS: How then can she be alive, having consented to this?

HERACLES: Ah! Do not weep for your wife till that time comes.

ADMETUS: Those who are about to die are dead, and the dead are nothing.

HERACLES: Men hold that to be and not to be are different things.

ADMETUS: You hold for one, Heracles, and I for the other.

HERACLES: Whom, then, do you mourn? Which of your friends is dead?

ADMETUS: A woman. We spoke of her just now.

HERACLES *(mistaking his meaning)*: A stranger? Or one born of your kin?

ADMETUS: A stranger, but one related to this house.

HERACLES: But how, then, did she chance to die in your house?

ADMETUS: When her father died she was sheltered here.

HERACLES: Alas! Would I had not found you in this grief, Admetus!

ADMETUS: What plan are you weaving with those words?

HERACLES: I shall go to the hearth of another friend.

ADMETUS: Not so, O King! This wrong must not be.

HERACLES *(hesitating)*: The coming of a guest is troublesome to those who mourn.

ADMETUS *(decisively)*: The dead are dead. Enter my house.

HERACLES: But it is shameful to feast among weeping friends.

ADMETUS: We shall put you in the guest-rooms, which are far apart.

HERACLES: Let me go, and I will give you a thousand thanks.

ADMETUS: No, you shall not go to another man's hearth. *(To a servant)* Guide him, and open for him the guest-rooms apart from the house.

(HERACLES enters the Palace by the guests' door; when he has gone in, ADMETUS turns to the other servants)

Close the inner door of the courtyard; it is unseemly that guests rejoicing at table should hear lamentations, and be saddened.

(The attendants go into the Palace.)

LEADER: What are you about? When such a calamity has fallen upon you, Admetus, have you the heart to entertain a guest? Are you mad?

ADMETUS: And if I had driven away a guest who came to my house and city, would you have praised me more? No, indeed! My misfortune would have been no less, and I inhospitable. One more ill would have been added to those I have if my house were called inhospitable. I myself find him the best of hosts when I enter the thirsty land of Argos.

LEADER: But why did you hide from him the fate that has befallen, if the man came as a friend, as you say?

ADMETUS: Never would he have entered my house if he had guessed my misfortune. To some, I know, I shall appear senseless in doing this, and they will blame me; but my roof knows not to reject or insult a guest.

(He goes into the Palace, as the CHORUS begins its song.)

CHORUS *(singing, strophe 1)*:
O house of a bountiful lord,
Ever open to many guests,
The God of Pytho,
Apollo of the beautiful lyre,
Deigned to dwell in you
And to live a shepherd in your lands!
On the slope of the hillsides
He played melodies of mating
On the Pipes of Pan to his herds.

(antistrophe 1)
And the dappled lynxes fed with them
In joy at your singing;
From the wooded vale of Orthrys
Came a yellow troop of lions;
To the sound of your lyre, O Phoebus,
Danced the dappled fawn
Moving on light feet
Beyond the high-crested pines,
Charmed by your sweet singing. . . .

(The funeral procession of ALCESTIS enters from the door of the women's quarters. The body, carried on a bier by men servants, is followed by

*ADMETUS and his two children. Behind them comes a train of attend-
ants and servants carrying the funeral offerings. All are in mourning.
ADMETUS addresses the CHORUS.)*

ADMETUS: O friendly presence of you men of Pherae! Now that the
body is prepared, and the servants bear it on high to the tomb and the
fire, do you, as is fitting, salute the dead as she goes forth on her last
journey.

*(PHERES, the father of ADMETUS, enters, followed by attendants bear-
ing funeral offerings.)*

LEADER OF THE CHORUS: But I see your father, tottering with an
old man's walk, and his followers bearing in their hands for your wife
garments as an offering to the dead.

PHERES: My son, I have come to share your sorrow, for the wife you
have lost was indeed noble and virtuous—none can deny it. But these
things must be endured, however intolerable they may be. Take these
garments, and let her descend under the earth. Her body must be
honoured, for she died to save your life, my son; she has not made me
childless, nor left me to be destroyed without you in my hapless old age;
and she has given glorious fame to all women by daring so noble a deed!
(He lifts his hand in salutation to the body of ALCESTIS.) O woman,
who saved my son, who raised me up when I had fallen, hail! Be happy
in the halls of Hades! I declare it—such marriages are profitable to
mankind; otherwise, it is foolish to marry.

ADMETUS *(furiously)*: It was not my wish that you should come to this
burial, and I deny that your presence is that of a friend! She shall never
wear these garments of yours; she needs not your gifts for her burial.
You should have grieved when I was about to die; but you stood aside,
and now do you come to wail over a corpse when you, an old man,
allowed a young woman to die? Were you in very truth father of this
body of mine? Did she, who claims to be and is called my mother, bring
me forth? Or was I bred of a slave's seed and secretly brought to your
wife's breast? You have proved what you are when it comes to the test,
and therefore I am not your begotten son; or you surpass all men in
cowardice, for, being at the very verge and end of life, you had neither
courage nor will to die for your son. But this you left to a woman, a
stranger, whom alone I hold as my father and my mother! Yet it had
been a beautiful deed in you to die for your son, and short indeed was
the time left you to live. She and I would have lived out our lives, and I
should not now be here alone lamenting my misery. . . .

LEADER: Admetus! The present misfortune is enough. Do not provoke
your father's spirit.

(ADMETUS turns angrily to depart, but PHERES prevents him.)

PHERES: My son, do you think you are pursuing some hireling Lydian
or Phrygian with your taunts? Do you know I am a Thessalian, a free
man lawfully begotten by a Thessalian father? You are over-insolent, and
you shall not leave thus, after wounding me with your boyish insults.

I indeed begot you, and bred you up to be lord of this land, but I am not bound to die for you. It is not a law of our ancestors or of Hellas that the fathers should die for the children! You were born to live your own life, whether miserable or fortunate; and what is due to you from me you have. You rule over many men, and I shall leave you many wide fields even as I received them from my own father. How, then, have I wronged you? Of what have I robbed you? Do not die for me, any more than I die for you. You love to look upon the light of day—do you think your father hates it? I tell myself that we are a long time underground and that life is short, but sweet. . . .

LEADER: These insults and those that went before suffice. Old man, cease to revile your son.

ADMETUS *(to PHERES)*: Speak on! I shall refute you. If the truth wounds you when you hear it you should not have wronged me.

PHERES: I should have wronged you far more if I had died for you.

ADMETUS: Dying is different for an old man. I am young.

PHERES: A man has but one life to live—his own.

ADMETUS: May you live longer than God!

PHERES: Do you curse your parents when they have done you no wrong?

ADMETUS: I see you are in love with long life.

PHERES: But you are not carrying her dead body in place of your own?

ADMETUS: It is the proof of your cowardice, O worst of men.

PHERES: You cannot say she died for me!

ADMETUS: Alas! May you one day need my help.

PHERES: Woo many women, so that more may die for you.

ADMETUS: To your shame be it—you who dared not die.

PHERES: Sweet is the daylight of the Gods, very sweet.

ADMETUS: Your spirit is mean, not a man's.

PHERES: Would you laugh to carry an old man's body to the grave?

ADMETUS: You will die infamous, whenever you die.

PHERES: It will matter little enough to me to hear ill of myself when I am dead!

ADMETUS: Alas! Alas! full of impudence is old age!

PHERES: She was not impudent, but foolish.

ADMETUS: Go! Leave me to bury her body.

PHERES *(turning away)*: I go. You, her murderer, will bury her—but soon you must render an account to her relatives. Acastus is not a man if he fails to avenge his sister's blood on you!

(PHERES goes out by the way he entered, followed by his attendants. ADMETUS gazes angrily after him.)

ADMETUS: Go with a curse, you, and she who dwells with you! Grow old, as you ought, childless though you have a child. You shall never return to this house. And if I could renounce your hearth as my father's by heralds, I would do it. But we—since this sorrow must be endured—let us go, and set her body on the funeral pyre.

(The Procession moves slowly along the stage, and is joined by the CHORUS. As they pass, the LEADER salutes the body of ALCESTIS.)

LEADER *(chanting)*: Alas! Alas! You who suffer for your courage, O noblest and best of women, hail! May Hermes of the Dead, may Hades, greet you kindly. If there are rewards for the dead, may you share them as you sit by the bride of the Lord of the Dead!

(The Procession has filed out. A servant in mourning hurries out from the guests' quarters.)

SERVANT: Many guests from every land, I know, have come to the Palace of Admetus, and I have set food before them, but never one worse than this guest have I welcomed to the hearth. First, though he saw our Lord was in mourning, he entered, and dared to pass through the gates. Then, knowing our misfortune, he did not soberly accept what was offered him, but if anything was not served to him he ordered us to bring it. In both hands he took a cup of ivy-wood, and drank the unmixed wine of the dark grape-mother, until he was encompassed and heated with the flame of wine. He crowned his head with myrtle sprays, howling discordant songs. There was he caring nothing for Admetus's misery, and we servants weeping for our Queen; and yet we hid our tear-laden eyes from the guest, for so Admetus had commanded. And now in the Palace I must entertain this stranger, some villainous thief and brigand, while she, the Queen I mourn, has gone from the house unfollowed, unsaluted, she who was as a mother to me and all us servants, for she sheltered us from a myriad troubles by softening her husband's wrath. Am I not right, then, to hate this stranger, who came to us in the midst of sorrow?

(HERACLES comes from the Palace. He is drunkenly merry, with a myrtle wreath on his head, and a large cup and wine-skin in his hands. He staggers a little.)

HERACLES: Hey, you! Why so solemn and anxious? A servant should not be sullen with guests, but greet them with a cheerful heart. You see before you a man who is your lord's friend, and you greet him with a gloomy, frowning face, because of your zeal about a strange woman's death. Come here, and let me make you a little wiser! *(With drunken gravity)* Know the nature of human life? Don't think you do. You couldn't. Listen to me. All mortals must die. Isn't one who knows if he'll be alive to-morrow morning. Who knows where Fortune will lead? Nobody can teach it. Nobody learn it by rules. So, rejoice in what you hear, and learn from me! Count each day as it comes as Life—and leave the rest to Fortune. Above all, honour the Love Goddess, sweetest of all the Gods to mortal men, a kindly goddess! Put all the rest aside. Trust in what I say, if you think I speak truth as I believe. Get rid of this gloom, rise superior to Fortune. Crown yourself with flowers and drink with me, won't you? I know the regular clink of the wine-cup will rouse you from darkness and gloom to another haven. Mortals should think mortal thoughts. To all solemn and frowning men, life I say is not life, but a disaster.

SERVANT: We know all that, but what we endure here to-day is far indeed from gladness and laughter.

HERACLES: But the dead woman was a stranger. Lament not over-much, then, for the Lords of this Palace are still alive.

SERVANT: How, alive? Do you not know the misery of this house?

HERACLES: Your lord did not lie to me?

SERVANT: He goes too far in hospitality!

HERACLES: But why should I suffer for a stranger's death?

SERVANT: It touches this house only too nearly.

HERACLES: Did he hide some misfortune from me?

SERVANT: Go in peace! The miseries of our lords concern us.

HERACLES: That speech does not imply mourning for a stranger!

SERVANT: No, or I should not have been disgusted to see you drinking.

HERACLES: Have I then been basely treated by my host?

SERVANT: You did not come to this house at a welcome hour. We are in mourning. You see my head is shaved and the black garments I wear.

HERACLES: But who, then, is dead? One of the children? The old father?

SERVANT: O stranger, Admetus no longer has a wife.

HERACLES: What! And yet I was received in this way?

SERVANT: He was ashamed to send you away from his house.

HERACLES: O hapless one! What a wife you have lost!

SERVANT: Not she alone, but all of us are lost.

HERACLES *(now completely sobered)*: I felt there was something when I saw his tear-wet eyes, his shaven head, his distracted look. But he persuaded me he was taking the body of a stranger to the grave. Against my will I entered these gates, and drank in the home of this generous man—and he in such grief! And shall I drink at such a time with garlands of flowers on my head? You, why did you not tell me that such misery had come upon this house? Where is he burying her? Where shall I find him?

SERVANT: Beside the straight road which leads to Larissa you will see a tomb of polished stone outside the walls. *(Returns to the servants' quarters.)*

HERACLES: O heart of me, much-enduring heart, O right arm, now indeed must you show what son was born to Zeus by Alcmena, the Tirynthian, daughter of Electryon! For I must save this dead woman, and bring back Alcestis to this house as a grace to Admetus. I shall watch for Death, the black-robed Lord of the Dead, and I know I shall find him near the tomb, drinking the blood of the sacrifices. If I can leap upon him from an ambush, seize him, grasp him in my arms, no power in the world shall tear his bruised sides from me until he has yielded up this woman. If I miss my prey, if he does not come near the bleeding sacrifice, I will go down to Kore and her lord in their sunless dwelling, and I will make my entreaty to them, and I know they will give me Alcestis to bring back to the hands of the host who welcomed me, who did not repulse me from his house, though he was smitten with heavy woe which most nobly he hid from me! Where would be a warmer welcome in Thessaly or in all the dwellings of Hellas? He shall not say he was generous to an ingrate!

(HERACLES goes out. Presently ADMETUS and his attendants, followed by the CHORUS, return from the burial of ALCESTIS.)

ADMETUS *(chanting)*: Alas!

Hateful approach, hateful sight of my widowed house! Oh me! Oh me! Alas! Whither shall I go? Where rest? What can I say? What refrain from saying? Why can I not die? Indeed my mother bore me for a hapless fate. I envy the dead, I long to be with them, theirs are the dwellings where I would be. Without pleasure I look upon the light of day and set my feet upon the earth—so precious a hostage has Death taken from me to deliver unto Hades!

CHORUS *chanting responsively with ADMETUS)*: Go forward,
Enter your house.

ADMETUS: Alas!

CHORUS: Your grief deserves our tears.

ADMETUS: O Gods!

CHORUS: I know you have entered into sorrow.

ADMETUS: Woe! Woe!

CHORUS: Yet you bring no aid to the dead.

ADMETUS: Oh me! Oh me!

CHORUS: Heavy shall it be for you
Never to look again
On the face of the woman you love.

ADMETUS: You bring to my mind the grief that breaks my heart. What sorrow is worse for a man than the loss of such a woman? I would I had never married, never shared my house with her. I envy the wifeless and the childless. They live but one life—what is suffering to them? But the sickness of children, bridal-beds ravished by Death—dreadful! when we might be wifeless and childless to the end.

CHORUS: Chance, dreadful Chance, has stricken you.

ADMETUS: Alas!

CHORUS: But you set no limit to your grief.

ADMETUS: Ah! Gods!

CHORUS: A heavy burden to bear, and yet....

ADMETUS: Woe! Woe!

CHORUS: Courage! You are not the first to lose....

ADMETUS: Oh me! Oh me!

CHORUS: A wife.
Different men
Fate crushes with different blows....

ADMETUS (*speaking*): O friends, whatsoever may be thought by others, to me it seems that my wife's fate is happier than mine. Now, no pain ever shall touch her again; she has reached the noble end of all her sufferings. But I, I who should have died, I have escaped my fate, only to drag out a wretched life. Only now do I perceive it. How shall I summon strength to enter this house? Whom shall I greet? Who will greet me in joy at my coming? Whither shall I turn my steps? I shall be driven forth by solitude when I see my bed widowed of my wife, empty the chairs on which she sat, a dusty floor beneath my roof, my children falling at my knees and calling for their mother, and the servants lamenting for the noble lady lost from the house! ...

(*He covers his head with his robe, and crouches in abject misery on the steps of his Palace.*)

CHORUS (*singing, strophe 1*):
I have lived with the Muses
And on lofty heights:
Many doctrines have I learned;
But Fate is above us all.
Nothing avails against Fate
Neither the Thracian tablets
Marked with Orphic symbols,
Nor the herbs given by Phoebus
To the children of Asclepius
To heal men of their sickness.

(*antistrophe 1*)
None can come near to her altars,
None worship her statues;
She regards not our sacrifice.
O sacred goddess,
Bear no more hardly upon me
Than in days overpast!
With a gesture Zeus judges,
But the sentence is yours.
Hard iron yields to your strength;
Your fierce will knows not gentleness....

(*ADMETUS is still crouched on the Palace steps, when HERACLES enters from the side, leading a veiled woman.*)

LEADER OF THE CHORUS: But see! The son of Alcmena, as I think, comes to your house.

(ADMETUS uncovers his head, and faces the newcomer.)

HERACLES: Admetus, a man should speak freely to his friends, and not keep reproaches silent in his heart. Since I was near you in your misfortune, should have wished to show myself your friend. But you did not tell me the dead body was your wife's, and you took me into your house as if you were in mourning only for a stranger. And I put a garland of flowers upon my head, and poured wine-offerings to the Gods, when your house was filled with lamentation. I blame you, yes, I blame you for this—but I will not upbraid you in your misfortune. Why I turned back and am here, I shall tell you. Take and keep this woman for me until I have slain the King of the Bistones and return here with the horses of Thrace. If ill happens to me—may I return safely!—I give her to you to serve in your house. With much striving I won her to my hands. On my way I found public games, worthy of athletes, and I have brought back this woman whom I won as the prize of victory. The winners of the easy tests had horses; heads of cattle were given to those who won in boxing and wrestling. Then came a woman as a prize. Since I was present, it would have been shameful for me to miss this glorious gain. Therefore, as I said, you must take care of this woman, whom I bring to you, not as one stolen but as the prize of my efforts. Perhaps in time you will approve of what I do.

ADMETUS: Not from disdain, nor to treat you as a foe, did I conceal my wife's fate from you. But if you had turned aside to another man's hearth, one more grief had been added to my sorrow. It was enough that I should weep my woe. This woman—O King, I beg it may be thus—enjoin some other Thessalian, one who is not in sorrow, to guard her. In Pherae there are many to welcome you. Do not remind me of my grief. Seeing her in my house, I could not restrain my tears. Add not a further anguish to my pain, for what I suffer is too great. And then—where could I harbour a young woman in my house? For she is young—I see by her clothes and jewels. Could she live with the men under my roof? How, then, could she remain chaste, if she moved to and fro among the young men? Heracles, it is not easy to restrain the young.... I am thinking of your interests.... Must I take her to my dead wife's room? How could I endure her to enter that bed? I fear a double reproach—from my people, who would accuse me of betraying my saviour to slip into another woman's bed, and from my dead wife, who deserves my respect, for which I must take care.

O woman, whosoever you may be, you have the form of Alcestis, and your body is like hers. Ah! By all the Gods, take her from my sight! Do not insult a broken man. When I look upon her—she seems my wife—my heart is torn asunder tears flow from my eyes. Miserable creature that I am, now taste the bitterness of my sorrow.

LEADER: I do not praise this meeting; but, whatever happens, we must accept the gifts of the Gods.

HERACLES: Oh, that I might bring your wife back into the light of day from the dwelling of the Under–Gods, as a gift of grace to you!

ADMETUS: I know you would wish this but to what end? The dead cannot return to the light of day.

HERACLES: Do not exaggerate, but bear this with decorum.

ADMETUS: Easier to advise than bear the test.

HERACLES: How will it aid you to lament for ever?

ADMETUS: I know, but my love whirls me away.

HERACLES: Love for the dead leads us to tears.

ADMETUS: I am overwhelmed beyond words.

HERACLES: You have lost a good wife, who denies it?

ADMETUS: So that for me there is no more pleasure in life.

HERACLES: Time will heal this open wound.

ADMETUS: You might say Time, if Time were death!

HERACLES: Another woman, a new marriage, shall console you.

ADMETUS: Oh, hush! What have you said? A thing unbelievable!

HERACLES: What! You will not marry? Your bed will remain widowed?

ADMETUS: No other woman shall ever lie at my side.

HERACLES: Do you think that avails the dead?

ADMETUS: Wherever she may be, I must do her honour.

HERACLES: I praise you but men will call you mad.

ADMETUS: Yet never more shall I be called a bridegroom.

HERACLES: I praise your faithful love to your wife.

ADMETUS: May I die if I betray her even when dead!

HERACLES (*offering him the veiled woman's hand*): Receive her then into your noble house.

ADMETUS: No, by Zeus who begot you, no!

HERACLES: Yet you will do wrong if you do not take her.

ADMETUS: If I do it, remorse will tear my heart.

HERACLES: Yield—perhaps it will be a good thing for you.

ADMETUS: Ah! If only you had not won her in the contest!

HERACLES: But I conquered and you conquered with me.

ADMETUS: It is true but let the woman go hence.

HERACLES: She shall go, if she must. But first ought she to go?

ADMETUS: She must—unless it would anger you.

HERACLES: There is good reason for my zeal.

ADMETUS: You have conquered then but not for my pleasure.

HERACLES: One day you will praise me for it, be persuaded.

ADMETUS *(to his attendants)*: Lead her in, since she must be received in this house.

HERACLES: No, I cannot leave such a woman to servants.

ADMETUS: Then lead her in yourself, if you wish.

HERACLES: I must leave her in your hands.

ADMETUS: I must not touch her—let her go into the house.

HERACLES: I trust only in your right hand.

ADMETUS: O King, you force me to this against my will.

HERACLES: Put forth your hand and take this woman.

ADMETUS *(turning aside his head)*: It is held out.

HERACLES: As if you were cutting off a Gorgon's head! Do you hold her?

ADMETUS: Yes.

HERACLES: Then keep her. You shall not deny that the son of Zeus is a grateful guest. *(Takes off the veil and shows ALCESTIS.)* Look at her, and see if she is not like your wife. And may joy put an end to all your sorrow!

ADMETUS *(drops her hand and starts back)*: O Gods! What am I to say? Unhoped-for wonder! Do I really look upon my wife? Or I am snared in the mockery of a God?

HERACLES: No, you look upon your wife indeed.

ADMETUS: Beware! May it not be some phantom from the Underworld?

HERACLES: Do not think your guest a sorcerer.

ADMETUS: But do I indeed look upon the wife I buried?

HERACLES: Yes—but I do not wonder at your mistrust.

ADMETUS: Can I touch, speak to her, as my living wife?

HERACLES: Speak to her—you have all you desired.

ADMETUS *(taking ALCESTIS in his arms)*: O face and body of the dearest of women! I have you once more, when I thought I should never see you again!

HERACLES: You have her—may the envy of the Gods be averted from you!

ADMETUS: O noble son of greatest Zeus, fortune be yours, and may your Father guard you! But how did you bring her back from the Underworld to the light of day?

HERACLES: By fighting with the spirit who was her master.

ADMETUS: Then did you contend with Death?

HERACLES: I hid by the tomb and leaped upon him.

ADMETUS: But why is she speechless?

HERACLES: She is still consecrated to the gods below. For three days, until she is purified, you may not hear her voice. Come, take her in. And pay your debt to me, Admetus, by showing your guests benceforth a true respect. Now I must go; I have work to do. Eurystheus is my master. Good-bye!

ADMETUS: Stay with us! Join in our feast and thanksgiving!

HERACLES: When I come back. But now I must lose no time.

ADMETUS: Good luck go with you, and bring you safe home!

Exit Heracles.

ADMETUS: I command our citizens and all the land to celebrate this joyful deliverance with dance and festival! Let every altar run with the fat of sacrifice! Our life is changed: a new and better day now rises. I confess that Fortune has been kind to me.

CHORUS: Gods manifest themselves in many forms,
Bring many matters to surprising ends;
The things we thought would happen do not happen;
Things unexpected God makes possible:
And that is what has happened here today!

Notes

1. *Schmucks?* Was Admetus a schmuck? Was Pheres a schmuck?

2. *The Star of Heracles.* Son of Jupiter and Alcmena, Hercules won immortality by accomplishing the twelve feats known as the labors of Hercules.

3. *A Guest.* Under Greek rules of hospitality, a host could not refuse a guest. Hercules returned the hospitality.

4. *The Betrayed Wife?* What will Alcestis' attitude be toward Admetus after her three days of purification?

5. *The Chorus.* What is the purpose of the chorus?

C. SHAKESPEARE

Shakespeare, as a poet and dramatist, dominates English and American literature. No greater tragedy writer has appeared since the Greek golden age of the 5th century B.C. No one can forget Falstaff, Richard III, Iago, Macbeth, Hamlet, and on and on. Shelley (*In Defence of Poetry*, reprinted in Chapter 5) considered Shakespeare's *Lear* to be unsurpassed. *See* PAUL W. KAHN, LAW AND LOVE—THE TRIALS OF KING LEAR (2000).

There is continuing controversy about the authorship of the Shakespearean plays. It seems fairly clear that the writer was not Shakespeare of Stratford-on-Avon. *See* DIANA PRICE, SHAKESPEARE'S UNORTHODOX BIOGRAPHY (2001). There is a strong case for believing Edward de Vere, the 17th Earl of Oxford, was the author. *See* CHARLTON OSBORN, THE MYSTERIOUS WILLIAM SHAKESPEARE (2d ed. 1992). Contemporary scholarship indicates that, at least in a number of the plays and particularly the histories, there may have been a consortium of writers. *See* GIORGIO MELCHIORI, KING EDWARD III (1998). In any event, wouldn't a rose by any other name smell as sweet?

Many of Shakespeare's plays are difficult to understand. MEASURE FOR MEASURE is especially problematic. What, or whom, does the Duke represent? The play falls short of a tragedy but is it a comedy? Or something else?

WILLIAM SHAKESPEARE
MEASURE FOR MEASURE

DRAMATIS PERSONAE

VINCENTIO, the Duke
ANGELO, the Deputy
ESCALUS, an ancient Lord
CLAUDIO, a young gentleman
LUCIO, a fantastic
Two other like Gentlemen
VARRIUS, a gentleman, servant to the Duke
PROVOST
THOMAS, friar
PETER, friar
A JUSTICE
ELBOW, a simple constable
FROTH, a foolish gentleman
POMPEY, a clown and servant to Mistress Overdone
ABHORSON, an executioner
BARNARDINE, a dissolute prisoner
ISABELLA, sister to Claudio
MARIANA, betrothed to Angelo
JULIET, beloved of Claudio
FRANCISCA, a nun
MISTRESS OVERDONE, a bawd
Lords, Officers, Citizens, Boy, and Attendants

ACT I, SCENE 1

The DUKE'S palace, Vienna.

Enter DUKE, ESCALUS, LORDS, and ATTENDANTS

DUKE: Escalus!

ESCALUS: My lord.

DUKE: Of government the properties to unfold
Would seem in me t' affect speech and discourse,
Since I am put to know that your own science
Exceeds, in that, the lists of all advice
My strength can give you; then no more remains

But that to your sufficiency, as your worth is able,
And let them work. The nature of our people,
Our city's institutions, and the terms
For common justice, y'are as pregnant in
As art and practice hath enriched any
That we remember. There is our commission,
From which we would not have you warp. Call hither,
I say, bid come before us, Angelo.   *Exit an ATTENDANT*
What figure of us think you he will bear?
For you must know we have with special soul
Elected him our absence to supply;
Lent him our terror, dress'd him with our love,
And given his deputation all the organs
Of our own power. What think you of it?

ESCALUS: If any in Vienna be of worth
To undergo such ample grace and honour,
It is Lord Angelo.

Enter ANGELO

DUKE: Look where he comes.

ANGELO: Always obedient to your Grace's will,
I come to know your pleasure.

DUKE: Angelo,
There is a kind of character in thy life
That to th' observer doth thy history
Fully unfold. Thyself and thy belongings
Are not thine own so proper as to waste
Thyself upon thy virtues, they on thee.
Heaven doth with us as we with torches do,
Not light them for themselves; for if our virtues
Did not go forth of us, 'twere all alike
As if we had them not. Spirits are not finely touch'd
But to fine issues; nor Nature never lends
The smallest scruple of her excellence
But, like a thrifty goddess, she determines
Herself the glory of a creditor,
Both thanks and use. But I do bend my speech
To one that can my part in him advertise.
Hold, therefore, Angelo:
In our remove be thou at full ourself;
Mortality and mercy in Vienna
Live in thy tongue and heart. Old Escalus,
Though first in question, is thy secondary.
Take thy commission.

ANGELO: Now, good my lord,
Let there be some more test made of my metal,
Before so noble and so great a figure
Be stamp'd upon it.

DUKE: No more evasion!
We have with a leaven'd and prepared choice
Proceeded to you; therefore take your honours.
Our haste from hence is of so quick condition
That it prefers itself, and leaves unquestion'd
Matters of needful value. We shall write to you,
As time and our concernings shall importune,
How it goes with us, and do look to know
What doth befall you here. So, fare you well.
To th' hopeful execution do I leave you
Of your commissions.

ANGELO: Yet give leave, my lord,
That we may bring you something on the way.

DUKE: My haste may not admit it;
Nor need you, on mine honour, have to do
With any scruple: your scope is as mine own,
So to enforce or qualify the laws
As to your soul seems good. Give me your hand;
I'll privily away. I love the people,
But do not like to stage me to their eyes;
Though it do well, I do not relish well
Their loud applause and Aves vehement;
Nor do I think the man of safe discretion
That does affect it. Once more, fare you well.

ANGELO: The heavens give safety to your purposes!

ESCALUS: Lead forth and bring you back in happiness!

DUKE: I thank you. Fare you well.   *Exit*

ESCALUS: I shall desire you, sir, to give me leave
To have free speech with you; and it concerns me
To look into the bottom of my place:
A pow'r I have, but of what strength and nature
I am not yet instructed.

ANGELO: 'Tis so with me. Let us withdraw together,
And we may soon our satisfaction have
Touching that point.

ESCALUS: I'll wait upon your honour.   *Exeunt*

SCENE 2

A street

Enter LUCIO and two other GENTLEMEN

LUCIO: If the Duke, with the other dukes, come not to composition with the King of Hungary, why then all the dukes fall upon the King.

FIRST GENTLEMAN: Heaven grant us its peace, but not the King of Hungary's!

SECOND GENTLEMAN: Amen.

LUCIO: Thou conclud'st like the sanctimonious pirate that went to sea with the Ten Commandments, but scrap'd one out of the table.

SECOND GENTLEMAN: 'Thou shalt not steal'?

LUCIO: Ay, that he raz'd.

FIRST GENTLEMAN: Why, 'twas a commandment to command the captain and all the rest from their functions: they put forth to steal. There's not a soldier of us all that, in the thanksgiving before meat, do relish the petition well that prays for peace.

SECOND GENTLEMAN: I never heard any soldier dislike it.

LUCIO: I believe thee; for I think thou never wast where grace was said.

SECOND GENTLEMAN: No? A dozen times at least.

FIRST GENTLEMAN: What, in metre?

LUCIO: In any proportion or in any language.

FIRST GENTLEMAN: I think, or in any religion.

LUCIO: Ay, why not? Grace is grace, despite of all controversy; as, for example, thou thyself art a wicked villain, despite of all grace.

FIRST GENTLEMAN: Well, there went but a pair of shears between us.

LUCIO: I grant; as there may between the lists and the velvet. Thou art the list.

FIRST GENTLEMAN: And thou the velvet; thou art good velvet; thou'rt a three-pil'd piece, I warrant thee. I had as lief be a list of an English kersey as be pil'd, as thou art pil'd, for a French velvet. Do I speak feelingly now?

LUCIO: I think thou dost; and, indeed, with most painful feeling of thy speech. I will, out of thine own confession, learn to begin thy health; but, whilst I live, forget to drink after thee.

FIRST GENTLEMAN: I think I have done myself wrong, have I not?

SECOND GENTLEMAN: Yes, that thou hast, whether thou art tainted or free.

Enter MISTRESS OVERDONE

LUCIO: Behold, behold, where Madam Mitigation comes! I have purchas'd as many diseases under her roof as come to—

SECOND GENTLEMAN: To what, I pray?

FIRST GENTLEMAN: Judge.

SECOND GENTLEMAN: To three thousand dolours a year.

FIRST GENTLEMAN: Ay, and more.

LUCIO: A French crown more.

FIRST GENTLEMAN: Thou art always figuring diseases in me, but thou art full of error; I am sound.

LUCIO: Nay, not, as one would say, healthy; but so sound as things that are hollow: thy bones are hollow; impiety has made a feast of thee.

FIRST GENTLEMAN: How now! which of your hips has the most profound sciatica?

MRS. OVERDONE: Well, well! there's one yonder arrested and carried to prison was worth five thousand of you all.

FIRST GENTLEMAN: Who's that, I pray thee?

MRS. OVERDONE: Marry, sir, that's Claudio, Signior Claudio.

FIRST GENTLEMAN: Claudio to prison? 'Tis not so.

MRS. OVERDONE: Nay, but I know 'tis so: I saw him arrested; saw him carried away; and, which is more, within these three days his head to be chopp'd off.

LUCIO: But, after all this fooling, I would not have it so. Art thou sure of this?

MRS. OVERDONE: I am too sure of it; and it is for getting Madam Julietta with child.

LUCIO: Believe me, this may be; he promis'd to meet me two hours since, and he was ever precise in promise-keeping.

SECOND GENTLEMAN: Besides, you know, it draws something near to the speech we had to such a purpose.

FIRST GENTLEMAN: But most of all agreeing with the proclamation.

LUCIO: Away; let's go learn the truth of it.

Exeunt LUCIO and GENTLEMEN

MRS. OVERDONE: Thus, what with the war, what with the sweat, what with the gallows, and what with poverty, I am custom-shrunk.

Enter POMPEY

How now! what's the news with you?

POMPEY: Yonder man is carried to prison.

MRS. OVERDONE: Well, what has he done?

POMPEY: A woman.

MRS. OVERDONE: But what's his offence?

POMPEY: Groping for trouts in a peculiar river.

MRS. OVERDONE: What! is there a maid with child by him?

POMPEY: No; but there's a woman with maid by him. You have not heard of the proclamation, have you?

MRS. OVERDONE: What proclamation, man?

POMPEY: All houses in the suburbs of Vienna must be pluck'd down.

MRS. OVERDONE: And what shall become of those in the city?

POMPEY: They shall stand for seed; they had gone down too, but that a wise burgher put in for them.

MRS. OVERDONE: But shall all our houses of resort in the suburbs be pull'd down?

POMPEY: To the ground, mistress.

MRS. OVERDONE: Why, here's a change indeed in the commonwealth! What shall become of me?

POMPEY: Come, fear not you: good counsellors lack no clients. Though you change your place you need not change your trade; I'll be your tapster still. Courage, there will be pity taken on you; you that have worn your eyes almost out in the service, you will be considered.

MRS. OVERDONE: What's to do here, Thomas Tapster? Let's withdraw.

POMPEY: Here comes Signior Claudio, led by the provost to prison; and there's Madam Juliet.

Exeunt

Enter PROVOST, CLAUDIO, JULIET, and OFFICERS; LUCIO following

CLAUDIO: Fellow, why dost thou show me thus to th' world?
Bear me to prison, where I am committed.

PROVOST: I do it not in evil disposition,
But from Lord Angelo by special charge.

CLAUDIO: Thus can the demigod Authority
Make us pay down for our offence by weight
The words of heaven: on whom it will, it will;
On whom it will not, so; yet still 'tis just.

LUCIO: Why, how now, Claudio, whence comes this restraint?

CLAUDIO: From too much liberty, my Lucio, liberty;
As surfeit is the father of much fast,
So every scope by the immoderate use
Turns to restraint. Our natures do pursue,
Like rats that ravin down their proper bane,
A thirsty evil; and when we drink we die.

LUCIO: If I could speak so wisely under an arrest, I would send for certain of my creditors; and yet, to say the truth, I had as lief have the foppery of freedom as the morality of imprisonment. What's thy offence, Claudio?

CLAUDIO: What but to speak of would offend again.

LUCIO: What, is't murder?

CLAUDIO: No.

LUCIO: Lechery?

CLAUDIO: Call it so.

PROVOST: Away, sir; you must go.

CLAUDIO: One word, good friend. Lucio, a word with you.

LUCIO: A hundred, if they'll do you any good. Is lechery so look'd after?

CLAUDIO: Thus stands it with me: upon a true contract
I got possession of Julietta's bed.
You know the lady; she is fast my wife,
Save that we do the denunciation lack
Of outward order; this we came not to,
Only for propagation of a dow'r
Remaining in the coffer of her friends.
From whom we thought it meet to hide our love
Till time had made them for us. But it chances
The stealth of our most mutual entertainment,
With character too gross, is writ on Juliet.

LUCIO: With child, perhaps?

CLAUDIO: Unhappily, even so.
And the new deputy now for the Duke—
Whether it be the fault and glimpse of newness,
Or whether that the body public be
A horse whereon the governor doth ride,
Who, newly in the seat, that it may know
He can command, lets it straight feel the spur;
Whether the tyranny be in his place,
Or in his eminence that fills it up,
I stagger in. But this new governor
Awakes me all the enrolled penalties
Which have, like unscour'd armour, hung by th' wall
So long that nineteen zodiacs have gone round
And none of them been worn; and, for a name,
Now puts the drowsy and neglected act
Freshly on me. 'Tis surely for a name.

LUCIO: I warrant it is; and thy head stands so tickle on thy shoulders that a milkmaid, if she be in love, may sigh it off. Send after the Duke, and appeal to him.

CLAUDIO: I have done so, but he's not to be found.
I prithee, Lucio, do me this kind service:
This day my sister should the cloister enter,
And there receive her approbation;
Acquaint her with the danger of my state;
Implore her, in my voice, that she make friends
To the strict deputy; bid herself assay him.
I have great hope in that; for in her youth
There is a prone and speechless dialect
Such as move men; beside, she hath prosperous art
When she will play with reason and discourse,
And well she can persuade.

LUCIO: I pray she may; as well for the encouragement of the like, which else would stand under grievous imposition, as for the enjoying of thy life, who I would be sorry should be thus foolishly lost at a game of tick-tack. I'll to her.

CLAUDIO: I thank you, good friend Lucio.

LUCIO: Within two hours.

CLAUDIO: Come, officer, away.

Exeunt

SCENE 3

A monastery

Enter DUKE and FRIAR THOMAS

DUKE: No, holy father; throw away that thought;
Believe not that the dribbling dart of love
Can pierce a complete bosom. Why I desire thee
To give me secret harbour hath a purpose
More grave and wrinkled than the aims and ends
Of burning youth.

FRIAR: May your Grace speak of it?

DUKE: My holy sir, none better knows than you
How I have ever lov'd the life removed,
And held in idle price to haunt assemblies
Where youth, and cost, a witless bravery keeps.
I have deliver'd to Lord Angelo,
A man of stricture and firm abstinence,
My absolute power and place here in Vienna,
And he supposes me travell'd to Poland;
For so I have strew'd it in the common ear,
And so it is received. Now, pious sir,
You will demand of me why I do this.

FRIAR: Gladly, my lord.

DUKE: We have strict statutes and most biting laws,
The needful bits and curbs to headstrong steeds,
Which for this fourteen years we have let slip;
Even like an o'ergrown lion in a cave,
That goes not out to prey. Now, as fond fathers,
Having bound up the threat'ning twigs of birch,
Only to stick it in their children's sight
For terror, not to use, in time the rod
Becomes more mock'd than fear'd; so our decrees,
Dead to infliction, to themselves are dead;
And liberty plucks justice by the nose;
The baby beats the nurse, and quite athwart
Goes all decorum.

FRIAR: It rested in your Grace

To unloose this tied-up justice when you pleas'd;
And it in you more dreadful would have seem'd
Than in Lord Angelo.

DUKE: I do fear, too dreadful.
Sith 'was my fault to give the people scope,
'Twould be my tyranny to strike and gall them
For what I bid them do; for we bid this be done,
When evil deeds have their permissive pass
And not the punishment. Therefore, indeed, my father,
I have on Angelo impos'd the office;
Who may, in th' ambush of my name, strike home,
And yet my nature never in the fight
To do in slander. And to behold his sway,
I will, as 'twere a brother of your order,
Visit both prince and people. Therefore, I prithee,
Supply me with the habit, and instruct me
How I may formally in person bear me
Like a true friar. More reasons for this action
At our more leisure shall I render you.
Only, this one: Lord Angelo is precise;
Stands at a guard with envy; scarce confesses
That his blood flows, or that his appetite
Is more to bread than stone. Hence shall we see,
If power change purpose, what our seemers be.   *Exeunt*

SCENE 4

A nunnery

Enter ISABELLA and FRANCISCA

ISABELLA: And have you nuns no farther privileges?

FRANCISCA: Are not these large enough?

ISABELLA: Yes, truly; I speak not as desiring more,
But rather wishing a more strict restraint
Upon the sisterhood, the votarists of Saint Clare.

LUCIO: [*Within*] Ho! Peace be in this place!

ISABELLA: Who's that which calls?

FRANCISCA: It is a man's voice. Gentle Isabella,
Turn you the key, and know his business of him:
You may, I may not; you are yet unsworn;
When you have vow'd, you must not speak with men
But in the presence of the prioress;
Then, if you speak, you must not show your face,
Or, if you show your face, you must not speak.
He calls again; I pray you answer him.   *Exit FRANCISCA*

ISABELLA: Peace and prosperity! Who is't that calls?

Enter LUCIO

LUCIO: Hail, virgin, if you be, as those cheek-roses
Proclaim you are no less. Can you so stead me
As bring me to the sight of Isabella,
A novice of this place, and the fair sister
To her unhappy brother Claudio?

ISABELLA: Why her 'unhappy brother'? Let me ask
The rather, for I now must make you know
I am that Isabella, and his sister.

LUCIO: Gentle and fair, your brother kindly greets you.
Not to be weary with you, he's in prison.

ISABELLA: Woe me! For what?

LUCIO: For that which, if myself might be his judge,
He should receive his punishment in thanks:
He hath got his friend with child.

ISABELLA: Sir, make me not your story.

LUCIO: It is true.
I would not, though 'tis my familiar sin
With maids to seem the lapwing, and to jest,
Tongue far from heart, play with all virgins so:
I hold you as a thing enskied and sainted,
By your renouncement an immortal spirit,
And to be talk'd with in sincerity,
As with a saint.

ISABELLA: You do blaspheme the good in mocking me.

LUCIO: Do not believe it. Fewness and truth, 'tis thus:
Your brother and his lover have embrac'd.
As those that feed grow full, as blossoming time
That from the seedness the bare fallow brings
To teeming foison, even so her plenteous womb
Expresseth his full tilth and husbandry.

ISABELLA: Some one with child by him? My cousin Juliet?

LUCIO: Is she your cousin?

ISABELLA: Adoptedly, as school-maids change their names
By vain though apt affection.

LUCIO: She it is.

ISABELLA: O, let him marry her!

LUCIO: This is the point.
The Duke is very strangely gone from hence;
Bore many gentlemen, myself being one,
In hand, and hope of action; but we do learn,
By those that know the very nerves of state,
His givings-out were of an infinite distance
From his true-meant design. Upon his place,
And with full line of his authority,

Governs Lord Angelo, a man whose blood
Is very snow-broth, one who never feels
The wanton stings and motions of the sense,
But doth rebate and blunt his natural edge
With profits of the mind, study and fast.
He, to give fear to use and liberty,
Which have for long run by the hideous law,
As mice by lions, hath pick'd out an act
Under whose heavy sense your brother's life
Falls into forfeit; he arrests him on it,
And follows close the rigour of the statute
To make him an example. All hope is gone,
Unless you have the grace by your fair prayer
To soften Angelo. And that's my pith of business
'Twixt you and your poor brother.

ISABELLA: Doth he so seek his life?

LUCIO: Has censur'd him
Already, and, as I hear, the Provost hath
A warrant for his execution.

ISABELLA: Alas! what poor ability's in me
To do him good?

LUCIO: Assay the pow'r you have.

ISABELLA: My power, alas, I doubt!

LUCIO: Our doubts are traitors,
And make us lose the good we oft might win
By fearing to attempt. Go to Lord Angelo,
And let him learn to know, when maidens sue,
Men give like gods; but when they weep and kneel,
All their petitions are as freely theirs
As they themselves would owe them.

ISABELLA: I'll see what I can do.

LUCIO: But speedily.

ISABELLA: I will about it straight:
No longer staying but to give the Mother
Notice of my affair. I humbly thank you.
Commend me to my brother; soon at night
I'll send him certain word of my success.

LUCIO: I take my leave of you.

ISABELLA: Good sir, adieu.   *Exeunt*

ACT II, SCENE 1

A hall in ANGELO'S house

Enter ANGELO, ESCALUS, a JUSTICE, PROVOST, OFFICERS, and other ATTENDANTS

ANGELO: We must not make a scarecrow of the law,
Setting it up to fear the birds of prey,
And let it keep one shape till custom make it
Their perch, and not their terror.

ESCALUS: Ay, but yet
Let us be keen, and rather cut a little
Than fall and bruise to death. Alas! this gentleman,
Whom I would save, had a most noble father.
Let but your honour know,
Whom I believe to be most strait in virtue,
That, in the working of your own affections,
Had time coher'd with place, or place with wishing,
Or that the resolute acting of our blood
Could have attain'd th' effect of your own purpose
Whether you had not sometime in your life
Err'd in this point which now you censure him,
And pull'd the law upon you.

ANGELO: 'Tis one thing to be tempted, Escalus,
Another thing to fall. I not deny
The jury, passing on the prisoner's life,
May in the sworn twelve have a thief or two
Guiltier than him they try. What's open made to justice,
That justice seizes. What knows the laws
That thieves do pass on thieves? 'Tis very pregnant,
The jewel that we find, we stoop and take't,
Because we see it; but what we do not see
We tread upon, and never think of it.
You may not so extenuate his offence
For I have had such faults; but rather tell me,
When I, that censure him, do so offend,
Let mine own judgment pattern out my death,
And nothing come in partial. Sir, he must die.

ESCALUS: Be it as your wisdom will.

ANGELO: Where is the Provost?

PROVOST: Here, if it like your honour.

ANGELO: See that Claudio
Be executed by nine to-morrow morning;
Bring him his confessor; let him be prepar'd;
For that's the utmost of his pilgrimage.   *Exit PROVOST*

ESCALUS: [*Aside*] Well, heaven forgive him! and forgive us all!
Some rise by sin, and some by virtue fall;
Some run from breaks of ice, and answer none,
And some condemned for a fault alone.

Enter ELBOW and OFFICERS with FROTH and POMPEY

ELBOW: Come, bring them away; if these be good people in a common-weal that do nothing but use their abuses in common houses, I know no law; bring them away.

ANGELO: How now, sir! What's your name, and what's the matter?

ELBOW: If it please your honour, I am the poor Duke's constable, and my name is Elbow; I do lean upon justice, sir, and do bring in here before your good honour two notorious benefactors.

ANGELO: Benefactors! Well what benefactors are they? Are they not malefactors?

ELBOW: If it please your honour, I know not well what they are; but precise villains they are, that I am sure of, and void of all profanation in the world that good Christians ought to have.

ESCALUS: This comes off well; here's a wise officer.

ANGELO: Go to; what quality are they of? Elbow is your name? Why dost thou not speak, Elbow?

POMPEY: He cannot, sir; he's out at elbow.

ANGELO: What are you, sir?

ELBOW: He, sir? A tapster, sir; parcel-bawd; one that serves a bad woman; whose house, sir, was, as they say, pluck'd down in the suburbs; and now she professes a hot-house, which, I think, is a very ill house too.

ESCALUS: How know you that?

ELBOW: My Wife, sir, whom I detest before heaven and your honour—

ESCALUS: How! thy wife!

ELBOW: Ay, sir; whom I thank heaven, is an honest woman.

ESCALUS: Dost thou detest her therefore?

ELBOW: I say, sir, I will detest myself also, as well as she, that this house, if it be not a bawd's house, it is pity of her life, for it is a naughty house.

ESCALUS: How dost thou know that, constable?

ELBOW: Marry, sir, by my wife; who, if she had been a woman cardinally given, might have been accus'd in fornication, adultery, and all uncleanliness there.

ESCALUS: By the woman's means?

ELBOW: Ay, sir, by Mistress Overdone's means; but as she spit in his face, so she defied him.

POMPEY: Sir, if it please your honour, this is not so.

ELBOW: Prove it before these varlets here, thou honourable man, prove it.

ESCALUS: Do you hear how he misplaces?

POMPEY: Sir, she came in great with child; and longing, saving your honour's reverence, for stew'd prunes. Sir, we had but two in the house, which at that very distant time stood, as it were, in a fruit dish, a dish of some three pence; your honours have seen such dishes; they are not China dishes, but very good dishes.

ESCALUS: Go to, go to; no matter for the dish, sir.

POMPEY: No, indeed, sir, not of a pin; you are therein in the right; but to the point. As I say, this Mistress Elbow, being, as I say, with child, and being great-bellied, and longing, as I said, for prunes; and having but two in the dish, as I said, Master Froth here, this very man, having eaten the rest, as I said, and, as I say, paying for them very honestly; for, as you know, Master Froth, I could not give you three pence again.

FROTH: No, indeed.

POMPEY: Very well; you being then, if you be rememb'red, cracking the stones of the foresaid prunes—

FROTH: Ay, so I did indeed.

POMPEY: Why, very well; I telling you then, if you be rememb'red, that such a one and such a one were past cure of the thing you wot of, unless they kept very good diet, as I told you.

FROTH: All this is true.

POMPEY: Why, very well then.

ESCALUS: Come, you are a tedious fool. To the purpose: what was done to Elbow's wife that he hath cause to complain of? Come me to what was done to her.

POMPEY: Sir, your honour cannot come to that yet.

ESCALUS: No, sir, nor I mean it not.

POMPEY: Sir, but you shall come to it, by your honour's leave. And, I beseech you, look into Master Froth here, sir, a man of fourscore pound a year; whose father died at Hallowmas—was't not at Hallowmas, Master Froth?

FROTH: All-hallond eve.

POMPEY: Why, very well; I hope here be truths. He, sir, sitting, as I say, in a lower chair, sir; 'twas in the Bunch of Grapes, where, indeed, you have a delight to sit, have you not?

FROTH: I have so; because it is an open room, and good for winter.

POMPEY: Why, very well then; I hope here be truths.

ANGELO: This will last out a night in Russia,
When nights are longest there; I'll take my leave,
And leave you to the hearing of the cause,
Hoping you'll find good cause to whip them all.

ESCALUS: I think no less. Good morrow to your lordship.

[*Exit ANGELO*] Now, sir, come on; what was done to Elbow's wife, once more?

POMPEY: Once, sir? There was nothing done to her once.

ELBOW: I beseech you, sir, ask him what this man did to my wife.

POMPEY: I beseech your honour, ask me.

ESCALUS: Well, sir, what did this gentleman to her?

POMPEY: I beseech you, sir, look in this gentleman's face. Good Master Froth, look upon his honour; 'tis for a good purpose. Doth your honour mark his face?

ESCALUS: Ay, sir, very well.

POMPEY: Nay, I beseech you, mark it well.

ESCALUS: Well, I do so.

POMPEY: Doth your honour see any harm in his face?

ESCALUS: Why, no.

POMPEY: I'll be suppos'd upon a book his face is the worst thing about him. Good then; if his face be the worst thing about him, how could Master Froth do the constable's wife any harm? I would know that of your honour.

ESCALUS: He's in the right, constable; what say you to it?

ELBOW: First, an it like you, the house is a respected house; next, this is a respected fellow; and his mistress is a respected woman.

POMPEY: By this hand, sir, his wife is a more respected person than any of us all.

ELBOW: Varlet, thou liest; thou liest, wicket varlet; the time is yet to come that she was ever respected with man, woman, or child.

POMPEY: Sir, she was respected with him before he married with her.

ESCALUS: Which is the wiser here, Justice or Iniquity? Is this true?

ELBOW: O thou caitiff! O thou varlet! O thou wicked Hannibal! I respected with her before I was married to her! If ever I was respected with her, or she with me, let not your worship think me the poor Duke's officer. Prove this, thou wicked Hannibal, or I'll have mine action of batt'ry on thee.

ESCALUS: If he took you a box o' th' ear, you might have your action of slander too.

ELBOW: Marry, I thank your good worship for it. What is't your worship's pleasure I shall do with this wicked caitiff?

ESCALUS: Truly, officer, because he hath some offences in him that thou wouldst discover if thou couldst, let him continue in his courses till thou know'st what they are.

ELBOW: Marry, I thank your worship for it. Thou seest, thou wicked varlet, now, what's come upon thee: thou art to continue now, thou varlet; thou art to continue.

ESCALUS: Where were you born, friend?

FROTH: Here in Vienna, sir.

ESCALUS: Are you of fourscore pounds a year?

FROTH: Yes, an't please you, sir.

ESCALUS: So. What trade are you of, sir?

POMPEY: A tapster, a poor widow's tapster.

ESCALUS: Your mistress' name?

POMPEY: Mistress Overdone.

ESCALUS: Hath she had any more than one husband?

POMPEY: Nine, sir; Overdone by the last.

ESCALUS: Nine! Come hither to me, Master Froth. Master Froth, I would not have you acquainted with tapsters: they will draw you, Master Froth, and you will hang them. Get you gone, and let me hear no more of you.

FROTH: I thank your worship. For mine own part, I never come into any room in a taphouse but I am drawn in.

ESCALUS: Well, no more of it, Master Froth; farewell. [*Exit FROTH*]

Come you hither to me, Master Tapster; what's your name, Master Tapster?

POMPEY: Pompey.

ESCALUS: What else?

POMPEY: Bum, sir.

ESCALUS: Troth, and your bum is the greatest thing about you; so that, in the beastliest sense, you are Pompey the Great. Pompey, you are partly a bawd, Pompey, howsoever you colour it in being a tapster. Are you not? Come, tell me true; it shall be the better for you.

POMPEY: Truly, sir, I am a poor fellow that would live.

ESCALUS: How would you live, Pompey, by being a bawd? What do you think of the trade, Pompey? Is it a lawful trade?

POMPEY: If the law would allow it, sir.

ESCALUS: But the law will not allow it, Pompey; nor it shall not be allowed in Vienna.

POMPEY: Does your worship mean to geld and splay all the youth of the city?

ESCALUS: No, Pompey.

POMPEY: Truly, sir, in my poor opinion, they will to't then. If your worship will take order for the drabs and the knaves, you need not to fear the bawds.

ESCALUS: There is pretty orders beginning, I can tell you: but it is but heading and hanging.

POMPEY: If you head and hang all that offend that way but for ten year together, you'll be glad to give out a commission for more heads; if this law hold in Vienna ten year, I'll rent the fairest house in it, after threepence a bay. If you live to see this come to pass, say Pompey told you so.

ESCALUS: Thank you, good Pompey; and, in requital of your prophecy, hark you: I advise you, let me not find you before me again upon any complaint whatsoever—no, not for dwelling where you do; if I do, Pompey, I shall beat you to your tent, and prove a shrewd Caesar to you; in plain dealing, Pompey, I shall have you whipt. So for this time, Pompey, fare you well.

POMPEY: I thank your worship for your good counsel; [*aside*] but I shall follow it as the flesh and fortune shall better determine.

Whip me? No, no; let carman whip his jade;

The valiant heart's not whipt out of his trade.   *Exit*

ESCALUS: Come hither to me, Master Elbow; come hither, Master Constable. How long have you been in this place of constable?

ELBOW: Seven year and a half, sir.

ESCALUS: I thought, by the readiness in the office, you had continued in it some time. You say seven years together?

ELBOW: And a half, sir.

ESCALUS: Alas, it hath been great pains to you! They do you wrong to put you so oft upon't. Are there not men in your ward sufficient to serve it?

ELBOW: Faith, sir, few of any wit in such matters; as they are chosen, they are glad to choose me for them; I do it for some piece of money, and go through with all.

ESCALUS: Look you, bring me in the names of some six or seven, the most sufficient of your parish.

ELBOW: To your worship's house, sir?

ESCALUS: To my house. Fare you well.   [*Exit ELBOW*]

What's o'clock, think you?

JUSTICE: Eleven, sir.

ESCALUS: I pray you home to dinner with me.

JUSTICE: I humbly thank you.

ESCALUS: It grieves me for the death of Claudio;
But there's no remedy.

JUSTICE: Lord Angelo is severe.

ESCALUS: It is but needful:
Mercy is not itself that oft looks so;
Pardon is still the nurse of second woe.
But yet, poor Claudio! There is no remedy.
Come, sir.   *Exeunt*

SCENE 2

Another room in ANGELO'S house

Enter PROVOST and a SERVANT

SERVANT: He's hearing of a cause; he will come straight.
I'll tell him of you.

PROVOST: Pray you do. [*Exit SERVANT*] I'll know
His pleasure; may be he will relent. Alas,
He hath but as offended in a dream!
All sects, all ages, smack of this vice; and he
To die for 't!

Enter ANGELO

ANGELO: Now, what's the matter, Provost?

PROVOST: Is it your will Claudio shall die to-morrow?

ANGELO: Did not I tell thee yea? Hadst thou not order?
Why dost thou ask again?

PROVOST: Lest I might be too rash;
Under your good correction, I have seen
When, after execution, judgment hath
Repented o'er his doom.

ANGELO: Go to; let that be mine.
Do you your office, or give up your place,
And you shall well be spar'd.

PROVOST: I crave your honour's pardon.
What shall be done, sir, with the groaning Juliet?
She's very near her hour.

ANGELO: Dispose of her
To some more fitter place, and that with speed.
Re-enter SERVANT

SERVANT: Here is the sister of the man condemn'd
Desires access to you.

ANGELO: Hath he a sister?

PROVOST: Ay, my good lord; a very virtuous maid,
And to be shortly of a sisterhood,
If not already.

ANGELO: Well, let her be admitted.   *Exit SERVANT*
See you the fornicatress be remov'd;
Let her have needful but not lavish means;
There shall be order for't.

Enter LUCIO and ISABELLA

PROVOST: [*Going*] Save your honour!

ANGELO: Stay a little while. [*To ISABELLA*] Y'are welcome; what's
your will?

ISABELLA: I am a woeful suitor to your honour,
Please but your honour hear me.

ANGELO: Well; what's your suit?

ISABELLA: There is a vice that most I do abhor,
And most desire should meet the blow of justice;
For which I would not plead, but that I must;
For which I must not plead, but that I am
At war 'twixt will and will not.

ANGELO: Well; the matter?

ISABELLA: I have a brother is condemn'd to die;
I do beseech you, let it be his fault,
And not my brother.

PROVOST: [*Aside*] Heaven give thee moving graces.

ANGELO: Condemn the fault and not the actor of it!
Why, every fault's condemn'd ere it be done;
Mine were the very cipher of a function,
To fine the faults whose fine stands in record,
And let go by the actor.

ISABELLA: O just but severe law!
I had a brother, then. Heaven keep your honour!

LUCIO: [*To ISABELLA*] Give't not o'er so; to him again, entreat him,
Kneel down before him, hang upon his gown;
You are too cold: if you should need a pin,
You could not with more tame a tongue desire it.
To him, I say.

ISABELLA: Must he needs die?

ANGELO: Maiden, no remedy.

ISABELLA: Yes; I do think that you might pardon him.
And neither heaven nor man grieve at the mercy.

ANGELO: I will not do't.

ISABELLA: But can you, if you would?

ANGELO: Look, what I will not, that I cannot do.

ISABELLA: But might you do't, and do the world no wrong,
If so your heart were touch'd with that remorse
As mine is to him?

ANGELO: He's sentenc'd; 'tis too late.

LUCIO: [*To ISABELLA*] You are too cold.

ISABELLA: Too late? Why, no; I, that do speak a word,
May call it back again. Well, believe this:
No ceremony that to great ones longs,
Not the king's crown nor the deputed sword,
The marshal's truncheon nor the judge's robe,
Become them with one half so good a grace

As mercy does.
If he had been as you, and you as he,
You would have slipp'd like him; but he, like you,
Would not have been so stern.

ANGELO: Pray you be gone.

ISABELLA: I would to heaven I had your potency,
And you were Isabel! Should it then be thus?
No; I would tell what 'twere to be a judge
And what a prisoner.

LUCIO: [*To ISABELLA*] Ay, touch him; there's the vein.

ANGELO: Your brother is a forfeit of the law,
And you but waste your words.

ISABELLA: Alas! Alas!
Why, all the souls that were were forfeit once;
And He that might the vantage best have took
Found out the remedy. How would you be
If He, which is the top of judgment, should
But judge you as you are? O, think on that;
And mercy then will breathe within your lips,
Like man new made.

ANGELO: Be you content, fair maid.
It is the law, not I, condemn your brother.
Were he my kinsman, brother, or my son,
It should be thus with him. He must die to-morrow.

ISABELLA: To-morrow! O, that's sudden! Spare him, spare him.
He's not prepar'd for death. Even for our kitchens
We kill the fowl of season; shall we serve heaven
With less respect than we do minister
To our gross selves? Good, good my lord, bethink you.
Who is it that hath died for this offence?
There's many have committed it.

LUCIO: [*Aside*] Ay, well said.

ANGELO: The law hath not been dead, though it hath slept.
Those many had not dar'd to do that evil
If the first that did th' edict infringe
Had answer'd for his deed. Now 'tis awake,
Takes note of what is done, and, like a prophet,
Looks in a glass that shows what future evils,
Either now or by remissness new conceiv'd,
And so in progress to be hatch'd and born,
Are now to have no successive degrees,
But here they live to end.

ISABELLA: Yet show some pity.

ANGELO: I show it most of all when I show justice;
For then I pity those I do not know,

Which a dismiss'd offence would after gall,
And do him right that, answering one foul wrong,
Lives not to act another. Be satisfied;
Your brother dies to-morrow; be content.

ISABELLA: So you must be the first that gives this sentence,
And he that suffers. O, it is excellent
To have a giant's strength! But it is tyrannous
To use it like a giant.

LUCIO: [*To ISABELLA*] That's well said.

ISABELLA: Could great men thunder
As Jove himself does, Jove would ne'er be quiet,
For every pelting petty officer
Would use his heaven for thunder,
Nothing but thunder. Merciful Heaven,
Thou rather, with thy sharp and sulphurous bolt,
Splits the unwedgeable and gnarled oak
Than the soft myrtle. But man, proud man,
Dress'd in a little brief authority,
Most ignorant of what he's most assur'd,
His glassy essence, like an angry ape,
Plays such fantastic tricks before high heaven
As makes the angels weep; who, with our spleens,
Would all themselves laugh mortal.

LUCIO: [*To ISABELLA*] O, to him, to him, wench! He will relent;
He's coming; I perceive 't.

PROVOST: [*Aside*] Pray heaven she win him.

ISABELLA: We cannot weigh our brother with ourself.
Great men may jest with saints: 'tis wit in them;
But in the less foul profanation.

LUCIO: [*To ISABELLA*] Thou'rt i' th' right, girl; more o' that.

ISABELLA: That in the captain's but a choleric word
Which in the soldier is flat blasphemy.

LUCIO: [*To ISABELLA*] Art avis'd o' that? More on't.

ANGELO: Why do you put these sayings upon me?

ISABELLA: Because authority, though it err like others,
Hath yet a kind of medicine in itself
That skins the vice o' th' top. Go to your bosom,
Knock there, and ask your heart what it doth know
That's like my brother's fault. If it confess
A natural guiltiness such as is his,
Let it not sound a thought upon your tongue
Against my brother's life.

ANGELO: [*Aside*] She speaks, and 'tis
Such sense that my sense breeds with it. Fare you well.

ISABELLA: Gentle my lord, turn back.

ANGELO: I will bethink me. Come again to-morrow.

ISABELLA: Hark how I'll bribe you; good my lord, turn back.

ANGELO: How, bribe me?

ISABELLA: Ay, with such gifts that heaven shall share with you.

LUCIO: [*To ISABELLA*] You had marr'd all else.

ISABELLA: Not with fond sicles of the tested gold,
Or stones, whose rate are either rich or poor
As fancy values them; but with true prayers
That shall be up at heaven and enter there
Ere sunrise, prayers from preserved souls,
From fasting maids, whose minds are dedicate
To nothing temporal.

ANGELO: Well; come to me to-morrow.

LUCIO: [*To ISABELLA*] Go to; 'tis well; away.

ISABELLA: Heaven keep your honour safe!

ANGELO: [*Aside*] Amen; for I
Am that way going to temptation
Where prayers cross.

ISABELLA: At what hour to-morrow
Shall I attend your lordship?

ANGELO: At any time 'fore noon.

ISABELLA: Save your honour!   *Exeunt all but ANGELO*

ANGELO: From thee; even from thy virtue!
What's this, what's this? Is this her fault or mine?
The tempter or the tempted, who sins most?
Ha!
Not she; nor doth she tempt; but it is I
That, lying by the violet in the sun,
Do as the carrion does, not as the flow'r,
Corrupt with virtuous season. Can it be
That modesty may more betray our sense
Than woman's lightness? Having waste ground enough,
Shall we desire to raze the sanctuary,
And pitch our evils there? O, fie, fie, fie!
What dost thou, or what art thou, Angelo?
Dost thou desire her foully for those things
That make her good? O, let her brother live!
Thieves for their robbery have authority
When judges steal themselves. What, do I love her,
That I desire to hear her speak again,
And feast upon her eyes? What is't I dream on?
O cunning enemy, that, to catch a saint,
With saints dost bait thy hook! Most dangerous

Is that temptation that doth goad us on
To sin in loving virtue. Never could the strumpet,
With all her double vigour, art and nature,
Once stir my temper; but this virtuous maid
Subdues me quite. Ever till now,
When men were fond, I smil'd and wond'red how.   *Exit*

SCENE 3

A prison

Enter, severally, DUKE, disguised as a FRIAR, and PROVOST

DUKE: Hail to you, Provost! so I think you are.

PROVOST: I am the Provost. What's your will, good friar?

DUKE: Bound by my charity and my blest order,
I come to visit the afflicted spirits
Here in the prison. Do me the common right
To let me see them, and to make me know
The nature of their crimes, that I may minister
To them accordingly.

PROVOST: I would do more than that, if more were needful.

Enter JULIET

Look, here comes one; a gentlewoman of mine,
Who, falling in the flaws of her own youth,
Hath blister'd her report. She is with child;
And he that got it, sentenc'd; a young man
More fit to do another such offence
Than die for this.

DUKE: When must he die?

PROVOST: As I do think, to-morrow.

[*To JULIET*] I have provided for you; stay awhile
And you shall be conducted.

DUKE: Repent you, fair one, of the sin you carry?

JULIET: I do; and bear the shame most patiently.

DUKE: I'll teach you how you shall arraign your conscience,
And try your penitence, if it be sound
Or hollowly put on.

JULIET: I'll gladly learn.

DUKE: Love you the man that wrong'd you?

JULIET: Yes, as I love the woman that wrong'd him.

DUKE: So then, it seems, your most offenceful act
Was mutually committed.

JULIET: Mutually.

DUKE: Then was your sin of heavier kind than his.

JULIET: I do confess it, and repent it, father.

DUKE: 'Tis meet so, daughter; but lest you do repent
As that the sin hath brought you to this shame,
Which sorrow is always toward ourselves, not heaven,
Showing we would not spare heaven as we love it,
But as we stand in fear—

JULIET: I do repent me as it is an evil,
And take the shame with joy.

DUKE: There rest.
Your partner, as I hear, must die to-morrow,
And I am going with instruction to him.
Grace go with you! Benedicite!   *Exit*

JULIET: Must die to-morrow! O, injurious law,
That respites me a life whose very comfort
Is still a dying horror!

PROVOST: 'Tis pity of him.   *Exeunt*

SCENE 4

ANGELO'S house

Enter ANGELO

ANGELO: When I would pray and think, I think and pray
To several subjects. Heaven hath my empty words,
Whilst my invention, hearing not my tongue,
Anchors on Isabel. Heaven in my mouth,
As if I did but only chew his name,
And in my heart the strong and swelling evil
Of my conception. The state whereon I studied
Is, like a good thing being often read,
Grown sere and tedious; yea, my gravity,
Wherein—let no man hear me—I take pride,
Could I with boot change for an idle plume
Which the air beats for vain. O place, O form,
How often dost thou with thy case, thy habit,
Wrench awe from fools, and tie the wiser souls
To thy false seeming! Blood, thou art blood.
Let's write "good angel" on the devil's horn;
'Tis not the devil's crest.

Enter SERVANT

How now, who's there?

SERVANT: One Isabel, a sister, desires access to you.

ANGELO: Teach her the way. [*Exit SERVANT*] O heavens!
Why does my blood thus muster to my heart,
Making both it unable for itself
And dispossessing all my other parts
Of necessary fitness?

So play the foolish throngs with one that swoons;
Come all to help him, and so stop the air
By which he should revive; and even so
The general subject to a well-wish'd king
Quit their own part, and in obsequious fondness
Crowd to his presence, where their untaught love
Must needs appear offence.

Enter ISABELLA

How now, fair maid?

ISABELLA: I am come to know your pleasure.

ANGELO: That you might know it would much better please me
Than to demand what 'tis. Your brother cannot live.

ISABELLA: Even so! Heaven keep your honour!

ANGELO: Yet may he live awhile, and, it may be,
As long as you or I; yet he must die.

ISABELLA: Under your sentence?

ANGELO: Yea.

ISABELLA: When? I beseech you; that in his reprieve,
Longer or shorter, he may be so fitted
That his soul sicken not.

ANGELO: Ha! Fie, these filthy vices! It were as good
To pardon him that hath from nature stol'n
A man already made, as to remit
Their saucy sweetness that do coin heaven's image
In stamps that are forbid; 'tis all as easy
Falsely to take away a life true made
As to put metal in restrained means
To make a false one.

ISABELLA: 'Tis set down so in heaven, but not in earth.

ANGELO: Say you so? Then I shall pose you quickly.
Which had you rather, that the most just law
Now took your brother's life; or, to redeem him,
Give up your body to such sweet uncleanness
As she that he hath stain'd?

ISABELLA: Sir, believe this:
I had rather give my body than my soul.

ANGELO: I talk not of your soul; our compell'd sins
Stand more for number than for accompt.

ISABELLA: How say you?

ANGELO: Nay, I'll not warrant that; for I can speak
Against the thing I say. Answer to this:
I, now the voice of the recorded law,
Pronounce a sentence on your brother's life;

Might there not be a charity in sin
To save this brother's life?

ISABELLA: Please you to do't,
I'll take it as a peril to my soul
It is no sin at all, but charity.

ANGELO: Pleas'd you to do't at peril of your soul,
Were equal poise of sin and charity.

ISABELLA: That I do beg his life, if it be sin,
Heaven let me bear it! You granting of my suit,
If that be sin, I'll make it my morn prayer
To have it added to the faults of mine,
And nothing of your answer.

ANGELO: Nay, but hear me;
Your sense pursues not mine; either you are ignorant
Or seem so, craftily; and that's not good.

ISABELLA: Let me be ignorant, and in nothing good
But graciously to know I am no better.

ANGELO: Thus wisdom wishes to appear most bright
When it doth tax itself; as these black masks
Proclaim an enshielded beauty ten times louder
Than beauty could, display'd. But mark me:
To be received plain, I'll speak more gross:
Your brother is to die.

ISABELLA: So.

ANGELO: And his offence is so, as it appears,
Accountant to the law upon that pain.

ISABELLA: True.

ANGELO: Admit no other way to save his life,
As I subscribe not that, nor any other,
But, in the loss of question, that you, his sister,
Finding yourself desir'd of such a person
Whose credit with the judge, or own great place,
Could fetch your brother from the manacles
Of the all-binding law; and that there were
No earthly mean to save him but that either
You must lay down the treasures of your body
To this supposed, or else to let him suffer:
What would you do?

ISABELLA: As much for my poor brother as myself;
That is, were I under the terms of death,
Th' impression of keen whips I'd wear as rubies,
And strip myself to death as to a bed
That longing have been sick for, ere I'd yield
My body up to shame.

ANGELO: Then must your brother die.

ISABELLA: And 'twere the cheaper way:
Better it were a brother died at once
Than that a sister, by redeeming him,
Should die for ever.

ANGELO: Were not you, then, as cruel as the sentence
That you have slander'd so?

ISABELLA: Ignominy in ransom and free pardon
Are of two houses: lawful mercy
Is nothing kin to foul redemption.

ANGELO: You seem'd of late to make the law a tyrant;
And rather prov'd the sliding of your brother
A merriment than a vice.

ISABELLA: O, pardon me, my lord! It oft falls out,
To have what we would have, we speak not what we mean:
I something do excuse the thing I hate
For his advantage that I dearly love.

ANGELO: We are all frail.

ISABELLA: Else let my brother die,
If not a fedary but only he
Owe and succeed thy weakness.

ANGELO: Nay, women are frail too.

ISABELLA: Ay, as the glasses where they view themselves,
Which are as easy broke as they make forms.
Women, help heaven! Men their creation mar
In profiting by them. Nay, call us ten times frail;
For we are soft as our complexions are,
And credulous to false prints.

ANGELO: I think it well;
And from this testimony of your own sex,
Since I suppose we are made to be no stronger
Than faults may shake our frames, let me be bold.
I do arrest your words. Be that you are,
That is, a woman; if you be more, you're none;
If you be one, as you are well express'd
By all external warrants, show it now
By putting on the destin'd livery.

ISABELLA: I have no tongue but one; gentle, my lord,
Let me intreat you speak the former language.

ANGELO: Plainly conceive, I love you.

ISABELLA: My brother did love Juliet,
And you tell me that he shall die for't.

ANGELO: He shall not, Isabel, if you give me love.

ISABELLA: I know your virtue hath a license in't,
Which seems a little fouler than it is,

To pluck on others.

ANGELO: Believe me, on mine honour,
My words express my purpose.

ISABELLA: Ha! little honour to be much believ'd,
And most pernicious purpose! Seeming, seeming!
I will proclaim thee, Angelo, look for't.
Sign me a present pardon for my brother
Or, with an outstretch'd throat, I'll tell the world aloud
What man thou art.

ANGELO: Who will believe thee, Isabel?
My unsoil'd name, th' austereness of my life,
My vouch against you, and my place i' th' state,
Will so your accusation overweigh
That you shall stifle in your own report,
And smell of calumny. I have begun,
And now I give my sensual race the rein:
Fit thy consent to my sharp appetite;
Lay by all nicety and prolixious blushes
That banish what they sue for; redeem thy brother
By yielding up thy body to my will;
Or else he must not only die the death,
But thy unkindness shall his death draw out
To ling'ring sufferance. Answer me to-morrow,
Or, by the affection that now guides me most,
I'll prove a tyrant to him. As for you,
Say what you can: my false o'erweighs your true.   *Exit*

ISABELLA: To whom should I complain? Did I tell this,
Who would believe me? O perilous mouths
That bear in them one and the self-same tongue
Either of condemnation or approof,
Bidding the law make curtsy to their will;
Hooking both right and wrong to th' appetite,
To follow as it draws! I'll to my brother.
Though he hath fall'n by prompture of the blood,
Yet hath he in him such a mind of honour
That, had he twenty heads to tender down
On twenty bloody blocks, he'd yield them up
Before his sister should her body stoop
To such abhorr'd pollution.
Then, Isabel, live chaste, and, brother, die:
More than our brother is our chastity.
I'll tell him yet of Angelo's request,
And fit his mind to death, for his soul's rest.   *Exit*

ACT III, SCENE 1

The prison

Enter DUKE, disguised as before, CLAUDIO, and PROVOST

DUKE: So, then you hope of pardon from Lord Angelo?

CLAUDIO: The miserable have no other medicine
But only hope:
I have hope to live, and am prepar'd to die.

DUKE: Be absolute for death; either death or life
Shall thereby be the sweeter. Reason thus with life.
If I do lose thee, I do lose a thing
That none but fools would keep. A breath thou art,
Servile to all the skyey influences,
That dost this habitation where thou keep'st
Hourly afflict. Merely, thou art Death's fool;
For him thou labour'st by thy flight to shun
And yet run'st toward him still. Thou art not noble;
For all th' accommodations that thou bear'st
Are nurs'd by baseness. Thou 'rt by no means valiant;
For thou dost fear the soft and tender fork
Of a poor worm. Thy best of rest is sleep,
And that thou oft provok'st; yet grossly fear'st
Thy death, which is no more. Thou art not thyself;
For thou exist'st on many a thousand grains
That issue out of dust. Happy thou art not;
For what thou hast not, still thou striv'st to get,
And what thou hast, forget'st. Thou art not certain;
For thy complexion shifts to strange effects,
After the moon. If thou art rich, thou'rt poor;
For, like an ass whose back with ingots bows,
Thou bear'st thy heavy riches but a journey,
And Death unloads thee. Friend hast thou none;
For thine own bowels which do call thee sire,
The mere effusion of thy proper loins,
Do curse the gout, serpigo, and the rheum,
For ending thee no sooner. Thou hast nor youth nor age,
But, as it were, an after-dinner's sleep,
Dreaming on both; for all thy blessed youth
Becomes as aged, and doth beg the alms
Of palsied eld; and when thou art old and rich,
Thou hast neither heat, affection, limb, nor beauty,
To make thy riches pleasant. What's yet in this
That bears the name of life? Yet in this life
Lie hid moe thousand deaths; yet death we fear,
That makes these odds all even.

CLAUDIO: I humbly thank you.
To sue to live, I find I seek to die;
And, seeking death, find life. Let it come on.

ISABELLA: [*Within*] What, ho! Peace here; grace and good company!

PROVOST: Who's there? Come in; the wish deserves a welcome.

DUKE: Dear sir, ere long I'll visit you again.

CLAUDIO: Most holy sir, I thank you.

Enter ISABELLA

ISABELLA: My business is a word or two with Claudio.

PROVOST: And very welcome. Look, signior, here's your sister.

DUKE: Provost, a word with you.

PROVOST: As many as you please.

DUKE: Bring me to hear them speak, where I may be conceal'd.

Exeunt DUKE and PROVOST

CLAUDIO: Now, sister, what's the comfort?

ISABELLA: Why,
As all comforts are; most good, most good, indeed.
Lord Angelo, having affairs to heaven,
Intends you for his swift ambassador,
Where you shall be an everlasting leiger.
Therefore, your best appointment make with speed;
To-morrow you set on.

CLAUDIO: Is there no remedy?

ISABELLA: None, but such remedy as, to save a head,
To cleave a heart in twain.

CLAUDIO: But is there any?

ISABELLA: Yes, brother, you may live:
There is a devilish mercy in the judge,
If you'll implore it, that will free your life,
But fetter you till death.

CLAUDIO: Perpetual durance?

ISABELLA: Ay, just; perpetual durance, a restraint,
Though all the world's vastidity you had,
To a determin'd scope.

CLAUDIO: But in what nature?

ISABELLA: In such a one as, you consenting to't,
Would bark your honour from that trunk you bear,
And leave you naked.

CLAUDIO: Let me know the point.

ISABELLA: O, I do fear thee, Claudio; and I quake,
Lest thou a feverous life shouldst entertain,
And six or seven winters more respect
Than a perpetual honour. Dar'st thou die?
The sense of death is most in apprehension;
And the poor beetle that we tread upon
In corporal sufferance finds a pang as great
As when a giant dies.

CLAUDIO: Why give you me this shame?

Think you I can a resolution fetch
From flow'ry tenderness? If I must die,
I will encounter darkness as a bride
And hug it in mine arms.

ISABELLA: There spake my brother; there my father's grave
Did utter forth a voice. Yes, thou must die:
Thou art too noble to conserve a life
In base appliances. This outward-sainted deputy,
Whose settled visage and deliberate word
Nips youth i' th' head, and follies doth enew
As falcon doth the fowl, is yet a devil;
His filth within being cast, he would appear
A pond as deep as hell.

CLAUDIO: The prenzie Angelo!

ISABELLA: O, 'tis the cunning livery of hell
The damned'st body to invest and cover
In precise guards! Dost thou think, Claudio,
If I would yield him my virginity
Thou mightst be freed?

CLAUDIO: O heavens! it cannot be.

ISABELLA: Yes, he would give't thee, from this rank offence,
So to offend him still. This night's the time
That I should do what I abhor to name,
Or else thou diest to-morrow.

CLAUDIO: Thou shalt not do't.

ISABELLA: O, were it but my life!
I'd throw it down for your deliverance
As frankly as a pin.

CLAUDIO: Thanks, dear Isabel.

ISABELLA: Be ready, Claudio, for your death to-morrow.

CLAUDIO: Yes. Has he affections in him
That thus can make him bite the law by th' nose
When he would force it? Sure it is no sin;
Or of the deadly seven it is the least.

ISABELLA: Which is the least?

CLAUDIO: If it were damnable, he being so wise,
Why would he for the momentary trick
Be perdurably fin'd? O Isabel!

ISABELLA: What says my brother?

CLAUDIO: Death is a fearful thing.

ISABELLA: And shamed life a hateful.

CLAUDIO: Ay, but to die, and go we know not where;
To lie in cold obstruction, and to rot;

This sensible warm motion to become
A kneaded clod; and the delighted spirit
To bathe in fiery floods or to reside
In thrilling region of thick-ribbed ice;
To be imprison'd in the viewless winds,
And blown with restless violence round about
The pendent world; or to be worse than worst
Of those that lawless and incertain thought
Imagine howling—'tis too horrible!
The weariest and most loathed worldly life
That age, ache, penury, and imprisonment,
Can lay on nature is a paradise
To what we fear of death.

ISABELLA: Alas, alas!

CLAUDIO: Sweet sister, let me live.
What sin you do to save a brother's life,
Nature dispenses with the deed so far
That it becomes a virtue.

ISABELLA: O you beast!
O faithless coward! O dishonest wretch!
Wilt thou be made a man out of my vice?
Is't not a kind of incest to take life
From thine own sister's shame? What should I think?
Heaven shield my mother play'd my father fair!
For such a warped slip of wilderness
Ne'er issu'd from his blood. Take my defiance;
Die; perish. Might but my bending down
Reprieve thee from thy fate, it should proceed.
I'll pray a thousand prayers for thy death,
No word to save thee.

CLAUDIO: Nay, hear me, Isabel.

ISABELLA: O fie, fie, fie!
Thy sin's not accidental, but a trade.
Mercy to thee would prove itself a bawd;
'Tis best that thou diest quickly.

CLAUDIO: O, hear me, Isabella.

Re-enter DUKE as FRIAR

DUKE: Vouchsafe a word, young sister, but one word.

ISABELLA: What is your will?

DUKE: Might you dispense with your leisure, I would by and by have some speech with you; the satisfaction I would require is likewise your own benefit.

ISABELLA: I have no superfluous leisure; my stay must be stolen out of other affairs; but I will attend you awhile.

[Walks apart]

DUKE: [*as FRIAR, taking CLAUDIO aside*] Son, I have overheard what hath pass'd between you and your sister. Angelo had never the purpose to corrupt her; only he hath made an assay of her virtue to practise his judgment with the disposition of natures. She, having the truth of honour in her, hath made him that gracious denial which he is most glad to receive. I am confessor to Angelo, and I know this to be true; therefore prepare yourself to death. Do not satisfy your resolution with hopes that are fallible; to-morrow you must die; go to your knees and make ready.

CLAUDIO: Let me ask my sister pardon. I am so out of love with life that I will sue to be rid of it.

DUKE: Hold you there. Farewell. [*Exit CLAUDIO*] Provost, a word with you.

Re-enter PROVOST

PROVOST: What's your will, father?

DUKE: That, now you are come, you will be gone. Leave me a while with the maid; my mind promises with my habit no loss shall touch her by my company.

PROVOST: In good time.   *Exit PROVOST*

DUKE: The hand that hath made you fair hath made you good; the goodness that is cheap in beauty makes beauty brief in goodness; but grace, being the soul of your complexion, shall keep the body of it ever fair. The assault that Angelo hath made to you, fortune hath convey'd to my understanding; and, but that frailty hath examples for his falling, I should wonder at Angelo. How will you do to content this substitute, and to save your brother?

ISABELLA: I am now going to resolve him; I had rather my brother die by the law than my son should be unlawfully born. But, O, how much is the good Duke deceiv'd in Angelo! If ever he return, and I can speak to him, I will open my lips in vain, or discover his government.

DUKE: That shall not be much amiss; yet, as the matter now stands, he will avoid your accusation: he made trial of you only. Therefore fasten your ear on my advisings; to the love I have in doing good a remedy presents itself. I do make myself believe that you may most uprighteously do a poor wronged lady a merited benefit; redeem your brother from the angry law; do no stain to your own gracious person; and much please the absent Duke, if peradventure he shall ever return to have hearing of this business.

ISABELLA: Let me hear you speak farther; I have spirit to do anything that appears not foul in the truth of my spirit.

DUKE: Virtue is bold, and goodness never fearful. Have you not heard speak of Mariana, the sister of Frederick, the great soldier who miscarried at sea?

ISABELLA: I have heard of the lady, and good words went with her name.

DUKE: She should this Angelo have married; was affianced to her by oath, and the nuptial appointed; between which time of the contract and limit of the solemnity her brother Frederick was wreck'd at sea, having in that perished vessel the dowry of his sister. But mark how heavily this befell to the poor gentlewoman: there she lost a noble and renowned brother, in his love toward her ever most kind and natural; with him the portion and sinew of her fortune, her marriage-dowry; with both, her combinate husband, this well-seeming Angelo.

ISABELLA: Can this be so? Did Angelo so leave her?

DUKE: Left her in her tears, and dried not one of them with his comfort; swallowed his vows whole, pretending in her discoveries of dishonour; in few, bestow'd her on her own lamentation, which she yet wears for his sake; and he, a marble to her tears, is washed with them, but relents not.

ISABELLA: What a merit were it in death to take this poor maid from the world! What corruption in this life that it will let this man live! But how out of this can she avail?

DUKE: It is a rupture that you may easily heal; and the cure of it not only saves your brother, but keeps you from dishonour in doing it.

ISABELLA: Show me how, good father.

DUKE: This forenamed maid hath yet in her the continuance of her first affection; his unjust unkindness, that in all reason should have quenched her love, hath, like an impediment in the current made it more violent and unruly. Go you to Angelo; answer his requiring with a plausible obedience; agree with his demands to the point; only refer yourself to this advantage: first, that your stay with him may not be long; that the time may have all shadow and silence in it; and the place answer to convenience. This being granted in course, and now follows all: we shall advise this wronged maid to stead up your appointment, go in your place. If the encounter acknowledge itself hereafter, it may compel him to her recompense; and here, by this, is your brother saved, your honour untainted, the poor Mariana advantaged, and the corrupt deputy scaled. The maid will I frame and make fit for his attempt. If you think well to carry this as you may, the doubleness of the benefit defends the deceit from reproof. What think you of it?

ISABELLA: The image of it gives me content already; and I trust it will grow to a most prosperous perfection.

DUKE: It lies much in your holding up. Haste you speedily to Angelo; if for this night he entreat you to his bed, give him promise of satisfaction. I will presently to Saint Luke's; there, at the moated grange, resides this dejected Mariana. At that place call upon me; and dispatch with Angelo, that it may be quickly.

ISABELLA: I thank you for this comfort. Fare you well, good father.

Exeunt severally

SCENE 2

The street before the prison

Enter, on one side, DUKE disguised as before; on the other, ELBOW, and OFFICERS with POMPEY

ELBOW: Nay, if there be no remedy for it, but that you will needs buy and sell men and women like beasts, we shall have all the world drink brown and white bastard.

DUKE: O heavens! what stuff is here?

POMPEY: 'Twas never merry world since, of two usuries, the merriest was put down, and the worser allow'd by order of law a furr'd gown to keep him warm; and furr'd with fox on lamb-skins too, to signify that craft, being richer than innocency, stands for the facing.

ELBOW: Come your way, sir. Bless you, good father friar.

DUKE: And you, good brother father. What offence hath this man made you, sir?

ELBOW: Marry, sir, he hath offended the law; and, sir, we take him to be a thief too, sir, for we have found upon him, sir, a strange picklock, which we have sent to the deputy.

DUKE: [*as FRIAR, to POMPEY*] Fie, sirrah, a bawd, a wicked bawd!
The evil that thou causest to be done,
That is thy means to live. Do thou but think
What 'tis to cram a maw or clothe a back
From such a filthy vice; say to thyself
"From their abominable and beastly touches
I drink, I eat, array myself, and live."
Canst thou believe thy living is a life,
So stinkingly depending? Go mend, go mend.

POMPEY: Indeed, it does stink in some sort, sir; but yet, sir, I would prove—

DUKE: Nay, if the devil have given thee proofs for sin,
Thou wilt prove his. Take him to prison, officer;
Correction and instruction must both work
Ere this rude beast will profit.

ELBOW: He must before the deputy, sir; he has given him warning. The deputy cannot abide a whoremaster; if he be a whoremonger, and comes before him, he were as good go a mile on his errand.

DUKE: That we were all, as some would seem to be,
From our faults, as his faults from seeming, free.

ELBOW: His neck will come to your waist—a cord, sir.

Enter LUCIO

POMPEY: I spy comfort; I cry bail. Here's a gentleman, and a friend of mine.

LUCIO: How now, noble Pompey! What, at the wheels of Caesar? Art thou led in triumph? What, is there none of Pygmalion's images, newly made woman, to be had now for putting the hand in the pocket and extracting it clutch'd? What reply, ha? What say'st thou to this tune, matter, and method? Is't not drown'd i' th' last rain, ha? What say'st thou, trot? Is the world as it was, man? Which is the way? Is it sad, and few words? or how? The trick of it?

DUKE: [*as FRIAR, aside*] Still thus, and thus; still worse!

LUCIO: [*to POMPEY*] How doth my dear morsel, thy mistress? Procures she still, ha?

POMPEY: Troth, sir, she hath eaten up all her beef, and she is herself in the tub.

LUCIO: Why, 'tis good; it is the right of it; it must be so; ever your fresh whore and your powder'd bawd—an unshunn'd consequence; it must be so. Art going to prison, Pompey?

POMPEY: Yes, faith, sir.

LUCIO: Why, 'tis not amiss, Pompey. Farewell; go, say I sent thee thither. For debt, Pompey, or how?

ELBOW: For being a bawd, for being a bawd.

LUCIO: Well, then, imprison him. If imprisonment be the due of a bawd, why, 'tis his right. Bawd is he doubtless, and of antiquity, too; bawd-born. Farewell, good Pompey. Commend me to the prison, Pompey. You will turn good husband now, Pompey; you will keep the house.

POMPEY: I hope, sir, your good worship will be my bail.

LUCIO: No, indeed, will I not, Pompey; it is not the wear. I will pray, Pompey, to increase your bondage. If you take it not patiently, why, your mettle is the more. Adieu trusty Pompey. Bless you, friar.

DUKE: And you.

LUCIO: Does Bridget paint still, Pompey, ha?

ELBOW: Come your ways, sir; come.

POMPEY: You will not bail me then, sir?

LUCIO: Then, Pompey, nor now. What news abroad, friar? What news?

ELBOW: Come your ways, sir; come.

LUCIO: Go to kennel, Pompey, go.

Exeunt ELBOW, POMPEY and OFFICERS

What news, friar, of the Duke?

DUKE: I know none. Can you tell me of any?

LUCIO: Some say he is with the Emperor of Russia; other some, he is in Rome; but where is he, think you?

DUKE: I know not where; but wheresoever, I wish him well.

LUCIO: It was a mad fantastical trick of him to steal from the state and usurp the beggary he was never born to. Lord Angelo dukes it well in his absence; he puts transgression to't.

DUKE: He does well in't.

LUCIO: A little more lenity to lechery would do no harm in him; something too crabbed that way, friar.

DUKE: It is too general a vice, and severity must cure it.

LUCIO: Yes, in good sooth, the vice is of a great kindred; it is well allied; but it is impossible to extirp it quite, friar, till eating and drinking be put down. They say this Angelo was not made by man and woman after this downright way of creation. Is it true, think you?

DUKE: How should he be made, then?

LUCIO: Some report a sea-maid spawn'd him; some, that he was begot between two stock-fishes. But it is certain that when he makes water his urine is congeal'd ice; that I know to be true. And he is a motion generative; that's infallible.

DUKE: You are pleasant, sir, and speak apace.

LUCIO: Why, what a ruthless thing is this in him, for the rebellion of a codpiece to take away the life of a man! Would the Duke that is absent have done this? Ere he would have hang'd a man for the getting a hundred bastards, he would have paid for the nursing a thousand. He had some feeling of the sport; he knew the service, and that instructed him to mercy.

DUKE: I never heard the absent Duke much detected for women; he was not inclin'd that way.

LUCIO: O, sir, you are deceiv'd.

DUKE: 'Tis not possible.

LUCIO: Who, not the Duke? Yes, your beggar of fifty; and his use was to put a ducat in her clack-dish. The Duke had crotchets in him. He would be drunk too; that let me inform you.

DUKE: You do him wrong, surely.

LUCIO: Sir, I was an inward of his. A shy fellow was the Duke; and I believe I know the cause of his withdrawing.

DUKE: What, I prithee, might be the cause?

LUCIO: No, pardon; 'tis a secret must be lock'd within the teeth and the lips; but this I can let you understand: the greater file of the subject held the Duke to be wise.

DUKE: Wise? Why, no question but he was.

LUCIO: A very superficial, ignorant, unweighing fellow.

DUKE: Either this is envy in you, folly, or mistaking; the very stream of his life, and the business he hath helmed, must, upon a warranted need, give him a better proclamation. Let him be but testimonied in his own bringings-forth, and he shall appear to the envious a scholar, a states-man, and a soldier. Therefore you speak unskilfully; or, if your knowl-edge be more, it is much dark'ned in your malice.

LUCIO: Sir, I know him, and I love him.

DUKE: Love talks with better knowledge, and knowledge with dearer love.

LUCIO: Come, sir, I know what I know.

DUKE: I can hardly believe that, since you know not what you speak. But, if ever the Duke return, as our prayers are he may, let me desire you to make your answer before him. If it be honest you have spoke, you have courage to maintain it; I am bound to call upon you; and I pray you your name?

LUCIO: Sir, my name is Lucio, well known to the Duke.

DUKE: He shall know you better, sir, if I may live to report you.

LUCIO: I fear you not.

DUKE: O, you hope the Duke will return no more; or you imagine me too unhurtful an opposite. But, indeed, I can do you little harm: you'll forswear this again.

LUCIO: I'll be hang'd first. Thou art deceiv'd in me, friar. But no more of this. Canst thou tell if Claudio die to-morrow or no?

DUKE: Why should he die, sir?

LUCIO: Why? For filling a bottle with a tun-dish. I would the Duke we talk of were return'd again. This ungenitur'd agent will unpeople the province with continency; sparrows must not build in his house-eaves because they are lecherous. The Duke yet would have dark deeds darkly answered; he would never bring them to light. Would he were return'd! Marry, this Claudio is condemned for untrussing. Farewell, good friar; I prithee pray for me. The Duke, I say to thee again, would eat mutton on Fridays. He's not past it yet; and, I say to thee, he would mouth with a beggar though she smelt brown bread and garlic. Say that I said so. Farewell.   *Exit*

DUKE: No might nor greatness in mortality
Can censure scape; back-wounding calumny
The whitest virtue strikes. What king so strong
Can tie the gall up in the slanderous tongue?
But who comes here?

Enter ESCALUS, PROVOST, and OFFICERS with MISTRESS OVER-DONE

ESCALUS: Go, away with her to prison.

MRS. OVERDONE: Good my lord, be good to me; your honour is accounted a merciful man; good my lord.

ESCALUS: Double and treble admonition, and still forfeit in the same kind! This would make mercy swear and play the tyrant.

PROVOST: A bawd of eleven years' continuance, may it please your honour.

MRS. OVERDONE: My lord, this is one Lucio's information against me. Mistress Kate Keepdown was with child by him in the Duke's time; he promis'd her marriage. His child is a year and a quarter old come Philip and Jacob; I have kept it myself; and see how he goes about to abuse me.

ESCALUS: That fellow is a fellow of much license. Let him be call'd before us. Away with her to prison. Go to; no more words. [*Exeunt OFFICERS with MISTRESS OVERDONE*] Provost, my brother Angelo will not be alter'd: Claudio must die to-morrow. Let him be furnish'd with divines, and have all charitable preparation. If my brother wrought by my pity, it should not be so with him.

PROVOST: So please you, this friar hath been with him, and advis'd him for th' entertainment of death.

ESCALUS: Good even, good father.

DUKE: Bliss and goodness on you!

ESCALUS: Of whence are you?

DUKE: Not of this country, though my chance is now
To use it for my time. I am a brother
Of gracious order, late come from the See
In special business from his Holiness.

ESCALUS: What news abroad i' th' world?

DUKE: None, but that there is so great a fever on goodness that the dissolution of it must cure it. Novelty is only in request; and, as it is, as dangerous to be aged in any kind of course as it is virtuous to be constant in any undertaking. There is scarce truth enough alive to make societies secure; but security enough to make fellowships accurst. Much upon this riddle runs the wisdom of the world. This news is old enough, yet it is every day's news. I pray you, sir, of what disposition was the Duke?

ESCALUS: One that, above all other strifes, contended especially to know himself.

DUKE: What pleasure was he given to?

ESCALUS: Rather rejoicing to see another merry than merry at any-thing which profess'd to make him rejoice; a gentleman of all temper-ance. But leave we him to his events, with a prayer they may prove prosperous; and let me desire to know how you find Claudio prepar'd. I am made to understand that you have lent him visitation.

DUKE: He professes to have received no sinister measure from his judge, but most willingly humbles himself to the determination of justice. Yet had he framed to himself, by the instruction of his frailty, many deceiving promises of life; which I, by my good leisure, have discredited to him, and now he is resolv'd to die.

ESCALUS: You have paid the heavens your function, and the prisoner the very debt of your calling. I have labour'd for the poor gentleman to the extremest shore of my modesty; but my brother justice have I found so severe that he hath forc'd me to tell him he is indeed Justice.

DUKE: If his own life answer the straitness of his proceeding, it shall become him well; wherein if he chance to fail, he hath sentenc'd himself.

ESCALUS: I am going to visit the prisoner. Fare you well.

DUKE: Peace be with you!

Exeunt ESCALUS and PROVOST
He who the sword of heaven will bear
Should be as holy as severe;
Pattern in himself to know,
Grace to stand, and virtue go;
More nor less to others paying
Than by self-offences weighing.
Shame to him whose cruel striking
Kills for faults of his own liking!
Twice treble shame on Angelo,
To weed my vice and let his grow!
O, what may man within him hide,
Though angel on the outward side!
How may likeness, made in crimes,
Make a practice on the times,
To draw with idle spiders' strings
Most ponderous and substantial things!
Craft against vice I must apply.
With Angelo to-night shall lie
His old betrothed but despised;
So disguise shall, by th' disguised,
Pay with falsehood false exacting,
And perform an old contracting.   *Exit*

ACT IV, SCENE 1

The moated grange at Saint Duke's

Enter MARIANA, and BOY singing

SONG
Take, O, take those lips away,
That so sweetly were forsworn;
And those eyes, the break of day,
Lights that do mislead the morn;
But my kisses bring again, bring again;
Seals of love, but seal'd in vain, seal'd in vain.

Enter DUKE, disguised as before

MARIANA: Break off thy song, and haste thee quick away;
Here comes a man of comfort, whose advice
Hath often still'd my brawling discontent.   *Exit BOY*

I cry you mercy, sir, and well could wish
You had not found me here so musical.
Let me excuse me, and believe me so,
My mirth it much displeas'd, but pleas'd my woe.

DUKE: 'Tis good; though music oft hath such a charm
To make bad good and good provoke to harm.
I pray you tell me hath anybody inquir'd for me here to-day. Much upon this time have I promis'd here to meet.

MARIANA: You have not been inquir'd after; I have sat here all day.

Enter ISABELLA

DUKE: I do constantly believe you. The time is come even now. I shall crave your forbearance a little. May be I will call upon you anon, for some advantage to yourself.

MARIANA: I am always bound to you.   *Exit*

DUKE: Very well met, and well come.
What is the news from this good deputy?

ISABELLA: He hath a garden circummur'd with brick,
Whose western side is with a vineyard back'd;
And to that vineyard is a planched gate
That makes his opening with this bigger key;
This other doth command a little door
Which from the vineyard to the garden leads.
There have I made my promise
Upon the heavy middle of the night
To call upon him.

DUKE: But shall you on your knowledge find this way?

ISABELLA: I have ta'en a due and wary note upon't;
With whispering and most guilty diligence,
In action all of precept, he did show me
The way twice o'er.

DUKE: Are there no other tokens
Between you 'greed concerning her observance?

ISABELLA: No, none, but only a repair i' th' dark;
And that I have possess'd him my most stay
Can be but brief; for I have made him know
I have a servant comes with me along,
That stays upon me; whose persuasion is
I come about my brother.

DUKE: 'Tis well borne up.
I have not yet made known to Mariana
A word of this. What ho, within! come forth.

Re-enter MARIANA

I pray you be acquainted with this maid;
She comes to do you good.

ISABELLA: I do desire the like.

DUKE: Do you persuade yourself that I respect you?

MARIANA: Good friar, I know you do, and have found it.

DUKE: Take, then, this your companion by the hand,
Who hath a story ready for your ear.
I shall attend your leisure; but make haste;
The vaporous night approaches.

MARIANA: Will't please you walk aside?

Exeunt MARIANA and ISABELLA

DUKE: O place and greatness! Millions of false eyes
Are stuck upon thee. Volumes of report
Run with these false, and most contrarious quest
Upon thy doings. Thousand escapes of wit
Make thee the father of their idle dream,
And rack thee in their fancies.

Re-enter MARIANA and ISABELLA

Welcome, how agreed?

ISABELLA: She'll take the enterprise upon her, father,
If you advise it.

DUKE: It is not my consent,
But my entreaty too.

ISABELLA: Little have you to say,
When you depart from him, but, soft and low,
"Remember now my brother."

MARIANA: Fear me not.

DUKE: Nor, gentle daughter, fear you not at all.
He is your husband on a pre-contract.
To bring you thus together 'tis no sin,
Sith that the justice of your title to him
Doth flourish the deceit. Come, let us go;
Our corn's to reap, for yet our tithe's to sow.   *Exeunt*

SCENE 2

The prison

Enter PROVOST and POMPEY

PROVOST: Come hither, sirrah. Can you cut off a man's head?

POMPEY: If the man be a bachelor, sir, I can; but if he be a married man, he's his wife's head, and I can never cut off a woman's head.

PROVOST: Come, sir, leave me your snatches and yield me a direct answer. To-morrow morning are to die Claudio and Barnardine. Here is in our prison a common executioner, who in his office lacks a helper; if you will take it on you to assist him, it shall redeem you from your gyves; if not, you shall have your full time of imprisonment, and your deliverance with an unpitied whipping, for you have been a notorious bawd.

POMPEY: Sir, I have been an unlawful bawd time out of mind; but yet I will be content to be a lawful hangman. I would be glad to receive some instructions from my fellow partner.

PROVOST: What ho, Abhorson! Where's Abhorson there?

Enter ABHORSON

ABHORSON: Do you call, sir?

PROVOST: Sirrah, here's a fellow will help you to-morrow in your execution. If you think it meet, compound with him by the year, and let him abide here with you; if not, use him for the present, and dismiss him. He cannot plead his estimation with you; he hath been a bawd.

ABHORSON: A bawd, sir? Fie upon him! He will discredit our mystery.

PROVOST: Go to, sir; you weigh equally; a feather will turn the scale.

Exit

POMPEY: Pray, sir, by your good favour—for surely, sir, a good favour you have but that you have a hanging look—do you call, sir, your occupation a mystery?

ABHORSON: Ay, sir; a mystery.

POMPEY: Painting, sir, I have heard say, is a mystery; and your whores, sir, being members of my occupation, using painting, do prove my occupation a mystery; but what mystery there should be in hanging, if I should be hang'd, I cannot imagine.

ABHORSON: Sir, it is a mystery.

POMPEY: Proof?

ABHORSON: Every true man's apparel fits your thief: if it be too little for your thief, your true man thinks it big enough; if it be too big for your thief, your thief thinks it little enough; so every true man's apparel fits your thief.

Re-enter PROVOST

PROVOST: Are you agreed?

POMPEY: Sir, I will serve him; for I do find your hangman is a more penitent trade than your bawd; he doth oftener ask forgiveness.

PROVOST: You, sirrah, provide your block and your axe to-morrow four o'clock.

ABHORSON: Come on, bawd; I will instruct thee in my trade; follow.

POMPEY: I do desire to learn, sir; and I hope, if you have occasion to use me for your own turn, you shall find me yare; for truly, sir, for your kindness I owe you a good turn.

PROVOST: Call hither Barnardine and Claudio.

Exeunt ABHORSON and POMPEY

Th' one has my pity; not a jot the other,
Being a murderer, though he were my brother.

Enter CLAUDIO

Look, here's the warrant, Claudio, for thy death;
'Tis now dead midnight, and by eight to-morrow
Thou must be made immortal. Where's Barnardine?

CLAUDIO: As fast lock'd up in sleep as guiltless labour
When it lies starkly in the traveller's bones.
He will not wake.

PROVOST: Who can do good on him?
Well, go, prepare yourself. [*Knocking within*] But hark, what noise?
Heaven give your spirits comfort!   *Exit CLAUDIO*

[*Knocking continues*] By and by.
I hope it is some pardon or reprieve
For the most gentle Claudio.

Enter DUKE, disguised as before
Welcome, father.

DUKE: The best and wholesom'st spirits of the night
Envelop you, good Provost! Who call'd here of late?

PROVOST: None, since the curfew rung.

DUKE: Not Isabel?

PROVOST: No.

DUKE: They will then, ere't be long.

PROVOST: What comfort is for Claudio?

DUKE: There's some in hope.

PROVOST: It is a bitter deputy.

DUKE: Not so, not so; his life is parallel'd
Even with the stroke and line of his great justice;
He doth with holy abstinence subdue
That in himself which he spurs on his pow'r
To qualify in others. Were he meal'd with that
Which he corrects, then were he tyrannous;
But this being so, he's just. [*Knocking within*] Now are they come.

Exit PROVOST

This is a gentle provost; seldom when
The steeled gaoler is the friend of men. [*Knocking within*]
How now, what noise! That spirit's possess'd with haste
That wounds th' unsisting postern with these strokes.

Re-enter PROVOST

PROVOST: There he must stay until the officer
Arise to let him in; he is call'd up.

DUKE: Have you no countermand for Claudio yet

But he must die to-morrow?

PROVOST: None, sir, none.

DUKE: As near the dawning, Provost, as it is,
You shall hear more ere morning.

PROVOST: Happily
You something know; yet I believe there comes
No countermand; no such example have we.
Besides, upon the very siege of justice,
Lord Angelo hath to the public ear
Profess'd the contrary.

Enter a MESSENGER

This is his lordship's man.

DUKE: And here comes Claudio's pardon.

MESSENGER: My lord hath sent you this note; and by me this further charge, that you swerve not from the smallest article of it, neither in time, matter, or other circumstance. Good morrow; for as I take it, it is almost day.

PROVOST: I shall obey him.   *Exit MESSENGER*

DUKE: [*Aside*] This is his pardon, purchas'd by such sin
For which the pardoner himself is in;
Hence hath offence his quick celerity,
When it is borne in high authority.
When vice makes mercy, mercy's so extended
That for the fault's love is th' offender friended.
Now, sir, what news?

PROVOST: I told you: Lord Angelo, belike thinking me remiss in mine office, awakens me with this unwonted putting-on; methinks strangely, for he hath not us'd it before.

DUKE: Pray you, let's hear.

PROVOST: [*Reads*] "Whatsoever you may hear to the contrary, let Claudio be executed by four of the clock, and, in the afternoon, Barnardine. For my better satisfaction, let me have Claudio's head sent me by five. Let this be duly performed, with a thought that more depends on it than we must yet deliver. Thus fail not to do your office, as you will answer it at your peril." What say you to this, sir?

DUKE: What is that Barnardine who is to be executed in th' afternoon?

PROVOST: A Bohemian born; but here nurs'd up and bred. One that is a prisoner nine years old.

DUKE: How came it that the absent Duke had not either deliver'd him to his liberty or executed him? I have heard it was ever his manner to do so.

PROVOST: His friends still wrought reprieves for him; and, indeed, his fact, till now in the government of Lord Angelo, came not to an undoubted proof.

DUKE: It is now apparent?

PROVOST: Most manifest, and not denied by himself.

DUKE: Hath he borne himself penitently in prison? How seems he to be touch'd?

PROVOST: A man that apprehends death no more dreadfully but as a drunken sleep; careless, reckless, and fearless, of what's past, present, or to come; insensible of mortality and desperately mortal.

DUKE: He wants advice.

PROVOST: He will hear none. He hath evermore had the liberty of the prison; give him leave to escape hence, he would not; drunk many times a day, if not many days entirely drunk. We have very oft awak'd him, as if to carry him to execution, and show'd him a seeming warrant for it; it hath not moved him at all.

DUKE: More of him anon. There is written in your brow, Provost, honesty and constancy. If I read it not truly, my ancient skill beguiles me; but in the boldness of my cunning I will lay myself in hazard. Claudio, whom here you have warrant to execute, is no greater forfeit to the law than Angelo who hath sentenc'd him. To make you understand this in a manifested effect, I crave but four days' respite; for the which you are to do me both a present and a dangerous courtesy.

PROVOST: Pray, sir, in what?

DUKE: In the delaying death.

PROVOST: Alack! How may I do it, having the hour limited, and an express command, under penalty, to deliver his head in the view of Angelo? I may make my case as Claudio's, to cross this in the smallest.

DUKE: By the vow of mine order, I warrant you, if my instructions may be your guide. Let this Barnardine be this morning executed, and his head borne to Angelo.

PROVOST: Angelo hath seen them both, and will discover the favour.

DUKE: O, death's a great disguiser; and you may add to it. Shave the head and tie the beard; and say it was the desire of the penitent to be so bar'd before his death. You know the course is common. If anything fall to you upon this more than thanks and good fortune, by the saint whom I profess, I will plead against it with my life.

PROVOST: Pardon me, good father; it is against my oath.

DUKE: Were you sworn to the Duke, or to the deputy?

PROVOST: To him and to his substitutes.

DUKE: You will think you have made no offence if the Duke avouch the justice of your dealing?

PROVOST: But what likelihood is in that?

DUKE: Not a resemblance, but a certainty. Yet since I see you fearful, that neither my coat, integrity, nor persuasion, can with ease attempt you, I will go further than I meant, to pluck all fears out of you. Look you, sir, here is the hand and seal of the Duke. You know the character, I doubt not; and the signet is not strange to you.

PROVOST: I know them both.

DUKE: The contents of this is the return of the Duke; you shall anon over-read it at your pleasure, where you shall find within these two days he will be here. This is a thing that Angelo knows not; for he this very day receives letters of strange tenour, perchance of the Duke's death, perchance entering into some monastery; but, by chance, nothing of what is writ. Look, th' unfolding star calls up the shepherd. Put not yourself into amazement how these things should be: all difficulties are but easy when they are known. Call your executioner, and off with Barnardine's head. I will give him a present shrift, and advise him for a better place. Yet you are amaz'd, but this shall absolutely resolve you. Come away; it is almost clear dawn.

Exeunt

SCENE 3

The prison

Enter POMPEY

POMPEY: I am as well acquainted here as I was in our house of profession; one would think it were Mistress Overdone's own house, for here be many of her old customers. First, here's young Master Rash; he's in for a commodity of brown paper and old ginger, nine score and seventeen pounds, of which he made five marks ready money. Marry, then ginger was not much in request, for the old women were all dead. Then is there here one Master Caper, at the suit of Master Threepile the mercer, for some four suits of peach-colour'd satin, which now peaches him a beggar. Then have we here young Dizy, and young Master Deepvow, and Master Copperspur, and Master Starvelackey, the rapier and dagger man, and young Dropheir that kill'd lusty Pudding, and Master Forthlight the tilter, and brave Master Shootie the great traveller, and wild Halfcan that stabb'd Pots, and, I think, forty more, all great doers in our trade, and are now "for the Lord's sake."

Enter ABHORSON

ABHORSON: Sirrah, bring Barnardine hither.

POMPEY: Master Barnardine! You must rise and be hang'd, Master Barnardine!

ABHORSON: What ho, Barnardine!

BARNARDINE: [*Within*] A pox o' your throats! Who makes that noise there? What are you?

POMPEY: Your friends, sir; the hangman. You must be so good, sir, to rise and be put to death.

BARNARDINE: [*Within*] Away, you rogue, away; I am sleepy.

ABHORSON: Tell him he must awake, and that quickly too.

POMPEY: Pray, Master Barnardine, awake till you are executed, and sleep afterwards.

ABHORSON: Go in to him, and fetch him out.

POMPEY: He is coming, sir, he is coming; I hear his straw rustle.

Enter BARNARDINE

ABHORSON: Is the axe upon the block, sirrah?

POMPEY: Very ready, sir.

BARNARDINE: How now, Abhorson, what's the news with you?

ABHORSON: Truly, sir, I would desire you to clap into your prayers; for, look you, the warrant's come.

BARNARDINE: You rogue, I have been drinking all night; I am not fitted for't.

POMPEY: O, the better, sir! For he that drinks all night and is hanged betimes in the morning may sleep the sounder all the next day.

Enter DUKE, disguised as before

ABHORSON: Look you, sir, here comes your ghostly father. Do we jest now, think you?

DUKE: [*To Barnardine*] Sir, induced by my charity, and hearing how hastily you are to depart, I am come to advise you, comfort you, and pray with you.

BARNARDINE: Friar, not I; I have been drinking hard all night, and I will have more time to prepare me, or they shall beat out my brains with billets. I will not consent to die this day, that's certain.

DUKE: O, Sir, you must; and therefore I beseech you look forward on the journey you shall go.

BARNARDINE: I swear I will not die to-day for any man's persuasion.

DUKE: But hear you—

BARNARDINE: Not a word; if you have anything to say to me, come to my ward; for thence will not I to-day.   *Exit*

DUKE: Unfit to live or die. O gravel heart!
After him, fellows; bring him to the block.

Exeunt ABHORSON and POMPEY

Enter PROVOST

PROVOST: Now, sir, how do you find the prisoner?

DUKE: A creature unprepar'd, unmeet for death;
And to transport him in the mind he is
Were damnable.

PROVOST: Here in the prison, father,

There died this morning of a cruel fever
One Ragozine, a most notorious pirate,
A man of Claudio's years; his beard and head
Just of his colour. What if we do omit
This reprobate till he were well inclin'd,
And satisfy the deputy with the visage
Of Ragozine, more like to Claudio?

DUKE: O, 'tis an accident that heaven provides!
Dispatch it presently; the hour draws on
Prefix'd by Angelo. See this be done,
And sent according to command; whiles I
Persuade this rude wretch willingly to die.

PROVOST: This shall be done, good father, presently.
But Barnardine must die this afternoon;
And how shall we continue Claudio,
To save me from the danger that might come
If he were known alive?

DUKE: Let this be done:
Put them in secret holds, both Barnardine and Claudio.
Ere twice the sun hath made his journal greeting
To the under generation, you shall find
Your safety manifested.

PROVOST: I am your free dependant.

DUKE: Quick, dispatch, and send the head to Angelo.

Exit PROVOST

Now will I write letters to Angelo—
The Provost, he shall bear them—whose contents
Shall witness to him I am near at home,
And that, by great injunctions, I am bound
To enter publicly. Him I'll desire
To meet me at the consecrated fount,
A league below the city; and from thence,
By cold gradation and well-balanc'd form.
We shall proceed with Angelo.

Re-enter PROVOST

PROVOST: Here is the head; I'll carry it myself.

DUKE: Convenient is it. Make a swift return;
For I would commune with you of such things
That want no ear but yours.

PROVOST: I'll make all speed.   *Exit*

ISABELLA: [*Within*] Peace, ho, be here!

DUKE: The tongue of Isabel. She's come to know
If yet her brother's pardon be come hither;
But I will keep her ignorant of her good,

To make her heavenly comforts of despair
When it is least expected.

Enter ISABELLA

ISABELLA: Ho, by your leave!

DUKE: Good morning to you, fair and gracious daughter.

ISABELLA: The better, given me by so holy a man.
Hath yet the deputy sent my brother's pardon?

DUKE: He hath releas'd him, Isabel, from the world.
His head is off and sent to Angelo.

ISABELLA: Nay, but it is not so.

DUKE: It is no other.
Show your wisdom, daughter, in your close patience,

ISABELLA: O, I will to him and pluck out his eyes!

DUKE: You shall not be admitted to his sight.

ISABELLA: Unhappy Claudio! Wretched Isabel!
Injurious world! Most damned Angelo!

DUKE: This nor hurts him nor profits you a jot;
Forbear it, therefore; give your cause to heaven.
Mark what I say, which you shall find
By every syllable a faithful verity.
The Duke comes home to-morrow. Nay, dry your eyes.
One of our convent, and his confessor,
Gives me this instance. Already he hath carried
Notice to Escalus and Angelo,
Who do prepare to meet him at the gates,
There to give up their pow'r. If you can, pace your wisdom
In that good path that I would wish it go,
And you shall have your bosom on this wretch,
Grace of the Duke, revenges to your heart,
And general honour.

ISABELLA: I am directed by you.

DUKE: This letter, then, to Friar Peter give;
'Tis that he sent me of the Duke's return.
Say, by this token, I desire his company
At Mariana's house to-night. Her cause and yours
I'll perfect him withal; and he shall bring you
Before the Duke; and to the head of Angelo
Accuse him home and home. For my poor self,
I am combined by a sacred vow,
And shall be absent. Wend you with this letter.
Command these fretting waters from your eyes
With a light heart; trust not my holy order,
If I pervert your course. Who's here?

Enter LUCIO

LUCIO: Good even. Friar, where's the Provost?

DUKE: Not within, sir.

LUCIO: O pretty Isabella, I am pale at mine heart to see thine eyes so red. Thou must be patient. I am fain to dine and sup with water and bran; I dare not for my head fill my belly; one fruitful meal would set me to't. But they say the Duke will be here to-morrow. By my troth, Isabel, I lov'd thy brother. If the old fantastical Duke of dark corners had been at home, he had lived.

Exit ISABELLA

DUKE: Sir, the Duke is marvellous little beholding to your reports; but the best is, he lives not in them.

LUCIO: Friar, thou knowest not the Duke so well as I do; he's a better woodman than thou tak'st him for.

DUKE: Well, you'll answer this one day. Fare ye well.

LUCIO: Nay, tarry; I'll go along with thee; I can tell thee pretty tales of the Duke.

DUKE: You have told me too many of him already, sir, if they be true; if not true, none were enough.

LUCIO: I was once before him for getting a wench with child.

DUKE: Did you such a thing?

LUCIO: Yes, marry, did I; but I was fain to forswear it: they would else have married me to the rotten medlar.

DUKE: Sir, your company is fairer than honest. Rest you well.

LUCIO: By my troth, I'll go with thee to the lane's end. If bawdy talk offend you, we'll have very little of it. Nay, friar, I am a kind of burr; I shall stick. *Exeunt*

SCENE 4

ANGELO'S house

Enter ANGELO and ESCALUS

ESCALUS: Every letter he hath writ hath disvouch'd other.

ANGELO: In most uneven and distracted manner. His actions show much like to madness; pray heaven his wisdom be not tainted! And why meet him at the gates, and redeliver our authorities there?

ESCALUS: I guess not.

ANGELO: And why should we proclaim it in an hour before his ent'ring that, if any crave redress of injustice, they should exhibit their petitions in the street?

ESCALUS: He shows his reason for that: to have a dispatch of complaints; and to deliver us from devices hereafter, which shall then have no power to stand against us.

ANGELO: Well, I beseech you, let it be proclaim'd;

Betimes i' th' morn I'll call you at your house;
Give notice to such men of sort and suit
As are to meet him.

ESCALUS: I shall, sir; fare you well.

ANGELO: Good night.   *Exit ESCALUS*
This deed unshapes me quite, makes me unpregnant
And dull to all proceedings. A deflow'red maid!
And by an eminent body that enforc'd
The law against it! But that her tender shame
Will not proclaim against her maiden loss,
How might she tongue me! Yet reason dares her no;
For my authority bears a so credent bulk
That no particular scandal once can touch
But it confounds the breather. He should have liv'd,
Save that his riotous youth, with dangerous sense,
Might in the times to come have ta'en revenge,
By so receiving a dishonour'd life
With ransom of such shame. Would yet he had liv'd!
Alack, when once our grace we have forgot,
Nothing goes right; we would, and we would not.   *Exit*

SCENE 5

Fields without the town

Enter DUKE in his own habit, and Friar PETER

DUKE: These letters at fit time deliver me. [*Giving letters*]
The Provost knows our purpose and our plot.
The matter being afoot, keep your instruction
And hold you ever to our special drift;
Though sometimes you do blench from this to that
As cause doth minister. Go, call at Flavius' house,
And tell him where I stay; give the like notice
To Valentinus, Rowland, and to Crassus,
And bid them bring the trumpets to the gate;
But send me Flavius first.

PETER: It shall be speeded well.   *Exit FRIAR*

Enter VARRIUS

DUKE: I thank thee, Varrius; thou hast made good haste.
Come, we will walk. There's other of our friends
Will greet us here anon. My gentle Varrius!   *Exeunt*

SCENE 6

A street near the city gate

Enter ISABELLA and MARIANA

ISABELLA: To speak so indirectly I am loath;
I would say the truth; but to accuse him so,

That is your part. Yet I am advis'd to do it;
He says, to veil full purpose.

MARIANA: Be rul'd by him.

ISABELLA: Besides, he tells me that, if peradventure
He speak against me on the adverse side,
I should not think it strange; for 'tis a physic
That's bitter to sweet end.

MARIANA: I would Friar Peter—

Enter FRIAR PETER

ISABELLA: O, peace! the friar is come.

PETER: Come, I have found you out a stand most fit,
Where you may have such vantage on the Duke
He shall not pass you. Twice have the trumpets sounded;
The generous and gravest citizens
Have hent the gates, and very near upon
The Duke is ent'ring; therefore, hence, away.   *Exeunt*

ACT V, SCENE 1

The city gate

*Enter at several doors DUKE, VARRIUS, LORDS, ANGELO, ESCALUS,
LUCIO, PROVOST, OFFICERS, and CITIZENS*

DUKE: My very worthy cousin, fairly met!
Our old and faithful friend, we are glad to see you.

ANGELO, ESCALUS: Happy return be to your royal Grace!

DUKE: Many and hearty thankings to you both.
We have made inquiry of you, and we hear
Such goodness of your justice that our soul
Cannot but yield you forth to public thanks,
Forerunning more requital.

ANGELO: You make my bonds still greater.

DUKE: O, your desert speaks loud; and I should wrong it
To lock it in the wards of covert bosom,
When it deserves, with characters of brass,
A forted residence 'gainst the tooth of time
And razure of oblivion. Give me your hand.
And let the subject see, to make them know
That outward courtesies would fain proclaim
Favours that keep within. Come, Escalus,
You must walk by us on our other hand,
And good supporters are you.

Enter FRIAR PETER and ISABELLA

PETER: Now is your time; speak loud, and kneel before him.

ISABELLA: Justice, O royal Duke! Vail your regard

Upon a wrong'd—I would fain have said a maid!
O worthy Prince, dishonour not your eye
By throwing it on any other object
Till you have heard me in my true complaint,
And given me justice, justice, justice, justice.

DUKE: Relate your wrongs. In what? By whom? Be brief.
Here is Lord Angelo shall give you justice;
Reveal yourself to him.

ISABELLA: O worthy Duke,
You bid me seek redemption of the devil!
Hear me yourself; for that which I must speak
Must either punish me, not being believ'd,
Or wring redress from you. Hear me, O, hear me, here!

ANGELO: My lord, her wits, I fear me, are not firm;
She hath been a suitor to me for her brother,
Cut off by course of justice.

ISABELLA: By course of justice!

ANGELO: And she will speak most bitterly and strange.

ISABELLA: Most strange, but yet most truly, will I speak.
That Angelo's forsworn, is it not strange?
That Angelo's a murderer, is't not strange?
That Angelo is an adulterous thief,
An hypocrite, a virgin-violator,
Is it not strange and strange?

DUKE: Nay, it is ten times strange.

ISABELLA: It is not truer he is Angelo
Than this is all as true as it is strange;
Nay, it is ten times true; for truth is truth
To th' end of reck'ning.

DUKE: Away with her. Poor soul,
She speaks this in th' infirmity of sense.

ISABELLA: O Prince! I conjure thee, as thou believ'st
There is another comfort than this world,
That thou neglect me not with that opinion
That I am touch'd with madness. Make not impossible
That which but seems unlike: 'tis not impossible
But one, the wicked'st caitiff on the ground,
May seem as shy, as grave, as just, as absolute,
As Angelo; even so may Angelo,
In all his dressings, characts, titles, forms,
Be an arch-villain. Believe it, royal Prince,
If he be less, he's nothing; but he's more,
Had I more name for badness.

DUKE: By mine honesty,
If she be mad, as I believe no other,

Her madness hath the oddest frame of sense,
Such a dependency of thing on thing,
As e'er I heard in madness.

ISABELLA: O gracious Duke,
Harp not on that; nor do not banish reason
For inequality; but let your reason serve
To make the truth appear where it seems hid,
And hide the false seems true.

DUKE: Many that are not mad
Have, sure, more lack of reason. What would you say?

ISABELLA: I am the sister of one Claudio,
Condemn'd upon the act of fornication
To lose his head; condemn'd by Angelo.
I, in probation of a sisterhood,
Was sent to by my brother; one Lucio
As then the messenger—

LUCIO: That's I, an't like your Grace.
I came to her from Claudio, and desir'd her
To try her gracious fortune with Lord Angelo
For her poor brother's pardon.

ISABELLA: That's he, indeed.

DUKE: You were not bid to speak.

LUCIO: No, my good lord;
Nor wish'd to hold my peace.

DUKE: I wish you now, then;
Pray you take note of it; and when you have
A business for yourself, pray heaven you then
Be perfect.

LUCIO: I warrant your honour.

DUKE: The warrant's for yourself; take heed to't.

ISABELLA: This gentleman told somewhat of my tale.

LUCIO: Right.

DUKE: It may be right; but you are i' the wrong
To speak before your time. Proceed.

ISABELLA: I went
To this pernicious caitiff deputy.

DUKE: That's somewhat madly spoken.

ISABELLA: Pardon it;
The phrase is to the matter.

DUKE: Mended again. The matter, proceed.

ISABELLA: In brief—to set the needless process by,
How I persuaded, how I pray'd, and kneel'd,
How he refell'd me, and how I replied,

For this was of much length—the vile conclusion
I now begin with grief and shame to utter:
He would not, but by gift of my chaste body
To his concupiscible intemperate lust,
Release my brother; and, after much debatement,
My sisterly remorse confutes mine honour,
And I did yield to him. But the next morn betimes,
His purpose surfeiting, he sends a warrant
For my poor brother's head.

DUKE: This is most likely!

ISABELLA: O that it were as like as it is true!

DUKE: By heaven, fond wretch, thou know'st not what thou speak'st,
Or else thou art suborn'd against his honour
In hateful practice. First, his integrity
Stands without blemish; next, it imports no reason
That with such vehemency he should pursue
Faults proper to himself. If he had so offended,
He would have weigh'd thy brother by himself,
And not have cut him off. Some one hath set you on;
Confess the truth, and say by whose advice
Thou cam'st here to complain.

ISABELLA: And is this all?
Then, O you blessed ministers above,
Keep me in patience; and, with ripened time,
Unfold the evil which is here wrapt up
In countenance! Heaven shield your Grace from woe,
As I, thus wrong'd, hence unbelieved go!

DUKE: I know you'd fain be gone. An officer!
To prison with her! Shall we thus permit
A blasting and a scandalous breath to fall
On him so near us? This needs must be a practice.
Who knew of your intent and coming hither?

ISABELLA: One that I would were here, Friar Lodowick.

DUKE: A ghostly father, belike. Who knows that Lodowick?

LUCIO: My lord, I know him; 'tis a meddling friar.
I do not like the man; had he been lay, my lord,
For certain words he spake against your Grace
In your retirement, I had swing'd him soundly.

DUKE: Words against me? This's a good friar, belike!
And to set on this wretched woman here
Against our substitute! Let this friar be found.

LUCIO: But yesternight, my lord, she and that friar,
I saw them at the prison; a saucy friar,
A very scurvy fellow.

PETER: Blessed be your royal Grace!

I have stood by, my lord, and I have heard
Your royal ear abus'd. First, hath this woman
Most wrongfully accus'd your substitute;
Who is as free from touch or soil with her
As she from one ungot.

DUKE: We did believe no less.
Know you that Friar Lodowick that she speaks of?

PETER: I know him for a man divine and holy;
Not scurvy, nor a temporary meddler,
As he's reported by this gentleman;
And, on my trust, a man that never yet
Did, as he vouches, misreport your Grace.

LUCIO: My lord, most villainously; believe it.

PETER: Well, he in time may come to clear himself;
But at this instant he is sick, my lord,
Of a strange fever. Upon his mere request—
Being come to knowledge that there was complaint
Intended 'gainst Lord Angelo—came I hither
To speak, as from his mouth, what he doth know
Is true and false; and what he, with his oath
And all probation, will make up full clear,
Whensoever he's convented. First, for this woman—
To justify this worthy nobleman,
So vulgarly and personally accus'd—
Her shall you hear disproved to her eyes,
Till she herself confess it.

DUKE: Good friar, let's hear it   *Exit ISABELLA guarded*
Do you not smile at this, Lord Angelo?
O heaven, the vanity of wretched fools!
Give us some seats. Come, cousin Angelo;
In this I'll be impartial; be you judge
Of your own cause.

Enter MARIANA veiled

Is this the witness, friar?
First let her show her face, and after speak.

MARIANA: Pardon, my lord; I will not show my face
Until my husband bid me.

DUKE: What, are you married?

MARIANA: No, my lord.

DUKE: Are you a maid?

MARIANA: No, my lord.

DUKE: A widow, then?

MARIANA: Neither, my lord.

DUKE: Why, you are nothing then; neither maid, widow, nor wife.

LUCIO: My lord, she may be a punk; for many of them are neither maid, widow, nor wife.

DUKE: Silence that fellow. I would he had some cause
To prattle for himself.

LUCIO: Well, my lord.

MARIANA: My lord, I do confess I ne'er was married,
And I confess, besides, I am no maid.
I have known my husband; yet my husband
Knows not that ever he knew me.

LUCIO: He was drunk, then, my lord; it can be no better.

DUKE: For the benefit of silence, would thou wert so too!

LUCIO: Well, my lord.

DUKE: This is no witness for Lord Angelo.

MARIANA: Now I come to't, my lord:
She that accuses him of fornication,
In self-same manner doth accuse my husband;
And charges him, my lord, with such a time
When I'll depose I had him in mine arms,
With all th' effect of love.

ANGELO: Charges she moe than me?

MARIANA: Not that I know.

DUKE: No? You say your husband.

MARIANA: Why, just, my lord, and that is Angelo,
Who thinks he knows that he ne'er knew my body,
But knows he thinks that he knows Isabel's.

ANGELO: This is a strange abuse. Let's see thy face.

MARIANA: My husband bids me; now I will unmask. [*Unveiling*]
This is that face, thou cruel Angelo,
Which once thou swor'st was worth the looking on;
This is the hand which, with a vow'd contract,
Was fast belock'd in thine; this is the body
That took away the match from Isabel,
And did supply thee at thy garden-house
In her imagin'd person.

DUKE: Know you this woman?

LUCIO: Carnally, she says.

DUKE: Sirrah, no more.

LUCIO: Enough, my lord.

ANGELO: My lord, I must confess I know this woman;
And five years since there was some speech of marriage
Betwixt myself and her; which was broke off,
Partly for that her promised proportions

Came short of composition; but in chief
For that her reputation was disvalued
In levity. Since which time of five years
I never spake with her, saw her, nor heard from her,
Upon my faith and honour.

MARIANA: Noble Prince,
As there comes light from heaven and words from breath,
As there is sense in truth and truth in virtue,
I am affianc'd this man's wife as strongly
As words could make up vows. And, my good lord,
But Tuesday night last gone, in's garden-house,
He knew me as a wife. As this is true,
Let me in safety raise me from my knees,
Or else for ever be confixed here,
A marble monument!

ANGELO: I did but smile till now.
Now, good my lord, give me the scope of justice;
My patience here is touch'd. I do perceive
These poor informal women are no more
But instruments of some more mightier member
That sets them on. Let me have way, my lord,
To find this practice out.

DUKE: Ay, with my heart;
And punish them to your height of pleasure.
Thou foolish friar, and thou pernicious woman,
Compact with her that's gone, think'st thou thy oaths,
Though they would swear down each particular saint,
Were testimonies against his worth and credit,
That's seal'd in approbation? You, Lord Escalus,
Sit with my cousin; lend him your kind pains
To find out this abuse, whence 'tis deriv'd.
There is another friar that set them on;
Let him be sent for.

PETER: Would he were here, my lord! For he indeed
Hath set the women on to this complaint.
Your provost knows the place where he abides,
And he may fetch him.

DUKE: Go, do it instantly.   *Exit PROVOST*

[*To ANGELO*] And you, my noble and well-warranted cousin,
Whom it concerns to hear this matter forth,
Do with your injuries as seems you best
In any chastisement. I for a while will leave you;
But stir not you till you have well determin'd
Upon these slanderers.

ESCALUS: My lord, we'll do it throughly.   *Exit DUKE*

Signior Lucio, did not you say you knew that Friar Lodowick to be a dishonest person?

LUCIO: "Cucullus non facit monachum": honest in nothing but in his clothes; and one that hath spoke most villainous speeches of the Duke.

ESCALUS: We shall entreat you to abide here till he come and enforce them against him. We shall find this friar a notable fellow.

LUCIO: As any in Vienna, on my word.

ESCALUS: Call that same Isabel here once again; I would speak with her. [*Exit an ATTENDANT*] Pray you, my lord, give me leave to question; you shall see how I'll handle her.

LUCIO: Not better than he, by her own report.

ESCALUS: Say you?

LUCIO: Marry, sir, I think, if you handled her privately, she would sooner confess; perchance, publicly, she'll be asham'd.

Re-enter OFFICERS with ISABELLA; and PROVOST with the DUKE in his friar's habit

ESCALUS: I will go darkly to work with her.

LUCIO: That's the way; for women are light at midnight.

ESCALUS: Come on, mistress; here's a gentlewoman denies all that you have said.

LUCIO: My lord, here comes the rascal I spoke of, here with the Provost.

ESCALUS: In very good time. Speak not you to him till we call upon you.

LUCIO: Mum.

ESCALUS: Come, sir; did you set these women on to slander Lord Angelo? They have confess'd you did.

DUKE: 'Tis false.

ESCALUS: How! Know you where you are?

DUKE: Respect to your great place! and let the devil
Be sometime honour'd for his burning throne!
Where is the Duke? 'Tis he should hear me speak.

ESCALUS: The Duke's in us; and we will hear you speak;
Look you speak justly.

DUKE: Boldly, at least. But, O, poor souls,
Come you to seek the lamb here of the fox,
Good night to your redress! Is the Duke gone?
Then is your cause gone too. The Duke's unjust
Thus to retort your manifest appeal,
And put your trial in the villain's mouth
Which here you come to accuse.

LUCIO: This is the rascal; this is he I spoke of.

ESCALUS: Why, thou unreverend and unhallowed friar,
Is't not enough thou hast suborn'd these women
To accuse this worthy man, but, in foul mouth,
And in the witness of his proper ear,
To call him villain; and then to glance from him
To th' Duke himself, to tax him with injustice?
Take him hence; to th' rack with him! We'll touze you
Joint by joint, but we will know his purpose.
What, "unjust"!

DUKE: Be not so hot; the Duke
Dare no more stretch this finger of mine than he
Dare rack his own; his subject am I not,
Nor here provincial. My business in this state
Made me a looker-on here in Vienna,
Where I have seen corruption boil and bubble
Till it o'errun the stew: laws for all faults,
But faults so countenanc'd that the strong statutes
Stand like the forfeits in a barber's shop,
As much in mock as mark.

ESCALUS: Slander to th' state! Away with him to prison!

ANGELO: What can you vouch against him, Signior Lucio?
Is this the man that you did tell us of?

LUCIO: 'Tis he, my lord. Come hither, goodman bald-pate. Do you know me?

DUKE: I remember you, sir, by the sound of your voice. I met you at the prison, in the absence of the Duke.

LUCIO: O did you so? And do you remember what you said of the Duke?

DUKE: Most notedly, sir.

LUCIO: Do you so, sir? And was the Duke a fleshmonger, a fool, and a coward, as you then reported him to be?

DUKE: You must, sir, change persons with me ere you make that my report; you, indeed, spoke so of him; and much more, much worse.

LUCIO: O thou damnable fellow! Did not I pluck thee by the nose for thy speeches?

DUKE: I protest I love the Duke as I love myself.

ANGELO: Hark how the villain would close now, after his treasonable abuses!

ESCALUS: Such a fellow is not to be talk'd withal. Away with him to prison! Where is the Provost? Away with him to prison! Lay bolts enough upon him; let him speak no more. Away with those giglets too, and with the other confederate companion!

[*The PROVOST seizes the DUKE*]

DUKE: Stay, sir; stay awhile.

ANGELO: What, resists he? Help him, Lucio.

LUCIO: Come, sir; come, sir; come, sir; foh, sir! Why, you bald-pated lying rascal, you must be hooded, must you? Show your knave's visage, with a pox to you! Show your sheep-biting face, and be hang'd an hour! Will't not off?

[*Pulls off the FRIAR'S hood and discovers the DUKE*]

DUKE: Thou art the first knave that e'er mad'st a duke.
First, Provost, let me bail these gentle three.

[*To Lucio*] Sneak not away, sir, for the friar and you
Must have a word anon. Lay hold on him.

LUCIO: This may prove worse than hanging.

DUKE: [*To ESCALUS*] What you have spoke I pardon; sit you down.
We'll borrow place of him. [*To ANGELO*] Sir, by your leave.
Hast thou or word, or wit, or impudence,
That yet can do thee office? If thou hast,
Rely upon it till my tale be heard,
And hold no longer out.

ANGELO: O my dread lord,
I should be guiltier than my guiltiness,
To think I can be undiscernible,
When I perceive your Grace, like pow'r divine,
Hath look'd upon my passes. Then, good Prince,
No longer session hold upon my shame,
But let my trial be mine own confession;
Immediate sentence then, and sequent death,
Is all the grace I beg.

DUKE: Come hither, Mariana.
Say, wast thou e'er contracted to this woman?

ANGELO: I was, my lord.

DUKE: Go, take her hence and marry her instantly.
Do you the office, friar; which consummate,
Return him here again. Go with him, Provost.

Exeunt ANGELO, MARIANA, FRIAR PETER, and PROVOST

ESCALUS: My lord, I am more amaz'd at his dishonour
Than at the strangeness of it.

DUKE: Come hither, Isabel.
Your friar is now your prince. As I was then
Advertising and holy to your business,
Not changing heart with habit, I am still
Attorney'd at your service.

ISABELLA: O, give me pardon,
That I, your vassal, have employ'd and pain'd
Your unknown sovereignty.

DUKE: You are pardon'd, Isabel.

And now, dear maid, be you as free to us.
Your brother's death, I know, sits at your heart;
And you may marvel why I obscur'd myself,
Labouring to save his life, and would not rather
Make rash remonstrance of my hidden pow'r
Than let him so be lost. O most kind maid,
It was the swift celerity of his death,
Which I did think with slower foot came on,
That brain'd my purpose. But peace be with him!
That life is better life, past fearing death,
Than that which lives to fear. Make it your comfort,
So happy is your brother.

ISABELLA: I do, my lord.

Re-enter ANGELO, MARIANA, FRIAR PETER, and PROVOST

DUKE: For this new-married man approaching here,
Whose salt imagination yet hath wrong'd
Your well-defended honour, you must pardon
For Mariana's sake; but as he adjudg'd your brother—
Being criminal in double violation
Of sacred chastity and of promise-breach,
Thereon dependent, for your brother's life—
The very mercy of the law cries out
Most audible, even from his proper tongue,
"An Angelo for Claudio, death for death!"
Haste still pays haste, and leisure answers leisure;
Like doth quit like, and Measure still for Measure.
Then, Angelo, thy fault's thus manifested,
Which, though thou wouldst deny, denies thee vantage.
We do condemn thee to the very block
Where Claudio stoop'd to death, and with like haste.
Away with him!

MARIANA: O my most gracious lord,
I hope you will not mock me with a husband.

DUKE: It is your husband mock'd you with a husband.
Consenting to the safeguard of your honour,
I thought your marriage fit; else imputation,
For that he knew you, might reproach your life,
And choke your good to come. For his possessions,
Although by confiscation they are ours,
We do instate and widow you withal
To buy you a better husband.

MARIANA: O my dear lord,
I crave no other, nor no better man.

DUKE: Never crave him; we are definitive.

MARIANA: Gentle my liege— [*Kneeling*]

DUKE: You do but lose your labour.

Away with him to death! [*To LUCIO*] Now, sir, to you.

MARIANA: O my good lord! Sweet Isabel, take my part;
Lend me your knees, and all my life to come
I'll lend you all my life to do you service.

DUKE: Against all sense you do importune her.
Should she kneel down in mercy of this fact,
Her brother's ghost his paved bed would break,
And take her hence in horror.

MARIANA: Isabel,
Sweet Isabel, do yet but kneel by me;
Hold up your hands, say nothing; I'll speak all.
They say best men are moulded out of faults;
And, for the most, become much more the better
For being a little bad; so may my husband.
O Isabel, will you not lend a knee?

DUKE: He dies for Claudio's death.

ISABELLA: [*Kneeling*] Most bounteous sir,
Look, if it please you, on this man condemn'd,
As if my brother liv'd. I partly think
A due sincerity govern'd his deeds
Till he did look on me; since it is so,
Let him not die. My brother had but justice,
In that he did the thing for which he died;
For Angelo,
His act did not o'ertake his bad intent,
And must be buried but as an intent
That perish'd by the way. Thoughts are no subjects;
Intents but merely thoughts.

MARIANA: Merely, my lord.

DUKE: Your suit's unprofitable; stand up, I say.
I have bethought me of another fault.
Provost, how came it Claudio was beheaded
At an unusual hour?

PROVOST: It was commanded so.

DUKE: Had you a special warrant for the deed?

PROVOST: No, my good lord; it was by private message.

DUKE: For which I do discharge you of your office;
Give up your keys.

PROVOST: Pardon me, noble lord;
I thought it was a fault, but knew it not;
Yet did repent me, after more advice;
For testimony whereof, one in the prison,
That should by private order else have died,
I have reserv'd alive.

DUKE: What's he?

PROVOST: His name is Barnardine.

DUKE: I would thou hadst done so by Claudio.
Go fetch him hither; let me look upon him.   *Exit PROVOST*

ESCALUS: I am sorry one so learned and so wise
As you, Lord Angelo, have still appear'd,
Should slip so grossly, both in the heat of blood
And lack of temper'd judgment afterward.

ANGELO: I am sorry that such sorrow I procure;
And so deep sticks it in my penitent heart
That I crave death more willingly than mercy;
'Tis my deserving, and I do entreat it.

*Re-enter PROVOST, with BARNARDINE, CLAUDIO (muffled) and JU-
LIET*

DUKE: Which is that Barnardine?

PROVOST: This, my lord.

DUKE: There was a friar told me of this man.
Sirrah, thou art said to have a stubborn soul,
That apprehends no further than this world,
And squar'st thy life according. Thou'rt condemn'd;
But, for those earthly faults, I quit them all,
And pray thee take this mercy to provide
For better times to come. Friar, advise him;
I leave him to your hand. What muffl'd fellow's that?

PROVOST: This is another prisoner that I sav'd,
Who should have died when Claudio lost his head;
As like almost to Claudio as himself. [*Unmuffles CLAUDIO*]

DUKE: [*To ISABELLA*] If he be like your brother, for his sake
Is he pardon'd; and for your lovely sake,
Give me your hand and say you will be mine,
He is my brother too. But fitter time for that.
By this Lord Angelo perceives he's safe;
Methinks I see a quick'ning in his eye.
Well, Angelo, your evil quits you well.
Look that you love your wife; her worth worth yours.
I find an apt remission in myself;
And yet here's one in place I cannot pardon.

[*To Lucio*] You, sirrah, that knew me for a fool, a coward,
One all of luxury, an ass, a madman!
Wherein have I so deserv'd of you
That you extol me thus?

LUCIO: Faith, my lord, I spoke it but according to the trick. If you will
hang me for it, you may; but I had rather it would please you I might be
whipt.

DUKE: Whipt first, sir, and hang'd after.
Proclaim it, Provost, round about the city,
If any woman wrong'd by this lewd fellow,
As I have heard him swear himself there's one
Whom he begot with child, let her appear,
And he shall marry her. The nuptial finish'd,
Let him be whipt and hang'd.

LUCIO: I beseech your Highness, do not marry me to a whore. Your Highness said even now I made you a duke; good my lord, do not recompense me in making me a cuckold.

DUKE: Upon mine honour, thou shalt marry her.
Thy slanders I forgive; and therewithal
Remit thy other forfeits. Take him to prison;
And see our pleasure herein executed.

LUCIO: Marrying a punk, my lord, is pressing to death, whipping, and hanging.

DUKE: Slandering a prince deserves it.

Exeunt OFFICERS with LUCIO

She, Claudio, that you wrong'd, look you restore.
Joy to you, Mariana! Love her, Angelo;
I have confess'd her, and I know her virtue.
Thanks, good friend Escalus, for thy much goodness;
There's more behind that is more gratulate.
Thanks, Provost, for thy care and secrecy;
We shall employ thee in a worthier place.
Forgive him, Angelo, that brought you home
The head of Ragozine for Claudio's:
Th' offence pardons itself. Dear Isabel,
I have a motion much imports your good;
Whereto if you'll a willing ear incline,
What's mine is yours, and what is yours is mine.
So, bring us to our palace, where we'll show
What's yet behind that's meet you all should know.

Exeunt

D. MODERN PLAYS

PYGMALION
George Bernard Shaw

ACT I

London at 11.15 p.m. Torrents of heavy summer rain. Cab whistles blowing frantically in all directions. Pedestrians running for shelter into the market and under the portico of St. Paul's Church (not Wren's cathedral but Inigo Jones's church in Covent Garden vegetable market), among them a lady and her daughter in evening dress. All are peering out gloomily at the rain, except one man with his back turned to the rest, wholly preoccupied with a notebook in which he is writing.

The church clock strikes the first quarter.

THE DAUGHTER *[in the space between the central pillars, close to the one on her left]* I'm getting chilled to the bone. What can Freddy be doing all this time? He's been gone twenty minutes.

THE MOTHER *[On her daughter's right]* Not so long. But he ought to have got us a cab by this.

A BYSTANDER *[on the lady's right]* He won't get no cab not until half-past eleven, missus, when they come back after dropping their theatre fares.

THE MOTHER. But we must have a cab. We can't stand here until half-past eleven. It's too bad.

THE BYSTANDER. Well, it ain't my fault, missus.

THE DAUGHTER. If Freddy had a bit of gumption, he would have got one at the theatre door.

THE MOTHER. What could he have done, poor boy?

THE DAUGHTER. Other people got cabs. Why couldn't he?

Freddy rushes in out of the rain from the Southampton Street side, and comes between them closing dripping umbrella. He is a young man of twenty, in evening dress, very wet around the ankles.

THE DAUGHTER. Well, haven't you got a cab?

FREDDY. There's not one to be had for love or money.

THE MOTHER. Oh, Freddy, there must be one. You can't have tried.

THE DAUGHTER. It's too tiresome. Do you expect us to go and get one ourselves?

FREDDY. I tell you they're all engaged. The rain was so sudden: nobody was prepared; and everybody had to take a cab. I've been to Charing Cross one way and nearly to Ludgate Circus the other; and they were all engaged.

THE MOTHER. Did you try Trafalgar Square?

FREDDY. There wasn't one at Trafalgar Square.

THE DAUGHTER. Did you try?

FREDDY. I tried as far as Charing Cross Station. Did you expect me to walk to Hammersmith?

THE DAUGHTER. You haven't tried at all.

THE MOTHER. You really are very helpless, Freddy. Go again; and don't come back until you have found a cab.

FREDDY. I shall simply get soaked for nothing.

THE DAUGHTER. And what about us? Are we to stay here all night in this draught, with next to nothing on. You selfish pig—

FREDDY. Oh, very well: I'll go, I'll go. *[He opens his umbrella and dashes off Strandwards, but comes into collision with a flower girl, who is hurrying in for shelter, knocking her basket out of her hands. A blinding flash of lightning, followed instantly by a rattling peal of thunder, orchestrates the incident].*

THE FLOWER GIRL. Nah then, Freddy: look wh' y' gowin, deah.

FREDDY. Sorry *[he rushes off].*

THE FLOWER GIRL *[picking up her scattered flowers and replacing them in the basket]* There's menners f' yer! Te-oo banches o voylets trod into the mad. *[She sits down on the plinth of the column, sorting her flowers, on the lady's right. She is not at all an attractive person. She is perhaps eighteen, perhaps twenty, hardly older. She wears a little sailor hat of black straw that has long been exposed to the dust and soot of London and has seldom if ever been brushed. Her hair needs washing rather badly: its mousy color can hardly be natural. She wears a shoddy black coat that reaches nearly to her knees and is shaped to her waist. She has a brown skirt with a coarse apron. Her boots are much the worse for wear. She is no doubt as clean as she can afford to be; but compared to the ladies she is very dirty. Her features are no worse than theirs; but their condition leaves something to be desired; and she needs the services of a dentist.]*

THE MOTHER. How do you know that my son's name is Freddy, pray?

THE FLOWER GIRL. Ow, eez ye-ooa san, is e? Wal, fewd dan y' de-ooty bawmz a mather should, eed now bettern to spawl a pore gel's flahrzn than ran awy athaht pyin. Will ye-oo py me f'them? *[Here, with apologies, this desperate attempt to represent her dialect without a phonetic alphabet must be abandoned as unintelligible outside London.]*

THE DAUGHTER. Do nothing of the sort, mother. The idea!

THE MOTHER. Please allow me, Clara. Have you any pennies?

THE DAUGHTER. No. I've nothing smaller than sixpence.

THE FLOWER GIRL *[hopefully]* I can give you change for a tanner, kind lady.

THE MOTHER *[to Clara]* Give it to me. *[Clara parts reluctantly.]* Now *[to the girl]* This is for your flowers.

THE FLOWER GIRL. Thank you kindly, lady.

THE DAUGHTER. Make her give you the change. These things are only a penny a bunch.

THE MOTHER. Do hold your tongue, Clara. *[To the girl]* You can keep the change.

THE FLOWER GIRL. Oh, thank you, lady.

THE MOTHER. Now tell me how you know that young gentleman's name.

THE FLOWER GIRL. I didn't.

THE MOTHER. I heard you call him by it. Don't try to deceive me.

THE FLOWER GIRL [protesting] Who's trying to deceive you? I called him Freddy or Charlie same as you might yourself if you was talking to a stranger and wished to be pleasant. [She sits down beside her basket.]

THE DAUGHTER. Sixpence thrown away! Really, mamma, you might have spared Freddy that. [She retreats in disgust behind the pillar.]

An elderly gentleman of the amiable military type rushes into shelter, and closes a dripping umbrella. He is in the same plight as Freddy, very wet about the ankles. He is in evening dress, with a light overcoat. He takes the place left vacant by the daughter's retirement.

THE GENTLEMAN. Phew!

THE MOTHER [to the gentleman] Oh, sir, is there any sign of its stopping?

THE GENTLEMAN. I'm afraid not. It started worse than ever about two minutes ago. [He goes to the plinth beside the flower girl; puts up his foot on it; and stoops to turn down his trouser ends.]

THE MOTHER. Oh, dear! [She retires sadly and joins her daughter.]

THE FLOWER GIRL [taking advantage of the military gentleman's proximity to establish friendly relations with him.] If it's worse it's a sign it's nearly over. So cheer up, Captain; and buy a flower off a poor girl.

THE GENTLEMAN. I'm sorry, I haven't any change.

THE FLOWER GIRL. I can give you change, Captain.

THE GENTLEMEN. For a sovereign? I've nothing less.

THE FLOWER GIRL. Garn! Oh do buy a flower off me, Captain. I can change half-a-crown. Take this for tuppence.

THE GENTLEMAN. Now don't be troublesome: there's a good girl. [Trying his pockets] I really haven't any change—Stop: here's three hapence, if that's any use to you [he retreats to the other pillar].

THE FLOWER GIRL [disappointed, but thinking three halfpence better than nothing] Thank you, sir.

THE BYSTANDER [to the girl] You be careful: give him a flower for it. There's a bloke here behind taking down every blessed word you're saying. [All turn to the man who is taking notes.]

THE FLOWER GIRL [springing up terrified] I ain't done nothing wrong by speaking to the gentleman. I've a right to sell flowers if I keep off the kerb. [Hysterically] I'm a respectable girl: so help me, I never spoke to him except to ask him to buy a flower off me.

General hubbub, mostly sympathetic to the flower girl, but deprecating her excessive sensibility. Cries of "Don't start hollerin. Who's hurting you? Nobody's going to touch you. What's the good of fussing? Steady on. Easy, easy, etc.," come from the elderly staid spectators, who pat her comfortingly. Less patient ones bid her shut her head, or ask her roughly what is wrong with her. A remoter group, not knowing what the matter *is, crowd in and increase the noise with question and answer: "What's the row? What she do? Where is he? A tec taking her down. What! him? Yes: him over there: Took money off the gentleman, etc." The flower girl, distraught and mobbed, breaks through them to the gentleman, crying wildly.*

Oh, sir, don't let him charge me. You dunno what it means to me. They'll take away my character and drive me on the streets for speaking to gentlemen. They—

THE NOTE TAKER *[coming forward on her right, the rest crowding after him]* There, there, there, there! who's hurting you, you silly girl? What do you take me for?

THE BYSTANDER. It's all right: he's a gentleman: look at his boots. *[Explaining to the note taker]* She thought you was a copper's nark, sir.

THE NOTE TAKER *[with quick interest]* What's a copper's nark?

THE BYSTANDER *[inapt at definition]* It's a—well, it's a copper's nark, as you might say. What else would you call it? A sort of informer.

THE FLOWER GIRL *[still hysterical]* I take my Bible oath I never said a word—

THE NOTE TAKER *[overbearing but good-humored]* Oh, shut up, shut up. Do I look like a policeman?

THE FLOWER GIRL *[far from reassured]* Then what did you take down my words for? How do I know whether you took me down right? You just shew me what you've wrote about me. *[The note taker opens his book and holds it steadily under her nose, though the pressure of the mob trying to read it over his shoulders would upset a weaker man.]* What's that? That ain't proper writing. I can't read that.

THE NOTE TAKER. I can. *[Reads, reproducing her pronunciation exactly]* "Cheer ap, Keptin; n' baw ya flahr orf a pore gel."

THE FLOWER GIRL *[much distressed]* It's because I called him Captain. I meant no harm. *[To the gentleman]* Oh, sir, don't let him lay a charge agen me for a word like that. You—

THE GENTLEMAN. Charge! I make no charge. *[To the note taker]* Really, sir, if you are a detective, you need not begin protecting me against molestation by young women until I ask you. Anybody could see that the girl meant no harm.

THE BYSTANDERS GENERALLY *[demonstrating against police espionage]* Course they could. What business is it of yours? You mind your own affairs. He wants promotion, he does. Taking down people's words! Girl never said a word to him. What harm if she did? Nice thing a girl can't shelter from the rain without being insulted, etc., etc., etc. *[She is conducted by the more sympathetic demonstrators back to her plinth, where she resumes her seat and struggles with her emotion.]*

THE BYSTANDER. He ain't a tec. Hes a blooming busybody: that's what he is. I tell you, look at his boots.

THE NOTE TAKER *[turning on him genially]* And how are all your people down at Selsey?

THE BYSTANDER *[suspiciously]* Who told you my people come from Selsey?

THE NOTE TAKER. Never you mind. They did. *[To the girl]* How do you come to be up so far east? You were born in Lisson Grove.

THE FLOWER GIRL *[appalled]* Oh, what harm is there in my leaving Lisson Grove? It wasn't fit for a pig to live in; and I had to pay four-and-six a week. *[In tears]* Oh, boo—hoo—oo—

THE NOTE TAKER. Live where you like; but stop that noise.

THE GENTLEMAN *[to the girl]* Come, come! he can't touch you: you have a right to live where you please.

A SARCASTIC BYSTANDER *[thrusting himself between the note taker and the gentleman]* Park Lane, for instance. I'd like to go into the Housing Question with you, I would.

THE FLOWER GIRL *[subsiding into a brooding melancholy over her basket, and talking very low-spiritedly to herself]* I'm a good girl, I am.

THE SARCASTIC BYSTANDER *[not attending to her]* Do you know where I come from?

THE NOTE TAKER *[promptly]* Hoxton.

Titterings. Popular interest in the note taker's performance increases.

THE SARCASTIC ONE *[amazed]* Well, who said I didn't? Bly me! You know everything, you do.

THE FLOWER GIRL *[still nursing her sense of injury]* Ain't no call to meddle with me, he ain't.

THE BYSTANDER *[to her]* Of course he ain't. Don't you stand it from him. *[To the note taker]* See here: what call have you to know about people what never offered to meddle with you? Where's your warrant?

SEVERAL BYSTANDERS *[encouraged by this seeming point of law]* Yes: where's your warrant?

THE FLOWER GIRL. Let him say what he likes. I don't want to have no truck with him.

THE BYSTANDER. You take us for dirt under your feet, don't you? Catch you taking liberties with a gentleman!

THE SARCASTIC BYSTANDER. Yes: tell him where he come from if you want to go fortune-telling.

THE NOTE TAKER. Cheltenham, Harrow, Cambridge, and India.

THE GENTLEMAN. Quite right. *[Great laughter. Reaction in the note taker's favor. Exclamations of "He knows all about it. Told him proper. Hear him tell the toff where he come from? etc."]* May I ask, sir, do you do this for your living at a music hall?

THE NOTE TAKER. I've thought of that. Perhaps I shall some day.

The rain has stopped; and the persons on the outside of the crowd begin to drop off.

THE FLOWER GIRL *[resenting the reaction]* He's no gentleman, he ain't, to interfere with a poor girl.

THE DAUGHTER *[out of patience, pushing her way rudely to the front and displacing the gentleman, who politely retires to the other side of the pillar]* What on earth is Freddy doing? I shall get pneumonia if I stay in this draught any longer.

THE NOTE TAKER *[to himself, hastily making a note of her pronunciation of "monia"]* Earlscourt.

THE DAUGHTER *[violently]* Will you please keep your impertinent remarks to yourself?

THE NOTE TAKER. Did I say that out loud? I didn't mean to. I beg your pardon. Your mother's Epsom, unmistakeably.

THE MOTHER *[advancing between her daughter and the note taker]* How very curious! I was brought up in Largelady Park, near Epsom.

THE NOTE TAKER *[uproariously amused]* Ha! ha! What a devil of a name! Excuse me. *[To the daughter]* You want a cab, do you?

THE DAUGHTER. Don't dare speak to me.

THE MOTHER. Oh, please, please Clara. *[Her daughter repudiates her with an angry shrug and retires haughtily.]* We should be so grateful to you, sir, if you found us a cab. *[The note taker produces a whistle.]* Oh, thank you. *[She joins her daughter.]*

The note taker blows a piercing blast.

THE SARCASTIC BYSTANDER. There! I knowed he was a plain-clothes copper.

THE BYSTANDER. That ain't a police whistle: that's a sporting whistle.

THE FLOWER GIRL *[still preoccupied with her wounded feelings]* He's no right to take away my character. My character is the same to me as any lady's.

THE NOTE TAKER. I don't know whether you've noticed it; but the rain stopped about two minutes ago.

THE BYSTANDER. So it has. Why didn't you say so before? and us losing our time listening to your silliness. *[He walks off towards the Strand.]*

THE SARCASTIC BYSTANDER. I can tell where you come from. You come from Anwell. Go back there.

THE NOTE TAKER *[helpfully]* Hanwell.

THE SARCASTIC BYSTANDER *[affecting great distinction of speech]* Thenk you, teacher. Haw haw! So long *[he touches his hat with mock respect and strolls off]*.

THE FLOWER GIRL. Frightening people like that! How would he like it himself?

THE MOTHER. It's quite fine now, Clara. We can walk to a motor bus. Come. *[She gathers her skirts above her ankles and hurries off towards the Strand.]*

THE DAUGHTER. But the cab—*[her mother is out of hearing]*. Oh, how tiresome! *[She follows angrily.]*

All the rest have gone except the note taker, the gentleman, and the flower girl, who sits arranging her basket, and still pitying herself in murmurs.

THE FLOWER GIRL. Poor girl! Hard enough for her to live without being worrited and chivied.

THE GENTLEMAN *[returning to his former place on the note taker's left]* How do you do it, if I may ask?

THE NOTE TAKER. Simply phonetics. The science of speech. That's my profession: also my hobby. Happy is the man who can make a living by his hobby! You can spot an Irishman or a Yorkshireman by his brogue. I can place any man within six miles. I can place him within two miles in London. Sometimes within two streets.

THE FLOWER GIRL. Ought to be ashamed of himself, unmanly coward!

THE GENTLEMAN. But is there a living in that?

THE NOTE TAKER. Oh yes. Quite a fat one. This is an age of upstarts. Men begin in Kentish Town with £80 a year, and end in Park Lane with a hundred thousand. They want to drop Kentish Town; but they give themselves away every time they open their mouths. Now I can teach them—

THE FLOWER GIRL. Let him mind his own business and leave a poor girl—

THE NOTE TAKER *[explosively]* Woman: cease this detestable boohooing instantly; or else seek the shelter of some other place of worship.

THE FLOWER GIRL *[with feeble defiance]* I've a right to be here if I like, same as you.

THE NOTE TAKER. A woman who utters such depressing and disgusting sounds has no right to be anywhere—no right to live. Remember that you are a human being with a soul and the divine gift of articulate speech: that your native language is the language of Shakespeare and Milton and The Bible; and don't sit there crooning like a bilious pigeon.

THE FLOWER GIRL *[quite overwhelmed, and looking up at him in mingled wonder and deprecation without daring to raise her head]* Ah-ah-ah-ow-ow-ow-oo!

THE NOTE TAKER *[whipping out his book]* Heavens! what a sound! *[He writes; then holds out the book and reads, reproducing her vowels exactly]* Ah-ah-ah-ow-ow-ow-oo!

THE FLOWER GIRL [*tickled by the performance, and laughing in spite of herself*] Garn!

THE NOTE TAKER. You see this creature with her kerbstone English: the English that will keep her in the gutter to the end of her days. Well, sir, in three months I could pass that girl off as a duchess at an ambassador's garden party. I could even get her a place as lady's maid or shop assistant, which requires better English. That's the sort of thing I do for commercial millionaires. And on the profits of it I do genuine scientific work in phonetics, and a little as a poet on Miltonic lines.

THE GENTLEMAN. I am myself a student of Indian dialects; and—

THE NOTE TAKER [*eagerly*] Are you? Do you know Colonel Pickering, the author of Spoken Sanskrit?

THE GENTLEMAN. I am Colonel Pickering. Who are you?

THE NOTE TAKER. Henry Higgins, author of Higgins's Universal Alphabet.

PICKERING [*with enthusiasm*] I came from India to meet you.

HIGGINS. I was going to India to meet you.

PICKERING. Where do you live?

HIGGINS. 27A Wimpole Street. Come and see me tomorrow.

PICKERING. I'm at the Carlton. Come with me now and let's have a jaw over some supper.

HIGGINS. Right you are.

THE FLOWER GIRL [*to Pickering, as he passes her*] Buy a flower, kind gentleman. I'm short for my lodging.

PICKERING. I really haven't any change. I'm sorry [*he goes away*].

HIGGINS [*shocked at girl's mendacity*] Liar. You said you could change half-a-crown.

THE FLOWER GIRL [*rising in desperation*] You ought to be stuffed with nails, you ought. [*Flinging the basket at his feet*] Take the whole blooming basket for sixpence.

The church clock strikes the second quarter.

HIGGINS [*hearing in it the voice of God, rebuking him for his Pharisaic want of charity to the poor girl*] A reminder. [*He raises his hat solemnly; then throws a handful of money into the basket and follows Pickering.*]

THE FLOWER GIRL [*picking up a half-crown*] Ah-ow-ooh! [*Picking up a couple of florins*] Aaah-ow-ooh! [*Picking up several coins*] Aaaaaah-ow-ooh! [*Picking up a half-sovereign*] Aaaaaaaaaaaah-ow-ooh!!!

FREDDY [*springing out of a taxicab*] Got one at last. Hallo! [*To the girl*] Where are the two ladies that were here?

THE FLOWER GIRL. They walked to the bus when the rain stopped.

FREDDY. And left me with a cab on my hands. Damnation!

THE FLOWER GIRL [*with grandeur*] Never you mind, young man. I'm going home in a taxi. [*She sails off to the cab. The driver puts his hand behind him and holds the door firmly shut against her. Quite understanding his mistrust, she shews him her handful of money.*] A taxi fare ain't no object to me, Charlie. [*He grins and opens the door.*] Here. What about the basket?

THE TAXIMAN. Give it here. Tuppence extra.

LIZA. No: I don't want nobody to see it. [*She crushes it into the cab and gets in, continuing the conversation through the window*] Goodbye, Freddy.

FREDDY [*dazedly raising his hat*] Goodbye.

TAXIMAN. Where to?

LIZA. Bucknem Pellis [Buckingham Palace].

TAXIMAN. What d'ye mean–Buchnam Pellis?

LIZA. Don't you know where it is? In the Green Park, where the King lives. Goodbye, Freddy. Don't let me keep you standing there. Goodbye.

FREDDY. Goodbye. [*He goes.*]

TAXIMAN. Here? What's this Bucknam Pellis? What business have you at Bucknam Pellis?

LIZA. Of course I haven't none. But I wasn't going to let him know that. You drive me home.

TAXIMAN. And where's home?

LIZA. Angel Court. Drury Lane, next to Meiklejohn's oil shop.

TAXIMAN. That sounds more like it, Judy. [*He drives off.*]

* * *

Let us follow the taxi to the entrance to Angel Court, a narrow little archway between two shops, one of them Meiklejohn's oil shop. When it stops there, Eliza gets out, dragging her basket with her.

LIZA. How much?

TAXIMAN [*indicating the taximeter*] Can't you read? A shilling.

LIZA. A shilling for two minutes!

TAXIMAN. Two minutes or ten: it's all the same.

LIZA. Well, I don't call it right.

TAXIMAN. Ever been in a taxi before?

LIZA [*with dignity*] Hundreds and thousands of times, young man.

TAXIMAN [*laughing at her*] Good for you, Judy. Keep the shilling, darling, with best love from all at home. Good luck! [*He drives off.*]

LIZA [*humiliated*] Impidence!

She picks up the basket and trudges up the alley with it to her lodging: a small room with very old wallpaper hanging loose in the damp places. A broken pane in the window is mended with paper. A portrait of a popular actor and a fashion plate of ladies' dresses, all wildly beyond poor Eliza's means, both torn from newspapers, are pinned up on the wall. A birdcage hangs in the window; but its tenant died long ago: it remains as a memorial only.

There are the only visible fixtures: the rest is the irreducible minimum of poverty's needs: a wretched bed heaped with all sorts of coverings that have any warmth in them, a draped packing case with a basin and jug on it and a little looking glass over it, a chair and table, the refuse of some suburban kitchen, and an American alarum clock on the shelf above the unused fireplace: the whole lighted with a gas lamp with a penny in the slot meter. Rent: four shillings a week.

Here Eliza, chronically weary, but too excited to go to bed, sits, counting her new riches and dreaming and planning what to do with them, until the gas goes out, when she enjoys for the first time the sensation of being able to put in another penny without grudging it. This prodigal mood does not extinguish her gnawing sense of the need for economy sufficiently to prevent her from calculating that she can dream and plan in bed more cheaply and warmly than sitting up without a fire. So she takes off her shawl and skirt and adds them to the miscellaneous bedclothes. Then she kicks off her shoes and gets into bed without any further change.

ACT II

Next day at 11 a.m., Higgins's laboratory in Wimpole Street.

HIGGINS *[as he shuts the last drawer]* Well, I think that's the whole show.

PICKERING. It's really amazing. I haven't taken half of it in, you know.

HIGGINS. Would you like to go over any of it again?

PICKERING *[rising and coming to the fireplace, where he plants himself with his back to the fire]* No, thank you; not now. I'm quite done up for this morning.

HIGGINS *[following him, and standing beside him on his left]* Tired of listening to sounds?

PICKERING. Yes. It's a fearful strain. I rather fancied myself because I can pronounce twenty-four distinct vowel sounds; but your hundred and thirty beat me. I can't hear a bit of difference between most of them.

HIGGINS *[chuckling, and going over to the piano to eat sweets]* Oh, that comes with practice. You hear no difference at first; but you keep on listening, and presently you find they're all as different as A from B. *[Mrs. Pearce looks in: she is Higgins's housekeeper]* What's the matter?

MRS. PEARCE [*hesitating, evidently perplexed*] A young woman wants to see you, sir.

HIGGINS. A young woman! What does she want?

MRS. PEARCE. Well, sir, she says you'll be glad to see her when you know what she's come about. She's quite a common girl, sir. Very common indeed. I should have sent her away, only I thought perhaps you wanted her to talk into your machines. I hope I've not done wrong; but really you see such queer people sometimes—you'll excuse me, I'm sure, sir—

HIGGINS. Oh, that's all right, Mrs. Pearce. Has she an interesting accent?

MRS. PEARCE. Oh, something dreadful, sir, really. I don't know how you can take an interest in it.

HIGGINS [*to Pickering*] Let's have her up. Shew her up, Mrs. Pearce [*he rushes across to his working table and picks out a cylinder to use on the phonograph*].

MRS. PEARCE [*only half resigned to it*] Very well, sir. It's for you to say. [*She goes downstairs.*]

HIGGINS. This is rather a bit of luck. I'll shew you how I make records. We'll set her talking; and I'll take it down first in Bell's Visible Speech; then in broad Romic; and then we'll get her on the phonograph so that you can turn her on as often as you like with the written transcript before you.

MRS. PEARCE [*returning*] This is the young woman, sir.

The flower girl enters in state. She has a hat with three ostrich feathers, orange, sky-blue, and red. She has a nearly clean apron, and the shoddy coat has been tidied a little. The pathos of this deplorable figure, with its innocent vanity and consequential air, touches Pickering, who has already straightened himself in the presence of Mrs. Pearce. But as to Higgins, the only distinction he makes between men and women is that when he is neither bullying nor exclaiming to the heavens against some featherweight cross, he coaxes women as a child coaxes its nurse when it wants to get anything out of her.

HIGGINS [*brusquely, recognizing her with unconcealed disappointment, and at once, babylike, making an intolerable grievance of it*] Why, this is the girl I jotted down last night. She's no use: I've got all the records I want of the Lisson Grove lingo; and I'm not going to waste another cylinder on it. [*To the girl*] Be off with you: I don't want you.

THE FLOWER GIRL. Don't you be so saucy. You ain't heard what I come for yet. [*To Mrs. Pearce, who is waiting at the door for further instruction*] Did you tell him I come in a taxi?

MRS. PEARCE. Nonsense, girl! what do you think a gentleman like Mr. Higgins cares what you came in?

THE FLOWER GIRL. Oh, we are proud! He ain't above giving lessons, not him: I heard him say so. Well, I ain't come here to ask for any compliment; and if my money's not good enough I can go elsewhere.

HIGGINS. Good enough for what?

THE FLOWER GIRL. Good enough for ye-oo. Now you know, don't you? I'm come to have lessons, I am. And to pay for em too: make no mistake.

HIGGINS [stupent] Well!!! [Recovering his breath with a gasp] What do you expect me to say to you?

THE FLOWER GIRL. Well, if you was a gentleman, you might ask me to sit down, I think. Don't I tell you I'm bringing you business?

HIGGINS. Pickering: shall we ask this baggage to sit down or shall we throw her out of the window?

THE FLOWER GIRL [running away in terror to the piano, where she turns at bay] Ah-ah-ah-ow-ow-ow-oo! [Wounded and whimpering] I won't be called a baggage when I've offered to pay like any lady.

[Motionless, the two men stare at her from the other side of the room, amazed.]

PICKERING [gently] What is it you want, my girl?

THE FLOWER GIRL. I want to be a lady in a flower shop stead of selling at the corner of Tottenham Court Road. But they won't take me unless I can talk more genteel. He said he could teach me. Well, here I am ready to pay him—not asking any favor—and he treats me as if I was dirt.

MRS. PEARCE. How can you be such a foolish ignorant girl as to think you could afford to pay Mr. Higgins?

THE FLOWER GIRL. Why shouldnt I? I know what lessons cost as well as you do; and I'm ready to pay.

HIGGINS. How much?

THE FLOWER GIRL [coming back to him, triumphant] Now you're talking! I thought you'd come off it when you saw a chance of getting back a bit of what you chucked at me last night. [Confidentially] You'd had a drop in, hadn't you?

HIGGINS [peremptorily] Sit down.

THE FLOWER GIRL. Oh, if you're going to make a compliment of it—

HIGGINS [thundering at her] Sit down.

MRS. PEARCE [severely] Sit down, girl. Do as you're told. [She places the stray chair near the hearthrug between Higgins and Pickering, and stands behind it waiting for the girl to sit down].

THE FLOWER GIRL. Ah-ah-ah-ow-ow-oo! [She stands, half rebellious, half bewildered.]

PICKERING [very courteous] Won't you sit down?

LIZA [coyly] Don't mind if I do. [She sits down. Pickering returns to the hearthrug.]

HIGGINS. What's your name?

THE FLOWER GIRL. Liza Doolittle.

HIGGINS [declaiming gravely]

　　Eliza, Elizabeth, Betsy and Bess,

　　They went to the woods to get a bird nes':

PICKERING. They found a nest with four eggs in it:

HIGGINS. They took one apiece, and left three in it.

They laugh heartily at their own wit.

LIZA. Oh, don't be silly.

MRS. PEARCE. You mustn't speak to the gentleman like that.

LIZA. Well, why won't he speak sensible to me?

HIGGINS. Come back to business. How much do you propose to pay me for the lessons?

LIZA. Oh, I know what's right. A lady friend of mine gets French lessons for eighteenpence an hour from a real French gentleman. Well, you wouldn't have the face to ask me the same for teaching me my own language as you would for French; so I won't give more than a shilling. Take it or leave it.

HIGGINS [walking up and down the room, rattling his keys and his cash in his pockets] You know, Pickering, if you consider a shilling, not as a simple shilling, but as a percentage of this girl's income, it works out as fully equivalent to sixty or seventy guineas from a millionaire.

PICKERING. How so?

HIGGINS. Figure it out. A millionaire has about £150 a day. She earns about half-a-crown.

LIZA [haughtily] Who told you I only—

HIGGINS [continuing] She offers me two-fifths of her day's income for a lesson. Two-fifths of a millionaire's income for a day would be somewhere about £60. It's handsome. By George, it's enormous! It's the biggest offer I ever had.

LIZA [rising, terrified] Sixty pounds! What are you talking about? I never offered you sixty pounds. Where would I get—

HIGGINS. Hold your tongue.

LIZA [weeping] But I ain't got sixty pounds. Oh—

MRS. PEARCE. Don't cry, you silly girl. Sit down. Nobody is going to touch your money.

HIGGINS. Somebody is going to touch you, with a broomstick, if you don't stop snivelling. Sit down.

LIZA [obeying slowly] Ah-ah-ah-ow-oo-o! One would think you was my father.

HIGGINS. If I decide to teach you, I'll be worse than two fathers to you. Here! [he offers her his silk handkerchief]

LIZA. What's this for?

HIGGINS. To wipe your eyes. To wipe any part of your face that feels moist. Remember: that's your handkerchief; and that's your sleeve. Don't mistake the one for the other if you wish to become a lady in a shop.

Liza, utterly bewildered, stares helplessly at him.

MRS. PEARCE. It's no use talking to her like that, Mr. Higgins: she doesn't understand you. Besides, you're quite wrong: she doesn't do it that way at all [she takes the handkerchief].

LIZA [snatching it] Here! You give me that handkerchief. He give it to me, not to you.

PICKERING [laughing] He did. I think it must be regarded as her property, Mrs. Pearce.

MRS. PEARCE [resigning herself] Serve you right, Mr. Higgins.

PICKERING. Higgins: I'm interested. What about the ambassador's garden party? I'll say you're the greatest teacher alive if you make that good. I'll bet you all the expenses of the experiment you can't do it. And I'll pay for the lessons.

LIZA. Oh, you are real good. Thank you, Captain.

HIGGINS [tempted, looking at her] It's almost irresistible. She's so deliciously low—so horribly dirty—

LIZA [protesting extremely] Ah-ah-ah-ah-ow-ow-oo-oo!!! I ain't dirty: I washed my face and hands afore I come, I did.

PICKERING. You're certainly not going to turn her head with flattery, Higgins.

MRS. PEARCE [uneasy] Oh, don't say that, sir: there's more ways than one of turning a girl's head; and nobody can do it better than Mr. Higgins, though he may not always mean it. I do hope, sir, you won't encourage him to do anything foolish.

HIGGINS [becoming excited as the idea grows on him] What is life but a series of inspired follies? The difficulty is to find them to do. Never lose a chance: it doesn't come every day. I shall make a duchess of this draggle-tailed guttersnipe.

LIZA [strongly deprecating this view of her] Ah-ah-ah-ow-ow-oo!

HIGGINS [carried away] Yes: in six months—in three if she has a good ear and a quick tongue—I'll take her anywhere and pass her off as anything. We'll start today: now! this moment! Take her away and clean her, Mrs. Pearce. Monkey Brand, if it won't come off any other way. Is there a good fire in the kitchen?

MRS. PEARCE [*protesting*] Yes; but—

HIGGINS [*storming on*] Take all her clothes off and burn them. Ring up Whiteley or somebody for new ones. Wrap her up in brown paper til they come.

LIZA. You're no gentleman, you're not, to talk of such things. I'm a good girl, I am; and I know what the like of you are, I do.

HIGGINS. We want none of your Lisson Grove prudery here, young woman. You've got to learn to behave like a duchess. Take her away, Mrs. Pearce. If she gives you any trouble wallop her.

LIZA [*springing up and running between Pickering and Mrs. Pearce for protection*] No! I'll call the police, I will.

MRS. PEARCE. But I've no place to put her.

HIGGINS. Put her in the dustbin.

LIZA. Ah-ah-ah-ow-ow-oo!

PICKERING. Oh come, Higgins! be reasonable.

MRS. PEARCE [*resolutely*] You must be reasonable, Mr. Higgins: really you must. You can't walk over everybody like this.

Higgins, thus scolded, subsides. The hurricane is succeeded by a zephyr of amiable surprise.

HIGGINS [*with professional exquisiteness of modulation*] I walk over everybody! My dear Mrs. Pearce, my dear Pickering, I never had the slightest intention of walking over anyone. All I propose is that we should be kind to this poor girl. We must help her to prepare and fit herself for her new station in life. If I did not express myself clearly it was because I did not wish to hurt her delicacy, or yours.

Liza, reassured, steals back to her chair.

MRS. PEARCE [*to Pickering*] Well, did you ever hear anything like that, sir?

PICKERING [*laughing heartily*] Never, Mrs. Pearce: never.

HIGGINS [*patiently*] What's the matter?

MRS. PEARCE. Well, the matter is, sir, that you can't take a girl up like that as if you were picking up a pebble on the beach.

HIGGINS. Why not?

MRS. PEARCE. Why not! But you don't know anything about her. What about her parents? She may be married.

LIZA. Garn!

HIGGINS. There! As the girl very properly says, Garn! Married indeed! Don't you know that a woman of that class looks a worn out drudge of fifty a year after she's married.

LIZA. Whood marry me?

HIGGINS [*suddenly resorting to the most thrillingly beautiful low tones in his best elocutionary style*] By George, Eliza, the streets will be strewn with the bodies of men shooting themselves for your sake before I've done with you.

MRS. PEARCE. Nonsense, sir. You mustn't talk like that to her.

LIZA [*rising and squaring herself determinedly*] I'm going away. He's off his chump, he is. I don't want no balmies teaching me.

HIGGINS [*wounded in his tenderest point by her insensibility to his elocution*] Oh, indeed! I'm mad, am I? Very well, Mrs. Pearce: you needn't order the new clothes for her. Throw her out.

LIZA [*whimpering*] Nah-ow. You got no right to touch me.

MRS. PEARCE. You see now what comes of being saucy. [*Indicating the door*] This way, please.

LIZA [*almost in tears*] I didn't want no clothes. I wouldn't have taken them [*she throws away the handkerchief*]. I can buy my own clothes.

HIGGINS [*deftly retrieving the handkerchief and intercepting her on her reluctant way to the door*] You're an ungrateful wicked girl. This is my return for offering to take you out of the gutter and dress you beautifully and make a lady of you.

MRS. PEARCE. Stop, Mr. Higgins. I won't allow it. It's you that are wicked. Go home to your parents, girl; and tell them to take better care of you.

LIZA. I ain't got no parents. They told me I was big enough to earn my own living and turned me out.

MRS. PEARCE. Where's your mother?

LIZA. I ain't got no mother. Her that turned me out was my sixth stepmother. But I done without them. And I'm a good girl, I am.

HIGGINS. Very well, then, what on earth is all this fuss about? The girl doesn't belong to anybody—is no use to anybody but me. [*He goes to Mrs. Pearce and begins coaxing.*] You can adopt her, Mrs. Pearce: I'm sure a daughter would be a great amusement to you. Now don't make any more fuss. Take her downstairs; and—

MRS. PEARCE. But what's to become of her? Is she to be paid anything? Do be sensible, sir.

HIGGINS. Oh, pay her whatever is necessary: put it down in the housekeeping book. [*Impatiently*] What on earth will she want with money? She'll have her food and her clothes. She'll only drink if you give her money.

LIZA [*turning on him*] Oh you are a brute. It's a lie: nobody ever saw the sign of liquor on me. [*She goes back to her chair and plants herself there defiantly.*]

PICKERING [*in good-humored remonstrance*] Does it occur to you, Higgins, that the girl has some feelings?

HIGGINS *[looking critically at her]* Oh no, I don't think so. Not any feelings that we need bother about. *[Cheerily]* Have you, Eliza?

LIZA. I got my feelings same as anyone else.

HIGGINS *[to Pickering, reflectively]* You see the difficulty?

PICKERING. Eh? What difficulty?

HIGGINS. To get her to talk grammar. The mere pronunciation is easy enough.

LIZA. I don't want to talk grammar. I want to talk like a lady.

MRS. PEARCE. Will you please keep to the point, Mr. Higgins. I want to know on what terms the girl is to be here. Is she to have any wages? And what is to become of her when you've finished your teaching? You must look ahead a little.

HIGGINS *[impatiently]* What's to become of her if I leave her in the gutter? Tell me that, Mrs. Pearce.

MRS. PEARCE. That's her own business, not yours, Mr. Higgins.

HIGGINS. Well, when I've done with her, we can throw her back into the gutter; and then it will be her own business again; so that's all right.

LIZA. Oh, you've no feeling heart in you: you don't care for nothing but yourself *[she rises and takes the floor resolutely]*. Here! I've had enough of this. I'm going *[making for the door]*. You ought to be ashamed of yourself, you ought.

HIGGINS *[snatching a chocolate cream from the piano, his eyes suddenly beginning to twinkle with mischief]* Have some chocolates, Eliza.

LIZA *[halting, tempted]* How do I know what might be in them? I've heard of girls being drugged by the like of you.

Higgins whips out his penknife; cuts a chocolate in two; puts one half into his mouth and bolts it; and offers her the other half.

HIGGINS. Pledge of good faith, Eliza. I eat one half: you eat the other. *[Liza opens her mouth to retort: he pops the half chocolate into it.]* You shall have boxes of them, barrels of them, every day. You shall live on them. Eh?

LIZA *[who has disposed of the chocolate after being nearly choked by it]* I wouldn't have ate it, only I'm too ladylike to take it out of my mouth.

HIGGINS. Listen, Eliza. I think you said you came in a taxi.

LIZA. Well, what if I did? I've as good a right to take a taxi as anyone else.

HIGGINS. You have, Eliza; and in future you shall have as many taxis as you want. You shall go up and down and round the town in a taxi every day. Think of that, Eliza.

MRS. PEARCE. Mr. Higgins: you're tempting the girl. It's not right. She should think of the future.

HIGGINS. At her age! Nonsense! Time enough to think of the future when you haven't any future to think of. No, Eliza: do as this lady does: think of other people's futures; but never think of your own. Think of chocolates, and taxis, and gold, and diamonds.

LIZA. No: I don't want no gold and no diamonds. I'm a good girl, I am. *[She sits down again, with an attempt at dignity.]*

HIGGINS. You shall remain so, Eliza, under the care of Mrs. Pearce. And you shall marry an officer in the Guards, with a beautiful moustache: the son of a marquis, who will disinherit him for marrying you, but will relent when he sees your beauty and goodness—

PICKERING. Excuse me, Higgins; but I really must interfere. Mrs. Pearce is quite right. If this girl is to put herself in your hands for six months for an experiment in teaching, she must understand thoroughly what she's doing.

HIGGINS. How can she? She's incapable of understanding anything. Besides, do any of us understand what we are doing? If we did, would we ever do it?

PICKERING. Very clever, Higgins; but not sound sense. *[To Eliza]* Miss Doolittle—

LIZA *[overwhelmed]* Ah-ah-ow-oo!

HIGGINS. There! That's all you get out of Eliza. Ah-ah-ow-oo! No use explaining. As a military man you ought to know that. Give her her orders: that's what she wants. Eliza: you are to live here for the next six months, learning how to speak beautifully, like a lady in a florist's shop. If you're good and do whatever you're told, you shall sleep in a proper bedroom, and have lots to eat, and money to buy chocolates and take rides in taxis. If you're naughty and idle you will sleep in the back kitchen among the black beetles, and be walloped by Mrs. Pearce with a broomstick. At the end of six months you shall go to Buckingham Palace in a carriage, beautifully dressed. If the King finds out you're not a lady, you will be taken by the police to the Tower of London, where your head will be cut off as a warning to other presumptuous flower girls. If you are not found out, you shall have a present of seven-and-sixpence to start life with as a lady in a shop. If you refuse this offer you will be a most ungrateful and wicked girl; and the angels will weep for you. *[To Pickering]* Now are you satisfied, Pickering? *[To Mrs. Pearce]* Can I put it more plainly and fairly, Mrs. Pearce?

MRS. PEARCE *[patiently]* I think you'd better let me speak to the girl properly in private. I don't know that I can take charge of her or consent to the arrangement at all. Of course I know you don't mean her any harm; but when you get what you call interested in people's accents, you never think or care what may happen to them or you. Come with me, Eliza.

HIGGINS. That's all right. Thank you, Mrs. Pearce. Bundle her off to the bath-room.

LIZA [*rising reluctantly and suspiciously*] You're a great bully, you are. I won't stay here if I don't like. I won't let nobody wallop me. I never asked to go to Bucknam Palace, I didn't. I was never in trouble with the police, not me. I'm a good girl—

MRS. PEARCE. Don't answer back, girl. You don't understand the gentleman. Come with me. [*She leads the way to the door, and holds it open for Eliza.*]

LIZA [*as she goes out*] Well, what I say is right. I won't go near the king, not if I'm going to have my head cut off. If I'd known what I was letting myself in for, I wouldn't have come here. I always been a good girl; and I never offered to say a word to him; and I don't owe him nothing; and I don't care; and I won't be put upon; and I have my feelings the same as anyone else—

Mrs. Pearce shuts the door; and Eliza's plaints are no longer audible. Pickering comes from the hearth to the chair and sits astride it with his arms on the back.

* * *

Eliza is taken upstairs to the third floor greatly to her surprise; for she expected to be taken down to the scullery. There Mrs. Pearce opens a door and takes her into a spare bedroom.

MRS. PEARCE. I will have to put you here. This will be your bedroom.

LIZA. Oh, I couldn't sleep here, missus. It's too good for the likes of me. I should be afraid to touch anything. I ain't a duchess yet, you know.

MRS. PEARCE. You have got to make yourself as clean as the room: then you won't be afraid of it. And you must call me Mrs. Pearce, not missus. [*She throws open the door of the dressing-room, now modernized as a bathroom*].

LIZA. Gawd! what's this? Is this where you wash clothes? Funny sort of copper I call it.

MRS. PEARCE. It is not a copper. This is where we wash ourselves, Eliza, and where I am going to wash you.

LIZA. You expect me to get into that and wet myself all over! Not me. I should catch my death. I knew a woman who did it every Saturday night; and she died of it.

MRS. PEARCE Mr. Higgins has the gentleman's bathroom downstairs; and he has a bath every morning, in cold water.

LIZA. Ugh! He's made of iron, that man.

MRS. PEARCE. If you are to sit with him and the Colonel and be taught you will have to do the same. They won't like the smell of you if you don't. But you can have the water as hot as you like. There are two taps: hot and cold.

LIZA [weeping] I couldn't. I durns't. It's not natural: it would kill me. I've never had a bath in my life: not what you'd call a proper one.

MRS. PEARCE. Well, don't you want to be clean and sweet and decent, like a lady? You know you can't be a nice girl inside if you're a dirty slut outside.

LIZA. Boohoo!!

MRS. PEARCE. Now stop crying and go back into your room and take off all your clothes. Then wrap yourself in this [taking down a gown from its peg and handing it to her] and come back to me. I will get the bath ready.

LIZA [all tears] I can't. I won't. I'm not used to it. I've never took off all my clothes before. It's not right: it's not decent.

MRS. PEARCE. Nonsense, child. Don't you take off all you clothes every night when you go to bed?

LIZA [amazed] No. Why should I? I should catch my death. Of course I take off my skirt.

MRS. PEARCE. Do you mean that you sleep in the underclothes you wear in the daytime?

LIZA. What else have I to sleep in?

MRS. PEARCE. You will never do that as long as you live here. I will get you a proper night dress.

LIZA. Do you mean change into cold things and lie awake shivering half the night? You want to kill me, you do.

MRS. PEARCE. I want to change you from a frowzy slut to a clean respectable girl fit to sit with the gentlemen in the study. Are you going to trust me and do what I tell you or be thrown out and sent back to your flower basket?

LIZA. But you don't know what the cold is to me. You don't know how I dread it.

MRS. PEARCE. Your bed won't be cold here: I will put a hot water bottle in it. [Pushing her into the bedroom] Off with you and undress.

LIZA. Oh, if only I'd a known what a dreadful thing it is to be clean I'd have never come. I didn't know when I was well off. I— [Mrs. Pearce pushes her through the door, but leaves it partly open lest her prisoner should take to flight.]

Mrs. Pearce puts on a pair of white rubber sleeves, and fills the bath, mixing hot and cold, and testing the result with the bath thermometer. She perfumes it with a handful of bath salts and adds a palmful of mustard. She then takes a formidable looking long handled scrubbing brush and soaps it profusely with a ball of scented soap.

Eliza comes back with nothing on but the bath gown huddled tightly around her, a piteous spectacle of abject terror.

MRS. PEARCE. Now come along. Take that thing off.

LIZA. Oh I couldn't, Mrs. Pearce: I reely couldn't. I never done such a thing.

MRS. PEARCE. Nonsense. Here: step in and tell me whether it's hot enough for you.

LIZA. Ah-oo! Ah-oo! It's too hot.

MRS. PEARCE. *[deftly snatching the gown away and throwing Eliza down on her back]* It won't hurt you. *[She sets to work with the scrubbing brush.]*

Eliza's screams are heartrending.

* * *

Meanwhile the Colonel has been having it out with Higgins about Eliza. Pickering has come from the hearth chair and seated himself astride of it with his arms on the back to cross-examine him.

PICKERING. Excuse the straight question, Higgins. Are you a man of good character where women are concerned?

HIGGINS *[moodily]* Have you ever met a man of good character where women are concerned?

PICKERING. Yes: very frequently.

HIGGINS *[dogmatically, lifting himself on his hands to the level of the piano, and sitting on it with a bounce]* Well, I haven't. I find that the moment I let a woman make friends with me, she becomes jealous, exacting, suspicious, and a damned nuisance. I find that the moment I let myself make friends with a woman, I become selfish and tyrannical. Women upset everything. When you let them into your life, you find that the woman is driving at one thing and you're driving at another.

PICKERING. At what, for example?

HIGGINS *[coming off the piano restlessly]* Oh, Lord knows! I suppose the woman wants to live her own life; and the man wants to live his; and each tries to drag the other on to the wrong track. One wants to go north and the other south; and the result is that both have to go east, though they both hate the east wind. *[He sits down on the bench at the keyboard.]* So here I am, a confirmed old bachelor, and likely to remain so.

PICKERING *[rising and standing over him gravely]* Come, Higgins! You know what I mean. If I'm to be in this business I shall feel responsible for that girl. I hope it's understood that no advantage is to be taken of her position.

HIGGINS. What! That thing! Sacred, I assure you. *[Rising to explain]* You see, she'll be a pupil; and teaching would be impossible unless pupils were sacred. I've taught scores of American millionairesses how to speak English: the best looking women in the world. I'm seasoned. They might as well be blocks of wood. I might as well be a block of wood. It's—

Mrs. Pearce opens the door. She has Eliza's hat in her hand. Pickering retires to the easy-chair at the hearth and sits down.

HIGGINS *[eagerly]* Well, Mrs. Pearce: is it all right?

MRS. PEARCE *[at the door]* I just wish to trouble you with a word, if I may, Mr. Higgins.

HIGGINS. Yes, certainly. Come in. *[She comes forward.]* Don't burn that, Mrs. Pearce. I'll keep it as a curiosity. *[He takes the hat.]*

MRS. PEARCE. Handle it carefully, sir, please. I had to promise her not to burn it; but I had better put it in the oven for a while.

HIGGINS *[putting it down hastily on the piano]* Oh! thank you. Well, what have you to say to me?

PICKERING. Am I in the way?

MRS. PEARCE. Not at all, sir. Mr. Higgins: will you please be very particular what you say before the girl?

HIGGINS *[sternly]* Of course. I'm always particular about what I say. Why do you say this to me?

MRS. PEARCE *[unmoved]* No, sir: you're not at all particular when you've mislaid anything or when you get a little impatient. Now it doesn't matter before me: I'm used to it. But you really must not swear before the girl.

HIGGINS *[indignantly]* I swear! *[Most emphatically]* I never swear. I detest the habit. What the devil do you mean?

MRS. PEARCE *[stolidly]* That's what I mean, sir. You swear a great deal too much. I don't mind your damning and blasting, and what the devil and where the devil and who the devil—

HIGGINS. Mrs. Pearce: this language from your lips! Really!

MRS. PEARCE *[not to be put off]*—but there is a certain word I must ask you not to use. The girl has just used it herself because the bath was too hot. It begins with the same letter as bath. She knows no better: she learnt it at her mother's knee. But she must not hear it from your lips.

HIGGINS *[loftily]* I cannot charge myself with having ever uttered it, Mrs. Pearce. *[She looks at him steadfastly. He adds, hiding an uneasy conscience with a judicial air]* Except perhaps in a moment of extreme and justifiable excitement.

MRS. PEARCE. Only this morning, sir, you applied it to your boots, to the butter, and to the brown bread.

HIGGINS. Oh, that! Mere alliteration, Mrs. Pearce, natural to a poet.

MRS. PEARCE. Well, sir, whatever you choose to call it, I beg you not to let the girl hear you repeat it.

HIGGINS. Oh, very well, very well. Is that all?

MRS. PEARCE. No, sir. We shall have to be very particular with this girl as to personal cleanliness.

HIGGINS. Certainly. Quite right. Most important.

MRS. PEARCE. I mean not to be slovenly about her dress or untidy in leaving things about.

HIGGINS [going to her solemnly] Just so. I intended to call your attention to that [He passes on to Pickering, who is enjoying the conversation immensely]. It is these little things that matter, Pickering. Take care of the pence and the pounds will take care of themselves is as true of personal habits as of money. [He comes to anchor on the hearthrug, with the air of a man in an unassailable position.]

MRS. PEARCE. Yes, sir. Then might I ask you not to come down to breakfast in your dressing-gown, or at any rate not to use it as a napkin to the extent you do, sir. And if you would be so good as not to eat everything off the same plate, and to remember not to put the porridge saucepan out of your hand on the clean tablecloth, it would be a better example to the girl. You know you nearly choked yourself with a fishbone in the jam only last week.

HIGGINS [routed from the hearthrug and drifting back to the piano] I may do these things sometimes in absence of mind; but surely I don't do them habitually. [Angrily] By the way: my dressing-gown smells most damnably of benzine.

MRS. PEARCE. No doubt it does, Mr. Higgins. But if you will wipe your fingers—

HIGGINS [yelling] Oh very well, very well: I'll wipe them in my hair in future.

MRS. PEARCE. I hope you're not offended, Mr. Higgins.

HIGGINS [shocked at finding himself thought capable of an unamiable sentiment] Not at all, not at all. You're quite right, Mrs. Pearce: I shall be particularly careful before the girl. Is that all?

MRS. PEARCE. No, sir. Might she use some of those Japanese dresses you brought from abroad? I really can't put her back into her old things.

HIGGINS. Certainly. Anything you like. Is that all?

MRS. PEARCE. Thank you, sir. That's all. [She goes out.]

HIGGINS. You know, Pickering, that woman has the most extraordinary ideas about me. Here I am, a shy, diffident sort of man. I've never been able to feel really grown-up and tremendous, like other chaps. And yet she's firmly persuaded that I'm an arbitrary overbearing bossing kind of person. I can't account for it.

Mrs. Pearce returns.

MRS. PEARCE. If you please, sir, the trouble's beginning already. There's a dustman downstairs, Alfred Doolittle, wants to see you. He says you have his daughter here.

PICKERING [rising] Phew! I say! [He retreats to the hearthrug.]

HIGGINS [promptly] Send the blackguard up.

MRS. PEARCE. Oh, very well, sir. *[She goes out.]*

PICKERING. He may not be a blackguard, Higgins.

HIGGINS. Nonsense. Of course he's a blackguard.

PICKERING. Whether he is or not, I'm afraid we shall have some trouble with him.

HIGGINS *[confidently]* Oh no: I think not. If there's any trouble he shall have it with me, not I with him. And we are sure to get something interesting out of him.

PICKERING. About the girl?

HIGGINS. No. I mean his dialect.

PICKERING. Oh!

MRS. PEARCE *[at the door]* Doolittle, sir. *[She admits Doolittle and retires.]*

Alfred Doolittle is an elderly but vigorous dustman, clad in the costume of his profession, including a hat with a back brim covering his neck and shoulders. He has well marked and rather interesting features, and seems equally free from fear and conscience. He has a remarkably expressive voice, the result of a habit of giving vent to his feelings without reserve. His present pose is that of wounded honor and stern resolution.

DOOLITTLE *[at the door, uncertain which of the two gentlemen is his man]* Professor Higgins?

HIGGINS. Here. Good morning. Sit down.

DOOLITTLE. Morning, Governor. *[He sits down magisterially]* I come about a very serious matter, Governor.

HIGGINS *[to Pickering]* Brought up in Hounslow. Mother Welsh, I should think. *[Doolittle opens his mouth, amazed. Higgins continues]* What do you want, Doolittle?

DOOLITTLE *[menacingly]* I want my daughter: that's what I want. See?

HIGGINS. Of course you do. You're her father, aren't you? You don't suppose anyone else wants her, do you? I'm glad to see you have some spark of family feeling left. She's upstairs. Take her away at once.

DOOLITTLE *[rising, fearfully taken aback]* What!

HIGGINS. Take her away. Do you suppose I'm going to keep your daughter for you?

DOOLITTLE *[remonstrating]* Now, now, look here, Governor. Is this reasonable? Is it fairity to take advantage of a man like this? The girl belongs to me. You got her. Where do I come in? *[He sits down again.]*

HIGGINS. Your daughter had the audacity to come to my house and ask me to teach her how to speak properly so that she could get a place in a flower-shop. This gentleman and my housekeeper have been here all the time. *[Bullying him]* How dare you come here and attempt to blackmail me? You sent her here on purpose.

DOOLITTLE *[protesting]* No, Governor.

HIGGINS. You must have. How else could you possibly know that she is here?

DOOLITTLE. Don't take a man up like that, Governor.

HIGGINS. The police shall take you up. This is a plant—a plot to extort money by threats. I shall telephone for the police *[he goes resolutely to the telephone and opens the directory.]*

DOOLITTLE. Have I asked you for a brass farthing? I leave it to the gentleman here: have I said a word about money?

HIGGINS *[throwing the book aside and marching down on Doolittle with a poser]* What else did you come for?

DOOLITTLE *[sweetly]* Well, what would a man come for? Be human, Governor.

HIGGINS *[disarmed]* Alfred: did you put her up to it?

DOOLITTLE. So help me, Governor, I never did. I take my Bible oath I ain't seen the girl these two months past.

HIGGINS. Then how did you know she was here?

DOOLITTLE *[most musical, most melancholy]* I'll tell you, Governor, if you'll only let me get a word in. I'm willing to tell you. I'm wanting to tell you. I'm waiting to tell you.

HIGGINS. Pickering: this chap has a certain natural gift of rhetoric. Observe the rhythm of his native woodnotes wild. "I'm willing to tell you: I'm wanting to tell you: I'm waiting to tell you." Sentimental rhetoric! That's the Welsh strain in him. It also accounts for his mendacity and dishonesty.

PICKERING. Oh, please, Higgins: I'm west country myself. *[To Doolittle]* How did you know the girl was here if you didn't send her?

DOOLITTLE. It was like this, Governor. The girl took a boy in the taxi to give him a jaunt. Son of her landlady, he is. He hung about on the chance of her giving him another ride home. Well, she sent him back for her luggage when she heard you was willing for her to stop here. I met the boy at the corner of Long Acre and Endell Street.

HIGGINS. Public house. Yes?

DOOLITTLE. The poor man's club, Governor: why shouldn't I?

PICKERING. Do let him tell his story, Higgins.

DOOLITTLE. He told me what was up. And I ask you, what was my feelings and my duty as a father? I says to the boy, "You bring me the luggage," I says—

PICKERING. Why didn't you go for it yourself?

DOOLITTLE. Landlady wouldn't have trusted me with it, Governor. She's that kind of woman: you know. I had to give the boy a penny afore he trusted me with it, the little swine. I brought it to her just to oblige you like, and make myself agreeable. That's all.

HIGGINS. How much luggage?

DOOLITTLE. Musical instrument, Governor. A few pictures, a trifle of jewelry, and a bird-cage. She said she didn't want no clothes. What was I to think from that, Governor? I ask you as a parent what was I to think?

HIGGINS. So you came to rescue her from worse than death, eh?

DOOLITTLE [appreciatively: relieved at being so well understood] Just so, Governor. That's right.

PICKERING. But why did you bring her luggage if you intended to take her away?

DOOLITTLE. Have I said a word about taking her away? Have I now?

HIGGINS [determinedly] You're going to take her away, double quick. [He crosses to the hearth and rings the bell.]

DOOLITTLE [rising] No, Governor. Don't say that. I'm not the man to stand in my girl's light. Here's a career opening for her, as you might say; and—

Mrs. Pearce opens the door and awaits orders.

HIGGINS. Mrs. Pearce: this is Eliza's father. He has come to take her away. Give her to him. [He goes back to the piano, with an air of washing his hands of the whole affair.]

DOOLITTLE. No. This is a misunderstanding. Listen here—

MRS. PEARCE. He can't take her away, Mr. Higgins: how can he? You told me to burn her clothes.

DOOLITTLE. That's right. I can't carry the girl through the streets like a blooming monkey, can I? I put it to you.

HIGGINS. You have put it to me that you want your daughter. Take your daughter. If she has no clothes go out and buy her some.

DOOLITTLE [desperate] Where's the clothes she come in? Did I burn them or did your missus here?

MRS. PEARCE. I am the housekeeper, if you please. I have sent for some clothes for your girl. When they come you can take her away. You can wait in the kitchen. This way, please.

Doolittle, much troubled, accompanies her to the door; then hesitates; finally turns confidentially to Higgins.

DOOLITTLE. Listen here, Governor. You and me is men of the world, ain't we?

HIGGINS. Oh! Men of the world, are we? You'd better go, Mrs. Pearce.

MRS. PEARCE. I think so, indeed, sir. [She goes, with dignity.]

PICKERING. The floor is yours, Mr. Doolittle.

DOOLITTLE *[to Pickering]* I thank you, Governor. *[To Higgins, who takes refuge on the piano bench, a little overwhelmed by the proximity of his visitor; for Doolittle has a professional flavor of dust about him.]* Well, the truth is, I've taken a sort of fancy to you, Governor; and if you want the girl, I'm not so set on having her back home again but what I might be open to an arrangement. Regarded in the light of a young woman, she's a fine handsome girl. As a daughter she's not worth her keep; and so I tell you straight. All I ask is my rights as a father; and you're the last man alive to expect me to let her go for nothing; for I can see you're one of the straight sort, Governor. Well, what's a five pound note to you? And what's Eliza to me? *[He returns to his chair and sits down judicially.]*

PICKERING. I think you ought to know, Doolittle, that Mr. Higgins's intentions are entirely honorable.

DOOLITTLE. Course they are, Governor. If I thought they wasn't, I'd ask fifty.

HIGGINS *[revolted]* Do you mean to say, you callous rascal, that you would sell your daughter for £50?

DOOLITTLE. Not in a general way I wouldn't; but to oblige a gentleman like you I'd do a good deal, I do assure you.

PICKERING. Have you no morals, man?

DOOLITTLE *[unabashed]* Can't afford them, Governor. Neither could you if you was as poor as me. Not that I mean any harm, you know. But if Liza is going to have a bit out of this, why not me too?

HIGGINS *[troubled]* I don't know what to do, Pickering. There can be no question that as a matter of morals it's a positive crime to give this chap a farthing. And yet I feel a sort of rough justice in his claim.

DOOLITTLE, That's it, Governor. That's all I say. A father's heart, as it were.

PICKERING. Well, I know the feeling; but really it seems hardly right—

DOOLITTLE. Don't say that, Governor. Don't look at it that way. What am I, Governors both? I ask you, what am I? I'm one of the undeserving poor: that's what I am. Think of what that means to a man. It means that he's up agen middle class morality all the time. If there's anything going, and I put in for a bit of it, it's always the same story: "You're undeserving; so you can't have it." But my needs is as great as the most deserving widows that ever got money out of six different charities in one week for the death of the same husband. I don't need less than a deserving man: I need more. I don't eat less hearty than him; and I drink a lot more. I want a bit of amusement, cause I'm a thinking man. I want cheerfulness and a song and a band when I feel low. Well, they charge me just the same for everything as they charge the deserving. What is middle class morality? Just an excuse for never giving me anything. Therefore, I ask you, as two gentlemen, not to play that game on me. I'm playing straight with you. I ain't pretending to be deserving.

I'm undeserving; and I mean to go on being undeserving. I like it; and that's the truth. Will you take advantage of a man's nature to do him out of the price of his own daughter what he's brought up and fed and clothed by the sweat of his brow until she's growed big enough to be interesting to you two gentlemen? Is five pounds unreasonable? I put it to you; and I leave it to you.

HIGGINS [rising, and going over to Pickering] Pickering: if we were to take this man in hand for three months, he could choose between a seat in the Cabinet and a popular pulpit in Wales.

PICKERING. What do you say to that, Doolittle?

DOOLITTLE. Not me, Governor, thank you kindly. I've heard all the preachers and all the prime ministers—for I'm a thinking man and game for politics or religion or social reform same as all the other amusements—and I tell you it's a dog's life anyway you look at it. Undeserving poverty is my line. Taking one station in society with another, it's—it's—well, it's the only one that has any ginger in it, to my taste.

HIGGINS. I suppose we must give him a fiver.

PICKERING. He'll make a bad use of it, I'm afraid.

DOOLITTLE. Not me, Governor, so help me I won't. Don't you be afraid that I'll save it and spare it and live idle on it. There won't be a penny of it left by Monday: I'll have to go to work same as if I'd never had it. It won't pauperize me, you bet. Just one good spree for myself and the missus, giving pleasure to ourselves and employment to others, and satisfaction to you to think it's not been throwed away. You couldn't spend it better.

HIGGINS [taking out his pocket book and coming between Doolittle and the piano] This is irresistible. Let's give him ten. [He offers two notes to the dustman.]

DOOLITTLE. No, Governor. She wouldn't have the heart to spend ten; and perhaps I shouldn't neither. Ten pounds is a lot of money: it makes a man feel prudent like; and then goodbye to happiness. You give me what I ask you, Governor: not a penny more, and not a penny less.

PICKERING. Why don't you marry that missus of yours? I rather draw the line at encouraging that sort of immorality.

DOOLITTLE. Tell her so, Governor: tell her so. I'm willing. It's me that suffers by it. I've no hold on her. I got to be agreeable to her. I got to give her presents. I got to buy her clothes something sinful. I'm a slave to that woman, Governor, just because I'm not her lawful husband. And she knows it too. Catch her marrying me! Take my advice, Governor: marry Eliza while she's young and don't know no better. If you don't you'll be sorry for it after. If you do, shell be sorry for it after; but better you than her, because you're a man, and she's only a woman and don't know how to be happy anyhow.

HIGGINS. Pickering: if we listen to this man another minute, we shall have no convictions left. [To Doolittle] Five pounds I think you said.

DOOLITTLE. Thank you kindly, Governor.

HIGGINS. You're sure you won't take ten?

DOOLITTLE. Not now. Another time, Governor.

HIGGINS [*handing him a five-pound note*] Here you are.

DOOLITTLE. Thank you, Governor. Good morning. [*He hurries to the door, anxious to get away with his booty. When he opens it he is confronted with a dainty and exquisitely clean young Japanese lady in a simple blue cotton kimono printed cunningly with small white jasmine blossoms. Mrs. Pearce is with her. He gets out of her way deferentially and apologizes.*] Beg pardon, miss.

THE JAPANESE LADY. Garn! Don't you know your own daughter?

DOOLITTLE		*all*		Bly me! it's Eliza!
HIGGINS	{	*exclaiming*	}	What's that? It's Eliza!
PICKERING		*simultaneously*		By Jove!

LIZA. Don't I look silly?

HIGGINS. Silly?

MRS. PEARCE [*at the door*] Now, Mr. Higgins, please don't say anything to make the girl conceited about herself.

HIGGINS [*conscientiously*] Oh! Quite right, Mrs. Pearce. [*To Eliza*] Yes: damned silly.

MRS. PEARCE. Please, sir.

HIGGINS [*correcting himself*] I mean extremely silly.

LIZA. I should look all right with my hat on. [*She takes up her hat; puts it on; and walks across the room to the fireplace with a fashionable air.*]

HIGGINS. A new fashion, by George! And it ought to look horrible!

DOOLITTLE [*with fatherly pride*] Well, I never thought she'd clean up as good looking as that, Governor. She's a credit to me, ain't she?

LIZA. I tell you, it's easy to clean up here. Hot and cold water on tap, just as much as you like, there is. Woolly towels, there is; and a towel horse so hot, it burns your fingers. Soft brushes to scrub yourself, and a wooden bowl of soap smelling like primroses. Now I know why ladies is so clean. Washing's a treat for them. Wish they saw what it is for the like of me!

HIGGINS. I'm glad the bath-room met with your approval.

LIZA. It didn't: not all of it; and I don't care who hears me say it. Mrs. Pearce knows.

HIGGINS. What was wrong, Mrs. Pearce?

MRS. PEARCE [*blandly*] Oh, nothing, sir. It doesn't matter.

LIZA. I had a good mind to break it. I didn't know which way to look. But I hung a towel over it, I did.

HIGGINS. Over what?

MRS. PEARCE. Over the looking-glass, sir.

HIGGINS. Doolittle: you have brought your daughter up too strictly.

DOOLITTLE. Me! I never brought her up at all, except to give her a lick of a strap now and again. Don't put it on me, Governor. She ain't accustomed to it, you see: that's all. But she'll soon pick up your free-and-easy ways.

LIZA. I'm a good girl, I am; and I won't pick up no free and easy ways.

HIGGINS. Eliza: if you say again that you're a good girl, your father shall take you home.

LIZA. Not him. You don't know my father. All he come here for was to touch you for some money to get drunk on.

DOOLITTLE. Well, what else would I want money for? To put into the plate in church, I suppose. [*She puts out her tongue at him. He is so incensed by this that Pickering presently finds it necessary to step between them.*] Don't you give me none of your lip; and don't let me hear you giving this gentleman any of it neither, or you'll hear from me about it. See?

HIGGINS. Have you any further advice to give her before you go, Doolittle? Your blessing, for instance.

DOOLITTLE. No, Governor: I ain't such a mug as to put up my children to all I know myself. Hard enough to hold them in without that. If you want Eliza's mind improved, Governor, you do it yourself with a strap. So long, gentlemen. [*He turns to go.*]

HIGGINS [*impressively*] Stop. You'll come regularly to see your daughter. It's your duty, you know. My brother is a clergyman; and he could help you in your talks with her.

DOOLITTLE [*evasively*] Certainly. I'll come, Governor. Not just this week, because I have a job at a distance. But later on you may depend on me. Afternoon, gentlemen. Afternoon, ma'am. [*He takes off his hat to Mrs. Pearce, who disdains the salutation and goes out. He winks at Higgins, thinking him probably a fellow-sufferer from Mrs. Pearce's difficult disposition, and follows her.*]

LIZA. Don't you believe the old liar. He'd as soon you set a bull-dog on him as a clergyman. You won't see him again in a hurry.

HIGGINS. I don't want to, Eliza. Do you?

LIZA. Not me. I don't want never to see him again, I don't. He's a disgrace to me, he is, collecting dust, instead of working at his trade.

PICKERING. What is his trade, Eliza?

LIZA. Talking money out of other people's pockets into his own. His proper trade's a navvy; and he works at it sometimes too—for exercise—and earns good money at it. Ain't you going to call me Miss Doolittle any more?

PICKERING. I beg your pardon, Miss Doolittle. It was a slip of the tongue.

LIZA. Oh, I don't mind; only it sounded so genteel. I should just like to take a taxi to the corner of Tottenham Court Road and get out there and tell it to wait for me, just to put the girls in their place a bit. I wouldn't speak to them, you know.

PICKERING. Better wait til we get you something really fashionable.

HIGGINS. Besides, you shouldn't cut your old friends now that you have risen in the world. That's what we call snobbery.

LIZA. You don't call the like of them my friends now, I should hope. They've took it out of me often enough with their ridicule when they had the chance; and now I mean to get a bit of my own back. But if I'm to have fashionable clothes, I'll wait. I should like to have some. Mrs. Pearce says you're going to give me some to wear in bed at night different to what I wear in the daytime; but it do seem a waste of money when you could get something to shew. Besides, I never could fancy changing into cold things on a winter night.

MRS. PEARCE [coming back] Now, Eliza. The new things have come for you to try on.

LIZA. Ah-ow-oo-ooh! [She rushes out.]

MRS. PEARCE [following her] Oh, don't rush about like that, girl [She shuts the door behind her.]

HIGGINS. Pickering: we have taken on a stiff job.

PICKERING [with conviction] Higgins: we have.

* * *

There seems to be some curiosity as to what Higgins's lessons to Eliza were like. Well, here is a sample: the first one.

Picture Eliza, in her new clothes, and feeling her inside put out of step by a lunch, dinner, and breakfast of a kind to which it is unaccustomed, seated with Higgins and the Colonel in the study, feeling like a hospital out-patient at a first encounter with the doctors.

Higgins, constitutionally unable to sit still, discomposes her still more by striding restlessly about. But for the reassuring presence and quietude of her friend the Colonel she would run for her life, even back to Drury lane.

HIGGINS. Say your alphabet.

LIZA. I know my alphabet. Do you think I know nothing? I don't need to be taught like a child.

HIGGINS. [thundering] Say your alphabet.

PICKERING. Say it, Miss Doolittle. You will understand presently. Do what he tells you; and let him teach you in his own way.

LIZA. Oh well, if you put it like that—Ahyee, b yee, c yee, d yee—

HIGGINS *[with the roar of a wounded lion]* Stop. Listen to this, Pickering. This is what we pay for as elementary education. This unfortunate animal has been locked up for nine years in school at our expense to teach her to speak and read the language of Shakespeare and Milton. And the result is Ahyee, B-yee, C-yee, D-yee. *[To Eliza]* Say, A, B, C, D.

LIZA *[almost in tears]* But I'm saying it. Ahyee, B-yee, C-yee—

HIGGINS. Stop. Say a cup of tea.

LIZA. A capp t-ee.

HIGGINS. Put your tongue forward until it squeezes against the top of your lower teeth. Now say cup.

LIZA. C-c-c—I can't. C-Cup.

PICKERING. Good. Splendid, Miss Doolittle.

HIGGINS. By Jupiter, she's done it at the first shot. Pickering: we shall make a duchess of her. *[To Eliza]* Now do you think you could possibly say tea? Not t-yee, mind: if you ever say b yee, c yee, d yee again you shall be dragged round the room three times by the hair of your head. *[Fortissimo]* T,T,T,T.

LIZA *[weeping]* I can't hear no difference cep that it sounds more genteel-like when you say it.

HIGGINS. Well, if you can hear that difference, what the devil are you crying for? Pickering: give her a chocolate.

PICKERING. No, no. Never mind crying a little, Miss Doolittle: you are doing very well; and the lessons won't hurt. I promise you I won't let him drag you round the room by your hair.

HIGGINS. Be off with you to Mrs. Pearce and tell her about it. Think about it. Try to do it by yourself: and keep your tongue well forward in your mouth instead of trying to roll it up and swallow it. Another lesson at half-past four this afternoon. Away with you.

Eliza, still sobbing, rushes from the room.

And that is the sort of ordeal poor Eliza has to go through for months before we meet her again on her first appearance in London society of the professional class.

ACT III

[*Henry Higgins decides to take Eliza to an "at-home" day at his mother's, who is receiving guests. The guests are of established (but impoverished) society: Mrs. Eynsford Hill, and her daughter and son Freddy (the same ones we met under the portico of St. Paul's Church at the beginning of the play).*

[*Mrs. Higgins is curious about Eliza. Henry tries to explain his "experiment" to her, and she, like Mrs. Pearce, is dubious. She wonders what will become of Eliza.*

[The Hills arrive, and so do Eliza and Col. Pickering. Eliza is stunningly beautiful, and her pronunciation impeccable, but unfortunately the substance of her conversation (when she gets beyond the topic of the weather) leaves something to be desired. Eliza, at Henry's urging, leaves early, taking a taxi. Freddy offers to walk her home, but Eliza responds: "Walk! Not bloody likely. I am going in a taxi."

[Freddy has fallen hopelessly in love with Eliza. Eds.]

Clearly Eliza will not pass as a duchess yet; and Higgins's bet remains unwon. But the six months are not yet exhausted; and just in time Eliza does actually pass as a princess. For a glimpse of how she did it imagine an Embassy in London one summer evening after dark. The hall door has an awning and a carpet across the sidewalk to the kerb, because a grand reception is in progress. A small crowd is lined up to see the guests arrive.

A Rolls–Royce car drives up. Pickering in evening dress, with medals and orders, alights, and hands out Eliza, in opera cloak, evening dress, diamonds, flowers, and all accessories. Higgins follows. The car drives off, and the three go up the steps and into the house, the door opening for them as they approach.

Inside the house they find themselves in a spacious hall from which the grand staircase rises. On the left are the arrangements for the gentlemen's cloaks. The male guests are depositing their hats and wraps there.

On the right is a door leading to the ladies' cloakroom. Ladies are going in cloaked and coming out in splendor. Pickering whispers to Eliza and points out the ladies' room. She goes into it. Higgins and Pickering take off their overcoats and take tickets for them from the attendant.

One of the guests, occupied in the same way, has his back turned. Having taken his ticket, he turns round and reveals himself as an important-looking young man with an astonishingly hairy face. He has an enormous moustache, flowing out into luxuriant whiskers. Waves of hair cluster on his brow. His hair is cropped closely at the back, and glows with oil. Otherwise he is very smart. He wears several worthless orders. He is evidently a foreigner, guessable as a whiskered Pandour from Hungary; but in spite of the ferocity of his moustache he is amiable and genially voluble.

Recognizing Higgins, he flings his arms wide apart and approaches him enthusiastically.

WHISKERS. Maestro, maestro *[he embraces Higgins and kisses him on both cheeks]*. You remember me?

HIGGINS. No I don't. Who the devil are you?

WHISKERS. I am your pupil: your first pupil, your best and greatest pupil. I am little Nepommuck, the marvellous boy. I have made your name famous throughout Europe. You teach me phonetic. You cannot forget ME.

HIGGINS. Why don't you shave?

NEPOMMUCK. I have not your imposing appearance, your chin, your brow. Nobody notices me when I shave. Now I am famous: they call me Hairy Faced Dick.

HIGGINS. And what are you doing here among all these swells?

NEPOMMUCK. I am interpreter. I speak 32 languages. I am indispensable at these international parties. You are great cockney specialist: you place a man anywhere in London the moment he opens his mouth. I place any man in Europe.

A footman hurries down the grand staircase and comes to Nepommuck.

FOOTMAN. You are wanted upstairs. Her excellency cannot understand the Greek gentleman.

NEPOMMUCK. Thank you, yes, immediately.

The footman goes and is lost in the crowd.

NEPOMMUCK *[to Higgins]* This Greek diplomatist pretends he cannot speak nor understand English. He cannot deceive me. He is the son of a Clerkenwell watchmaker. He speaks English so villainously that he dare not utter a word of it without betraying his origin. I help him to pretend; but I make him pay through the nose. I make them all pay. Ha ha! *[He hurries upstairs.]*

PICKERING. Is this fellow really an expert? Can he find out Eliza and blackmail her?

HIGGINS. We shall see. If he finds her out I lose my bet.

Eliza comes from the cloakroom and joins them.

PICKERING. Well, Eliza, now for it. Are you ready?

LIZA. Are you nervous, Colonel?

PICKERING. Frightfully. I feel exactly as I felt before my first battle. It's the first time that frightens.

LIZA. It's not the first time for me, Colonel. I have done this fifty times—hundreds of times—in my little piggery in Angel Court in my daydreams. I am in a dream now. Promise me not to let Professor Higgins wake me; for if he does I shall forget everything and talk as I used to in Drury Lane.

PICKERING. Not a word, Higgins. *[To Eliza]* Now ready?

LIZA. Ready.

PICKERING. Go.

They mount the stairs, Higgins last. Pickering whispers to the footman on the first landing.

FIRST LANDING FOOTMAN. Miss Doolittle, Colonel Pickering, Professor Higgins.

SECOND LANDING FOOTMAN. Miss Doolittle, Colonel Pickering, Professor Higgins.

At the top of the staircase the Ambassador and his wife with Nepommuck at her elbow, are receiving.

HOSTESS *[taking Eliza's hand]* How d'ye do?

HOST *[same play]* How d'ye do? How d'ye do, Pickering?

LIZA *[with a beautiful gravity that awes her hostess]* How do you do? *[She passes on to the drawing room.]*

HOSTESS. Is that your adopted daughter, Colonel Pickering? She will make a wonderful sensation.

PICKERING. Most kind of you to invite her for me. *[He passes on.]*

HOSTESS *[to Nepommuck]* Find out all about her.

NEPOMMUCK *[bowing]* Excellency—*[he goes into the crowd.]*

HOST. How d'ye do, Higgins? You have a rival here tonight. He introduced himself as your pupil. Is he any good?

HIGGINS. He can learn a language in a fortnight—knows dozens of them. A sure mark of a fool. As a phonetician, no good whatever.

HOSTESS. How d'ye do, Professor?

HIGGINS. How do you do? Fearful bore for you, this sort of thing. Forgive my part in it. *[He passes on.]*

In the drawing room and its suite of salons the reception is in full swing. Eliza passes through. She is so intent on her ordeal that she walks like a somnambulist in a desert instead of a débutante in a fashionable crowd. They stop talking to look at her, admiring her dress, her jewels, and her strangely attractive self. Some of the younger ones at the back stand on their chairs to see.

The Host and Hostess come in from the staircase and mingle with their guests. Higgins, gloomy and contemptuous of the whole business, comes into the group where they are chatting.

HOSTESS. Ah, here is Professor Higgins: he will tell us. Tell us all about the wonderful young lady, Professor.

HIGGINS *[almost morosely]* What wonderful young lady?

HOSTESS. You know very well. They tell me there has been nothing like her in London since people stood on their chairs to look at Mrs. Langtry.

Nepommuck joins the group, full of news.

HOSTESS. Ah, here you are at last, Nepommuck. Have you found all about the Doolittle lady?

NEPOMMUCK. I have found out all about her. She is a fraud.

HOSTESS. A fraud! Oh no.

NEPOMMUCK. YES, yes. She cannot deceive me. Her name cannot be Doolittle.

HIGGINS. Why?

NEPOMMUCK. Because Doolittle is an English name. And she is not English.

HOSTESS. Oh, nonsense! She speaks English perfectly.

NEPOMMUCK. Too perfectly. Can you shew me any English woman who speaks English as it should be spoken? Only foreigners who have been taught to speak it speak it well.

HOSTESS. Certainly she terrified me by the way she said How d'ye do. I had a schoolmistress who talked like that; and I was mortally afraid of her. But if she is not English what is she?

NEPOMMUCK. Hungarian.

ALL THE REST. Hungarian!

NEPOMMUCK. Hungarian. And of royal blood. I am Hungarian. My blood is royal.

HIGGINS. Did you speak to her in Hungarian?

NEPOMMUCK. I did. She was very clever. She said "Please speak to me in English: I do not understand French." French! She pretends not to know the difference between Hungarian and French. Impossible: she knows both.

HIGGINS. And the blood royal? How did you find that out?

NEPOMMUCK. Instinct, maestro, instinct. Only the Magyar races can produce that air of the divine right, those resolute eyes. She is a princess.

HOST. What do you say, Professor?

HIGGINS. I say an ordinary London girl out of the gutter and taught to speak by an expert. I place her in Drury Lane.

NEPOMMUCK. Ha ha ha! Oh, maestro, maestro, you are mad on the subject of cockney dialects. The London gutter is the whole world for you.

HIGGINS *[to the Hostess]* What does your Excellency say?

HOSTESS. Oh, of course I agree with Nepommuck. She must be a princess at least.

HOST. Not necessarily legitimate, of course. Morganatic perhaps. But that is undoubtedly her class.

HIGGINS. I stick to my opinion.

HOSTESS. Oh, you are incorrigible.

The group breaks up, leaving Higgins isolated. Pickering joins him.

PICKERING. Where is Eliza? We must keep an eye on her.

Eliza joins them.

LIZA. I don't think I can bear much more. The people all stare at me. An old lady just told me I speak exactly like Queen Victoria. I am sorry I have lost your bet. I have done my best; but nothing can make me the same as these people.

PICKERING. You have not lost it, my dear. You have won it ten times over.

HIGGINS. Let us get out of this. I have had enough of chattering to these fools.

PICKERING. Eliza is tired; and I am hungry. Let us clear out and have supper somewhere.

ACT IV

The Wimpole Street laboratory, midnight. Nobody in the room. The clock on the mantelpiece strikes twelve. The fire is not alight: it is a summer night.

Presently Higgins and Pickering are heard on the stairs.

HIGGINS *[calling down to Pickering]* I say, Pick: lock up, will you. I shan't be going out again.

PICKERING. Right. Can Mrs. Pearce go to bed? We don't want anything more, do we?

HIGGINS. Lord, no!

Eliza opens the door and is seen on the lighted landing in opera cloak, brilliant evening dress, and diamonds, with fan, flowers, and all accessories. She comes to the hearth, and switches on the electric lights there. She is tired: her pallor contrasts strongly with her dark eyes and hair; and her expression is almost tragic. She takes off her cloak; puts her fan and flowers on the piano; and sits down on the bench, brooding and silent. Higgins, in evening dress, with overcoat and hat, comes in, carrying a smoking jacket which he has picked up downstairs. He takes off the hat and overcoat; throws them carelessly on the newspaper stand; disposes of his coat in the same way; puts on the smoking jacket; and throws himself wearily into the easy-chair at the hearth. Pickering, similarly attired, comes in. He also takes off his hat and overcoat, and is about to throw them on Higgins' when he hesitates.

PICKERING. I say: Mrs. Pearce will row if we leave these things lying about in the drawing-room.

HIGGINS. Oh, chuck them over the bannisters into the hall. She'll find them there in the morning and put them away all right. She'll think we were drunk.

PICKERING. We are, slightly. Are there any letters?

HIGGINS. I didn't look. *[Pickering takes the overcoats and hats and goes down stairs. Higgins begins half singing, half yawning an air from* La Fanciulla del Golden West. *Suddenly he stops and exclaims]* I wonder where the devil my slippers are!

Eliza looks at him darkly; then rises suddenly and leaves the room.

Higgins yawns again, and resumes his song.

Pickering returns, with the contents of the letter-box in his hand.

PICKERING. Only circulars, and this coroneted billet-doux for you. *[He throws the circulars into the fender, and posts himself on the hearthrug, with his back to the grate.]*

HIGGINS *[glancing at the billet-doux]* Money-lender. *[He throws the letter after the circulars].*

[Eliza returns with a pair of large down-at-heel slippers. She places them on the carpet before Higgins, and sits as before without a word.]

HIGGINS *[yawning again]* Oh Lord! What an evening! What a crew! What a silly tomfoolery! *[He raises his shoe to unlace it, and catches sight of the slippers. He stops unlacing and looks at them as if they had appeared there of their own accord.]* Oh! they're there, are they?

PICKERING *[stretching himself]* Well, I feel a bit tired. It's been a long day. The garden party, a dinner party, and the opera! Rather too much of a good thing. But you've won your bet, Higgins. Eliza did the trick, and something to spare, eh?

HIGGINS *[fervently]* Thank God it's over!

Eliza flinches violently; but they take no notice of her; and she recovers herself and sits stonily as before.

PICKERING. Were you nervous at the garden party? I was. Eliza didn't seem a bit nervous.

HIGGINS. Oh, she wasn't nervous. I knew she'd be all right. No: it's the strain of putting the job through all these months that has told on me. It was interesting enough at first, while we were at the phonetics; but after that I got deadly sick of it. If I hadn't backed myself to do it I should have chucked the whole thing up two months ago. It was a silly notion: the whole thing has been a bore.

PICKERING. Oh come! the garden party was frightfully exciting. My heart began beating like anything.

HIGGINS. Yes, for the first three minutes. But when I saw we were going to win hands down, I felt like a bear in a cage, hanging about doing nothing. The dinner was worse: sitting gorging there for over an hour, with nobody but a damned fool of a fashionable woman to talk to! I tell you, Pickering, never again for me. No more artificial duchesses. The whole thing has been simple purgatory.

PICKERING. You've never been broken in properly to the social routine. *[Strolling over to the piano]* I rather enjoy dipping into it occasionally myself: it makes me feel young again. Anyhow, it was a great success: an immense success. I was quite frightened once or twice because Eliza was doing it so well. You see, lots of the real people can't do it at all: they're such fools that they think style comes by nature to people in their position; and so they never learn. There's always something professional about doing a thing superlatively well.

HIGGINS. Yes: that's what drives me mad: the silly people don't know their own silly business. *[Rising]* However, it's over and done with; and now I can go to bed at last without dreading tomorrow.

Eliza's beauty becomes murderous.

PICKERING. I think I shall turn in too. Still, it's been a great occasion: a triumph for you. Good-night. *[He goes.]*

HIGGINS *[following him]* Good-night. *[Over his shoulder, at the door]* Put out the lights, Eliza; and tell Mrs. Pearce not to make coffee for me in the morning: I'll take tea. *[He goes out.]*

Eliza tries to control herself and feel indifferent as she rises and walks across to the hearth to switch off the lights. By the time she gets there she is on the point of screaming. She sits down in Higgins's chair and holds on hard to the arms. Finally she gives way and flings herself furiously on the floor, raging.

HIGGINS *[in despairing wrath outside]* What the devil have I done with my slippers? *[He appears at the door.]*

LIZA *[snatching up the slippers, and hurling them at him one after the other with all her force]* There are your slippers. And there. Take your slippers; and may you never have a day's luck with them!

HIGGINS *[astounded]* What on earth—! *[He comes to her.]* What's the matter? Get up. *[He pulls her up.]* Anything wrong?

LIZA *[breathless]* Nothing wrong—with you. I've won your bet for you, haven't I? That's enough for you. I don't matter, I suppose.

HIGGINS. You won my bet! You! Presumptuous insect! I won it. What did you throw those slippers at me for?

LIZA. Because I wanted to smash your face. I'd like to kill you, you selfish brute. Why didn't you leave me where you picked me out of—in the gutter? You thank God it's all over, and that now you can throw me back again there, do you? *[She crisps her fingers frantically.]*

HIGGINS *[looking at her in cool wonder]* The creature is nervous, after all.

LIZA *[gives a suffocated scream of fury, and instinctively darts her nails at his face.]*

HIGGINS *[catching her wrists]* Ah! would you? Claws in, you cat. How dare you shew your temper to me? Sit down and be quiet. *[He throws her roughly into the easy-chair.]*

LIZA *[crushed by superior strength and weight]* What's to become of me? What's to become of me?

HIGGINS. How the devil do I know what's to become of you? What does it matter what becomes of you?

LIZA. You don't care. I know you don't care. You wouldn't care if I was dead. I'm nothing to you—not so much as them slippers.

HIGGINS *[thundering]* Those slippers.

LIZA [with bitter submission] Those slippers. I didn't think it made any difference now.

A pause. Eliza hopeless and crushed. Higgins a little uneasy.

HIGGINS [in his loftiest manner] Why have you begun going on like this? May I ask whether you complain of your treatment here?

LIZA. No.

HIGGINS. Has anybody behaved badly to you? Colonel Pickering? Mrs. Pearce? Any of the servants?

LIZA. No.

HIGGINS. I presume you don't pretend that I have treated you badly.

LIZA. No.

HIGGINS. I am glad to hear it. [He moderates his tone] Perhaps you're tired after the strain of the day. Will you have a glass of champagne? [He moves towards the door.]

LIZA. No. [Recollecting her manners] Thank you.

HIGGINS [good-humored again] This has been coming on you for some days. I suppose it was natural for you to be anxious about the garden party. But that's all over now. [He pats her kindly on the shoulder. She writhes.] There's nothing more to worry about.

LIZA. No. Nothing more for you to worry about. [She suddenly rises and gets away from him by going to the piano bench, where she sits and hides her face.] Oh God! I wish I was dead.

HIGGINS [staring after her in sincere surprise] Why? in heaven's name, why? [Reasonably, going to her] Listen to me, Eliza. All this irritation is purely subjective.

LIZA. I don't understand. I'm too ignorant.

HIGGINS. It's only imagination. Low spirits and nothing else. Nobody's hurting you. Nothing's wrong. You go to bed like a good girl and sleep it off. Have a little cry and say your prayers: that will make you comfortable.

LIZA. I heard your prayers. "Thank God it's all over!"

HIGGINS [impatiently] Well, don't you thank God it's all over? Now you are free and can do what you like.

LIZA [pulling herself together in desperation] What am I fit for? What have you left me fit for? Where am I to go? What am I to do? What's to become of me?

HIGGINS [enlightened, but not at all impressed] Oh, that's what's worrying you, is it? [He thrusts his hands into his pockets, and walks about in his usual manner, rattling the contents of his pockets, as if condescending to a trivial subject out of pure kindness.] I shouldn't bother about it if I were you. I should imagine you won't have much difficulty in settling yourself somewhere or other, though I hadn't quite realized that you were going away. [She looks quickly at him: he does not *look at her, but examines the dessert stand on the piano and decides that he will eat an apple.]* You might marry, you know. *[He bites a large piece out of the apple, and munches it noisily.]* You see, Eliza, all men are not confirmed old bachelors like me and the Colonel. Most men are the marrying sort (poor devils!); and you're not bad-looking; it's quite a pleasure to look at you sometimes—not now, of course, because you're crying and looking as ugly as the very devil; but when you're all right and quite yourself, you're what I should call attractive. That is, to the people in the marrying line, you understand. You go to bed and have a good nice rest; and then get up and look at yourself in the glass; and you won't feel so cheap.

Eliza again looks at him, speechless, and does not stir.

The look is quite lost on him: he eats his apple with a dreamy expression of happiness, as it is quite a good one.

HIGGINS *[a genial afterthought occurring to him]* I daresay my mother could find some chap or other who would do very well.

LIZA. We were above that at the corner of Tottenham Court Road.

HIGGINS *[waking up]* What do you mean?

LIZA. I sold flowers. I didn't sell myself. Now you've made a lady of me I'm not fit to sell anything else. I wish you'd left me where you found me.

HIGGINS *[slinging the core of the apple decisively into the grate]* Tosh, Eliza. Don't you insult human relations by dragging all this cant about buying and selling into it. You needn't marry the fellow if you don't like him.

LIZA. What else am I to do?

HIGGINS. Oh, lots of things. What about your old idea of a florist's shop? Pickering could set you up in one: he's lots of money. *[Chuckling]* He'll have to pay for all those togs you have been wearing today; and that, with the hire of the jewellery, will make a big hole in two hundred pounds. Why, six months ago you would have thought it the millennium to have a flower shop of your own. Come! you'll be all right. I must clear off to bed: I'm devilish sleepy. By the way, I came down for something: I forget what it was.

LIZA. Your slippers.

HIGGINS. Oh yes, of course. You shied them at me. *[He picks them up, and is going out when she rises and speaks to him.]*

LIZA. Before you go, sir—

HIGGINS *[dropping the slippers in his surprise at her calling him Sir]* Eh?

LIZA. Do my clothes belong to me or to Colonel Pickering?

HIGGINS *[coming back into the room as if her question were the very climax of unreason]* What the devil use would they be to Pickering?

LIZA. He might want them for the next girl you pick up to experiment on.

HIGGINS *[shocked and hurt]* Is that the way you feel towards us?

LIZA. I don't want to hear anything more about that. All I want to know is whether anything belongs to me. My own clothes were burnt.

HIGGINS. But what does it matter? Why need you start bothering about that in the middle of the night?

LIZA. I want to know what I may take away with me. I don't want to be accused of stealing.

HIGGINS *[now deeply wounded]* Stealing! You shouldn't have said that, Eliza. That shews a want of feeling.

LIZA. I'm sorry. I'm only a common ignorant girl; and in my station I have to be careful. There can't be any feelings between the like of you and the like of me. Please will you tell me what belongs to me and what doesn't?

HIGGINS *[very sulky]* You may take the whole damned houseful if you like. Except the jewels. They're hired. Will that satisfy you? *[He turns on his heel and is about to go in extreme dudgeon.]*

LIZA *[drinking in his emotion like nectar, and nagging him to provoke a further supply]* Stop, please. *[She takes off her jewels.]* Will you take these to your room and keep them safe? I don't want to run the risk of their being missing.

HIGGINS *[furious]* Hand them over. *[She puts them into his hands.]* If these belonged to me instead of to the jeweler, I'd ram them down your ungrateful throat. *[He perfunctorily thrusts them into his pockets, unconsciously decorating himself with the protruding ends of the chains.]*

LIZA *[taking a ring off]* This ring isn't the jewelers: it's the one you bought me in Brighton. I don't want it now. *[Higgins dashes the ring violently into the fireplace, and turns on her so threateningly that she crouches over the piano with her hands over her face, and exclaims]* Don't you hit me.

HIGGINS. Hit you! You infamous creature, how dare you accuse me of such a thing? It is you who have hit me. You have wounded me to the heart.

LIZA *[thrilling with hidden joy]* I'm glad. I've got a little of my own back, anyhow.

HIGGINS *[with dignity, in his finest professional style]* You have caused me to lose my temper: a thing that has hardly ever happened to me before. I prefer to say nothing more tonight. I am going to bed.

LIZA *[pertly]* You'd better leave a note for Mrs. Pearce about the coffee; for she won't be told by me.

HIGGINS *[formally]* Damn Mrs. Pearce; and damn the coffee; and damn you; and damn my own folly in having lavished hard-earned knowledge and the treasure of my regard and intimacy on a heartless guttersnipe.

[*He goes out with impressive decorum, and spoils it by slamming the door savagely.*]

Eliza goes down on her knees on the hearthrug to look for the ring. When she finds it she considers for a moment what to do with it. Finally she flings it down on the dessert stand and goes upstairs in a tearing rage.

[*Eliza goes to her room, changes her clothes, puts on some walking shoes, takes her vanity bag, and walks out of the house.*

[*Outside she meets lovesick Freddy, who has been gazing at Eliza's second floor room. They kiss and ride around town together in a taxi for the rest of the night. In the morning Eliza goes to Mrs. Higgins's house. Eds.*]

ACT V

Mrs. Higgins's drawing-room. She is at her writing-table as before. The parlor-maid comes in.

THE PARLOR-MAID [*at the door*] Mr. Henry, ma'am, is downstairs with Colonel Pickering.

MRS. HIGGINS. Well, shew them up.

THE PARLOR-MAID. They're using the telephone, ma'am. Telephoning to the police, I think.

MRS. HIGGINS. What!

THE PARLOR-MAID [*coming further in and lowering her voice*] Mr. Henry's in a state, ma'am. I thought I'd better tell you.

MRS. HIGGINS. If you had told me that Mr. Henry was not in a state it would have been more surprising. Tell them to come up when they've finished with the police. I suppose he's lost something.

THE PARLOR-MAID. Yes, ma'am [*going*].

MRS. HIGGINS. Go upstairs and tell Miss Doolittle that Mr. Henry and the Colonel are here. Ask her not to come down till I send for her.

THE PARLOR-MAID. Yes, ma'am.

Higgins bursts in. He is, as the parlor-maid has said, in a state.

HIGGINS. Look here, mother: here's a confounded thing!

MRS. HIGGINS. Yes, dear. Good-morning. [*He checks his impatience and kisses her, whilst the parlor-maid goes out.*] What is it?

HIGGINS. Eliza's bolted.

MRS. HIGGINS [*calmly continuing her writing*] You must have frightened her.

HIGGINS. Frightened her! nonsense! She was left last night, as usual, to turn out the lights and all that; and instead of going to bed she changed her clothes and went right off: her bed wasn't slept in. She came in a cab for her things before seven this morning; and that fool Mrs. Pearce let her have them without telling me a word about it. What am I to do?

MRS. HIGGINS. Do without, I'm afraid, Henry. The girl has a perfect right to leave if she chooses.

HIGGINS *[wandering distractedly across the room]* But I can't find anything. I don't know what appointments I've got. I'm—*[Pickering comes in. Mrs. Higgins puts down her pen and turns away from the writing-table.]*

PICKERING *[shaking hands]* Good-morning, Mrs. Higgins. Has Henry told you? *[He sits down on the ottoman.]*

HIGGINS. What does that ass of an inspector say? Have you offered a reward?

MRS. HIGGINS *[rising in indignant amazement]* You don't mean to say you have set the police after Eliza?

HIGGINS. Of course. What are the police for? What else could we do? *[He sits in the Elizabethan chair.]*

PICKERING. The inspector made a lot of difficulties. I really think he suspected us of some improper purpose.

MRS. HIGGINS. Well, of course he did. What right have you to go to the police and give the girl's name as if she were a thief, or a lost umbrella, or something? Really! *[She sits down again, deeply vexed.]*

HIGGINS. But we want to find her.

PICKERING. We can't let her go like this, you know, Mrs. Higgins. What were we to do?

MRS. HIGGINS. You have no more sense, either of you, than two children. Why—

The parlor-maid comes in and breaks off the conversation.

THE PARLOR-MAID. Mr. Henry: a gentleman wants to see you very particular. He's been sent on from Wimpole Street.

HIGGINS. Oh, bother! I can't see anyone now. Who is it?

THE PARLOR-MAID. A Mr. Doolittle, sir.

PICKERING. Doolittle! Do you mean the dustman?

THE PARLOR-MAID. Dustman! Oh no, sir: a gentleman.

HIGGINS *[springing up excitedly]* By George, Pick, it's some relative of hers that she's gone to. Somebody we know nothing about. *[To the parlor-maid]* Send him up, quick.

THE PARLOR-MAID. Yes, sir *[She goes]*.

HIGGINS *[eagerly, going to his mother]* Genteel relatives! now we shall hear something. *[He sits down in the Chippendale chair.]*

MRS. HIGGINS. Do you know any of her people?

PICKERING. Only her father: the fellow we told you about.

THE PARLOR-MAID *[announcing]* Mr. Doolittle. *[She withdraws.]*

Doolittle enters. He is brilliantly dressed in a new fashionable frock-coat, with white waistcoat and grey trousers. A flower in his buttonhole, a dazzling silk hat, and patent leather shoes complete the effect. He is too concerned with the business he has come on to notice Mrs. Higgins. He walks straight to Higgins, and accosts him with vehement reproach.

DOOLITTLE *[indicating his own person]* See here! Do you see this? You done this.

HIGGINS. Done what, man?

DOOLITTLE. This, I tell you. Look at it. Look at this hat. Look at this coat.

PICKERING. Has Eliza been buying you clothes?

DOOLITTLE. Eliza! not she. Not half. Why would she buy me clothes?

MRS. HIGGINS. Good-morning, Mr. Doolittle. Won't you sit down?

DOOLITTLE *[taken aback as he becomes conscious that he has forgotten his hostess]* Asking your pardon, ma'am. *[He approaches her and shakes her proffered hand]*. Thank you. *[He sits down on the ottoman, on Pickering's right.]* I am that full of what has happened to me that I can't think of anything else.

HIGGINS. What the dickens has happened to you?

DOOLITTLE. I shouldn't mind if it had only happened to me: anything might happen to anybody and nobody to blame but Providence, as you might say. But this is something that you done to me: yes, you, Henry Higgins.

HIGGINS. Have you found Eliza? That's the point.

DOOLITTLE. Have you lost her?

HIGGINS. Yes.

DOOLITTLE. You have all the luck, you have. I ain't found her; but she'll find me quick enough now after what you done to me.

MRS. HIGGINS. But what has my son done to you, Mr. Doolittle?

DOOLITTLE. Done to me! Ruined me. Destroyed my happiness. Tied me up and delivered me into the hands of middle class morality.

HIGGINS *[rising intolerantly and standing over Doolittle]* You're raving. You're drunk. You're mad. I gave you five pounds. After that I had two conversations with you, at half-a-crown an hour. I've never seen you since.

DOOLITTLE. Oh! Drunk! am I? Mad! am I? Tell me this. Did you or did you not write a letter to an old blighter in America that was giving five millions to found Moral Reform Societies all over the world, and that wanted you to invent a universal language for him?

HIGGINS. What! Ezra D. Wannafeller! He's dead. *[He sits down again carelessly.]*

DOOLITTLE. Yes: he's dead; and I'm done for. Now did you or did you not write a letter to him to say that the most original moralist at present in England, to the best of your knowledge, was Alfred Doolittle, a common dustman.

HIGGINS. Oh, after your last visit I remember making some silly joke of the kind.

DOOLITTLE. Ah! you may well call it a silly joke. It put the lid on me right enough. Just give him the chance he wanted to shew that Americans is not like us: that they recognize and respect merit in every class of life, however humble. Them words is in his blooming will, in which, Henry Higgins, thanks to your silly joking, he leaves me a share in his Pre-digested Cheese Trust worth three thousand a year on condition that I lecture for his Wannafeller Moral Reform World League as often as they ask me up to six times a year.

HIGGINS. The devil he does! Whew! *[Brightening suddenly]* What a lark!

PICKERING. A safe thing for you, Doolittle. They won't ask you twice.

DOOLITTLE. It ain't the lecturing I mind. I'll lecture them blue in the face, I will, and not turn a hair. It's making a gentleman of me that I object to. Who asked him to make a gentleman of me? I was happy. I was free. I touched pretty nigh everybody for money when I wanted it, same as I touched you, Henry Higgins. Now I am worrited; tied neck and heels; and everybody touches me for money. It's a fine thing for you, says my solicitor. Is it? says I. You mean it's a good thing for you, I says. When I was a poor man and had a solicitor once when they found a pram in the dust cart, he got me off, and got shut of me and got me shut of him as quick as he could. Same with the doctors: used to shove me out of the hospital before I could hardly stand on my legs, and nothing to pay. Now they finds out that I'm not a healthy man and can't live unless they looks after me twice a day. In the house I'm not let do a hand's turn for myself: somebody else must do it and touch me for it. A year ago I hadn't a relative in the world except two or three that wouldn't speak to me. Now I've fifty, and not a decent weeks wages among the lot of them. I have to live for others and not for myself: that's middle class morality. You talk of losing Eliza. Don't you be anxious: I bet she's on my doorstep by this: she that could support herself easy by selling flowers if I wasn't respectable. And the next one to touch me will be you, Henry Higgins. I'll have to learn to speak middle class language from you, instead of speaking proper English. That's where you'll come in; and I daresay that's what you done it for.

MRS. HIGGINS. But, my dear Mr. Doolittle, you need not suffer all this if you are really in earnest. Nobody can force you to accept this bequest. You can repudiate it. Isn't that so, Colonel Pickering?

PICKERING. I believe so.

DOOLITTLE *[softening his manner in deference to her sex]* That's the tragedy of it, ma'am. It's easy to say chuck it; but I haven't the nerve.

Which of us has? We're all intimidated. Intimidated, ma'am: that's what we are. What is there for me if I chuck it but the workhouse in my old age? I have to dye my hair already to keep my job as a dustman. If I was one of the deserving poor, and had put by a bit, I could chuck it; but then why should I, acause the deserving poor might as well be millionaires for all the happiness they ever has. They don't know what happiness is. But I, as one of the undeserving poor, have nothing between me and the pauper's uniform but this here blasted three thousand a year that shoves me into the middle class. (Excuse the expression, ma'am: you'd use it yourself if you had my provocation.) They've got you every way you turn: it's a choice between the Skilly of the workhouse and the Char Bydis of the middle class; and I haven't the nerve for the workhouse. Intimidated: that's what I am. Broke. Bought up. Happier men than me will call for my dust, and touch me for their tip; and I'll look on helpless, and envy them. And that's what your son has brought me to. *[He is overcome by emotion.]*

MRS. HIGGINS. Well, I'm very glad you're not going to do anything foolish, Mr. Doolittle. For this solves the problem of Eliza's future. You can provide for her now.

DOOLITTLE *[with melancholy resignation]* Yes, ma'am: I'm expected to provide for everyone now, out of three thousand a year.

HIGGINS *[jumping up]* Nonsense! he can't provide for her. He shan't provide for her. She doesn't belong to him. I paid him five pounds for her. Doolittle: either you're an honest man or a rogue.

DOOLITTLE *[tolerantly]* A little of both, Henry, like the rest of us: a little of both.

HIGGINS. Well, you took that money for the girl; and you have no right to take her as well.

MRS. HIGGINS. Henry: don't be absurd. If you really want to know where Eliza is, she is upstairs.

HIGGINS *[amazed]* Upstairs!!! Then I shall jolly soon fetch her downstairs. *[He makes resolutely for the door.]*

MRS. HIGGINS *[rising and following him]* Be quiet, Henry. Sit down.

HIGGINS. I—

MRS. HIGGINS. Sit down, dear; and listen to me.

HIGGINS. Oh very well, very well, very well. *[He throws himself ungraciously on the ottoman, with his face towards the windows.]* But I think you might have told me this half an hour ago.

MRS. HIGGINS. Eliza came to me this morning. She passed the night partly walking about in a rage, partly trying to throw herself into the river and being afraid to, and partly in the Carlton Hotel. She told me of the brutal way you two treated her.

HIGGINS *[bounding up again]* What!

PICKERING [*rising also*] My dear Mrs. Higgins, she's been telling you stories. We didn't treat her brutally. We hardly said a word to her; and we parted on particularly good terms. [*Turning on Higgins.*] Higgins, did you bully her after I went to bed?

HIGGINS. Just the other way about. She threw my slippers in my face. She behaved in the most outrageous way. I never gave her the slightest provocation. The slippers came bang into my face the moment I entered the room—before I had uttered a word. And used perfectly awful language.

PICKERING [*astonished*] But why? What did we do to her?

MRS. HIGGINS. I think I know pretty well what you did. The girl is naturally rather affectionate, I think. Isn't she, Mr. Doolittle?

DOOLITTLE. Very tender-hearted, ma'am. Takes after me.

MRS. HIGGINS. Just so. She had become attached to you both. She worked very hard for you, Henry! I don't think you quite realize what anything in the nature of brain work means to a girl like that. Well, it seems that when the great day of trial came, and she did this wonderful thing for you without making a single mistake, you two sat there and never said a word to her, but talked together of how glad you were that it was all over and how you had been bored with the whole thing. And then you were surprised because she threw your slippers at you! I should have thrown the fire-irons at you.

HIGGINS. We said nothing except that we were tired and wanted to go to bed. Did we, Pick?

PICKERING [*shrugging his shoulders*] That was all.

MRS. HIGGINS [*ironically*] Quite sure?

PICKERING. Absolutely. Really, that was all.

MRS. HIGGINS. You didn't thank her, or pet her, or admire her, or tell her how splendid she'd been.

HIGGINS [*impatiently*] But she knew all about that. We didn't make speeches to her, if that's what you mean.

PICKERING [*conscience stricken*] Perhaps we were a little inconsiderate. Is she very angry?

MRS. HIGGINS [*returning to her place at the writing-table*] Well, I'm afraid she won't go back to Wimpole Street, especially now that Mr. Doolittle is able to keep up the position you have thrust on her; but she says she is quite willing to meet you on friendly terms and to let bygones be bygones.

HIGGINS [*furious*] Is she, by George? Ho!

MRS. HIGGINS. If you promise to behave yourself, Henry, I'll ask her to come down. If not, go home; for you have taken up quite enough of my time.

HIGGINS. Oh, all right. Very well. Pick: you behave yourself. Let us put on our best Sunday manners for this creature that we picked out of the mud. *[He flings himself sulkily into the Elizabethan chair.]*

DOOLITTLE *[remonstrating]* Now, now, Henry Higgins! have some consideration for my feelings as a middle class man.

MRS. HIGGINS. Remember your promise, Henry. *[She presses the bell-button on the writing-table.]* Mr. Doolittle: will you be so good as to step out on the balcony for a moment. I don't want Eliza to have the shock of your news until she has made it up with these two gentlemen. Would you mind?

DOOLITTLE. As you wish, lady. Anything to help Henry to keep her off my hands. *[He disappears through the window.]*

The parlor-maid answers the bell. Pickering sits down in Doolittle's place.

MRS. HIGGINS. Ask Miss Doolittle to come down, please.

THE PARLOR-MAID. Yes, ma'am. *[She goes out].*

MRS. HIGGINS. Now, Henry: be good.

HIGGINS. I am behaving myself perfectly.

PICKERING. He is doing his best, Mrs. Higgins.

A pause. Higgins throws back his head; stretches out his legs; and begins to whistle.

MRS. HIGGINS. Henry, dearest, you don't look at all nice in that attitude.

HIGGINS *[pulling himself together]* I was not trying to look nice, mother.

MRS. HIGGINS. It doesn't matter, dear. I only wanted to make you speak.

HIGGINS. Why?

MRS. HIGGINS. Because you can't speak and whistle at the same time.

Higgins groans. Another very trying pause.

HIGGINS *[springing up, out of patience]* Where the devil is that girl? Are we to wait here all day?

Eliza enters, sunny, self-possessed, and giving a staggeringly convincing exhibition of ease of manner. She carries a little work-basket, and is very much at home. Pickering is too much taken aback to rise.

LIZA. How do you do, Professor Higgins? Are you quite well?

HIGGINS *[choking]* Am I— *[He can say no more].*

LIZA. But of course you are: you are never ill. So glad to see you again, Colonel Pickering. *[He rises hastily; and they shake hands.]* Quite chilly this morning, isn't it? *[She sits down on his left. He sits beside her.]*

HIGGINS. Don't you dare try this game on me. I taught it to you; and it doesn't take me in. Get up and come home; and don't be a fool.

Eliza takes a piece of needlework from her basket, and begins to stitch at it, without taking the least notice of this outburst.

MRS. HIGGINS. Very nicely put, indeed, Henry. No woman could resist such an invitation.

HIGGINS. You let her alone, mother. Let her speak for herself. You will jolly soon see whether she has an idea that I haven't put into her head or a word that I haven't put into her mouth. I tell you I have created this thing out of the squashed cabbage leaves of Covent Garden; and now she pretends to play the fine lady with me.

MRS. HIGGINS *[placidly]* Yes, dear; but you'll sit down, won't you?

Higgins sits down again, savagely.

LIZA *[to Pickering, taking no apparent notice of Higgins, and working away deftly]* Will you drop me altogether now that the experiment is over, Colonel Pickering?

PICKERING. Oh don't. You mustn't think of it as an experiment. It shocks me, somehow.

LIZA. Oh, I'm only a squashed cabbage leaf—

PICKERING *[impulsively]* No.

LIZA *[continuing quietly]*—but I owe so much to you that I should be very unhappy if you forgot me.

PICKERING. It's very kind of you to say so, Miss Doolittle.

LIZA. It's not because you paid for my dresses. I know you are generous to everybody with money. But it was from you that I learnt really nice manners; and that is what makes one a lady, isn't it? You see it was so very difficult for me with the example of Professor Higgins always before me. I was brought up to be just like him, unable to control myself, and using bad language on the slightest provocation. And I should never have known that ladies and gentlemen didn't behave like that if you hadn't been there.

HIGGINS. Well!!

PICKERING. Oh, that's only his way, you know. He doesn't mean it.

LIZA. Oh, I didn't mean it either, when I was a flower girl. It was only my way. But you see I did it; and that's what makes the difference after all.

PICKERING. No doubt. Still, he taught you to speak; and I couldn't have done that, you know.

LIZA *[trivially]* Of course: that is his profession.

HIGGINS. Damnation!

LIZA *[continuing]* It was just like learning to dance in the fashionable way: there was nothing more than that in it. But do you know what began my real education?

PICKERING. What?

LIZA *[stopping her work for a moment]* Your calling me Miss Doolittle that day when I first came to Wimpole Street. That was the beginning of self-respect for me. *[She resumes her stitching.]* And there were a hundred little things you never noticed, because they came naturally to you. Things about standing up and taking off your hat and opening the door—

PICKERING. Oh, that was nothing.

LIZA. Yes: things that shewed you thought and felt about me as if I were something better than a scullery-maid; though of course I know you would have been just the same to a scullery-maid if she had been let in the drawing-room. You never took off your boots in the dining room when I was there.

PICKERING. You mustn't mind that. Higgins takes off his boots all over the place.

LIZA. I know. I am not blaming him. It is his way, isn't it? But it made such a difference to me that you didn't do it. You see, really and truly, apart from the things anyone can pick up (the dressing and the proper way of speaking, and so on), the difference between a lady and a flower girl is not how she behaves, but how she's treated. I shall always be a flower girl to Professor Higgins, because he always treats me as a flower girl, and always will; but I know I can be a lady to you, because you always treat me as a lady, and always will.

MRS. HIGGINS. Please don't grind your teeth, Henry.

PICKERING. Well, this is really very nice of you, Miss Doolittle.

LIZA. I should like you to call me Eliza, now, if you would.

PICKERING. Thank you. Eliza, of course.

LIZA. And I should like Professor Higgins to call me Miss Doolittle.

HIGGINS. I'll see you damned first.

MRS. HIGGINS. Henry! Henry!

PICKERING *[laughing]* Why don't you slang back at him? Don't stand it. It would do him a lot of good.

LIZA. I can't. I could have done it once; but now I can't go back to it. Last night, when I was wandering about, a girl spoke to me; and I tried to get back into the old way with her; but it was no use. You told me, you know, that when a child is brought to a foreign country, it picks up the language in a few weeks, and forgets its own. Well, I am a child in your country. I have forgotten my own language, and can speak nothing but yours. That's the real break-off with the corner of Tottenham Court Road. Leaving Wimpole Street finishes it.

PICKERING *[much alarmed]* Oh! but you're coming back to Wimpole Street, aren't you? You'll forgive Higgins?

HIGGINS *[rising]* Forgive! Will she, by George! Let her go. Let her find out how she can get on without us. She will relapse into the gutter in three weeks without me at her elbow.

Doolittle appears at the centre window. With a look of dignified reproach at Higgins, he comes slowly and silently to his daughter, who, with her back to the window, is unconscious of his approach.

PICKERING. He's incorrigible, Eliza. You won't relapse, will you?

LIZA. No: Not now. Never again. I have learnt my lesson. I don't believe I could utter one of the old sounds if I tried. *[Doolittle touches her on her left shoulder. She drops her work, losing her self-possession utterly at the spectacle of her father's splendor]* A-a-a-a-a-ah-ow-ooh!

HIGGINS *[with a crow of triumph]* Aha! Just so. A-a-a-a-ahowooh! A-a-a-a-ahowooh! A-a-a-a-ahowooh! Victory! Victory! *[He throws himself on the divan, folding his arms, and spraddling arrogantly.]*

DOOLITTLE. Can you blame the girl? Don't look at me like that, Eliza. It ain't my fault. I've come into some money.

LIZA. You must have touched a millionaire this time, dad.

DOOLITTLE. I have. But I'm dressed something special today. I'm going to St. George's, Hanover Square. Your stepmother is going to marry me.

LIZA *[angrily]* You're going to let yourself down to marry that low common woman!

PICKERING *[quietly]* He ought to, Eliza. *[To Doolittle]* Why has she changed her mind?

DOOLITTLE *[sadly]* Intimidated, Governor. Intimidated. Middle class morality claims its victim. Won't you put on your hat, Liza, and come and see me turned off?

LIZA. If the Colonel says I must, I—I'll *[almost sobbing]* I'll demean myself. And get insulted for my pains, like enough.

DOOLITTLE. Don't be afraid: she never comes to words with anyone now, poor woman! respectability has broke all the spirit out of her.

PICKERING *[squeezing Eliza's elbow gently]* Be kind to them, Eliza. Make the best of it.

LIZA *[forcing a little smile for him through her vexation]* Oh well, just to shew there's no ill feeling. I'll be back in a moment. *[She goes out.]*

DOOLITTLE *[sitting down beside Pickering]* I feel uncommon nervous about the ceremony, Colonel. I wish you'd come and see me through it.

PICKERING. But you've been through it before, man. You were married to Eliza's mother.

DOOLITTLE. Who told you that, Colonel?

PICKERING. Well, nobody told me. But I concluded—naturally—

DOOLITTLE. No: that ain't the natural way, Colonel: it's only the middle class way. My way was always the undeserving way. But don't say nothing to Eliza. She don't know: I always had a delicacy about telling her.

PICKERING. Quite right. We'll leave it so, if you don't mind.

DOOLITTLE. And you'll come to the church, Colonel, and put me through straight?

PICKERING. With pleasure. As far as a bachelor can.

MRS. HIGGINS. May I come, Mr. Doolittle? I should be very sorry to miss your wedding.

DOOLITTLE. I should indeed be honored by your condescension, ma'am; and my poor old woman would take it as a tremenjous compliment. She's been very low, thinking of the happy days that are no more.

MRS. HIGGINS *[rising]* I'll order the carriage and get ready. *[The men rise, except Higgins.]* I shan't be more than fifteen minutes. *[As she goes to the door Eliza comes in, hatted and buttoning her gloves.]* I'm going to the church to see your father married, Eliza. You had better come in the brougham with me. Colonel Pickering can go on with the bridegroom.

Mrs. Higgins goes out. Eliza comes to the middle of the room between the centre window and the ottoman. Pickering joins her.

DOOLITTLE. Bridegroom! What a word! It makes a man realize his position, somehow. *[He takes up his hat and goes towards the door.]*

PICKERING. Before I go, Eliza, do forgive him and come back to us.

LIZA. I don't think papa would allow me. Would you, dad?

DOOLITTLE *[sad but magnanimous]* They played you off very cunning, Eliza, them two sportsmen. If it had been only one of them, you could have nailed him. But you see, there was two; and one of them chaperoned the other, as you might say. *[To Pickering]* It was artful of you, Colonel; but I bear no malice: I should have done the same myself. I been the victim of one woman after another all my life; and I don't grudge you two getting the better of Eliza. I shan't interfere. It's time for us to go, Colonel. So long, Henry. See you in St. George's, Eliza. *[He goes out.]*

PICKERING *[coaxing]* Do stay with us, Eliza. *[He follows Doolittle.]*

Eliza goes out on the balcony to avoid being alone with Higgins. He rises and joins her there. She immediately comes back into the room and makes for the door; but he goes along the balcony quickly and gets his back to the door before she reaches it.

HIGGINS. Well, Eliza, you've had a bit of your own back, as you call it. Have you had enough? and are you going to be reasonable? Or do you want any more?

LIZA. You want me back only to pick up your slippers and put up with your tempers and fetch and carry for you.

HIGGINS. I haven't said I wanted you back at all.

LIZA. Oh, indeed. Then what are we talking about?

HIGGINS. About you, not about me. If you come back I shall treat you just as I have always treated you. I can't change my nature; and I don't intend to change my manners. My manners are exactly the same as Colonel Pickering's.

LIZA. That's not true. He treats a flower girl as if she was a duchess.

HIGGINS. And I treat a duchess as if she was a flower girl.

LIZA. I see. *[She turns away composedly, and sits on the ottoman, facing the window.]* The same to everybody.

HIGGINS. Just so.

LIZA. Like father.

HIGGINS *[grinning, a little taken down]* Without accepting the comparison at all points, Eliza, it's quite true that your father is not a snob, and that he will be quite at home in any station of life to which his eccentric destiny may call him. *[Seriously]* The great secret, Eliza, is not having bad manners or good manners or any other particular sort of manners, but having the same manner for all human souls: in short, behaving as if you were in Heaven, where there are no third-class carriages, and one soul is as good as another.

LIZA. Amen. You are a born preacher.

HIGGINS *[irritated]* The question is not whether I treat you rudely, but whether you ever heard me treat anyone else better.

LIZA *[with sudden sincerity]* I don't care how you treat me. I don't mind your swearing at me. I don't mind a black eye: I've had one before this. But *[standing up and facing him]* I won't be passed over.

HIGGINS. Then get out of my way; for I won't stop for you. You talk about me as if I were a motor bus.

LIZA. So you are a motor bus: all bounce and go, and no consideration for anyone. But I can do without you: don't think I can't.

HIGGINS. I know you can. I told you you could.

LIZA *[wounded, getting away from him to the other side of the ottoman with her face to the hearth]* I know you did, you brute. You wanted to get rid of me.

HIGGINS. Liar.

LIZA. Thank you. *[She sits down with dignity.]*

HIGGINS. You never asked yourself, I suppose, whether I could do without you.

LIZA *[earnestly]* Don't you try to get round me. You'll have to do without me.

HIGGINS *[arrogant]* I can do without anybody. I have my own soul: my own spark of divine fire. But *[with sudden humility]* I shall miss you, Eliza. *[He sits down near her on the ottoman.]* I have learnt something from your idiotic notions: I confess that humbly and gratefully. And I have grown accustomed to your voice and appearance. I like them, rather.

LIZA. Well, you have both of them on your gramophone and in your book of photographs. When you feel lonely without me, you can turn the machine on. It's got no feelings to hurt.

HIGGINS. I can't turn your soul on. Leave me those feelings; and you can take away the voice and the face. They are not you.

LIZA. Oh, you are a devil. You can twist the heart in a girl as easy as some could twist her arms to hurt her. Mrs. Pearce warned me. Time and again she has wanted to leave you; and you always got round her at the last minute. And you don't care a bit for her. And you don't care a bit for me.

HIGGINS. I care for life, for humanity; and you are a part of it that has come my way and been built into my house. What more can you or anyone ask?

LIZA. I won't care for anybody that doesn't care for me.

HIGGINS. Commercial principles, Eliza. Like [reproducing her Covent Garden pronunciation with professional exactness] s'yollin voylets, isn't it?

LIZA. Don't sneer at me. It's mean to sneer at me.

HIGGINS. I have never sneered in my life. Sneering doesn't become either the human face or the human soul. I am expressing my righteous contempt for commercialism. I don't and won't trade in affection. You call me a brute because you couldn't buy a claim on me by fetching my slippers and finding my spectacles. You were a fool: I think a woman fetching a mans slippers is a disgusting sight: did I ever fetch your slippers? I think a good deal more of you for throwing them in my face. No use slaving for me and then saying you want to be cared for: who cares for a slave? If you come back, come back for the sake of good fellowship; for you'll get nothing else. You've had a thousand times as much out of me as I have out of you; and if you dare to set up your little dogs tricks of fetching and carrying slippers against my creation of a Duchess Eliza, I'll slam the door in your silly face.

LIZA. What did you do it for if you didn't care for me?

HIGGINS [heartily] Why, because it was my job.

LIZA. You never thought of the trouble it would make for me.

HIGGINS. Would the world ever have been made if its maker had been afraid of making trouble? Making life means making trouble. There's only one way of escaping trouble; and that's killing things. Cowards, you notice, are always shrieking to have troublesome people killed.

LIZA. I'm no preacher: I don't notice things like that. I notice that you don't notice me.

HIGGINS *[jumping up and walking about intolerantly]* Eliza: you're an idiot. I waste the treasures of my Miltonic mind by spreading them before you. Once for all, understand that I go my way and do my work without caring twopence what happens to either of us. I am not intimidated, like your father and your stepmother. So you can come back or go to the devil: which you please.

LIZA. What am I to come back for?

HIGGINS *[bouncing up on his knees on the ottoman and leaning over it to her]* For the fun of it. That's why I took you on.

LIZA *[with averted face]* And you may throw me out tomorrow if I don't do everything you want me to?

HIGGINS. Yes; and you may walk out tomorrow if I don't do everything you want me to.

LIZA. And live with my stepmother?

HIGGINS. Yes, or sell flowers.

LIZA. Oh! if I only could go back to my flower basket! I should be independent of both you and father and all the world! Why did you take my independence from me? Why did I give it up? I'm a slave now, for all my fine clothes.

HIGGINS. Not a bit. I'll adopt you as my daughter and settle money on you if you like. Or would you rather marry Pickering?

LIZA *[looking fiercely round at him]* I wouldn't marry you if you asked me; and you're nearer my age than what he is.

HIGGINS *[gently]* Than he is: not "than what he is."

LIZA *[losing her temper and rising]* I'll talk as I like. You're not my teacher now.

HIGGINS *[reflectively]* I don't suppose Pickering would, though. He's as confirmed an old bachelor as I am.

LIZA. That's not what I want; and don't you think it. I've always had chaps enough wanting me that way. Freddy Hill writes to me twice and three times a day, sheets and sheets.

HIGGINS *[disagreeably surprised]* Damn his impudence! *[He recoils and finds himself sitting on his heels.]*

LIZA. He has a right to if he likes, poor lad. And he does love me.

HIGGINS *[getting off the ottoman]* You have no right to encourage him.

LIZA. Every girl has a right to be loved.

HIGGINS. What! By fools like that?

LIZA. Freddy's not a fool. And if he's weak and poor and wants me, maybe he'd make me happier than my betters that bully me and don't want me.

HIGGINS. Can he make anything of you? That's the point.

LIZA. Perhaps I could make something of him. But I never thought of us making anything of one another; and you never think of anything else. I only want to be natural.

HIGGINS. In short, you want me to be as infatuated about you as Freddy? Is that it?

LIZA. No I don't. That's not the sort of feeling I want from you. And don't you be too sure of yourself or of me. I could have been a bad girl if I'd liked. I've seen more of some things than you, for all your learning. Girls like me can drag gentlemen down to make love to them easy enough. And they wish each other dead the next minute.

HIGGINS. Of course they do. Then what in thunder are we quarrelling about?

LIZA [much troubled] I want a little kindness. I know I'm a common ignorant girl, and you a book-learned gentleman; but I'm not dirt under your feet. What I done [correcting herself] what I did was not for the dresses and the taxis: I did it because we were pleasant together and I come—came—to care for you; not to want you to make love to me, and not forgetting the difference between us, but more friendly like.

HIGGINS. Well, of course. That's just how I feel. And how Pickering feels. Eliza: you're a fool.

LIZA. That's not a proper answer to give me [she sinks on the chair at the writing-table in tears].

HIGGINS. It's all you'll get until you stop being a common idiot. If you're going to be a lady, you'll have to give up feeling neglected if the men you know don't spend half their time snivelling over you and the other half giving you black eyes. If you can't stand the coldness of my sort of life, and the strain of it, go back to the gutter. Work til you are more a brute than a human being; and then cuddle and squabble and drink til you fall asleep. Oh, it's a fine life, the life of the gutter. It's real: it's warm: it's violent: you can feel it through the thickest skin: you can taste it and smell it without any training or any work. Not like Science and Literature and Classical Music and Philosophy and Art. You find me cold, unfeeling, selfish, don't you? Very well: be off with you to the sort of people you like. Marry some sentimental hog or other with lots of money, and a thick pair of lips to kiss you with and a thick pair of boots to kick you with. If you can't appreciate what you've got, you'd better get what you can appreciate.

LIZA [desperate] Oh, you are a cruel tyrant. I can't talk to you: you turn everything against me: I'm always in the wrong. But you know very well all the time that you're nothing but a bully. You know I can't go back to the gutter, as you call it, and that I have no real friends in the world but you and the Colonel. You know well I couldn't bear to live with a low common man after you two; and it's wicked and cruel of you to insult me by pretending I could. You think I must go back to Wimpole Street because I have nowhere else to go but father's. But don't you be too sure that you have me under your feet to be trampled on and talked down. I'll marry Freddy, I will, as soon as he's able to support me.

HIGGINS *[sitting down beside her]* Rubbish! you shall marry an ambassador. You shall marry the Governor-General of India or the Lord-Lieutenant of Ireland, or somebody who wants a deputy-queen. I'm not going to have my masterpiece thrown away on Freddy.

LIZA. You think I like you to say that. But I haven't forgot what you said a minute ago; and I won't be coaxed round as if I was a baby or a puppy. If I can't have kindness, I'll have independence.

HIGGINS. Independence? That's middle class blasphemy. We are all dependent on one another, every soul of us on earth.

LIZA *[rising determinedly]* I'll let you see whether I'm dependent on you. If you can preach, I can teach. I'll go and be a teacher.

HIGGINS. What'll you teach, in heaven's name?

LIZA. What you taught me. I'll teach phonetics.

HIGGINS. Ha! Ha! Ha!

LIZA. I'll offer myself as an assistant to Professor Nepommuck.

HIGGINS *[rising in a fury]* What! That impostor! that humbug! that toadying ignoramus! Teach him my methods! my discoveries! You take one step in his direction and I'll wring your neck. *[He lays hands on her.]* Do you hear?

LIZA *[defiantly non-resistant]* Wring away. What do I care? I knew you'd strike me some day. *[He lets her go, stamping with rage at having forgotten himself, and recoils so hastily that he stumbles back into his seat on the ottoman.]* Aha! Now I know how to deal with you. What a fool I was not to think of it before! You can't take away the knowledge you gave me. You said I had a finer ear than you. And I can be civil and kind to people, which is more than you can. Aha! That's done you, Henry Higgins, it has. Now I don't care that *[snapping her fingers]* for your bullying and your big talk. I'll advertize it in the papers that your duchess is only a flower girl that you taught, and that she'll teach anybody to be a duchess just the same in six months for a thousand guineas. Oh, when I think of myself crawling under your feet and being trampled on and called names, when all the time I had only to lift up my finger to be as good as you, I could just kick myself.

HIGGINS *[wondering at her]* You damned impudent slut, you! But it's better than snivelling; better than fetching slippers and finding spectacles, isn't it? *[Rising]* By George, Eliza, I said I'd make a woman of you; and I have. I like you like this.

LIZA. Yes: you turn round and make up to me now that I'm not afraid of you, and can do without you.

HIGGINS. Of course I do, you little fool. Five minutes ago you were like a millstone round my neck. Now you're a tower of strength: a consort battleship. You and I and Pickering will be three old bachelors together instead of only two men and a silly girl.

Mrs. Higgins returns, dressed for the wedding. Eliza instantly becomes cool and elegant.

MRS. HIGGINS. The carriage is waiting, Eliza. Are you ready?

LIZA. Quite. Is the Professor coming?

MRS. HIGGINS. Certainly not. He can't behave himself in church. He makes remarks out loud all the time on the clergyman's pronunciation.

LIZA. Then I shall not see you again, Professor. Good bye. *[She goes to the door.]*

MRS. HIGGINS *[coming to Higgins]* Good-bye, dear.

HIGGINS. Good-bye, mother. *[He is about to kiss her, when he recollects something.]* Oh, by the way, Eliza, order a ham and a Stilton cheese, will you? And buy me a pair of reindeer gloves, number eights, and a tie to match that new suit of mine, at Eale & Binmans. You can choose the color. *[His cheerful, careless, vigorous voice shows that he is incorrigible.]*

LIZA *[disdainfully]* Buy them yourself. *[She sweeps out].*

MRS. HIGGINS. I'm afraid you've spoiled that girl, Henry. But never mind, dear: I'll buy you the tie and gloves.

HIGGINS *[sunnily]* Oh, don't bother. She'll buy 'em all right enough. Good-bye.

They kiss. Mrs. Higgins runs out. Higgins, left alone, rattles his cash in his pocket; chuckles; and disports himself in a highly self-satisfied manner.

Notes

1. *Speech*. In Great Britain, accent is closely identified with class. For example, the Beatles' Liverpudlian accents identified them as "working class." The United States arguably has a much less rigid class structure than does Great Britain, but is there still a hierarchy of speech in the United States?

2. *Postscript*. Shaw could not resist writing a postscript to the play, in which he clarified that Eliza married Freddy and established a successful flower shop. She continued "to meddle in the housekeeping at Wimpole Street in spite of the shop and her own family.... [S]he has never got out of the habit of nagging Higgins.... She snaps his head off on the faintest provocation.... Galatea never does quite like Pygmalion: his relation to her is too godlike to be altogether agreeable." Shaw, however, ignores the fact that in the Greek myth Pygmalion falls hopelessly in love with Galatea, his artistic creation. What are we to make of this distinction between the play and the myth?

3. *Domestic Violence*. *Pygmalion* was subsequently adapted as the immensely popular musical, *My Fair Lady*. The musical treats the relationship between Henry Higgins and Eliza Doolittle as a romantic love story.

Does Shaw here portray their relationship as a romantic one? Their relationship is certainly volatile; several passages hint at violence between them. What's going on here? Is Shaw suggesting that the potential for violence accompanies romantic passion?

DIRTY WORK AT THE CROSSROADS
OR
TEMPTED, TRIED, AND TRUE
Bill Johnson

ACT ONE

SCENE: A country garden on the banks of the Mill River, near Totoket, Connecticut. Set in the Gay 'Nineties.

AT RISE: MUNRO MURGATROYD and MOOKIE MAGUGGINS are discovered up Left. MUNRO is an artist and wears the usual Bohemian costume: tam, smock, flowing tie. He is pain'ting a landscape on an easel. Has pallet and brushes. MOOKIE, the hired man, sits on a stump, chewing a straw, watching him.

MUSIC: A country air such as "Pop Goes the Weasel" or "Turkey in the Straw." Bird calls and whistles.

MUNRO. *(After a few moments of work, stands back and observes the painting)* At last! It is finished! How do you like it, Mookie?

MOOKIE. *(Looking at it)* Wunnerful, by gum! So real, it looks like a pitcher onna calendar.

MUNRO. Your rapture speaks well for your artistic inclinations; you have quite a taste for the fine arts, Mookie Maguggins.

MOOKIE. *(Chewing straw pensively)* Waal, sor, dunno nothin' 'bout the reefined arts like you calls 'em, but take thet thar cow—*(Points to cow in painting)* 'Tis the mooin' image o' the Widow Lovelace.

MUNRO. *(Laughing)* Ha, ha! Come now, you do not think it resembles your employer too much?

MOOKIE. 'Tis an unnateral cow, sor. I kin almos' hear her moo.

MUNRO. Yes, I flatter myself I am rather good at cows.

MOOKIE. So'm I—at milkin' 'em.

MUNRO. Do you think Miss Nellie will enjoy it, Mookie?

MOOKIE. Be it fur her ye're paintin' it, Mister Murgatroyd?

MUNRO. It is indeed.

MOOKIE. Bless you, sor—she'll love it. Miz Nellie allus was a gal fur pitchers.

MUNRO. She appreciates the fine arts, then?

MOOKIE. Thet she does. Miz Nellie's as smart as a buggy whip, an' twicet as handsome.

MUNRO. Your enthusiasm does you credit. Miss Nellie is certainly very accomplished for a simple country maiden. She plays beautifully.

MOOKIE. Plays beautifully? Why, sor, she kin make a pianner talk, she kin. Not as she can't do ordinary fireworks such as pickin' a chune to pieces and a-puttin' it together agin. Ah, but when she plays some simple old ditty, like "When You and I was Young, Magee," it takes sech a hold o' my heart thet I gets so overcome, I has to go into the barn an' have a cry. *(Starts sniffling)* Boo-hoo. It makes me cry, even to think o' her piano-playin'. Boo-hoo! Boo-hoo!

MUNRO. *(Aside)* Simple lout. But I can use him for my purposes. *(To Mookie)* Your young Mistress must be very popular with the country rustics, eh, Mookie?

MOOKIE. Bless you, sor. She c'ld be engaged twicet-over. But a mighty partic'lar gal is our Miz Nellie. Cal'late thar'll be no other man fur her save Adam Oakhart.

MUSIC: ADAM'S theme.

MUNRO. Adam Oakhart, the blacksmith's son?

MOOKIE. Aye, sor—and what a handy man he is around the livery stable.

MUNRO. He loves Miss Nellie?

MOOKIE. Ever since they was children, Mister Murgatroyd. They growed up together, hand in hand. He's as brave as she be lovely.

MUNRO. Are they— *(Aside)* Oh, cursed word—engaged?

MOOKIE. Engaged hard an' fast—as solid as the roots o' thet stump. *(Points to stump.)*

MUNRO. And there is to be a wedding?

MOOKIE. *(Nods)* Whenna goldenrod blooms in September, sor. Thet's Miz Nellie's favor't posey, the goldenrod. *(Sneezes)* Ker-choo! Cain't even think o' thet thar goldenrod 'thout kerchooin'. Kerchoo! Ker-choo! *(Pulls out red handkerchief and wipes his nose.)*

MUNRO. *(To the audience)* So, the beautiful Nellie Lovelace would wed the humble blacksmith's son? Never! Little does she know my purpose. *(Packs colors and brushes in paint-box.)*

MOOKIE. 'Course, since ye come to visit here this summer, Mister Murgatroyd, an' took lodgin' in her mother's house, Miz Nellie ain't thought so much o' Adam as she useter. Cal'late she's taken by your fast city ways. But come September, and ye return to Bridgeport.

MUNRO. *(Triumphantly)* And I shall return to Bridgeport, Master Mookie.

MOOKIE. Good for you, sor.

MUNRO. *(Aside)* But not alone, ah no, not alone. Nellie shall be mine. I defy all others. *(Aloud)* Here, Mookie, will you carry my easel into the house? I wish to sit on yonder bank, and contemplate the rolling river. Ah, how I glory in the majesty of nature. *(Looks at backdrop.)*

MUSIC: Spring song. Bird calls.

MOOKIE. *(Picking up paraphernalia)* Shall I carry the pitcher, sor?

MUNRO. *(Turning)* Do you think you can manage it?

MOOKIE. *(Holding out one arm in a circle)* If ye'll fit it in here, sor, so on'y the edges touches—I won' go near the cow what's wet.

MUNRO. *(Loads him down with easel, palette, paint-box and canvas)* There, you're more than loaded.

MOOKIE. Hur, hur! Thet I am, sor—loaded like a gun. *(Crosses toward house)* Ye gotta treat me with care, sor.

MUNRO. Treat you with care, Mookie?

MOOKIE. Yis sor, or I might go off! *(Laughs with rustic glee)* Haw! Haw! Haw! *(Exits door in house.)*

MUNRO. *(To the audience)* What a chowderhead he is! What a simple country bumpkin! But the girl, Nellie, daughter of the Widow Lovelace, is always present in my thoughts. I shall sit here on the bank of the river and contemplate her. *(Sits on rock at river's edge)* I sleep but to dream of her beautiful hair, her eyes, deep languid pools, her teeth, shining stars, her—her— *(Changes tone)* I swear I will have her. She shall be mine! Vain, simpleheaded beauty! How can she resist me? Have I not the charms of an Adonis? Am I not a man of the world? True, I have not a penny to my name, but what then? Cannot my face be my fortune? This farm of the Widow Lovelace is a valuable property. I have it on secret information that the new railroad is coming this way, will cross Mill River, somewhere near this point. So, what better way to fortune than marrying one? Especially when it comes in a form as soft and rosy as Nellie's. *(Rises triumphantly)* Her form and fortune shall be mine, I swear it! Mine, hard and fast *(Clenching fist)*. Hard and fast.

MUSIC: Mysterioso. IDA'S theme. She enters from Right in a boat; this is the painted profile of a canoe, which she carries waist-high with her, legs masked by the ground-row. "Paddles" to Center.

IDA. Ah, Munro Murgatroyd, as I live and breathe!

MUNRO. *(Startled)* Eh! What? Ida! You here?

IDA. Yes, Ida Rhinegold.

MUNRO. *(Assisting her from boat. A step should be placed behind ground-row so she may step from boat to rock at river's bank)* Did anyone see you? *(He is worried.)*

IDA. No, I rowed across the river. I am living in New Haven. I heard rumors you were here, boarding with the Widow Lovelace. What devilment now, Munro Murgatroyd?

MUNRO. But I thought you were still at Green Oaks, that you were—

IDA. That I was put away for good, or so you hoped, eh, Munro?

MUNRO. Why, Ida, you speak like a fool. Are you not my wife? *MUSIC: Chord.*

IDA. Yes, I am your wife—but not an acknowledged one. And did you not have me shut up in Green Oaks Asylum, pretending I was insane?

MUNRO. Come, come, Ida. Let bygones be bygones. There is work for both of us here.

IDA. Dirty work, I warrant. That's the only kind you ever had a hand in.

MUNRO. You shall judge for yourself, Ida. Look around you. Is this not a beautiful farm?

MUSIC: Spring Song.

IDA. *(Gazing about her)* And since when have you, born and bred in city ways, taken a liking for the bucolic life?

MUNRO. Since I discovered— *(Lowers voice cautiously)* —the New York, New Haven Railroad is coming this way.

IDA. A railroad coming to this hole? What on earth for?

MUNRO. Never mind. They are taking options on property for the right of way. This spot is the narrowest on the river. They must bridge it here. I have only to acquire this farm; and I hold the New York, New Haven, right where I want them—in the palm of my hand! *(Holds up palm and rubs it.)*

IDA. *(Examining his hand)* Still not a callus on them, I see.

MUNRO. I always keep my hands soft and clean. You know that, Ida.

IDA. Yes. I also know that some of the dirtiest work in this world is done by the whitest of hands.

MUNRO. Ha! You are no one to boast! Queen of the New Haven campus.

IDA. I was once, Munro Murgatroyd. Before you came into my life, I was as pure as the driven snow, the apple of my father's eye, the hope of my mother's old age.

MUSIC: Specialty solo by IDA.

ALL THAT GLITTERS IS NOT GOLD
Just an ivy covered cottage with a brooklet running near,
Just an aged couple seated in the door;
Sadly thinking of their Ida, to their fond hearts ever dear,
In wounded pride she left them years before;
And as they stood at parting there, the couple old and gray,
They begged her not to leave them all alone;
"If you leave us," said the father: "you may regret some day,
Remember, child. the motto in your home."

CHORUS

All is not gold that glitters;
All is not pure that shines,
Follow your mother's teachings,
And happiness will be thine;

Lovers may seek your favor,
Boast of their wealth untold,
But all through your life, remember, child,
All that glitters is not gold.

The verse and music for this song may be found in "Weep Some More, My Lady" by Sigmund Spaeth.

MUNRO. *(At conclusion of song)* Enough of this moralizing. We must make plans for the future. We must obtain this farm.

IDA. How? You have no money, you're nothing but a penniless artist. For years you lived on my meager earnings as a music hall entertainer.

MUNRO. Listen carefully. This property is owned by the Widow Lovelace. She has an only daughter, Nellie, a simple country lass. I have only to marry Nellie—

IDA. But you cannot marry her—you are my husband in the sight of heaven.

MUNRO. Of course I am, Ida, but think what it will mean: Riches, travel, gowns. You have only to remain silent until I have secured the farm.

IDA. And how do you propose to do that?

MUNRO. Having married Nellie, I come into control of her property. I will immediately sell it to the railroad, and have her committed to Green Oaks.

IDA. *(Bitterly)* As you did me.

MUNRO. Then you and I, Ida, shall spend the rest of our lives in luxury and wealth, traveling on the continent, visiting Paris, living a life of ease.

IDA. You paint a pretty picture. You always did—with your tongue. But what about the Widow Lovelace? Did you not say the property belonged to her?

MUNRO. *(Cautiously)* The Widow Lovelace is not long for this world, I promise you that.

IDA. *(Frightened)* Not—not murder? No, no, Munro—not that!

MUNRO. *(Smoothly)* Murder is an ugly word, Ida. I would prefer you did not use it. Shall we say, the Widow Lovelace, shortly after drinking her afternoon tea some sunny day, will be taken ill—mortally ill?

IDA. *(Half in praise)* You villain, you!

MUNRO. Come, Ida—you will assist me?

IDA. I dare not trust you, Munro.

MUNRO. You must! Time is of the essence. Even now the railroad agents are coming this way. The girl must flee with me tonight.

IDA. Tonight?

MUNRO. You shall bend her to my will. She is in love with a village swain. It will be easy for you, with your slinking, knowing ways, to win him away. Then Nellie, heartbroken, shall need comforting, and who better than I to comfort her?

IDA. You old comforter, you.

MUNRO. I tell you, Ida, with your assistance, the girl is mine. *(IDA snorts)* For a short time only, I promise.

IDA. How can I trust you?

MUNRO. *(His voice rises in menace)* You have no other choice, unless—

IDA. Unless what, Munro Murgatroyd?

MUNRO. Unless you would return to Green Oaks, the abode of the alcoholic insane. You forget I am your husband, and have your commitment papers. I did it once, and I can do it again.

IDA. You villain! You have me in your clutches. Very well, then, I consent.

MUNRO. Good!

IDA. Now tell me the part I am to play in this unholy drama.

MUNRO. Walk down to the crossroads—that path there, *(Points Left)* and make the acquaintance of one Adam Oakhart. You will find him in the livery stable.

IDA. I go. *(Crosses down Left)* But when it is done, *(To audience)* beware how you play me false! *(Exits Left)*

MUSIC: IDA's theme.

MUNRO. *(Looking after her)* The devil take her! *(To the audience)* If she wasn't so useful to my plans, I'd slit her windpipe tonight. I'm sick of her gush, but her part will soon be played. Then *(gesture of throat-cutting)* skullit!

MUSIC: WIDOW'S theme.

WIDOW. *(Bustles on from house, carrying tray of tea-things)* Ah, good afternoon, Mister Murgatroyd. Skeets botherin' you? *(Puts tray on table.)*

MUNRO. *(Graciously)* Good-afternoon, Widow Lovelace. Permit me to assist you. I fear that tray is far too heavy. *(Takes tray from her, a few inches from table, and puts it down.)*

WIDOW. Sakes! I'm used to fetchin' an' carryin'. Thanky just the same. Thought I'd have my tea out here. It's such a smilin' day. Won't you jine me? *(Sits at table.)*

MUNRO. Thank you. Nothing would give me more pleasure. *(Aside, as WIDOW arranges cups and saucers)* Now is my chance. A few drops from this vial, in her tea, and then— *(Takes tiny vial from pocket surreptitiously.)*

WIDOW. Have you seen my Nellie?

MUNRO. No. I have been occupied with my pain'ting all afternoon.

WIDOW. She said she was a-goin' down to the livery stable. Sakes, I do wish she wouldn't spend so much time there. She comes home with such an air. But sakes, she's a gal and in love with Adam Oakhart, and a fine, handsome lad he is, too. Come, sit down.

MUNRO sits opposite her. She pours from empty teapot.

MUNRO. Widow Lovelace, I have a confession to make.

WIDOW. A confession? Sakes! Wait'll I fix your tea. How many lumps?

MUNRO. Seven.

WIDOW. *(Counting lumps of sugar into his cup)* One, two three, four— How many months you been boardin' with us, Mr. Murgatroyd?

MUNRO. Two.

WIDOW. *(Miscounting lumps)* Two, three, four, five, six—how much longer you calc'latin' on stayin'?

MUNRO. Just one.

WIDOW. One? *(Miscounting all over)* Two, three, four, five, six, and one is seven. There you are. *(Gives him tea)* Hope it's sweet enough. They's cream in that pitcher.

MUNRO. Thank you. *(Sips tea; makes face)* There's only one thing sweeter, Mrs. Lovelace.

WIDOW. What's that? *(Cup to lips.)*

MUNRO. Your daughter, Nellie. I love her.

WIDOW. *(Sputters and chokes)* Sakes alive! *(Puts down cup.)*

MUNRO. I know that I am older than she, and wiser in the ways of the world. But I have tired of the town beauties with their faded cheeks and artificial bloom. Who knows what this fresh, innocent girl may make of me?

WIDOW. No, no, say no more. Nellie is not for the likes of you. She is promised to Adam Oakhart.

MUNRO. Mrs. Lovelace, you may think this but the passing fancy of a summer boarder but it is not so. I love your daughter, Nellie, and she loves me.

WIDOW. No, no, 'tis false. Nellie is true to Adam.

MUNRO. Not so, she has written me letters.

WIDOW. Letters?

MUNRO. Letters declaring her love.

WIDOW. I cannot believe it. Show me one.

MUNRO. *(Aside)* Curses! I have no letters. Nellie has never shown the slightest romantic interest. *(Aloud)* I have them in my bureau. I will show them to you later. *(Aside)* One may be easily forged.

WIDOW. Sir, I do not like this at all. I am a poor, ignorant woman, but I am not so ignorant that I don't know what I am, and what you are.

MUNRO. *(Haughtily)* Explain yourself, madam.

WIDOW. Only this, sir. I gave you the advantage of my home, and you have taken advantage of my little Nellie.

MUNRO. But I love your daughter; I want her for my own.

WIDOW. Never, by fair means or foul. And now, sir, I must ask you to make other living arrangements. Your presence here is no longer wanted. *(Rises haughtily, turning back on him.)*

MUNRO. *(Soothingly)* There, there, good Mother. Perhaps we are overexcited. *(Pours contents of vial into tea)* Let us talk no more of the matter now. Won't you drink your tea?

WIDOW. *(Coldly)* Yes, thanky. The shock of this news has made me faint. *(He hands her cup of tea. She raises it to her lips, then lowers it)* You are a man of the world, Mr. Murgatroyd. You will find women everywhere more adapted to your requirements, but Nellie, little Nellie, is like some timid wildflower growing sheltered in the woods. Transplanted, she would fade and die. *(She drinks.)*

MUNRO. *(Aside)* It will take effect within the hour. *(Aloud)* Perhaps you are right, good Mother. Perhaps Nellie is not for me. *(WIDOW coughs and chokes)* Are you ill, good Mother?

WIDOW. 'Tis nothing. 'Twill pass. Sakes, but I feel drowsy. I will go in and lay down. When Nellie comes, will you send her to me? *(Aside)* I'll question her about this collegian's advances.

MUNRO. Certainly, certainly. Here, let me assist you, good Mother! *(Takes her arm and they exit into house.)*

MUSIC: First sad and in a minor key, then it brightens into NELLIE's theme.

NELLIE. *(Enters Left swinging bonnet in one hand, bouquet of wild flowers in other)* I know Adam doesn't love me, or he wouldn't have looked at that woman. It shows his ill-breeding. He's nothing like Mr. Murgatroyd. Now there's a fine gentleman for you. He even went to college. Adam Oakhart isn't fit to black his boots. *(Stamps foot petulantly.)*

MUSIC: MUNRO'S theme.

MUNRO. *(Re-enters from house. Has removed artist's smock and beret; wears smoking jacket, no hat. Aside)* The noble girl seems put out a bit. *(Aloud)* Ah, good afternoon, Miss Nellie. May I say dear Miss Nellie? *(Crosses to her.)*

NELLIE. Good-afternoon, Mr. Murgatroyd. And you may say anything you wish.

MUNRO. What lovely posies! May I have one?

NELLIE. Of course! *(Holds up bouquet.)*

MUNRO. From your tender hand? *(Holds out lapel)* You will place it here for me?

NELLIE. *(Doing so)* It's only a daisy.

MUNRO. *(Looking down at NELLIE)* Only a daisy? A lovely, pure-white daisy, in the cool, clear bloom of spring. How refreshing you are.

NELLIE. How pretty you phrase things. I grow so tired of—of other people and their coarse ways.

MUNRO. Let me tell you of Bridgeport, Nellie.

NELLIE. Bridgeport, the big city! Oh, how I'd love to live there.

MUNRO. You shall, Nellie, with me. You have only to say the word.

NELLIE. *(Drawing herself up proudly)* Sir! I know I am only a country girl, not used to city ways, but that does not permit you to insult me.

MUNRO. Insult you, Nellie? Never. Ah, little do you understand me, if you think that. No, Nellie, I love you. From that first tender moment when I saw you, swinging on the barnyard gate, calling the pigs, I loved you. From that first idle hour as we wandered through the haylofts hunting eggs, from those first few mornings when you served me flapjacks, cooked with your own fair hand, and sweetened with your own sweet smile, have I loved you. Now I throw myself at your feet. *(Kneels)* I ask you, beg you, plead with you to be my bride.

NELLIE. No, no, that can never be. I love another; have from tenderest infancy been promised to Adam Oakhart.

MUNRO. *(Rising. Bitterly)* Adam Oakhart! He does not love you.

NELLIE. *(Angrily)* How dare you!

MUNRO. *(Humbly)* Nellie, forgive me. I would spare you this—but have you not heard of the notorious Ida Rhinegold?

NELLIE. Ida Rhinegold, the famous college widow?

MUNRO. None other.

NELLIE. Why do you mention her vile name to me?

MUNRO. Forgive me for sullying your ears, but this you must know: She is an old flame of Adam Oakhart's. He met her on a visit to New Haven.

NELLIE. *(Aghast)* Adam false to me? I cannot believe it.

MUNRO. Then look yonder! *(Points Left)* Believe your own eyes.

NELLIE. *(Looking Left)* Adam approaches. He is walking with that strange woman. He is assisting her up the garden path. *(To MUNRO)* Tell me, Mr. Murgatroyd, is that the notorious Ida Rhinegold?

MUNRO. None other.

NELLIE. *(Looking off-stage)* He takes her arm. He smiles at her tenderly. Oh, Adam, Adam! Oh, my Adam! *(Weeps.)*

MUNRO. Come, my little one, you are distraught. You must be brave. You must not let him see you weeping.

NELLIE. *(Drying her eyes with a quick jab of her handkerchief)* You are right. Thank you for your counsel, Munro. No, Adam Oakhart shall never see me weeping. *(Bursts into tears)* Boo-hoo! Boo-hoo! Boo-hoo! *(Rushes off Right)*

MUNRO. Nellie! Wait! Nellie! *(Crosses up, then to audience)* The game is mine! Ha! Ha! Ha! *(Leers and exits Right)*

MUSIC: MUNRO's theme, then changing into ADAM's theme—a heroic motif.

ADAM enters Left with IDA on his arm. He is the noble heroic type, but bashful, countrified in manner.

IDA. I find these country lanes quite unsuitable to my town-bred feet. Thank you for the generous use of your arm.

ADAM. Quite all right, marm. Glad to be of service. Is this where you left your boat?

IDA. Yes, it is moored to the river bank yonder.

ADAM. This is the Widow Lovelace's cottage. Do you know her?

IDA. No, I know no one in these parts. I was merely taking a paddle on the river when I sprung a leak. I am sure that you can help me.

ADAM. Horses is my line, but I'll do my best. *(Starts up Center)*

IDA. But wait—I would talk with you.

ADAM. *(Turning)* Yes, marm?

IDA. *(Coquettishly)* Tell me, are all the men of this neighborhood as handsome and stalwart as you? But no, that could not be. Otherwise Connecticut would be populated by Greek gods.

ADAM. *(Shyly)* Oh, I ain't so handsome, marm. There's lots more handsome 'n me. Take Buchanan for one.

IDA. Buchanan?

ADAM. My horse, and he's as purty a piece of horseflesh as you ever set eyes on. You should see his eyes—they're soft an' gentle like— *(Looks about for a comparison)* that velvet. His mane is long and silky as—your hair. His hocks are like—your ankles.

IDA. *(Pretending anger)* Sir, you insult me. How dare you compare me with a horse?

ADAM. Oh, no, marm—no offense meant—rather a compliment.

IDA. You have not seen my ankle. How can you then compare it with Buchanan's?

ADAM. You're right, marm. I shouldn't have spoke so hasty.

IDA. But wait, we can easily remedy that. You shall see my ankle. Then tell me which is most beautiful. *(Puts foot on stump or rock.)*

NELLIE appears Right and watches.

ADAM. *(Embarrassed)* Oh, no, marm, that won't be necessary. *(Turns away, blushing.)*

IDA. Come now, you aren't afraid, are you? Afraid of a pretty woman's ankle, or shall I say a woman's pretty ankle? *(Starts pulling her skirt slowly.)*

NELLIE. *(Aside)* If he looks, he is not the man I thought him.

IDA. Come, come—not afraid? *(Reveals her ankle.)*

ADAM slowly overcomes his shyness, turns and looks.

NELLIE. *(Aghast. Aside)* Lost! Lost! *(Exits Right)*

IDA. Well? Has the cat got your tongue? What do you think of it?

ADAM. *(Gulping)* Nice, marm, nice enough. But Buchanan's tendons—

IDA. *(Angrily; standing erect)* You fool! How can you prefer a horse's ankles to a woman's?

ADAM. Oh, I don't, marm. Nellie has awful nice hocks.

IDA. Another horse, I presume?

ADAM. Oh, no, marm. Nellie's the mos' elegant, the mos' talented, the mos' wunnerful gal in the world. When the goldenrod blooms, we're to be wed. *(Sighs ecstatically.)*

IDA. *(Suddenly)* Ouch!

ADAM. What is it, marm?

IDA. *(Running about, slapping at the air)* A bee! A bee! I'm mortally afraid of bees. Save me! Save me! *(Faints.)*

ADAM. *(Concerned)* That's all right, marm. I'm here. Don't be afeard. *(She collapses in his arms. He gulps)* Gosh!

NELLIE. *(Enters Right on the arm of MUNRO)* Well! I hope we are not intruding? Come, Munro.

ADAM. Hello, Nellie. Gosh, you're just in time. Help me.

NELLIE. *(Crossing Left)* Help you indeed! You seem to be doing very well without me. Come, Munro—we will leave Mr. Oakhart to his own devices. *(Exits Left)*

MUNRO. Ha! Ha! Ha! Indeed yes. Boys will be boys! *(Gives high-sign to the "fainting" IDA, then follows NELLIE out Left)*

IDA. *(After winking at MUNRO, she slowly revives)* Where am I? Where am I?

ADAM. *(Nervously)* You're right here. New Haven County, Connecticut.

IDA. In your arms?

ADAM. Calc'late so.

IDA. *(Drawing away haughtily)* How dare you take advantage of my indisposition? Unloose me, sir, or I shall scream for help. Hel—!

ADAM. Shush, shush—please don't scream. I don't think Nellie would understand. I've got to go after her and the summer boarder. *(Starts up Left)*

IDA. *(Screaming)* Help! Help!

ADAM. *(Running back and forth, distracted)* Don't scream! Nellie! Don't scream! Nellie!

MUNRO. *(Re-enters)* Did I hear a cry for help?

IDA: This son of a blacksmith took advantage of me!

MUNRO. *(Pretending righteous anger)* Why, you cur! A poor, innocent, defenseless woman—one of nature's tenderest creatures, and you insulted her! Why, if I had my way, you'd be whipped out of the county.

ADAM. Now wait a minute, stranger. You ain't got the straight o' this.

MUNRO. Ha, ha! The old story—a man taking advantage of a woman's simple courtesy. Thank heaven, I arrived in time. Now be off with you, before I forget I'm a gentleman. *(Points Left)*

ADAM. But the lady asked me to fix her boat.

MUNRO. Fix her boat? A likely story. Be off with you, or shall I summon Miss Nellie and pour in her delicate ears the story of your wicked perfidy!

ADAM. *(Upset)* No, no, don't tell Nellie. I'll go, I'll go—but when I've got this whole thing figgered out, I'll return. There's somep'n around here that smells, and I don' mean the livery stable.

MUNRO. *(Pointing dramatically)* Go!

ADAM. *(To the front)* Oh, woman, woman, strangest of all creations. How can man ever hope to understand you? *(He exits Left)*

MUSIC: ADAM'S theme in minor key.

IDA. *(Laughing heartlessly)* Silly bumpkin!

MUNRO. Good work, Ida. You managed well.

IDA. And the girl? The silly simpering Nellie?

MUNRO. Mine, all mine! But you must help me further. Convince her she must go with me tonight. Advise her for her own good. Ha! Ha! Ha! And have her put it in writing.

IDA. But what influence can I, a stranger, have upon her?

MUNRO. She is like all women, easily led. Weak and vain at the best of times.

IDA. She is won already by your fine town-bred ways?

MUNRO. If only she will forget Adam Oakhart.

IDA. He loves her better than his horse. He loves her as I once thought you loved me—and the loss of her will break his heart.

MUNRO. What matter, that? This night, then? Tonight—her acceptance in writing.

IDA. Why in writing?

MUNRO. Two reasons—one as evidence she accompanies me willingly, in case her stout-hearted swain should seek to interfere. Second, to show her doubting, dying mother that I am in truth in possession of such a letter. You understand?

IDA. Only too well. You would ruin her character.

MUNRO. Character, my dear Ida, is a gentleman's stock in trade. You have spent all yours. I never had any. *(Up Left)* I will send her to you. Do your work well. And diamonds shall be yours. *(Exits Left)*

IDA. *(Alone)* I'll do my work well, but not for love of you, Munro Murgatroyd. *(Looks Left)* She is in the clouds! And threatening clouds they are, too. *(Comes down stage)* I will get her to write two lines—and then, the reward! Dresses and gold and diamonds are precious in my eyes. They set my gipsy blood aglow! But revenge for the world's wrongs is sweet, sweeter than diamonds. She will leave her home—and then—then the public exposure, the shame that I have known. And all Ida Rhinegold's doings. All her doings! All her doings!

Specialty solo by IDA, "The Gipsy's Warning," may be inserted here if desired.

NELLIE. *(Enters Left at conclusion of specialty)* What? You here, and alone. Where is Adam?

IDA. He fled, after basely insulting me.

NELLIE. Insulted you—how?

IDA. He asked me to be his wife.

NELLIE. *(Proudly)* I do not believe you.

IDA. *(Shrugs)* What matter? I refused his rude advances.

NELLIE. Adam loves me, or did so once. Now, I hardly know.

IDA. *(Turning on her sharply)* You're a stupid fool! Did I not see you walking with Munro Murgatroyd?

NELLE. You know him?

IDA. Only by reputation. *(Aside)* And what a reputation—99 and 44/100ths percent bad. *(Aloud)* What a fortunate girl you are!

NELLIE. Fortunate?

IDA. To have Munro Murgatroyd at your feet. Think of what he presents—a life of brilliance, traveling about from place to place, plenty of dresses and gold and diamonds. *(Aside)* What a fool she is to believe it!

NELLIE. You think I should accept his offer—accompany him to Bridgeport?

IDA. By all means.

NELLIE. But it would break my poor mother's heart. And Adam, what about Adam?

IDA. Adam? What life does he offer? A home in a livery stable. Toiling from morning to night, rags, wretchedness, without one ray of hope to lighten the gloom.

NELLIE. Don't talk like that.

IDA. You must be mad to lose this opportunity. Why not write one line to Mr. Murgatroyd, to say that you will go with him?

NELLIE. *(Troubled)* I can't! I can't!

IDA. Have you no pride? Have you no spirit? Is it pity you have in your heart for Adam Oakhart? Pity, when you saw him with your own two eyes ogling me?

NELLIE. *(Furiously)* You are right! I will go to Bridgeport! *MUSIC: Chord.*

IDA. Good. Write Murgatroyd a note now.

NELLIE. Why should I write? He is close by.

IDA. Why? Because no well-bred Bridgeport lady accepts a gentleman's propositions verbally.

NELLIE. No? Then where is pen and paper? *(Starts toward house.)*

IDA. Here. *(Opens purse)* I carry it in my reticule. I have always found it pays to get proposals in writing.

NELLIE. Not one of them newfangled pens?

IDA. *(Displaying crude fountain pen)* Yes, one of the latest inventions. They call them "fountains."

NELLIE. One more of the city's refinements.

IDA. I also have paper and an envelope. A lady should always be prepared. *(They go to the table. IDA arranges paper and pen so that NELLIE may write.)*

NELLIE. *(Sitting at table; takes pen)* Is this how you hold it?

IDA. *(Adjusting pen in her hand)* Now write.

NELLIE. How should I begin it? "Dear Mr. Murgatroyd"?

IDA. No, no. "Dearest Munro."

NELLIE. But that's so familiar.

IDA. And what could be more familiar than going with a man to Bridgeport?

NELLIE. *(Writes the letter, pausing from time to time. IDA watching triumphantly over her shoulder)* "Dearest Munro. I am doing wrongly, very wrongly, but I trust to your honor and the love you say you bear me. I will fly, but take me away tonight so that I may never look on the faces here again. I trust to you. Do not let me trust in vain." *(To IDA)* Oh, he will marry me, won't he?

IDA. He is a gentleman, and he will keep his word. *(NELLIE rises)* Stay and sign it! *(NELLIE does so with a great flourish, then addresses envelope)* That's done. So far, so well. *(Seals letter in envelope.)*

NELLIE. *(Changing her mind)* No, no! Give it back. I cannot send that letter.

IDA. I'll take care of it. *(Holds letter from her.)*

MOOKIE. *(Enters from house. NELLIE appeals to IDA with a pleading gesture)* Beg pardon, Miz Nellie, I was agoin' ta— *(Sees IDA, who looks at him, angrily)* Oh! *(Aside)* Them two must be up to somep'n. I don't like the looks o' that black-eyed gal. She's got bad eyes. When she fixes 'em at me, I feels quite mercerized.

IDA. *(To MOOKIE)* Come here. You will deliver this message to Mr. Murgatroyd. You will find him yonder—with the pigs. *(Points Left)*

MOOKIE. *(Timidly, afraid of IDA; takes letter)* Wan' me to take this—to the pigs?

IDA. And don't let anyone see you deliver it.

MOOKIE. *(Business of being frightened)* Not let anyone see me—oh !

IDA. Here's a dime for you—take it— *(Impatiently)* Take it! *(Takes dime from coin purse strapped around leg.)*

MOOKIE. *(Registers frightened comedy through all this business)* Should I, Miz Nellie?

NELLIE. As you wish, only—I'd really rather.

IDA. *(To NELLIE)* Good courage, come with me. It will be all right, dear. *(Leads her to house.)*

MOOKIE. *(Watching NELLIE, scratching his head, confused. As NELLIE reaches door she turns and holds out her hand for the letter hopelessly.)* What? Does she want the dime?

IDA. *(Drawing NELLIE off)* All will be well. Keep a stiff upper lip. Come, I'll help you pack. *(They exit into house.)*

MOOKIE. *(Alone)* They's somep'n up. What did she go and gimme a dime for? Ladies don't give gentlemens dimes lessen somep'ns up. I knows that fur a fack, 'cause once me an' my gal, Maria. Wait, I'll tell you about it.

MUSIC: Specialty solo by MOOKIE.

OH, FRED, TELL THEM TO STOP
No doubt you have heard of the Great Fancy Fair
That used to take place ev'ry day.
Well, I thought for amusement I'd take my gal there,
To pass a dull hour away.
We went in, you must know, and saw Barnum's great show,
Van Amburgh's Menagerie as well.
There were round-a-bouts, swings and all kinds of things.
Forget the day I never shall.

CHORUS

Oh, Mook! Tell them to stop
That was the cry of Maria.
But the more she said, "Whoa!" they said, "Let it go!"
And the swing went a little bit higher.

*The complete words and music will be found in "Read 'Em and Weep,"
by Sigmund Spaeth. At conclusion of song, MOOKIE holds up letter and
examines it curiously.*

MOOKIE. I wunner what's inside? I allus was cur'ous, awful cur'ous. So
was Mother, she was cur'ous too. Awful scraggy writin' on the outside.
(Laughs) Hur, hur, hur! Ain't nobody about. *(Goes to table; seats self)*
These stick onwelopes will open if ye bite 'em. I seen the postmaster
do't. *(Laughs and bites flap with teeth)* Now it's beginnin' to come—
handsome. *(Works to get envelope open. WIDOW enters from house;
watches him)* Now! *(WIDOW slaps him on shoulder)* Oh, murder! *(Jumps
up and runs Left)*

WIDOW. What be you doin' there, Mookie?

MOOKIE. Nothin', marm. *(Tries to hide letter.)*

WIDOW. What ails you? Have you gone mad? Sakes alive!

MOOKIE. No, marm. Ain't got brains enough to go mad.

WIDOW. Then what are you hidin' behind your back?

MOOKIE. Nothin', marm, nothin'. See, nothin'. *(Keeps letter in one hand
behind his back; shows the other.)*

WIDOW. Let's see t'other hand.

MOOKIE. *(Puts hand behind back; switches letter; shows other hand)*
Still nothin', marm, on'y more so.

WIDOW. I saw you. You was readin' a letter.

MOOKIE. *(Bringing it out)* Yes, marm. Like Ananias, I kin not tell a lie.
On'y a letter for Mr. Murgatroyd, marm.

WIDOW. *(Concerned)* Mr. Murgatroyd? Who from?

MOOKIE tries to read envelope.

ADAM. *(Enters Left)* I cannot stand this any longer. I must see Nellie
and explain. *(Sees WIDOW; touches hat)* Evenin', marm.

WIDOW. Oh, Adam! Tell me what this letter is. Mookie can't read and I
haven't my specs.

ADAM. *(Going Right)* Of course. Let me see the letter, Mookie. *(Takes it;
starts)* Nellie's handwriting. *(Shocked, fingers the envelope nervously, not
knowing whether to open it or not.)*

WIDOW. *(Anguished)* Nellie writing to Mr. Murgatroyd? Then what he
said is true.

ADAM. What did he say, marm?

WIDOW. He said—he said. But better read the letter, Adam. I grow
faint. *(Hand to brow, sinks in chair.)*

ADAM. *(Aside)* I see it all now. Sending him love notes! Oh, what a fool
I've been!

MOOKIE. What does it mean? Good gals don' write letters to summer
boarders.

WIDOW. I'll know what it says. *(Calls)* Nellie! Nellie, come here.

NELLIE and IDA enter from house.

MOOKIE. *(Crying)* Boo-hoo! Boo-hoo—it's all my doin's. Poor Miz Nellie.

NELLIE. Yes, Mother?

WIDOW. This letter from you to Mr. Murgatroyd. What is it?

NELLIE. *(Anguished)* Oh, Mother—

WIDOW. What does it mean? That what he told me was true? *(NELLIE hangs her head in shame)* Answer me, child, answer me— *(NELLIE droops lower)* It is true! *(Grasps bosom)* My heart! My heart! *(Faints.)*

NELLIE. *(Going to her, comforting her)* Mother!

WIDOW. *(Reviving slightly)* Stay away; I will not have your hands touching me.

NELLIE. But you're ill.

WARN CURTAIN.

WIDOW. Mookie will help me. Even though he be no kin of mine, he is loyal and honest and good. Can you say as much? Look me in the eye and say as much?

NELLIE. *(She tries to face her mother but is compelled to avert her head)* Oh, Mother!

MUNRO appears up stage, Left, unseen by OTHERS.

WIDOW. What does the letter say, Adam?

MUNRO. *(Aside)* 'Tis better than I expected. My triumph has come at last. The mother dying, the girl shamed before the world.

IDA goes to him. They shake hands gleefully.

ADAM. *(Opening letter)* It is not mine to read.

WIDOW. Read it. I would know the truth before I die. *(Pants heavily.)*

MUSIC: Sad, melancholy theme.

ADAM. *(Pretends to read, but the letter hangs in his hand as he makes up as he goes along)* Dear Mr. Murgatroyd: You ask me if I will go away from home. I own I have been dazzled by the thought of a grander home than I could ever hope for, in Bridgeport. But if I go away I would break two hearts that love me better than life. I have been wavering, but I am strong now, all the stronger for temptation. My decision is irrevocable. I will not leave my happy home! *(Tears up letter.)*

WIDOW. Nellie! *(Opens arms joyfully.)*

NELLIE. Mother! *(They embrace.)*

WIDOW. I die content! *(She dies.)*

NELLIE. Oh! Adam—? *(Holds out her arms to him, pleading. He turns his back, spurning her)* Mother! *(Buries head in mother's shoulders, sobbing.)*

CURTAIN

The Curtain falls, then rises disclosing the characters frozen in a tableau. WIDOW and NELLIE at table. MOOKIE wiping eyes with red handkerchief. ADAM down Left, his back to them, dropping bits of the letter. MUNRO and IDA upstage, pictures of angry scorn.

MUNRO. Curses! Foiled! *(Gnashing his teeth.)*

CURTAIN

ACT TWO, SCENE I

[Poor Nellie's mother is dead, and Nellie is eking out a living by renting rooms. Adam has disappeared, no one knows where, but it is rumored he has gone to the city to drown his sorrows in drink. Nellie spurned Murgatroyd, and he too has disappeared. Only Mookie remains to support Nellie in her sorrow.

[Mrs. Asterbilt, her daughter Leonie, and their French maid Fleurette come to Nellie's house seeking rooms. Mrs. Asterbilt is trying to get Leonie out of the clutches of Murgatroyd, with whom Leonie fell madly in love when he kissed her on a train while in a tunnel.

[Murgatroyd has followed them there, hoping to steal Leonie away. Fleurette agrees to arrange a tryst. But Nellie learns from Leonie about her love for Murgatroyd, and vows to save her from a fate worse than death.

[Meantime, Ida reappears (having been released from prison or the asylum), and vows to blackmail Mrs. Asterbilt by revealing that the latter had been committed to an asylum for dipsomania—unless Mrs. Asterbilt will consent to Leonie's marriage to Murgatroyd. She steadfastly refuses to consent. Murgatroyd, learning that Leonie's mother has been a dipsomaniac, throws over Leonie. Eds.]

SCENE II

[A brief flirtation between Mookie and Fleurette begins the scene. Adam, disheveled and drunken, returns at nightfall to gain a glimpse of Nellie. Mookie tries to get him to sober up.

[Ida returns, intending to commit suicide by jumping into the River near Nellie's house. Adam intervenes and urges her to turn to religion with him. He picks up her purse and goes to get his horse. While he is gone, Mrs. Asterbilt, who has begun drinking again, comes out of Nellie's house and stabs Ida, who falls into the river. Mrs. Asterbilt leaves, Adam returns, and Murgatroyd appears on the scene to declare to the whole world that Adam has murdered Ida. Nellie cannot believe his guilt. Eds.]

ACT THREE, SCENE I

[Adam has been arrested for Ida's murder, and languishes in jail. Nellie has sold the farm to the railroad in order to hire attorneys to defend Adam. She has succeeded in getting Mookie a job at the county

jail, and Mookie departs, carrying his valise and wearing his Sunday best.

[*Shortly after Mookie's departure, Murgatroyd appears and proposes to Nellie. He promises not to testify against Adam if she will marry him (Murgatroyd). But she detests Murgatroyd and spurns his advances. He then attempts to take her by force, but Mookie reappears and knocks Murgatroyd to the ground. Murgatroyd rises, dusts himself off, and departs, promising to be "horribly revenged." Mookie then leaves, telling Nellie to telegraph if ever she needs him. Eds.*]

SCENE II

[*The time: several years later. A railroad crosses the river on a trestle. Nellie's home has been converted into a signal house with a sign on it reading "N.Y., N.H. & H. R.R." Nellie has a daughter, little Nell, born of Nellie's marriage to Adam while he was languishing in jail. Nellie has been hired by the railroad as crossing watch-woman, and lives with her little daughter in the signal house. Sound effect of departing train. Nellie is discovered, standing on the track Left, looking out toward the audience. She wears a ragged old shawl, her hair is drawn back tight, and she waves a red signal flag. Eds.*]

NELLIE. Yonder goes the five-fifteen—now no other train until the six o'clock express. *(Crosses to house)* How strange it all seems! Once my happy childhood home; now a railroad crossing and signal station. How kind it was of the New York, New Haven and Hartford, in my hour of distress, to give me a position as crossing watch-woman. Who says corporations are heartless? *(Leans flag against house)* All my inheritance spent in Adam's defense—without result. He could not break through the horrible evidence of that villain, Munro. I will not even think his wretched name. At least Adam and I were married by the chaplain in the prison. I have his child to comfort me, sweet Little Nell! *(Calls)* Little Nellie! Nellie, come to Mama, dear.

LITTLE NELL. *(Enters from house with toy. She can be a small girl or child of any age. Very childish and cute in manner with a lisping voice)* Yes, Mama.

NELLIE. Dear, bright, smiling little girl! How she reminds me of my mother.

LITTLE NELL. Mama, will I go to heaven when I die?

NELLIE. Of course, dearest. All good little girls go to heaven.

LITTLE NELL. Even when they don't have daddies?

NELLIE. Poor, blighted, lonesome little child! Never to know a father's caress. *(Wipes eyes.)*

LITTLE NELL. Mother, what makes you cry? Don't cry any more. It makes me want to cry, too.

NELLIE. Yes, I must be brave. She must never know the truth about her father. I'm not crying, dear. See, I'm not crying any more. I'm laughing! I'm laughing! *(Exits hysterically, Right)*

LITTLE NELL. Poor, dear Mother. When she dies she'll surely go to heaven. Parson *(Insert name of local minister)* told me so, and he never tells fibs.

Song by LITTLE NELL.

NOBODY'S DARLING
Out in this cold world alone,
Playing around on the tracks,
Asking a penny for bread,
Begging for things that I lacks,
Fatherless, friendless and poor,
Nothing but sorrow I see.
I am nobody's darling,
Nobody cares for me.

CHORUS

Nobody's darling on earth,
Heaven will merciful be.
There I am somebody's darling.
Somebody cares for me.

Other verses and music in "Weep Some More, My Lady."

NELLIE. *(Re-enters at conclusion of song)* Now you must go inside, dear. I will be in shortly. As soon as I have flagged the Express. It is growing dark. *(LIGHTS start to dim.)*

LITTLE NELL. Yes, Mama. Will you sing to me?

NELLIE. Yes, dear, climb into your little trundle bed, and Mother will come and sing. *(LITTLE NELL goes into house)* Even though your heart is breaking, you must sing.

MOOKIE. *(Off Left)* Miz Oakhart! Miz Oakhart!

NELLIE. Ah, my old friend, Mookie Maguggins, now Sheriff of this County.

MOOKIE. *(Rushes in Left, puffing. He wears hunting suit and big star badge; gun in holster on hip.)* Has the six o'clock flyer come through yet?

NELLIE. Why, no, Mookie. It isn't time.

MOOKIE. That's good. I was afearin' we'd missed it.

NELLIE. Missed it, Mookie? But the six o'clock express does not stop here—except on signal.

MOOKIE. I got a special order to flag it. *(Shows paper)* I'm takin' a prisoner to state penitentuary.

NELLIE. Yes, this gives me the necessary authority to flag the express. Where is your prisoner, poor fellow?

MOOKIE. I left him yonder—handcuffed to the tree.

NELLIE. But Mookie, you cannot leave a man handcuffed to a tree, with the night air falling. That's cruel. No matter what he has done. What if it should rain?

MOOKIE. Won't matter much to this prisoner, marm. He's on his way to be hung.

NELLIE. Hung? How dreadful! Anyone I know?

MOOKIE. *(Sadly)* Yes, Miz Oakhart, yore husband.

NELLIE. *(Surprised)* Adam—here—with you?

MOOKIE. It's him all right, marm. We got orders today to transfer him to the state penitentuary.

NELLIE. Then his last appeal has failed?

MOOKIE. That it has. Nothin' left for him now but the gallus.

NELLIE. *(Hiding face in hands)* Oh, Mookie, how awful!

MOOKIE. I'm on'y doin' my sworn duty, marm. Ye can't blame me.

NELLIE. I do not blame you, good Mookie. You are only doing your duty. But surely I may speak to him, to murmur my last farewell?

MOOKIE. Can't be done, marm. Clean agin orders. You see, he's an exter-special criminal—he's a murderer. We're more pertickler about them.

NELLIE. But surely, Mookie, you do not believe those calumnies?

MOOKIE. No'm, can't say as I do—but the law's the law, an' I'm paid to withold it.

NELLIE. *(Pleading)* Mookie, do you love me?

MOOKIE. 'Course I loves you, marm, in a respectable sort of way. You was always good to me.

NELLIE. Then, you will do a great thing for my sake?

MOOKIE. Let you see yore husband? 'Course I will! What do you think I come early for?

NELLIE. Thank you, good Mookie, but it is much more than that I am asking.

MOOKIE. More than that? What could be more than that?

NELLIE. *(Cautiously)* Mookie—prisoners have escaped before now.

MOOKIE. Escaped?

NELLIE. Why not this one? *(Aside)* I must not shrink from saving him at any cost. Oh, it will break my heart. I shall die, I shall die. *(To him)* Oh, help me, Mookie. For my sake, go counter to your duty. *(Kneeling)* My old friend Mookie, save him, and my life shall be devoted to you.

MOOKIE. Oh, Miz Nellie—you don't know what ye're sayin'.

NELLIE. *(Clasping his legs)* Save his life and take mine! All the State asks is an eye for an eye. Take my eye! Take my tooth! Spare Adam's!

MOOKIE. If I consent, they will blame me.

NELLIE. No, no, they will believe you are on the train—until too late. I will keep him hidden here until the search is abandoned—then when all is calm he can make his escape to Canada.

MOOKIE. You mean I'm to pertend he jumped off the train?

NELLIE. Yes, yes, good Mookie. They will never find him—and you will not be blamed. Say yes, Mookie, say yes.

MOOKIE. *(After a long pause as he wavers)* Yes, Miz Nellie. You was good to ol' Bess an' me. I'll repay you.

NELLIE. *(Rises)* Thank you, thank you. We must make haste. Bring him here. I'll hide him in the cellar.

MOOKIE. I'll do it. I'll do it, by cracky. I never was a man to hold with corporal punishment. *(Exits Left)*

NELLIE. *(Elated)* Oh, joy! Oh, rapture! Fate has intervened. Fate has shown the way. *(MOOKIE reenters with ADAM in handcuffs. He wears striped convict suit)* Adam, my husband! *(Rushes to him. They embrace.)*

ADAM. Nellie, what bitter fate allows us to meet?

NELLIE. No, no, Adam, look up! All is well.

ADAM. *(Sadly)* All is not well, Nellie. The shadow of these stripes has entered into my blood, and the very garments of crime make me feel as those who wear them more justly.

NELLIE. Listen carefully. Mookie is going to permit your escape.

ADAM. Escape? *(To MOOKIE)* Do you mean it?

MOOKIE. Aye. *(Removes handcuffs.)*

ADAM. Heaven bless you.

NELLIE. Come. I will conceal you in our cellar until all search is past. There you may make acquaintance of our daughter. *(Leads him to house.)*

ADAM. A daughter, you say? We have a daughter? Oh, rapture! Mookie, I cannot thank you now—but some day, when I have proved my innocence, you shall not repent it.

NELLIE. This way, Adam, love, husband! *(They go into the house.)*

MOOKIE. Waal now, by cracky—reckon I've gone an' done it. Gone counter to my sworn oath of office. But then, arter all, what's an oath of office? jest a lot of 'fishial cuss-words. *(Postman's WHISTLE off Left)* I snum, there's the postman. He gets here late. I'll go see if he's got any mail for Nellie. *(Exits Left)*

NELLIE. *(Re-enters from house)* Thank heaven, he is carefully preserved in the fruit-cellar. Now I must go about my duties as though nothing untoward had occurred.

MOOKIE. *(Re-enters with letter)* A letter for you, Miz Oakhart. The postman just give it to me. It's from some foreign land— *(Reads postmark)* Lost Angels, Californ-eye-a.

NELLIE. Thank you, Mookie. *(Takes letter)* Now who could be writing me from California? *(Opens letter. Reads signature)* Amazement! It's from Leonie Asterbilt! Why would she be writing me? *(Reads hastily. Is amazed.)*

MOOKIE. Does she say anything about Flour-teatea?

NELLIE. *(Great surprise at what she reads)* But this is incredible news. Mookie, listen: *(Reads)* "I write to tell of my bereavement. My mother has passed away. On her deathbed she confessed to a dreadful crime. On the night preceding our departure from your abode, she stabbed Ida Rhinegold and flung her body into the river. My only hope is no one has suffered for the deed for which she alone was guilty. Signed, Leonie Asterbilt." *(To MOOKIE)* Heaven has answered my prayers.

MOOKIE. Thet means Adam is innocent, always has been. Thet letter proves it.

NELLIE. *(Joyfully)* Yes, oh, yes! Mookie, hasten to the town; bring the authorities here. Tell them I have proof of Adam's guiltlessness.

MOOKIE. Yep, I'll do that, Miz Nellie, but ye better let me have that letter.

NELLIE. No, no—it is priceless. I dare not let it from me.

MOOKIE. Be of good cheer. I'll return within the hour! *(Exits Left)*

NELLIE. I knew the truth would come to light some day, but I never suspected Mrs. Asterbilt of so foul a crime. She must have done it in a drunken frenzy. Let me read the letter again. *(Reads.)*

MUNRO. *(Off Left)* Help! Help!

MUSIC: MUNRO's theme.

NELLIE. I hear a voice crying over there. *(Looks up Left)* Who could it be? Some strange man's crawling on the ground.

MUNRO. *(Crawls on Left He is dressed like a hobo, ragged, patched clothes, half-shaven and dirty)* Water! Water!

NELLIE. He is hurt! He is dying! *(Gets dipper of water from bucket near house)* Here, drink.

MUNRO. Thank you, thank you. *(Drinks greedily.)*

NELLIE. Who are you?

MUNRO. A hungry and footsore stranger—a dying man. More! More!

NELLIE. *(Returning to bucket with dipper)* Some poor old tramp who has been thrown from a passing train by a cruel brakeman. Poor fellow!

MUNRO. Water! Water!

NELLIE. *(Returning)* Unfortunate wretch. Today in my joy, my heart overflows with kindness.

MUNRO. *(After drinking)* That brings strength to me. I am a man once more. I was dying, you've saved my life. Yes! *(Gets up)* It brings the blood back to my heart. Now I can face my pursuers.

NELLIE. *(Growing fearful)* Who are you? *(She shrinks away.)*

MUNRO. *(Viciously)* Why do you shrink from me like all the rest?

NELLIE. *(Aside)* Munro Murgatroyd.

MUNRO. Are you so timid that the sight of a poor starved, footsore fellow creature frightens you? What is there to fear from me? *(Recognizes her)* Ah! Nellie Lovelace?

NELLIE. Nellie Oakhart! I am Adam Oakhart's wife. What evil chance has brought you here?

MUNRO. Still the same proud Nellie. *(Looks around)* And yet your circumstances seem strangely altered. Your garden of goldenrod now a railroad crossing, your beautiful cottage a signal station.

NELLIE. I have remained faithful, Munro. Can you say as much?

MUNRO. So my rival still holds your affections. You still love the vile murderer.

NELLIE. Oh, no, murderer no more. I have here the full confession of the crime, given on their deathbed by the one who did the deed. *(Holds up letter.)*

MUNRO. Do you speak true? Yes, I can tell that by your eyes. Foiled, beaten everywhere! Where is the blacksmith's son?

NELLIE. This letter has just come. Even now I am expecting the proper authorities, who will order Adam's release.

MUNRO. You are alone. You hold in your hands the confession which will make him free again. If it were destroyed, all proof— *(Seizes NELLIE.)*

NELLIE. Let me go! Help! Help! *(Agitato as they struggle.)*

LITTLE NELL. *(Rushes in from house)* Mama, what is it? What are you doing with that awful man?

NELLIE. Run, child—fetch your father!

LITTLE NELL. Father, dear Father! *(Exits into house.)*

MUNRO. *(Having obtained letter)* So he is here with you—my rival already free?

ADAM. *(Enters from house, followed by LITTLE NELL)* What is it, Nellie?

MUNRO. And in convict garb? As I live and breathe! Isn't he the handsome creature? Ha, ha, ha!

ADAM. Who is this man? Wait, I recognize that bitter laugh.

NELLIE. Beware, Adam, beware! It is our deadly enemy, Munro Murgatroyd. He has in his possession a letter proving your innocence.

ADAM. Give it to me, sir.

MUNRO. Give it to you? Ha, ha, ha! *(Puts it in pocket.)*

ADAM. *(Advancing)* Munro Murgatroyd, I'm beginning to think you don't like me.

MUNRO. Stand back! *(Draws gun)* Don't like you? You are the bitterest curse of my life. My first revenge broke down and you escaped. Now I have you in my power.

NELLIE. No, no. Have mercy, mercy!

MUNRO. Mercy? Never!

NELLIE. What are you going to do?

MUNRO. There is one bullet in this gun. It is for him who I hate.

LITTLE NELL. **Whom** you hate. *(Goes to him.)*

MUNRO. Or perhaps for this little grammarian here. Yes! *(Grabs LIT-TLE NELL.)*

NELLIE. *(Screaming)* Look out!

MUNRO. Stand back! Come one step closer, and the bullet shall be hers. *(Holds onto the child, pointing the gun at her.)*

ADAM. You villain!

MUNRO. Now I have you all in my power. Adam shall die—but not with my single bullet—not so the guilt shall be mine—but a nameless death, the death of an escaping convict. Child, find a piece of rope.

NELLIE. What are you going to do?

LITTLE NELL. There's a piece over here.

MUNRO. Bring it to me. Adam Oakhart, to the railroad track.

NELLIE. Not that! Not that!

MUNRO. Do as I command, or the bullet shall be your child's. *(Points gun at LITTLE NELL, who has found a piece of rope.)*

ADAM. He has us in his power. *(Goes to tracks.)*

MUNRO. *(To LITTLE NELL)* That's fine, thank you. Give it to your mother.

LITTLE NELL. Here, Mama. What are we going to do? *(Gives her the rope.)*

NELLIE. What would you have me do?

MUNRO. Bind your husband to the railroad track, at the peril of your child's life.

NELLIE. No, no!

ADAM. Do as he says, Nellie. There's no reasoning with such a viper. *(Lays down on track.)*

NELLIE. No, no, anything else, anything—but don't make me do that.

MUNRO. Bind him to the tracks, even as I shall bind you to my will.

ADAM. Obey him, Nellie—what is my useless life compared to Little Nell's?

MUSIC: Sad and melancholy. NELLIE binds ADAM to the tie.

MUNRO. Make the knots tight. I am watching you. *(Keeps gun on LITTLE NELL.)*

NELLIE. Adam! My poor Adam! Saved only to be lost again!

ADAM. I die willingly to save you, Nellie.

NELLIE. Save me from what? A fate worse than death?

MUNRO. *(Laughing)* Ha, ha, ha!

NELLIE. Man, man, have you no pity in your soul?

MUNRO. None, for the proud Nellie Lovelace. Revenge and cruelty has always been my mastering emotion. Even as a child, I'd pluck the wings from moths and watch them squirm.

LITTLE NELL. You nasty man! *(Kicks him.)*

MUNRO. You little brat! *(Nurses bruise.)*

NELLIE. *(Shouting)* Run, Nellie, run into the woods and hide.

LITTLE NELL runs away off Right.

MUNRO. Stop! *(Points gun; fires off Right; NELLIE screams; rushes to him)* Curses! I missed!

NELLIE. Thank heaven, at least she is free from harm.

MUNRO. Be not so sure. I heard wolves howling before.

NELLIE. Even a wolf would have more compassion than you.

MUNRO. Is he bound?

NELLIE. Yes. May I kiss him farewell?

MUNRO. Do so—one last embrace. Never let it be said Munro Murgatroyd wasn't as good as a wolf.

MUSIC: Doloroso.

ADAM. *(As NELLIE kisses him tenderly on the brow)* Farewell, my Nellie, farewell.

Train WHISTLE in distance.

NELLIE. Ah, the train! *(Tries to unfasten rope.)*

MUNRO. Oh, no, you don't! *(Pulls her away from track.)*

NELLIE. Let me go!

MUNRO. *(Draws her Right)* Come with me, Nellie. We shall retire into the house—there to watch from yonder window.

NELLIE. *(Trying to get free)* No, no, not that!

MUNRO. Yes, that! Come, my dear Nellie, come! *(Gathers her up in his arms.)*

NELLIE. Help!!

ADAM. *(Straining at his ropes)* Villain, vile villain! Is there no power on earth to stay your purpose? Has heaven deserted the poor blacksmith's son?

NELLIE. *(As MUNRO carries her toward house)* Adam! Love! Husband!

MUNRO. So now, my proud beauty, I have you in my power. Who is to say me nay? Who? Who?

Cuckoo CLOCK off Right "cuckoos" six times. MUNRO carries NELLIE into the house and closes the door.

MUSIC: Furioso.

TRAIN is heard approaching. ADAM struggles to get free. NELLIE and MUNRO are seen through the window, struggling. The lights are very dim. The stage is dark.

ADAM. *(Writhing)* Is there no help, in heaven or on earth?

MOOKIE. *(Enters Left)* Thet there is, sor—on earth. *MUSIC: Chord.*

ADAM. Quick, Mookie, free me.

MOOKIE. That I will, sor. What devil did this? Don't tell me. I kin guess—Old Duckbottom. *(Starts to untie ropes.)*

TRAIN comes nearer.

MUNRO. *(Enters from house. Aside)* Ah, the cunning rascal; he thinks to defeat my purpose! *(Locks door behind him. Finds noose of rope; steals up behind MOOKIE. Neither of the MEN see him.)*

MOOKIE. Keep yore chin up, Adam. I'll have you loose quicker'n yeast.

MUNRO. *(Lassoing MOOKIE)* Oh, yeah?

MOOKIE. Waylaid!

MUNRO. Little do you know the power of Munro Murgatroyd. Now, my friend, our ancient score shall be settled too. *(Binds MOOKIE to track)* The world shall believe both the keeper and the convict died in an attempted escape.

NELLIE. *(Beating on door from inside)* Let me out! Let me out!

WARN CURTAIN.

MUNRO. Never! This is my hour of triumph. *(Completes work; starts to move Right, only to discover foot is caught in track)* My foot! *(Struggles to free himself)* I am caught! Caught in my own trap! Help! Help! *(Struggles to get leg loose.)*

TRAIN louder.

NELLIE. Help! Help!

ADAM. *(Calling)* Nellie! Quickly! Cut our bonds!

NELLIE. I cannot! I am locked within! *(Pounds on door.)*

ADAM. Our last hope has gone! Is this then to be the end?

IDA. *(Off Right)* Courage, Adam Oakhart, courage! *(Enters Right paddling boat as in Act One.)*

MUNRO. Whose voice is that?

IDA. It is I! Ida Rhinegold.

MUNRO. Ida? Is this some spectre come to haunt me? Some shade of my wretched past?

IDA. Not so, Munro. I am flesh and blood.

MUNRO. Then loose me quickly. There is not a moment to lose. Any moment the train will sweep across the trestle.

IDA. *(Scornfully)* Loose you, vile villain! I would see you burn in the darkest flames below. Adam Oakhart alone shall have my succor. *(Goes to him.)*

ADAM. No, no, there is not a moment to lose. Free Mookie first.

MOOKIE. After you, Adam, after you.

IDA starts to work on ADAM's bonds. TRAIN whistles.

MUNRO. Save me! Have mercy! Mercy!

IDA. *(Laughing)* Ha, ha, ha!

MOOKIE. Look out!!

The TRAIN is seen coming across the trestle. This is done only by a light which is gradually unmasked so it grows bigger and brighter as the sound of the rushing train thunders in the ears.

QUICK CURTAIN

LIGHTS come up dimly on picture: ADAM stands near house with NELLIE in his arms; LITTLE NELL clings to his leg, MOOKIE and IDA stand near tracks, looking down at body of MUNRO, still on tracks, over which a sheet has been thrown.

ADAM. Nellie, look up. The danger is past. *(WARN CURTAIN.)*

NELLIE. You are safe, dear husband?

ADAM. Yes, all are saved, except, except— *(Glances at MUNRO.)*

MOOKIE. Mr. Duckbottom! Now he's on'y half a man. Hur! Hur! Hur! *(Laughs heartily.)*

NELLIE. A cruel fate, even for a villain. Perhaps he really didn't mean any harm.

ADAM. Good, kind, tender Nellie—always forgiving her enemies. *(Kisses her tenderly, then puts her down.)*

NELLIE. And whom am I to thank for this great service?

IDA. *(Coming down)* Me. Ida Rhinegold.

NELLIE. Then you are not dead?

IDA. No. When I was shoved into the river, I struck out. Being a pretty good swimmer—I was once a bathing beauty—I reached the opposite shore. Weak and wounded, I knew not my identity. I was taken to a convent of good sisters, and only this morning recovered my memory. I set out for here—the rest, you know.

NELLIE. Dear, good Ida! You came most opportunely.

ADAM. *(Taking NELLIE's hand, they come to footlights)* All the clouds of our life have passed away, and now no gloom obscures the future, no shadow flecks the presence of my brave, my tempted, my tried, yet ever true Nellie.

MUSIC: "Oh, What a Pal was Mary."

CURTAIN

Notes

1. *Melodrama.* At one time the term melodrama was applied generally to opera. It came to mean a play, usually accompanied by music, with emphasis on spectacle and sensation designed to stimulate the audience's emotions.

Melodrama as an established art form reached its height in the 1890s. It is little performed today, although, like other art forms, it may someday see a startling revival.

The melodrama art form was characterized by broad, sweeping gestures. The actors almost spoke in sign language with their bodies. Asides and soliloquies were spoken directly to the audience. The performance was usually interspersed with songs, and the lead characters (hero, villain, etc.) had identifiable musical themes announcing their entrance. In moments of agitation there would be agitated background music, etc. Not unlike the modern-day movie.

The melodrama was fast-paced and far-fetched. But the actors were always required to be sincere. They had to be caught up in the plot, in order to take the audience with them in a willing suspension of disbelief.

Dirty Work at the Crossroads is a typical example of the melodrama genre.

2. *Drama.* In a sense all drama is melodramatic. In that regard, review the plays of this chapter. A close cousin, farce, thrived throughout the nineteenth century. Lincoln was watching a popular farce, *Our American Cousin*, by Tom Taylor, when he was assassinated by John Wilkes Booth at Ford's Theater on April 14, 1865.

3. *The Law in Melodrama.* What is the role of law in *Dirty Work at the Crossroads*? Why would a number of legal motifs be woven into such a far-fetched and emotionally overwrought play?

4. *The Olio.* There were *entr'acte* performances in the melodrama, usually songs by the actors or others. One such olio is *Come Home, Father*, given below. This song was written by Henry Clay Work (1832–1884), and became a mainstay of the prohibitionist movement. Work also wrote *Grandfather's Clock* and *Marching Through Georgia*.

Wags may do the song humorously, with the drunken father at a bar table and a son entering with lantern in hand. In this portrayal, the chimes in the steeple may be ahead on each hour by one gong.

Or the song may be sung very seriously indeed.

COME HOME, FATHER

1. Father, dear father, come home with me now!

    The clock in the steeple strikes one.

    You said you were coming right home from the shop

    As soon as your day's work was done.

    Our fire has gone out, our house is all dark,

    And mother's been watching since tea,

    With poor brother Benny so sick in her arms,

    And no one to help her but me.

    CHORUS

    Come home, come home, come home!

    Please, Father, dear Father, come home!

    Hear the sweet voice of the child,

    Which the night winds repeat as they roam!

    Oh, who could resist this most plaintive of prayers?

    Please, Father, dear Father, come home!

2. Father, dear father, come home with me now!

    The clock in the steeple strikes two;

    The night has grown colder, and Benny is worse—

    But he has been calling for you.

    Indeed he is worse—Ma says he will die—

    Perhaps before morning shall dawn;

    And this is the message she sent me to bring—

    "Come quickly, or he will be gone."

    (repeat CHORUS)

3. Father, dear father, come home with me now!

    The clock in the steeple strikes three;

    The house is so lonely!—the hours are so long

    For poor weeping mother and me.

    Yes, we are alone—poor Benny is dead,

    And gone with the angels of light;

    And these were the very last words that he said—

    "I want to kiss Papa good night."

    (repeat CHORUS)

CHAPTER FIVE

POEMS

A. INTRODUCTION

The study of poetry can provide the most valuable skill for the study of law. Poetic language, like legal language, is very compact. The syntax and structure must be examined with great care. Word choice is critical to the writer's meaning. No word is extraneous.

Poems, like law stories, have a beginning and an end. Everything must be judged by its order in the sequence of events. But poems, like law, can sometimes take you by surprise and begin *in medias res*. Or, the beginning may foretell the end, and the ending may redound to the beginning. It is up to the good lawyer to determine whether a resolution has been achieved.

Poems are often tightly ordered in rhyme scheme, meter, and word play. Order is a primary characteristic of the law. Poems, like the law, are usually difficult to understand. A poem generally can never be resolved to a single meaning. Lawyers pretend that the law can be, but in their hearts they know otherwise. Who has ever captured that leprechaun, the reasonable person? Who can identify a true *res ipsa loquitur*? Would anyone be so intrepid as to define insanity, or free speech, with precision? Potter Stewart admitted more about the law than he probably realized when, in *Jacobellis v. Ohio*, 378 U.S. 184, 84 S.Ct. 1676, 12 L.Ed.2d 793 (1964), he said he could not define pornography, but "I know it when I see it." The lawyer may find it difficult to comprehend reality through a perspective of negative capability, or suspended judgment, but the poet exists always in such an environment of suspension.

Perhaps the hallmark of poetry is that it rises to a level of communication far above that ordinarily attempted by prose. Poetry, first and foremost, sings in the mind of the hearer. It is onomatopoetic. Good prose can be poetic, however, and so can good law.

B. HUMOR

POST HOC
Anon.

There once was a young man from Ealing,
Who took a train down to Wheeling;
A sign on the door
Said "Don't spit on the floor,"
So he lay down and spat on the ceiling.

PRODUCTS LIABILITY
Anon.

There once was lady in tort,
Who brought some new stretch pants for sport;
A spider therein
Did bite her rear end,
"But whose fault was that?" cried the court!

Notes

1. *The Limerick.* The limerick is as ancient as the sonnet, and as complicated in structure. It goes 3, 3, 2, 2, 3 in meter, and A A B B A in rhyme scheme. Which is the most difficult to understand: the limerick, the sonnet, or the law?

2. *Post Hoc.* Why didn't the young man spit on the wall, instead of undertaking the rather strenuous task of spitting on the ceiling? Would he have spat at all, had there been no sign on the door?

3. *Products Liability.* This limerick is loosely based on *Flippo v. Mode O'Day Frock Shops of Hollywood, Inc.*, 248 Ark. 1, 449 S.W.2d 692 (1970).

LOVE
Anon.

There's the wonderful love of a beautiful maid,
And the love of a staunch true man,
And the love of a baby that's unafraid—
All have existed since time began.
But the most wonderful love, the Love of all loves,
Even greater than the love for Mother,
Is the infinite, tenderest, passionate love
Of one dead drunk for another.

SONNETS
William Shakespeare
116

Let me not to the marriage of true minds
Admit impediments. Love is not love
Which alters when it alteration finds,
Or bends with the remover to remove.
O no, it is an ever-fixèd mark
That looks on tempests and is never shaken;
It is the star to every wand'ring bark,
Whose worth's unknown, although his height be taken.
Love's not time's fool, though rosy lips and cheeks
Within his bending sickle's compass come.
Love alters not with his brief hours and weeks,
But bears it out ev'n to the edge of doom.
    If this be error and upon me proved,
    I never writ, nor no man ever loved.

130

My mistress' eyes are nothing like the sun—
Coral is far more red than her lips' red—
If snow be white, why then her breasts are dun—
If hairs be wires, black wires grow on her head:
I have seen roses damasked, red and white,
But no such roses see I in her cheeks,
And in some perfumes is there more delight
Than in the breath that from my mistress reeks.
I love to hear her speak, yet will I know
That music hath a far more pleasing sound.
I grant I never saw a goddess go;
My mistress when she walks treads on the ground.
    And yet by heav'n I think my love as rare
    As any she belied with false compare.

138

When my love swears that she is made of truth,
I do believe her though I know she lies,
That she might think me some untutored youth,
Unlearned in the world's false subtleties.
Thus vainly thinking that she thinks me young,
Although she knows my days are past the best,
Simply I credit her false-speaking tongue:
On both sides thus is simple truth suppressed.
But wherefore says she not she is unjust?
And wherefore say not I that I am old?
O love's best habit is in seeming trust,

And age in love loves not to have years told.
 Therefore I lie with her, and she with me,
 And in our faults by lies we flattered be.

128

How oft, when thou my music music play'st
Upon that blessèd wood whose motion sounds
With thy sweet fingers when thou gently sway'st
The wiry concord that mine ear confounds,
Do I envy those jacks that nimble leap
To kiss the tender inward of thy hand,
Whilst my poor lips, which should that harvest reap,
At the wood's boldness by thee blushing stand.
To be so tickled they would change their state
And situation with those dancing chips.
O'er whom thy fingers walk with gentle gait,
Making dead wood more blest than living lips.
 Since saucy jacks so happy are in this,
 Give them thy fingers, me thy lips to kiss.

Note

1. *Sonnet 116 and Sonnet 130.* Sonnet 116 is normally interpreted as a love poem. Alternatively, it can be read as a rather stiff-necked, moralizing pronouncement of an uncompromising prude. Or again, the final couplet suggests a humorous bent of the writing. Could the author have intended all three interpretations?

Conversely, Sonnet 130 has a dramatic reverse effect. The writer appears to be kidding his beloved until the final couplet: her beauty is as rare as any of the things to which she has been falsely compared.

Did you know that "she" was often used as a noun meaning "woman" in early modern English, so that "a she" or "any she" can mean "any woman"? Does this knowledge change your reading of the final couplet?

Discuss the different ways the word "lies" is used in Sonnet 138. Give several examples of such wordplay in contemporary literature. Is such word play ever relevant to law?

THE NAMING OF CATS
T.S. Eliot

The Naming of Cats is a difficult matter,
It isn't just one of your holiday games;
You may think at first I'm as mad as a hatter
When I tell you, a cat must have three different names.
First of all, there's the name that the family use daily,
Such as Peter, Augustus, Alonzo, or James,
Such as Victor or Jonathan, George or Bill Bailey—

All of them sensible everyday names.
There are fancier names if you think they sound sweet-
er,
Some for gentlemen, some for the dames:
Such as Plato, Admetus, Electra, Demeter—
But all of them sensible everyday names.
But I tell you, a cat needs a name that's particular,
A name that's peculiar, and more dignified,
Else how can he keep up his tail perpendicular,
Or spread out his whiskers, or cherish his pride?
Of names of this kind, I can give you a quorum,
Such as Munkustrap, Quaxo, or Coricopat,
Such as Bombalurina, or else Jellylorum—
Names that never belong to more than one cat.
But above and beyond there's still one name left over,
And that is the name that you never will guess;
The name that no human research can discover—
But THE CAT HIMSELF KNOWS, and will never
confess.
When you notice a cat in profound meditation,
The reason, I tell you, is always the same:
His mind is engaged in a rapt contemplation
Of the thought, of the thought, of the thought of his
name:
His ineffable effable
Effanineffable
Deep and inscrutable singular Name.

Notes

1. *The Poet.* Eliot's *Waste Land* as well as most of his other writings depicts a depressing, lost world. Yet his series of poems about cats is light and playful. What does this contrast of views suggest about the author's outlook on life?

2. *The Play.* If you have seen the musical *Cats*, did your reading of this poem echo the music or the staging accompanying this poem in the play? If so, how does that echo affect your enjoyment of the poem? Can you present the poem differently from how it is presented in the play?

3. *The People.* Do people have "[e]ffanineffable/ Deep and inscrutable singular name(s)"? Consider this quote from the psychologist D.W. Winnicott: "At the centre of each person is an incommunicado element and this is sacred and most worthy of preservation."

JANET WAKING
John Crowe Ransom

Beautifully Janet slept
Till it was deeply morning. She woke then
And thought about her dainty-feathered hen,

To see how it had kept.

One kiss she gave to her mother.
Only a small one gave she to her daddy
Who would have kissed each curl of his shining baby;
No kiss at all for her brother.

"Old Chucky, old Chucky!" she cried,
Running across the world upon the grass
To Chucky's house, and listening. But alas,
Her Chucky had died.

It was a transmogrifying bee
Came droning down on Chucky's old bald head
And sat and put the poison. It scarcely bled,
But how exceedingly

And purply did the knot
Swell with the venom and communicate
Its rigor! Now the poor comb stood up straight
But Chucky did not.

So there was Janet
Kneeling on the wet grass, crying her brown hen
(Translated far beyond the daughters of men)
To rise and walk upon it.

And weeping fast as she had breath
Janet implored us, "Wake her from her sleep!"
And would not be instructed in how deep
Was the forgetful kingdom of death.

Notes

1. *The Forgetful Kingdom of Death.* Ransom's poem, "Janet Waking," could equally well have been placed under the heading of "Death" or of "Youth." Which heading should it have been placed under? If it is placed under the heading of humor, what sort of humor is involved?

Do you oftentimes find in law, and in life, that a subject should be placed under a different heading than that which it is given?

2. *Style.* How does the style of "Janet Waking" compare to the style of the poems by Shakespeare and Eliot? Isn't "Janet" rather prosaic? Can you identify specific aspects of this poem that distinguish it from Shakespeare's sonnets or Eliot's poem?

C. AGING

PUSH ME, PLEASE
Anon.

Which I didn't. Perhaps, were he a child,
I would have done; but he was in his sixties,

Sitting in the hall, in the nursing home,
In his wheelchair, waiting for someone to help;
Why me? I knew him from nobody else.
Like the priest and Levite, I later felt,
My chance to help was now forever gone.
When I came back, the next day, he was gone too.

Note

1. *Literary References*. This poem radiates Biblical references to the New Testament. "Inasmuch as ye have done it unto one of the least of these...." *Matthew* 25:40. See also the parable of the Good Samaritan, *Luke* 10:33–37.

The priest and the Levite in *Luke* may well have feared the possible adverse legal consequences of providing aid to a stranger.

THE FOLLY OF BEING COMFORTED
William Butler Yeats

One that is ever kind said yesterday:
"Your well-beloved's hair has threads of grey,
And little shadows come about her eyes;
Time can but make it was easier to be wise
Though now it seem impossible, and so
All that you need is patience."
                    Heart cries, "No,
I have not a crumb of comfort, not a grain.
Time can but make her beauty over again:
Because of that great nobleness of hers
The fire that stirs about her, when she stirs,
Burns but more clearly. O she had not these ways
When all the wild summer was in her gaze."
Heart! O heart! If she'd but turn her head,
You'd know the folly of being comforted.

Notes

1. *Comfort*. Is the would-be comforter like a lawyer? Is the uncomforted meant to appear unrealistic?

2. *Heart*. Is the word "heart" in this poem intended to be read literally or figuratively? How do you know Yeats's intention? Is the "Heart" in line 7 identical to the "heart" and "head" in line 13? Read the poem with the three "hearts" having identical meaning and again with the three "hearts" each having a different meaning.

SONNET 63
William Shakespeare

Against my love shall be, as I am now,
With time's injurious hand crushed and o'erworn,
When hours have drained his blood and filled his brow
With lines and wrinkles, when his youthful morn
Hath travelled on to age's steepy night,
And all those beauties whereof now he's king
Are vanishing or vanished out of sight,
Stealing away the treasure of his spring—
For such a time do I now fortify
Against confounding age's cruel knife,
That he shall never cut from memory
My sweet love's beauty, though my lover's life.
    His beauty shall in these black lines be seen,
    And they shall live, and he in them still green.

Note

1. *Against.* What does the word "against" mean in line 1? Can the phrase "my love" in line 1 be read in more than one way? What point is Shakespeare making in line 12 by distinguishing "[m]y sweet love's beauty" from "my lover's life"?

SONNET 73
William Shakespeare

That time of year thou mayst in me behold
When yellow leaves, or none, or few, do hang
Upon those boughs which shake against the cold,
Bare ruin'd choirs, where late the sweet birds sang.
In me thou see'st the twilight of such day
As after sunset fadeth in the west;
Which by and by black night doth take away,
Death's second self, that seals up all in rest.
In me thou see'st the glowing of such fire,
That on the ashes of his youth doth lie,
As the death-bed whereon it must expire
Consum'd with that which it was nourish'd by.
    This thou perceiv'st, which makes thy love more strong,
    To love that well which thou must leave ere long.

Note

1. *Imagery.* This sonnet contains a number of striking images that are justly famous. Catalog the images or phrases that appeal to you and explain their appeal.

D. DEATH

O CAPTAIN! MY CAPTAIN!
Walt Whitman

O Captain! my Captain! our fearful trip is done;
The ship has weather'd every rack, the prize we sought
is won;
The port is near, the bells I hear, the people all
exulting,
While follow eyes the steady keel, the vessel grim and
daring:
But O heart! heart! heart!
O the bleeding drops of red,
Where on the deck my Captain lies,
Fallen cold and dead.

O Captain! my Captain! rise up and hear the bells;
Rise up——for you the flag is flung——for you the
bugle trills;
For you bouquets and ribbon'd wreaths——for you the
shores a-crowding;
For you they call, the swaying mass, their eager faces
turning;
Here Captain! dear father!
This arm beneath your head;
It is some dream that on the deck,
You've fallen cold and dead.

My Captain does not answer, his lips are pale and still;
My father does not feel my arm, he has no pulse nor
will;
The ship is anchor'd safe and sound, its voyage closed
and done;
From fearful trip, the victor ship, comes in with object
won;
Exult, O shores, and ring, O bells!
But I, with mournful tread,
Walk the deck my Captain lies,
Fallen cold and dead.

Notes

1. *Lincoln.* This poem memorializes the death of Lincoln. Whitman
wrote a longer, deeply melancholy elegy for Lincoln, "When Lilacs Last in
the Dooryard Bloom'd." Could you tell—if you did not already know—that
the "Captain" of this poem was intended to refer to Lincoln?

2. *The Metaphor.* Explain how the extended metaphor of the poem
works as a reference to Lincoln. Are there others to whom the poem could
apply?

SONNET 126
William Shakespeare

O thou, my lovely boy, who in thy pow'r
Dost hold Time's fickle glass, his sickle hour,
Who hast by waning grown, and therein show'st
Thy lovers withering, as thy sweet self grow'st—
If Nature, sovereign mistress over wrack,
As thou goest onwards, still will pluck thee back,
She keeps thee to this purpose, that her skill
May time disgrace and wretched minutes kill.
Yet fear her, O thou minion of her pleasure;
She may detain, but not still keep, her treasure.
Her audit, though delay'd, answer'd must be,
And her quietus is to render thee.

Notes

1. *The Truncated Sonnet.* While no. 126 is included within Shakespeare's collection of 154 sonnets, strictly speaking it is not a sonnet since it lacks the final couplet. The flaming love of the earlier sonnets has gone completely sour, and it is as if the poet could not bring himself to complete the poem.

2. *Quietus.* What metaphor is deployed in lines 11–12 here? Does that metaphor come too late to be meaningful?

THE BLACK SNAKE
Mary Oliver

When the black snake
flashed onto the morning road,
and the truck could not swerve—
death, that is how it happens.

Now he lies looped and useless
as an old bicycle tire.
I stop the car
and carry him to the bushes.

He is as cool and gleaming
as a braided whip, he is as beautiful and quiet
as a dead brother.
I leave him under the leaves

and drive on, thinking
about *death*: its sudddenness,
its terrible weight,
its certain coming. Yet under

reason burns a brighter fire, which the bones
have always preferred.

It is the story of endless good fortune.
It says to oblivion: not me!

It is the light at the center of every cell.
It is what sent the snake coiling and flowing forward
happily all spring through the green leaves before
he came to the road.

Note

1. *The Serpent.* This poem is taken from the author's collection of poems entitled *Twelve Moons* (1979). The poem makes us remember how we must admire all of Nature's creatures.

DO NOT GO GENTLE INTO THAT GOOD NIGHT
Dylan Thomas

Do not go gentle into that good night,
Old age should burn and rave at close of day;
Rage, rage against the dying of the light.

Though wise men at their end know dark is right,
Because their words had forked no lightning they
Do not go gentle into that good night.

Good men, the last wave by, crying how bright
Their frail deeds might have danced in a green bay,
Rage, rage against the dying of the light.

Wild men who caught and sang the sun in flight,
And learn, too late, they grieved it on its way,
Do not go gentle into that good night.

Grave men, near death, who see with blinding sight
Blind eyes could blaze like meteors and be gay,
Rage, rage against the dying of the light.

And you, my father, there on the sad height,
Curse, bless, me now with your fierce tears, I pray.
Do not go gentle into that good night.
Rage, rage against the dying of the light.

E.　DESOLATION

THE SICK ROSE
William Blake

O Rose, thou art sick!
The invisible worm
That flies in the night,
In the howling storm,
Has found out thy bed
Of crimson joy,

And his dark secret love
Does thy life destroy.

Note

1. *Flowers*. If there is one thing this poem is not about, it is not about horticulture ... is it? Note that the rose is addressed in the second person familiar.

The last line invites an accent on every syllable. Some might be tempted to lighten the accent on the first syllable of "destroy," but the alliteration of "Does" does not allow that. The effect is hammer-like, like driving nails into a coffin. This effect contrasts sharply with the flying sound of the invisible worm in the howling storm. The difference is between the onset of a fatal illness, and the conclusion of the illness.

PSALM 137
King James Bible

¹ By the rivers of Babylon, there we sat down, yea, we wept, when we remembered Zion.

² We hanged our harps upon the willows in the midst thereof.

³ For there they that carried us away captive required of us a song; and they that wasted us required of us mirth, saying, Sing us one of the songs of Zion.

⁴ How shall we sing the LORD's song in a strange land?

⁵ If I forget thee, O Jerusalem, let my right hand forget her cunning.

⁶ If I do not remember thee, let my tongue cleave to the roof of my mouth; if I prefer not Jerusalem above my chief joy.

⁷ Remember, O LORD, the children of Edom in the day of Jerusalem; who said, Rase it, rase it, even to the foundation thereof.

⁸ O daughter of Babylon, who art to be destroyed; happy shall he be, that rewardeth thee as thou hast served us.

⁹ Happy shall he be, that taketh and dasheth thy little ones against the stones.

Note

1. *In a Strange Land*. There are few more poignant lines than that of verse 4: "How shall we sing the Lord's song in a strange land?" Can this poignancy be reconciled with verse 9?

Note the sinister sibilance of the final phrase of verse 3. The same "s" sound turns to one of sorrow in the following verse. In view of this remarkable parallel, yet strikingly dissonant, use of the same consonant sound in verses 3 and 4, it is apparent that onomatopoeia is not inherent in sounds alone.

PSALM 42
King James Bible

[1] As the hart panteth after the water brooks, so panteth my soul after thee, O God.

[2] My soul thirsteth for God, for the living God: when shall I come and appear before God?

[3] My tears have been my meat day and night, while they continually say unto me, Where is thy God?

[4] When I remember these things, I pour out my soul in me: for I had gone with the multitude, I went with them to the house of God, with the voice of joy and praise, with a multitude that kept holyday.

[5] Why art thou cast down, O my soul? and why art thou disquieted in me? hope thou in God: for I shall yet praise him for the help of his countenance.

[6] O my God, my soul is cast down within me: therefore will I remember thee from the land of Jordan, and of the Hermonites, from the hill Mizar.

[7] Deep calleth unto deep at the noise of thy waterspouts: all thy waves and thy billows are gone over me.

[8] Yet the LORD will command his lovingkindness in the daytime, and in the night his song shall be with me, and my prayer unto the God of my life.

[9] I will say unto God my rock, Why hast thou forgotten me? why go I mourning because of the oppression of the enemy?

[10] As with a sword in my bones, mine enemies reproach me; while they say daily unto me, Where is thy God?

[11] Why art thou cast down, O my soul? and why art thou disquieted within me? hope thou in God: for I shall yet praise him, who is the health of my countenance, and my God.

Note

1. *Concreteness.* One of the things that makes the King James Bible so great is its striking use of concrete imagery. "As the hart panteth ... so panteth my soul." The psalmist's tears have been his "meat day and night." In verse 5 the psalmist's soul is "cast down," in the same way that a rock might be thrown to the ground.

Vernacular speech usually has this concrete quality. The King James achieves the remarkable feat of combining the common vernacular with a loftiness of tone and theme.

THE CLOD AND THE PEBBLE
William Blake

"Love seeketh not itself to please,
Nor for itself hath any care,
But for another gives its ease,
And builds a Heaven in Hell's despair."

So sung a little Clod of Clay
Trodden with the cattle's feet,
But a Pebble of the brook
Warbled out these metres meet:

"Love seeketh only self to please,
To bind another to its delight,
Joys in another's loss of ease,
And builds a Hell in Heaven's despite."

Note

1.   *Ambiguity*. Why does Blake choose a clod to praise love, and a pebble to condemn it?

SONG
William Blake

How sweet I roam'd from field to field,
And tasted all the summer's pride,
'Till I the prince of love beheld,
Who in the sunny beams did glide!

He shew'd me lilies for my hair,
And blushing roses for my brow;
He led me through his gardens fair,
Where all his golden pleasures grow.

With sweet May dews my wings were wet,
And Phœœbus fir'd my vocal rage;
He caught me in his silken net,
And shut me in his golden cage.

He loves to sit and hear me sing,
Then, laughing, sports and plays with me;
Then stretches out my golden wing,
And mocks my loss of liberty.

Notes

1.   *Love*. Who is the "prince of love"?

2.   *Liberty*. What is the "loss of liberty" referred to in the last line?

LONDON
William Blake

I wander thro' each charter'd street,
Near where the charter'd Thames does flow,
And mark in every face I meet
Marks of weakness, marks of woe.

In every cry of every Man,
In every Infant's cry of fear,
In every voice, in every ban,
The mind-forg'd manacles I hear.

How the Chimney-sweeper's cry
Every black'ning Church appalls;
And the hapless Soldier's sigh
Runs in blood down Palace walls.

But most thro' midnight streets I hear
How the youthful Harlot's curse
Blasts the new born Infant's tear,
And blights with plagues the Marriage hearse.

Notes

1. *Charter'd Street.* A law student in our class said he thought the law word "chartered" seemed extraneous to the poem. Is it? Give three relevant meanings of the word. Which meaning, in your view, is the most correct? Does the word "chartered" have overtones of "charnel"? Why?

2. *Corporations.* Corporations are "chartered." How are corporations relevant to the poem?

I NEVER HEAR THE WORD "ESCAPE"
Emily Dickinson

I never hear the word "escape"
Without a quicker blood,
A sudden expectation,
A flying attitude.
I never hear of prisons broad
By soldiers battered down,
But I tug childish at my bars,—
Only to fail again!

THE REVELATION OF SAINT JOHN THE DIVINE
CHAPTER 18

King James Bible

[1] And after these things I saw another angel come down from heaven, having great power; and the earth was lightened with his glory.

[2] And he cried mightily with a strong voice, saying, Babylon the great is fallen, is fallen, and is become the habitation of devils, and the hold of every foul spirit, and a cage of every unclean and hateful bird.

[3] For all nations have drunk of the wine of the wrath of her fornication, and the kings of the earth have committed fornication with her, and the merchants of the earth are waxed rich through the abundance of her delicacies.

[4] And I heard another voice from heaven, saying, Come out of her, my people, that ye be not partakers of her sins, and that ye receive not of her plagues.

[5] For her sins have reached unto heaven, and God hath remembered her iniquities.

[6] Reward her even as she rewarded you, and double unto her double according to her works: in the cup which she hath filled fill to her double.

[7] How much she hath glorified herself, and lived deliciously, so much torment and sorrow give her: for she saith in her heart, I sit a queen, and am no widow, and shall see no sorrow.

[8] Therefore shall her plagues come in one day, death, and mourning, and famine; and she shall be utterly burned with fire: for strong is the LORD God who judgeth her.

[9] And the kings of the earth, who have committed fornication and lived deliciously with her, shall bewail her, and lament for her, when they shall see the smoke of her burning,

[10] Standing afar off for the fear of her torment, saying, Alas, alas, that great city Babylon, that mighty city! for in one hour is thy judgment come.

[11] And the merchants of the earth shall weep and mourn over her; for no man buyeth their merchandise any more:

[12] The merchandise of gold, and silver, and precious stones, and of pearls, and fine linen, and purple, and silk, and scarlet, and all thyine wood, and all manner vessels of ivory, and all manner vessels of most precious wood, and of brass, and iron, and marble,

[13] And cinnamon, and odours, and ointments, and frankincense, and wine, and oil, and fine flour, and wheat, and beasts, and sheep, and horses, and chariots, and slaves, and souls of men.

[14] And the fruits that thy soul lusted after are departed from thee, and all things which were dainty and goodly are departed from thee, and thou shalt find them no more at all.

[15] The merchants of these things, which were made rich by her, shall stand afar off for the fear of her torment, weeping and wailing,

[16] And saying, Alas, alas, that great city, that was clothed in fine linen, and purple, and scarlet, and decked with gold, and precious stones, and pearls!

[17] For in one hour so great riches is come to nought. And every shipmaster, and all the company in ships, and sailors, and as many as trade by sea, stood afar off,

[18] And cried when they saw the smoke of her burning, saying, What city is like unto this great city!

[19] And they cast dust on their heads, and cried, weeping and wailing, saying, Alas, alas, that great city, wherein were made rich all that had ships in the sea by reason of her costliness! for in one hour is she made desolate.

[20] Rejoice over her, thou heaven, and ye holy apostles and prophets; for God hath avenged you on her.

[21] And a mighty angel took up a stone like a great millstone, and cast it into the sea, saying, Thus with violence shall that great city Babylon be thrown down, and shall be found no more at all.

[22] And the voice of harpers, and musicians, and of pipers, and trumpeters, shall be heard no more at all in thee; and no craftsman, of whatsoever craft he be, shall be found any more in thee; and the sound of a millstone shall be heard no more at all in thee;

[23] And the light of a candle shall shine no more at all in thee; and the voice of the bridegroom and of the bride shall be heard no more at all in thee: for thy merchants were the great men of the earth; for by thy sorceries were all nations deceived.

[24] And in her was found the blood of prophets, and of saints, and of all that were slain upon the earth.

BEREFT
Robert Frost

Where had I heard this wind before
Change like this to a deepening roar?
What would it take my standing there for,
Holding open a restive door,
Looking down hill to a frothy shore?
Summer was past and the day was past.
Sombre clouds in the west were massed.
Out in the porch's sagging floor,
Leaves got up in a coil and hissed,

Blindly struck at my knee and missed.
Something sinister in the tone
Told me my secret must be known:
Word I was in the house alone
Somehow must have gotten abroad,
Word I was in my life alone,
Word I had no one left but God.

Note

1. *Rhyme and Meter.* Frost begins with five rhyming lines, followed by a couplet, and then a one-line return to the first rhyme. After that, there are two couplets, concluding with a quatrain of A B A B, with the A's being the same word and the B's being a half rhyme. The two "alone's" in the final quatrain reflect in meaning and rhyme a desperate attempt to hold together the disintegrating rhyme scheme.

The four-beat meter encourages a caesura in the middle of each line. This repetitive, lonesome beat is broken by frequent switches from the iambic to the trochee. This switching picks up the sound of ordinary speech, for which Frost's poetry is noted. The final two lines are starkly spondaic— except for a single iamb, standing alone.

This complicated kind of interrelation between sound and sense characterizes good prose, as well as good poetry. The good lawyer is aware of this interrelation.

SONNET 49
William Shakespeare

Against that time, (if ever that time come),
When I shall see thee frown on my defects,
Whenas thy love hath cast his utmost sum,
Call'd to that audit by advised respects—
Against that time when thou shalt strangely pass,
And scarcely greet me with that sun thine eye,
When love converted from the thing it was
Shall reasons find of settled gravity—
Against that time do I ensconce me here
Within the knowledge of mine own desert,
And this my hand against myself uprear,
To guard the lawful reasons on thy part—
    To leave poor me thou hast the strength of laws,
    Since why to love I can allege no cause.

SONNET 87
William Shakespeare

Farewell, thou art too dear for my possessing,
And like enough thou know'st thy estimate.
The charter of thy worth gives thee releasing;

My bonds in thee are all determinate.
For how do I hold thee but by thy granting,
And for that riches where is my deserving?
The cause of this fair gift in me is wanting,
And so my patent back again is swerving.
Thyself thou gav'st, thy own worth then not knowing,
Or me, to whom thou gavest it, else mistaking;
So thy great gift, upon misprision growing,
Comes home again, on better judgment making.
    Thus have I had thee, as a dream doth flatter:
    In sleep a king, but waking no such matter.

SONNET 69
William Shakespeare

Those parts of thee that the world's eye doth view
Want nothing that the thoughts of hearts can mend.
All tongues, the voice of souls, give thee that due,
Utt'ring bare truth, ev'n so as foes commend.
Thy outward thus with outward praise is crowned,
But those same tongues that give thee so thine own,
In other accents do this praise confound
By seeing farther than the eye hath shown.
They look into the beauty of thy mind,
And that in guess they measure by thy deeds;
Then, churls, their thoughts—although their eyes were kind—
To thy fair flow'r add the rank smell of weeds;
    But why thy odor matcheth not thy show,
    The soil is this, that thou dost common grow.

Note

1. *Imagery and Word Meaning.* Sonnets 49 and 87 are filled with legal imagery, used by one who has no legal claim on his beloved. The last line of no. 49 picks up the desolate reply of Lear to his daughters Goneril and Reagan, when they ask why he needs an entourage of knights in his retirement: "O, reason not the need! Our basest beggars are in the poorest things superfluous." *King Lear,* Act II, sc. iv, ll. 264–265.

No. 69 concludes, "The soil is this, that thou dost common grow." The word "soil" here is used in the sense of "stain" (e.g., "you have soiled your shirt"). The *Oxford English Dictionary* gives an additional sixteenth-century meaning, "solution." Is the author thus using "soil" as a double entendre?

What does the word "common" mean, both today and in the sixteenthth century? The *OED* is a wonderful source of insight into the vocabulary of pre–21st-century works of literature.

Does it matter what the word meant at the time the work was written? Or is the only relevant meaning today's meaning? The United States

Supreme Court has grown fond of using dictionaries as an aid to statutory interpretation. Which dictionary should they use? One that is contemporaneous with the passage of an act? Or its amendment, even if the word in question is not revised? Or one that is contemporary with the facts of the case under consideration?

NEVER GIVE ALL THE HEART
William Butler Yeats

Never give all the heart, for love
Will hardly seem worth thinking of
To passionate women if it seem
Certain, and they never dream
That it fades out from kiss to kiss;
For everything that's lovely is
But a brief, dreamy, kind delight.
O never give the heart outright,
For they, for all smooth lips can say,
Have given their hearts up to the play.
And who could play it well enough
If deaf and dumb and blind with love?
He that made this knows all the cost,
For he gave all his heart and lost.

Notes

1. *Another Case of Mis-Categorization?* Is this not a humorous poem—at least until the last couplet? Compare "Janet Waking" in the section on humor.

2. *Sonnet.* Did you recognize Yeats' poem as a sonnet? How does Yeats' invocation of that form—surely a conscious choice—affect the meaning of the poem? Compare the final couplet to that of Shakespeare's Sonnet 87 above. Why does Yeats refer to himself as "he who made this" rather than "I"?

3. *Maude Gonne.* In your experience is this poem true? Is your answer affected by the knowledge that Yeats was in love with an Irish revolutionary, Maud Gonne, for 6 years and proposed marriage to her numerous times, but was rejected each time?

MY LIFE CLOSED TWICE
Emily Dickinson

My life closed twice before its close;
It yet remains to see
If Immortality unveil
A third event to me,

So huge, so hopeless to conceive,
As these that twice befell.

Parting is all we know of heaven,
And all we need of hell.

WILLIAM SHAKESPEARE
MACBETH
Act V Scene 5

She should have died hereafter;
There would have been a time for such a word.
To-morrow, and to-morrow, and to-morrow
Creeps in this petty pace from day to day
To the last syllable of recorded time;
And all our yesterdays have lighted fools
The way to dusty death. Out, out, brief candle!
Life's but a walking shadow, a poor player,
That struts and frets his hour upon the stage
And then is heard no more. It is a tale
Told by an idiot, full of sound and fury,
Signifying nothing.

Note

1. *Passion.* If there is one thing that characterizes the great Shakespeare, it is his ability to evoke passion even on behalf of characters that are not likeable. In the above scene, Macbeth has just been told of the death of Lady Macbeth. In the next scene, just before his own death, Macbeth laments: "They have tied me to a stake. I cannot fly,/But bear-like I must fight the course."

In *King John,* Act III, scene 4, Constance, the not very likeable mother of Arthur, on learning of the imprisonment of her son and having a premonition of his death, expresses the lament of every bereaved mother:

Grief fills the room up of my absent child,
Lies in his bed, walks up and down with me,
Puts on his pretty looks, repeats his words,
Remembers me of all his gracious parts,
Stuffs out his vacant garments with his form;
Then, have I reason to be fond of grief?

On the night before his defeat at the Battle of Bosworth, Richard III dreams of his own impending death and awakes to deliver a terrifying, schizophrenic monologue (Act V, scene 3):

I shall despair. These is no creature loves me,
And if I die, no soul will pity me.
And, wherefore should they, since I myself
Find in myself no pity to myself?

When Lear discovers, in the final scene of the play, that Cordelia is dead, he delivers what some believe to be the most pathetic line in all of literature. Reversing the iamb for the trochee in the second line, he mourns for all bereaved parents of all times:

And thou no breath at all? Thou'lt come no more,
Never, never, never, never, never!

DOVER BEACH
Matthew Arnold

The sea is calm tonight,
The tide is full, the moon lies fair
Upon the straits;—on the French coast the light
Gleams and is gone; the cliffs of England stand,
Glimmering and vast, out in the tranquil bay.
Come to the window, sweet is the night-air!
Only, from the long line of spray
Where the sea meets the moon-blanched land,
Listen! you hear the grating roar
Of pebbles which the waves draw back, and fling,
At their return, up the high strand,
Begin, and cease, and then again begin,
With tremulous cadence slow, and bring
The eternal note of sadness in.

Sophocles long ago
Heard it on the Aegean, and it brought
Into his mind the turbid ebb and flow
Of human misery; we
Find also in the sound a thought,
Hearing it by this distant northern sea.

The Sea of Faith
Was once, too, at the full, and round earth's shore
Lay like the folds of a bright girdle furled.
But now I only hear
Its melancholy, long, withdrawing roar,
Retreating, to the breath
Of the night-wind, down the vast edges drear
And naked shingles of the world.

Ah, love, let us be true
To one another! for the world, which seems
To lie before us like a land of dreams,
So various, so beautiful, so new,
Hath really neither joy, nor love, nor light,
Nor certitude, nor peace, nor help for pain;
And we are here as on a darkling plain
Swept with confused alarms of struggle and flight,
Where ignorant armies clash by night.

ACQUAINTED WITH THE NIGHT
Robert Frost

I have been one acquainted with the night.
I have walked out in rain—and back in rain.
I have outwalked the furthest city light.

I have looked down the saddest city lane.
I have passed by the watchman on his beat
And dropped my eyes, unwilling to explain.

I have stood still and stopped the sound of feet
When far away an interrupted cry
Came over houses from another street,

But not to call me back or say good-bye;
And further still at an unearthly height
One luminary clock against the sky

Proclaimed the time was neither wrong nor right.
I have been one acquainted with the night.

THE WORLD IS TOO MUCH WITH US
William Wordsworth

The World is too much with us; late and soon,
Getting and spending, we lay waste our powers:
Little we see in Nature that is ours;
We have given our hearts away, a sordid boon!
This Sea that bares her bosom to the moon;
The winds that will be howling at all hours;
And are up-gathered now like sleeping flowers;
For this, for everything, we are out of tune;
It moves us not.—Great God! I'd rather be
A pagan suckled in a creed outworn;
So might I, standing on this pleasant lea,
Have glimpses that would make me less forlorn;
Have sight of Proteus rising from the sea;
Or hear old Triton blow his wreathèd horn.

Notes

1. *Sea of Faith.* What is the Sea of Faith referred to by Arnold in "Dover Beach"? Give at least three possibilities.

2. *Darkling Plain.* The final stanza of "Dover Beach" is justly famous; the poetry in this stanza is beautiful while the content is depressing. Is this contrast a paradox? If so, how do you explain it?

3. *Luminary Clock.* What is the "luminary clock" referred to by Frost in "Acquainted with the Night"? Give at least three possibilities.

4. *Stanza.* The final stanza of "Acquainted with the Night" has only two lines, instead of three as do the preceding stanzas. What is the effect of this change in form?

5. *Getting and Spending.* According to Wordsworth in "The World Is Too Much With Us," what powers are we laying waste by "getting and spending"?

6. *Proteus & Triton.* What is the significance of the mythological allusions in the final two lines of Wordworth's poem? Try rewriting the poem from "Great God! I'd rather be" in your own terms.

I REASON, EARTH IS SHORT
Emily Dickinson

I reason, earth is short,
And anguish absolute.
And many hurt;
But what of that?

I reason, we could die:
The best vitality
Cannot excel decay;
But what of that?

I reason that in heaven
Somehow, it will be even,
Some new equation given;
But what of that?

PAIN HAS AN ELEMENT OF BLANK
Emily Dickinson

Pain has an element of blank;
It cannot recollect
When it began, or if there were
A day when it was not.

It has no future but itself,
Its infinite realms contain
Its past, enlightened to perceive
New periods of pain.

Note

1. *Translation.* Are the words "pain" and "blank," in the second poem by Dickinson, onomatopoeic? Why?

What does the poet mean by the question, "But what of that?" Give three different paraphrases of the question. Give three different oral readings of the question.

F. THE FALL

PARADISE LOST

BOOK IX
John Milton

The Argument

Satan having compast the Earth, with meditated guile returns as a mist by Night into Paradise, enters into the Serpent sleeping. Adam and Eve in the Morning go forth to their labours, which Eve proposes to divide in several places, each labouring apart: Adam consents not, alleging the danger, lest that Enemy, of whom they were forewarn'd, should attempt her found alone: Eve loath to be thought not circumspect or firm enough, urges her going apart, the rather desirous to make trial of her strength; Adam at last yields: The Serpent finds her alone; his subtle approach, first gazing, then speaking, with much flattery extolling Eve above all other Creatures. Eve wond'ring to hear the Serpent speak, asks how he attain'd both human speech and understanding not till now; the Serpent answers, that by tasting of a certain Tree in the Garden he attain'd to Speech and Reason, till then void of both: Eve requires him to bring her to that Tree, and finds it to be the Tree of Knowledge forbidden: The Serpent now grown bolder, with many wiles and arguments induces her at length to eat; she pleas'd with the taste deliberates awhile whether to impart thereof to Adam or not, at last brings him of the Fruit, relates what persuaded her to eat thereof: Adam at first amaz'd, but perceiving her lost, resolves through vehemence of love to perish with her; and extenuating the trespass, eats also of the Fruit: The effects thereof in them both; they seek to cover their nakedness; then fall into variance and accusation of one another.

No more of talk where God or Angel guest
With Man, as with his friend, familiar us'd
To sit indulgent, and with him partake
Rural repast, permitting him the while
Venial discourse unblam'd. I now must change
Those notes to tragic—foul distrust, and breach
Disloyal on the part of Man, revolt
And disobedience; on the part of Heav'n,
Now alienated, distance and distaste,
Anger and just rebuke, and judgment giv'n,
That brought into this World a world of woe,
Sin and her shadow Death, and Misery,
Death's harbinger. Sad task! yet argument
Not less but more heroic than the wrath
Of stern Achilles on his foe pursu'd
Thrice fugitive about Troy wall; or rage
Of Turnus for Lavinia disespous'd;
Or Neptune's ire, or Juno's, that so long

Perplex'd the Greek, and Cytherea's son:
If answerable style I can obtain
Of my celestial patroness, who deigns
Her nightly visitation unimplor'd,
And dictates to me slumb'ring, or inspires
Easy my unpremeditated verse:
Since first this subject for heroic song
Pleas'd me, long choosing and beginning late,
Not sedulous by nature to indite
Wars, hitherto the only argument
Heroic deem'd, chief maistry to dissect
With long and tedious havoc fabl'd knights
In battles feign'd—the better fortitude
Of patience and heroic martyrdom
Unsung; or to describe races and games,
Or tilting furniture, emblazon'd shields,
Impreses quaint, caparisons and steeds,
Bases and tinsel trappings, gorgeous knights
At joust and tournament; then marshall'd feast
Serv'd up in hall with sewers and seneschals,
The skill of artifice or office mean:
Not that which justly gives heroic name
To person or to poem. Me, of these
Nor skill'd nor studious, higher argument
Remains, sufficient of itself to raise
That name, unless an age too late, or cold
Climate, or years, damp my intended wing
Depress'd; and much they may if all be mine,
Not hers who brings it nightly to my ear.

        The sun was sunk, and after him the star
Of Hesperus, whose office is to bring
Twilight upon the earth, short arbiter
'Twixt day and night, and now from end to end
Night's hemisphere had veil'd the horizon round,
When Satan, who late fled before the threats
Of Gabriel out of Eden, now improv'd
In meditated fraud and malice, bent
On Man's destruction, maugre what might hap
Of heavier on himself, fearless return'd.
By night he fled, and at midnight return'd
From compassing the earth, cautious of day
Since Uriel, Regent of the Sun, descried
His entrance and forewarn'd the Cherubim
That kept their watch. Thence, full of anguish, driv'n,
The space of seven continu'd nights he rode
With darkness—thrice the equinoctial line
He circl'd, four times cross'd the car of Night
From pole to pole, traversing each colure—

On the eighth return'd and, on the coast averse
From entrance or cherubic watch, by stealth
Found unsuspected way. There was a place
(Now not, though Sin, not Time, first wrought the change)
Where Tigris, at the foot of Paradise,
Into a gulf shot under ground, till part
Rose up a fountain by the Tree of Life.
In with the river sunk and with it rose
Satan, involv'd in rising mist; then sought
Where to lie hid. Sea he had search'd and land
From Eden over Pontus, and the pool
Maeotis, up beyond the river Ob;
Downward as far antarctic; and, in length,
West from Orontes to the ocean barr'd
At Darien; thence to the land where flows
Ganges and Indus. Thus the orb he roam'd
With narrow search, and with inspection deep
Consider'd every creature, which of all
Most opportune might serve his wiles, and found
The serpent subtlest beast of all the field.
Him, after long debate, irresolute
Of thoughts revolv'd, his final sentence chose
Fit vessel, fittest imp of fraud, in whom
To enter, and his dark suggestions hide
From sharpest sight; for in the wily snake,
Whatever sleights, none would suspicious mark
As from his wit and native subtlety
Proceeding, which, in other beasts observ'd,
Doubt might beget of diabolic pow'r
Active within beyond the sense of brute.
Thus he resolv'd, but first from inward grief
His bursting passion into plaints thus pour'd:

      "O Earth, how like to Heav'n, if not preferr'd
More justly, seat worthier of Gods, as built
With second thoughts, reforming what was old!
For what God after better worse would build?
Terrestrial Heav'n, danc'd round by other heav'ns
That shine, yet bear their bright officious lamps
Light above light, for thee alone as seems,
In thee concentring all their precious beams
Of sacred influence! As God in Heav'n
Is centre, yet extends to all, so thou
Centring receiv'st from all those orbs; in thee,
Not in themselves, all their known virtue appears,
Productive in herb, plant, and nobler birth
Of creatures animate with gradual life
Of growth, sense, reason, all summ'd up in Man.
With what delight could I have walk'd thee round,

If I could joy in aught—sweet interchange
Of hill and valley, rivers, woods, and plains,
Now land, now sea, and shores with forest crown'd,
Rocks, dens, and caves! But I in none of these
Find place or refuge; and the more I see
Pleasures about me, so much more I feel
Torment within me, as from the hateful siege
Of contraries: all good to me becomes
Bane, and in Heav'n much worse would be my state.
But neither here seek I, no, nor in Heav'n,
To dwell, unless by mast'ring Heav'n's Supreme;
Nor hope to be myself less miserable
By what I seek, but others to make such
As I, though thereby worse to me redound—
For only in destroying I find ease
To my relentless thoughts; and him destroy'd,
Or won to what may work his utter loss,
For whom all this was made, all this will soon
Follow, as to him link'd in weal or woe:
In woe then, that destruction wide may range!
To me shall be the glory sole among
The infernal Powers, in one day to have marr'd
What he, Almighty styl'd, six nights and days
Continu'd making, and who knows how long
Before had been contriving? though perhaps
Not longer than since I in one night freed
From servitude inglorious well-nigh half
Th' angelic name, and thinner left the throng
Of his adorers. He, to be aveng'd,
And to repair his numbers thus impair'd—
Whether such virtue, spent of old, now fail'd
More Angels to create, if they at least
Are his created, or to spite us more,
Determin'd to advance into our room
A creature form'd of earth, and him endow,
Exalted from so base original,
With heav'nly spoils, our spoils. What he decreed
He effected: Man he made, and for him built
Magnificent this World, and Earth his seat,
Him Lord pronounc'd, and, O indignity!
Subjected to his service Angel-wings
And flaming ministers, to watch and tend
Their earthy charge. Of these the vigilance
I dread, and to elude, thus wrapt in mist
Of midnight vapour glide obscure, and pry
In every bush and brake where hap may find
The serpent sleeping, in whose mazy folds
To hide me and the dark intent I bring.
O foul descent! that I, who erst contended

With Gods to sit the highest, am now constrain'd
Into a beast, and, mix'd with bestial slime,
This essence to incarnate and imbrute,
That to the highth of Deity aspir'd!
But what will not ambition and revenge
Descend to? Who aspires must down as low
As high he soar'd, obnoxious first or last
To basest things. Revenge, at first though sweet,
Bitter ere long back on itself recoils;
Let it; I reck not, so it light well aim'd,
Since higher I fall short, on him who next
Provokes my envy, this new favourite
Of Heav'n, this Man of clay, son of despite,
Whom us the more to spite, his Maker rais'd
From dust: spite then with spite is best repaid."

   So saying, through each thicket, dank or dry,
Like a black mist low-creeping, he held on
His midnight search where soonest he might find
The serpent. Him fast sleeping soon he found,
In labyrinth of many a round self-roll'd,
His head the midst, well stor'd with subtle wiles:
Not yet in horrid shade or dismal den,
Nor nocent yet, but on the grassy herb,
Fearless, unfear'd, he slept. In at his mouth
The Devil enter'd, and his brutal sense
In heart or head possessing, soon inspir'd
With act intelligential, but his sleep
Disturb'd not, waiting close th' approach of morn.
Now, when as sacred light began to dawn
In Eden on the humid flow'rs, that breath'd
Their morning incense, when all things that breathe
From th' Earth's great altar send up silent praise
To the Creator, and his nostrils fill
With grateful smell, forth came the human pair,
And join'd their vocal worship to the quire
Of creatures wanting voice; that done, partake
The season, prime for sweetest scents and airs;
Then commune how that day they best may ply
Their growing work: for much their work outgrew
The hands' dispatch of two gard'ning so wide.
And Eve first to her husband thus began:

   "Adam, well may we labour still to dress
This garden, still to tend plant, herb, and flow'r,
Our pleasant task enjoin'd; but till more hands
Aid us the work under our labour grows,
Luxurious by restraint: what we by day
Lop overgrown, or prune or prop or bind,
One night or two with wanton growth derides,

Tending to wild. Thou, therefore, now advise,
Or hear what to my mind first thoughts present,
Let us divide our labours, thou where choice
Leads thee, or where most needs, whether to wind
The woodbine round this arbour, or direct
The clasping ivy where to climb, while I,
In yonder spring of roses intermix'd
With myrtle, find what to redress till noon;
For while so near each other thus all day
Our task we choose, what wonder if so near
Looks intervene and smiles, or objects new
Casual discourse draw on, which intermits
Our day's work, brought to little though begun
Early, and th' hour of supper comes unearn'd!"

   To whom mild answer Adam thus returned:
"Sole Eve, associate sole, to me beyond
Compare above all living creatures dear!
Well hast thou motion'd, well thy thoughts employ'd,
How we might best fulfil the work which here
God hath assign'd us, nor of me shalt pass
Unprais'd; for nothing lovelier can be found
In woman than to study household good,
And good works in her husband to promote.
Yet not so strictly hath our Lord impos'd
Labour as to debar us when we need
Refreshment, whether food or talk between,
Food of the mind, or this sweet intercourse
Of looks and smiles; for smiles from reason flow,
To brute denied, and are of love the food,
Love not the lowest end of human life.
For not to irksome toil, but to delight,
He made us, and delight to reason join'd.
These paths and bowers doubt not but our joint hands
Will keep from wilderness with ease, as wide
As we need walk, till younger hands ere long
Assist us. But if much converse perhaps
Thee satiate, to short absence I could yield;
For solitude sometimes is best society,
And short retirement urges sweet return.
But other doubt possesses me, lest harm
Befall thee, sever'd from me; for thou know'st
What hath been warn'd us; what malicious foe,
Envying our happiness, and of his own
Despairing, seeks to work us woe and shame
By sly assault; and somewhere nigh at hand
Watches, no doubt, with greedy hope to find
His wish and best advantage, us asunder,
Hopeless to circumvent us join'd, where each

To other speedy aid might lend at need.
Whether his first design be to withdraw
Our fealty from God, or to disturb
Conjugal love—than which perhaps no bliss
Enjoy'd by us excites his envy more—
Or this or worse, leave not the faithful side
That gave thee being, still shades thee and protects.
The wife, where danger or dishonour lurks,
Safest and seemliest by her husband stays,
Who guards her, or with her the worst endures."

      To whom the virgin majesty of Eve,
As one who loves, and some unkindness meets,
With sweet austere composure thus replied:
"Offspring of Heav'n and Earth, and all Earth's lord!
That such an enemy we have, who seeks
Our ruin, both by thee inform'd I learn,
And from the parting Angel overheard
As in a shady nook I stood behind
Just then return'd at shut of evening flow'rs.
But that thou shouldst my firmness therefore doubt
To God or thee, because we have a foe
May tempt it, I expected not to hear.
His violence thou fear'st not, being such
As we, not capable of death or pain,
Can either not receive or can repel.
His fraud is then thy fear; which plain infers
Thy equal fear that my firm faith and love
Can by his fraud be shak'n or seduc'd:
Thoughts—which how found they harbour in thy breast,
Adam?—misthought of her to thee so dear!"

      To whom with healing words Adam replied:
"Daughter of God and Man, immortal Eve!—
For such thou art, from sin and blame entire—
Not diffident of thee do I dissuade
Thy absence from my sight, but to avoid
Th' attempt itself, intended by our foe.
For he who tempts, though in vain, at least asperses
The tempted with dishonour foul, suppos'd
Not incorruptible of faith, not proof
Against temptation. Thou thyself with scorn
And anger wouldst resent the offer'd wrong,
Though ineffectual found; misdeem not, then,
If such affront I labour to avert
From thee alone, which on us both at once
The enemy, though bold, will hardly dare,
Or, daring, first on me th' assault shall light.
Nor thou his malice and false guile contemn—
Subtle he needs must be who could seduce

Angels—nor think superfluous other's aid.
I from the influence of thy looks receive
Access in every virtue—in thy sight
More wise, more watchful, stronger, if need were
Of outward strength; while shame, thou looking on,
Shame to be overcome or overreach'd,
Would utmost vigour raise, and rais'd unite.
Why shouldst not thou like sense within thee feel
When I am present, and thy trial choose
With me, best witness of thy virtue tried?"

    So spake domestic Adam in his care
And matrimonial love; but Eve, who thought
Less attributed to her faith sincere,
Thus her reply with accent sweet renew'd:

    "If this be our condition, thus to dwell
In narrow circuit strait'n'd by a foe,
Subtle or violent, we not endu'd
Single with like defence wherever met,
How are we happy, still in fear of harm?
But harm precedes not sin: only our foe
Tempting affronts us with his foul esteem
Of our integrity; his foul esteem
Sticks no dishonour on our front, but turns
Foul on himself. Then wherefore shunn'd or fear'd
By us, who rather double honour gain
From his surmise prov'd false, find peace within,
Favour from Heav'n, our witness, from th' event?
And what is faith, love, virtue, unassay'd
Alone, without exterior help sustain'd?
Let us not then suspect our happy state
Left so imperfect by the Maker wise
As not secure to single or combin'd:
Frail is our happiness, if this be so,
And Eden were no Eden, thus expos'd."

    To whom thus Adam fervently replied:
"O Woman, best are all things as the will
Of God ordain'd them; his creating hand
Nothing imperfect or deficient left
Of all that he created, much less Man
Or aught that might his happy state secure,
Secure from outward force. Within himself
The danger lies, yet lies within his power:
Against his will he can receive no harm.
But God left free the will; for what obeys
Reason is free, and reason he made right,
But bid her well beware and still erect,
Lest, by some fair appearing good surpris'd,
She dictate false and misinform the will

To do what God expressly hath forbid.
Not then mistrust, but tender love, enjoins
That I should mind thee oft, and mind thou me.
Firm we subsist, yet possible to swerve,
Since reason not impossibly may meet
Some specious object by the foe suborn'd
And fall into deception unaware,
Not keeping strictest watch as she was warn'd.
Seek not temptation, then, which to avoid
Were better—and most likely if from me
Thou sever not. Trial will come unsought.
Wouldst thou approve thy constancy, approve
First thy obedience; th' other who can know?
Not seeing thee attempted, who attest?
But if thou think trial unsought may find
Us both securer than thus warn'd thou seem'st,
Go; for thy stay, not free, absents thee more.
Go in thy native innocence; rely
On what thou hast of virtue, summon all;
For God towards thee hath done his part: do thine."

      So spake the Patriarch of Mankind; but Eve
Persisted; yet submiss, though last, replied:
"With thy permission, then, and thus forewarn'd,
Chiefly by what thy own last reasoning words
Touch'd only, that our trial when least sought
May find us both perhaps far less prepar'd,
The willinger I go, nor much expect
A foe so proud will first the weaker seek—
So bent, the more shall shame him his repulse."

      Thus saying, from her husband's hand her hand
Soft she withdrew, and, like a wood-nymph light,
Oread or Dryad or of Delia's train,
Betook her to the groves; but Delia's self
In gait surpass'd and goddess-like deport,
Though not as she with bow and quiver arm'd,
But with such gard'ning tools as art, yet rude,
Guiltless of fire had form'd, or Angels brought.
To Pales or Pomona, thus adorn'd,
Likest she seem'd, Pomona when she fled
Vertumnus, or to Ceres in her prime,
Yet virgin of Proserpina from Jove.
Her long with ardent look his eye pursu'd
Delighted, but desiring more her stay;
Oft he to her his charge of quick return
Repeated; she to him as oft engag'd
To be return'd by noon amid the bower,
And all things in best order to invite
Noontide repast or afternoon's repose.

O much deceiv'd, much failing, hapless Eve,
Of thy presum'd return! event perverse!
Thou never from that hour in Paradise
Found'st either sweet repast or sound repose;
Such ambush, hid among sweet flowers and shades,
Waited with hellish rancour imminent
To intercept thy way, or send thee back
Despoil'd of innocence, of faith, of bliss.
For now, and since first break of dawn, the Fiend,
Mere serpent in appearance, forth was come,
And on his quest where likeliest he might find
The only two of mankind, but in them
The whole included race, his purpos'd prey.
In bower and field he sought, where any tuft
Of grove or garden-plot more pleasant lay,
Their tendance or plantation for delight,
By fountain or by shady rivulet
He sought them both, but wish'd his hap might find
Eve separate: he wish'd, but not with hope
Of what so seldom chanc'd, when to his wish,
Beyond his hope, Eve separate he spies,
Veil'd in a cloud of fragrance where she stood
Half-spied, so thick the roses bushing round
About her glow'd, oft stooping to support
Each flower of tender stalk whose head, though gay
Carnation, purple, azure, or speck'd with gold,
Hung drooping unsustain'd. Them she upstays
Gently with myrtle band, mindless the while
Herself, though fairest unsupported flow'r,
From her best prop so far, and storm so nigh.
Nearer he drew, and many a walk travers'd
Of stateliest covert, cedar, pine, or palm;
Then voluble and bold, now hid, now seen
Among thick-wov'n arborets and flow'rs
Imborder'd on each bank, the hand of Eve:
Spot more delicious than those gardens feign'd
Or of reviv'd Adonis, or renown'd
Alcinous, host of old Laertes' son,
Or that, not mystic, where the sapient king
Held dalliance with his fair Egyptian spouse.
Much he the place admir'd, the person more.
As one who, long in populous city pent,
Where houses thick and sewers annoy the air,
Forth issuing on a summer's morn, to breathe
Among the pleasant villages and farms
Adjoin'd, from each thing met conceives delight,
The smell of grain, or tedded grass, or kine,
Or dairy, each rural sight, each rural sound;
If chance with nymph-like step fair virgin pass,

What pleasing seem'd, for her now pleases more,
She most, and in her look sums all delight.
Such pleasure took the Serpent to behold
This flow'ry plat, the sweet recess of Eve
Thus early, thus alone; her heav'nly form
Angelic, but more soft and feminine,
Her graceful innocence, her every air
Of gesture or least action, overaw'd
His malice, and with rapine sweet bereav'd
His fierceness of the fierce intent it brought;
That space the Evil One abstracted stood
From his own evil, and for the time remain'd
Stupidly good, of enmity disarm'd,
Of guile, of hate, of envy, of revenge;
But the hot Hell that always in him burns,
Though in mid Heav'n, soon ended his delight,
And tortures him now more, the more he sees
Of pleasure not for him ordain'd: then soon
Fierce hate he recollects, and all his thoughts
Of mischief, gratulating, thus excites:

       "Thoughts, whither have ye led me? with what sweet
Compulsion thus transported to forget
What hither brought us? Hate, not love, nor hope
Of Paradise for Hell, hope here to taste
Of pleasure, but all pleasure to destroy,
Save what is in destroying, other joy
To me is lost. Then let me not let pass
Occasion which now smiles. Behold alone
The Woman, opportune to all attempts;
Her husband—for I view far round—not nigh,
Whose higher intellectual more I shun,
And strength, of courage haughty, and of limb
Heroic built, though of terrestrial mould:
Foe not informidable, exempt from wound,
I not; so much hath Hell debas'd, and pain
Enfeebl'd me, to what I was in Heav'n.
She fair, divinely fair, fit love for Gods;
Not terrible, though terror be in love
And beauty, not approach'd by stronger hate,
Hate stronger under show of love well feign'd,
The way which to her ruin now I tend."

       So spake the Enemy of Mankind, enclos'd
In serpent, inmate bad, and toward Eve
Address'd his way, not with indented wave
Prone on the ground, as since, but on his rear,
Circular base of rising folds that tow'r'd
Fold above fold, a surging maze, his head
Crested aloft, and carbuncle his eyes;

With burnished neck of verdant gold, erect
Amidst his circling spires that on the grass
Floated redundant: pleasing was his shape
And lovely, never since of serpent kind
Lovelier, not those that in Illyria chang'd
Hermione and Cadmus, or the God
In Epidaurus; nor to which transform'd
Ammonian Jove, or Capitoline, was seen,
He with Olympias, this with her who bore
Scipio, the heighth of Rome. With tract oblique
At first, as one who sought access but fear'd
To interrupt, sidelong he works his way.
As when a ship, by skilful steersman wrought
Nigh river's mouth or foreland, where the wind
Veers oft, as oft so steers and shifts her sail,
So varied he, and of his tortuous train
Curl'd many a wanton wreath in sight of Eve,
To lure her eye; She busied, heard the sound
Of rustling leaves, but minded not, as us'd
To such disport before her through the field
From every beast, more duteous at her call
Than at Circean call the herd disguis'd.
He, bolder now, uncall'd before her stood,
But as in gaze admiring: Oft he bow'd
His turret crest and sleek enamell'd neck,
Fawning, and lick'd the ground whereon she trod.
His gentle dumb expression turn'd at length
The eye of Eve to mark his play; he, glad
Of her attention gain'd, with serpent-tongue
Organic, or impulse of vocal air,
His fraudulent temptation thus began:
"Wonder not, sovran mistress, if perhaps
Thou canst who art sole wonder, much less arm
Thy looks, the heav'n of mildness, with disdain,
Displeas'd that I approach thee thus and gaze
Insatiate, I thus single, nor have fear'd
Thy awful brow, more awful thus retir'd.
Fairest resemblance of thy Maker fair,
Thee all things living gaze on, all things thine
By gift, and thy celestial beauty adore,
With ravishment beheld, there best beheld
Where universally admir'd; but here,
In this enclosure wild, these beasts among,
Beholders rude and shallow to discern
Half what in thee is fair, one man except
Who sees thee (and what is one?) who shouldst be seen
A Goddess among Gods, ador'd and serv'd
By Angels numberless, thy daily train?"

So gloz'd the Tempter, and his proem tun'd;
Into the heart of Eve his words made way,
Though at the voice much marvelling; at length,
Not unamaz'd, she thus in answer spake:
"What may this mean? Language of man pronounc'd
By tongue of brute, and human sense express'd?
The first at least of these I thought denied
To beasts, whom God on their creation-day
Created mute to all articulate sound;
The latter I demur, for in their looks
Much reason, and in their actions, oft appears.
Thee, Serpent, subtlest beast of all the field
I knew, but not with human voice endu'd;
Redouble then this miracle, and say
How cam'st thou speakable of mute, and how
To me so friendly grown above the rest
Of brutal kind that daily are in sight?
Say, for such wonder claims attention due."

To whom the guileful Tempter thus replied:
"Empress of this fair World, resplendent Eve!
Easy to me it is to tell thee all
What thou command'st, and right thou shouldst be obey'd:
I was at first as other beasts that graze
The trodden herb, of abject thoughts and low
As was my food, nor aught but food discern'd
Or sex, and apprehended nothing high:
Till on a day roving the field, I chanc'd
A goodly tree far distant to behold,
Loaden with fruit of fairest colours mix'd,
Ruddy and gold. I nearer drew to gaze,
When from the boughs a savoury odour blown,
Grateful to appetite, more pleas'd my sense
Than smell of sweetest fennel, or the teats
Of ewe or goat dropping with milk at ev'n,
Unsuck'd of lamb or kid, that tend their play.
To satisfy the sharp desire I had
Of tasting those fair apples, I resolv'd
Not to defer; hunger and thirst at once,
Powerful persuaders, quick'n'd at the scent
Of that alluring fruit, urg'd me so keen.
About the mossy trunk I wound me soon;
For high from ground the branches would require
Thy utmost reach or Adam's: round the tree
All other beasts that saw, with like desire
Longing and envying stood, but could not reach.
Amid the tree now got where plenty hung
Tempting so nigh, to pluck and eat my fill
I spar'd not; for such pleasure till that hour

At feed or fountain never had I found.
Sated at length, ere long I might perceive
Strange alteration in me, to degree
Of reason in my inward powers, and speech
Wanted not long, though to this shape retain'd.
Thenceforth to speculations high or deep
I turn'd my thoughts, and with capacious mind
Consider'd all things visible in Heav'n,
Or Earth, or Middle, all things fair and good;
But all that fair and good in thy divine
Semblance, and in thy beauty's heav'nly ray,
United I beheld; no fair to thine
Equivalent or second, which compell'd
Me thus, though importune perhaps, to come
And gaze, and worship thee of right declar'd
Sovran of creatures, universal Dame!"
So talk'd the spirited sly Snake; and Eve,
Yet more amaz'd, unwary thus replied:

      "Serpent, thy overpraising leaves in doubt
The virtue of that fruit, in thee first prov'd:
But say, where grows the tree, from hence how far?
For many are the trees of God that grow
In Paradise, and various, yet unknown
To us; in such abundance lies our choice
As leaves a greater store of fruit untouch'd,
Still hanging incorruptible, till men
Grow up to their provision, and more hands
Help to disburden Nature of her bearth."

      To whom the wily Adder, blithe and glad,
"Empress, the way is ready and not long:
Beyond a row of myrtles, on a flat
Fast by a fountain, one small thicket past
Of blowing myrrh and balm; If thou accept
My conduct, I can bring thee thither soon."

      "Lead, then," said Eve. He, leading, swiftly roll'd
In tangles, and made intricate seem straight,
To mischief swift. Hope elevates, and joy
Brightens his crest. As when a wand'ring fire,
Compact of unctuous vapour which the night
Condenses, and the cold environs round,
Kindl'd through agitation to a flame,
Which oft, they say, some evil spirit attends,
Hovering and blazing with delusive light,
Misleads th' amaz'd night-wanderer from his way
To bogs and mires, and oft through pond or pool,
There swallow'd up and lost, from succour far:
So glister'd the dire Snake, and into fraud
Led Eve, our credulous Mother, to the Tree

Of Prohibition, root of all our woe;
Which when she saw, thus to her guide she spake:

      "Serpent, we might have spar'd our coming hither,
Fruitless to me, though fruit be here to excess,
The credit of whose virtue rest with thee,
Wondrous indeed, if cause of such effects.
But of this tree we may not taste nor touch;
God so commanded, and left that command
Sole daughter of his voice; the rest, we live
Law to ourselves, our reason is our law."

      To whom the Tempter guilefully replied:
"Indeed! Hath God then said that of the fruit
Of all these garden-trees ye shall not eat,
Yet lords declar'd of all in earth or air?"

      To whom thus Eve, yet sinless: "Of the fruit
Of each tree in the garden we may eat;
But of the fruit of this fair tree, amidst
The garden, God hath said, 'Ye shall not eat
Thereof, nor shall ye touch it, lest ye die."

      She scarce had said, though brief, when now more bold
The Tempter, but with show of zeal and love
To Man, and indignation at his wrong,
New part puts on, and as to passion mov'd,
Fluctuates disturb'd, yet comely, and in act
Rais'd, as of some great matter to begin.
As when of old some orator renown'd
In Athens or free Rome, where eloquence
Flourish'd, since mute, to some great cause address'd,
Stood in himself collected, while each part,
Motion, each act, won audience ere the tongue
Sometimes in heighth began, as no delay
Of preface brooking through his zeal of right.
So standing, moving, or to heighth upgrown,
The Tempter, all impassion'd, thus began.

      "O sacred, wise, and wisdom-giving Plant,
Mother of science! now I feel thy power
Within me clear, not only to discern
Things in their causes, but to trace the ways
Of highest agents, deem'd however wise.
Queen of this Universe! do not believe
Those rigid threats of death; ye shall not die.
How should ye? by the fruit? it gives you life
To knowledge: By the Threat'ner? look on me,
Me who have touch'd and tasted, yet both live,
And life more perfect have attain'd than Fate
Meant me, by vent'ring higher than my lot.
Shall that be shut to Man which to the beast

Is open? or will God incense his ire
For such a petty trespass, and not praise
Rather your dauntless virtue, whom the pain
Of death denounc'd, whatever thing death be,
Deterr'd not from achieving what might lead
To happier life, knowledge of good and evil?
Of good, how just? of evil, if what is evil
Be real, why not known, since easier shunn'd?
God therefore cannot hurt ye, and be just;
Not just, not God; not fear'd then, nor obey'd:
Your fear itself of death removes the fear.
Why then was this forbid? Why but to awe,
Why but to keep ye low and ignorant,
His worshippers; he knows that in the day
Ye eat thereof your eyes, that seem so clear,
Yet are but dim, shall perfectly be then
Open'd and clear'd, and ye shall be as Gods,
Knowing both good and evil as they know.
That ye should be as Gods, since I as Man,
Internal Man, is but proportion meet,
I, of brute, human; ye, of human, Gods.
So ye shall die, perhaps, by putting off
Human, to put on Gods, death to be wish'd,
Though threat'n'd, which no worse than this can bring.
And what are Gods, that Man may not become
As they, participating godlike food?
The Gods are first, and that advantage use
On our belief, that all from them proceeds;
I question it; for this fair earth I see,
Warm'd by the sun, producing every kind,
Them nothing: If they all things, who enclos'd
Knowledge of good and evil in this tree,
That whoso eats thereof forthwith attains
Wisdom without their leave? and wherein lies
Th' offence, that Man should thus attain to know?
What can your knowledge hurt him, or this tree
Impart against his will, if all be his?
Or is it envy? and can envy dwell
In Heav'nly breasts? These, these and many more
Causes import your need of this fair fruit.
Goddess humane, reach then and freely taste.''

He ended; and his words, replete with guile,
Into her heart too easy entrance won:
Fix'd on the fruit she gaz'd, which to behold
Might tempt alone; and in her ears the sound
Yet rung of his persuasive words, impregn'd
With reason, to her seeming, and with truth;
Meanwhile the hour of noon drew on and wak'd

An eager appetite, rais'd by the smell
So savoury of that fruit, which with desire,
Inclinable now grown to touch or taste,
Solicited her longing eye; yet first,
Pausing a while, thus to herself she mus'd:

      "Great are thy virtues, doubtless, best of fruits,
Though kept from Man, and worthy to be admir'd,
Whose taste, too long forborne, at first assay
Gave elocution to the mute, and taught
The tongue not made for speech to speak thy praise:
Thy praise he also who forbids thy use
Conceals not from us, naming thee the Tree
Of Knowledge, knowledge both of good and evil;
Forbids us then to taste, but his forbidding
Commends thee more, while it infers the good
By thee communicated, and our want:
For good unknown sure is not had, or had
And yet unknown, is as not had at all.
In plain, then, what forbids he but to know,
Forbids us good, forbids us to be wise?
Such prohibitions bind not. But if Death
Bind us with after-bands, what profits then
Our inward freedom? In the day we eat
Of this fair fruit, our doom is we shall die.
How dies the Serpent? He hath eat'n, and lives
And knows and speaks and reasons and discerns,
Irrational till then. For us alone
Was death invented? or to us denied
This intellectual food, for beasts reserv'd?
For beasts it seems; yet that one beast which first
Hath tasted envies not, but brings with joy
The good befall'n him, author unsuspect,
Friendly to Man, far from deceit or guile.
What fear I then? rather, what know to fear
Under this ignorance of good and evil,
Of God or death, of law or penalty?
Here grows the cure of all: this fruit divine,
Fair to the eye, inviting to the taste,
Of virtue to make wise: What hinders then
To reach and feed at once both body and mind?"

      So saying, her rash hand in evil hour
Forth-reaching to the fruit, she pluck'd, she ate:
Earth felt the wound, and Nature from her seat,
Sighing through all her works, gave signs of woe
That all was lost. Back to the thicket slunk
The guilty Serpent, and well might; for Eve,
Intent now wholly on her taste, naught else
Regarded, such delight till then, as seem'd,

In fruit she never tasted, whether true
Or fancied so through expectation high
Of knowledge, nor was Godhead from her thought.
Greedily she ingorg'd without restraint,
And knew not eating death: Satiate at length,
And height'n'd as with wine, jocund and boon,
Thus to herself she pleasingly began:

       "O sovran, virtuous, precious of all trees
In Paradise, of operation blest
To sapience, hitherto obscur'd, infam'd,
And thy fair fruit let hang, as to no end
Created; but henceforth my early care,
Not without song each morning, and due praise,
Shall tend thee, and the fertile burden ease
Of thy full branches, offer'd free to all:
Till, dieted by thee, I grow mature
In knowledge, as the Gods who all things know;
Though others envy what they cannot give;
For had the gift been theirs, it had not here
Thus grown. Experience, next to thee I owe
Best guide; not following thee, I had remain'd
In ignorance; thou open'st Wisdom's way
And giv'st access, though secret she retire.
And I perhaps am secret; Heav'n is high,
High, and remote to see from thence distinct
Each thing on Earth; and other care perhaps
May have diverted from continual watch
Our great Forbidder, safe with all his spies
About him. But to Adam in what sort
Shall I appear? Shall I to him make known
As yet my change, and give him to partake
Full happiness with me, or rather not,
But keep the odds of knowledge in my power
Without copartner? so to add what wants
In female sex, the more to draw his love,
And render me more equal, and perhaps,
A thing not undesirable, sometime
Superior; for, inferior, who is free?
This may be well; but what if God have seen,
And death ensue? Then I shall be no more;
And Adam, wedded to another Eve,
Shall live with her enjoying, I extinct;
A death to think. Confirm'd then, I resolve,
Adam shall share with me in bliss or woe:
So dear I love him that with him all deaths
I could endure, without him live no life."

       So saying, from the tree her step she turn'd,
But first low reverence done as to the Power

That dwelt within, whose presence had infus'd
Into the plant sciential sap, deriv'd
From nectar, drink of Gods. Adam the while,
Waiting desirous her return, had wove
Of choicest flow'rs a garland, to adorn
Her tresses and her rural labours crown,
As reapers oft are wont their harvest queen.
Great joy he promis'd to his thoughts, and new
Solace in her return, so long delay'd;
Yet oft his heart, divine of something ill,
Misgave him; he the falt'ring measure felt,
And forth to meet her went, the way she took
That morn when first they parted; by the Tree
Of Knowledge he must pass; there he her met,
Scarce from the tree returning; in her hand
A bough of fairest fruit that downy smil'd,
New gather'd, and ambrosial smell diffus'd.
To him she hasted; in her face excuse
Came prologue, and apology to prompt,
Which with bland words at will she thus addrest:

      "Hast thou not wonder'd, Adam, at my stay?
Thee I have miss'd, and thought it long, depriv'd
Thy presence, agony of love till now
Not felt, nor shall be twice, for never more
Mean I to try, what rash untri'd I sought,
The pain of absence from thy sight. But strange
Hath been the cause, and wonderful to hear:
This tree is not, as we are told, a tree
Of danger tasted, nor to evil unknown
Op'ning the way, but of divine effect
To open eyes and make them Gods who taste;
And hath been tasted such: the Serpent wise,
Or not restrain'd as we, or not obeying,
Hath eat'n of the fruit, and is become
Not dead, as we are threat'n'd, but thenceforth
Endu'd with human voice and human sense,
Reasoning to admiration, and with me
Persuasively hath so prevail'd that I
Have also tasted, and have also found
Th' effects to correspond, opener mine eyes,
Dim erst, dilated spirits, ampler heart,
And growing up to Godhead, which for thee
Chiefly I sought, without thee can despise.
For bliss, as thou hast part, to me is bliss,
Tedious unshar'd with thee, and odious soon.
Thou therefore also taste, that equal lot
May join us, equal joy, as equal love;
Lest thou not tasting, different degree

Disjoin us, and I then too late renounce
Deity for thee, when Fate will not permit.''

        Thus Eve with count'nance blithe her story told;
But in her cheek distemper flushing glow'd.
On th' other side, Adam, soon as he heard
The fatal trespass done by Eve, amaz'd,
Astonied stood and blank, while horror chill
Ran through his veins and all his joints relax'd;
From his slack hand the garland wreath'd for Eve
Down dropp'd, and all the faded roses shed.
Speechless he stood and pale, till thus at length
First to himself he inward silence broke:

        ''O fairest of creation, last and best
Of all God's works, creature in whom excell'd
Whatever can to sight or thought be form'd,
Holy, divine, good, amiable, or sweet!
How art thou lost, how on a sudden lost,
Defac'd, deflow'r'd, and now to death devote?
Rather how hast thou yielded to transgress
The strict forbiddance, how to violate
The sacred fruit forbidd'n! Some cursed fraud
Of enemy hath beguil'd thee, yet unknown,
And me with thee hath ruin'd, for with thee
Certain my resolution is to die;
How can I live without thee, how forgo
Thy sweet converse, and love so dearly join'd,
To live again in these wild woods forlorn?
Should God create another Eve, and I
Another rib afford, yet loss of thee
Would never from my heart; no no; I feel
The link of nature draw me: flesh of flesh,
Bone of my bone thou art, and from thy state
Mine never shall be parted, bliss or woe.''

        So having said, as one from sad dismay
Recomforted and, after thoughts disturb'd,
Submitting to what seem'd remediless,
Thus in calm mood his words to Eve he turn'd:

        ''Bold deed thou hast presum'd, advent'rous Eve,
And peril great provok'd, who thus hast dar'd
Had it been only coveting to eye
That sacred fruit, sacred to abstinence,
Much more to taste it under ban to touch.
But past who can recall, or done undo?
Not God Omnipotent, nor Fate, Yet so
Perhaps thou shalt not die, perhaps the fact
Is not so heinous now, foretasted fruit,
Profan'd first by the Serpent, by him first

Made common and unhallow'd ere your taste;
Nor yet on him found deadly, he yet lives,
Lives, as thou saidst, and gains to live as Man,
Higher degree of life, inducement strong
To us, as likely tasting to attain
Proportional ascent; which cannot be
But to be Gods or Angels demi-gods.
Nor can I think that God, Creator wise,
Though threat'ning, will in earnest so destroy
Us, his prime creatures, dignified so high,
Set over all his works, which in our fall,
For us created, needs with us must fail,
Dependent made; So God shall uncreate,
Be frustrate, do, undo, and labour lose,
Not well conceiv'd of God; who, though his power
Creation could repeat, yet would be loath
Us to abolish, lest the Adversary
Triumph and say: 'Fickle their state whom God
Most favours; who can please him long? Me first
He ruin'd, now mankind; whom will he next?'
Matter of scorn not to be given the Foe.
However, I with thee have fix'd my lot,
Certain to undergo like doom, if death
Consort with thee, death is to me as life;
So forcible within my heart I feel
The bond of Nature draw me to my own,
My own in thee, for what thou art is mine;
Our state cannot be sever'd, we are one,
One flesh; to lose thee were to lose myself."

So Adam, and thus Eve to him replied:
"O glorious trial of exceeding love,
Illustrious evidence, example high!
Engaging me to emulate but, short
Of thy perfection, how shall I attain?,
Adam, from whose dear side I boast me sprung,
And gladly of our union hear thee speak,
One heart, one soul in both; whereof good proof
This day affords, declaring thee resolv'd,
Rather than death, or aught than death more dread,
Shall separate us, link'd in love so dear,
To undergo with me one guilt, one crime,
If any be, of tasting this fair fruit,
Whose virtue, for of good still good proceeds,
Direct, or by occasion hath presented
This happy trial of thy love, which else
So eminently never had been known.
Were it I thought death menac'd would ensue
This my attempt, I would sustain alone

The worst, and not persuade thee, rather die
Deserted than oblige thee with a fact
Pernicious to thy peace, chiefly assur'd
Remarkably so late of thy so true,
So faithful, love unequall'd; but I feel
Far otherwise th' event, not death, but life
Augmented, op'n'd eyes, new hopes, new joys,
Taste so divine that what of sweet before
Hath touch'd my sense flat seems to this and harsh.
On my experience, Adam, freely taste,
And fear of death deliver to the winds."

So saying, she embrac'd him, and for joy
Tenderly wept, much won that he his love
Had so ennobl'd, as of choice to incur
Divine displeasure for her sake, or death.
In recompense (for such compliance bad
Such recompense best merits) from the bough
She gave him of that fair enticing fruit
With liberal hand; he scrupl'd not to eat,
Against his better knowledge, not deceiv'd,
But fondly overcome with female charm.
Earth trembl'd from her entrails, as again
In pangs, and Nature gave a second groan;
Sky lour'd and, muttering thunder, some sad drops
Wept at completing of the mortal sin
Original; while Adam took no thought,
Eating his fill, nor Eve to iterate
Her former trespass fear'd, the more to soothe
Him with her lov'd society, that now,
As with new wine intoxicated both
They swim in mirth, and fancy that they feel
Divinity within them breeding wings
Wherewith to scorn the Earth: but that false fruit
Far other operation first display'd,
Carnal desire inflaming, he on Eve
Began to cast lascivious eyes, she him
As wantonly repaid: in lust they burn:
Till Adam thus 'gan Eve to dalliance move:

"Eve, now I see thou art exact of taste
And elegant, of sapience no small part,
Since to each meaning savour we apply,
And palate call judicious; I the praise
Yield thee, so well this day thou hast purvey'd.
Much pleasure we have lost, while we abstain'd
From this delightful fruit, nor known till now
True relish, tasting; If such pleasure be
In things to us forbidd'n, it might be wish'd
For this one tree had been forbidden ten.

But come; so well refresh'd, now let us play,
As meet is after such delicious fare;
For never did thy beauty since the day
I saw thee first and wedded thee, adorn'd
With all perfections, so inflame my sense
With ardour to enjoy thee, fairer now
Than ever, bounty of this virtuous tree!''

        So said he, and forbore not glance or toy
Of amorous intent, well understood
Of Eve, whose eye darted contagious fire.
Her hand he seiz'd, and to a shady bank,
Thick overhead with verdant roof embow'r'd,
He led her, nothing loath; flow'rs were the couch,
Pansies and violets and asphodel,
And hyacinth, Earth's freshest, softest lap.
There they their fill of love and love's disport
Took largely, of their mutual guilt the seal,
The solace of their sin, till dewy sleep
Oppress'd them, wearied with their amorous play.
Soon as the force of that fallacious fruit,
That with exhilarating vapour bland
About their spirits had play'd and inmost powers
Made err, was now exhal'd, and grosser sleep
Bred of unkindly fumes, with conscious dreams
Encumber'd, now had left them, up they rose
As from unrest, and each the other viewing,
Soon found their eyes how op'n'd, and their minds
How dark'n'd; innocence, that as a veil
Had shadow'd them from knowing ill, was gone,
Just confidence, and native righteousness,
And honour from about them, naked left
To guilty Shame; he cover'd, but his robe
Uncover'd more. So rose the Danite strong,
Herculean Samson, from the harlot-lap
Of Philistean Dalilah, and wak'd
Shorn of his strength, they destitute and bare
Of all their virtue: silent, and in face
Confounded, long they sat, as struck'n mute;
Till Adam, though not less than Eve abash'd,
At length gave utterance to these words constrain'd:

        "O Eve, in evil hour thou didst give ear
To that false Worm, of whomsoever taught
To counterfeit Man's voice, true in our Fall,
False in our promis'd rising; since our eyes
Op'n'd we find indeed, and find we know
Both good and evil, good lost, and evil got,
Bad fruit of knowledge, if this be to know,
Which leaves us naked thus, of honour void,

Of innocence, of faith, of purity,
Our wonted ornaments now soil'd and stain'd,
And in our faces evident the signs
Of foul concupiscence; whence evil store;
Even shame, the last of evils; of the first
Be sure then. How shall I behold the face
Henceforth of God or Angel, erst with joy
And rapture so oft beheld? those heav'nly shapes
Will dazzle now this earthly, with their blaze
Insufferably bright. O might I here
In solitude live savage, in some glade
Obscur'd, where highest woods impenetrable
To star or sunlight, spread their umbrage broad,
And brown as evening; Cover me, ye pines,
Ye cedars, with innumerable boughs
Hide me, where I may never see them more.
But let us now, as in bad plight, devise
What best may for the present serve to hide
The parts of each from other that seem most
To shame obnoxious, and unseemliest seen,
Some tree, whose broad smooth leaves, together sew'd,
And girded on our loins, may cover round
Those middle parts, that this new comer, Shame,
There sit not and reproach us as unclean."

   So counsell'd he, and both together went
Into the thickest wood, there soon they chose
The figtree, not that kind for fruit renown'd,
But such as at this day, to Indians known,
In Malabar or Decan spreads her arms
Branching so broad and long that in the ground
The bended twigs take root, and daughters grow
About the mother tree, a pillar'd shade
High overarch'd, and echoing walks between;
There oft the Indian herdsman, shunning heat,
Shelters in cool, and tends his pasturing herds
At loopholes cut through thickest shade: Those leaves
They gather'd, broad as Amazonian targe,
And with what skill they had together sew'd,
To gird their waist, vain covering if to hide
Their guilt and dreaded shame; O how unlike
To that first naked glory. Such of late
Columbus found th' American, so girt
With feather'd cincture, naked else and wild,
Among the trees on isles and woody shores.
Thus fenc'd and, as they thought, their shame in part
Cover'd, but not at rest or ease of mind,
They sat them down to weep, nor only tears
Rain'd at their eyes, but high winds worse within

Began to rise, high passions, anger, hate,
Mistrust, suspicion, discord, and shook sore
Their inward state of mind, calm region once
And full of peace, now toss'd and turbulent:
For Understanding rul'd not, and the Will
Heard not her lore, both in subjection now
To sensual Appetite, who, from beneath
Usurping over sovran Reason, claim'd
Superior sway: From thus distemper'd breast
Adam, estrang'd in look and alter'd style,
Speech intermitted, thus to Eve renew'd:

      "Would thou hadst heark'n'd to my words, and stay'd
With me, as I besought thee, when that strange
Desire of wand'ring, this unhappy morn,
I know not whence possess'd thee; we had then
Remain'd still happy, not, as now, despoil'd
Of all our good, sham'd, naked, miserable.
Let none henceforth seek needless cause to approve
‚The faith they owe; when earnestly they seek
Such proof, conclude they then begin to fail."

      To whom, soon mov'd with touch of blame, thus Eve:
"What words have pass'd thy lips, Adam severe,
Imput'st thou that to my default, or will,
Of wandering, as thou call'st it, which who knows
But might as ill have happ'n'd thou being by,
Or to thyself perhaps: Hadst thou been there,
Or here th' attempt, thou couldst not have discern'd
Fraud in the Serpent, speaking as he spake,
No ground of enmity between us known,
Why he should mean me ill or seek to harm.
Was I to have never parted from thy side?
As good have grown there still, a lifeless rib.
Being as I am, why didst not thou, the head,
Command me absolutely not to go,
Going into such danger, as thou said'st?
Too facile then, thou didst not much gainsay,
Nay, didst permit, approve, and fair dismiss.
Hadst thou been firm and fix'd in thy dissent,
Neither had I transgress'd, nor thou with me."

      To whom then first incens'd Adam replied:
"Is this the love, is this the recompense
Of mine to thee, ingrateful Eve, express't
Immutable when thou wert lost, not I,
Who might have liv'd and joy'd immortal bliss,
Yet willingly chose rather death with thee:
And am I now upbraided as the cause
Of thy transgressing? not enough severe,

It seems, in thy restraint: What could I more?
I warn'd thee, I admonish'd thee, foretold
The danger and the lurking enemy
That lay in wait; beyond this had been force,
And force upon free will hath here no place.
But confidence then bore thee on, secure
Either to meet no danger or to find
Matter of glorious trial; and perhaps
I also err'd in overmuch admiring
What seem'd in thee so perfect that I thought
No evil durst attempt thee, but I rue
That error now, which is become my crime,
And thou th' accuser. Thus it shall befall
Him who, to worth in women overtrusting,
Lets her will rule; restraint she will not brook,
And, left to herself, if evil thence ensue,
She first his weak indulgence will accuse."

Thus they in mutual accusation spent
The fruitless hours, but neither self-condemning,
And of their vain contest appear'd no end.

Notes

1. *This Verse.* Milton's *Paradise Lost* was first published in 1667. He added the following explanatory comments in 1668:

> The Measure is English Heroic Verse without Rhyme, as that of Homer in Greek, and of Virgil in Latin; Rhyme being no necessary Adjunct or true Ornament of Poem or good Verse, in longer works especially, but the Invention of a barabarous Age, to set off wretched matter and lame Meter, grac't indeed since by the use of some famous modern Poets, carried away by Custom, but much to their own vexation, hindrance, and constraint to express many things otherwise, and for the most part worse than they would have expresst them. Not without cause therefore some both Italian and Spanish poets of prime note have rejected Rhyme both in longer and shorter Works, as have also long since our best English Tragedies, as a thing of itself, to all judicious ears, trivial and of no true musical delight; which consists only in apt Numbers, fit quantity of Syllables, and the sense variously drawn out from one Verse into another, not in the jingling sound of like endings, a fault avoided by the learned Ancients both in Poetry and all good Oratory. This neglect then of Rhyme so little is to be taken for a defect, though it may seem so perhaps to vulgar Readers, that it rather is to be esteem'd an example set, the first in English, of ancient liberty recover'd to Heroic Poem from the troublesome and modern bondage of Rhyming.

Is Milton right about rhyme? How does your reaction to the following poem affect your answer?

THE RAVEN
Edgar Allen Poe

Once upon a midnight dreary, while I pondered, weak and weary,
Over many a quaint and curious volume of forgotten lore—
While I nodded, nearly napping, suddenly there came a tapping,
As of some one gently rapping, rapping at my chamber door.
" 'Tis some visitor," I muttered, "tapping at my chamber door—
Only this, and nothing more."

Ah, distinctly I remember it was in the bleak December;
And each separate dying ember wrought its ghost upon the floor.
Eagerly I wished the morrow;—vainly I had sought to borrow
From my books surcease of sorrow—sorrow for the lost Lenore—
For the rare and radiant maiden whom the angels name Lenore—
Nameless *here* for evermore.

And the silken sad uncertain rustling of each purple curtain
Thrilled me—filled me with fantastic terrors never felt before;
So that now, to still the beating of my heart, I stood repeating
" 'Tis some visitor entreating entrance at my chamber door—
Some late visitor entreating entrance at my chamber door;—
This it is, and nothing more."

Presently my soul grew stronger; hesitating then no longer,
"Sir," said I, "or Madam, truly your forgiveness I implore;
But the fact is I was napping, and so gently you came rapping,
And so faintly you came tapping, tapping at my chamber door,
That I scarce was sure I heard you"—here I opened
    wide the door;—
Darkness there and nothing more.

Deep into that darkness peering, long I stood there wondering,
    fearing,
Doubting, dreaming dreams no mortal ever dared to dream before;
But the silence was unbroken, and the darkness gave no token,
And the only word there spoken was the whispered word, "Lenore!"
This I whispered, and an echo murmured back the word,
    "Lenore!"—
Merely this, and nothing more.

Back into the chamber turning, all my soul within me burning,
Soon I heard again a tapping somewhat louder than before.
"Surely," said I, "surely that is something at my window lattice;
Let me see, then, what thereat is, and this mystery explore—

Let my heart be still a moment and this mystery explore;—
'Tis the wind and nothing more!''

Open here I flung the shutter, when, with many a flirt and flutter,
In there stepped a stately raven of the saintly days of yore.
Not the least obeisance made he; not an instant stopped or stayed
    he;
But, with mien of lord or lady, perched above my chamber door—
Perched upon a bust of Pallas just above my chamber door—
Perched, and sat, and nothing more.

Then this ebony bird beguiling my sad fancy into smiling,
By the grave and stern decorum of the countenance it wore,
"Though thy crest be shorn and shaven, thou," I said, "art sure no
    craven,
Ghastly grim and ancient raven wandering from the Nightly shore—
Tell me what thy lordly name is on the Night's Plutonian shore!''
Quoth the raven "Nevermore.''

Much I marvelled this ungainly fowl to hear discourse so plainly,
Though its answer little meaning—little relevancy bore;
For we cannot help agreeing that no living human being
Ever yet was blessed with seeing bird above his chamber door—
Bird or beast upon the sculptured bust above his chamber door,
With such name as "Nevermore.''

But the raven, sitting lonely on the placid bust, spoke only
That one word, as if his soul in that one word he did outpour.
Nothing farther then he uttered—not a feather then he fluttered—
Till I scarcely more than muttered "Other friends have flown
    before—
On the morrow *he* will leave me, as my hopes have flown before.''
Then the bird said "Nevermore.''

Startled at the stillness broken by reply so aptly spoken,
"Doubtless," said I, "what it utters is its only stock and store
Caught from some unhappy master whom unmerciful Disaster
Followed fast and followed faster till his songs one burden bore—
Till the dirges of his Hope that melancholy burden bore
Of "Never—nevermore.''

But the raven still beguiling all my sad soul into smiling,
Straight I wheeled a cushioned seat in front of bird, and bust and
    door;
Then, upon the velvet sinking, I betook myself to linking
Fancy unto fancy, thinking what this ominous bird of yore—
What this grim, ungainly, ghastly, gaunt and ominous bird of yore
Meant in croaking "Nevermore.''

This I sat engaged in guessing, but no syllable expressing
To the fowl whose fiery eyes now burned into my bosom's core;
This and more I sat divining, with my head at ease reclining
On the cushion's velvet lining that the lamplight gloated o'er,
But whose velvet violet lining with the lamplight gloating o'er,
She shall press, ah, nevermore!

Then, methought, the air grew denser, perfumed from an unseen
    censer
Swung by Seraphim whose foot-falls tinkled on the tufted floor.
"Wretch," I cried, "thy God hath lent thee—by these angels he hath
    sent thee
Respite—respite and nepenthe from thy memories of Lenore;
Quaff, oh quaff this kind nepenthe and forget this lost Lenore!"
Quoth the raven, "Nevermore."

"Prophet!" said I, "thing of evil!—prophet still, if bird or devil!—
Whether Tempter sent, or whether tempest tossed thee here ashore,
Desolate yet all undaunted, on this desert land enchanted—
On this home by Horror haunted—tell me truly, I implore—
Is there—*is* there balm in Gilead?—tell me—tell me, I implore!"
Quoth the raven, "Nevermore."

"Prophet!" said I, "thing of evil—prophet still, if bird or devil!
By that Heaven that bends above us—by that God we both adore—
Tell this soul with sorrow laden if, within the distant Aidenn,
It shall clasp a sainted maiden whom the angels name Lenore—
Clasp a rare and radiant maiden whom the angels name Lenore."
Quoth the raven, "Nevermore."

"Be that word our sign of parting, bird or fiend!" I shrieked,
    upstarting—
"Get thee back into the tempest and the Night's Plutonian shore!
Leave no black plume as a token of that lie thy soul hath spoken!
Leave my loneliness unbroken!—quit the bust above my door!
Take thy beak from out my heart, and take thy form from off my
    door!"
Quoth the raven, "Nevermore."

And the raven, never flitting, still is sitting, still is sitting
On the pallid bust of Pallas just above my chamber door;
And his eyes have all the seeming of a demon's that is dreaming,
And the lamp-light o'er him streaming throws his shadow on the
    floor;
And my soul from out that shadow that lies floating on the floor
Shall be lifted—nevermore!

Notes

1. *Reading Poetry*. Milton uses enjambment, or the run-over line, so frequently that the verse line is largely undetectable when this epic poem is read aloud. The major poetic features which Milton retains are the iambic pentameter—which he adheres to religiously—and poetic imagery that places the poem among the very greatest classics of the English language.

Many students find Milton difficult to read. Many legal texts, such as statutes and contracts, are likewise difficult to read, yet they certainly do not share with Milton the iambic pentameter and rich classical allusions. Can you identify the features that make Milton hard to read? Are those the same features that make some legal texts hard to read? Is it worth reading them (Milton or legal texts) anyway? Why or why not? With Milton—as with Shakespeare and Chaucer—an annotated version can be very helpful. In the case of Milton, Bullfinch's *Mythology* is also a very helpful aid.

2. *Milton the Lawyer*. The "arguments" between Adam and Eve, and between Satan and Eve, in Book IX are enough to bedazzle the best of legal minds.

3. *Reverberations*. It is no accident that the "argument" between Adam and Eve immediately precedes that between Satan and Eve. Satan would, if he could, supplant Adam in Eve's affections. Indeed, the flattery and respect which Satan displays toward Eve's physical beauty and native intelligence make Adam seem something of a dunce by comparison. Mark Twain emphasizes this comparison in his *Extracts From Adam's Diary*, *Passage From Satan's Diary*, and *Passage From Eve's Diary*.

Another such echo can be found in Books II and III of *Paradise Lost*. In Book II Satan debates with his cohorts in hell how best to proceed against God. In Book III God debates with his Son in heaven how best to proceed against Satan. It is quite clear that God and Satan are jockeying for the leadership position throughout this epic.

4. *The Fall*. It is disingenuous to believe that God did not expect Adam and Eve to eat of the Tree of Knowledge of Good and Evil. He foresaw the Fall, as Milton makes clear in Book III. How else could Adam and Eve have achieved freedom of choice without exercising that freedom? Something of the same idea is expressed in the *Book of Job*: How could God, or Job, ever know Job's faithfulness unless that faith were put to the fullest test? Thus, we may conclude that true knowledge and understanding come at a very high price.

G. FATE

THE SECOND COMING
William Butler Yeats

Turning and turning in the widening gyre
The falcon cannot hear the falconer;
Things fall apart, the centre cannot hold;
Mere anarchy is loosed upon the world,
The blood-dimmed tide is loosed, and everywhere
The ceremony of innocence is drowned;
The best lack all conviction, while the worst
Are full of passionate intensity.

Surely some revelation is at hand;
Surely the Second Coming is at hand.
The Second Coming! Hardly are those words out
When a vast image out of *Spiritus Mundi*
Troubles my sight: somewhere in the sands of the
desert
A shape with lion body and the head of a man,
A gaze blank and pitiless as the sun,
Is moving its slow thighs, while all about it
Reel shadows of the indignant desert birds.
The darkness drops again; but now I know
That twenty centuries of stony sleep
Were vexed to nightmare by a rocking cradle,
And what rough beast, its hour come round at last,
Slouches towards Bethlehem to be born?

Note

1. *Bethlehem.* Presumably the rough beast has already been born, or otherwise it wouldn't be slouching towards Bethlehem. What, then, is the purpose of Bethlehem? Is the beast the "shape" with the blank and pitiless gaze? Is the beast the baby Jesus, who vexed to nightmare twenty centuries of stony sleep? Why does the beast slouch?

STOPPING BY WOODS ON A SNOWY EVENING
Robert Frost

Whose woods these are I think I know.
His house is in the village though;
He will not see me stopping here
To watch his woods fill up with snow.

My little horse must think it queer
To stop without a farmhouse near
Between the woods and frozen lake
The darkest evening of the year.

He gives his harness bells a shake
To ask if there is some mistake.
The only other sound's the sweep
Of easy wind and downy flake.

The woods are lovely, dark and deep.
But I have promises to keep,
And miles to go before I sleep,
And miles to go before I sleep.

Note

1. *Fate.* Fate implies an inevitable outcome. Does fate dictate that the one who stops by the woods on a snowy evening must keep his promises? If so, then why does fate have that one stop and admire the woods, so "lovely, dark and deep," even though his little horse thinks there must be some mistake?

DESIGN
Robert Frost

I found a dimpled spider, fat and white,
On a white heal-all, holding up a moth
Like a white piece of rigid satin cloth—
Assorted characters of death and blight
Mixed ready to begin the morning right,
Like the ingredients of a witches' broth—
A snow-drop spider, a flower like a froth,
And dead wings carried like a paper kite.
What had that flower to do with being white,
The wayside blue and innocent heal-all?
What brought the kindred spider to that height,
Then steered the white moth thither in the night?
What but design of darkness to appall?—
If design govern in a thing so small.

Notes

1. *Colors.* Frost has a field day with colors in this poem. White, so often the symbol of innocence and purity, here symbolizes death. The blue, innocent heal-all, is a sepulcher rather than a source of healing. And darkness brought the white moth to its white doom.

2. *Design.* The poem questions whether fate governs "a thing so small" as the death of a moth. The question encompasses much more than the moth, however. Reconsider Virginia Woolf's *The Death of the Moth*, in Chapter Two.

APPARENTLY WITH NO SURPRISE
Emily Dickinson

Apparently with no surprise
To any happy flower,
The frost beheads it at its play
In accidental power.
The blond assassin passes on,
The sun proceeds unmoved
To measure off another day
For an approving God.

Note

1. *With No Surprise.* The death of "any happy flower" by the killing frost is "apparently" of no surprise to the flower. Can death be of any surprise to anyone?

The blond assassin apparently acts under the eye of "an approving God." Compare *King Lear*, Act IV, scene 1: "As flies to wanton boys, are we to the gods; They kill us for their sport."

H. ETERNITY

BECAUSE I COULD NOT STOP FOR DEATH
Emily Dickinson

Because I could not stop for Death,
He kindly stopped for me;
The carriage held but just ourselves
And Immortality.

We slowly drove, he knew no haste,
And I had put away
My labor, and my leisure too,
For his civility.

We passed the school where children played
Their lessons scarcely done;
We passed the fields of gazing grain,
We passed the setting sun.

We paused before a house that seemed
A swelling of the ground;
The roof was scarcely visible,
The cornice but a mound.

Since then 'tis centuries; but each
Feels shorter than the day
I first surmised the horses' heads
Were toward eternity.

Notes

1. *Death.* Why do you suppose Dickinson describes death as kind and civil?

2. *The Antimony.* The dictionary describes an antimony as "a contradiction between two apparent equal valid principles," or "a fundamental and apparently unresolvable conflict or contradiction." *Merriam-Webster's Collegiate Dictionary* 51 (10th ed. 1998). Is the concept of eternity an antimony? Eternity is presumably never-ending. But is it possible to conceive of anything—time, space, or what have you—without an end?

The logician may have grave trouble with antimony. Should the poet? the lawyer?

THE LAST NIGHT THAT SHE LIVED
Emily Dickinson

The last night that she lived,
It was a common night,
Except the dying; this to us
Made nature different.

We noticed smallest things,—
Things overlooked before,
By this great light upon our minds
Italicized, as 'twere.

That others could exist
While she must finish quite,
A jealousy for her arose
So nearly infinite.

We waited while she passed;
It was a narrow time,
Too jostled were our souls to speak,
At length the notice came.

She mentioned, and forgot;
Then lightly as a reed
Bent to the water, shivered scarce,
Consented, and was dead.

And we, we placed the hair,
And drew the head erect;
And then an awful leisure was,
Our faith to regulate.

Notes

1. *The Awful Leisure.* It is understandable why there was an "awful leisure." But why the need to regulate "[o]ur faith"?

2. *Untitled.* Emily Dickinson did not give titles to her poems. Why do you suppose she did not? By way of comparison, recall that Shakespeare did

not title his sonnets. Do you think Dickinson and Shakespeare had the same reason for not using titles?

O DO NOT LOVE TOO LONG
William Butler Yeats

Sweetheart, do not love too long:
I loved long and long,
And grew to be out of fashion
Like an old song.
All through the years of our youth
Neither could have known
Their own thought from the other's,
We were so much at one.
But O, in a minute she changed—
O do not love too long,
Or you will grow out of fashion
Like an old song.

Note

1. *Love.* Should love last for eternity? Recall Shakespeare's Sonnet 116.

LA DIVINA COMMEDIA
Dante

This epic by Dante is considered one of the greatest pieces of literature of all times. It is in three parts: the *Inferno*, *Purgatory*, and *Paradise*. The great poet Virgil conducts Dante through the Inferno (Hell) and Purgatory.

The following is a description by Dante of the inscription which he found at the Gate of Hell:

"Per me si va nella città dolente;

per me si va nell' eterno dolore;

per me si va tra la perduta gente.

Guistizia mosse il mio alto Fattore;

fecemi la divina Potestate,

la somma Sapienza e il primo Amore.

Dinanzi a me non fur cose create,

se non eterne, ed io eterno duro:

lasciate ogni speranza, voi ch' entrate."

"Through me is the way into the doleful city;

through me the way into the eternal pain;

through me the way among the people lost.

Justice moved my High Maker; Divine Power

made me, Wisdom Supreme, and Primal Love.

Before me were no things created, but eternal; and eternal I endure: leave all hope, ye that enter."

At the end of the third book (*Paradiso*), Dante is permitted to look upon God:

O luce eterna, che sola in te sidi, sola t'intendi, e, da te intelletta ed intendente te, ami ed arridi!

O Light eternal who only in thyself abidest, only thyself dost understand, and self-understanding, turnest love on and smilest at thyself!

I. CATACLYSM

THE BRAIN WITHIN ITS GROOVE
Emily Dickinson

The brain within its groove
Runs evenly and true;
But let a splinter swerve,
'Twere easier for you
To put the water back
When floods have slit the hills,
And scooped a turnpike for themselves,
And blotted out the mills!

Notes

1. *Insanity.* Who understands insanity—one of the most common features of the human species? Is this poem about insanity? Is "splinter" a subject-noun or an adjective?

2. *Rhyme and Rhythm.* Dickinson was fond of slant rhyme. Probably the first and third lines qualify as slant rhymes. Slant rhyme is a compromise between full rhyme, and Milton's rejection of rhyme altogether in *Paradise Lost.*

Lines 5 and 7 lack any rhyme whatever, and line 7 breaks the tetrameter rhythm. The effect is to create the broken sound of the flood, once the splinter has swerved.

J. HAUGHTINESS

ISAIAH
CHAPTER 3
King James Bible

¹ For, behold, the Lord, the Lord of hosts, doth take away from Jerusalem and from Judah the stay and the staff, the whole stay of bread, and the whole stay of water,

² The mighty man, and the man of war, the judge, and the prophet, and the prudent, and the ancient,

³ The captain of fifty, and the honourable man, and the counsellor, and the cunning artificer, and the eloquent orator.

⁴ And I will give children to be their princes, and babes shall rule over them.

⁵ And the people shall be oppressed, every one by another, and every one by his neighbour: the child shall behave himself proudly against the ancient, and the base against the honourable.

⁶ When a man shall take hold of his brother of the house of his father, saying, Thou hast clothing, be thou our ruler, and let this ruin be under thy hand:

⁷ In that day shall he swear, saying, I will not be an healer; for in my house is neither bread nor clothing: make me not a ruler of the people.

⁸ For Jerusalem is ruined, and Judah is fallen: because their tongue and their doings are against the LORD, to provoke the eyes of his glory.

⁹ The shew of their countenance doth witness against them; and they declare their sin as Sodom, they hide it not. Woe unto their soul! for they have rewarded evil unto themselves.

¹⁰ Say ye to the righteous, that it shall be well with him: for they shall eat the fruit of their doings.

¹¹ Woe unto the wicked! it shall be ill with him: for the reward of his hands shall be given him.

¹² As for my people, children are their oppressors, and women rule over them. O my people, they which lead thee cause thee to err, and destroy the way of thy paths.

¹³ The LORD standeth up to plead, and standeth to judge the people.

¹⁴ The LORD will enter into judgment with the ancients of his people, and the princes thereof: for ye have eaten up the vineyard; the spoil of the poor is in your houses.

¹⁵ What mean ye that ye beat my people to pieces, and grind the faces of the poor? saith the Lord GOD of hosts.

¹⁶ Moreover the LORD saith, Because the daughters of Zion are haughty, and walk with stretched forth necks and wanton eyes, walking and mincing as they go, and making a tinkling with their feet:

¹⁷ Therefore the Lord will smite with a scab the crown of the head of the daughters of Zion, and the LORD will discover their secret parts.

¹⁸ In that day the Lord will take away the bravery of their tinkling ornaments about their feet, and their cauls, and their round tires like the moon,

¹⁹ The chains, and the bracelets, and the mufflers,

²⁰ The bonnets, and the ornaments of the legs, and the headbands, and the tablets, and the earrings,

²¹ The rings, and nose jewels,

²² The changeable suits of apparel, and the mantles, and the wimples, and the crisping pins,

²³ The glasses, and the fine linen, and the hoods, and the vails.

[24] And it shall come to pass, that instead of sweet smell there shall be stink; and instead of a girdle a rent; and instead of well set hair baldness; and instead of a stomacher a girding of sackcloth; and burning instead of beauty.

[25] Thy men shall fall by the sword, and thy mighty in the war.

[26] And her gates shall lament and mourn; and she being desolate shall sit upon the ground.

Notes

1. *Chauvinism.* Are verses 16–24 of *Isaiah* chapter 3 merely an example of male chauvinist piggism? Would the effect be different if the verses had been written by a woman?

Note that women are not the only ones who come in for a shellacking in the chapter. *See, e.g.,* verses 2–3, 15.

2. *Imagery.* Whatever else one may think about this chapter, the chapter presents an outstanding example of the brilliant imagery of the King James Bibles. Rather than just provoking the Lord, his people have provoked "the eyes of his glory," verse 8. The wicked have "beat my people to pieces," and ground "the faces of the poor," verse 15. Who can ever forget the daughters of Zion, walking "with stretched forth necks" and with "tinkling ornaments about their feet," verses 16, 18?

K. IRONY

THE SCHOLARS
William Butler Yeats

Bald heads forgetful of their sins,
Old, learned, respectable bald heads
Edit and annotate the lines
That young men, tossing on their beds,
Rhymed out in love's despair
To flatter beauty's ignorant ear.

All shuffle there; all cough in ink;
All wear the carpet with their shoes;
All think what other people think;
All know the man their neighbor knows.
Lord, what would they say
Did their Catullus walk that way?

NO SECOND TROY
William Buter Yeats

Why should I blame her that she filled my days
With misery, or that she would of late
Have taught to ignorant men most violent ways,

Or hurled the little streets upon the great,
Had they but courage equal to desire?
What could have made her peaceful with a mind
That nobleness made simple as a fire,
With beauty like a tightened bow, a kind
That is not natural in an age like this,
Being high and solitary and most stern?
Why, what could she have done, being what she is?
Was there another Troy for her to burn?

WHEN HELEN LIVED
William Butler Yeats

We have cried in our despair
That men desert,
For some trivial affair
Or noisy, insolent sport,
Beauty that we have won
From bitterest hours;
Yet we, had we walked within
Those topless towers
Where Helen walked with her boy,
Had given but as the rest
Of the men and women of Troy,
A word and jest.

Notes

1. *Irony*. Irony has been defined as "a subtly humorous perception of inconsistency, in which an apparently straightforward statement or event is undermined by its context to give it a very different significance." CHRIS BALDICK, OXFORD CONCISE DICTIONARY OF LITERARY TERMS 130 (2001). "Lord, what would they say" if Catullus walked that way? Nothing? "Why should I blame her . . . being what she is"? We have won beauty from "bitterest hours"; yet, had we walked within the "topless towers" of Troy, we would have given a word or jest where Helen walked with her "boy" (Paris). These are all ironic statements. Explain why.

2. *Catallus*. A great Roman lyric poet, Catallus (87–54? BC) introduced many Greek rhythms into Latin literature, and had a profound influence on later poets such as Ovid and Horace, and on Elizabethan and Caroline poetry. Catullus fell disastrously in love with the beautiful, gifted, and unscrupulous Clodius. Bankrupt financially and emotionally, Catallus died at about the age of thirty-three. BENÉT'S READER'S ENCYCLOPEDIA 168 (3d ed. 1987).

3. *Helen*. Yeats' second Helen poem reflects admirably the great debate in Shakespeare's *Troilus and Cressida*, Act II, scene 2.

L. HOPE

LYCIDAS
John Milton

Yet once more, O ye Laurels, and once more
Ye Myrtles brown, with Ivy never sere,
I come to pluck your berries harsh and crude,
And with forc'd fingers rude,
Shatter your leaves before the mellowing year.
Bitter constraint, and sad occasion dear,
Compels me to disturb your season due;
For Lycidas is dead, dead ere his prime,
Young Lycidas, and hath not left his peer.
Who would not sing for Lycidas? he knew
Himself to sing, and build the lofty rhyme.
He must not float upon his wat'ry bier
Unwept, and welter to the parching wind,
Without the meed of some melodious tear.

Begin, then, Sisters of the Sacred Well,
That from beneath the seat of Jove doth spring,
Begin, and somewhat loudly sweep the string.
Hence with denial vain, and coy excuse:
So may some gentle Muse
With lucky words favour my destin'd urn,
And, as he passes, turn,
And bid fair peace be to my sable shroud!
For we were nurst upon the self-same hill,
Fed the same flock, by fountain, shade, and rill;

Together both, ere the high lawns appear'd
Under the opening eye-lids of the morn,
We drove a-field, and both together heard
What time the gray-fly winds her sultry horn,
Batt'ning our flocks with the fresh dews of night,
Oft till the Star that rose, at Ev'ning, bright
Toward Heaven's descent had slop'd his westering
wheel.
Meanwhile the rural ditties were not mute,
Temper'd to the Oaten Flute;
Rough Satyrs danc'd, and Fauns with clov'n heel,
From the glad sound would not be absent long,
And old Damætas lov'd to hear our song.

But O the heavy change, now thou art gone,
Now thou art gone, and never must return!
Thee, Shepherd, thee the Woods, and desert Caves,
With wilde Thyme and the gadding Vine o'ergrown,
And all their echoes mourn.
The Willows, and the Hazle Copses green,

Shall now no more be seen
Fanning their joyous Leaves to thy soft layes.
As killing as the Canker to the Rose,
Or Taint-worm to the weanling Herds that graze,
Or Frost to Flowers, that their gay wardrobe wear,
When first the white thorn blows;
Such, Lycidas, thy loss to Shepherd's ear.

Where were ye, Nymphs, when the remorseless deep
Clos'd o'er the head of your lov'd Lycidas?
For neither were ye playing on the steep,
Where your old Bards, the famous Druids lie,
Nor on the shaggy top of Mona high,
Nor yet where Deva spreads her wizard stream:
Ay me, I fondly dream!
Had ye been there—for what could that have done?
What could the Muse herself that Orpheus bore,
The Muse herself, for her enchanting son
Whom universal Nature did lament,
When, by the rout that made the hideous roar,
His goary visage down the stream was sent,
Down the swift Hebrus to the Lesbian shore.

Alas! what boots it with uncessant care
To tend the homely, slighted Shepherd's trade,
And strictly meditate the thankless Muse?
Were it not better done as others use,
To sport with Amaryllis in the shade,
Or with the tangles of Neæra's hair?
Fame is the spur that the clear spirit doth raise
(That last infirmity of Noble mind)
To scorn delights, and live laborious days;
But the fair Guerdon when we hope to find,
And think to burst out into sudden blaze,
Comes the blind Fury with th'abhorrèd shears,
And slits the thin-spun life. "But not the praise,"
Phoebus repli'd, and touch'd my trembling ears;
"Fame is no plant that grows on mortal soil,
Nor in the glistering foil
Set off to the world, nor in broad rumour lies,
But lives and spreads aloft by those pure eyes,
And perfect witness of all-judging Jove;
As he pronounces lastly on each deed,
Of so much fame in Heav'n expect thy meed."

O fountain Arethuse, and thou honour'd floud,
Smooth-sliding Mincius, crown'd with vocal reeds,
That strain I heard was of a higher mood:
But now my Oat proceeds,
And listens to the Herald of the Sea
That came in Neptune's plea,

He ask'd the Waves, and ask'd the felon winds,
What hard mishap hath doom'd this gentle swain?
And question'd every gust of rugged wings
That blows from off each beakèd Promontory:
They knew not of his story,
And sage Hippotades their answer brings,
That not a blast was from his dungeon stray'd,
The air was calm, and on the level brine,
Sleek Panope with all her sisters play'd.
It was that fatall and perfidious Bark
Built in th'eclipse, and rigg'd with curses dark,
That sunk so low that sacred head of thine.

Next Camus, reverend Sire, went footing slow,
His Mantle hairy, and his Bonnet sedge,
Inwrought with figures dim, and on the edge
Like to that sanguine flower inscrib'd with woe.
"Ah! Who hath reft," quoth he, "my dearest pledge?"
Last came, and last did go,
The Pilot of the Galilean lake,
Two massy Keys he bore of metals twain,
(The Golden opes, the Iron shuts amain).
He shook his miter'd locks, and stern bespake:
"How well could I have spar'd for thee, young swain,
Enow of such as for their bellies' sake,
Creep, and intrude, and climb into the fold?
Of other care they little reck'ning make,
Than how to scramble at the shearers' feast,
And shove away the worthy bidden guest.
Blind mouths! that scarce themselves know how to hold
A Sheep-hook, or have learn'd ought else the least
That to the faithful Herdman's art belongs!
What recks it them? What need they? They are sped;
And when they list, their lean and flashy songs
Grate on their scrannel Pipes of wretched straw;
The hungry Sheep look up, and are not fed,
But swoln with wind, and the rank mist they draw,
Rot inwardly, and foul contagion spread;
Besides what the grim Wolf with privy paw
Daily devours apace, and nothing said;
But that two-handed engine at the door
Stands ready to smite once, and smite no more."

Return Alphéus, the dread voice is past
That shrunk thy streams; Return Sicilian Muse,
And call the Vales, and bid them hither cast
Their Bells, and Flowerets of a thousand hues.
Ye valleys low where the mild whispers use,
Of shades, and wanton winds, and gushing brooks,
On whose fresh lap the swart Star sparely looks,

Throw hither all your quaint enameld eyes,
That on the green turf suck the honied showres,
And purple all the ground with vernal flowers.
Bring the rathe Primrose that forsaken dies.
The tufted Crow-toe, and pale Jessamine,
The white Pink, and the Pansie freakt with jet,
The glowing Violet,
The Musk-rose, and the well attir'd Woodbine,
With Cowslips wan that hang the pensive head,
And every flower that sad embroidery wears;
Bid Amaranthus all his beauty shed,
And Daffadillies fill their cups with tears,
To strew the laureat Hearse where Lycid lies.
For so, to interpose a little ease,
Let our frail thoughts dally with false surmise.
Ay me! Whilst thee the shores and sounding Seas
Wash far away, where ere thy bones are hurled,
Whether beyond the stormy Hebrides,
Where thou, perhaps, under the whelming tide
Visit'st the bottom of the monstrous world;
Or whether thou, to our moist vows deny'd,
Sleep'st by the fable of Bellerus old,
Where the great vision of the guarded Mount
Looks toward Namancos and Bayona's hold:
Look homeward Angel, now, and melt with ruth;
And, O ye Dolphins, waft the hapless youth.

Weep no more, woeful Shepherds, weep no more,
For Lycidas, your sorrow, is not dead,
Sunk though he be beneath the watery floor:
So sinks the day-star in the Ocean bed,
And yet anon repairs his drooping head,
And tricks his beams, and with new-spangled Ore,
Flames in the forehead of the morning sky:
So Lycidas, sunk low, but mounted high,
Through the dear might of Him that walk'd the waves
Where, other groves and other streams along,
With Nectar pure his oozy Locks he laves,
And hears the unexpressive nuptial Song,
In the blest Kingdoms meek of Joy and Love.
There entertain him all the Saints above,
In solemn troops, and sweet Societies,
That sing, and singing in their glory move,
And wipe the tears forever from his eyes.
Now, Lycidas, the Shepherds weep no more;
Henceforth thou art the Genius of the shore,
In thy large recompense, and shalt be good
To all that wander in that perilous flood.

Thus sang the uncouth Swain to the oaks and rills,

While the still morn went out with Sandals gray,
He touch'd the tender stops of various Quills,
With eager thought warbling his Dorick lay:
And now the Sun had stretch'd out all the hills,
And now was dropt into the Western bay;
At last he rose, and twitch'd his Mantle blue:
Tomorrow to fresh Woods, and Pastures new.

Note

1. *Elegy.* This is a poem written by Milton at age 29, in honor of
his college friend Edward King who was drowned at sea. The name of
the poem is taken from that of a shepherd in Virgil's third *Bucolic.*

While an elegy is a poem of mourning in honor of the dead, this
poem is nevertheless strikingly hopeful. After recognizing that true fame
is found only in heaven, castigating the corruption of the church, and the
blind luck of chance, Milton then gives a paean to the glory of flowers (l.
134 *et seq.*) almost unmatched in English literature. He ends on a note of
great hope and faith: "Look homeward Angel ... And wipe the tears
forever from his eyes." And so the shepherd rose, "and twitch'd his
Mantle blue: Tomorrow to fresh Woods, and Pasture new."

HOPE (I)
Emily Dickinson

Hope is the thing with feathers
That perches in the soul,
And sings the tune without words
And never stops and all,

And sweetest in the gale is heard;
And sore must be the storm
That could abash the little bird
That kept so many warm.

I've heard it in the chillest land,
And on the strangest sea;
Yet, never in extremity,
It asked a crumb of me.

HOPE (II)
Emily Dickinson

Hope is a subtle glutton;
He feeds upon the fair;
And yet, inspected closely,
What abstinence is there!

His is the halcyon table
That never seats but one,
And whatsoever is consumed

The same amounts remain.

Notes

1. *Ambiguity Personified.* In the first poem, hope is eulogized as that dear support made famous by I *Corinthians* 13:13.

In the second poem, hope is personified as a "subtle glutton": whatsoever he consumes, the "same amounts remain."

How can Dickinson entertain both these views of hope?

Why, in the last line of the second poem, does the poet use the word "amounts," in the plural?

2. *Subtle Glutton.* What is a subtle glutton? Write a prose paraphrase of the poem. Can you capture its substance? Notice that "subtle" and "glutton" share the short "u" sound, along with the gutteral consonant sounds of "l" & "t." These sounds contrast with the bright sound of "hope," with its long "o" and sharp "p." Are there other noteworthy sounds in the poem? How do these sounds add, if at all, to the meaning?

M. IMMORTALITY

SONNET 18
William Shakespeare

Shall I compare thee to a summer's day?
Thou art more lovely and more temperate:
Rough winds do shake the darling buds of May,
And summer's lease hath all too short a date;
Sometime too hot the eye of heaven shines,
And often is his gold complexion dimmed;
And every fair from fair sometime declines,
By chance or nature's changing course untrimmed:
But thy eternal summer shall not fade,
Nor lose possession of that fair thou ow'st,
Nor shall death brag thou wand'rest in his shade,
When in eternal lines to time thou grow'st.
    So long as men can breathe or eyes can see,
    So long lives this, and this gives life to thee.

ODE ON A GRECIAN URN
John Keats

1

Thou still unravish'd bride of quietness,
Thou foster-child of silence and slow time,
Sylvan historian, who canst thus express
A flowery tale more sweetly than our rhyme:
What leaf-fring'd legend haunts about thy shape

Of deities or mortals, or of both,
In Tempe or the dales of Arcady?
What men or gods are these? What maidens loth?
What mad pursuit? What struggle to escape?
What pipes and timbrels? What wild ecstasy?

2

Heard melodies are sweet, but those unheard
Are sweeter; therefore, ye soft pipes, play on;
Not to the sensual ear, but, more endear'd,
Pipe to the spirit ditties of no tone:
Fair youth, beneath the trees, thou canst not leave
Thy song, nor ever can those trees be bare;
Bold Lover, never, never canst thou kiss,
Though winning near the goal—yet, do not grieve;
She cannot fade, though thou hast not thy bliss,
For ever wilt thou love, and she be fair!

3

Ah, happy, happy boughs! that cannot shed
Your leaves, nor ever bid the Spring adieu;
And, happy melodist, unwearied,
For ever piping songs for ever new;
More happy love! more happy, happy love!
For ever warm and still to be enjoy'd,
For ever panting, and for ever young;
All breathing human passion far above,
That leaves a heart high-sorrowful and cloy'd,
A burning forehead, and a parching tongue.

4

Who are these to the sacrifice?
To what green altar, O mysterious priest,
Lead'st thou that heifer lowing at the skies,
And all her silken flanks with garlands drest?
What little town by river or sea shore,
Or mountain-built with peaceful citadel,
Is emptied of this folk, this pious morn?
And, little town, thy streets for evermore
Will silent be; and not a soul to tell
Why thou art desolate, can e'er return.

5

O Attic shape! Fair attitude! with brede
Of marble men and maidens overwrought,
With forest branches and the trodden weed;
Thou, silent form, dost tease us out of thought
As doth eternity: Cold Pastoral!
When old age shall this generation waste,
Thou shalt remain, in midst of other woe

Than ours, a friend to man, to whom thou say'st,
"Beauty is truth, truth beauty,—that is all
Ye know on earth, and all ye need to know."

OAK TREE BEDIZENED WITH BIRDS
31 12 01
Anon.

The old oak stands towering in our front yard
Gnarled and bent nearly two hundred years old
And you gone only twice as much forward
As now stands that tree so strong and so bold

When suddenly six flocks of birds flew in
Tacking east on their way toward the south
Singing in thundering small voices thin
Seeming thousands landing like a bright cloud

In that old oak bedizened now with birds
Where yellow leaves or none or few did hang
Now filled with lovely singing choirs of birds
Filling my glowing heart as they did sing

Oh Shakespeare if we sing like angel birds
Then neither time nor love shall pale our words

SONNET 146
William Shakespeare

Poor soul, the center of my sinful earth,
. . . . these rebel pow'rs that thee array,
Why dost thou pine within and suffer dearth,
Painting thy outward walls so costly gay?
Why so large cost, having so short a lease,
Dost thou upon thy fading mansion spend?
Shall worms, inheritors of this excess,
Eat up thy charge? Is this thy body's end?
Then, soul, live thou upon thy servant's loss,
And let that pine to aggravate thy store:
Buy terms divine in selling hours of dross;
Within be fed, without be rich no more.
    So shalt thou feed on death, that feeds on men,
    And death once dead, there's no more dying then.

ODE TO A NIGHTINGALE
John Keats

My heart aches, and a drowsy numbness pains
My sense, as though of hemlock I had drunk,
Or emptied some dull opiate to the drains
One minute past, and Lethe-wards had sunk:

'Tis not through envy of thy happy lot,
But being too happy in thine happiness,—
That thou, light-winged Dryad of the trees
In some melodious plot
Of beechen green, and shadows numberless,
Singest of summer in full-throated ease.

O, for a draught of vintage! that hath been
Cool'd a long age in the deep-delved earth,
Tasting of Flora and the country green,
Dance, and Provençal song, and sunburnt mirth!
O for a beaker full of the warm South,
Full of the true, the blushful Hippocrene,
With beaded bubbles winking at the brim,
And purple-stainèd mouth;
That I might drink, and leave the world unseen,
And with thee fade away into the forest dim:

Fade far away, dissolve, and quite forget
What thou among the leaves hast never known,
The weariness, the fever, and the fret
Here, where men sit and hear each other groan;
Where palsy shakes a few, sad, last gray hairs,
Where youth grows pale, and spectre-thin, and dies;
Where but to think is to be full of sorrow
And leaden-eyed despairs,
Where Beauty cannot keep her lustrous eyes,
Or new Love pine at them beyond to-morrow.

Away! away! for I will fly to thee,
Not charioted by Bacchus and his pards,
But on the viewless wings of Poesy,
Though the dull brain perplexes and retards:
Already with thee! tender is the night,
And haply the Queen-Moon is on her throne,
Cluster'd around by all her starry Fays;
But here there is no light,
Save what from heaven is with the breezes blown
Through verdurous glooms and winding mossy ways.

I cannot see what flowers are at my feet,
Nor what soft incense hangs upon the boughs,
But, in embalmed darkness, guess each sweet
Wherewith the seasonable month endows
The grass, the thicket, and the fruit-tree wild;
White hawthorn, and the pastoral eglantine;
Fast fading violets cover'd up in leaves;
And mid-May's eldest child,
The coming musk-rose, full of dewy wine,
The murmurous haunt of flies on summer eves.

Darkling I listen; and, for many a time

I have been half in love with easeful Death,
Call'd him soft names in many a musèd rhyme,
To take into the air my quiet breath;
Now more than ever seems it rich to die,
To cease upon the midnight with no pain,
While thou art pouring forth thy soul abroad
In such an ecstasy!
Still wouldst thou sing, and I have ears in vain—
To thy high requiem become a sod.

Thou wast not born for death, immortal Bird!
No hungry generations tread thee down;
The voice I hear this passing night was heard
In ancient days by emperor and clown:
Perhaps the self-same song that found a path
Through the sad heart of Ruth, when, sick for home,
She stood in tears amid the alien corn;
The same that oft-times hath
Charm'd magic casements, opening on the foam
Of perilous seas, in faery lands forlorn.

Forlorn! the very word is like a bell
To toll me back from thee to my sole self!
Adieu! the fancy cannot cheat so well
As she is fam'd to do, deceiving elf.
Adieu! adieu! thy plaintive anthem fades
Past the near meadows, over the still stream,
Up the hill-side; and now 'tis buried deep
In the next valley-glades:
Was it a vision, or a waking dream?
Fled is that music:—Do I wake or sleep?

Notes

1. *Sonnet 18.* Can art capture beauty?

2. *Grecian Urn.* What is the sound, or sense, of line 14: "Pipe to the spirit ditties of no tone"?

3. *Oak Tree.* This poem has obvious references to Shakespeare's Sonnet 73. Note that the poem is dated on the last day of the year. What is the effect of having no punctuation?

4. *Sonnet 146.* This sonnet has strong overtones of Christian belief. Compare I *Corinthians* 15:54–55.

5. *The Nightingale.* The voice of the nightingale, which usually sings at night, is unsurpassed in its musical liquidity.

John Keats died of tuberculosis at age 26. His odes to melancholy, to a grecian urn, to psyche, and to a nightingale, are considered to be among the finest poems in English literature.

N. LOVE

THE DIVINE IMAGE
William Blake

To Mercy, Pity, Peace, and Love
All pray in their distress;
And to these virtues of delight
Return their thankfulness.

For Mercy, Pity, Peace and Love
Is God, our father dear,
And Mercy, Pity, Peace, and Love
Is Man, his child and care.

For Mercy has a human heart,
Pity a human face,
And Love, the human form divine,
And Peace, the human dress.

Then every man, of every clime,
That prays in his distress,
Prays to the human form divine,
Love, Mercy, Pity, Peace.

And all must love the human form,
In heathen, turk, or jew;
Where Mercy, Love, & Pity dwell
There God is dwelling too.

ISAIAH
CHAPTER 40:1–11
King James Bible

¹ Comfort ye, comfort ye my people, saith your God.

² Speak ye comfortably to Jerusalem, and cry unto her, that her warfare is accomplished, that her iniquity is pardoned: for she hath received of the LORD's hand double for all her sins.

³ The voice of him that crieth in the wilderness, Prepare ye the way of the LORD, make straight in the desert a highway for our God.

⁴ Every valley shall be exalted, and every mountain and hill shall be made low: and the crooked shall be made straight, and the rough places plain:

⁵ And the glory of the LORD shall be revealed, and all flesh shall see it together: for the mouth of the LORD hath spoken it.

⁶ The voice said, Cry. And he said, What shall I cry? All flesh is grass, and all the goodliness thereof is as the flower of the field:

⁷ The grass withereth, the flower fadeth: because the spirit of the LORD bloweth upon it: surely the people is grass.

⁸ The grass withereth, the flower fadeth: but the word of our God shall stand for ever.

⁹ O Zion, that bringest good tidings, get thee up into the high mountain; O Jerusalem, that bringest good tidings, lift up thy voice with strength; lift it up, be not afraid; say unto the cities of Judah, Behold your God!

¹⁰ Behold, the Lord GOD will come with strong hand, and his arm shall rule for him: behold, his reward is with him, and his work before him.

¹¹ He shall feed his flock like a shepherd: he shall gather the lambs with his arm, and carry them in his bosom, and shall gently lead those that are with young.

THE GUITARIST TUNES UP
Frances Cornford

With what attentive courtesy he bent
Over his instrument;
Not as a lordly conquerer who could
Command both wire and wood,
But as a man with a loved woman might,
Inquiring with delight
What slight essential things she had to say
Before they started, he and she, to play.

SONNET 66
William Shakespeare

Tir'd with all these, for restful death I cry,
As to behold desert a beggar born,
And needy nothing trimmed in jollity,
And purest faith unhappily forsworn,
And gilded honor shamefully misplaced,
And maiden virtue rudely strumpeted,
And right perfection wrongfully disgraced,
And strength by limping sway disabled,
And art made tongue-tied by authority,
And folly, doctor-like, controlling skill,
And simple truth miscalled simplicity,
And captive good attending captain ill.
    Tir'd with all these, from these would I be gone,
    Save that to die, I leave my love alone.

SONNET 29
William Shakespeare

When in disgrace with fortune and men's eyes,
I all alone beweep my outcast state,

And trouble deaf heav'n with my bootless cries,
And look upon myself and curse my fate,
Wishing my like to one more rich in hope,
Featured like him, like him with friends possessed,
Desiring this man's art, and that man's scope,
With what I most enjoy contented least;
Yet in these thoughts myself almost despising.
Haply I think on thee, and then my state,
Like to the lark at break of day arising
From sullen earth, sings hymns at heaven's gate;
    For thy sweet love rememb'red such wealth brings,
    That then I scorn to change my state with kings.

A RED, RED ROSE
Robert Burns

O my Luve's like a red, red rose,
    That's newly sprung in June;
O my Luve's like the melodie
    That's sweetly play'd in tune.

As fair art thou, my bonnie lass,
    So deep in luve am I;
And I will love thee still, my Dear,
    Till a' the seas gang dry.

Till a' the seas gang dry, my Dear,
    And the rocks melt wi' the sun:
I will love thee still, my Dear,
    While the sands o' life shall run.

And fare thee weel, my only Luve!
    And fare thee weel, a while!
And I will come again, my Luve,
    Tho' it were ten thousand mile!

1 CORINTHIANS
CHAPTER 13
King James Bible

[1] Though I speak with the tongues of men and of angels, and have not charity, I am become as sounding brass, or a tinkling cymbal.

[2] And though I have the gift of prophecy, and understand all mysteries, and all knowledge; and though I have all faith, so that I could remove mountains, and have not charity, I am nothing.

[3] And though I bestow all my goods to feed the poor, and though I give my body to be burned, and have not charity, it profiteth me nothing.

[4] Charity suffereth long, and is kind; charity envieth not; charity vaunteth not itself, is not puffed up,

[5] Doth not behave itself unseemly, seeketh not her own, is not easily provoked, thinketh no evil;

[6] Rejoiceth not in iniquity, but rejoiceth in the truth;

[7] Beareth all things, believeth all things, hopeth all things, endureth all things.

[8] Charity never faileth: but whether there be prophecies, they shall fail; whether there be tongues, they shall cease; whether there be knowledge, it shall vanish away.

[9] For we know in part, and we prophesy in part.

[10] But when that which is perfect is come, then that which is in part shall be done away.

[11] When I was a child, I spake as a child, I understood as a child, I thought as a child: but when I became a man, I put away childish things.

[12] For now we see through a glass, darkly; but then face to face: now I know in part; but then shall I know even as also I am known.

[13] And now abideth faith, hope, charity, these three; but the greatest of these is charity.

Notes

1. *Charity.* Most modern versions of the Bible replace the word "charity" with the word "love." Which is more accurate? More poetic?

2. *Definitions.* We asked our students on a law and literature final exam to define justice, with reference to at least two of the works we had read during the semester. Most said they could not define the term. Some boldly asserted that it was getting your just deserts (or desserts, as a number of students said). But that definition, of course, was no more helpful than the non-definition.

We asked them if justice was synonymous with fairness. About half said yes, and half said no.

We did not mention mercy, nor did they either.

Is it the plight of the lawyer, and of the poet, never to be able to define the essential terms of their profession?

Is it the plight of mankind never to be able to define love?

O. MERCY

WILLIAM SHAKESPEARE
THE MERCHANT OF VENICE
ACT IV SCENE 1

PORTIA. The quality of mercy is not strain'd,
It droppeth as the gentle rain from heaven
Upon the place beneath. It is twice blest:
It blesseth him that gives and him that takes.

'Tis mightiest in the mightiest; it becomes
The thronèd monarch better than his crown.
His sceptre shows the force of temporal power,
The attribute to awe and majesty
Wherein doth sit the dread and fear of kings;
But mercy is above this sceptred sway.
It is enthroned in the hearts of kings;
It is an attribute to God himself;
And earthly power doth then show likest God's
When mercy seasons justice. Therefore, Jew,
Though justice be thy plea, consider this:
That, in the course of justice, none of us
Should see salvation. We do pray for mercy,
And that same prayer doth teach us all to render
The deeds of mercy.

Note

1. *Mercy and Justice.* This speech by Portia is probably one of Shakespeare's most well-known speeches. Yet, little mercy is shown in the end to Shylock, to whom the speech is directed. In fact it is very doubtful that he receives justice, or fairness.

A distinguished German scholar said a few years ago that *The Merchant of Venice* has been played in post-World War II Germany as a play sympathetic to the Jews. When we told the class about the scholar's statement, the Jews grimaced wryly.

Could you play Shylock sympathetically? How should the other characters then be played?

P. POETRY

It may seem strange to have a section called poetry, in a chapter on poems. This section, however, can be viewed as self-regarding. Here the writers and critics of poetry examine what it is we do when we create poetry.

ROBERT PINSKY, THE SOUNDS OF POETRY (1998), explores in a very readable manner the formal rhythm and vernacular accent in poetry, and the ways in which these two play off each other to create complex meanings. He explores the relation between the formal line and the informal enjambment or run-over effects of reading and hearing a poem.

In trying to understand the sense of a poem, Pinsky says, "[O]ne can begin to form a judgment about how [a poem] should sound, and therefore what arrangement in lines best brings out those vocal rhythms for the reader." *Id.* at 46. Conversely, by studying the sound of a line of poetry, "you get the information of the line as well as the information of the syntax." *Id.* at 36. *See also* GEORGE T. WRIGHT, HEARING THE MEASURES (2001).

In an attempt to get at the substantive meaning of what poetry is, Percy Bysshe Shelley (1792–1822) wrote the classic paean to poetry in his essay, *A Defence of Poetry* (1821). The following extracts from that essay, and summary thereof, are intended to give a flavor of Shelley's conception of poetry. A reading of the entire essay is heartily commended, to get the full impact of Shelley's conception.

At the beginning of the essay, Shelley contrasts reason and imagination:

> [T]he former may be considered as mind contemplating the relations borne by one thought to another, however produced; and the latter, as mind acting upon those thoughts so as to colour them with its own light, and composing from them as from elements, other thoughts, each containing within itself the principle of its own integrity.... Reason is the enumeration of quantities already known; imagination is the perception of the value of those quantities, both separately and as a whole.... Reason is to imagination as the instrument to the agent, as the body to the spirit, as the shadow to the substance.
>
> Poetry, in a general sense, may be defined to be "the expression of the imagination:" and poetry is connate with the origin of man.

He makes the astounding statement that the discovery of language is tantamount to the discovery of poetry:

> In the infancy of society every author is necessarily a poet, because language itself is poetry; and to be a poet is to apprehend the true and the beautiful, in a word, the good which exists in the relation, subsisting, first between existence and perception, and secondly between perception and expression.

The poet "not only beholds intensely the present as it is," but "participates in the eternal, the infinite, and the one."

He explores the relation of poetry to other forms of expression:

> Language, colour, form, and religious and civil habits of action, are all the instruments and materials of poetry; they may be called poetry by that figure of speech which considers the effect as a synonyme of the cause. But poetry in a more restricted sense expresses those arrangements of language, and especially metrical language, which are created by that imperial faculty, whose throne is curtained within the invisible nature of man. And this springs from the nature itself of language, which is a more direct representation of the actions and passions of our internal being, and is susceptible of more various and delicate combinations, than colour, form, or motion, and is more plastic and obedient to the control of that faculty of which it is the creation. For language is arbitrarily produced by the imagination, and has relation to thoughts alone; but all other materials, instruments, and conditions of art, have relations among each other, which limit and interpose between conception and expression.

Then he examines the peculiar relation of sound to meaning in poetry:

> Sounds as well as thoughts have relation both between each other and towards that which they represent, and a perception of the order of those relations has always been found connected with a perception of the order of the relations of thought. Hence the language of poets has ever affected a certain uniform and harmonious recurrence of sound, without which it were not poetry, and which is scarcely less indispensable to the communication of its influence, than the words themselves, without reference to that peculiar order. Hence the vanity of translation; it were as wise to cast a violet into a crucible that you might discover the formal principle of its colour and odour, as seek to transfuse from one language into another the creations of a poet. (The plant must spring again from its seed, or it will bear no flower—and this is the burthen of the curse of Babel.)

The distinction between poets and prose writers, he says, "is a vulgar error.... Plato was essentially a poet—the truth and splendour of his imagery, and the melody of his language, are the most intense that it is possible to conceive." A single sentence, or even a single word, may be poetry:

> The parts of a composition may be poetical, without the composition as a whole being a poem. A single sentence may be considered as a whole, though it may be found in the midst of a series of unassimilated portions; a single word may even be a spark of inexhaustible thought. And thus all the great historians, Herodotus, Plutarch, Livy, were poets; and although the plan of these writers, especially that of Livy, restrained them from developing this faculty in its highest degree, they made copious and ample amends for their subjection, by filling all the interstices of their subjects with living images.

He contrasts a story and a poem:

> A poem is the very image of life expressed in its eternal truth. There is this difference between a story and a poem, that a story is a catalogue of detached facts, which have no other connexion than time, place, circumstance, cause, and effect; the other is the creation of actions according to the unchangeable forms of human nature, as existing in the mind of the Creator, which is itself the image of all other minds. The one is partial, and applies only to a definite period of time, and a certain combination of events which can never again recur; the other is universal, and contains within itself the germ of a relation to whatever motives or actions have place in the possible varieties of human nature. Time, which destroys the beauty and the use of the story of particular facts, stripped of the poetry which should invest them, augments that of poetry, and forever develops new and wonderful applications of the eternal truth which it contains. Hence epitomes have been called the moths of just history; they eat out the poetry of it. A story of particular facts is as a mirror

which obscures and distorts that which should be beautiful: poetry is a mirror which makes beautiful that which is distorted.

In the beginning, he says, neither the poets nor their auditors "were aware of the excellence of poetry," for poetry "acts in a divine and unapprehended manner, above and beyond consciousness." Only later generations came to "contemplate and measure the might, cause and effect [of poetry and consciousness] in all the strength and splendour of their union."

He makes the remarkable statement that few poets

of the highest class have chosen to exhibit the beauty of their conceptions in its naked truth and splendour; and it is doubtful whether the alloy of costume, habit, & c., be not necessary to temper this planetary music for mortal ears.... Poetry is a sword of lightning, ever unsheathed, which consumes the scabbard that would contain it.... [W]hen composition begins, inspiration is already on the decline, and the most glorious poetry that has ever been communicated to the world is probably a feeble shadow of the original conceptions of the poet.

Shelley contrasts poetry with morality, or ethical science:

Ethical science arranges the elements which poetry has created, and propounds schemes and proposes examples of civil and domestic life; nor is it for want of admirable doctrines that men hate, despise and censure, and deceive, and subjugate one another. But poetry acts in another and diviner manner. It awakens and enlarges the mind itself by rendering it the receptacle of a thousand unapprehended combinations of thought. Poetry lifts the veil from the hidden beauty of the world, and makes familiar objects be as if they were not familiar; it reproduces all that it represents, and the impersonations clothed in its Elysian light stand thenceforward in the minds of those who have once contemplated them, as memorial of that gentle and exalted content which extends itself over all thoughts and actions with which it coexists. The great secret of morals is love; or a going out of our own nature, and an identification of ourselves with the beautiful which exists in thought, action, or person, not our own. A man, to be greatly good, must imagine intensely and comprehensively; he must put himself in the place of another and of many others; the pains and pleasures of his species must become his own. The great instrument of moral good is the imagination; and poetry administers to the effect by acting upon the cause. Poetry enlarges the circumference of the imagination by replenishing it with thoughts of ever new delight, which have the power of attracting and assimilating to their own nature all other thoughts, and which form new intervals and interstices whose void for ever craves fresh food. Poetry strengthens the faculty which is the organ of the moral nature of man, in the same manner as exercise strengthens a limb. A poet therefore would do ill to embody his own conceptions of right and wrong, which are usually those of his place and time, in his poetical creations, which participate in neither.

He compares poetry and drama, as it developed in the heyday of classical Athens:

It was at the period here adverted to, that the drama had its birth; and however a succeeding writer may have equalled or surpassed those few great specimens of the Athenian drama which have been preserved to us, it is indisputable that the art itself never was understood or practised according to the true philosophy of it, as at Athens. For the Athenians employed language, action, music, painting, the dance, and religious institutions, to produce a common effect in the representation of the highest idealisms of passion and of power; each division in the art was made perfect in its kind by artists of the most consummate skill, and was disciplined into a beautiful proportion and unity one towards the other.

Moving to Shakespeare, Shelley says *King Lear* "may be judged to be the most perfect specimen of the dramatic art existing in the world." In the drama "of the highest order there is little food for censure or hatred; it teaches rather self-knowledge and self-respect."

He gives other examples of high poetry. "Jesus Christ divulged the sacred and eternal truths ... to mankind, and Christianity, in its abstract purity, became the exoteric expression of the esoteric doctrines of the poetry and wisdom of antiquity."

The abolition of personal slavery "is the basis of the highest political hope that it can enter into the mind of man to conceive. The freedom of women produced the poetry of sexual love." Dante "understood the secret things of love even more than Petrarch. His *Vita Nuova* is an inexhaustible fountain of purity of sentiment and language.... His apotheosis of Beatrice in Paradise, and the gradations of his own love and her loveliness, by which as by steps he feigns himself to have ascended to the throne of the Supreme Cause, is the most glorious imagination of modern poetry."

Shelley makes a surprising evaluation of Milton's *Paradise Lost*:

Milton's Devil as a moral being is as far superior to his God, as one who perseveres in some purpose which he has conceived to be excellent in spite of adversity and torture, is to one who in the cold security of undoubted triumph inflicts the most horrible revenge upon his enemy, not from any mistaken notion of inducing him to repent of a perseverance in enmity, but with the alleged design of exasperating him to deserve new torments. Milton has so far violated the popular creed (if this shall be judged to be a violation) as to have alleged no superiority of his god over his devil. And this bold neglect of a direct moral purpose is the most decisive proof of the supremacy of Milton's genius.

Although Shelley portrays poetry as good, this portrayal is not so simple as to exclude the dark side of life:

Sorrow, terror, anguish, despair itself, are often the chosen expressions of an approximation to the highest good. Our sympathy in tragic fiction depends on this principle; tragedy delights by affording a shadow of that pleasure which exists in pain. This is the source also of the melancholy which is inseparable from the sweetest melody. The pleasure that is in sorrow is sweeter than the pleasure of pleasure itself. And hence the saying, "It is better to go to the house of mourning than to the house of mirth." Not that this highest species of pleasure is necessarily linked with pain. The delight of love and friendship, the ecstacy of the admiration of nature, the joy of the perception and still more of the creation of poetry, is often wholly unalloyed.

The production and assurance of pleasure in this highest sense is true utility. Those who produce and preserve this pleasure are poets or poetical philosophers.

Nor is poetry necessarily connected to morality, as that term is commonly understood:

Let us assume that Homer was a drunkard, that Virgil was a flatterer, that Horace was a coward, that Tasso was a madman, that Lord Bacon was a peculator, that Raphael was a libertine, that Spenser was a poet laureate. It is inconsistent with this division of our subject to cite living poets, but posterity has done ample justice to the great names now referred to. Their errors have been weighed and found to have been dust in the balance; if their sins "were as scarlet, they are now white as snow:" They have been washed in the blood of the mediator and redeemer, time. Observe in what a ludicrous chaos the imputations of real or fictitious crime have been confused in the contemporary calumnies against poetry and poets; consider how little is, as it appears—or appears, as it is; look to your own motives, and judge not, lest ye be judged.

Shelley is particularly acerbic in his criticism of utilitarians (read "lawyers"?):

But poets have been challenged to resign the civic crown to reasoners and mechanists, on another plea. It is admitted that the exercise of the imagination is most delightful, but it is alleged that of reason is more useful. Let us examine, as the grounds of this distinction, what is here meant by utility. Pleasure or good, in a general sense, is that which the consciousness of a sensitive and intelligent being seeks, and in which, when found, it acquiesces. There are two kinds of pleasure, one durable, universal and permanent; the other transitory and particular. Utility may either express the means of producing the former or the latter. In the former sense, whatever strengthens and purifies the affections, enlarges the imagination, and adds spirit to sense, is useful. But a narrower meaning may be assigned to the word utility, confining it to express that which banishes the importunity of the wants of our animal nature, the surrounding men with security of life, the dispersing the grosser delusions of superstition, and the conciliating such a degree of mutual forbearance among men as may consist with the motives of personal advantage.

Undoubtedly the promoters of utility, in this limited sense, have their appointed office in society. They follow the footsteps of poets, and copy the sketches of their creations into the book of common life. They make space, and give time. Their exertions are of the highest value, so long as they confine their administration of the concerns of the inferior powers of our nature within the limits due to the superior ones. But while the sceptic destroys gross superstitions, let him spare to deface, as some of the French writers have defaced, the eternal truths charactered upon the imaginations of men. Whilst the mechanist abridges, and the political economist combines, labour, let them beware that their speculations, for want of correspondence with those first principles which belong to the imagination, do not tend, as they have in modern England, to exasperate at once the extremes of luxury and want. They have exemplified the saying, "To him that hath, more shall be given; and from him that hath not, the little that he hath shall be taken away." The rich have become richer, and the poor have become poorer; and the vessel of the state is driven between the Scylla and Charybdis of anarchy and despotism. Such are the effects which must ever flow from an unmitigated exercise of the calculating faculty.

Nor is he any less critical of science, or analytical reasoning:

But it exceeds all imagination to conceive what would have been the moral condition of the world if neither Dante, Petrarch, Boccaccio, Chaucer, Shakespeare, Calderon, Lord Bacon, nor Milton, had ever existed; if Raphael and Michael Angelo had never been born; if the Hebrew poetry had never been translated; if a revival of the study of Greek literature had never taken place; if no monuments of ancient sculpture had been handed down to us; and if the poetry of the religion of the ancient world had been extinguished together with its belief. The human mind could never, except by the intervention of these excitements, have been awakened to the invention of the grosser sciences, and that application of analytical reasoning to the aberrations of society, which it is now attempted to exalt over the direct expression of the inventive and creative faculty itself.

We have more moral, political, and historical wisdom, than we know how to reduce into practice; we have more scientific and economical knowledge than can be accommodated to the just distribution of the produce which it multiplies. The poetry, in these systems of thought, is concealed by the accumulation of facts and calculating processes. There is no want of knowledge respecting what is wisest and best in morals, government, and political economy, or at least what is wiser and better than what men now practise and endure. But we let "I *dare not* wait upon I *would*, like the poor cat in the adage." We want the creative faculty to imagine that which we know; we want the generous impulse to act that which we imagine; we want the poetry of life: our calculations have outrun conception; we have eaten more than we can digest. The cultivation of those sciences which have enlarged the limits of the empire of man over the external world, has, for want of the poetical faculty, proportionally circumscribed those of the internal world; and man, having enslaved the elements, remains himself a slave. To what but cultivation of the mechanical arts in a degree disproportioned to the presence of the creative faculty, which is the basis of all knowledge, is to be attributed to the abuse of all invention for abridging and combining labour, to the exasperation of the inequality of mankind? From what other cause has it arisen that the discoveries which should have lightened, have added a weight to the curse imposed on Adam? Poetry, and the principle of Self, of which money is the visible incarnation, are the God and Mammon of the world.

Poetry, Shelley says, is like a fountain:

A great poem is a fountain for ever overflowing with the waters of wisdom and delight; and after one person and one age has exhausted all its divine effluence which their peculiar relations enable them to share, another and yet another succeeds, and new relations are ever developed, the source of an unforeseen and unconceived delight.

It "arises from within, like the colour of a flower which fades and changes as it is developed, and the conscious portions over our nature are unprophetic either of its approach or its departure.... Poetry is the record of the best and happiest moments of the happiest and best minds."

In a brilliant insight, he says that poetry "purges from our inward sight the film of familiarity which obscures from us the wonder of our being,"

For the benefit of all lawyers, Shelley concludes:

The most unfailing herald, companion, and follower of the awakening of a great people to work a beneficial change in opinion or institution, is poetry. At such periods there is an accumulation of the power of communicating and receiving intense and impassioned conceptions respecting man and nature. The persons in whom this power resides, may often as far as regards many portions of their nature, have little apparent correspondence with that spirit of good of which they are the ministers. But even whilst they deny and abjure, they are yet compelled to serve, the power which is seated on the throne of their own soul. It is impossible to read the compositions of the most celebrated writers of the present day without being startled with the electric life which burns within their words. They measure the circumference and sound the depths of human nature with a comprehensive and all-penetrating spirit, and they are themselves perhaps the most sincerely astonished at its manifestations; for it is less their spirit than the spirit of the age. Poets are the hierophants of unapprehended inspirations; the mirrors of gigantic shadows which futurity casts upon the present; the words which express what they understand not; the trumpets which sing to battle and feel not what they inspire; the influence which is moved not, but moves. Poets are the unacknowledged legislators of the world.

JOHN
CHAPTER 1
King James Bible

[1] In the beginning was the Word, and the Word was with God, and the Word was God.

[2] The same was in the beginning with God.

[3] All things were made by him; and without him was not any thing made that was made.

[4] In him was life; and the life was the light of men.

[5] And the light shineth in darkness; and the darkness comprehended it not.

TO A SKYLARK
Percy Bysshe Shelley

Hail to thee, blithe spirit!
Bird thou never wert—
That from heaven or near it
Pourest thy full heart
In profuse strains of unpremeditated art.

Higher still and higher
From the earth thou springest,
Like a cloud of fire;
The blue deep thou wingest,
And singing still dost soar, and soaring ever singest.

In the golden light'ning
Of the sunken sun,
O'er which clouds are bright'ning,
Thou dost float and run,
Like an unbodied joy whose race is just begun.

The pale purple even
Melts around thy flight;
Like a star of heaven,
In the broad daylight
Thou art unseen, but yet I hear thy shrill delight—

Keen as are the arrows
Of that silver sphere
Whose intense lamp narrows
In the white dawn clear,
Until we hardly see, we feel that it is there.

All the earth and air
With thy voice is loud,
As when night is bare,
From one lonely cloud
The moon rains out her beams, and heaven is over-
flow'd.

What thou art we know not;
What is most like thee?
From rainbow clouds there flow not
Drops so bright to see,
As from thy presence showers a rain of melody:—

Like a poet hidden
In the light of thought,
Singing hymns unbidden,
Till the world is wrought
To sympathy with hopes and fears it heeded not:

Like a high-born maiden
In a palace tower
Soothing her love-laden
Soul in secret hour
With music sweet as love, which overflows her bower:

Like a glow-worm golden
In a dell of dew,
Scattering unbeholden
Its aerial hue
Among the flowers and grass which screen it from the
view:

Like a rose embower'd
In its own green leaves,
By warm winds deflower'd,
Till the scent it gives
Makes faint with too much sweet those heavy-wingèd
thieves.

Sound of vernal showers
On the twinkling grass,
Rain-awaken'd flowers—
All that ever was
Joyous and clear and fresh—thy music doth surpass.

Teach us, sprite or bird,
What sweet thoughts are thine:
I have never heard
Praise of love or wine
That panted forth a flood of rapture so divine.

Chorus hymeneal,
Or triumphal chant,
Match'd with thine would be all

But an empty vaunt—
A thing wherein we feel there is some hidden want.

What objects are the fountains
Of thy happy strain?
What fields, or waves, or mountains?
What shapes of sky or plain?
What love of thine own kind? what ignorance of pain?

With thy clear keen joyance
Languor cannot be:
Shadow of annoyance
Never came near thee:
Thou lovest, but ne'er knew love's sad satiety.

Waking or asleep,
Thou of death must deem
Things more true and deep
Than we mortals dream,
Or how could thy notes flow in such a crystal stream?

We look before and after,
And pine for what is not:
Our sincerest laughter
With some pain is fraught;
Our sweetest songs are those that tell of saddest
thought.

Yet, if we could scorn
Hate and pride and fear,
If we were things born
Not to shed a tear,
I know not how thy joy we ever should come near.

Better than all measures
Of delightful sound,
Better than all treasures
That in books are found,
Thy skill to poet were, thou scorner of the ground!

Teach me half the gladness
That thy brain must know;
Such harmonious madness
From my lips would flow,
The world should listen then, as I am listening now.

Note

1. *Comparing Birds.* Which is more beautiful, Keats' nightingale or Shelley's skylark? One sings of immortality, and the other outflies imagination.

THERE IS NO FRIGATE LIKE A BOOK
Emily Dickinson

There is no frigate like a book
  To take us lands away,
Nor any coursers like a page
  of prancing poetry.

This traverse may the poorest take
  Without oppress of toll;
How frugal is the chariot
  That bears a human soul!

Note

1. *Imagery.* The poet compares a book to a frigate, poetry to a prancing courser, and literature to a chariot. Why these very strong symbols?

WORDS
William Butler Yeats

I had this thought a while ago,
"My darling cannot understand
What I have done, or what would do
In this blind bitter land."

And I grew weary of the sun
Until my thoughts cleared up again,
Remembering that the best I have done
Was done to make it plain;

That every year I have cried, "At length
My darling understands it all,
Because I have come into my strength,
And words obey my call";

That had she done so who can say
What would have shaken from the sieve?
I might have thrown poor words away
And been content to live.

Notes

1. *Poetry.* The poet seems to suggest that love is more powerful than words that "obey my call." Or does he? Compare the role of Prospero in Shakespeare's *The Tempest*, Act V, scene 1.

2. *Obedience and Obeisance.* Lawyers' tools are words. Each of us would all wish to claim that "words obey my call." Do words obey your call? Do words respect you, and you them? Explain.

ARS POETICA
Archibald MacLeish

A poem should be palpable and mute
As a globed fruit,

Dumb
As old medallions to the thumb,

Silent as the sleeve-worn stone
Of casement ledges where the moss has grown—

A poem should be wordless
As the flight of birds.

A poem should be motionless in time
As the moon climbs,

Leaving, as the moon releases
Twig by twig the night-entangled trees,

Leaving as the moon behind in winter leaves,
Memory by memory the mind—

A poem should be motionless in time
As the moon climbs.

A poem should be equal to:
Not true.

For all the history of grief
An empty doorway and a maple leaf.

For love
The leaning grasses and two lights above the sea—

A poem should not mean
But be.

Note

1. *Sound and Sense.* Surely MacLeish does not mean that a poem should have no meaning. Then what does he mean?

Is it possible to describe a good legal opinion as not meaning, but being? Compare *Luke* 18:9–14.

ON FIRST LOOKING INTO CHAPMAN'S HOMER
John Keats

Much have I traveled in the realms of gold,
    And many goodly states and kingdoms seen;
    Round many western islands have I been
Which bards in fealty to Apollo hold.
Oft of one wide expanse had I been told
    That deep-browed Homer ruled as his demense;
    Yet did I never breathe its pure serene

Till I heard Chapman speak out loud and bold:
Then felt I like some watcher of the skies
    When a new planet swims into his ken;
Or like stout Cortez when with eagle eyes
    He stared at the Pacific—and all his men
Looked at each other with a wild surmise—
    Silent, upon a peak in Darien.

AN ESSAY ON CRITICISM
Alexander Pope

. . . .

True ease in writing comes from art, not chance,
As those move easiest have learned to dance.
'Tis not enough no harshness gives offense,
The sound must seem an echo to the sense:
Soft is the strain when Zephyr gently blows,
And the smooth stream in smoother numbers flows:
But when loud surges lash the sounding shore,
The hoarse, rough verse should like the torrent roar:
When Ajax strives some rock's vast weight to throw,
The line too labors, and the words move slow;
Not so, when swift Camilla scours the plain,
Flies o'er th' unbending corn, and skims along the
main.
Hear how Timotheus' varied lays surprise,
And bid alternate passions fall and rise!

. . . .

ON THE LATE MASSACRE IN PIEDMONT
John Milton

Avenge, O Lord, they slaughtered saints, whose bones
Lie scattered on the Alpine mountains cold;
Ev'n them who kept thy truth so pure of old,
When all our fathers worshipped stocks and stones,
Forget not: in thy book record their groans
Who were thy sheep, and in their ancient fold
Slain by the bloody Piedmontese, that rolled
Mother with infant down the rocks. Their moans
The vales redoubled to the hills, and they
To heav'n. Their martyred blood and ashes sow
O'er all th' Italian fields, where still doth sway
The triple Tyrant that from these may grow
A hundredfold, who, having learnt thy way,
Early may fly the Babylonian woe.

Note

1. *Their Moans.* Does Milton's sonnet illustrate Pope's point? Does this sonnet be, rather than mean?

PSALM 96
King James Bible

[1] O sing unto the LORD a new song: sing unto the LORD, all the earth.

[2] Sing unto the LORD, bless his name; shew forth his salvation from day to day.

[3] Declare his glory among the heathen, his wonders among all people.

[4] For the LORD is great, and greatly to be praised: he is to be feared above all gods.

[5] For all the gods of the nations are idols: but the LORD made the heavens.

[6] Honour and majesty are before him: strength and beauty are in his sanctuary.

[7] Give unto the LORD, O ye kindreds of the people, give unto the LORD glory and strength.

[8] Give unto the LORD the glory due unto his name: bring an offering, and come into his courts.

[9] O worship the LORD in the beauty of holiness: fear before him, all the earth.

[10] Say among the heathen that the LORD reigneth: the world also shall be established that it shall not be moved: he shall judge the people righteously.

[11] Let the heavens rejoice, and let the earth be glad; let the sea roar, and the fulness thereof.

[12] Let the field be joyful, and all that is therein: then shall all the trees of the wood rejoice

[13] Before the LORD: for he cometh, for he cometh to judge the earth: he shall judge the world with righteousness, and the people with his truth.

Note

1. *Repetition.* One of the major poetic devices in Psalm 96 is repetition—not the simple repetition of words but the complex interrelationship of sounds and structure. Trace out in detail these interrelationships.

Q. SOLITUDE

THE SNOW MAN
Wallace Stevens

One must have a mind of winter
To regard the frost and the boughs
Of the pine-trees crusted with snow,

And have been cold a long time
To behold the junipers shagged with ice,
The spruces rough in the distant glitter

Of the January sun, and not to think
Of any misery in the sound of the wind,
In the sound of a few leaves,

Which is the sound of the land
Full of the same wind
That is blowing in the same bare place

For the listener, who listens in the snow,
And, nothing himself, beholds
Nothing that is not there and the nothing that is.

Note

1. *Double Entendre*? The listener who listens in the snow "beholds." Does he do so by listening?

The listener beholds "[n]othing that is not there," and "the nothing that is." How could he behold nothing? What is it that the listener is not beholding?

SHE DWELT AMONG THE UNTRODDEN WAYS
William Wordsworth

She dwelt among the untrodden ways
    Beside the springs of Dove,
A Maid whom there were none to praise
    And very few to love:

A violet by a mossy stone
    Half hidden from the eye!
—Fair as a star, when only one
    Is shining in the sky.

She lived unknown, and few could know
    When Lucy ceased to be;
But she is in her grave, and, oh,
    The difference to me!

THE SOLITARY REAPER
William Wordsworth

Behold her, single in the field,
Yon solitary Highland lass!
Reaping and singing by herself;
Stop here, or gently pass!
Alone she cuts and binds the grain,
And sings a melancholy strain;
O listen! for the vale profound
Is overflowing with the sound.

No nightingale did ever chaunt
More welcome notes to weary bands
Of travelers in some shady haunt
Among Arabian sands.
A voice so thrilling ne'er was heard
In springtime from the cuckoo-bird,
Breaking the silence of the seas
Among the farthest Hebrides.

Will no one tell me what she sings?—
Perhaps the plaintive numbers flow
For old, unhappy, far-off things,
And battles long ago.
Or is it some more humble lay,
Familiar matter of today?
Some natural sorrow, loss, or pain,
That has been, and may be again?

Whate'er the theme, the maiden sang
As if her song could have no ending;
I saw her singing at her work,
And o'er the sickle bending—
I listened, motionless and still;
And, as I mounted up the hill,
The music in my heart I bore
Long after it was heard no more.

I WANDERED LONELY AS A CLOUD
William Wordsworth

I wandered lonely as a cloud
That floats on high o'er vales and hills,
When all at once I saw a crowd,
A host, of golden daffodils;
Beside the lake, beneath the trees,
Fluttering and dancing in the breeze.

Continuous as the stars that shine
And twinkle on the milky way,

They stretched in never-ending line
Along the margin of a bay:
Ten thousand saw I at a glance,
Tossing their heads in sprightly dance.

The waves beside them danced; but they
Out-did the sparkling waves in glee:
A poet could not but be gay,
In such a jocund company:
I gazed—and gazed—but little thought
What wealth the show to me had brought:

For oft, when on my couch I lie
In vacant or in pensive mood,
They flash upon that inward eye
Which is the bliss of solitude;
And then my heart with pleasure fills,
And dances with the daffodils.

A SLUMBER DID MY SPIRIT SEAL
William Wordsworth

A slumber did my spirit seal;
I had no human fears:
She seemed a thing that could not feel
The touch of earthly years.

No motion has she now, no force;
She neither hears nor sees;
Rolled round in earth's diurnal course,
With rocks, and stones, and trees.

Note

1. *Nature.* Wordsworth's poems display an acute awareness of nature, combined with a spiritual consciousness. They also use traditional poetic meter and rhyme. This combination of qualities may account for the popularity of Wordworth's poetry throughout the years. What appeals to you about these poems, if anything?

R. LIBIDO

SONG OF SOLOMON
King James Bible

CHAPTER 1

[1] The song of songs, which is Solomon's.

[2] Let him kiss me with the kisses of his mouth: for thy love is better than wine.

[3] Because of the savour of thy good ointments thy name is as ointment poured forth, therefore do the virgins love thee.

⁴ Draw me, we will run after thee: the king hath brought me into his chambers: we will be glad and rejoice in thee, we will remember thy love more than wine: the upright love thee.

⁵ I am black, but comely, O ye daughters of Jerusalem, as the tents of Kedar, as the curtains of Solomon.

⁶ Look not upon me, because I am black, because the sun hath looked upon me: my mother's children were angry with me; they made me the keeper of the vineyards; but mine own vineyard have I not kept.

⁷ Tell me, O thou whom my soul loveth, where thou feedest, where thou makest thy flock to rest at noon: for why should I be as one that turneth aside by the flocks of thy companions?

⁸ If thou know not, O thou fairest among women, go thy way forth by the footsteps of the flock, and feed thy kids beside the shepherds' tents.

⁹ I have compared thee, O my love, to a company of horses in Pharaoh's chariots.

¹⁰ Thy cheeks are comely with rows of jewels, thy neck with chains of gold.

¹¹ We will make thee borders of gold with studs of silver.

¹² While the king sitteth at his table, my spikenard sendeth forth the smell thereof.

¹³ A bundle of myrrh is my wellbeloved unto me; he shall lie all night betwixt my breasts.

¹⁴ My beloved is unto me as a cluster of camphire in the vineyards of En-gedi.

¹⁵ Behold, thou art fair, my love; behold, thou art fair; thou hast doves' eyes.

¹⁶ Behold, thou art fair, my beloved, yea, pleasant: also our bed is green.

¹⁷ The beams of our house are cedar, and our rafters of fir.

CHAPTER 2

¹ I am the rose of Sharon, and the lily of the valleys.

² As the lily among thorns, so is my love among the daughters.

³ As the apple tree among the trees of the wood, so is my beloved among the sons. I sat down under his shadow with great delight, and his fruit was sweet to my taste.

⁴ He brought me to the banqueting house, and his banner over me was love.

⁵ Stay me with flagons, comfort me with apples: for I am sick of love.

⁶ His left hand is under my head, and his right hand doth embrace me.

[7] I charge you, O ye daughters of Jerusalem, by the roes, and by the hinds of the field, that ye stir not up, nor awake my love, till he please.

[8] The voice of my beloved! behold, he cometh leaping upon the mountains, skipping upon the hills.

[9] My beloved is like a roe or a young hart: behold, he standeth behind our wall, he looketh forth at the windows, shewing himself through the lattice.

[10] My beloved spake, and said unto me, Rise up, my love, my fair one, and come away.

[11] For, lo, the winter is past, the rain is over and gone;

[12] The flowers appear on the earth; the time of the singing of birds is come, and the voice of the turtle is heard in our land;

[13] The fig tree putteth forth her green figs, and the vines with the tender grape give a good smell. Arise, my love, my fair one, and come away.

[14] O my dove, that art in the clefts of the rock, in the secret places of the stairs, let me see thy countenance, let me hear thy voice; for sweet is thy voice, and thy countenance is comely.

[15] Take us the foxes, the little foxes, that spoil the vines: for our vines have tender grapes.

[16] My beloved is mine, and I am his: he feedeth among the lilies.

[17] Until the day break, and the shadows flee away, turn, my beloved, and be thou like a roe or a young hart upon the mountains of Bether.

CHAPTER 3

[1] By night on my bed I sought him whom my soul loveth: I sought him, but I found him not.

[2] I will rise now, and go about the city in the streets, and in the broad ways I will seek him whom my soul loveth: I sought him, but I found him not.

[3] The watchmen that go about the city found me: to whom I said, Saw ye him whom my soul loveth?

[4] It was but a little that I passed from them, but I found him whom my soul loveth: I held him, and would not let him go, until I had brought him into my mother's house, and into the chamber of her that conceived me.

[5] I charge you, O ye daughters of Jerusalem, by the roes, and by the hinds of the field, that ye stir not up, nor awake my love, till he please.

[6] Who is this that cometh out of the wilderness like pillars of smoke, perfumed with myrrh and frankincense, with all powders of the merchant?

[7] Behold his bed, which is Solomon's; threescore valiant men are about it, of the valiant of Israel.

[8] They all hold swords, being expert in war: every man hath his sword upon his thigh because of fear in the night.

[9] King Solomon made himself a chariot of the wood of Lebanon.

[10] He made the pillars thereof of silver, the bottom thereof of gold, the covering of it of purple, the midst thereof being paved with love, for the daughters of Jerusalem.

[11] Go forth, O ye daughters of Zion, and behold king Solomon with the crown wherewith his mother crowned him in the day of his espousals, and in the day of the gladness of his heart.

CHAPTER 4

[1] Behold, thou art fair, my love; behold, thou art fair; thou hast doves' eyes within thy locks: thy hair is as a flock of goats, that appear from mount Gilead.

[2] Thy teeth are like a flock of sheep that are even shorn, which came up from the washing; whereof every one bear twins, and none is barren among them.

[3] Thy lips are like a thread of scarlet, and thy speech is comely: thy temples are like a piece of a pomegranate within thy locks.

[4] Thy neck is like the tower of David builded for an armoury, whereon there hang a thousand bucklers, all shields of mighty men.

[5] Thy two breasts are like two young roes that are twins, which feed among the lilies.

[6] Until the day break, and the shadows flee away, I will get me to the mountain of myrrh, and to the hill of frankincense.

[7] Thou art all fair, my love; there is no spot in thee.

[8] Come with me from Lebanon, my spouse, with me from Lebanon: look from the top of Amana, from the top of Shenir and Hermon, from the lions' dens, from the mountains of the leopards.

[9] Thou hast ravished my heart, my sister, my spouse; thou hast ravished my heart with one of thine eyes, with one chain of thy neck.

[10] How fair is thy love, my sister, my spouse! how much better is thy love than wine! and the smell of thine ointments than all spices!

[11] Thy lips, O my spouse, drop as the honeycomb: honey and milk are under thy tongue; and the smell of thy garments is like the smell of Lebanon.

[12] A garden inclosed is my sister, my spouse; a spring shut up, a fountain sealed.

[13] Thy plants are an orchard of pomegranates, with pleasant fruits; camphire, with spikenard,

[14] Spikenard and saffron; calamus and cinnamon, with all trees of frankincense; myrrh and aloes, with all the chief spices:

[15] A fountain of gardens, a well of living waters, and streams from Lebanon.

[16] Awake, O north wind; and come, thou south; blow upon my garden, that the spices thereof may flow out. Let my beloved come into his garden, and eat his pleasant fruits.

CHAPTER 5

[1] I am come into my garden, my sister, my spouse: I have gathered my myrrh with my spice; I have eaten my honeycomb with my honey; I have drunk my wine with my milk: eat, O friends; drink, yea, drink abundantly, O beloved.

[2] I sleep, but my heart waketh: it is the voice of my beloved that knocketh, saying, Open to me, my sister, my love, my dove, my undefiled: for my head is filled with dew, and my locks with the drops of the night.

[3] I have put off my coat; how shall I put it on? I have washed my feet; how shall I defile them?

[4] My beloved put in his hand by the hole of the door, and my bowels were moved for him.

[5] I rose up to open to my beloved; and my hands dropped with myrrh, and my fingers with sweet smelling myrrh, upon the handles of the lock.

[6] I opened to my beloved; but my beloved had withdrawn himself, and was gone: my soul failed when he spake: I sought him, but I could not find him; I called him, but he gave me no answer.

[7] The watchmen that went about the city found me, they smote me, they wounded me; the keepers of the walls took away my veil from me.

[8] I charge you, O daughters of Jerusalem, if ye find my beloved, that ye tell him, that I am sick of love.

[9] What is thy beloved more than another beloved, O thou fairest among women? what is thy beloved more than another beloved, that thou dost so charge us?

[10] My beloved is white and ruddy, the chiefest among ten thousand.

[11] His head is as the most fine gold, his locks are bushy, and black as a raven.

[12] His eyes are as the eyes of doves by the rivers of waters, washed with milk, and fitly set.

[13] His cheeks are as a bed of spices, as sweet flowers: his lips like lilies, dropping sweet smelling myrrh.

[14] His hands are as gold rings set with the beryl: his belly is as bright ivory overlaid with sapphires.

[15] His legs are as pillars of marble, set upon sockets of fine gold: his countenance is as Lebanon, excellent as the cedars.

¹⁶ His mouth is most sweet: yea, he is altogether lovely. This is my beloved, and this is my friend, O daughters of Jerusalem.

CHAPTER 6

¹ Whither is thy beloved gone, O thou fairest among women? whither is thy beloved turned aside? that we may seek him with thee.

² My beloved is gone down into his garden, to the beds of spices, to feed in the gardens, and to gather lilies.

³ I am my beloved's, and my beloved is mine: he feedeth among the lilies.

⁴ Thou art beautiful, O my love, as Tirzah, comely as Jerusalem, terrible as an army with banners.

⁵ Turn away thine eyes from me, for they have overcome me: thy hair is as a flock of goats that appear from Gilead.

⁶ Thy teeth are as a flock of sheep which go up from the washing, whereof every one beareth twins, and there is not one barren among them.

⁷ As a piece of a pomegranate are thy temples within thy locks.

⁸ There are threescore queens, and fourscore concubines, and virgins without number.

⁹ My dove, my undefiled is but one; she is the only one of her mother, she is the choice one of her that bare her. The daughters saw her, and blessed her; yea, the queens and the concubines, and they praised her.

¹⁰ Who is she that looketh forth as the morning, fair as the moon, clear as the sun, and terrible as an army with banners?

¹¹ I went down into the garden of nuts to see the fruits of the valley, and to see whether the vine flourished, and the pomegranates budded.

¹² Or ever I was aware, my soul made me like the chariots of Amminadib.

¹³ Return, return, O Shulamite; return, return, that we may look upon thee. What will ye see in the Shulamite? As it were the company of two armies.

CHAPTER 7

¹ How beautiful are thy feet with shoes, O prince's daughter! the joints of thy thighs are like jewels, the work of the hands of a cunning workman.

² Thy navel is like a round goblet, which wanteth not liquor: thy belly is like an heap of wheat set about with lilies.

³ Thy two breasts are like two young roes that are twins.

[4] Thy neck is as a tower of ivory; thine eyes like the fishpools in Heshbon, by the gate of Bath-rabbim: thy nose is as the tower of Lebanon which looketh toward Damascus.

[5] Thine head upon thee is like Carmel, and the hair of thine head like purple; the king is held in the galleries.

[6] How fair and how pleasant art thou, O love, for delights!

[7] This thy stature is like to a palm tree, and thy breasts to clusters of grapes.

[8] I said, I will go up to the palm tree, I will take hold of the boughs thereof: now also thy breasts shall be as clusters of the vine, and the smell of thy nose like apples;

[9] And the roof of thy mouth like the best wine for my beloved, that goeth down sweetly, causing the lips of those that are asleep to speak.

[10] I am my beloved's, and his desire is toward me.

[11] Come, my beloved, let us go forth into the field; let us lodge in the villages.

[12] Let us get up early to the vineyards; let us see if the vine flourish, whether the tender grape appear, and the pomegranates bud forth: there will I give thee my loves.

[13] The mandrakes give a smell, and at our gates are all manner of pleasant fruits, new and old, which I have laid up for thee, O my beloved.

CHAPTER 8

[1] O that thou wert as my brother, that sucked the breasts of my mother! when I should find thee without, I would kiss thee; yea, I should not be despised.

[2] I would lead thee, and bring thee into my mother's house, who would instruct me: I would cause thee to drink of spiced wine of the juice of my pomegranate.

[3] His left hand should be under my head, and his right hand should embrace me.

[4] I charge you, O daughters of Jerusalem, that ye stir not up, nor awake my love, until he please.

[5] Who is this that cometh up from the wilderness, leaning upon her beloved? I raised thee up under the apple tree: there thy mother brought thee forth: there she brought thee forth that bare thee.

[6] Set me as a seal upon thine heart, as a seal upon thine arm: for love is strong as death; jealousy is cruel as the grave: the coals thereof are coals of fire, which hath a most vehement flame.

[7] Many waters cannot quench love, neither can the floods drown it: if a man would give all the substance of his house for love, it would utterly be contemned.

⁸ We have a little sister, and she hath no breasts: what shall we do for our sister in the day when she shall be spoken for?

⁹ If she be a wall, we will build upon her a palace of silver: and if she be a door, we will inclose her with boards of cedar.

¹⁰ I am a wall, and my breasts like towers: then was I in his eyes as one that found favour.

¹¹ Solomon had a vineyard at Baal-hamon; he let out the vineyard unto keepers; every one for the fruit thereof was to bring a thousand pieces of silver.

¹² My vineyard, which is mine, is before me: thou, O Solomon, must have a thousand, and those that keep the fruit thereof two hundred.

¹³ Thou that dwellest in the gardens, the companions hearken to thy voice: cause me to hear it.

¹⁴ Make haste, my beloved, and be thou like to a roe or to a young hart upon the mountains of spices.

Note

1. *The Song of Songs.* No one quite understands why the *Song of Songs* is included in the Bible, which is allegedly a book of moral instruction. One writer suggests that it got included because it was associated with "the venerated name of Solomon," E.S. Bates, The Bible As Living Literature 771 (1936). The book is dated from the fourth century B.C., however, and "was certainly not by Solomon." *Id. See also* R. Alter & F. Kermode, Eds., The Literary Guide To The Bible fn. 14 ("Third–Fourth Centuries B.C.E. The evidence is linguistic (Persian and Greek loan words) and stylistic.") Later Christian writers, says Bates, have tried to justify *The Song* "as a far fetched allegory of the love of Christ for his Church," *supra*. Bates describes the book as a "fragmentary wedding idyll," and attempts to break the book down into its various speakers—Solomon, the Shulamite, the Brothers, the Chorus. *Id.* at 771–85.

Francis Landy in his essay on *The Song of Songs*, pp. 305–319, in The Literary Guide, *supra*, notes the extraordinary sensuousness of the book. "Sight and smell are the dominant sensations of the Song." *Id.* at 310. Some of the metaphors of the *The Song*, he says, "are wonderfully perplexing, sometimes surreal in their juxtaposition of extreme incongruities, their baroque development, their cultivation of disproportion." *Id.* at 309. Do you agree with this evaluation of the metaphors?

SONNET 129
William Shakespeare

Th'expence of Spirit in a waste of shame

Is lust in action, and till action, lust
Is perjured, murd'rous, bloody, full of blame,
Savage, extreme, rude, cruel, not to trust,
Enjoyed no sooner but despisèd straight,

> Past reason hunted, and no sooner had,
> Past reason hated as a swallowed bait,
> On purpose laid to make the taker mad;
> Made in pursuit and in possession so,
> Had, having, and in quest to have, extreme,
> A bliss in proof, and proved, a very woe,
> Before a joy proposed, behind, a dream,
>
> > All this the world well knows, yet none knowes well
> > To shun the heav'n that leads men to this hell.

Note

1. *A Love Sonnet*? What is this poem doing in Shakespeare's love sonnets?

Compare Claudio's description to Lucio, in *Measure for Measure* Act I scene 2, of his fornication with Juliet: "Our natures do pursue, Like rats that ravin down their proper bane, A thirsty evil, and when we drink we die." One of the most vicious attacks on sex in all of literature is that of Lear, *King Lear*, Act IV scene 6, when he realizes the full perfidy of his daughters Goneril and Regan:

> Behold yond simp'ring dame,
> Whose face between her forks presages snow,
> That minces virtue, and does shake the head
> To hear of pleasure's name;
> The fitchew, nor the spoiled horse, goes to't
> With a more riotous appetite.
> Down from the waist they are Centaurs,
> Though women all above,
> But to the girdle do the gods inherit,
> Beneath is all the fiends'.
> There's hell, there's darkness, there is the sulphurous pit,
> Burning, scalding, stench, consumption. Fie, fie, fie!
> Pah, pah! Give me an ounce of civet, good apothecary,
> sweeten my imagination. There's money for thee.

THE SUN RISING
John Donne

> Busy old fool, unruly Sun,
> Why dost thou thus,
> Through windows, and through curtains, call on us?
> Must to thy motions lovers' seasons run?
> Saucy pedantic wretch, go chide
> Late schoolboys, and sour prentices,
> Go tell court-huntsmen that the king will ride,
> Call country ants to harvest offices;
> Love, all alike, no season knows, nor clime,

Nor hours, days, months, which are the rags of time.

    Thy beams, so reverend and strong
    Why shouldst thou think?
I could eclipse and cloud them with a wink,
But that I would not lose her sight so long;
    If her eyes have not blinded thine,
    Look, and tomorrow late tell me
Whether both th' Indias of spice and mine
Be where thou left'st them, or lie here with me.
Ask for those kings whom thou saw'st yesterday,
And thou shalt hear: "All here in one bed lay."

    She's all states, and all princes I,
    Nothing else is.
Princes do but play us; compar'd to this,
All honour's mimic, all wealth alchemy.
    Thou, sun, art half as happy 's we,
    In that the world's contracted thus;
Thine age asks ease, and since thy duties be
To warm the world, that's done in warming us.
Shine here to us, and thou art everywhere;
This bed thy centre is, these walls, thy sphere.

S.   REPENTANCE

PSALM 51
King James Bible

[1] Have mercy upon me, O God, according to thy lovingkindness: according unto the multitude of thy tender mercies blot out my transgressions.

[2] Wash me throughly from mine iniquity, and cleanse me from my sin.

[3] For I acknowledge my transgressions: and my sin is ever before me.

[4] Against thee, thee only, have I sinned, and done this evil in thy sight: that thou mightest be justified when thou speakest, and be clear when thou judgest.

[5] Behold, I was shapen in iniquity; and in sin did my mother conceive me.

[6] Behold, thou desirest truth in the inward parts: and in the hidden part thou shalt make me to know wisdom.

[7] Purge me with hyssop, and I shall be clean: wash me, and I shall be whiter than snow.

[8] Make me to hear joy and gladness; that the bones which thou hast broken may rejoice.

[9] Hide thy face from my sins, and blot out all mine iniquities.

[10] Create in me a clean heart, O God; and renew a right spirit within me.

[11] Cast me not away from thy presence; and take not thy holy spirit from me.

[12] Restore unto me the joy of thy salvation; and uphold me with thy free spirit.

[13] Then will I teach transgressors thy ways; and sinners shall be converted unto thee.

[14] Deliver me from bloodguiltiness, O God, thou God of my salvation: and my tongue shall sing aloud of thy righteousness.

[15] O LORD, open thou my lips; and my mouth shall shew forth thy praise.

[16] For thou desirest not sacrifice; else would I give it: thou delightest not in burnt offering.

[17] The sacrifices of God are a broken spirit: a broken and a contrite heart, O God, thou wilt not despise.

[18] Do good in thy good pleasure unto Zion: build thou the walls of Jerusalem.

[19] Then shalt thou be pleased with the sacrifices of righteousness, with burnt offering and whole burnt offering: then shall they offer bullocks upon thine altar.

PSALM 139
King James Bible

[1] O LORD, thou hast searched me, and known me.

[2] Thou knowest my downsitting and mine uprising, thou understandest my thought afar off.

[3] Thou compassest my path and my lying down, and art acquainted with all my ways.

[4] For there is not a word in my tongue, but, lo, O LORD, thou knowest it altogether.

[5] Thou hast beset me behind and before, and laid thine hand upon me.

[6] Such knowledge is too wonderful for me; it is high, I cannot attain unto it.

[7] Whither shall I go from thy spirit? or whither shall I flee from thy presence?

[8] If I ascend up into heaven, thou art there: if I make my bed in hell, behold, thou art there.

[9] If I take the wings of the morning, and dwell in the uttermost parts of the sea;

¹⁰ Even there shall thy hand lead me, and thy right hand shall hold me.

¹¹ If I say, Surely the darkness shall cover me; even the night shall be light about me.

¹² Yea, the darkness hideth not from thee; but the night shineth as the day: the darkness and the light are both alike to thee.

¹³ For thou hast possessed my reins: thou hast covered me in my mother's womb.

¹⁴ I will praise thee; for I am fearfully and wonderfully made: marvellous are thy works; and that my soul knoweth right well.

¹⁵ My substance was not hid from thee, when I was made in secret, and curiously wrought in the lowest parts of the earth.

¹⁶ Thine eyes did see my substance, yet being unperfect; and in thy book all my members were written, which in continuance were fashioned, when as yet there was none of them.

¹⁷ How precious also are thy thoughts unto me, O God! how great is the sum of them!

¹⁸ If I should count them, they are more in number than the sand: when I awake, I am still with thee.

¹⁹ Surely thou wilt slay the wicked, O God: depart from me therefore, ye bloody men.

²⁰ For they speak against thee wickedly, and thine enemies take thy name in vain.

²¹ Do not I hate them, O LORD, that hate thee? and am not I grieved with those that rise up against thee?

²² I hate them with perfect hatred: I count them mine enemies.

²³ Search me, O God, and know my heart: try me, and know my thoughts:

²⁴ And see if there be any wicked way in me, and lead me in the way everlasting.

Note

1. *The Psalms.* For a fine, concise, readable analysis of the psalms, see MARY ELLEN CHASE, THE PSALMS FOR THE COMMON READER (1962). Professor Chase has the highest opinion of Psalm 139. She calls it a psalm of thanksgiving, a psalm of meditation and reflection, a psalm of gratitude, and a psalm of wonder. *Id.* at 44. Surely it is also a psalm of repentance, since the psalmist begs God to search him for his sinful thoughts. "Whither shall I go from thy spirit? or whither shall I flee from thy presence?" He cannot escape God, even if he makes his bed in hell.

Professor Chase says: "Perhaps among all the writers of the Psalms this man is the most appealing. His very effervescence is intoxicating; and we wish it had been our good fortune to have known him, wherever he lived, whoever he was." *Id.* at 45.

T. PRAISE

PSALM 66
King James Bible

[1] Make a joyful noise unto God, all ye lands:

[2] Sing forth the honour of his name: make his praise glorious.

[3] Say unto God, How terrible art thou in thy works! through the greatness of thy power shall thine enemies submit themselves unto thee.

[4] All the earth shall worship thee, and shall sing unto thee; they shall sing to thy name. Selah.

[5] Come and see the works of God: he is terrible in his doing toward the children of men.

[6] He turned the sea into dry land: they went through the flood on foot: there did we rejoice in him.

[7] He ruleth by his power for ever; his eyes behold the nations: let not the rebellious exalt themselves. Selah.

[8] O bless our God, ye people, and make the voice of his praise to be heard:

[9] Which holdeth our soul in life, and suffereth not our feet to be moved.

[10] For thou, O God, hast proved us: thou hast tried us, as silver is tried.

[11] Thou broughtest us into the net; thou laidst affliction upon our loins.

[12] Thou hast caused men to ride over our heads; we went through fire and through water: but thou broughtest us out into a wealthy place.

[13] I will go into thy house with burnt offerings: I will pay thee my vows,

[14] Which my lips have uttered, and my mouth hath spoken, when I was in trouble.

[15] I will offer unto thee burnt sacrifices of fatlings, with the incense of rams; I will offer bullocks with goats. Selah.

[16] Come and hear, all ye that fear God, and I will declare what he hath done for my soul.

[17] I cried unto him with my mouth, and he was extolled with my tongue.

[18] If I regard iniquity in my heart, the LORD will not hear me:

[19] But verily God hath heard me; he hath attended to the voice of my prayer.

[20] Blessed be God, which hath not turned away my prayer, nor his mercy from me.

PSALM 104
King James Bible

[1] Bless the Lord, O my soul. O Lord my God, thou art very great; thou art clothed with honour and majesty.

[2] Who coverest thyself with light as with a garment: who stretchest out the heavens like a curtain:

[3] Who layeth the beams of his chambers in the waters: who maketh the clouds his chariot: who walketh upon the wings of the wind:

[4] Who maketh his angels spirits; his ministers a flaming fire:

[5] Who laid the foundations of the earth, that it should not be removed for ever.

[6] Thou coveredst it with the deep as with a garment: the waters stood above the mountains.

[7] At thy rebuke they fled; at the voice of thy thunder they hasted away.

[8] They go up by the mountains; they go down by the valleys unto the place which thou hast founded for them.

[9] Thou hast set a bound that they may not pass over; that they turn not again to cover the earth.

[10] He sendeth the springs into the valleys, which run among the hills.

[11] They give drink to every beast of the field: the wild asses quench their thirst.

[12] By them shall the fowls of the heaven have their habitation, which sing among the branches.

[13] He watereth the hills from his chambers: the earth is satisfied with the fruit of thy works.

[14] He causeth the grass to grow for the cattle, and herb for the service of man: that he may bring forth food out of the earth;

[15] And wine that maketh glad the heart of man, and oil to make his face to shine, and bread which strengtheneth man's heart.

[16] The trees of the Lord are full of sap; the cedars of Lebanon, which he hath planted;

[17] Where the birds make their nests: as for the stork, the fir trees are her house.

[18] The high hills are a refuge for the wild goats; and the rocks for the conies.

[19] He appointed the moon for seasons: the sun knoweth his going down.

[20] Thou makest darkness, and it is night: wherein all the beasts of the forest do creep forth.

[21] The young lions roar after their prey, and seek their meat from God.

[22] The sun ariseth, they gather themselves together, and lay them down in their dens.

[23] Man goeth forth unto his work and to his labour until the evening.

[24] O LORD, how manifold are thy works! in wisdom hast thou made them all: the earth is full of thy riches.

[25] So is this great and wide sea, wherein are things creeping innumerable, both small and great beasts.

[26] There go the ships: there is that leviathan, whom thou hast made to play therein.

[27] These wait all upon thee; that thou mayest give them their meat in due season.

[28] That thou givest them they gather: thou openest thine hand, they are filled with good.

[29] Thou hidest thy face, they are troubled: thou takest away their breath, they die, and return to their dust.

[30] Thou sendest forth thy spirit, they are created: and thou renewest the face of the earth.

[31] The glory of the LORD shall endure for ever: the LORD shall rejoice in his works.

[32] He looketh on the earth, and it trembleth: he toucheth the hills, and they smoke.

[33] I will sing unto the LORD as long as I live: I will sing praise to my God while I have my being.

[34] My meditation of him shall be sweet: I will be glad in the LORD.

[35] Let the sinners be consumed out of the earth, and let the wicked be no more. Bless thou the LORD, O my soul. Praise ye the LORD.

PSALM 114
King James Bible

[1] When Israel went out of Egypt, the house of Jacob from a people of strange language;

[2] Judah was his sanctuary, and Israel his dominion.

[3] The sea saw it, and fled: Jordan was driven back.

[4] The mountains skipped like rams, and the little hills like lambs.

[5] What ailed thee, O thou sea, that thou fleddest? thou Jordan, that thou wast driven back?

[6] Ye mountains, that ye skipped like rams; and ye little hills, like lambs?

[7] Tremble, thou earth, at the presence of the LORD, at the presence of the God of Jacob;

[8] Which turned the rock into a standing water, the flint into a fountain of waters.

PSALM 150
King James Bible

[1] Praise ye the LORD. Praise God in his sanctuary: praise him in the firmament of his power.

[2] Praise him for his mighty acts: praise him according to his excellent greatness.

[3] Praise him with the sound of the trumpet: praise him with the psaltery and harp.

[4] Praise him with the timbrel and dance: praise him with stringed instruments and organs.

[5] Praise him upon the loud cymbals: praise him upon the high sounding cymbals.

[6] Let every thing that hath breath praise the LORD. Praise ye the LORD.

U. SPIRIT

HE WISHES FOR THE CLOTHS OF HEAVEN
William Butler Yeats

Had I the heavens' embroidered cloths,
Enwrought with golden and silver light,
The blue and the dim and the dark cloths
Of night and light and the half-light,
I would spread the cloths under your feet:
But I, being poor, have only my dreams;
I have spread my dreams under your feet;
Tread softly because you tread on my dreams.

SHE WAS A PHANTOM OF DELIGHT
William Wordsworth

She was a Phantom of delight
When first she gleam'd upon my sight;
A lovely Apparition, sent
To be a moment's ornament:
Her eyes as stars of twilight fair;
Like twilight's, too, her dusky hair;
But all things else about her drawn
From May-time and the cheerful dawn;

A dancing shape, an image gay,
To haunt, to startle, and waylay.

I saw her upon nearer view,
A Spirit, yet a Woman too!
Her household motions light and free,
And steps of virgin liberty;
A countenance in which did meet
Sweet records, promises as sweet;
A creature not too bright or good
For human nature's daily food,
For transient sorrows, simple wiles,
Praise, blame, love, kisses, tears, and smiles.

And now I see with eye serene
The very pulse of the machine;
A being breathing thoughtful breath,
A traveller between life and death:
The reason firm, the temperate will,
Endurance, foresight, strength, and skill;
A perfect Woman, nobly plann'd
To warn, to comfort, and command;
And yet a Spirit still, and bright
With something of an angel light.

V. TIME

TO HIS COY MISTRESS
Andrew Marvell

Had we but world enough, and time,
This coyness, Lady, were no crime
We would sit down and think which way
To walk and pass our long love's day.
Thou by the Indian Ganges' side
Shouldst rubies find: I by the tide
Of Humber would complain. I would
Love you ten years before the Flood,
And you should, if you please, refuse
Till the conversion of the Jews.
My vegetable love should grow
Vaster than empires, and more slow;
An hundred years should go to praise
Thine eyes and on thy forehead gaze;
Two hundred to adore each breast,
But thirty thousand to the rest;
An age at least to every part,
And the last age should show your heart.
For, Lady, you deserve this state,
Nor would I love at lower rate.

But at my back I always hear
Time's wingèd chariot hurrying near;
And yonder all before us lie
Deserts of vast eternity.
Thy beauty shall no more be found,
Nor, in thy marble vault, shall sound
My echoing song: then worms shall try
That long preserved virginity,
And your quaint honour turn to dust,
And into ashes all my lust:
The grave's a fine and private place,
But none, I think, do there embrace.

Now therefore, while the youthful hue
Sits on thy skin like morning dew,
And while thy willing soul transpires
At every pore with instant fires,
Now let us sport us while we may,
And now, like amorous birds of prey,
Rather at once our time devour
Than languish in his slow-chapt power.
Let us roll all our strength and all
Our sweetness up into one ball,
And tear our pleasures with rough strife
Thorough the iron gates of life:
Thus, though we cannot make our sun
Stand still, yet we will make him run.

Note

1. *Coyness.* This poem is written on a very light note. Indeed, it resembles Robert Herrick's "Gather Ye Rosebuds While Ye May."

Yet, hardly halfway through Marvell's light-hearted poem is one of the most somber couplets in all of Western literature.

But at my back I always hear
Time's wingèd chariot hurrying near;

Compare John Crowe Ransom's poem, "Janet Waking," in section B of this chapter.

W. GOD

THE WINDHOVER
Gerard Manley Hopkins

I caught this morning morning's minion, king-
    dom of daylight's dauphin, dapple-dawn-drawn Falcon, in
    his riding
Of the rolling level underneath him steady air, and striding

High there, how he rung upon the rein of a wimpling wing
In his ecstasy! then off, off forth on swing,
    As a skate's heel sweeps smooth on a bow-bend: the hurl
    and gliding
    Rebuffed the big wind. My heart in hiding
Stirred for a bird,—the achieve of; the mastery of the thing!

Brute beauty and valour and act, oh, air, pride, plume, here
    Buckle! AND the fire that breaks from thee then, a billion
    Times told lovelier, more dangerous, O my chevalier!

    No wonder of it: shéer plód makes plough down sillion
Shine, and blue-bleak embers, ah my dear,
    Fall, gall themselves, and gash gold-vermillion.

GOD'S GRANDEUR
Gerard Manley Hopkins

The world is charged with the grandeur of God.
    It will flame out, like shining from shook foil;
    It gathers to a greatness, like the ooze of oil
Crushed. Why do men then now not reck his rod?
Generations have trod, have trod, have trod;
    And all is seared with trade; bleared, smeared with toil;
    And wears man's smudge and shares man's smell: the soil
Is bare now, nor can foot feel, being shod.

And for all this, nature is never spent;
    There lives the dearest freshness deep down things;
And though the last lights off the black West went
    Oh, morning, at the brown brink eastward, springs—
Because the Holy Ghost over the bent
    World broods with warm breast and with ah! bright wings.

PSALM 8
King James Bible

[1] O Lord our Lord, how excellent is thy name in all the earth! who hast set thy glory above the heavens.

[2] Out of the mouth of babes and sucklings hast thou ordained strength because of thine enemies, that thou mightest still the enemy and the avenger.

[3] When I consider thy heavens, the work of thy fingers, the moon and the stars, which thou hast ordained;

[4] What is man, that thou art mindful of him? and the son of man, that thou visitest him?

[5] For thou hast made him a little lower than the angels, and hast crowned him with glory and honour.

[6] Thou madest him to have dominion over the works of thy hands; thou hast put all things under his feet:

[7] All sheep and oxen, yea, and the beasts of the field;

[8] The fowl of the air, and the fish of the sea, and whatsoever passeth through the paths of the seas.

[9] O LORD our LORD, how excellent is thy name in all the earth!

PSALM 27
King James Bible

[1] The LORD is my light and my salvation; whom shall I fear? the LORD is the strength of my life; of whom shall I be afraid?

[2] When the wicked, even mine enemies and my foes, came upon me to eat up my flesh, they stumbled and fell.

[3] Though an host should encamp against me, my heart shall not fear: though war should rise against me, in this will I be confident.

[4] One thing have I desired of the LORD, that will I seek after; that I may dwell in the house of the LORD all the days of my life, to behold the beauty of the LORD, and to inquire in his temple.

[5] For in the time of trouble he shall hide me in his pavilion: in the secret of his tabernacle shall he hide me; he shall set me up upon a rock.

[6] And now shall mine head be lifted up above mine enemies round about me: therefore will I offer in his tabernacle sacrifices of joy; I will sing, yea, I will sing praises unto the LORD.

[7] Hear, O LORD, when I cry with my voice: have mercy also upon me, and answer me.

[8] When thou saidst, Seek ye my face; my heart said unto thee, Thy face, LORD, will I seek.

[9] Hide not thy face far from me; put not thy servant away in anger: thou hast been my help; leave me not, neither forsake me, O God of my salvation.

[10] When my father and my mother forsake me, then the LORD will take me up.

[11] Teach me thy way, O LORD, and lead me in a plain path, because of mine enemies.

[12] Deliver me not over unto the will of mine enemies: for false witnesses are risen up against me, and such as breathe out cruelty.

[13] I had fainted, unless I had believed to see the goodness of the LORD in the land of the living.

[14] Wait on the LORD: be of good courage, and he shall strengthen thine heart: wait, I say, on the LORD.

JOB
CHAPTER 38
King James Bible

[1] Then the LORD answered Job out of the whirlwind, and said,

[2] Who is this that darkeneth counsel by words without knowledge?

[3] Gird up now thy loins like a man; for I will demand of thee, and answer thou me.

[4] Where wast thou when I laid the foundations of the earth? declare, if thou hast understanding.

[5] Who hath laid the measures thereof, if thou knowest? or who hath stretched the line upon it?

[6] Whereupon are the foundations thereof fastened? or who laid the corner stone thereof;

[7] When the morning stars sang together, and all the sons of God shouted for joy?

[8] Or who shut up the sea with doors, when it brake forth, as if it had issued out of the womb?

[9] When I made the cloud the garment thereof, and thick darkness a swaddlingband for it,

[10] And brake up for it my decreed place, and set bars and doors,

[11] And said, Hitherto shalt thou come, but no further: and here shall thy proud waves be stayed?

[12] Hast thou commanded the morning since thy days; and caused the dayspring to know his place;

[13] That it might take hold of the ends of the earth, that the wicked might be shaken out of it?

[14] It is turned as clay to the seal; and they stand as a garment.

[15] And from the wicked their light is withholden, and the high arm shall be broken.

[16] Hast thou entered into the springs of the sea? or hast thou walked in the search of the depth?

[17] Have the gates of death been opened unto thee? or hast thou seen the doors of the shadow of death?

[18] Hast thou perceived the breadth of the earth? declare if thou knowest it all.

[19] Where is the way where light dwelleth? and as for darkness, where is the place thereof,

[20] That thou shouldest take it to the bound thereof, and that thou shouldest know the paths to the house thereof?

²¹ Knowest thou it, because thou wast then born? or because the number of thy days is great?

²² Hast thou entered into the treasures of the snow? or hast thou seen the treasures of the hail,

²³ Which I have reserved against the time of trouble, against the day of battle and war?

²⁴ By what way is the light parted, which scattereth the east wind upon the earth?

²⁵ Who hath divided a watercourse for the overflowing of waters, or a way for the lightning of thunder;

²⁶ To cause it to rain on the earth, where no man is; on the wilderness, wherein there is no man;

²⁷ To satisfy the desolate and waste ground; and to cause the bud of the tender herb to spring forth?

²⁸ Hath the rain a father? or who hath begotten the drops of dew?

²⁹ Out of whose womb came the ice? and the hoary frost of heaven, who hath gendered it?

³⁰ The waters are hid as with a stone, and the face of the deep is frozen.

³¹ Canst thou bind the sweet influences of Pleiades, or loose the bands of Orion?

³² Canst thou bring forth Mazzaroth in his season? or canst thou guide Arcturus with his sons?

³³ Knowest thou the ordinances of heaven? canst thou set the dominion thereof in the earth?

³⁴ Canst thou lift up thy voice to the clouds, that abundance of waters may cover thee?

³⁵ Canst thou send lightnings, that they may go, and say unto thee, Here we are?

³⁶ Who hath put wisdom in the inward parts? or who hath given understanding to the heart?

³⁷ Who can number the clouds in wisdom? or who can stay the bottles of heaven,

³⁸ When the dust groweth into hardness, and the clods cleave fast together?

³⁹ Wilt thou hunt the prey for the lion? or fill the appetite of the young lions,

⁴⁰ When they couch in their dens, and abide in the covert to lie in wait?

⁴¹ Who provideth for the raven his food? when his young ones cry unto God, they wander for lack of meat.

BATTER MY HEART, THREE–PERSONED GOD
John Donne

Batter my heart, three-person'd God, for you
As yet but knock, breathe, shine, and seek to mend;
That I may rise and stand, o'erthrow me, and bend
Your force to break, blow, burn, and make me new.
I, like an usurp'd town, to another due,
Labor to admit you, but oh, to no end;
Reason, your viceroy in me, me should defend,
But is captived, and proves weak or untrue.
Yet dearly I love you, and would be loved fain,
But am betrothed unto your enemy;
Divorce me, untie or break that knot again,
Take me to you, imprison me, for I,
Except you enthrall me, never shall be free,
Nor ever chaste, except you ravish me.

GOD IS A DISTANT, STATELY LOVER
Emily Dickinson

God is a distant, stately Lover—
Woos, as he states us, by his son:
Verily, a vicarious courtship—
Miles, and Priscilla, were such an one,

But, lest the Soul, like fair Priscilla,
Choose the Envoy and spurn the Groom,
Vouches, with hyperbolic archness,
Miles, and John Alden were Synonym.

ON HIS BLINDNESS
John Milton

When I consider how my light is spent
E're half my days in this dark world and wide,
And that one talent which is death to hide
Lodged with me useless, though my Soul more bent
To serve therewith my Maker, and present
My true account, lest he returning chide,
"Doth God exact day-labour, light denied?"
I fondly ask. But patience to prevent
That murmur, soon replies, "God doth not need
Either man's work or his own gifts. Who best
Bear his mild yoke, they serve him best. His State
Is kingly: thousands at his bidding speed,
And post o'er land and ocean without rest:
They also serve who only stand and wait."

THE TYGER
William Blake

Tyger! Tyger! burning bright
In the forests of the night,
What immortal hand or eye
Could frame thy fearful symmetry?

In what distant deeps or skies
Burnt the fire of thine eyes?
On what wings dare he aspire?
What the hand dare seize the fire?

And what shoulder, and what art,
Could twist the sinews of thy heart?
And when thy heart began to beat,
What dread hand? and what dread feet?

What the hammer? what the chain?
In what furnace was thy brain?
What the anvil? what dread grasp
Dare its deadly terrors clasp?

When the stars threw down their spears,
And water'd heaven with their tears,
Did he smile his work to see?
Did he who made the Lamb make thee?

Tyger! Tyger! burning bright
In the forests of the night,
What immortal hand or eye,
Dare frame thy fearful symmetry?

Note

1. *The Omnipotent.* A discussion of God can hardly be avoided in a course that deals, inter alia, with *Paradise Lost* and the book of *Job*. Satan throws down the ultimate challenge to Eve in Book IX, l. 701 of *Paradise Lost*. "Not just, not God; nor fear'd then, nor obey'd." On the other hand, as God makes amply clear to Job in chapters 38–41 of the book of *Job*, how can man ever understand the ways of God? *See* Søren Kiekegaard, Fear and Trembling (1843).

Suppose we rephrase Satan's challenge: "Not just, not man." But how can man be just, if he has other unjust persons to live with? For that matter, how can God be just if he has Satan to contend with? The difference is that God, unlike man, is omnipotent, and can work his will for absolute good. On the other hand, as Lord Acton said in a letter to Bishop Creighton (5 April 1887), "Power tends to corrupt and absolute power corrupts absolutely."

Is it any surprise, then, that our students are unable to define justice?

X. COMFORT

PSALM 84
King James Bible

[1] How amiable are thy tabernacles, O Lord of hosts!

[2] My soul longeth, yea, even fainteth for the courts of the Lord: my heart and my flesh crieth out for the living God.

[3] Yea, the sparrow hath found an house, and the swallow a nest for herself, where she may lay her young, even thine altars, O Lord of hosts, my King, and my God.

[4] Blessed are they that dwell in thy house: they will be still praising thee. Selah.

[5] Blessed is the man whose strength is in thee; in whose heart are the ways of them.

[6] Who passing through the valley of Baca make it a well; the rain also filleth the pools.

[7] They go from strength to strength, every one of them in Zion appeareth before God.

[8] O Lord God of hosts, hear my prayer: give ear, O God of Jacob. Selah.

[9] Behold, O God our shield, and look upon the face of thine anointed.

[10] For a day in thy courts is better than a thousand. I had rather be a doorkeeper in the house of my God, than to dwell in the tents of wickedness.

[11] For the Lord God is a sun and shield: the Lord will give grace and glory: no good thing will he withhold from them that walk uprightly.

[12] O Lord of hosts, blessed is the man that trusteth in thee.

PSALM 91
King James Bible

[1] He that dwelleth in the secret place of the most High shall abide under the shadow of the Almighty.

[2] I will say of the Lord, He is my refuge and my fortress: my God; in him will I trust.

[3] Surely he shall deliver thee from the snare of the fowler, and from the noisome pestilence.

[4] He shall cover thee with his feathers, and under his wings shalt thou trust: his truth shall be thy shield and buckler.

[5] Thou shalt not be afraid for the terror by night; nor for the arrow that flieth by day;

[6] Nor for the pestilence that walketh in darkness; nor for the destruction that wasteth at noonday.

⁷ A thousand shall fall at thy side, and ten thousand at thy right hand; but it shall not come nigh thee.

⁸ Only with thine eyes shalt thou behold and see the reward of the wicked.

⁹ Because thou hast made the L<small>ORD</small>, which is my refuge, even the most High, thy habitation;

¹⁰ There shall no evil befall thee, neither shall any plague come nigh thy dwelling.

¹¹ For he shall give his angels charge over thee, to keep thee in all thy ways.

¹² They shall bear thee up in their hands, lest thou dash thy foot against a stone.

¹³ Thou shalt tread upon the lion and adder: the young lion and the dragon shalt thou trample under feet.

¹⁴ Because he hath set his love upon me, therefore will I deliver him: I will set him on high, because he hath known my name.

¹⁵ He shall call upon me, and I will answer him: I will be with him in trouble; I will deliver him, and honour him.

¹⁶ With long life will I satisfy him, and shew him my salvation.

PSALM 46
King James Bible

¹ God is our refuge and strength, a very present help in trouble.

² Therefore will not we fear, though the earth be removed, and though the mountains be carried into the midst of the sea;

³ Though the waters thereof roar and be troubled, though the mountains shake with the swelling thereof. Selah.

⁴ There is a river, the streams whereof shall make glad the city of God, the holy place of the tabernacles of the most High.

⁵ God is in the midst of her; she shall not be moved: God shall help her, and that right early.

⁶ The heathen raged, the kingdoms were moved: he uttered his voice, the earth melted.

⁷ The L<small>ORD</small> of hosts is with us; the God of Jacob is our refuge. Selah.

⁸ Come, behold the works of the L<small>ORD</small>, what desolations he hath made in the earth.

⁹ He maketh wars to cease unto the end of the earth; he breaketh the bow, and cutteth the spear in sunder; he burneth the chariot in the fire.

¹⁰ Be still, and know that I am God: I will be exalted among the heathen, I will be exalted in the earth.

¹¹ The L<small>ORD</small> of hosts is with us; the God of Jacob is our refuge. Selah.

ISAIAH
CHAPTER 11:1–9
King James Bible

¹ And there shall come forth a rod out of the stem of Jesse, and a Branch shall grow out of his roots:

² And the spirit of the LORD shall rest upon him, the spirit of wisdom and understanding, the spirit of counsel and might, the spirit of knowledge and of the fear of the LORD;

³ And shall make him of quick understanding in the fear of the LORD: and he shall not judge after the sight of his eyes, neither reprove after the hearing of his ears:

⁴ But with righteousness shall he judge the poor, and reprove with equity for the meek of the earth: and he shall smite the earth with the rod of his mouth, and with the breath of his lips shall he slay the wicked.

⁵ And righteousness shall be the girdle of his loins, and faithfulness the girdle of his reins.

⁶ The wolf also shall dwell with the lamb, and the leopard shall lie down with the kid; and the calf and the young lion and the fatling together; and a little child shall lead them.

⁷ And the cow and the bear shall feed; their young ones shall lie down together: and the lion shall eat straw like the ox.

⁸ And the sucking child shall play on the hole of the asp, and the weaned child shall put his hand on the cockatrice' den.

⁹ They shall not hurt nor destroy in all my holy mountain: for the earth shall be full of the knowledge of the LORD, as the waters cover the sea.

ISAIAH
CHAPTER 2:1–5
King James Bible

¹ The word that Isaiah the son of Amoz saw concerning Judah and Jerusalem.

² And it shall come to pass in the last days, that the mountain of the LORD's house shall be established in the top of the mountains, and shall be exalted above the hills; and all nations shall flow unto it.

³ And many people shall go and say, Come ye, and let us go up to the mountain of the LORD, to the house of the God of Jacob; and he will teach us of his ways, and we will walk in his paths: for out of Zion shall go forth the law, and the word of the LORD from Jerusalem.

⁴ And he shall judge among the nations, and shall rebuke many people: and they shall beat their swords into plowshares, and their spears into pruninghooks: nation shall not lift up sword against nation, neither shall they learn war any more.

[5] O house of Jacob, come ye, and let us walk in the light of the LORD.

Note

1. *Isaiah 2:4.* In the garden of the United Nations in New York City is a statue of a man holding a hammer, given by the U.S.S.R. in 1959. It bears the inscription: "We Shall Beat Swords Into Plowshares."

On the outside wall of the United Nations General Headquarters is engraved the motto of the United Nations:

> AND THEY SHALL BEAT THEIR
> SWORDS INTO PLOWSHARES, AND
> THEIR SPEARS INTO PRUNINGHOOKS:
> NATION SHALL NOT LIFT UP SWORD
> AGAINST NATION, NEITHER SHALL
> THEY LEARN WAR ANY MORE.

Y. YOUTH

I HEAR AMERICA SINGING
Walt Whitman

I hear America singing, the varied carols I hear;
Those of mechanics, each one singing his, as it should be, blithe and strong,
The carpenter singing his as he measures his plank or beam,
The mason singing his as he makes ready for work, or leaves off work,
The boatman singing what belongs to him in his boat the deckhand singing on the steamboat deck,
The shoemaker singing as he sits on his bench, the hatter singing as he stands,
The wood-cutter's song, the ploughboy's, on his way in the morning, or at the noon intermission or at sundown,
The delicious singing of the mother, or of the young wife at work, or of the girl sewing or washing,
Each singing what belongs to her, and to none else,
The day what belongs to the day, at night, the party of young fellows, robust, friendly,
Singing, with open mouths, their strong melodious songs.

DOWN BY THE SALLEY GARDENS
William Butler Yeats

Down by the salley gardens my love and I did meet;
She passed the salley gardens with little snow-white feet.
She bid me take love easy, as the leaves grow on the tree;
But I, being young and foolish, with her would not agree.
In a field by the river my love and I did stand,
And on my leaning shoulder she laid her snow-white hand.

She bid me take life easy, as the grass grows on the weirs;
But I was young and foolish, and now am full of tears.

THE CHIMNEY SWEEPER
William Blake

When my mother died I was very young,
And my father sold me while yet my tongue
Could scarcely cry " 'weep! 'weep! 'weep! 'weep!''
So your chimneys I sweep, and in soot I sleep.

There's little Tom Dacre, who cried when his head,
That curl'd like a lamb's back, was shav'd; so I said,
"Hush, Tom! never mind it, for when your head's bare
You know that the soot cannot spoil your white hair."

And so he was quiet, and that very night
As Tom was a-sleeping, he had such a sight!
That thousands of sweepers, Dick, Joe, Ned, and Jack,
Were all of them lock'd up in coffins of black.

And by came an Angel who had a bright key,
And he open'd the coffins and set them all free;
Then down a green plain leaping, laughing, they run,
And wash in a river, and shine in the sun.

Then naked and white, all their bags left behind,
They rise upon clouds and sport in the wind;
And the Angel told Tom, if he'd be a good boy,
He'd have God for his father, and never want joy.

And so Tom awoke, and we rose in the dark,
And got with our bags and our brushes to work.
Though the morning was cold, Tom was happy and warm;
So if all do their duty they need not fear harm.

THE OXEN
Thomas Hardy

Christmas Eve, and twelve of the clock.
"Now they are all on their knees,"
An elder said as we sat in a flock
By the embers in hearthside ease.

We pictured the meek mild creatures where
They dwelt in their strawy pen,
Nor did it occur to one of us there
To doubt they were kneeling then.

So fair a fancy few would weave
In these years! Yet, I feel,
If someone said on Christmas Eve,
"Come; see the oxen kneel

"In the lonely barton by yonder coomb
Our childhood used to know,"
I should go with him in the gloom,
Hoping it might be so.

FERN HILL
Dylan Thomas

Now as I was young and easy under the apple boughs
About the lilting house and happy as the grass was green,
The night above the dingle starry,
Time let me hail and climb

Golden in the heydays of his eyes,
And honoured among wagons I was prince of the apple towns
And once below a time I lordly had the trees and leaves
Trail with daisies and barley
Down the rivers of the windfall light.

And as I was green and carefree, famous among the barns
About the happy yard and singing as the farm was home,
In the sun that is young once only,
Time let me play and be
Golden in the mercy of his means,
And green and golden I was huntsman and herdsman, the calves
Sang to my horn, the foxes on the hills barked clear and cold,
And the sabbath rang slowly
In the pebbles of the holy streams.

All the sun long it was running, it was lovely, the hay
Fields high as the house, the tunes from the chimneys, it was air
And playing, lovely and watery
And fire green as grass.
And nightly under the simple stars
As I rode to sleep the owls were bearing the farm away,
All the moon long I heard, blessed among stables, the nightjars
Flying with the ricks, and the horses
Flashing into the dark.

And then to awake, and the farm, like a wanderer white
With the dew, come back, the cock on his shoulder: it was all
Shining, it was Adam and maiden,
The sky gathered again
And the sun grew round that very day.
So it must have been after the birth of the simple light
In the first, spinning place, the spellbound horses walking warm
Out of the whinnying green stable
On to the fields of praise.
And honoured among foxes and pheasants by the gay house

Under the new made clouds and happy as the heart was long,
In the sun born over and over,
I ran my heedless ways,
My wishes raced through the house high hay
And nothing I cared, at my sky blue trades, that time allows
In all his tuneful turning so few and such morning songs
Before the children green and golden
Follow him out of grace,

Nothing I cared, in the lamb white days, that time would take me
Up to the swallow thronged loft by the shadow of my hand,
In the moon that is always rising,
Nor that riding to sleep
I should hear him fly with the high fields
And wake to the farm forever fled from the childless land.
Oh as I was young and easy in the mercy of his means,
Time held me green and dying
Though I sang in my chains like the sea.

WE REAL COOL
Gwendolyn Brooks

We real cool. We
Left school. We

Lurk late. We
Strike straight. We

Sing sin. We
Thin gin. We

Jazz June. We
Die soon.

PICTURES FROM BREUGHEL
William Carlos Williams

This is a schoolyard
crowded
with children

of all ages near a village
on a small stream
meandering by

where some boys
are swimming
bare-ass

or climbing a tree in leaf
everything
is motion

elder women are looking
after the small
fry

a play wedding a
christening
nearby one leans

hollering
into
an empty hogshead

Note

1.   *Stasis.* Compare the verb structure of Williams' poem with that of Lincoln's *Second Inaugural Address* in Chapter One. Compare the punctuation of the poem with that of "Oak Tree Bedizened" in section M of this chapter. Are these characteristics of Williams' poem (stasis, and lack of punctuation) contrapuntal?

Z.   NATURE

PSALM 121
King James Bible

[1] I will lift up mine eyes unto the hills, from whence cometh my help.

[2] My help cometh from the LORD, which made heaven and earth.

[3] He will not suffer thy foot to be moved: he that keepeth thee will not slumber.

[4] Behold, he that keepeth Israel shall neither slumber nor sleep.

[5] The LORD is thy keeper: the LORD is thy shade upon thy right hand.

[6] The sun shall not smite thee by day, nor the moon by night.

[7] The LORD shall preserve thee from all evil: he shall preserve thy soul.

[8] The LORD shall preserve thy going out and thy coming in from this time forth, and even for evermore.

PSALM 23
King James Bible

[1] The LORD is my shepherd; I shall not want.

[2] He maketh me to lie down in green pastures: he leadeth me beside the still waters.

[3] He restoreth my soul: he leadeth me in the paths of righteousness for his name's sake.

[4] Yea, though I walk through the valley of the shadow of death, I will fear no evil: for thou art with me; thy rod and thy staff they comfort me.

[5] Thou preparest a table before me in the presence of mine enemies: thou anointest my head with oil; my cup runneth over.

[6] Surely goodness and mercy shall follow me all the days of my life: and I will dwell in the house of the LORD for ever.

THE CANTERBURY TALES
Geoffrey Chaucer

THE GENERAL PROLOGUE
(Excerpt)

Whan that Aprille with his shoures soote
The droghte of March hath perced to the roote,
And bathed every veyne in swich licour
Of which vertu engendered is the flour;
When Zephirus with his sweete breeth
Inspired hath in every holt and heeth
The tendre croppes, and the yonge sonne
Hath in the Ram his halve cours yronne,
And smale foweles maken melodye,
That slepen al the nyght with open ye
(So priketh hem nature in hir corages);
Thanne longen folk to goon on pilgrimages,
And palmers for to seken straunge strondes,
To ferne halwes, kowthe in sondry londes;
And specially from every shires ende
Of Engleond to Canterbury they wende,
The hooly blisful martir for to seke,
That hem hath holpen whan that they were seeke.

TO AUTUMN
John Keats

Season of mists and mellow fruitfulness,
Close bosom-friend of the maturing sun;
Conspiring with him how to load and bless
With fruit the vines that round the thatch-eves run;
To bend with apples the moss'd cottage-trees,
And fill all fruit with ripeness to the core;
To swell the gourd, and plump the hazel shells
With a sweet kernel; to set budding more,
And still more, later flowers for the bees,
Until they think warm days will never cease,
For Summer has o'er-brimm'd their clammy cells.

Who hath not seen thee oft amid thy store?
Sometimes whoever seeks abroad may find
Thee sitting careless on a granary floor,
Thy hair soft-lifted by the winnowing wind;
Or on a half-reap'd furrow sound asleep,

Drows'd with the fume of poppies, while thy hook
Spares the next swath and all its twined flowers:
And sometimes like a gleaner thou dost keep
Steady thy laden head across a brook;
Or by a cyder-press, with patient look,
Thou watchest the last oozings hours by hours.

Where are the songs of Spring? Ay, where are they?
Think not of them, thou hast thy music too,—
While barred clouds bloom the soft-dying day,
And touch the stubble-plains with rosy hue;
Then in a wailful choir the small gnats mourn
Among the river sallows, borne aloft
Or sinking as the light wind lives or dies;
And full-grown lambs loud bleat from hilly bourn;
Hedge-crickets sing; and now with treble soft
The red-breast whistles from a garden-croft;
And gathering swallows twitter in the skies.

THE CAT AND THE MOON
William Butler Yeats

The cat went here and there
And the moon spun round like a top,
And the nearest kin of the moon,
The creeping cat, looked up.
Black Minnaloushe stared at the moon,
For, wander and wail as he would,
The pure cold light in the sky
Troubled his animal blood.
Minnaloushe runs in the grass
Lifting his delicate feet.
Do you dance, Minnaloushe, do you dance?

When two close kindred meet,
What better than call a dance?
Maybe the moon may learn,
Tired of that courtly fashion,
A new dance turn.
Minnaloushe creeps through the grass
From moonlit place to place,
The sacred moon overhead
Has taken a new phase.
Does Minnaloushe know that his pupils
Will pass from change to change,
And that from round to crescent,
From crescent to round they range?
Minnaloushe creeps through the grass
Alone, important and wise,
And lifts to the changing moon
His changing eyes.

DUST OF SNOW
Robert Frost

The way a crow
Shook down on me
The dust of snow
From a hemlock tree

Has given my heart
A change of mood
And saved some part
Of a day I had rued.

IN JUST
E.E. Cummings

in Just-
spring   when the world is mud-
luscious the little
lame balloonman

whistles   far   and wee

and eddieandbill come
running from marbles and
piracies and it's
spring

when the world is puddle-wonderful

the queer
old balloonman whistles
far   and   wee
and bettyandisbel come dancing

from hop-scotch and jump-rope and

it's
spring
and
    the

        goat-footed

balloonMan   whistles
far
and
wee

WHEN SERPENTS BARGAIN FOR THE RIGHT TO SQUIRM
E.E. Cummings

when serpents bargain for the right to squirm
and the sun strikes to gain a living wage—
when thorns regard their roses with alarm
and rainbows are insured against old age

when every thrush may sing no new moon in
if all screech-owls have not okayed his voice
—and any wave signs on the dotted line
or else an ocean is compelled to close

when the oak begs permission of the birch
to make an acorn—valleys accuse their
mountains of having altitude—and march
denounces april as a saboteur

then we'll believe in that incredible
unanimal mankind(and not until)

NOTHING GOLD CAN STAY
Robert Frost

Nature's first green is gold,
Her hardest hue to hold.
Her early leaf's a flower;
But only so an hour.
Then leaf subsides to leaf.
So Eden sank to grief,
So dawn goes down to day.
Nothing gold can stay.

HAD I THE CHOICE
Walt Whitman

Had I the choice to tally greatest bards,
To limn their portraits, stately, beautiful, and emulate at will,
Homer with all his wars and warriors—Hector, Achilles, Ajax,
Or Shakespeare's woe-entangled Hamlet, Lear, Othello—Tennyson's
fair ladies
Meter or wit the best, or choice conceit to wield in perfect rhyme,
delight of singers;
These, these, O seas, all these I'd gladly barter,
Would you the undulation of one wave, its trick to me transfer,
Or breathe one breath of yours upon my verse,
And leave its odor there.

TWO JAPANESE HAIKU

The lightning flashes!
And slashing through the darkness,
A night-heron's screech.

Matsuo Bashô

The falling flower
I saw drift back to the branch
Was a butterfly.

Moritake

Note

1. *Haiku.* The haiku, a Japanese poetic form, consists of three lines with five, seven, and five syllables, respectively. A haiku evokes a complete impression of mood through the juxtaposition of a natural physical element. Bashô was the greatest practitioner of the art form. The poem by Moritake reflects the Buddhist proverb that the fallen leaf never returns to its branch.

AN INDIAN WALKS IN ME
Marilou Awiakta

An Indian walks in me.
She steps so firmly in my mind
that when I stand against the pine
I know we share the inner light
of the star that shines on me.
She taught me this, my Cherokee,
when I was a spindly child.
And rustling in dry forest leaves
I heard her say, "These speak."
She said the same of sighing wind,
of hawk descending on the hare
and Mother's care to draw
the cover snug around me,
of copperhead coiled on the stone
and blackberries warming in the sun—
"These speak."   I listened ...
Long before I learned the
universal turn of atoms, I heard
the Spirit's song that binds us
all as one. And no more
could I follow any rule
that split my soul.
My Cherokee left me no sign
except in hair and cheek
and this firm step of mind

that seeks the whole
in strength and peace.

Note

1. *Abiding Appalachia.* Marilou Awiakta is a Cherokee/Appalachian poet and essayist, who grew up in Oak Ridge, Tennessee, site of the secret Manhattan Project during World War II. This poem is from her collection, *Abiding Appalachia: Where Mountain and Atom Meet*, in which she explores her three heritages—Cherokee, Appalachian, and scientific. Awiakta's logo, which she designed, signifies the balancing of her three heritages through the law of respect, a law symbolized by the Cherokee Little Deer in atomic orbits. All of us who "seek the whole" in our lives can identify with this symbol. It is a fitting way to close a text on law and literature.

Author and Title Index

———

-A-

-B-

761

-K-

-L-

-M-

†